SECURITY

An Introduction

SECURITY

An Introduction

Philip P. Purpura, CPP

CRC Press
Taylor & Francis Group
Boca Raton   London   New York

CRC Press is an imprint of the
Taylor & Francis Group, an **informa** business

CRC Press
Taylor & Francis Group
6000 Broken Sound Parkway NW, Suite 300
Boca Raton, FL 33487-2742

© 2011 by Taylor and Francis Group, LLC
CRC Press is an imprint of Taylor & Francis Group, an Informa business

No claim to original U.S. Government works

Printed in the United States of America on acid-free paper
10 9 8 7 6 5 4 3 2 1

International Standard Book Number: 978-1-4200-9283-7 (Hardback)

Library of Congress Cataloging-in-Publication Data

Purpura, Philip P., 1950-
    Security : an introduction / Philip P. Purpura.
        p. cm.
    Includes bibliographical references and index.
    ISBN 978-1-4200-9283-7 (hbk. : alk. paper)
    1. Private security services. 2. Crime prevention. 3. Security systems. I. Title.

HV8290.P874 2011
363.3--dc22   2010032014

Visit the Taylor & Francis Web site at
http://www.taylorandfrancis.com

and the CRC Press Web site at
http://www.crcpress.com

To My Family

To the millions of security, public safety, military, and other
professionals who strive to create a safe and secure world.

Contents

SECTION I   The History and Profession of Security

SECTION II Protecting People and Assets

SECTION III Risk and All-Hazards Protection

CHAPTER 12—Protection of Critical Infrastructures and Key Resources 501

SECTION IV The Future

Preface

Security has emerged as a profession supported through associations whose members are involved in training, certifications, and codes of ethics; a history and body of knowledge in books, periodicals, and other sources; and college and university academic programs that produce graduates who possess skills and competencies relevant to the security profession.

Our complex world has made the study of security equally complex. As security professionals strive to protect people and assets, they are faced with enormous and varied challenges involving local, state, national, and international threats and hazards. At the same time, many resources are available to security professionals to assist them in their duties. Examples are education and training programs, books and periodicals, the Internet, peers, associations, government, and standards and guidelines.

Security has become increasingly diverse and specialized. We can no longer narrowly view offenders as being threats only from the outside, who can be thwarted through perimeter access controls and patrols. The reality is that the threat may also be from within—on the premises every day, for instance, as a disgruntled employee or a spy. Simultaneously, the Internet and information technology (IT) systems have resulted in serious vulnerabilities. In addition, security is an essential component of comprehensive protection when an entity is faced with a variety of hazards which are not criminal in nature, such as adverse weather or a utility failure.

Security: An Introduction provides information about the security profession, the business of security, and how to protect people and assets. An emphasis is placed on history, terminology, theory, methodology, and practical strategies of protection. This book applies several techniques to guide the student and/or professional toward enhanced security competencies and skills.

Each chapter begins with learning objectives. A list of key terms follows to guide the reader toward important concepts in the body of knowledge of security. Within each chapter, the key terms are in bold and defined. At the beginning of each chapter, a quiz primes the reader's mind and increases curiosity to facilitate learning. An introduction opens the chapter content. As the chapter is studied, the reader will see various aids that will not only help him or her learn chapter content, but also to apply the knowledge, think creatively in a challenging environment, and understand the profession. This is accomplished through informative boxes on select topics, issues boxes, legal cases, boxes on actual events entitled "Do Not Make These Mistakes," global perspectives, informative sidebars, critical thinking questions in sidebars, and boxes on the varied careers in security. A summary ends the main body of each chapter, followed by discussion questions that reinforce chapter content and point the reader toward debating issues that influence decision making in the security profession. To assist the reader in further understanding how the chapter content is applied in the "real world," practical applications are presented next that pose challenges that security practitioners encounter. Organizations and Web addresses follow to provide sources for additional information and research. Each chapter ends with references from a variety of sources and perspectives.

Security: An Introduction includes a methodology of security. In the security profession, there is a need to possess the knowledge, skill, and ability to explain what is being done in security work, how, to whom, why, where, and when. Such explanations may occur when a security practitioner seeks funding for security or is involved in litigation. An objective of this book is to influence security professionals, researchers, and others toward an ever-expanding, comprehensive body of knowledge of security methodology.

Theory and practical applications are linked in the chapters. "Security-relevant criminology" is explained and emphasized to draw from the mass of theories and research from criminology and related disciplines that have relevance to security and its objectives of protecting people, assets, and operations. On the practical side, security at a variety of sites—from state fairs to biosafety labs—is explained to help the reader understand security vulnerabilities and what can be done to enhance protection.

Besides covering introductory "body of knowledge" security information, topics unique to this book include the following:

- Contexts of security
- Battles of Matewan and Blair Mountain

- 2001 anthrax attacks and Dr. Bruce Ivins
- Mercenaries
- Outlaw private security companies
- Benefits of a college education
- Cautions when reading security periodicals
- Security methodology
- Security business proposals
- Security master plans
- Security-relevant criminology with applications to actual security challenges
- Crime mapping
- Site plan review process
- Fingerprint versus name-based records
- Infinity screening
- LEED standards versus security
- Cyber reconnaissance
- Cases of espionage against the U.S. military
- Cyber warfare
- The legal limits of investigating a business competitor
- Computer forensics
- CSI effect
- Safeguarding undercover investigators
- Transnational internal investigations
- Enterprise risk management
- Enterprise resilience
- Safe-area bombing
- True first responders
- ASIS SPC. 1-2009
- Medical surge
- Access point database checks
- Methodologies of futures studies
- Globalization of hazard
- Infrastructure-to-vehicle communications

The book is divided into four parts: Section I, "The History and Profession of Security," includes Chapters 1–3. Chapter 1, "Definition, Role, and History of Security," defines security, explains the contexts of security, and traces the historical development of security. Chapter 2, "Security in an Environment of Threats, Terrorism, and All-Hazards," concentrates on the serious threats and hazards that confront security practitioners and organizations. Chapter 3, "The Profession and Business of Security," describes the characteristics that support security as a profession, the security industry and its regulation, training and education, and career opportunities.

Section II, "Protecting People and Assets," includes Chapters 4–10. Chapter 4, "Security Methodology," provides a foundation for security planning and the implementation of security strategies through theory, research, and practical business and security tools. Chapter 5, "Security Strategies," explains the many paths to enhanced security, such as security layers, redundancy, and force multipliers. This chapter also describes problems and countermeasures relevant to violence, theft, and drugs in the workplace. Chapter 6, "Personnel Security," focuses on the "insider threat" and countermeasures, preemployment screening, methods of countering complacency and inattention by security practitioners, and strategies of executive and personnel protection. Chapter 7, "Physical Security," includes the topics of standards, information technology and physical security, electronic security systems, entry control systems, lock and key systems, protection for doors and windows, lighting, and closed-circuit television systems. Chapter 8, "Information and Information Technology Security," describes information as an asset, laws pertaining to information protection, threats to information technology and data, cyber warfare, information security, the protection of information technology, communications security, spying, and competitive intelligence. Chapter 9, "Security Law and Liabilities," includes an introduction to the legal system; arrest, search, and seizure law; and electronic evidence. Chapter 10, "Investigations," provides an overview of the investigative process and the skills required for successful investigations. The chapter describes investigative guidelines for fraud, internal theft, shoplifting, and robbery.

Section III, "Risk and All-Hazards Protection," includes Chapters 11 and 12. Chapter 11, "Enterprise Risk Management and Resilience," explains risk management in the private and public sectors, enterprise risk management, enterprise security risk management, natural disasters, human-made disasters, business continuity, enterprise resilience, emergency management, life safety, and fire protection. Chapter 12, "Protection of Critical Infrastructures and Key Resources," describes the history of these vital assets, the National Infrastructure Protection Plan, methodologies of assessing vulnerabilities, and individual critical infrastructures/key resources. Section IV, "The Future," consists of the final chapter. Chapter 13, "Twenty-First Century Security," offers methodologies for anticipating the future, applications to security, predictions from the World Future Society, and emerging technologies.

Security is a profession characterized by many challenges and issues. These include the definition of security; guidelines, standards, regulations, and laws; professionalism; the application of security personnel, policies and procedures, and technology; and the adequacy of security.

After reading and understanding of the contents of this book, the author hopes that the reader will possess an increased ability to protect people, assets, organizations, and our nation.

Acknowledgments

I am grateful for the many people who supported the writing of this book. My family is at the top of the list. I appreciate the patience and loving support of my wife, Amyie, during the long hours of research and writing required for this book. Laura Purpura, a daughter, provided superb editorial and typing assistance. Another daughter, Alaine Purpura, also provided assistance as the project became overwhelming and deadlines approached. The editorial team at Taylor & Francis/CRC Press—specifically Mark Listewnik and Stephanie Morkert—are recognized for their skills and support. I am thankful for the security professionals who answered questions and provided information and the colleagues, librarians, and others who provided input. Special thanks go to the reviewers who provided helpful feedback to improve this book; they are Kenneth Christopher, DPA professor in the Criminal Justice Department at Park University, Parkville, Missouri and Scott Nelson, former Deputy Assistant Director/Inspector FBI and currently, president Security & Risk Management Group, LLC.

About the Author

Philip P. Purpura, Certified Protection Professional, is director of the Security and Justice Institute and coordinator of the Security for Houses of Worship Project in South Carolina. He has taught security and criminal justice courses for more than thirty years. He serves on the ASIS International Council on Academic Programs. Purpura has practical experience as an expert witness, consultant, security manager, investigator, and police officer. He is the author of seven other books: *Security & Loss Prevention: An Introduction*, 5th ed. (Boston: Elsevier Butterworth-Heinemann, 2008); *Security Handbook*, 2nd ed. (Boston: Elsevier Butterworth-Heinemann, 2003), translated into Spanish and Chinese (Albany, NY: Delmar, 1991); *Terrorism & Homeland Security: An Introduction with Applications* (Boston: Elsevier Butterworth-Heinemann, 2007); *Police & Community: Concepts & Cases* (Needham, MA: Allyn & Bacon, 2001); *Criminal Justice: An Introduction* (Boston: Butterworth-Heinemann, 1997); *Retail Security & Shrinkage Protection* (Boston: Butterworth-Heinemann, 1993); and *Modern Security & Loss Prevention Management* (Boston: Butterworth, 1989). Purpura has also been a contributing editor to three security periodicals; written numerous articles published in journals, magazines, and newsletters; and been involved in a variety of editorial projects for publishers. He holds bachelor's and master's degrees in criminal justice from the University of Dayton and Eastern Kentucky University, respectively. He has also studied in Europe, Asia, and the former Soviet Union.

Section I

The History and Profession of Security

Chapter 1

Definition, Role, and History of Security

Chapter Learning Objectives

After reading this chapter, you should be able to:

1. Write a definition of security
2. Explain why it is difficult to differentiate *private security* and *public police and public security*
3. Describe the contexts of security
4. Explain at least two major roles of security
5. Discuss at least five benefits of studying history
6. Understand at least five trends in the historical development of security
7. Trace the history of security from prehistoric times to the Peelian Reform Movement
8. Describe the history of security in the United States
9. Examine the formation of the security industry in the United States

Terms to Know

security
private security
public police and public security

privatization
private justice
contexts of security
security methodology
security strategies
security officer
contract security company
proprietary security
Laws of Hammurabi
Great Wall of China
polis
Praetorian Guard
vigiles
feudalism
frankpledge system
tithing
Magna Carta
Statute of Westminster
Nicolas-Gabriel de La Reynie
Eugène François Vidocq
fence
Henry Fielding
Bow Street Runners
Sir Robert Peel
Allan Pinkerton
Henry Wells and William Fargo
Edwin Holmes
Washington Perry Brink
William J. Burns
J. Edgar Hoover
Homestead, Pennsylvania, strike
Baldwin–Felts Detective Agency
Battle of Matewan
Battle of Blair Mountain
National Industrial Security Program
George R. Wackenhut

QUIZ

This quiz serves to prime the reader's mind and begin the reading, thinking, and studying processes for this chapter. The answers to all of the questions are found within this chapter.

1. Why is the distinction between *private security* and *public police and public security* becoming increasingly blurred?
2. Does federal law require applicant screening and training for all private security officers in the United States, or does the responsibility fall to the states?
3. Did the Great Wall of China succeed in providing security and protection from invading armies?
4. The concepts and security practices that form the basis for modern American security can be traced to which country?
5. During the 1800s, before Allan Pinkerton developed his security business, what great advantage did bank and train robbers exploit to succeed in their crimes?
6. What agency was responsible for the security and protection of President Lincoln when he was assassinated?

Introduction

This chapter provides a foundation for the reader by defining basic terms, discussing the various contexts in which *security* is applied, and explaining the roles of the security function in organizations and what security practitioners seek to accomplish and how. In addition, the history of security is presented so that we can learn the progression of security and how it has been applied through the centuries.

Security Defined

Security is the quality or state of being secure. It is freedom from danger, and it implies safety—freedom from fear or anxiety (Merriam–Webster Online Dictionary, 2008).

The term *security* was first used in popular English literature sometime prior to A.D. 1050. The etymology of *security* is as follows: "Security \Se cu ri ty\, noun; plural Securities. [Latin securitas: compare to French s[`e] curit[`e]...]" (Webster's Online Dictionary, 2008).

The subject of this book focuses on security methodology and strategies to protect people, assets, buildings, and operations at businesses, institutions, and other organizations. An entity often has an individual and/or department responsible for the security function. In an entity, security management plans, implements, and monitors a variety of protection strategies, such as security officers, access controls, alarm systems, and investigations.

ISSUE

Can *Private Security* and *Public Police and Public Security* Be Differentiated?

To assist the reader, a definition of each term is presented, followed by general distinctions between each and explanations as to why the distinctions are becoming blurred.

Private security is defined by the "Report of the Task Force on Private Security" (U.S. Department of Justice 1976, 4) as follows: "Private security includes those self-employed individuals and privately funded business entities and organizations providing security-related services to specific clientele for a fee, for the individual or entity that retains or employs them, or for themselves, in order to protect their persons, private property, or interests from varied hazards." The report (U.S. Department of Justice 1976, 3) also states: "A universally acceptable and explicit definition is difficult to construct because private security is not only identified with the performance of certain functions and activities of a public nature, but also encompasses many activities for the private sector." Figure 1.1 shows a private security officer patrolling in a public location.

Private security personnel give attention to following company policies and procedures and satisfying the protection needs of their customers or clients. They emphasize prevention of crime. The role of private security is continuously expanding (e.g., information and information technology

FIGURE 1.1 **Private security officer in a public place. (® Shutterstock.com. With permission.)**

security, protection against terrorism) and being integrated throughout organizations, as described in this and other chapters.

Public police and public security refer to government-funded (i.e., tax dollars) law enforcement and security efforts that concentrate on public locations and citizens in general. Public police agencies and many levels and types of government bodies have become more involved in public security efforts since the September 11, 2001, terrorist attacks. These public police agencies and other government bodies are on the local, state, and federal levels, including the military branches. Whereas most public police officers focus on law enforcement, other officers may have public security duties, such as protecting a police building and other government buildings. Governments also employ nonuniformed security specialists who are involved in security duties, but they may also be law enforcement officers and make arrests when appropriate. For instance, on the federal level, the U.S. Secret Service and the U.S. Marshal's Service are heavily involved in public security duties, but they also make arrests. The former protects dignitaries, while the latter protects courthouses and witnesses. The Federal Bureau of Investigation (FBI) is a dominant law enforcement agency with broad domestic and international jurisdiction to control crime and enhance security. The FBI's National Security Branch focuses on counterterrorism, counterintelligence, and intelligence while also providing intelligence to state and local police. The U.S. Department of Homeland Security also plays a major role in law enforcement and security efforts, as explained in the next chapter.

ASIS International (2005, 4) states: "Many people think of the security field as being synonymous with the private sector, and to a large extent, that is true. However, there are many security opportunities in government agencies, particularly at the federal level. Public sector security personnel perform many of the same functions as their proprietary counterparts in the private sector."

A distinction between *private security* and *public police and public security* is becoming increasingly difficult, as both of these sectors (i.e., private sector/business and public sector/government) are taking on characteristics of the other. For example, privately employed security officers are sometimes provided with special police commissions by government to enhance their arrest powers. At the same time, since the 9/11 attacks, public police have increasingly studied and applied private security methods. In addition, numerous locations are protected through partnerships that combine public police and private security services, and both sectors may train together and share information and resources to improve effectiveness. A city's central business district may be protected by such a partnership. As another illustration, we see police substations at shopping malls protected by private security.

Private security is seen at many businesses, institutions, and other locations. A corporation, for example, may establish its own proprietary security force. An alternative is for the corporation to contract the security function to an outside security service firm. Either way, the corporation pays for its security at its private location. On the other hand, public policing and public security are paid for through tax dollars and serve public locations. Increasingly, we are seeing exceptions to these generalizations. For instance, numerous government entities (e.g., courthouses, schools, and military bases) are protected by contract security firms, often because it is argued that it is less expensive than employing government workers, who typically receive better pay, benefits, and pensions. This is known as **privatization**.

Public college campuses are known to employ various types (also called *classes*, such as Class I, II, and III, depending on the state where the college is located) of police and security personnel. Examples are regular police officers with full academy training and full arrest powers; another class of police officers with less training and limited arrest powers who may focus on traffic and parking; and contract security officers who are assigned to access points at roads and buildings, observe closed-circuit television (CCTV) monitors, and perform other duties.

Although those who provide public security and public policing are paid through tax dollars and serve the public, they may, in the course of their work, serve private-sector needs. This is illustrated when a public police officer works with neighborhood businesses in an effort to prevent robberies through security surveys and other security strategies.

Public police often work part-time ("moonlight") at private-sector locations. Depending on state law, they may be permitted to wear their uniform and equipment, typically paid for through tax dollars, in this part-time capacity. In addition, many retired police officers work in private security.

Traditionally, public police have been "reactive." A crime occurs, and they quickly respond to investigate. Traditionally, private security has prevented crime. Businesses exist to make a profit and seek to avoid becoming a "mini criminal justice system." Arrests are deemphasized in the private sector. Today, public police are increasingly "proactive." They seek to control crime prior to its occurrence through data systems that provide quick information on subjects stopped on the street, through crime analysis units and software that anticipate crime, and through citizen crime prevention programs, such as Neighborhood Watch. This proactive approach intensified following the 9/11 terrorist attacks; public police and other government agencies have become much more involved in public security through, for example, countersurveillance (e.g., watching for adversaries who may be conducting surveillance of potential targets or victims) and emergency planning.

In reference to legal issues, private security personnel generally possess citizen-arrest powers from legislative statutes, unless government provides them with additional arrest powers and broader jurisdiction to exercise arrest powers. (Arrest powers are covered in Chapter 9.) Public police and public security personnel are also granted their arrest powers through legislative statutes; these powers of arrest, search and seizure, surveillance, and questioning of suspects are greater than those powers granted to private security personnel. At the same time, public police and public security personnel are controlled more by federal and state constitutions than private security practitioners, who are often controlled by government regulation of the security industry and fear of a lawsuit.

Another distinguishing characteristic of private versus public personnel is training. Generally, private personnel, especially the entry-level security officer, receives much less training than, say, a public police officer. There are exceptions to this generalization, as seen, for example, with the training of private-sector nuclear security officers.

The private and public sectors also show differences in the way they process suspected criminal cases. A police officer may arrest a subject and take the subject to jail for processing, and a prosecutor will decide whether enough evidence is available for successful prosecution of the case. A corporation, for example, may produce evidence of embezzlement from an internal corporate investigation. Public police may be contacted. Alternatively, the suspected employee may be handled through what has been termed **private justice**, whereby the matter is settled internally to avoid bad publicity, without reporting the evidence to public police. This avenue does have its legal pitfalls. For instance, a suspect may be fired based upon weak evidence, and a civil suit may result.

Interestingly, history shows periods where either the private sector or public sector increased in importance because the other did not keep up with protection needs. For example, the Peelian Reform Movement in England revolutionized public police and public security because of the ineffectiveness of private security. In the past few decades, private security has filled gaps because of the inadequacies of public police and public security. Illustrations include the needs of businesses to protect against computer crime and disasters.

In conclusion, it is sometimes difficult to differentiate the sectors. To assist the reader in differentiating the sectors, these questions can be asked: Where does the money originate from (e.g., tax dollars or private sector) to pay the practitioner's salary? What arrest powers does the practitioner hold?

Critical Thinking

In the United States, should we prohibit all private security and maintain only public police and public security? Why or why not?

The Contexts of Security

The **contexts of security** refer to the different ways in which the term *security* is described by various disciplines as it is applied in specific environments. Although the meaning of the term may differ depending on the particular discipline and environment, we are better able to understand the term through diverse contexts. Webster's Online Dictionary (2008) offers a variety of contexts of security, as described next.

Besides the context described in the previous paragraphs, in the context of information technology (IT), security protects computers and their services from all natural and human-made hazards and provides an assurance that the computer performs its critical functions correctly; it also includes protection against unauthorized modification, destruction, and denial of services.

Our government seeks to protect our nation through homeland security and national security. Although both are intertwined, the former concentrates on domestic protection, civil defense and emergency preparedness, and the protection of infrastructure, whereas the latter focuses on the protection of our nation through armed forces and protection of our global interests.

In a military context, security is: "The condition achieved when designated information, material, personnel, activities and installations are protected against espionage, sabotage, subversion and terrorism, as well as against loss or unauthorized disclosure."

The private sector (i.e., business) uses the term *security* in various contexts: "The collateral that is given, deposited, or pledged to guarantee an obligation or the payment of a debt." In other words, security is property that a creditor can claim if a loan is not paid. Bankers are hesitant to lend without good security from a customer.

The term *securities* is common to the financial and investment industries. "Securities are tradable interests representing financial value. They are often represented by a certificate. They include shares of corporate stock or mutual funds, bonds issued by corporations or governmental agencies, stock options and other derivative securities, limited partnership units, and various other formal 'investment instruments (Economic Expert, 2009).'" The Securities and Exchange Commission (SEC), a government agency that regulates federal securities laws and the securities industry and stock markets, refers to "any instrument commonly known as a 'security'" (Section 3a item 10 of the Securities and Exchange Act of 1934).

The Roles of Security

The fundamental role of security is to protect people, assets, buildings, and operations. Businesses, institutions, and other organizations naturally seek peace and tranquility in the workplace so that objectives can be accomplished with minimum interruption.

Among the roles of security is the application of various methodologies to produce the most efficient and effective security strategies for optimum protection and return on investment. Security executives and managers apply various security methodologies and strategies that result in plans fulfilled by security personnel such as security officers and investigators. Chapter 4 explains security methodologies, and it is followed by Chapter 5 on security strategies. Here, we cover the "big picture" to assist the reader in understanding the beginning point from which security is implemented.

Security Methodology

Security methodology refers to the study of the methods, principles, and postulates applied by the security discipline. The methodology of a discipline includes theories, concepts, ideas, rationales, and philosophical assumptions. Examples of security methodologies are: a security survey of a building that pinpoints weaknesses in protection and assists in planning improved security; the theory and concepts of crime prevention through environmental design, whereby architectural design inhibits criminal behavior; and the principle that the least number of access points at a building increases protection. Methodology serves as a foundation and set of tools for planning and implementing security strategies.

Security Strategies

Security strategies develop from security methodology and focus on management application of human resources, information technology, physical security, policies and procedures, emergency response and recovery, investigations, and other components of security for optimum utilization and advantage.

The basic objectives and strategies of security are: deterrence, deception, detection, delay, denial, mitigation, and response. Security *deters* when offenders observe security personnel and physical security (e.g., CCTV and access controls) and avoid the potential target while seeking a weaker target. *Deception* tricks an adversary into seeing a target as less desirable. If an offender chooses to victimize a particular location, security should be in place to *detect* intrusion. Strategies for detection include an intrusion alarm system, CCTV, and security officers. Physical security, such as a fence and locks, *delay* an offender and possibly force the offender to forgo the attack and seek another victim. In addition, a delay may provide enough time for detection and *response* by security officers or public police. If an offender continues to try to penetrate a target to gain access, formidable security (e.g., a strong, steel door or, in the case of computer security, firewalls and other strategies) can *deny* access. *Mitigation* refers to reducing the impact of an adverse event, such as retailers making frequent bank deposits to reduce the take in case of robbery or burglary.

Security strategies not only focus on perimeter protection and preventing offenders from gaining access, but also on protecting against many other threats and hazards. These include violence, internal theft, computer crime, fraud, espionage, substance abuse, fire, accidents, terrorism, and natural and human-made disasters.

The Pervasive and Global Role of Security

Senior executives in organizations who understand the importance of security for business survival influence the role of security. In such organizations, security operations are integrated with many corporate functions (e.g., risk management, information technology, human resources, legal, audit, facilities, business continuity, and safety).

Within a corporation, security may be directed by senior management to develop itself into a profit center or else face outsourcing. In other words, security management must sell services to generate revenue. Otherwise, the security department will be dissolved, security personnel will be unemployed, and the corporation will seek the services of a contract security firm. Examples of services that an in-house corporate security department can possibly offer to other businesses for a profit are training, patrol, and investigations.

Security within an organization is linked to external organizations that provide assistance when unfortunate events occur. If a criminal investigation is required or an arrest is to be made, businesses work in conjunction with police and prosecutors. Security personnel may testify in a criminal case. If a fire, accident, or other emergency occurs on the premises, various government agencies respond, and security typically plays a role in protecting the injured and the scene, directing traffic, and assisting with an investigation.

For corporations with business interests in multiple countries, the role of security can be global. Protection may be required for employees, corporate sites, and assets, wherever they may be, even in transit.

As stated earlier, although the term *private security* is used in the security literature, there is a huge amount of *public security*. Federal, state, and local governments, as well as the military, maintain huge numbers of personnel, and expend enormous resources, on security. In addition, government bodies maintain contracts with private security businesses for protection services.

YOUR CAREER IN SECURITY

Security Officer

Security officer, often referred to by the less professional term, *security guard*, is an employment title that involves the protection of people, assets, buildings, and operations. The title spans many types of workplaces, and the position varies substantially in terms of requirements, training, duties, and pay. **Contract security companies** that provide a protection service (i.e., uniformed security officers) to businesses, institutions, and other organizations employ most security officers. These contract firms vary in terms of professionalism, ethics, intensity of background checks of applicants, turnover, and other factors. To protect the public, each state has a

---

regulatory unit, often within a state police agency, that requires the license and registration of contract firms, criminal background checks of owners, and adherence to laws and regulations. Security officers are regulated in a similar way.

Many businesses and institutions (e.g., hospitals, colleges) maintain their own security force. Known as **proprietary security**, or in-house security, the following services are provided from within the organization, rather than contracting them to an outside firm: screening applicants, training, providing uniforms and equipment, and supervision. States often require proprietary security organizations and security officers to be licensed and registered.

An organization may opt for a combination of contract and proprietary security, often referred to as a *hybrid security operation*. For example, maintaining an in-house security manager can reinforce consistency of security operations when there is turnover of security contractors and/or contract security officers. Colleges and other government entities, for instance, employ commissioned police officers to perform certain duties (e.g., conduct investigations and make arrests), while employing contract security officers to perform duties requiring less training (e.g., observing CCTV monitors).

Debate has raged for decades over which is superior—contract or proprietary security officers. It has been argued that the hiring of a contract firm is both less expensive and less time consuming for a business as it concentrates on its core operations. On the other hand, security may suffer if there is high turnover of contract security officers, which is a problem in this industry. The turnover of proprietary security officers is often less than that of contract security officers. Of course, there are exceptions to these generalizations.

Nature of the Work

Security officers perform an array of duties at stationary posts, such as doors and gates, and while on patrol by foot or vehicle. They may check the credentials of people and vehicles and inspect packages. Besides *observing* and *reporting* numerous types of events, they monitor sensors and CCTV cameras, interview witnesses and victims, write reports, direct traffic, supervise parking, perform crowd control, and, depending on the employer, issue traffic citations, make arrests, and testify in court.

The specific job duties depend on employer needs. A mall or theater often requires the protection of people and property in parking lots. Security personnel at transportation systems (e.g., air, rail, truck, port) protect passengers, employees, vehicles, freight, equipment, and buildings; they may employ canine units, metal detectors, and sensors to detect weapons of mass destruction.

A major duty of security officers, spanning virtually all security environments, is positive relations with the customers they serve and protect. This entails courtesy, respect, and self-control, even when the officer is faced with a difficult customer during a stressful event. For example, a customer may resent security controls. As a security officer, could you act professionally if a customer curses you because he is upset about security policies and procedures that limit his access to a controlled area or prohibit him from parking in a certain parking space? Training helps officers to prepare for such events.

Requirements

There is no federal law mandating applicant screening and training for all security officers in the United States. However, certain industries, such as aviation and nuclear power, are required under federal law to maintain strict applicant screening and intense training for security personnel. States differ on screening (usually a criminal records check), licensing, registration, and training hours required.

The American Society for Industrial Security (ASIS) International has written the "Private Security Officer Selection and Training" guideline. This is a voluntary guideline recommending employment screening criteria for security officers and 48 hours of training within the first 100 days of employment (ASIS International 2004).

Generally, there are minimal educational and experience requirements for entry-level security officer positions. Employers often prefer to hire applicants with at least a high school diploma for armed positions. To improve professionalism and reduce liability, employers typically provide one or more of the following types of training: in-class, on-line, and on-the-job. Topics for training include laws of arrest and search and seizure, customer relations, crime prevention, safety and fire protection, emergencies, and information for the particular workplace.

Armed officers receive more training than unarmed officers because of the potential for liability. State law usually mandates specific hours of training for armed officers. Topics include safety, firearms, use of force, and weapons retention. Periodically, officers qualify with their weapons on a firing range (U.S. Department of Labor 2008).

Security officers must be honest and have integrity. They should possess good judgment skills while following company policies and procedures. When emergencies occur, they must take charge, until relieved by a superior, to ensure the safety of people and property.

A major challenge for security officers is to remain alert during routine day-to-day duties. For example, officers must remain attentive when studying and verifying the credentials presented by a person at an access point, while watching CCTV monitors, or during late night or early morning shift work.

Salary

Employment opportunities for security officers are expected to grow faster than the average for all occupations. Presently, there are over one million security officers in the United States, and the projected employment is 1,216,000 by 2016. The salary varies widely, depending on geographic location, industry, education, and experience. The U.S. Department of Labor (2008) estimated that median annual salaries ranged from $21,530 to $27,130 in 2006. Security officers in certain industries earn higher pay, such as at nuclear power plants. In 2008, employer Web sites showed a salary range of between $42,500 and $54,700 per year, plus benefits, for armed nuclear security officers. Today, there are thousands of security practitioners who began their careers as entry-level security officers, advanced, and are today earning salaries from $50,000 to $100,000 and above.

Advice

Experience as an entry-level security officer is beneficial for multiple reasons: It helps individuals decide whether they have an interest in the security profession; the employment experience and training can be placed on a resume to build one's background; advancement opportunities may develop to supervisory positions, specialized positions, or the public sector; and the practitioner may decide to establish a contract security business. Many security organizations offer a multiplicity of services, besides security officers, that can be perceived as avenues for advancement. These include undercover investigations, background checks on employment applicants, polygraph examinations, executive protection, risk analysis, consulting, and corporate training.

The History of Security

Security challenges have faced humans throughout history. The need for security resulted from many threats such as wild beasts, an invading tribe or army, criminals, or human-made or natural disasters. Similar to earlier generations, present-day societies, governments, organizations, families, and individuals face security challenges. Today, we face enormous security challenges as global populations increase and the competition for resources intensifies. Although this book concentrates on protecting people, assets, buildings, and operations in businesses, institutions, and organizations, such protection does not exist in a vacuum, and it is affected by global events.

Critical Thinking

Do you think we face security challenges today that are more serious than at any other time in history? Was there a time in history when security challenges were more serious than today?

The Importance of History

There are many reasons for studying history (Stearns 2007). Here, the priority is its relevance to security. To begin with, history assists us in understanding change. Although change can be traumatic, it is an inevitable part of life. We should meet change with a positive view and try our best to work with it, although it can be challenging. Change can be beneficial, and what was perceived earlier in a negative light may produce positive results.

Security practitioners face challenging changes in the form of new technology, new types of crimes, a host of evolving threats and hazards, and political, social, and economic transformations. In addition, security practitioners face changes in the organizations they serve, often resulting from external forces. Examples might be a new type of crime committed against a corporation or a budget cut in security because of an economic slowdown.

History helps us to understand the past, the present, how our world evolved, and how to anticipate the future. By learning from others, we can study examples of success and avoid mistakes. History is filled with over-confident ideas and plans that, when implemented, resulted in failure and disaster. In our effort to anticipate the future, history serves as an important variable in planning.

Because we are bombarded with headlines of national and international events on a daily basis, knowledge of history is indispensable to the security practitioner. History helps us to look beyond the headlines. Security planning is enhanced by interpreting the significance of events with an understanding of history. A security manager responsible for several retail outlets in a city will be unlikely to overreact from heavy media coverage and sensationalism over a spike in robberies of retail stores in the city during December if the manager is aware that such a spike occurs every year during the holidays. However, the manager will still maintain security strategies, monitor the crimes, and look for significant changes from previous holiday seasons. If a security director of a global corporation learns of unrest in a country containing corporate personnel and interests, further fact gathering and planning will likely follow, with the history of the country being an important part of the input.

History provides a base from which we can interpret various contexts and perspectives. For instance, the definition of terrorism has changed over time and varies depending on the person defining it. In addition, it is often said that "one person's terrorist is another person's freedom fighter." Another example is security. Since the 9/11 attacks, there has been a renewed interest in security and its importance. Prior to the 9/11 attacks, many people often found security annoying; however, now there is greater understanding of its goal of increasing safety, even though it can still be an inconvenience.

History offers ethical guidelines. By studying dilemmas and adversity faced by others, and the decisions they made, we can gain perspectives on appropriate behavior.

History can help us to reduce stress. If we understand why certain events occurred in the past, then if such events occur in our work, we can possibly avoid the stress of trying to figure out why the events occurred. For instance, if a corporate investigator works long hours with police and prosecutors preparing evidence for a case, but the defendant is acquitted because of violations of the defendant's constitutional rights, knowledge of the history and application of the Bill of Rights—the first ten amendments to the U.S. Constitution—will serve as input for understanding why the defendant was acquitted.

History assists us in understanding our world, organizations, and individuals. It helps us as we seek to understand obvious and ulterior motives, conduct investigations and research, and draw conclusions and take action.

Trends in the Historical Development of Security

The historical development of security reveals several trends that are cyclical in nature (Christman et al. 2003, 20):

1. Private security initiatives generally precede government initiatives. The inadequacies of government protection services are often an opportunity for private security services.
2. Public- and private-sector security play a role in class struggles and attempts to control the underclass (have-nots). (See the coverage on miner unions in a subsequent box.)
3. There is a strong relationship between commerce and security needs. Each type of business (e.g., transportation, utilities, and Internet) differs in its risks and security needs.
4. Demographics (e.g., population size and age distribution) affect law enforcement and security. Immigrants who do not understand the language and culture of their newly adopted country create security challenges. A resort community has different protection needs than a campus.
5. The military has exerted an influence over security, police, and fire departments. Examples are the use of a paramilitary organizational structure and chain of command (e.g., sergeants, lieutenants, and so forth).
6. Security methods are generally a step behind the latest innovative methods of criminals.
7. Frequently, security initiatives follow serious losses. The losses from the 9/11 attacks serve as an example.

8. Serious losses can lead to the need for mutual protection. Homeland security is one example, whereby various levels of government and the private sector united for enhanced protection.

Prehistoric Times and Early History

During prehistoric times, when humans banded together for protection, they employed security strategies that were somewhat similar to security strategies applied in later centuries and today. Figure 1.2 illustrates how cave dwellers implemented layered security strategies that presented multiple obstacles for adversaries and beasts. These included a cave that was at a high elevation for safety and observation, a narrow path to the cave along steep cliffs, fire, dogs to provide an alarm warning through barking and to attack intruders, and armed sentries.

In early civilizations, as humans interacted, conflict resulted in retaliatory action. Revenge became the norm. Attempts were made to curb the cycle of violence through civil justice, whereby victims were compensated for their losses. As economies developed, laws were needed to protect people and property. The **Laws of Hammurabi**, King of Babylon (1900 B.C.), became the first written laws. They specified responsibilities of the individual to the group, civil law between individuals, penalties for violations, and *lex talionis*—the principle that equal injury could be inflicted for the injury suffered ("an eye for an eye").

FIGURE 1.2   Cave dwellers employed security strategies that were somewhat similar to security strategies applied in later centuries and today. (Art by Julie Helms. With permission.)

FIGURE 1.3   The Great Wall of China was a grand security fortification that did not live up to its expectation of protection against invading armies. (® Shutterstock. com. With permission.)

As early civilizations developed, huge walls and fortifications were built with inexpensive labor. The **Great Wall of China** (Figure 1.3), built between the seventh and fourth century B.C., is the longest structure ever built, at over 4,000 miles. It was designed to protect against invading armies and barbarians. This massive structure consisted primarily of passes, signal towers, and walls. Passes were 30-foot-high strongholds permitting access through a gate and located at major roads and trade routes. Signal towers were often built on hilltops and used for military communications that consisted of smoke signals during the day and fire or lanterns during the night. The walls were 23 to 26 feet high and were constructed of a variety of materials (e.g., stone, wood), depending on what was available in the area. The designers of the Great Wall had high aspirations of protection; however, it was unable to withstand a major attack (Encyclopedia Britannica 2008).

Many other civilizations used walls for protection. Ancient Greece, for example, is known for the **polis**, also referred to as a city-state, which originated about 600–500 B.C. It included a city, surrounding farmland, and a central fortress for protection.

The designers of Ancient Rome knew the importance of security. The city was constructed on seven hills, which enhanced defenses, with a view of the Tiber River, and about 15 miles from the sea. Roman legions were employed to fight wars and to maintain domestic order. Augustus, the first emperor of Rome (27 B.C.–A.D. 14), formed the **Praetorian Guard** to protect the emperor and his property. This protection force, also referred to as *urban cohorts*, is credited with being an early and effective police force and was assigned to the city to maintain law and order. Later, Augustus formed nonmilitary **vigiles**, resembling night watchmen. They functioned as police and firefighters (Post and Kingsbury 1977; Ursic and Pagano 1974).

The Anglo-Saxon period in England (A.D. 500–1066) is noteworthy because its customs of protection are still applied today. This was a time when the Romans were unable to conquer England. Security and law enforcement were a community responsibility. When a crime occurred, a "hue and cry" was sounded as the community banded together to capture the offender. Today, we have citizen arrest and *posse comitatus* (i.e., an authority requesting citizens to assist with stopping unlawful behavior).

When the Greek and Roman empires fell, Europe entered the Middle Ages (A.D. 400–1500). It was a time of slowly developing commercial and urban activity and royal power. **Feudalism** dominated this era and entailed overlords providing security to farmers and the granting of land for military service. A major form of security was the castle, a fortification with thick, high walls, towers, a drawbridge, and a moat (Figure 1.4).

The **frankpledge system** reached England from France (A.D. 600–900), and it brought about communal responsibility for security and justice. Ten families formed a **tithing**, and ten tithings formed a "hundred," supervised by a constable appointed by local nobility. Ten "hundreds" equaled a "shire," under the power of a "reeve" who was appointed by the king to enforce royal law and to collect taxes.

FIGURE 1.4 **Castle with moat built during the Middle Ages. (® Shutterstock.com. With permission.)**

In A.D. 1066, William, the Duke of Normandy (presently France), defeated England. He brought about several changes: He weakened the tithing system, centralized government and security, made a crime an offense against the state (rather than against the individual), and separated law enforcement and judicial roles. King William divided England into fifty-five military districts, also called *shires*, and a military officer, also called a *reeve*, was assigned to each. The word *sheriff* eventually evolved from the use of *shire* and *reeve*.

When King John reigned, beginning in 1199, he became a brutal monarch who was hated by many. In 1215, he was forced to sign the **Magna Carta**, which emphasized a distinction between national and local government, restored local political power to communities, and provided civil liberties, such as due process and trial by jury, that are part of the Bill of Rights within the U.S. Constitution (Purpura 2001, 8).

By 1285, the need for community protection became such a major problem that King Edward I issued the **Statute of Westminster**, which established a police and justice system. In addition, a "watch and ward" was organized for night duty (watch) to supplement constables who worked during the day (ward). All men were required to participate. The Statute of Westminster also required all males between 15 and 60 years of age to have a weapon in their home. Essentially, community responsibility and the "hue and cry" resurfaced.

During the 1600s, in England, increasing trade and business required security for goods. A variety of private police forces were formed, such as merchant police and dock police. In addition, a reward system was established to draw the public into reporting criminals.

England is not the only country that contributed to the history and development of security and policing. For example, in 1666, King Louis XIV of France appointed **Nicolas-Gabriel de La Reynie** to the position of lieutenant of police. As an innovator, de La Reynie developed crime prevention through preventive patrol, street lighting, and hygiene (maintaining clean streets and medical examinations of prostitutes). Paris police excelled in investigations. By the end of the 1800s, Paris police investigators were world renowned. Interestingly, while France emphasized criminal intelligence, informants, and plainclothes police, England and the United States concentrated on uniformed police to avoid criticism for domestic spying (Stead 1983, 14–15).

Eugène François Vidocq, a French soldier, criminal, and privateer (i.e., a private warship authorized by a country to attack foreign shipping), formed the first detective agency, *Le bureau des renseignements* (Office of Intelligence), in 1833. He hired ex-convicts, and authorities tried to close his business many times. Vidocq was finally arrested in 1842 for unlawful imprisonment and taking money under false pretenses after he solved an embezzlement case. He was sentenced to five years, but the

Court of Appeals released him. Vidocq is credited with introducing innovations such as record keeping, criminology, and ballistics to the investigative process. He was first to make plaster casts of shoe impressions for evidence. He also created indelible ink and unalterable bond paper (Wikipedia 2008).

In England, during the 1700s and the Industrial Revolution, urbanization and related problems (e.g., slave labor in factories, slums, poverty, homelessness, and crime) increased pressure to curb crime and protect business interests. Although taxes were used to pay for watchmen, criminals prowled the streets with impunity. The crime problems included prostitution, juvenile delinquency, counterfeiting, and use of a **fence** (i.e., a criminal who buys and sells stolen items). Merchants and other citizens of London had to resort to arming themselves and setting wolf traps to catch burglars (Germann et al. 1974, 59). The wealthy were able to afford servants and others to provide security. If a theft occurred, a thief-taker (or thief-catcher) could be hired. Originally, a thief-taker would be paid to recover stolen items and capture the thief. The thief-taker was usually an experienced constable, knowledgeable of the underworld, and capable of recovering the stolen items. Eventually, recoveries were made, and the thief remained anonymous. Unfortunately, this strategy was also transformed by some of the thief-takers into a thriving, illegal business enterprise. A thief-taker would hold some of the items as a supplement to payment, and the thief would not be brought to justice. Jonathan Wild was a notorious thief-taker who operated his endeavor for seven years. His illegal business plan was to not only locate stolen items, but to hire a group of thieves who stole on demand. Then, he would seek a commission to "find" the property. He was also responsible for the arrest and execution of numerous felons. Wild was successful in his illegal business, advertised himself as "Thief-taker General" of London, and lived in luxury until his execution (Johnson et al. 2008, 215).

Henry Fielding, a trendsetter in crime prevention through police action, was appointed magistrate in London in 1748 and formed the **Bow Street Runners**, often referred to as the first detective unit. This unit was paid a salary and was not dependent on compensation for the recovery of stolen items. Fielding's strategy was to dispatch the unit immediately to a crime scene upon being notified to improve the chances for an apprehension of the criminal. Fielding was a writer who became famous as the author of *Tom Jones*, a description of life in England in the 1700s. He also wrote about crime prevention and published the *Covent Garden Gazette*, which publicized descriptions of criminals and their methods of operation; readers were asked to report on suspected criminals (Johnson et al. 2008, 216).

FIGURE 1.5   British police officer ("Bobbie"). (® Shutterstock.com. With permission.)

By the 1800s, crime was rampant in England, with numerous crimes punishable by hanging, even for petty offenses such as stealing food or picking pockets. The death penalty did not deter crime. In addition, London was without an organized system of law enforcement. **Sir Robert Peel** assumed the office of home secretary in 1822 and emphasized the need for a professional police force. Many English citizens feared that a public police force would infringe upon their rights. To appease the citizenry, Peel offered to reform the criminal law and reduce the number of death-penalty crimes in exchange for a professional police force that would be unarmed and engage in preventive patrol to reduce crime. Following seven years of heated debate to gain support, Peel's Metropolitan Police Act was passed by Parliament. Opposition continued, and an assassination attempt on Peel by Daniel M'Naghten went wrong when he shot and killed Peel's secretary by mistake. The police were called "Peelers" and "Blue Devils," and then "Bobbies," after Sir Robert Peel (Figure 1.5). Although controversial, Peel's new system revolutionized policing and was copied around the globe (Purpura 1997, 118).

PRINCIPLES OF THE METROPOLITAN POLICE ACT OF 1829

Sir Robert Peel established the first modern police force in London in 1829 (Gaines and Miller 2009, 136). The Peelian Principles have been applied to police departments worldwide, and the ideas behind select principles also apply to security in businesses.

1. The police force must be organized along military lines.
2. Police administrators and officers must be under government control.
3. Emphasis must be placed on hiring qualified persons and training them properly.
4. New police officers must complete a probationary period; if they fail to meet standards during this time, they will not be hired as permanent officers.
5. Police personnel should be assigned to specific areas of the city for a specific time period.
6. Police headquarters must be centrally located in the city.
7. Police officers must maintain a proper appearance at all times in order to gain and keep the respect of citizens.
8. Individual police officers should be able to control their temper and refrain from violence whenever possible.
9. Police records must be kept in order to measure police effectiveness.

Critical Thinking

In reference to public policing, which Peelian Principle do you view as most important? Which do you view as least important? Which of the Peelian Principles is most helpful to business security?

The Development of Security in the United States

The concepts and security practices that form the basis for modern American security can be traced to early England (U.S. Department of Justice 1976, 30–38). Colonists settling in a new and alien land banded together under a system of mutual protection and accountability that stemmed from early Anglo-Saxon time. Prior to American independence, protection of the colonists and their property was the responsibility of town constables and sheriffs, supplemented in many towns, in English tradition, with watchmen who would patrol the streets at night. These watchmen remained familiar figures and constituted the primary security measure until the establishment of full-time police departments in the mid-1800s.

To ensure adequate protection, most local governments formalized the watch system and required each adult male inhabitant to serve a period as a watchman. A watchman's tour of duty usually began at 9 or 10 P.M. and ended at sunrise. During their tours of duty, the watchmen often encountered fires, Indian attacks, wild animals, runaway slaves, thieves, and grave robbers. They were expected to cope with these incidents and maintain order by quelling disturbances, arresting drunks, and enforcing the curfew. The watchman's job became increasingly difficult as industrialization and urbanization spread. Without training or legal support, and with little or no pay, most of those chosen to stand duty as watchmen would hire others to perform this unpleasant, thankless task. In addition, men convicted of petty crimes were sentenced to duty as watchmen. Although the task of protecting their communities had become more difficult and demanding, watchmen were vilified and downgraded in the eyes of their fellow colonists.

As security problems kept pace with the rapid growth of the country, public pressure mounted for increased and more effective protection. Attempts were made to add daytime complements to support and supplement the night watchmen, but it soon became apparent that the watch system was neither adequate nor efficient. This realization led to the formation of organized public police departments with full-time, paid personnel. These departments were modeled on the work of Sir Robert Peel. The earliest formal public police department in the United States can be traced to Boston (1838) and New York City (1844), and by 1856 police departments had been set up in Detroit, Cincinnati, Chicago, San Francisco, Los Angeles, Philadelphia, and Dallas. Although these early police departments were generally inefficient and often corrupt—and their personnel poorly trained—they represented a vast improvement over the watchman system. As the United States expanded west, and in rural areas in the East, sheriffs, marshals, and constables provided law enforcement over huge geographic areas. The sparsely settled frontier also required protection from bands of criminals and Indians. Military forts were scattered throughout the frontier and provided security to those in the fort or nearby.

The emergence of public police departments, however, did not mean the end of private citizen involvement in security. Public law enforcement agencies were in their early stage of development and could not keep pace with the mounting problem of crime in their communities. The incidence of crimes against property had become severe. The coupling of these facts forced industrial and business organizations to recognize the need for some form of effective security to protect their assets. Thus, in the 1850s, major components of the private security industry were developed in answer to this need.

Allan Pinkerton, who was born in Scotland, emigrated to the United States and served as a deputy sheriff in counties in Illinois before becoming the first police detective in Chicago. He formed the North West Police Agency in 1855 to provide protection for six Midwestern railroads, and in 1857 he formed the Pinkerton Protection Patrol to provide a private watchman service. Pinkerton agents tracked outlaws such as Jesse James, Butch Cassidy, and the Sundance Kid. (In a later era, their exploits would be recounted in popular movies.) Allan Pinkerton became widely known as a superb investigator. In addition, he saw a "hole in the market" and a business potential for security services that crossed jurisdictional lines because, when criminals robbed banks and trains and then crossed county and state borders, the local police were often unable or unwilling to leave their jurisdiction to pursue them. For more than 50 years, Pinkerton was the only company in the country engaged in interstate activities, especially the provision of security for many of the railroads. Pinkerton's company also provided security for industrial concerns and was hired as an intelligence-gathering unit for the Union Army. His company tried to obtain the job of protecting President Lincoln, but failed. The U.S. Secret Service did not exist at the time; protection was provided by the Washington, D.C., Police Department when Lincoln was assassinated (Johnson et al. 2008, 260). The Pinkerton company logo, an eye with the words "we never sleep," encouraged the term "private eye." Today, Pinkerton is still a thriving security company.

> During the mid-1800s, Allan Pinkerton saw a "hole in the market" and a business potential for security services that crossed jurisdictional lines because, when criminals robbed banks and trains and then crossed county and state borders, the local police were often unable or unwilling to leave their jurisdiction to pursue them.

As the United States grew and expanded west during the 1800s, another security need developed in the form of protection for the transportation of cash and other valuables. In 1852, **Henry Wells and William Fargo** capitalized on this market through Wells Fargo and Company. The early operation of this groundbreaking business is illustrated in many television programs and movies in which a stagecoach is under attack by a band of criminals or Indians, and a "shotgun rider" provides security as he tries to protect passengers and the strongbox.

Edwin Holmes began the first central-office burglar-alarm-monitoring operation in 1859, which evolved into Holmes Protection, Inc. When the American District Telegraph Company (ADT) was formed in 1874, the use of alarms and detection devices spread to provide protective services through the use of messengers and telegraph lines. By 1889, the use of electric protection for industrial and commercial enterprises in New York City was well established.

In 1859, **Washington Perry Brink** formed his trucking and package-delivery service in Chicago. He transported his first payroll in 1891, thereby initiating armored-car and courier service. By 1900, Brink had acquired a fleet of 85 wagons. Seventy-five years later, his security business was grossing more than $50 million in revenue each year.

During the 1800s, with the westward expansion of the United States, railroad lines moved into sparsely settled territories that had little or no public law enforcement. Trains were subject to attack by Indians and roving bands of outlaws who robbed passengers, stole cargo, dynamited track structures, and disrupted communications. In an effort to provide adequate protection of goods and passengers from constant dangers, various state legislatures passed railway police acts that enabled private railroads to establish proprietary security force with full police powers and broad jurisdictional reach. In many towns and territories, the railway police provided the only protective services until government units and law enforcement agencies were established. By 1914, U.S. railway police numbered about 14,000. Although railway police have been associated with public law enforcement for a long time, they are, in fact, private security forces granted law enforcement powers.

At the beginning of the 1900s, labor unions began to proliferate and to use strikes as a forceful tool for change. Because many factories were located in areas that had no effective public police force capable of maintaining order, private security agencies were called in by management to quell the disturbances surrounding strikes and to protect lives and property. During this period, two firms were established that became major security corporations. In 1909, Baker Industries, Inc., entered the businesses of fire control and burglary-detection equipment. That same year, the head of the FBI's predecessor agency, the Bureau of Investigation, formed the **William J. Burns** International Detective Agency and worked with the American Banking Association. During this time, the FBI was developing, and when **J. Edgar Hoover** became its director in 1924, the FBI evolved into a premier law enforcement agency noted for excellence in professionalism, training, scientific crime detection, and the ability to solve difficult crimes.

LABOR UNIONS VERSUS CORPORATIONS, SECURITY COMPANIES, POLICE AGENCIES, THE NATIONAL GUARD, AND U.S. MILITARY FORCES

During the late 1800s, as industry expanded in the United States, workers strived to improve their working conditions and pay. At the same time, management in corporations resisted the emerging demands of workers and unions. Labor unrest, strikes, and violence occurred frequently. To deal with these problems, corporations periodically hired security companies to protect assets and serve as strikebreakers. The violence from both sides focused national attention on the demands of workers and the brutality of the confrontations.

One of the most famous examples of these confrontations was the **Homestead, Pennsylvania, strike** of 1892. Henry Frick, an industrialist, hired a large Pinkerton security force to regain control of Andrew Carnegie's steel mill during a lockout (i.e., the closing of a business to resist the demands of workers) at Homestead. A gun battle ensued between strikers and the Pinkerton security force. Three security people and five workers were killed, in addition to numerous other casualties on both sides. The image of the Pinkerton firm and its employees was further tarnished when they surrendered and federal troops took over the plant. National attention to the violence resulted in "anti-Pinkertonism" laws that curbed the use of security companies in certain states and by the federal government.

Other security companies and industries also had their image tarnished from labor strife. For example, Henry Ford and his motor company were caught up in violent confrontations with workers in Michigan.

Virginia and West Virginia were among the states that were hotbeds of violence over labor issues, especially in the mining industry. The **Baldwin–Felts Detective Agency** played a role in such violence. William Baldwin and Thomas Felts founded their agency in the 1890s, with offices in Richmond, Virginia, and Bluefield, West Virginia. The company focused on crime (e.g., robbery) against railroads and coal-mine security (union busting, according to many), and it worked for the state of Virginia because Virginia had no state police at the time.

In the **Battle of Matewan**, on May 19, 1920, a confrontation developed between the Stone Mountain Mining Company and its Baldwin–Felts detectives versus Mayor Cabell Testerman, Chief of Police Sid Hatfield, and the citizens of Matewan, West Virginia. The issue involved evictions of striking workers from rented housing owned by the mining company. Hatfield urged citizens to arm themselves. A gunfight resulted in the death of two miners, Mayor Testerman, and seven Baldwin–Felts detectives, including Albert and Lee Felts, brothers of Thomas Felts. Kilkeary (2005) wrote: "Tom Felts'[s] lust for vengeance would rank right up there with another local but much better known vendetta—the Hatfields and McCoys."

Following the violence at Matewan, union membership increased, as did dynamite attacks of non-union mines and miners' tent colonies. The violence and deaths caused the governor to declare martial law. During this time, Sid Hatfield and several miners were indicted for the deaths of the Baldwin–Felts detectives, but they were acquitted by a sympathetic jury in Mingo County. Four Baldwin–Felts detectives were indicted for the death of Mayor Testerman and two miners, but they were acquitted in Greenbriar County, where miners were few. Later, Hatfield and thirty miners were charged with conspiracy linked to other acts of violence. On the day of the trial, August 1, 1921, the local sheriff, also a Hatfield, left the area to vacation at a resort in Virginia. When Sid Hatfield and a fellow defendant, Ed Chambers, arrived at the McDowell County courthouse for the trial, Baldwin–Felts detectives waited at the top of the steps, and as Hatfield approached, he was shot four times and killed. Chambers was also killed. The detectives claimed self-defense, and the case was never prosecuted (Kilkeary 2005).

Because Hatfield had become a hero to many miners, a large crowd gathered at the state capital in Charleston, West Virginia, to protest the killings. Union leaders urged the miners to fight. By August 24, 1921, about 5,000 men began to march toward Logan County, a non-union coal area. Security forces, police, and other West Virginia resources were unable to stop the march, so Governor Morgan requested federal troops from President Harding. Under the threat of being charged with treason, many of the marchers continued, and they took four Logan County deputies prisoner. Casualties mounted on both sides, and National Guard troops brought in planes to drop bombs. On September 1, President Harding finally dispatched federal troops from Fort Thomas, Kentucky, and an air squadron from Langley Field near Washington, D.C. The threat of fighting U.S. military forces caused the miners to surrender on Blair Mountain, West Virginia. During the violence, twelve miners and four men from the Logan County Sheriff's group were killed. Most of those who surrendered were escorted to trains to take them home. The leaders of the miners were indicted, but the prosecutions were not successful. The governor pardoned two individuals convicted of murdering Logan County deputies after serving three years of their eleven-year sentences. The defeat of the miners at the **Battle of Blair Mountain** interrupted union organizing in the Southern coalfields. However, in 1933, the National Industrial Recovery Act protected unions, and membership increased again (West Virginia State Archives 2007).

During the late 1800s and early 1900s, many local and state police agencies were formed in response to clashes among ethnic groups and labor–management unrest. Industrialists were especially interested in the formation of police agencies to be applied as strikebreakers. The Pennsylvania State Police, for example, was established in 1905 to combat striking coal miners, protect the coal industry, and safeguard "scabs"—non-union workers who were willing to replace the striking miners (Purpura 2001, 12–16).

Industry Formation

Prior to and during World War I, the concern for security intensified in U.S. industry, due not only to urbanization and industrial growth, but also to sabotage and espionage by politically active nationalists. Security services expanded to meet the demands, but tapered off when demands lessened after the war, reaching a low point during the Depression era.

Following World War I, there were significant developments in private security. A Burglary Protection Council was formed and held its first meeting in 1921, the results of which thrust Underwriters' Laboratories into the business of establishing specifications for, testing of, and certifying burglar-alarm systems and devices. This milestone was significant because consumers could look for standards of quality when seeking security services.

During the 1940s, World War II proved to be a significant catalyst in the growth of the private security industry. Prior to the awarding of national defense contracts, the federal government required that munitions contractors implement stringent and comprehensive security measures to protect classified materials and defense secrets from sabotage and espionage. The FBI assisted in establishing these security programs. Additionally, the federal government granted the status of auxiliary military police to more than 200,000 plant watchmen. Their primary duties included protection of war goods and products, supplies, equipment, and personnel. Local law enforcement agencies were responsible for their training. Because of the heightened emphasis on security within the government/military sphere, industry became increasingly aware of the need for security and its value in protection of their assets.

In 1952, the Korean War and the Cold War led to the formation of the Industrial Defense Program, now named the **National Industrial Security Program** (NISP). The NISP, operated by the Department of Defense (DOD), assists thousands of defense contractors in maintaining personnel, information, and physical security to protect against crimes such as espionage and sabotage.

The use of private security services and products expanded from the area of defense contractors to encompass all segments of the private and public sectors. For example, in 1954, **George R. Wackenhut** and three other former FBI agents formed the Wackenhut Corporation as a private investigative and contract security firm. By the 1970s, this firm had established itself as the third-largest contract guard and investigative agency in the country. The company also provided central-station alarms, screening of passengers in airports, and security services for the Trans-Alaska Pipeline.

Wackenhut achieved its growth, in large part, through the acquisition of smaller contract security firms, as did the William J. Burns International Detective Agency. Baker Industries used this technique (notably in the acquisition of Wells Fargo) to expand beyond its electronic-detection and equipment origins into guard, armored car, patrol, and investigation services. Burns used its acquisitions and industry reputation to move into central-station alarms and electronic security equipment. Pinkerton's, on the other hand, concentrated on guard and investigative services and achieved most of its growth internally.

Proprietary security, although not as visible as contract and other forms of security, has experienced equal if not greater growth. In this case, companies established an in-house security organization, rather than contracting the work to an outside security service firm. From an historical perspective, the greatest growth occurred because of World Wars I and II, with increased government concern and regulations for heightened security directed toward companies with government contracts for military equipment and supplies. Another major factor for the growth of proprietary security has been the increased awareness by companies of the importance of crime reduction and prevention. In response to this need, both small and large companies have increased proprietary security functions.

Technological Impact

Technology has played an important role in the growth of the private security industry. For example, with the application of advanced technology to the security industry, even one of the oldest security devices, the lock, was subject to revolutionary changes: combination locks, delayed-action time locks (e.g., inability to open a safe until a preset time has elapsed), combination locks with surveillance and electronic controls, and access-control systems that use the technology of television and computers.

The same advances in electronics technology that improved the quality of television and radio had significant impact upon the security market, broadening it to include additional consumer areas. This new technology fostered the development of integrated security systems operated by computers that control not only access, but also refrigeration, heating, air-conditioning, fire detection, and other services. Technological advances have reduced component cost and size, leading to the introduction of security measures now commonly in use, such as low-light-level, closed-circuit television cameras (CCTV) and electronic article-surveillance devices.

Security Trade Associations

The growth of private security services and products has been accompanied by a growth in security-related national trade associations. Early security trade organizations and security committees or divisions of major national associations included the American Bankers Association, the Association of American Railroads, the National Association of Manufacturers, the American Hotel and Motel Association, the American Transportation Association, and the National Retail Merchants Association. There are also numerous state and regional security associations. The trade associations cover the full range of private security activities such as alarms, armored cars, credit card fraud, private detectives, computer security, educational security, detection of deception, insurance, and security equipment. The American Society for Industrial Security (ASIS) International, a professional society with a membership of security supervisors and managers, has made significant contributions to the professionalism of the security industry. To further the objectives of crime prevention and the protection of assets, ASIS is concerned with all aspects of security in the private sector and emphasizes the education and professionalism of its members through publications, workshops, seminars, and certifications. Chapter 3 provides more information on security trade associations.

ISSUE

Should Federal Property Be Protected by Government Officers or Contract Security Officers?

The Congressional Research Service prepared a report for members and committees of Congress on issues related to this question (Reese 2007). The following information is based on that report.

The Federal Protective Service (FPS) a division of the U.S. Immigration Customs Enforcement (ICE) in the Department of Homeland Security (DHS), protects federal government property, all people on the premises, and property leased by the General Services Administration (GSA). The FPS employs over 15,000 contract security officers and 950 FPS law enforcement officers. The DHS is in favor of reassigning the 950 FPS law enforcement officers into other ICE entities and maintaining the protection of federal property solely by contract security officers.

Under current statutory provisions, FPS law enforcement officers are authorized to:

- Enforce federal laws and regulations
- Carry firearms
- Make arrests
- Serve warrants and subpoenas
- Conduct investigations on and off federal property

The DHS inspector general (DHS IG) notes that contract security officer services "represent the single largest item in the FPS operating budget, with an estimated FY2006 budget of $487 million." FPS security officers perform building access controls, ID checks, monitoring of physical security (e.g., alarms, CCTV), and patrols.

The National Capital Region (NCR) contracts with 54 contract security companies supplying 5,700 officers at 125 federal facilities. FPS requires background checks, medical and drug screening, and basic and refresher training. FPS issues task orders to the contractors, including post locations, hours, and whether officers are to be armed. FPS requires proper licenses, certifications, and permits. Arrest powers of security officers vary with the government entity that they are protecting and the particular building.

An audit of the NCR's FPS security contracts by the DHS IG found that the FPS has become increasingly dependent on contract security officers, that the contracts are not being monitored adequately, and that contract violations exist. Violations include unarmed officers working at armed posts, an officer with a felony conviction, and officers without the required security clearances. Such lapses can result in increased risks and payment for services not received.

On January 3, 2007, the National Association of Security Companies (NASCO), a trade association representing the security industry, organized and hosted the first meeting of its working group to study the tasks performed by security officers and law enforcement officers for the federal and commercial markets. The purpose was to produce "best practices" guidelines for security. NASCO states that its objectives are to establish a definition of security officers, identify security functions and tasks, and validate the functions for contract and training requirements.

In Congress, the House of Representatives, through 2008 DHS appropriations, states that no funds will support any activity that reduces the number of FPS law enforcement officers unless the FPS director provides a report to state and local police on how they may be affected by the downsizing. The report must contain the number and types of cases handled by the FPS in the previous two fiscal years and how security needs are to be addressed in the future. The House is to receive a copy of the report, especially since it is concerned about any downsizing.

The Senate passed legislation requiring the DHS secretary to ensure that there are not fewer than 1,200 FPS law enforcement officers protecting federal buildings, and that adjustments in budgeting for contractor security services be made to ensure full funding for the 1,200 officers.

Critical Thinking

Should federal government property be protected solely by contract security officers? Why or why not?
(Refer to "Your Career in Security: Security Officer," earlier in this chapter, for related information.)

Summary

Government has become increasingly involved in security since the 9/11 attacks, and differentiating *private security* and *public police and public security* can be challenging. Security can be understood under various contexts, which helps us to grasp its meaning.

The fundamental role of security is to protect people, assets, buildings, and operations. A professional security practitioner manages and implements a security program by applying various methodologies to produce the most efficient and effective security strategies for optimum protection and return on investment. Security officers observe, report, and perform an array of duties at stationary posts and while on patrol by foot or vehicle.

There are several practical benefits of studying history for students of security and security practitioners. Humans have faced security challenges throughout history, and the private and public sectors have shared the task of providing security and protection. Early history shows tribes uniting for protection. Self-protection and private protection have a long history. Early private security efforts in England were inadequate as crime increased, so government stepped in, and the Peelian Reform Movement revolutionized policing worldwide. As crime became overwhelming for public policing globally, the limited resources of government forced citizens and merchants to protect themselves, and private security grew. Many individuals, and their innovative ideas and hard work, produced a thriving security industry that helps to protect our society today.

Discussion Questions

1. How can we differentiate *private security* and *public police and public security*? What questions can we ask to distinguish these two sectors?
2. What are the roles of security today and what do you think the roles will be in the future?
3. Why is knowledge of history important to students of security and security practitioners?
4. How are the security strategies of prehistoric times and early civilizations similar to the security strategies applied today?
5. England is not the only country that contributed to the history and development of security and policing. What contributions did France make?
6. In reference to the Peelian Principles, if you were on an advisory panel from the business community assisting Sir Robert Peel with finalizing the principles, what recommendations would you make so the police can play a role in improving business security?
7. In reference to the box entitled "Labor Unions versus Corporations, Security Companies, Police Agencies, the National Guard, and U.S. Military Forces," why were so many resources expended to try to stop unions? What are your views of the actions of both union members and the Baldwin–Felts Detective Agency?

Animal Liberation Front (ALF)
People for the Ethical Treatment of Animals (PETA)
Earth Liberation Front (ELF)
Christian Identity Movement
state-sponsored terrorism
Oklahoma City bombing
Ruby Ridge incident
Waco incident
2001 anthrax attacks
secondary device
improvised explosive device (IED)
soft target
hard target
Aum Shinrikyo cult
radiological dispersion device or dirty bomb
Defense Against Weapons of Mass Destruction Act of 1996
Antiterrorism and Effective Death Penalty Act of 1996
USA Patriot Act of 2001
USA Patriot Improvement and Reauthorization Act of 2005
Homeland Security Act of 2002
Department of Homeland Security (DHS)
Intelligence Reform and Terrorism Prevention Act of 2004
Implementing Recommendations of the 9/11 Commission Act of 2007
UN Counterterrorism Implementation Task Force
International Atomic Energy Agency
World Health Organization
Interpol
homeland security
Federal Emergency Management Agency (FEMA)
all-hazards preparedness concept
Katrina disaster
National Response Framework (NRF)
National Incident Management System (NIMS)

QUIZ

This quiz serves to prime the reader's mind and begin the reading, thinking, and studying processes for this chapter. The answers to all of the questions are found within this chapter.

1. In reference to the protection of assets and people, which of the two is generally a higher priority for protection by security practitioners?
2. What does it mean to protect a company's brand?

3. Name one famous person who could be labeled a terrorist during one era who became a legitimate government leader during a subsequent era.
4. What are the four major types of weapons of mass destruction?
5. How many terrorist bombings occurred at the World Trade Center in New York City prior to the September 11, 2001, attacks?
6. How many commercial passenger jets were hijacked by terrorists on September 11, 2001, and how many landed safely?
7. What is all-hazards protection?
8. What is the name of the devastating hurricane that flooded New Orleans in 2005 and was followed by an inept response from the Federal Emergency Management Agency (FEMA) and other government bodies?

Introduction

We live in a dangerous world of many threats and hazards, and we learn of people killed or injured and property stolen or destroyed from a host of sources. At the same time, we all differ in our behavior in trying to avoid losses. Most people practice various forms of security and safety in their personal lives, such as locking homes and vehicles, wearing a shoulder harness when driving a vehicle, and trying to avoid setting the house on fire when cooking.

Both the private and public sectors spend enormous sums of money and resources seeking to prevent deaths, injuries, theft, and property damage from a host of threats and hazards. Whether in business or government, personnel are hired to perform protection functions. This chapter explains broad categories of threats and hazards that face our nation and organizations. The beginning of the chapter explains threats and hazards facing both security practitioners and the security function, and it goes on to explain what security practitioners have on their minds as they prioritize their duties. Then, an emphasis is placed on the problem of terrorism, homeland security, and all-hazards protection, because these topics receive much attention, and security professionals must seek to understand how these subjects and related issues affect their protection programs and their duties.

THREATS AND HAZARDS DEFINED

A **threat** is "an expression of intention to inflict evil, injury, or damage; one that threatens; [and] an indication of something impending" (Merriam–Webster Online Dictionary 2008). It is described as "something that is a source of danger," "a warning that something unpleasant is imminent," "a declaration of an intention or a determination to inflict harm on another," [and] "a person who inspires fear or dread." "A threat is also an explicit or implicit message from a person to another that the first will cause something bad to happen to the other, often except when certain demands are met." (Webster's Online Dictionary 2008).

A **hazard** is "a source of danger," "a chance event," [and an] "accident" (Merriam–Webster Online Dictionary 2008). Other definitions are "an unknown and unpredictable phenomenon that causes an event to result one way rather than another"; "the probability of the occurrence of a disaster caused by a natural phenomenon (earthquake, cyclone), or by failure of manmade sources of energy (nuclear reactor, industrial explosion) or by uncontrolled human activity (overgrazing, heavy traffic, conflict)." "In a broader sense, includes vulnerability, elements at risk and the consequences of risk." (Webster's Online Dictionary 2008).

Threats and Hazards

What are the priorities of security practitioners as they perform their job duties? Although the title of this chapter contains the words *terrorism* and *all-hazards*, security practitioners are concerned with a broad spectrum of threats, hazards, and issues, as described next.

A top priority of security executives is to protect people in the workplace, consisting of employees, customers, visitors, contractors, vendors, and others. The threats and hazards facing people are numerous. Examples are crimes, fires, accidents, and natural and human-made disasters. Periodically, we read about an employee, student, or outsider who commits murder in the workplace (Figure 2.1). In 2007, the **Virginia Tech massacre** became the worst mass-murder event at a school in U.S. history; in this rare event, a student with mental health problems killed 32 people before committing suicide. In 2008, the **Mumbai attacks** in India added even more challenges to the threat of active shooters. Ten heavily armed terrorists arrived by small boat in this city, known as India's financial capital, and positioned themselves at a hotel and other busy locations, before killing nearly 200 people. (Chapter 5 provides more information on the active shooter threat.) It is the job and responsibility of management to develop programs and strategies to deal with violence. In reference to fires, management typically establishes life-safety plans consisting of training, evacuation drills, and other strategies. Management promotes safety through training in the application of safe techniques, use of safety equipment, development of effective policies and procedures, and other methods. If a serious weather hazard approaches (e.g., hurricane), the value of preplanning and preparation becomes evident. The National Strategy for Homeland Security (White House 2007b) reports

FIGURE 2.1 **Violence in the workplace is a serious threat, and security practitioners work to protect people. (® Shutterstock.com. With permission.)**

that in the United States floods are the most frequently occurring natural disaster and the leading cause of property damage and death from natural disasters over the past century; over 800 tornadoes are reported annually, causing about 80 deaths, 1,500 injuries, and serious property damage; and 39 states face significant risk of earthquake.

Besides the top priority of protecting people in the workplace, the protection of assets is another major function of security. It includes protection of buildings, equipment, inventory, vehicles, information, money, and securities.

A serious threat to employer assets is internal theft and fraud. Estimated annual losses vary with the source, but are generally in the billions of dollars for each. Furthermore, one serious case of internal theft or fraud can result in business failure. Dishonest employees are the major culprits behind internal theft and they steal a variety of items from the workplace, such as merchandise, money, information, and equipment. Imagine the annual losses if, say, 300 employees at a manufacturing plant each stole one item (e.g., raw material, finished product, or tool) per week. Fraud involves deceit by the offender. Examples include an employee padding an expense account for travel, a bookkeeper or accountant manipulating financial records to embezzle money, or executives fabricating information in financial statements to make a company look profitable when the company is actually in financial difficulties. The infamous **Enron Corporation** case caused financial havoc for many people because executives used fraudulent accounting methods to hide debt and show unsuccessful investments as profitable. Employees and investors saw their multibillion dollar investments largely disappear as the energy company filed for bankruptcy. Among the lessons from this financial disaster are that employees should never place all of their retirement savings in one company and should be leery about compensation through company stock that may one day be almost worthless. In 2006, Kenneth Lay, Enron's founder, was convicted of fraud. One month following his conviction, he died of a heart attack before he was sentenced. Other Enron executives were successfully prosecuted and sentenced to prison. (Chapter 10 provides additional information on internal theft and fraud.)

A business's continued survival may very well depend on information assets and information security. Information assets include secret formulas or recipes, proprietary manufacturing processes or designs, and data. Theft of information can result in business failure and, in the defense industry, it could compromise national security. Business and military competition on a global scale has made certain information extremely valuable, which has led to a proliferation of spies in the ranks of foreign students, engineers, business people, and others. McCourt (2008, 16) notes that foreign competitors, whether sponsored by businesses or a military organization, have been successful in stealing secrets and that America's competitive advantage has been eroded. He writes that China and Russia are at the top of the list of the most aggressive nations.

The U.S. Department of Justice (2008a) reported that Xiaodong Meng—44 years old, a software engineer born in China and a resident of Cupertino, California—was sentenced to two years in prison for violating the Economic Espionage (EE) Act of 1996. Meng committed economic espionage by misappropriating a trade secret from his former employer, Quantum3D, Inc., with the intent to benefit the People's Republic of China (PRC) Navy Research Center in Beijing. He illegally exported to the PRC visual simulation software used to train U.S. military pilots who use night visual sensor equipment. Other EE cases include *United States v. Dongfan "Greg" Chung* (2008), *United States v. Lan Lee and Yuefei Ge* (2007), *United States v. Fei Ye and Ming Zhong* (2002), and *United States v. Okamoto and Serizawa* (2001).

Besides the need for information security, the information technology (IT) that holds the information and data is subject to a host of threats and hazards. These include hackers, disgruntled employees, spies, and natural and human-made disasters. Furthermore, protection is required for the privacy of personal information held in IT systems, as required by several laws. The traditional security executive that focuses on the management of security officers and physical security must work with IT specialists and business-continuity specialists to ensure that IT is protected and survives adverse events. (Chapter 8 covers information and IT security.)

Transnational crime is a serious threat to organizations and individuals. Albanese (2005, 561) defines it as follows: "Offenses in which the planning and execution of the crime involve more than one country." This crime may be initiated in one country and impact people or organizations in another country. It can involve a border crossing or the use of the Internet between countries. Examples of transnational crime are trafficking of humans, illegal drugs, and arms across borders; credit card fraud between countries (often using the Internet); and international terrorism.

In describing the problem of transnational crime, Hayes et al. (2008, 38) write of three specific threats: e-crime, money laundering, and counterfeiting. **E-crime**, also referred to as *computer crime* or *cybercrime*, refers to crime involving a computer or network. Modern IT is leveraged by transnational criminals and organized crime groups to commit identity theft, financial crimes, and other offenses. A resident of Los Angeles may have his or her identity and/or credit card information stolen by an individual or organized crime group working out of Moscow, who then sells the information to someone living in Mexico City. In another example, a business in Chicago may ship goods to a bogus business in Berlin that presents bogus credit information. The offender keeps the goods and avoids paying the bill. Because multiple jurisdictions characterize transnational crime, investigation and prosecution are difficult.

Money laundering is defined by Albanese (2005, 559) as follows: "A method of 'washing' illegally obtained money (e.g., from drugs or gambling proceeds) by making it appear as if the money were earned legally as part of a legitimate business." Because money laundering is used to fund terrorist activity, it is prohibited by the USA Patriot Act (among other laws), and the requirements (e.g., reporting suspicious financial activities) apply to banks, securities dealers, the insurance industry, casinos, and other businesses.

Counterfeiting, which is described in greater detail below, is a $500-billion illegal business. Between October 2005 and September 2006, the Department of Homeland Security made 14,000 seizures of counterfeit goods valued at $155 million (U.S. Immigration and Customs Enforcement 2007). The U.S. Secret Service focuses on currency counterfeiting, which is another global problem.

Another threat is harm to a brand that can cause serious financial difficulties to a business. A **brand** is a corporate asset, and it refers to a company's good name and reputation as represented through a product or service. A company's brand can be threatened in several ways. In 1982, the **Tylenol scare** occurred when seven people died after taking this over-the-counter medication that they had bought in a retail store. The Tylenol had been laced with cyanide. Johnson & Johnson recalled 31 million bottles of Tylenol, and drugmakers globally introduced tamper-resistant packaging. In another threat to a brand, the supertanker **Exxon *Valdez*** spilled 10 million gallons of oil in 1989 when it ran aground in Alaska. Exxon was criticized for being slow to respond to the disaster. It paid out billions of dollars in cleanup costs and damages. In 2010, the **BP oil spill** in the Gulf of Mexico far surpassed the spill and environmental damage of the Exxon *Valdez* event. In 2006, food from Taco Bell caused hundreds of people to be sick from *E. coli*. The company temporarily closed 60 stores, cleaned the stores, and restocked food (Nazarov 2007, 37). Harm to a brand can also result from hackers or others who steal private customer information (e.g., credit card numbers). This occurred with TJX, the parent company of T.J. Maxx and other stores, which was criticized for waiting too long to inform millions of customers of the breach. Counterfeiting of products also harms a brand. Just about any product can be subject to **counterfeiting**, which is the production of a fake to represent a genuine item. Examples are clothing, auto parts, and drugs. If a counterfeit product—labeled with a legitimate company name—fails, the legitimate company's brand is tarnished.

Another way to understand threats to an organization is to study the role of security in investigations of adverse events. Examples include not only investigations of internal theft, illegal drug use, and other crimes in the workplace, but also allegations of unethical conduct, sexual harassment, verbal threats, and unauthorized firearms on the premises.

Litigation against an employer is another unfortunate event that may involve the security function. A private investigation may be required to collect the facts of a case. The types of cases are numerous and could include a person supposedly injured on the premises, allegations of a defective product manufactured by the employer, or allegations of sexual harassment. In addition, the security function itself may be subject to litigation from allegations of inadequate security from a person victimized on the premises or from security personnel purportedly making errors in their duties.

A security practitioner's duties and the security function are linked to a variety of adverse occurrences affecting the workplace that a novice to the security profession may find unusual. For instance, if a power outage occurs, plans should be in place for backup power to continue business operations and to maintain the protection function of physical security systems. Imagine the criticism a security executive would receive if no contingency plans were in place when electronic access controls at a building failed and locked out employees who were seeking to begin the workday. Management would be very concerned about the financial costs of such an event. A security executive may also be linked to issues of environmental protection. If an employee is polluting the environment and violates environmental laws, the security executive, if knowledgeable of the violations, becomes part of the problem if the employee is not reported to management and authorities.

Critical Thinking

With so many threats and hazards facing security executives, how are they able to fulfill their job responsibilities?

ISSUE

What Are the Priorities of Security Practitioners?

Thus far, in this chapter, we have explained numerous threats and hazards facing security practitioners and the security function. However, what issues and concerns are on the minds of security executives? What are their priorities? Is protection against terrorism their top priority?

Editors of security periodicals regularly garner the views of security executives on a host of issues. The editors of *Corporate Security* (Security Executive Forum 2003) found varied opinions from security executives on the threat of terrorism. One vice president over security at a broadcasting company was more concerned about violence in the workplace than terrorism. Another security executive maintained a similar view and was particularly concerned about threats from employees, former employees, and spouses of employees. Security executives for an oil and gas company and a financial institution saw risks to IT as the most serious threats. A security specialist at a vacation resort viewed employee theft, fraud, and workplace violence as the greatest threats. At the same time, other security executives viewed protection against terrorism as a top priority. One health-care security director noted that the greatest threats are to the nation's infrastructure, specifically electricity, water, and transportation. A director of security for a food company emphasized bioterrorism and our vulnerable food supply as major concerns.

Bill Zalud (2008, 22–30), a top security editor, queried security executives and found a variety of concerns. While technology is leveraged to bring value to the business enterprise, there is pressure from senior management for security staff to perform security duties that are outside the traditional framework (e.g., managing the internal mail system). Another issue is regulatory compliance, which is a growing job function. This entails working with auditors to strengthen organizational integrity. Because of financial scandals and privacy issues, government has enacted laws to reduce corruption and protect privacy. Security and IT executives must work together to see that the organization complies with laws and regulations.

Zalud (2008, 22–30) found that the concern about terrorism has resulted in enhanced emergency plans to protect against bombs, computer crimes, weapons of mass destruction, and other threats. One executive quipped that, in nonglobal companies, complacency has set in about the threat of terrorism. However, prior to a disaster striking, there is a general consensus that training, testing of plans, and application of best practices are vital. If security management is to be effective, it must integrate with internal (e.g., safety, risk management) and external (e.g., fire department, emergency management) groups. An additional major issue is how well the groups function together when planning and responding to an incident.

Zalud (2008, 22–30) also wrote of other issues of concern to security executives. These include support for the security program from senior executives and customer service. The former involves security being aligned with business goals and a security budget that fulfills protection needs. The latter focuses on the protection of both internal customers (i.e., employees) and external customers (i.e., members of the public who produce sales).

Another issue focuses on economic conditions. Layoffs can create tension and violence in the workplace. High unemployment may cause individuals to commit property and other crimes to survive. Security professionals must be flexible and respond to changing security needs.

Terrorism

The topics of terrorism and the September 11, 2001, attacks are often in the news and on the minds of security practitioners in both the private and public sectors. Because of the serious threat it imposes, security students and practitioners should have a foundation of understanding of the problem of terrorism and countermeasures. In addition, practitioners must seek to understand how terrorism and related issues affect their protection programs and their duties.

The Difficulty of Defining Terrorism

There is no agreement on the definition of terrorism. It is a political term with definitions emanating from differing political perspectives, and the definition changes over time. It is often said that "one person's terrorist is another person's freedom fighter." In other words, your perspective on terrorism depends on "which side of the fence you are on."

In 1946, a group of Jews in Palestine, known as the Irgun, were involved in bombings as a strategy to end British occupation of the area. The Irgun was led by Menachem Begin, and the group bombed Jerusalem's King David Hotel, which housed British Army Headquarters. The bombing killed 91 people, affected the British occupation, and within two years, Israel became a nation. Interestingly, Begin became prime minister of Israel. What we have here is a person labeled a terrorist at one time and a legitimate government leader at another (Weinzierl 2004, 35).

CRITICAL THINKING

From the British perspective, was George Washington, leader of the American Revolution, a terrorist? Do American publications about George Washington refer to him as a terrorist or as the father of our country?

Here are definitions of **terrorism** from multiple sources as we seek to understand its meaning:

> From federal law, U.S. Code Title 22, Ch. 38, Para. 2656f(d): "Terrorism means premeditated, politically motivated violence perpetrated against noncombatant targets by subnational groups or clandestine agents."
>
> From the Federal Bureau of Investigation (2008): "Terrorism is the unlawful use of force or violence against persons or property to intimidate or coerce a government, the civilian population, or any segment thereof, in furtherance of political or social objectives."
>
> From the Council of Arab Ministers of the Interior and the Council of Arab Ministers of Justice (1998): "Any act or threat of violence, whatever its motives or purposes, that occurs in the advancement of an individual or collective criminal agenda and seeking to sow panic among people, causing fear by harming them, or placing their lives, liberty or security in danger, or seeking to cause damage to the environment or to public or private installations or property or to occupying or seizing them, or seeking to jeopardize national resources."

Terrorism: A History of Violence

Terrorism has existed since ancient times. Poland (2005, 26–27) refers to the **Zealots** and the **Sicarii**, who were Jewish groups in Palestine that confronted the Roman occupation during the first century. Their terrorist strategy was unexpected stabbings of Romans when large crowds gathered. The large crowds provided cover and escape, and the surprise attacks instilled widespread fear. Poland sees history repeating itself, because the Zealots and the Sicarii sought to provoke Romans into repression and reprisals to make authorities appear brutal. This also occurred with British forces against Catholics in Ireland (from the 1500s to the 1900s) and Jews in Palestine (1940s).

Weinzierl (2004, 31–32) writes about the **Assassins**, another religious group that applied terrorist methods. This group existed during the 1000s and 1100s and is linked to the long history of the Shiite Muslims of the Middle East. The Assassins fought Sunni Muslims over religious and/or political differences, and this conflict persists today (e.g., in Iraq). A Shiite murder of a Sunni leader today, as yesterday, is considered a holy act praised by God. This same mind-set holds true of other religious groups throughout history. Not only did the Assassins stab enemies unexpectedly, they are also known for their creative terrorist methods, especially the use of deception, disguise, and the suicide attack.

The **French Revolution** (1789–1799), which resulted in a major transformation of the society and political system of France, is an interesting and significant part of the history of terrorism (Kaiser 2008; Weinberg and Davis 1989, 24–25). Between 1793 and 1794, the Reign of Terror sought to end the power and wealth of the French monarch as people starved in the streets and taxes increased. Maximilien Robespierre, a lawyer, led this movement, known as the radical Jacobin government. As thousands of "enemies" were executed by guillotine, he espoused the idea that terror was good for justice and democracy. Robespierre claimed that constitutional government would be sought once fear and repression destroyed the enemies of the Revolution. He led the Committee of Public Safety that controlled the police and the Revolutionary Tribunal that tried cases and sentenced the guilty. The Jacobin government also enacted the Law of Suspects, used to charge counterrevolutionaries with "crimes against liberty." In other words, resistance to Jacobin doctrine meant punishment. At the beginning of the Reign of Terror, terrorism was viewed in a positive light, but as Robespierre fingered more "enemies," he was himself criticized and executed. Although the terror ended and the term *terrorism* took on negative connotations, the movement inspired revolution and anarchy worldwide.

The French Revolution had global appeal to those who were dissatisfied with the political, social, and economic conditions in their own country. Anarchist groups sought change through violent revolution in many countries.

The **Russian Narodnaya Volya**, meaning "people's will," was a nineteenth-century revolutionary group that viewed terrorism as the best strategy for political reform and eliminating the autocratic czar. The group assassinated Alexander II in 1881 in a bombing. The assassination caused a wave of anti-terrorist sentiment. The perpetrators were arrested and hanged, and the group was quashed (Zalman 2008).

In May of 1886, in Chicago, workers from the McCormick Harvesting Machine Company began a strike to secure an 8-hour work day. While police protected strikebreakers, violence erupted and one person was killed. The next day, a large rally was planned at **Haymarket Square** (a farmer's market) by anarchist leaders to protest alleged police brutality. During the rally, as police tried to disperse the crowd, a pipe bomb was thrown into the police ranks, killing seven and injuring over 60 others. The police fired into the crowd, killing four. There was no evidence of who threw the bomb, but police arrested eight anarchist leaders. Illinois law stated that anyone inciting a murder was guilty of that murder. In the hysteria that followed the bombing, a jury found the men guilty and sentenced them to death.

Although the event resulted in international interest, four of the anarchists were hung a year after the trial. Louis Lingg, a 21-year old carpenter, committed suicide in his cell by exploding a dynamite stick in his mouth. The other three remained in prison and were eventually pardoned by the governor. The Haymarket incident inspired others to protest authorities (Zinn 1995, 265–266).

The assassination of Archduke Franz Ferdinand and his wife in 1914, illustrates how one terrorist incident can alter world history (Simonsen and Spindlove 2004, 165). The assassin, Gavrilo Princip, was a member of the Young Bosnia movement of Serbs, Croats, and Bosnian Muslims seeking independence for Slavic peoples from Austria–Hungary. He was also a member of the Black Hand, a group that sought nationalist goals through assassination. When the archduke and his wife were in Sarajevo to watch a military exercise, members of the Black Hand lined the route with instructions to try to kill the archduke. One assassin threw a hand grenade, but missed when the driver of the archduke's car accelerated. Because occupants of another car and spectators were injured, the archduke and his wife headed to a hospital to visit the victims. On the way, Princip and the archduke's vehicle crossed paths and Princip shot the archduke in the neck and his wife in the abdomen. This incident had a profound impact on millions of people. The assassination caused Austria–Hungary to take action against Serbia, and then a complex web of alliances led to World War I.

In 1917, the **Bolsheviks** overthrew the czar, which led to communism, the dominant political ideology of the Soviet Union until its collapse in 1991. Because of opposition to Bolshevik rule in 1918, a period of terror by the Bolsheviks began. The church in Russia also became a target of terror. By 1939, all the clergy and many worshippers had been shot or forced to labor camps. Only about 500 churches remained from an original 50,000 (Simonsen and Spindlove 2004, 153). From 1922 until his death in 1953, Joseph Stalin ruled the Soviet Union with "an iron fist." The Great Purge, a form of state terrorism at the end of the 1930s, resulted in the deaths of millions of Soviets through execution or at labor camps in Siberia. The exact number of those killed is disputed.

Prior to World War I, terrorism was generally of the revolutionary, left wing, extremist type. To counter such movements and violence, right-wing groups formed (Weinzierl 2004, 34). **Left-wing politics** seek change because of discontent over such issues as inequality and injustice. The methods applied to bring about change include publications, peaceful protest, and violence by extremists. **Right-wing politics** consist of conservative viewpoints and avoiding change. The methods applied are similar to those used by left wingers.

It is important to understand that when we speak of left-wing and right-wing ideologies, there is violent extremism at both ends of the political spectrum. Think of a horizontal line with violent (left wing) extremists at the very end of the line to the left, and violent (right wing) extremists to the very end of the line to the right. Moderates are in the middle of the line, lean to either the right or left depending on their viewpoints, and are generally nonviolent. Terrorists are often referred to as extremists. Examples of violent, right-wing extremist groups are the Ku Klux Klan (KKK) and neo-Nazis.

Throughout the twentieth century, left-wing groups typically favored the ideology of **communism**. The theory behind it espouses equality and care for all citizens and government ownership of property and production. The reality, as seen in the former Soviet Union, was an unequal society with a privileged class (i.e., Communist Party members) and a government that stifled free enterprise (i.e., the driving force of the U.S. capitalist system that permits businesspeople to make a profit with minimal government interference). The Soviet Union adhered to a communist system through much of the twentieth century, but collapsed in 1991 because of economic reasons. Former Soviet republics now contain characteristics of capitalism.

Classifying Terrorist Groups

Terrorists and terrorist groups can be classified in many ways. Dyson (2001, 20–31), for example, refers to not only *left-wing* and *right-wing extremism*, but also *single-issue* or *special-interest terrorism* that concentrates on a single argument (e.g., abortion, animal rights), *religious terrorism* that acts in the name of God, *national* or *ethnic terrorism* that fights for a homeland and/or other rights, and *race-based* or *hate terrorism* that victimizes a particular group.

Classifications of terrorism are subject to overlap. For instance, a terrorist group with strong religious and ethnic ties typically focuses violence, hate, and intolerance on another religious and ethnic group.

Gurr (1989) uses a four-category classification of terrorism: *vigilante terrorism* involves citizens victimizing other citizens (e.g., KKK); *insurgent terrorism* seeks political change (e.g., the insurgency in Iraq following the 2003 U.S.-led invasion); *transnational terrorism* begins in one country and ends in another (e.g., 9/11 attacks); and *state terrorism*, whereby a government applies violence against its own people (e.g., Nazis against Jews during World War II).

Conflicts in the Name of Religion

Conflict over religion has existed for centuries. The **Crusades** involved Western European Christians traveling to the Holy Lands for a series of military campaigns during the Middle Ages to capture Palestine (the area where Jesus lived) from the Muslims. Jerusalem and the surrounding area were alternately controlled by both sides as each side claimed victories (Figure 2.2). Since the Crusades, hundreds of wars and campaigns

FIGURE 2.2 Jerusalem, today, a city of multiple religions. (® Shutterstock.com. With permission.)

to exterminate specific groups over religious and ethnic differences have occurred. A major benefit of the Crusades was an increase in trade between Europe and the Middle East (Simonsen and Spindlove 2004, 32–33).

Today, religious and ethnic conflict continues, and the Middle East remains a hotbed of violence. In addition, it is difficult to ascertain whether a terrorist group is more concerned about a religious agenda or a political agenda.

A summary of **Islam** is appropriate here to reduce misconceptions about this religion and its ties to terrorism (IslamicInformation.net, 2008). **Muslims** are believers in Islam, and they number about 1 billion people; over eighty percent of Muslims are not Arabs. They live in the Middle East, Asia, Africa, and other parts of the world. Although most Arabs are Muslims, there are Arabs who are Christians, Jews, and other religions. *Muslim* means "someone who submits to the will of God." The Islamic faith is based upon the doctrine preached by the Prophet Muhammad (A.D. 600s), who was an Arab born in Mecca and became God's messenger. Muslims worship God (Allah). The Koran parallels the Bible in that it contains religious teachings. Judgment day determines whether Muslims go to heaven or hell. Although terrorism is condemned by most Muslims, Islam refers to **jihad**, meaning "holy war," whereby defending Islam to the death provides a place in heaven. Centuries of conflict over Islamic religious doctrine have led to violence that continues today. The larger sect, **Sunni**, outnumber the **Shiite** in the Middle East; these groups differ in their religious teaching, besides having political differences. Prior to the ouster of Saddam Hussein by U.S.-led forces in 2003, the Sunnis dominated politics in Iraq. Following the war, Shiites gained control (backed by U.S.-led forces), often in violent clashes with Sunnis.

Another important topic relevant to conflict in the name of religion is the ongoing violence between Israelis and Palestinians. During ancient times, Judea was the home of the Jewish people, and it was conquered by the Romans, who changed the name to Palestine. Arabs then conquered Palestine and held it for many years. To counter Arab control over Palestine, the Zionist movement developed. **Zionism** refers to returning Jews to the homeland. The 1917 British Balfour Declaration paved the way for a homeland for Jews in Palestine. Repeated violence occurred between Jews and Arab Palestinians during British control of the area. The United Nations intervened and divided Palestine into an Arab state and a Jewish state, with Jerusalem controlled by multinational authorities. Violence continued. In 1948, the country of Israel was born, and fighting erupted again. Arab countries refused to recognize Israel. Several wars broke out, and terrorism and reprisals continue today. Each side blames the other for hostilities (Isseroff 2007).

Causes of Terrorism

At this point, the reader can probably hypothesize about the causes of terrorism. A major cause is perceived injustice by an individual or group. The injustices can result from poverty and economic disparity, religious or political repression, or discrimination and racism. An additional cause is a threat to a group's culture or religion by another group. In the case of state terrorism, a government may victimize a specific group because the group is gaining political strength.

Social scientists generally agree that most terrorists are not mentally ill (Clayton et al. 2003). According to Crenshaw (1990), terrorism is a logical political choice among options. She argues for a **rational-choice approach** to studying terrorism so that we can understand the circumstances and decision-making processes of terrorists. Sociologists explain terrorism as a response to weak social-structural conditions, such as limited civil liberties and inadequate government services (Calhoun et al. 2001, 27). When a group becomes powerless to correct injustices, its members may resort to terrorism. Another sociological approach to understanding terrorism is **relative deprivation theory**. It refers to a group's frustrations as the expectations of its members are destroyed by disappointments and they compare their unfortunate state with those who are more fortunate.

International Terrorism

The Federal Bureau of Investigation (2008) defines **international terrorism** as follows: "**International terrorism** is the unlawful use of force or violence committed by a group or individual, who has some connection to a foreign power or whose activities transcend national boundaries, against persons or property to intimidate or coerce a government, the civilian population, or any segment thereof, in furtherance of political or social objectives."

The measurement of terrorism is plagued by methodological problems, such as inconsistency in both the use of terminology and in reporting. In addition, the measurement of terrorism may reflect the management of counterterrorism (e.g., definition of terrorism, what to report, and what not to report) more so than the actual extent of terrorism (Purpura 2007, 86). At the current time, the U.S. government is working to improve the measurement of terrorism.

The U.S. Department of State is a major source of information on terrorism. It publishes "Country Reports on Terrorism" containing U.S. policy and programs as well as a list and descriptions of foreign terrorist organizations (FTOs). Groups listed as FTOs are Al-Qaeda, Hezbollah, Hamas, the Revolutionary Armed Forces of Columbia (FARC), and several others.

The U.S. Department of State (2008a) reported that **Al-Qaeda** and associated networks remain the greatest threat to the United States and its allies. Al-Qaeda has regrouped in Pakistan, near the border with Afghanistan. The group is adaptive to counterterrorism, creative, and seeks weapons of mass destruction. Al-Qaeda continues to target Western Europe and the United States through affiliates in the Middle East, Africa, and Europe. The **Taliban,** who were forced out of Afghanistan by the United States following the 9/11 attacks, today remain a threat inside Afghanistan and Pakistan. They try to maintain safe havens inside Pakistan; some link themselves to Al-Qaeda; and both groups are involved in terrorism and clashes with government forces in both Afghanistan and Pakistan. The United States, North Atlantic Treaty Organization (NATO), and other allied forces have a presence in Afghanistan.

Al-Qaeda was established by Osama bin Ladin in the late 1980s to unite Sunni Islamic extremists to fight the Soviets who occupied Afghanistan. Following the Soviet defeat in Afghanistan, Al-Qaeda directed its attention globally against the West and other non-Islamics. Al-Qaeda is a decentralized terror network and a global movement of a variety of groups. The total number of Al-Qaeda members is difficult to determine; the U.S. Department of State estimates several thousand members and associates. Al-Qaeda has been involved in numerous terrorist attacks, the most famous being the 9/11 attacks.

The U.S. Department of State sees Iran as the most significant state sponsor of terrorism, with Hezbollah as a key player in Iranian plans. Syria is also a supporter of Hezbollah.

In Columbia, the FARC illustrates the growing connection between terrorism and other criminal activity. The FARC holds hundreds of hostages from kidnappings and earns money from narcotics trafficking.

The **National Counterterrorism Center** (NCTC), in the Office of the Director of National Intelligence, publishes data on terrorist attacks worldwide. (The data was previously reported, with methodological problems, by the U.S. Department of State.) The NCTC was established following the 9/11 attacks because of problems of intelligence coordination and sharing among government agencies. Its goals are to integrate intelligence, plan, advise top leaders, and eliminate the terrorist threat at home and abroad.

The "2007 Report on Terrorism" (National Counterterrorism Center 2008) listed the following data:

- About 14,499 attacks in 2007 resulted in over 22,000 deaths, mostly Muslims in Iraq. This was approximately the same number of attacks as in 2006, but fatalities rose 16 percent.
- Of the 14,499 reported terrorist attacks in 2007, almost 43 percent occurred in Iraq.
- Increased fighting in Afghanistan resulted in 1,127 attacks, an increase of 16 percent from 2006.
- Violence in or near Somalia, Kenya, and Niger rose 96 percent in 2007, with 835 attacks.
- Attacks dropped 42 percent in the Western Hemisphere.
- Al-Qaeda in Iraq (AQI) claimed attacks with the highest casualty totals.
- Terrorist attacks declined 57 percent in Iraq from May to December 2007.
- The Taliban claimed the most attacks.
- Conventional weapons (e.g., bombs and small arms) were employed in most attacks.

The National Intelligence Council (NIC), reporting to the director of National Intelligence (DNI), provides the president and senior leaders with analyses of foreign policy issues and intelligence information. A National Intelligence Council (2007) publication, "The Terrorist Threat to the U.S. Homeland," described the following threats:

- The United States faces a persistent threat from Al-Qaeda. The group is innovative, seeks to overcome security obstacles, and will continue to try to acquire weapons of mass destruction.
- A radical Muslim terrorist threat exists in the United States, as evidenced by arrests of a small number of these extremists on U.S. soil. However, the threat is not as severe as in Europe.
- The Lebanese Hezbollah, which has attacked the United States overseas, may attack the homeland if Iran or the group itself is threatened by the United States.
- Other, non-Muslim terrorist groups, often called "single issue" groups by the FBI, will probably attack domestically over the next three years.

- Globalization trends and technological advances will continue to enable small groups to communicate their extremist views and mobilize resources for an attack without requiring an organizational structure, training facilities, or a leader.

The U.S. strategy of counterterrorism includes working to protect the population, winning political support, conducting special operations to control terrorism, and cooperating with allies. The United States and its allies have disrupted numerous terrorist plots since the 9/11 attacks. For example, in 2003, a senior Al-Qaeda operative was stopped from plotting to hijack commercial airplanes to attack targets on the East Coast, and in 2006, British authorities broke up an Al-Qaeda plot to blow up passenger airplanes flying to the United States (White House 2007a).

On Christmas day, 2009, Al-Qaeda terrorist plans unfolded again when a Nigerian flew from Lagos to Amsterdam and then Detroit. While the passenger jet approached Detroit, he attempted to set off a bomb from a six-inch package of powder and a syringe of liquid sewn into his underwear. Passengers heard a popping noise, smelled a strange odor, and subdued him as his pants and the side of the plane caught fire. The device could have destroyed the plane, but it failed. The U.S. intelligence community was criticized following this incident because the terrorist was on a U.S. list of suspected terrorist suspects, but not on the no-fly list. The offender was indicted in federal court on charges that included attempted murder of 289 passengers (CNN 2010). This incident has similarities to the case of Richard Reid, a British citizen who was trained as a terrorist in Afghanistan. In 2003, he was tried and sentenced to life in prison in a federal court for trying to blow up a passenger jet traveling from Paris to Miami in 2001. An airline attendant observed Reid trying to light a fuse for a bomb hidden in his shoe.

THE 9/16 AND 9/11 ATTACKS

A terrorist incident at the heart of New York's financial district killed more people than what most citizens imagined possible from terrorism. It left Americans facing an unknown enemy and the belief that the attack was an act of war. Americans felt that their world had changed irrevocably. Similar to the September 11, 2001, terrorist attacks, this earlier attack in New York's financial district, on Wall Street, occurred on September 16, 1920. As workers flooded streets on their lunch break, a horse-drawn cart, loaded with a bomb, exploded and killed 40 people while injuring many others. To Americans, the attack seemed unbelievable, horrible, and an illustration of our violent world. Although the September 11, 2001, attacks were much more deadly and destructive, similar feelings and questions emerged following the 9/16 and 9/11 terrorist attacks of America's financial center: How should the United States respond? How do we balance security and constitutional rights? Who is responsible for the attack? In the 9/16 bombing, the attack seemed to be a new type of violence, designed to kill as many innocent people as possible, and a symbolic assault on American power—similar to the 9/11 attacks.

Following the 9/16 attacks, suspicion focused on anarchists, communists, and "alien scum from the cesspools and sewers of the Old World," wrote the *Washington Post*. Authorities faced a major embarrassment because no terrorist was ever arrested for the crime, not even a scapegoat. In addition, democracy suffered as anarchists and communists were deprived of constitutional rights and immigrant groups were targeted by hate and discrimination (Gage 2001).

The discussion that follows focuses on the September 11, 2001, attacks at the World Trade Center (WTC), which included two 110-story skyscrapers. However, to understand this attack, it is important to explain the earlier **1993 World Trade Center attack**. On February 26, 1993, a bomb planted in a rental truck exploded in the basement parking garage of WTC Tower One. The large bomb was composed of over 1,000 pounds of nitrogen fertilizer, a fuse terminating in lead azide as the initiator, plus three metal cylinders of compressed hydrogen gas. The massive explosion killed six people, injured more than a thousand, and over 50,000 people were evacuated from the building (Simonsen and Spindlove 2004, 45). The 110-story building did not collapse, and the damage was repaired.

Unfortunately, the **September 11, 2001, attacks** (Figure 2.3) will go down in history as the most brilliant, enormously successful, and cost-effective terrorist attacks thus far. A mere 19 terrorists, with expenses of about $400,000 to $500,000, killed almost 3,000 people; totally destroyed two skyscrapers (and damaged nearby buildings and infrastructure) and four commercial airliners; severely damaged the Pentagon (home of the U.S. Department of Defense); sparked wars in Afghanistan and Iraq; caused over a trillion dollars to be spent on wars, counterterrorism, recovery from damage, victim compensation, and other expenses; and affected world history.

On the morning of September 11, 2001, 19 well-trained Al-Qaeda terrorists used deception, fraud, and stealthy methods to hijack four commercial passenger jets. They were armed with box cutters, small knives, and pepper spray. To instill fear, they cut the throats of some crew members and passengers and claimed to have a bomb. (Incidentally, before 9/11, training for air travel included complying with hijacker demands and negotiation. Today, in a 9/11 type of scenario, creative methods [e.g., weapons] must be applied by victims who may have to "kill or be killed.") The terrorists selected long-distance flights, since a large amount of fuel would be in the jets for maximum explosions, effectively transforming the jets into "cruise missiles."

United Airlines Flight 175 and American Airlines Flight 11 took off from Logan Airport in Boston for Los Angeles. When the terrorists gained control of the jets, both went off course and headed to New York City. At 8:45 a.m.,

FIGURE 2.3   Ground Zero, New York City, following the 9/11 terrorist attacks. (*Source:* U.S. Navy photo by Chief Photographer's Mate Eric J. Tilford.)

Flight 11 crashed into the North Tower of the WTC. Twenty minutes later, as many were watching what they thought was an accident, Flight 175 hit the South Tower. Because of the intensity of the jet fuel fire, those on the floors above the impact sites could not escape and waited for their time to die. Over 90 countries lost citizens, and 411 public safety personnel—who had entered the buildings to help during the emergency—died when the buildings collapsed. Others had a chance to escape.

United Flight 93, from Newark International Airport, was on its way to San Francisco when it was hijacked. As passengers on cell phones learned of the WTC attacks, they fought to control the jet, but it crashed in a rural area near Pittsburgh, killing everyone. American Airlines Flight 77 took off from Washington Dulles Airport for Los Angeles. The jet was hijacked, diverted toward the Pentagon, and crashed into it, killing all on board and 55 military personnel at the Pentagon.

Many reasons have been advanced to explain why the 9/11 attacks occurred. No single reason alone can explain the cause of the attacks. U.S. foreign policy, especially in the Middle East, and the support of Israel, has been blamed. Another explanation is the radicalization of the Afghan jihad that forced the Soviets out of Afghanistan and helped develop Al-Qaeda under Osama bin Laden. This success against the Soviets provided confidence in Al-Qaeda to battle another superpower—the United States. The conflict over religious differences (i.e., Muslims versus Christians and Jews) and the need to purify Islam, according to Al-Qaeda, are other perspectives (Bergen 2006).

Domestic Terrorism

The Federal Bureau of Investigation (2008) defines **domestic terrorism** as follows: "Domestic terrorism involves groups or individuals who are based and operate entirely in the United States and Puerto Rico without foreign direction and whose acts are directed at elements of the U.S. Government or population."

An example of a domestic terrorist cell planning an attack is as follows. In 2008, a former inmate of New Folsom Prison in California, Levar Washington, 30 years old, was sentenced to 22 years in federal prison for his role in a domestic terrorist cell planning to attack U.S. military and Jewish facilities in the Los Angeles area. Washington was recruited into the cell while in prison by Kevin James, who formed the terrorist group and required members to swear an oath of loyalty and obedience to James and the cell. Upon release from prison, cell members committed about a dozen armed robberies to raise money for the attacks. When police linked cell members to a robbery, a search of their apartment turned up a James-authored statement to be given to the media following a planned deadly attack. It read in part: "This incident is the first in a series of incidents to come in a plight to defend and propagate traditional Islam in its purity." The press release also warned "sincere Muslims" to avoid targets that support the Israeli state (U.S. Department of Justice 2008b).

Shane (2010) writes that the rash of terrorist plots in the United States during 2009 were not part of a united, well-organized and financed Al-Qaeda group, but "a scattered, uncoordinated group of amateurs who displayed more fervor than skill. The weapons were old-fashioned guns and explosives—in several cases, duds supplied by FBI informants—with no trace of the biological or radiological poisons, let alone the nuclear bombs, that have long been the ultimate fear." There were ten jihadist plots or attacks inside the United States in 2009. The deadliest was carried out by Major Nidal Malik Hasan, a U.S. Army psychiatrist at Fort Hood, Texas. Shane notes that 14 of the approximately 14,000 murders in the United States in 2009 resulted from jihadist attacks—13 at Fort Hood and another at an armed forces recruiting station in Little Rock, Arkansas.

To understand the different types of domestic terrorists, also known as "homegrown terrorists," Griset and Mahan (2003, 85–93) offer five categories.

Critical Thinking

Do you think the terrorist threat is overblown? In the future, do you think terrorists will use weapons of mass destruction or continue to use firearms and explosives? Explain your answer.

As noted previously, classifications are subject to overlap. A group's characteristics may span multiple categories, and a group may be difficult to place in any one category. In addition, terrorist groups constantly split and form new groups; older groups may become inactive permanently or "sleep" before becoming active again, and the viewpoints of terrorists change.

Left-wing groups were especially popular during the 1960s and 1970s. These groups often adhered to Marxism (i.e., the political ideology of Karl Marx that is the foundation of communism). They were against the Vietnam War and were proponents of civil rights. Although not all left-wing groups espouse violence or terrorism, during this era, those groups that became involved in violence were the Students for a Democratic Society (SDS), the Weather Underground Organization, the May 19 Communist Organization, the Black Panthers, and the Armed Forces for National Liberation (to seek independence for Puerto Rico from the United States). Shootouts with police and bombings characterized the violence.

Anarchists and *ecoterrorists* (together as one category, according to Griset and Mahan) espouse violence to reach their objectives. The anarchists, a term more popular in the 1800s and 1900s, opposed both Marxism and capitalism and favored revolution, but they had no plan for a replacement of the government. **Ecoterrorists** seek to preserve nature from human destruction. The FBI considers ecoterrorists as the number-one domestic threat because they continue their attacks in the United States. The **Animal Liberation Front (ALF)** and **People for the Ethical Treatment of Animals (PETA)** are concerned with animal rights, not eating animals, vegetarianism, and stopping research involving animals (Figure 2.4). The **Earth Liberation Front (ELF)** focuses on stopping environmental damage caused by humans. Arson has been a major weapon to try to halt development of rural lands. The FBI estimates that over $100 million in damage has resulted from arson by ecoterrorists. They are "leaderless," operate alone or in small groups, and are difficult to penetrate (Fox News 2008).

Racial supremacy (a third category) and *religious extremists* (a fourth category) are right wing, and each category may overlap the other. The KKK, neo-Nazi Aryan Nation, and skinheads are examples of racial supremacist groups. Religious extremists include the **Christian Identity Movement** that believes Jews are the offspring of the devil, and considers all nonwhites to be the "beasts in the field." There is an obvious connection between Christian

FIGURE 2.4   The Animal Liberation Front (ALF) and People for the Ethical Treatment of Animals (PETA) are concerned about the rights of animals, such as during research. (® Shutterstock.com. With permission.)

Identity and blatant racism. For this group, survival in the future is accomplished through the grace of God, their intellect, and stockpiled food and weapons (Baysinger 2006).

The fifth category is **state-sponsored terrorism**. This perspective includes U.S. government laws, policies, and actions against Native American Indians and the formation of police agencies and subsequent police action to curb the labor movement, as described in Chapter 1.

OKLAHOMA CITY BOMBING

The **Oklahoma City bombing** occurred on April 19, 1995, when Timothy McVeigh drove a rented Ryder truck containing 5,000 pounds of ammonium nitrate fertilizer, nitromethane, and a diesel fuel mixture to the front of the nine-story Alfred P. Murrah Federal Building. He parked near the building day-care center after lighting multiple fuses, locked the vehicle, and walked to his getaway vehicle. The bombing killed 168 people and injured 853. Nineteen children were killed, including fifteen from the day-care center. The blast destroyed about one-third of the building and damaged over 200 nearby buildings. This was the deadliest terrorist attack in the United States prior to the 9/11 attacks.

Less than two hours after the explosion, McVeigh was stopped by an Oklahoma state trooper for driving a vehicle without a license plate and was then arrested for having a concealed weapon. Later in the day, he was linked to the bombing via the vehicle identification on an axle from the destroyed

Ryder truck he had rented. In 1997, McVeigh was found guilty of murder and conspiracy and sentenced to death. He was executed by lethal injection on June 11, 2001, at the U.S. penitentiary in Terre Haute, Indiana. Terry Nichols, a coconspirator, was tried, found guilty, and sentenced to life without parole. Michael Fortier, another coconspirator, agreed to testify against McVeigh, received a light sentence, was released into the U.S. Witness Protection Program, and received a new identity (Wikipedia 2008).

Investigators revealed that McVeigh and Nichols were members of a right-wing militia movement and bombed the federal building in retaliation for the Ruby Ridge and Waco events. In the **Ruby Ridge incident** in 1992, Randy Weaver, a white supremacist, was under siege at his Idaho home for trying to sell illegal firearms. During the siege, a U.S. marshal, Weaver's pregnant wife, and Weaver's son were killed. Weaver finally surrendered amid much publicity over the incident, which became a symbol of right-wing struggles. In the **Waco incident** in 1993, the Bureau of Alcohol, Tobacco, and Firearms (ATF) made tragic mistakes in trying to arrest David Koresh, a religious leader, at his compound in Waco, Texas, for illegal firearms. The first assault on the compound resulted in four ATF agents being killed, 20 injured, and an unknown number of Branch Davidian casualties in the compound. The FBI then took control of the operation, cutting off electricity and water to the compound, and shining bright lights and playing loud music at night. Some members of the religious sect came out and surrendered, while others continued to wait for a message from God. After a standoff of 51 days, tear gas was fired into the compound. This was followed by the sound of explosions and the sight of intense smoke as the buildings became engulfed in flame. Seventy-five people (mostly women and children) died, and nine survived (Combs 2003, 178–179). A subsequent investigation indicated that the inhabitants of the compound set the fires.

2001 ANTHRAX ATTACKS: WAS THE TERRORIST A GOVERNMENT SCIENTIST?

Anthrax is a fatal infectious disease resulting from the bacterium known as *Bacillus anthracis*. Although the bacterium is found in the ground, human cases of infection are unusual. Infection takes place through a wound on the skin, causing a skin ulcer; through inhalation, causing respiratory failure; and through ingestion, causing vomiting and diarrhea. A strong dose of antibiotics fights the disease.

Anthrax is classified as a biological weapon. It is difficult to produce, requiring scientific expertise and equipment, but several countries possess it, including the United States.

The **2001 anthrax attacks** occurred soon after the September 11, 2001, terrorist attacks. Letters containing anthrax (in the form of a white powder) were sent via U.S. mail to employees of the news media and to members of Congress. This was the first case of a biological attack using anthrax. Twenty-two people were harmed by the anthrax in various states, half by skin contact and half by inhalation. Five died from inhaling anthrax. The disruption and cleanup at postal facilities and other locations was expensive (U.S. General Accounting Office 2003).

Many investigative questions surfaced during the anthrax investigation. Was one person responsible, or was it a conspiracy? Did a foreign government sponsor the attacks? Where and how was the anthrax produced?

Hundreds of federal agents worked on the case in the fall of 2001, with Al-Qaeda being the primary suspect group responsible for the attacks. Later, it was theorized that the offender was a government biodefense scientist. The FBI focused on Dr. Steven Hatfield and applied pressure on him through surveillance, publicized searches, and questioning (Shane and Lichtblau 2008). In 2002, they even searched several ponds for evidence near the Fort Detrick, Maryland, biodefense laboratory where Hatfield worked. Little did they know that an older man, Dr. Bruce Ivins, handing out coffee and sandwiches at one of the ponds as a Red Cross volunteer, would become a prime suspect five years later. Incidentally, when FBI agents at one of the ponds learned he worked at the lab, they asked him to leave, and he did so without protest. As for Dr. Hatfield, in 2008, a federal judge ruled that the FBI had no evidence linking him to the anthrax attacks, and he received a settlement from the government of $2.83 million and an annuity of $150,000 (Ripley 2008, 30–31).

Dr. Ivins was born in Ohio, educated at the University of Cincinnati, and worked at the Fort Detrick lab for 28 years. His work focused on vaccines for anthrax. Ivins was married, with two adopted children, and he played the keyboard at church. During 2000, his mental health was deteriorating, and he and his fellow scientists were under pressure because of problems developing an anthrax vaccine. Ivins was in counseling, hospitalized twice for depression, and one of his counselors said he had threatened to kill colleagues. A female counselor of Dr. Ivins's completed an application for a protective order and wrote that he had stalked her, threatened to kill her, and had a history of homicidal threats. Although Ivins cooperated with FBI agents during interviews and passed at least two polygraph tests, the government saw multiple motives for his involvement with the anthrax attacks. With Ivins's anthrax work under pressure, the attacks elevated his field of study to a major national security issue, resulting in an increase in funding and prestige. In addition, as part of a group of inventors of an anthrax vaccine, he could have possibly collected patent royalties. In 2003, Ivins and his colleagues received the Decoration of Exceptional Civilian Service from the Defense Department (Ripley 2008).

As the FBI was gathering more and more evidence against Dr. Ivins, and as federal prosecutors were about to indict him and seek the death penalty, he apparently committed suicide on July 29, 2008, at the age of 62. The FBI and federal prosecutors were then under pressure to release details of the case. They declared that they could prove the case beyond a reasonable doubt and that Ivins was the sole perpetrator of the attacks. The evidence was circumstantial (i.e., based upon conclusions) rather than direct (i.e., stronger evidence, without needing to draw conclusions, such as eyewitnesses). One strong piece of circumstantial evidence was lab records showing Ivins had worked unusually late on the nights prior to the anthrax letters being mailed out. Investigators reported that the envelopes used in the attacks had a printing defect and had been sold in Maryland and Virginia in 2001, including a location where Ivins had a post office box under an assumed name. He also wrote letters to members of Congress and the news media, sometimes under assumed names, and all the anthrax letters were sent to such targets. A review of his e-mails showed anger and frustration over anthrax vaccine research, and the language used in those e-mails was linked to the attack letters (Shane and Lichtblau 2008).

The arguments against the government's case are also compelling. Authorities admitted that over 100 people had access to the same supply of anthrax found in the attack letters. Searches of Ivins's home and vehicles showed no evidence of anthrax. The government could not prove that he traveled to Princeton, New Jersey, where the letters were mailed. Two bioterrorism experts, who studied available FBI evidence in response to a request from the *New York Times*, claimed that the FBI needed to release more scientific evidence for the experts to draw conclusions. The FBI also chose not to release the results of handwriting analysis of the attack letters (Shane and Lichtblau 2008).

Critical Thinking

Do you think authorities could have proven their case against Dr. Bruce Ivins beyond a reasonable doubt? Do you think federal authorities accused the wrong person, again, in the anthrax attacks?

Terrorist Attacks and Weapons

Terrorists apply various types of violence. These include bombings, suicide bombings, armed assaults with small arms, kidnappings, hostage taking (Figure 2.5), hijackings, and assassinations. Suicide bombings are especially effective as a "poor person's smart bomb," because the bomb can be delivered to a specific target and detonated at a precise moment. In addition, no escape plan is needed, and a terrorist group does not have to be concerned about the bomber giving up information upon being apprehended and subjected to interrogation.

Terrorists are especially devious in their attacks. They may detonate a bomb, wait for police or other first responders and a crowd to gather, and

**FIGURE 2.5   Terrorists apply various types of violence, such as hostage taking. (®
Shutterstock.com. With permission.)**

then detonate a **secondary device**. In addition, they may detonate several
bombs at one time. Terrorists are also creative and place bombs in almost
anything (e.g., a book, wheelchair, computer, motorcycle, or a dead body).
A bomb constructed from household and readily available items is known
as an **improvised explosive device** (IED). Unfortunately, instructions on
bomb making are easily available on the Web.

Terrorists have the advantage of surprise; they can attack without warning at a time of their own choosing. Another advantage is in target selection.
There are an almost infinite number of **soft targets**, which are locations with
limited security that make penetration and attack easy. Examples are buses,
trains, retail shopping malls, schools and colleges, hospitals, and houses of
worship. **Hard targets** maintain formidable security that presents difficult
obstacles for adversaries. Examples are military facilities, prisons and jails,
nuclear plants, and airports.

Terrorists employ a variety of methods to recruit attackers. They manipulate
the media, apply propaganda, use the Internet, make speeches and write publications, and interact in schools and houses of worship to influence others.

Weapons of Mass Destruction

The weapons generating the most fear are **weapons of mass destruction**
(WMD), because they have the potential to cause enormous casualties.
Although four major types of WMD are chemical, biological, radiological,

and nuclear, creative terrorists may use our own assets to create a WMD. An example is the 9/11 attacks; however, many other scenarios are possible, such as placing a bomb on a rail car filled with chemicals as it enters a city.

The chemical attacks of World War I, as German and Allied forces gassed each other, illustrate the horror of chemical warfare. Saddam Hussein, the former leader of Iraq, gassed his own people in 1987 and 1988 to suppress a revolt by the Kurds. In Japan, in 1995, the **Aum Shinrikyo cult** released the nerve agent sarin on five trains bound for central Tokyo. This chemical attack caused 12 deaths and about 6,000 injuries.

Most chemical agents are inhaled to cause harm. Examples are chlorine and cyanide. Blister agents (e.g., sulfur mustard) harm the skin, eyes, lungs, and digestive system. Nerve agents, such as sarin, cause many harmful symptoms to multiple organs of the body. Irritating agents temporarily incapacitate; examples are tear gas, Mace, and pepper spray.

Biological weapons have existed for hundreds of years, even in crude forms. Infected corpses, food, and other hosts containing disease were sent from one enemy to another to spread disease and kill. Symptoms are similar to the flu, prior to death. Examples of biological agents are viruses, bacteria (e.g., anthrax), rickettsiae, fungi, and toxins.

Radioactive material is not protected well within our society or globally. It is used to treat cancer, sterilize food, and serves other useful purposes in several industries. A **radiological dispersion device** or **dirty bomb** consists of radioactive material attached to a conventional bomb or IED. The harm to humans and destruction from such a device depends on the grade of the radioactive material. An explosion can render an area dangerous for humans, and victims can develop cancer.

Terrorists may be able to acquire a small nuclear weapon through the black market. These weapons are sometimes referred to as *backpack nuclear weapons* because they can fit in a backpack. Larger devices can be placed in cargo containers or other modes of transportation. Casualties could amount to hundreds of thousands of dead, $1 trillion in damage, and widespread panic. Government countermeasures include eliminating and securing nuclear stockpiles worldwide in cooperation with other governments, screening incoming cargo, and enhancing response teams to disarm devices (Hall 2008).

Research by Shelley (2006) shows that nuclear smuggling is rarely detected because it occurs through professionals and well-established contraband-smuggling networks, facilitated by corruption and without fear of apprehension by smugglers. She notes that technical solutions, such as detectors, may be ineffective when shipments are "protected" by corrupt officials. More attention needs to be paid to the crime and terrorist networks that facilitate trade in contraband. Shelley relates the case of former Russian minister of atomic energy, Yevgeny Adamov, who misused funds from the United States to safeguard nuclear sites. He was extradited from Switzerland to Russia for trial. Shelley wrote that the Russian phrase that "the fish rots from the head" applies to the Russian nuclear industry, where Adamov provided no incentive for his subordinates to maintain integrity.

Security practitioners should be mindful of the impact of WMD on business operations. Although explosive weapons are more likely to be used by terrorists, at the same time, WMD attacks will occur in the future, and the consequences will likely be catastrophic. There are many potential scenarios, and terrorists are creative. For example, the detonation of a "dirty bomb" or the release of a chemical or biological weapon in an office building or business district would have enormous consequences for people, assets, and business operations. If a seaport were attacked, businesses connected to a supply chain linked to the seaport would face serious problems. Later chapters cover relevant topics (e.g., infrastructure protection and business continuity).

National Strategies

The executive branch of the federal government prepares and updates several national strategies to protect the United States and its citizens, assets, and interests. A major strategy is the "National Security Strategy" (White House 2006a). It includes the goals of human dignity for all, defeating terrorism, defusing regional conflicts, reducing the threat of WMD, and facilitating global economic growth and democracy. Other national strategies include those that focus on national defense, WMD, cyberspace, illegal drugs, and money laundering.

The "National Strategy for Combating Terrorism" (White House 2006b) concentrates on four priorities: preventing terrorist attacks, denying WMD to rogue states and terrorists, denying terrorists the support and sanctuary of rogue states, and denying terrorists control of any nation they would use as a base for attacks.

The U.S. Department of State (2008b) is the diplomatic arm of the U.S. government. Its Office of the Coordinator for Counterterrorism leads a worldwide effort to combat terrorism through diplomacy, economic power, intelligence, law enforcement, and the armed forces. The office, among other bodies of government (e.g., Department of Defense), implements the goals of the "National Strategy for Combating Terrorism."

Another national strategy is the "National Strategy for Homeland Security" (White House 2007b). It has four major goals: prevent and disrupt terrorist attacks; protect citizens, critical infrastructure, and key resources; respond to and recover from incidents; and continue to enhance our capabilities. This strategy not only focuses on the risk of terrorism, but also risks from natural disasters, including diseases and hazards such as hurricanes and earthquakes, and human-made accidents. This strategy recognizes that homeland security is a national effort of cooperation among all levels of government, the private and nonprofit sectors, and individual citizens. International partners are also vital. Critical of homeland security prior to the 9/11 attacks, this strategy noted the patchwork of efforts to protect the United States among numerous bodies of government and the lack of a unified, cooperative approach.

There was a failure of our system in detecting the 9/11 attacks. This failure of our law enforcement and intelligence agencies, often working in isolation from one another when they had "pieces of the puzzle" to expose the 9/11 plans of attack, is the major reason for the creation of the Department of Homeland Security and a director of national intelligence.

ISSUE

Why Was the Federal Government Inept Prior to and during the 9/11 Attacks?

The National Commission on Terrorist Attacks upon the United States was created by Congress and President George W. Bush in 2002 to study the 9/11 attacks and provide recommendations to improve security. The "9/11 Commission Report" of the National Commission (2004) was highly critical of U.S. government bodies and their actions and inaction prior to, during, and following the 9/11 attacks. Major criticisms are listed next.

- There was a lack of coordination and communications between the Federal Aviation Administration (this agency regulates civil aviation to promote safety) and the military.
- The FBI, CIA, and other agencies failed at sharing intelligence for the greater good.
- The terrorists studied security weaknesses and exploited them.
- There was a failure of "imagination." Leaders did not think about the creativity and capabilities of Al-Qaeda.
- The Clinton and pre-9/11 Bush administrations and Congress did not consider terrorism as a high-priority concern, and they did not protect the borders as a national security issue.
- Airline employees were trained to comply with hijacker demands and to avoid confrontation.

Major statements and recommendations by the Commission are listed next.

- Following the 9/11 attacks, U.S. military action was correct in pursuing Al-Qaeda and ousting the Taliban from Afghanistan for providing a safe haven for Al-Qaeda. Multiple strategies must continue, namely diplomacy, economic policy, foreign aid, intelligence, covert action, law enforcement, and homeland defense.

- The enemy is not the Islamic faith, but a perversion of it by extremists who practice intolerance and combine religion and politics, while distorting both.
- Establish a National Counterterrorism Center (NCTC) to facilitate unity and cooperation among government agencies (e.g., FBI, CIA, and others). Appoint a national intelligence director to manage the NCTC. (These recommendations were implemented.)

Federal Legislation for Counterterrorism and All-Hazards Protection

In democratic societies, a dilemma persists when government takes action to control both terrorism and the effects of a disaster. A balance must be struck between police powers and the control of citizens versus constitutional rights. For instance, to counter terrorism, how much power should be granted to law enforcement officials to conduct searches, seize evidence, interview suspects, and confine them? In the event of a pandemic (i.e., outbreak of a disease over a large population), how much power should be exercised by government authorities to quarantine citizens to control the spread of disease? These types of questions generate considerable controversy in democratic nations as laws are enacted to deal with terrorism and all-hazards. Here we name and explain major, relevant federal laws.

The **Defense Against Weapons of Mass Destruction Act of 1996**, also called Nunn-Lugar, was enacted by Congress in response to three terrorist attacks: the first World Trade Center bombing in 1993, the Oklahoma City bombing in 1995, and the Tokyo subway chemical attack in 1995. This legislation aimed to improve federal government preparedness activities, training, and equipment for first responders to help them respond to WMD.

The **Antiterrorism and Effective Death Penalty Act of 1996** was designed to prevent terrorist acts, improve counterterrorism, and increase punishments for guilty offenders. Provisions of this 1996 Act include support for the death penalty when a terrorist act causes death, power to the secretary of state to establish a formal list of Foreign Terrorist Organizations (FTOs), and prohibition of financial support within the United States for international terrorist groups.

Once the 9/11 attacks occurred, government action against terrorism became much more intense. The nation was in shock, and government leaders knew that a strong response was necessary. A major enactment that generated much controversy was the **USA Patriot Act of 2001**. This 2001 Act not only enhanced law enforcement powers to investigate terrorist suspects, but it covered a wide variety of provisions, such as electronic surveillance, money laundering, protection of borders, rewards for information, improvements in intelligence, critical infrastructure protection, and victim compensation. Because of concerns over constitutional rights, lawmakers included sunset provisions in the law so that expanded police powers would expire in four years. In 2006, with terrorist cells in the United States still being exposed and prosecuted, President George W. Bush signed the **USA Patriot Improvement and Reauthorization Act of 2005**. The 2001 Act was provided with four more years of life with some minor modifications.

Another major piece of legislation from Congress following the 9/11 attacks was the **Homeland Security Act of 2002**. This 2002 Act resulted in a massive reorganization of the federal government. It established the **Department of Homeland Security (DHS)** as an agency of the executive branch of government, with a DHS secretary who reports to the president.

The **Intelligence Reform and Terrorism Prevention Act of 2004** answered the call to reform the intelligence community because of the intelligence failures prior to the 9/11 attacks. The purpose of the 2004 Act was to modernize the intelligence community and make it more unified, coordinated, and effective. A transformation was needed for intelligence to not only focus on foreign countries and their policies, strategies, economies, technology, and military capabilities, but also terrorist recruitment, training, strategies, and weapons. As recommended by the 9/11 Commission, the 2004 Act established a director of national security and the National Counterterrorism Center (NCTC).

Another federal law resulting from the 9/11 Commission was the **Implementing Recommendations of the 9/11 Commission Act of 2007** (Public Law 110-53). This law contains many of the commission's recommendations and is broad in scope. Besides homeland security and emergency management grants, this law includes provisions to improve communications among first responders, intelligence sharing, preventing terrorist travel, private-sector preparedness, and critical infrastructure security (especially for transportation).

Other federal laws have been enacted since the 9/11 attacks to counter terrorism and promote all-hazards protection. In addition, executive orders from the president and state laws have strengthened security and protection.

GLOBAL PERSPECTIVE: UNITED NATIONS COUNTERTERRORISM

For many years, the United Nations (UN) has been seeking to develop global counterterrorism strategies in agreement with member states. On September 8, 2006, the UN General Assembly finally adopted strategies that member states can apply to "address the conditions conducive to the spread of terrorism, prevent and combat terrorism and strengthen their individual and collective capacity to do so, and protect human rights and uphold the rule of law while countering terrorism" (United Nations 2007). The **UN Counterterrorism Implementation Task Force** (CTITF) coordinates efforts of at least two dozen UN entities. The task force established working groups to facilitate the following:

- Developing an integrated, cooperative strategy among member states
- Offering member states assistance in identifying how radicalization and extremism may lead to terrorism and ideas for prevention
- Countering the use of the Internet to facilitate terrorism
- Protecting human rights during counterterrorism actions
- Developing and sharing best practices to protect terrorist targets
- Developing and sharing best practices to support the victims of terrorism
- Developing strategies and standards to curb the financing of terrorism

To reduce the conditions that help to spread terrorism, the UN facilitates peace agreements in numerous conflicts. It also established the Mediation Support Unit and the Peacebuilding Support Office. The UN promotes dialogue among cultures and religions, as well as tolerance.

UN activities to prevent and combat terrorism are further explained here. The UN develops legal instruments that provide a legal framework for multilateral actions and to criminalize acts of terrorism. Technical assistance is also available. The UN requires states to impose sanctions (e.g., assets freeze, travel ban, and an arms embargo) on individuals and entities that associate with Al-Qaeda, Osama Bin Laden, and/or the Taliban. UN military and police units involved in peacekeeping operations seek to maintain security while limiting terrorism operations. To strengthen the security of nuclear and other radioactive materials, the (UN) **International Atomic Energy Agency** supports states through nuclear security plans. A bioincident database is used by the UN to detail biological incidents where a biological agent threatened to harm or did harm humans, livestock, or agricultural assets. By promoting adherence to the Chemical Weapons Convention, the UN contributes to counterterrorism. The UN assists states in promoting security at chemical facilities and responding to attacks on such. It has inventoried and secured thousands of tons of chemical agents and former chemical weapons production facilities. The UN also has programs in place to protect civil aviation, travel documents, and the maritime industry. The **World Health Organization**, another component of the UN, responds to all public health emergencies of international significance. It develops standards, conducts training, maintains an alert system, performs risk assessments, and mobilizes specialists.

Although the International Criminal Police Organization (Interpol) is not a component of the UN, it is a member of the CTITF. **Interpol** was created in 1923, and it is the world's largest police organization, headquartered in Lyon, France, with 186 member countries. Its purpose is to create a safer world by facilitating cooperation among organizations that prevent and counter international crime, even between nations that have no diplomatic relations. Interpol offers databases for police, crisis management services, training, and publications. Its staff is from about 80 countries, and it is funded by member countries, based upon a formula. The budget in 2008 was 47.6 million euros (Interpol 2008).

Interpol's role with the CTITF is to function through a special task force, facilitate the exchange of best practices and operational information, and identify terrorists and their methods (e.g., recruitment, training, and financing). Interpol operates a global database on wanted individuals, fingerprints, DNA profiles, photos, stolen and lost travel documents, and other information available to police and border checkpoints worldwide. It also has the capability to dispatch on-site Incident Response Teams following a terrorist attack.

The UN Department of Safety and Security coordinates the protection of UN staff, assets, and operations at duty stations globally. The UN Interregional Crime and Justice Research Institute provides support and training to member states involved in security preparations for such events as the Olympic Games and high-level summits.

Homeland Security

The executive branch of the federal government (White House 2007b, 3) defines **homeland security** as "a concerted national effort to prevent terrorist attacks within the United States, reduce America's vulnerability to terrorism, and minimize the damage and recover from attacks that do occur."

There is no universally acceptable definition of homeland security. The many definitions that do exist are influenced by the writer's background. Practitioners in security, law enforcement, the fire service, emergency management, the military, and other vocations each view homeland security differently. In addition, homeland security changes as serious events unfold and the public and politicians respond.

Bellavita (2008) writes of multiple definitions of homeland security based on claims of what it should emphasize. His perspectives include all hazards, terrorism, national security, and government efforts to curb civil liberties. He notes that each definition represents a set of interests, a need for resources, and an effort to develop a niche in homeland security. Four of his definitions follow, each based upon a different perspective.

- All-hazards perspective: "Homeland security is a concerted national effort to prevent and disrupt terrorist attacks, protect against man-made and natural hazards, and respond to and recover from incidents that do occur."

- Terrorism perspective: "Homeland security is a concerted national effort by federal, state and local governments, by the private sector, and by individuals to prevent terrorist attacks within the United States, reduce America's vulnerability to terrorism, and minimize the damage and recover from attacks that do occur."
- National security perspective: "Homeland security is an element of national security that works with the other instruments of national power to protect the sovereignty, territory, domestic population, and critical infrastructure of the United States against threats and aggression."
- Government efforts to curb civil liberties perspective: "Homeland security is a symbol used to justify government efforts to curtail civil liberties."

Department of Homeland Security

The Department of Homeland Security (DHS) employs about 180,000 men and women who work to protect the United States from a variety of threats and hazards. DHS strategic goals are as follows (U.S. Department of Homeland Security 2007):

- *Awareness*: Identify threats, determine impacts, and disseminate information
- *Prevention*: Detect, deter, and mitigate threats
- *Protection*: Safeguard people, assets, critical infrastructure, and the economy from terrorism, natural disasters, and other emergencies
- *Response*: Coordinate assistance when adverse events occur
- *Recovery*: Coordinate the restoration of communities following adverse events
- *Service*: Facilitate lawful trade, travel, and immigration
- *Organizational excellence*: Create a culture that promotes DHS employees as the most important resource and enhance their effectiveness

The DHS strives to fulfill these strategic goals. They are benchmarks for DHS management and employees. At the same time, the DHS has been subject to criticism from several quarters. These include the Government Accountability Office, the DHS Office of Inspector General, private interest groups, the public, the media, and politicians. Feedback is important to the DHS, as with other entities, because it helps it to improve its efficiency and effectiveness.

The major organizational components of the DHS are listed next.

- The *Directorate for National Protection and Programs* works to reduce the risks facing our nation through an integrated approach that includes physical and virtual threats.

- The *Directorate for Science and Technology* conducts research and development and provides agencies at all levels of government with technologies to protect the homeland.
- The *Directorate for Management* is responsible for DHS budgets, accounting, human resources, IT systems, facilities and equipment, and performance measures.
- The *Office of Policy* focuses on policy formulation and coordination and planning. (Policies guide employees in their decisions.)
- The *Office of Health Affairs* prepares and responds to events related to medical emergencies (e.g., an outbreak of a disease).
- The *Office of Intelligence and Analysis* collects information and intelligence to study threats to the United States.
- The *Office of Operations Coordination* monitors the security of the United States on a daily basis and works with units in the DHS, state governors, law enforcement partners, the private sector, and others.
- The *Transportation Security Administration* (TSA) protects the transportation systems (e.g., aviation) of the United States.
- *Customs and Border Protection* (CBP) secures U.S. borders, prevents contraband from entering and leaving, and facilitates legitimate travel of people and things through the borders.
- *Immigration and Customs Enforcement* (ICE) is the largest investigative component of the DHS and is responsible for immigration and customs law enforcement within the United States.
- *Citizenship and Immigration Services* administers immigration and naturalization (i.e., approves citizenship) adjudication functions and implements policies and priorities.
- The *Federal Emergency Management Agency* (FEMA) prepares the United States for hazardous events, responds to events, and aids in recovery.
- The *U.S. Secret Service* protects the president and other dignitaries and investigates counterfeiting and other financial crimes. It also focuses on identity theft, computer fraud, and computer-based attacks on financial, banking, and telecommunications infrastructure.
- The *Federal Law Enforcement Training Center* trains law enforcement professionals.
- The *Coast Guard* focuses on safety and rescue on waterways; on environmental protection; and on security at ports, waterways, along the coast, and on international waters (Figure 2.6).

FIGURE 2.6   **U.S. Coast Guard on homeland security patrol in New York City harbor. (*Source:* U.S. Coast Guard photo by Petty Officer Tom Sperduto.)**

Federal Emergency Management Agency and All-Hazards Protection

In 1979, because of the fragmentation of federal, state, and local agencies responsible for the management of disasters, and the inadequate response when disasters occurred, the administration of President Jimmy Carter established the **Federal Emergency Management Agency (FEMA)** through Executive Order 12127. This order was designed to unify emergency preparedness, mitigation, and response into one agency, with a director who would report directly to the president. President Carter appointed, and the Senate confirmed, John Macy as the first director of FEMA in 1979. Macy was a career civil servant with wide experience who stressed the similarities between natural hazards preparedness and civil defense against enemy attacks. This resulted in the development of an "all-hazards" approach to emergencies. The **all-hazards preparedness concept** focuses on similarities in the preparation for a variety of hazards, whether an earthquake, terrorist attack, or other emergency. However, Purpura (2007, 250) notes:

> The all-hazards approach seeks to maximize the efficiency and cost effectiveness of emergency management efforts through a realization that different risks and disasters contain similarities that can benefit, to a certain degree, from generic approaches to emergency management. However, there is a point at which generic emergency management must divide into specialized emergency management. For example, the detonation of a "dirty-bomb" or

an approaching hurricane necessitates evacuation; however, the victims and the scene of these disasters require markedly different expertise, treatment, and equipment.

Although the all-hazards preparedness concept became widely known and applied, problems of emergency management persisted. Hurricane Hugo struck the Southeast in 1989 and became the worst hurricane in a decade, causing 85 deaths and $15 billion in damage to South Carolina, North Carolina, and other locations. The FEMA response was so inadequate that Senator Ernest Hollings, from South Carolina, called the agency the "sorriest bunch of bureaucratic jackasses." Adding to the challenges of emergency management and all-hazards protection, the first World Trade Center bombing in 1993 began a rethinking of how our government agencies should respond to terrorist attacks. A major answer occurred following the 9/11 attacks with the establishment of the DHS in 2002, with FEMA placed within the DHS. Unfortunately, the **Katrina disaster** of 2005 created another "black eye" for FEMA because the all-hazards national response plan failed. Government response was slow, while victims of the disaster suffered. Hurricane Katrina caused 1,833 deaths, $125 billion in damage, a flood in New Orleans, and destruction along Gulf Coast states. It was the most expensive natural disaster in U.S. history (Blanchard 2007).

The Katrina disaster showed the need for revision of the National Response Plan (NRP) that was created in 2004 by the federal government following the 9/11 attacks, and the need for all-hazards protection. The NRP reflected the federal government's efforts to develop a unified and coordinated emergency response to disasters, but it required improvement. In 2008, the **National Response Framework (NRF)** replaced the NRP, which was criticized for placing too much emphasis on *federal* government response to emergencies. In the NRF, in coordination with the DHS and FEMA, more weight is placed on *local*, *county*, and *state* preparedness and response. A key change in the NRF is the elimination of the term "Incident of National Significance" as specified in the NRP, which played a role in the slow response to hurricane Katrina because government executives waited for this declaration before responding. It caused an arbitrary and confusing trigger point for response. The NRF complements the **National Incident Management System (NIMS)** that emphasizes *standardization* in terminology; planning; training; response; unified command structure, equipment, information management, and forms; and other areas of emergency management. The NIMS helps all levels of government and the private sector to work together more efficiently and effectively. It also contains principles, best practices, and organizational processes.

It is important to note the vital and major role of local and state governments in homeland security, protecting critical infrastructure, and responding to emergencies. Every day, local police, fire, emergency medical, and other services respond to calls for service to save lives, care for victims, and protect property. These local, public safety agencies are more likely to be on the scene of a disaster much faster than federal agencies.

YOUR CAREER IN SECURITY

Government Security

Although this book emphasizes private sector (i.e., business) security, which employs millions of people, public sector (i.e., government) security also employs millions of people in criminal justice agencies, and government agencies in general, on the federal, state, and local levels, plus the military branches. Jails and prisons have traditionally maintained strict security to prevent escapes. Violence at courthouses and law enforcement agencies has resulted in enhanced security. In addition, military facilities worldwide, obviously require strict security, whether in a combat zone or not. Today, management in government buildings of all types must consider threats and hazards in the environment and take action to protect people, assets, the building itself, and operations.

Following the September 11, 2001, terrorist attacks, the U.S. Department of Homeland Security (DHS) was created to protect America, and it consolidated 22 federal agencies, with about 170,000 employees, within one organization (U.S. Department of Labor 2008). Many other federal government agencies, not within the DHS, contend with security issues. Examples are the Federal Bureau of Investigation, the Central Intelligence Agency, the U.S. Postal Service, and the U.S. Marshals Service.

Besides federal agencies, state and local government agencies are also concerned about homeland security issues. States, cities, and counties typically have some type of homeland security and/or emergency management department.

Nature of the Work

Government security work involves many types of duties. Besides government security officers assigned to access points and patrol, another category of security employee, the security specialist, conducts security surveys and risk analyses to determine how to improve security at buildings. An additional category, investigators and agents, respond to incidents of crime, threats, issues of national security, and other problems. Investigations may occur on the premises—or anywhere in the world—to gather facts, intelligence, and evidence, so that superiors can decide on various courses of action, such as firing an employee; improving policies, procedures, and security; making an arrest; or contacting another nation for assistance.

Once government security personnel gather facts through interviewing, stationary or moving surveillance, performing studies of the status of security, and other methods, they prepare reports for their supervisors. Preparing reports and completing standard organizational forms (i.e., the "paperwork") consumes a lot of time for government security personnel, as with other occupations. (This is something rarely seen on television programs.)

Preparation of a report may be followed by a presentation of the report to others. This may entail verbal and visual (e.g., photos and PowerPoint) reports to management, conducting a training class, or testifying at a hearing or trial.

The day-to-day tasks of practitioners employed in government security include "desk work," such as making and responding to telephone calls, preparing and responding to e-mails, and conducting research on the Web or through restricted government information systems. Working with coworkers is essential and involves meetings to plan security, raids, investigations, and other duties. Supervisors and managers usually spend a lot of time in their offices.

Fieldwork away from the office includes interviewing victims, witnesses, and suspects; visiting a site for a security assessment; or making an arrest and transporting the arrestee to jail. Attending training programs is an essential aspect of the job, as in other professions.

Government security practitioners must always be available for emergencies. They often work various shifts, and they may travel frequently. Federal and state employees in certain positions must relocate periodically.

Government security work can be dangerous and stressful at times. Practitioners must be alert and cautious. The work can affect the private lives of practitioners.

Government security includes many specializations and opportunities for advancement. Examples include crime prevention, physical security, personnel security, information security, information technology (IT) security, special weapons and tactics (SWAT), special response units for weapons of mass destruction (WMD), investigations, counterterrorism, intelligence, and counterintelligence.

Requirements

Applicants for entry-level positions in government security go through an extensive screening process that checks physical and personal qualifications. Honesty and integrity are valued, as well as excellent written and verbal communications skills. An interview and background investigation are typical. Depending on the employer, a variety of tests may be administered, such as a cognitive-ability test (to measure an applicant's verbal, quantitative, and reasoning abilities); tests that measure hearing, vision, strength, and agility; medical examination; polygraph examination; drug test; and psychological evaluation.

The education and experience requirements differ among agencies. Because government security positions are competitive and require many skills, an associate or bachelor's degree enhances an applicant's opportunities. Federal agencies often require a bachelor's degree (although not all positions require it) and experience. Once an applicant is screened and hired, the next step is training at an academy or specialized school. Topics include law, use of force, firearms, surveillance techniques, security, terrorism, and many other subjects.

Salary

Because of the threat of crime, including terrorism, and other security issues that the United States faces domestically and abroad, the employment prospects in government security are excellent. In reference to U.S. Department of Labor (2008) research on the salaries of detectives and investigators, who often perform security-related duties, median annual earnings in 2006, were $69,510 in the federal government, $49,370 in state government, and $52,520 in local government, plus overtime and benefits. Other government employees who perform security duties and are employed by local, state, and federal agencies, and the military, receive a broad range of salaries, many comparable to the above figures, especially if they are in specialized units or in supervisory or management positions.

Advice

If you have an interest in a particular government agency, conduct research on the Web. It contains a wealth of information on specific agency history, requirements, screening, training, job duties, specializations, advancement, earnings, and openings.

Summary

The numerous threats and hazards that face organizations include crimes, fires, accidents, and natural and human-made disasters. It is the responsibility of security practitioners to ascertain vulnerabilities and priorities, and to plan and implement strategies of protection for people, assets, and operations. Examples of questions of importance are: Is the business high profile (e.g., critical infrastructure and/or subject to controversy)? In what geographic area(s) is business conducted? Where are suppliers and customers located? What transportation systems are linked to the business? How are IT systems protected? What are the vulnerabilities of business locations, and what events and disasters have occurred in the past?

Although protection against terrorism may not be a top priority for a security practitioner, a basic knowledge of this complex topic, as explained in this chapter, is important because one major incident can have major repercussions. Years ago, events occurring on the other side of the globe often had limited, if any, consequences at home. Today, the opposite is true. The global economy is affected by many events, threats, and hazards that occur on a regular basis.

A major public-sector strategy at all levels of government to protect against a variety of adverse events is called *all-hazards protection*. The last section of this chapter explained government action against terrorism and government all-hazards protection. The remainder of this book emphasizes private-sector protection from a variety of threats and hazards.

Discussion Questions

1. Generally, what do you think are the most serious threats and hazards facing organizations and the security function?
2. What factors would make a security executive more or less concerned about the threat of terrorism?
3. Why is terrorism such a difficult term to define?
4. What are your suggestions for improving the U.S. response to terrorism?
5. How does terrorism affect businesses and business security?
6. How much reliance should a business place on local and state public safety agencies and FEMA when a disaster strikes?
7. What are your suggestions for improving government (i.e., local, state, and federal) preparation and response to disasters?

Practical Applications

2A. You are a uniformed security officer on duty in an office-building lobby. What do you do upon noticing a man holding a knife to the throat of a female employee?

2B. As a security investigator for a company that manufactures expensive handbags and other items for women, your superior requests that you apply all of your time and effort to the problem of counterfeiting of the company's handbags. What is your plan of action to investigate these crimes, gather evidence, contact the police to seek arrests and prosecution, and prevent the manufacture and sales of the fake items?

2C. You are a security executive for a major international corporation based in the United States that manufactures chemicals. Your supervisor requests your presence at a meeting tomorrow on a new business venture for the corporation in Algeria. You will be asked about the overall security and safety situation in Algeria. Following your research on Algeria at the U.S. Department of State Web site and other sites, what do you say?

2D. As a newly hired assistant to the director of security for a retail chain, your first major assignment is to prepare a manual for your superior to be used as a guide in the event of a natural disaster in the geographic region where the stores are located. What organizations do you list in the manual as points of contact for the director?

Internet Connections

Animal Liberation Front: www.animalliberationfront.com/.

Brand Protection Alliance: www.brandprotectionalliance.com/about/about-us.html.

Center for Defense Information: www.cdi.org.

Centers for Disease Control (CDC): www.bt.cdc.gov.

Center for the Study of Terrorism and Political Violence: www.st-andrews.ac.uk/intrel/research/cstpv/.

Central Intelligence Agency: www.cia.gov.

Earth Liberation Front: http://earth-liberation-front.org.

Federal Bureau of Investigation: www.fbi.gov.

Federal Emergency Management Agency: www.fema.gov.

Government Accountability Office: www.gao.gov.

Hezbollah: www.hezbollah.org/.

International Institute for Counter-Terrorism: www.ict.org.il/.

Interpol: www.interpol.int/Default.asp.

Islamic Resistance Movement-HAMAS: www.hamasonline.com.

National Commission on Terrorist Attacks upon the United States: www.9-11commission.gov.

National Consortium for the Study of Terrorism and Responses to Terror: http://www.start.umd.edu/about/.

National Counterterrorism Center: www.nctc.gov.

Office of the President: www.whitehouse.gov.

Overseas Security Advisory Council (OSAC): www.OSAC.gov.

People for the Ethical Treatment of Animals: www.peta.org/.

Popular Front for the Liberation of Palestine: members.tripod.com/~freepalestine.

Project for the Research of Islamist Movements: www.e-prism.org/pages/1/.

Southern Poverty Law Center: www.splcenter.org.

Terrorism Research Center: www.terrorism.com.

United Kingdom Security Service (MI5): www.mi5.gov.uk.

United Nations: www.un.org.

U.S. Department of Defense: www.defenselink.mil.

U.S. Department of Homeland Security: www.dhs.gov.

U.S. Department of State: www.state.gov.

U.S. Secret Service: www.secretservice.gov.

White Aryan Resistance: www.resist.com/.

World Health Organization: http://www.who.int/en/.

References

Albanese, J. 2005. *Criminal justice*. 3rd ed. Boston: Allyn & Bacon.

Baysinger, T. 2006. Right-wing group characteristics and ideology. *Homeland Security Affairs* 2 (July).

Bellavita, C. 2008. Changing homeland security: What is homeland security? *Homeland Security Affairs* 4 (June).

Bergen, P. 2006. What were the causes of 9/11? New America Foundation. www.newamerica.net/publications.

Blanchard, B. 2007. Billion dollar U.S. disasters. training.fema.gov/.

Calhoun, C., et al. 2001. *Understanding sociology*. New York: Glencoe-McGraw-Hill.

Clayton, C., et al. 2003. Terrorism as group violence. In *Terrorism: strategies for intervention*, ed. H. Hall. Binghamton, NY: Haworth Press.

CNN. 2010. Airplane bomb suspect indicted (January 6, 2010). www.cnn.com/2010/CRIME/01/06/detroit.bomb/index.html?iref=allsearch.

Combs, C. 2003. *Terrorism in the twenty-first century*. 3rd ed. Upper Saddle River, NJ: Prentice Hall.

Council of Arab Ministers of the Interior and the Council of Arab Ministers of Justice. 1998. The Arab Convention for the suppression of terrorism. www.al-bab.com.

Crenshaw, M. 1990. The logic of terrorism: Terrorist behavior as a product of strategic choice. In *Terrorism: Strategies for intervention*, ed. H. Hall. Binghamton, NY: Haworth Press.

Dyson, W. 2001. *Terrorism: An investigator's handbook*. Cincinnati: Anderson.

Federal Bureau of Investigation. 2008. Terrorism. http://denver.fbi.gov/nfip.htm.

Fox News. 2008. FBI: Eco-terrorism remains no. 1 domestic terror threat (March 31). www.foxnews.com.

Gage, B. 2001. What happened when Wall Street was bombed in 1920? *History News Service*. http://historynewsnetwork.org.

Griset, P., and S. Mahan. 2003. *Terrorism in perspective*. Thousand Oaks, CA: Sage.

Gurr, T. 1989. Political terrorism: Historical antecedents and contemporary trends. In *Violence in America: Protest, rebellion, and reform*, ed. T. Gurr. Newbury Park, CA: Sage.

Hall, M. 2008. Experts to testify of "growing" nuke threat to U.S. *USA Today* (April 9). www.usatoday.com/.

Hayes, B., et al. 2008. The forces of change. *Security* 5 (April):44.

Interpol. 2008. About Interpol. www.interpol.int/Public/ICPO/default.asp.

IslamicInformation.net. 2008. Islam in a Nutshell. www.islamicinformation.net/2008/05/islamic-guide-islam-in-nutshell.html.

Kaiser, T. 2008. French Revolution. Encarta Online Encyclopedia. http://encarta.msn.com.

Laqueur, W. 2003. *The History of Zionism*. New York: Tauris Publishing.

McCourt, M. 2008. Keeping up with new threats. *Security* 45 (March):16.

Merriam–Webster On-line Dictionary. Threat. Hazard. 2008. www.merriam-webster.com.

National Commission on Terrorist Attacks upon the United States. 2004. The 9/11 Commission Report. http://govinfo.library.unt.edu/9/11.

National Counterterrorism Center. 2008. 2007 Report on terrorism (April 30). www.nctc.gov.

National Intelligence Council. 2007. The terrorist threat to the U.S. homeland (July). www.hsdl.org.

Nazarov, A. 2007. Stormy weather: Protecting your brand. *Information Security* 10 (July/August):37.

Poland, J. 2005. *Understanding terrorism: Groups, strategies, and responses*. 2nd ed. Englewood Cliffs, NJ: Prentice Hall.

Purpura, P. 2007. *Terrorism and homeland security: An introduction with applications.* Burlington, MA: Elsevier.

Ripley, A. 2008. The anthrax files. *Time,* 172 (August 18):30–31.

Security Executive Forum. 2003. Not everyone sees preventing terrorist attacks as job 1 for corporate security. *Corporate Security* 29 (November 30).

Shane, S. 2010. A year of terror plots, through a second prism. *New York Times* (January 13). www.nytimes.com/2010/01/13.

Shane, S., and E. Lichtblau. 2008. Officials say documents tie scientist to anthrax attack. *New York Times* (August 7). www.nytimes.com/2008/08/07.

Shelley, L. 2006. Trafficking in nuclear materials: Criminals and terrorists. *Global Crime* 7 (August-November).

Simonsen, C., and J. Spindlove. 2004. *Terrorism today.* 2nd ed. Upper Saddle River, NJ: Prentice Hall.

United Nations. 2007. Fact sheet: Implementing the global counter-terrorism strategy (December). www.un.org/terrorism/.

U.S. Department of Homeland Security. 2007. Strategic plan: Securing our homeland. www.dhs.gov/xabout/strategicplan/.

U.S. Department of Justice. 2008a. Chinese national sentenced for economic espionage. www.usdoj.gov/opa/pr/2008/June/08-nsd-545.html.

U.S. Department of Justice. 2008b. Man involved in domestic terrorism plot targeting military and Jewish facilities sentenced to 22 years (June 23). www.usdoj.gov.

U.S. Department of Labor. 2008. Occupational outlook handbook 2008–2009. www.bls.gov.

U.S. Department of State. 2008a. Country reports on terrorism. www.state.gov/s/ct/rls/crt/2007/103704.htm.

U.S. Department of State. 2008b. Mission of the Office of the Coordinator for Counterterrorism. www.state.gov.

U.S. General Accounting Office. 2003. Public health response to anthrax incidents of 2001. www.gao.gov.

U.S. Immigration and Customs Enforcement. 2007. Counterfeit goods seizures up 83% in FY 2006 (January 11). www.ice.gov/pi/news/newsreleases/articles/070111washingtondc.htm.

Webster's On-line Dictionary. Threat. Hazard. 2008. www.websters-online-dictionary.org.

Weinberg, L., and P. Davis. 1989. *Introduction to political terrorism.* New York: McGraw-Hill.

Weinzierl, J. 2004. Terrorism: Its origin and history. In *Understanding terrorism: Threats in an uncertain world,* ed. A. Nyatepe-Coo and D. Zeisler-Vralsted. Upper Saddle River, NJ: Pearson Prentice Hall.

White House. 2006a. National Security Strategy (March). www.whitehouse.gov/nsc/nss/2006/.

White House. 2006b. National Strategy for Combating Terrorism (September). www.whitehouse.gov/nsc/nsct/2006/.

White House. 2007a. Fact sheet: Combating terrorism worldwide. www.whitehouse.gov/news/releases/2007/08/print/20070806-1.html.

White House. 2007b. National Strategy for Homeland Security (October). www.whitehouse.gov.

Wikipedia. 2008. Oklahoma City bombing. http://en.wikipedia.org/?title=Oklahoma_City_bombing.

Zalman, A. 2008. Terrorism issues. *Narodnaya Volya* (The people's will). http://terrorism. about.com/od/groupsleader1/p/NarodnayaVolya.htm.

Zalud, B. 2008. Nightmare or opportunity: Top leaders talk it out. *Security* 45 (January):22–30.

Zinn, H. 1995. *A people's history of the United States.* New York: HarperCollins.

Chapter **3**

The Profession and Business of Security

Chapter Learning Objectives

After reading this chapter, you should be able to:

1. Explain the characteristics of a profession
2. Describe the scope of the business of security
3. Discuss the business of security and its relationship to privatization
4. List, describe, compare, and contrast four security associations
5. Examine the meaning and importance of ethics
6. Explain how the security industry is regulated
7. Differentiate training and higher education in relation to the security profession
8. Identify and describe career opportunities in the security profession

Terms to Know

security professional
professional relationships
body of knowledge
National Association of Security Companies
privatization

outsourcing
mercenary
professionalism
International Foundation for Protection Officers (IFPO)
ASIS International
Security Industry Association
National Burglar & Fire Alarm Association
ethics
International Association of Security and Investigative Regulators
Council on Licensure, Enforcement and Regulation
Private Security Officer Employment Authorization Act of 2004
training
instructional systems design
job analysis

QUIZ

This quiz serves to prime the reader's mind and begin the reading, thinking, and studying processes for this chapter. The answers to all of the questions are found within this chapter.

1. Is the business of security a multimillion or a multibillion dollar industry?
2. Are the largest security companies operating in the United States headquartered in other countries?
3. Is it true that professional security associations in the United States are controlled by government agencies?
4. Can a person hold more than one professional certification at one time?
5. What type of group prepares codes of ethics?
6. Why does government regulate the security industry?
7. What are the benefits of a higher education?

Introduction

Suppose you develop an interest in the security vocation and set a goal of becoming a security professional. This goal may occur as a student or as an employee in another vocation. People enter the security field for various reasons, such as the interest it generates, the need for a new career because of retirement, the need for employment, or another reason. A **security professional** is an individual of higher moral character than the general public who is employed in the security vocation and seeks multiple avenues of career development to enhance knowledge, skills, and capabilities to provide the best possible protection for customers.

To assist us in understanding a profession, DeGeorge (1990, 382–383) offers insight through four criteria:

1. A profession performs a needed service helpful to society.
2. A profession is characterized by specialized knowledge and advanced education.
3. Members of a profession decide who can become a member under what requirements and the criteria for banning a member from the profession.
4. Members are held to higher standards than the general public.

Another avenue to understand a profession is through **professional relationships**. Bayles (1995) offers guidance on this topic through his explanation of a professional's relationships and interactions with clients, colleagues, the profession, and oneself.

Bayles sees clients as the top priority. As in other fields, a security professional strives to understand and serve client (customer) needs. Customer satisfaction is earned through quality service, including follow-up on requests from customers and responding to telephone calls and e-mails. Otherwise, a business may not survive, and jobs may be lost. Whether working as a security officer, a security manager in a corporation, or a manager in a contract security business, the goal is to serve the customer. If customer needs are not satisfied, personnel may be replaced, and a new security contract company may be sought as a replacement.

Another professional relationship is with colleagues (Figure 3.1). These include coworkers, superiors, subordinates, and professionals in other organizations. Enormous benefits result from interaction with colleagues. Examples are learning from each other, avoiding mistakes, helping each other, sharing intelligence, and holding fellowship to enhance the working environment.

A profession itself is the third relationship. In the security profession, there are many associations that serve beneficial functions, as described in this chapter. Examples include developing ethical guidelines for members, offering educational programs, and conducting research—all to improve the profession.

Oneself makes up the fourth relationship. This pertains to making the best possible decisions on personal relationships, finances, physical fitness, eating habits, and many other personal decisions. Professionals are sometimes so consumed by their vocation that their personal lives and relationships suffer. This can occur due to job responsibilities that are overwhelming.

It is difficult to pinpoint when the security vocation became a profession. As in other professions, several components are required, all of which came together to advance the field of security to make it the profession it

FIGURE 3.1   **Security is a team effort. (® Shutterstock.com. With permission.)**

is today. To begin with, a **body of knowledge** is well established through many books, periodicals, reports, and other publications. Although there is a need for more quality research in this profession, security journals regularly publish research results. Several security associations put forth enormous efforts to advance this profession through educational programs, research projects, publications, certifications, a code of ethics, and guidelines and best practices. In addition, colleges and universities offer degree and nondegree programs in security. These components characterize the security profession in many countries, besides the United States. *This chapter expands on these components of the security profession and offers the reader building blocks to become a security professional.* The major topics of this chapter are the security industry, privatization, security associations, ethics, regulation of the industry and profession, training, higher education, and career opportunities.

The Business of Security

Because of the serious threats and hazards facing our world, security is a huge multibillion-dollar global industry with millions of career opportunities (Figure 3.2). The Freedonia Group (2008a), an industry market research company that studies investment opportunities for business clients, reported that the demand for private security contract services in the United States would grow 4.7 percent annually to $65.9 billion in 2012. The study of this 2007 $52.3-billion industry attributes the projected growth to "high perceived risks of crime and low expectations of public safety help." The fastest

FIGURE 3.2   The security industry offers a wide variety of services and products. (® Shutterstock.com. With permission.)

growing segments of the industry are projected to be security consulting, preemployment screening, systems integration, and guarding.

The global market for private security contract services is projected to grow 7.3 percent annually through 2010, exceeding $160 billion. In 2005, the revenues were $113 billion. Contract guarding consistently remains the largest segment of the market, with 40 percent of total revenues. This study by the Freedonia Group (2006) includes services such as guard, alarm monitoring, prison management, consulting, and private investigations. The best business opportunities, according to Freedonia, are in alarm monitoring, systems integration, and consulting.

The Freedonia Group (2008b) reported that the U.S. electronic security products and systems market is projected to increase 7.8 percent annually to $15.6 billion in 2012. Access-control systems will show the strongest growth because of technological innovations such as biometric identification.

The Freedonia Group (2008c) projections for global demand for security equipment foresee 7.8 percent annual growth through 2012 to over $90 billion. In 2007, the revenues were $62.1 billion. This study includes access controls, closed-circuit TV (CCTV), alarms, and locks.

The business of security is promoted by security industry groups that facilitate initiatives that result in increases in spending on security systems and services to create a safer world and increase profits for the security industry. For example, the Security Industry Association (SIA), as in other industries, maintains a legislative agenda and lobbies Congress. The SIA agenda includes ensuring that Congress fully funds post-9/11 laws (e.g., Implementing Recommendations of the 9/11 Commission Act of 2007) and provides tax incentives for investments in physical security. In addition, the SIA works to improve its position in advising government (e.g., White House and Department of Homeland Security) through advisory committees, and it seeks to ensure that end users have quality security training (Erickson 2008, 40).

Another example of an industry group that promotes the security industry is the **National Association of Security Companies** (NASCO). This association represents contract security services and participates in the creation and revision of federal and state legislation affecting this industry. Each year, NASCO holds a "Contract Security Summit and Hill Day" in Washington, D.C., to enable private security executives to interact with government officials. Many industry issues are discussed during this annual event, for instance, the management and performance of the Federal Protective Service (see Chapter 1) that employs thousands of contract security officers at government buildings around the country. NASCO is interested in the continued use of contract security by the Federal Protective Service (Kepner 2008, 10–12).

The business of security is linked to the homeland security market, which includes a wide variety of products and services that support homeland security. Market research firms that study the business of security or the business of homeland security are challenged because of the overlap and difficulty in separating these markets. For example, "U.S. Homeland Security (Government and Private) Market Outlook, 2007–2011," Homeland Security Research (2007), reported that the private sector would purchase $28.5 billion of homeland security products and services from the homeland security industry between 2007 and 2011. The report contained such titles as "Guard Service HLS (Homeland Security) Market Forecast" and "Software and Cyber Security HLS Market Forecast."

Because of the serious threats and hazards facing our world, security is a huge multibillion dollar global industry with millions of career opportunities.

ISSUE

Is Homeland Security Affected by Contract Security Companies in the United States Headquartered in Other Countries?

Zalud et al. (2008, 72) report that the five largest contract security ("guard") firms, including revenue (in millions of dollars) and employees, are: Securitas North America (2800/93,000), Group 4 Securicor (Wackenhut) (1900/36,000), Allied Barton (1200/50,400), U.S. Security Associates (575/24,000), and Guardsmark (564/19,467).

In 1999, Securitas purchased Pinkerton's Inc., and the following year, it purchased several more U.S. companies, including Burns International. Securitas works with 80 percent of the Fortune 1000 companies, plays a significant role in protecting critical infrastructure in the United States, and has operations in over 30 countries worldwide. It was founded in 1934, and its headquarters is in Stockholm, Sweden.

In 2004, Group 4 Falck merged with Securicor to form G4S, which employs over 500,000 people in more than 100 countries. The company offers security and financial services and owns Wackenhut Corporation, a leader in security services. G4S is headquartered in Sussex, England.

Critical Thinking

What are your views of security companies headquartered outside of the U.S. protecting critical infrastructure inside the United States?

Privatization

Another important topic of the business of security is **privatization**. It refers to organizational tasks and job functions, formerly accomplished by government, that are accomplished by a business for a profit. Privatization exists at local, state, and federal levels of government, and it includes a wide variety of activities, such as janitorial, food, and security services. Privatization can be confused with a company contracting work to a service business (e.g., contract security). When a company contracts work to an outside service business, it is referred to as **outsourcing**, and a company often does this to concentrate on its core business and to reduce costs.

U.S. privatization in war zones and against terrorism has expanded since the beginning of the wars in Iraq and Afghanistan. Privatization includes companies that offer not only food, transport services, supplies, and pest control, as examples, but also former military personnel to supplement U.S. armed forces. Singer (2007, 2) notes the difficulty of pinpointing the exact number of private-sector workers supporting U.S. forces in Iraq. He refers to a U.S. Central Command estimate of 100,000 in 2006, but mentions researchers who claim the figure is a WAG, meaning "wild ass guess." According to Singer, a 2007 Department of Defense report found 180,000 private employees in Iraq, while 160,000 troops were in the country during the "surge" of U.S. forces. One company noted by Singer is Halliburton, with a contract of $20.1 billion to support U.S. troops. Singer views the U.S. government as unable to carry out operations without private contractors.

Glanz (2008) reports on a study by the Special Inspector General for Iraq Reconstruction, an independent federal agency, which showed that 310 private security companies received contracts from U.S. agencies to provide security for U.S. and Iraqi officials, facilities, and convoys between 2003 and 2008. The list contains not only familiar names such as Blackwater and DynCorp, but also contractors from such nations as Romania, the Czech Republic, the Philippines, Cyprus, and Uganda. The use of contractors in war zones is often viewed by governments as cost effective and efficient.

Traditionally, the term **mercenary** has been used to describe a war fighter who is available to nations to fight in exchange for a salary. This term is difficult to define, and it has negative connotations because of how nations have applied mercenaries and related violence. The benefits of nations hiring private companies (or mercenaries) to serve military needs include gaining additional soldiers and expertise, less training required, limited impact on government from casualties of private soldiers and atrocities committed by them, and not having to fund a larger standing military when hostilities end.

Global private security companies offer services to the U.S. Department of State, other government bodies, corporations, nonprofit groups, and individuals. Such security services are applied to protect people, assets, supplies, convoys, buildings, business interests, and volunteers (e.g., aid workers helping displaced people near a war zone) from, as examples, an insurgency, a terrorist group, organized criminals, or a disaster.

The UN Working Group on the use of mercenaries (United Nations Office at Geneva 2008) states:

> Many private military and security companies at the national, regional and international levels currently operate without effective oversight and accountability.... A growing number of such companies in conflict-ridden areas, such as Afghanistan, Iraq and Columbia, are recruiting former military and policemen from developing countries as "security guards." However, once they engage in low intensity armed conflict or post-conflict situations, they become in fact "military armed private soldiers."

The UN Working Group argued that "military armed private soldiers" are essentially mercenaries and implicated in human-rights abuses. Although hiring governments may grant immunity from prosecution and typically lack the resources to regulate mercenaries, the responsibility for human-rights abuses rests with the hiring government, the mercenaries, and the country from which the mercenaries originate, according to the Working Group. In addition, the Working Group calls for all nations to ratify the "International Convention Against the Recruitment, Use, Financing and Training of Mercenaries."

Blackwater USA, a security company founded by a press-shy former Navy Seal and former U.S. Department of State officials, has received a lot of media attention over violence in Iraq. A Congressional report by Democrats states that the company, while guarding U.S. diplomats, has been involved in nearly 200 shootings in Iraq. In certain cases, weapons were fired from vehicles without stopping to check on casualties or assist the wounded. The company is reported to have paid victims' families (in one case $15,000) and sought to cover up other shootings. For instance, the State Department helped a Blackwater employee to flee Iraq soon after killing, while drunk, a bodyguard of one of Iraq's two vice presidents. In another case, Blackwater personnel were involved in a shooting in a Baghdad square that resulted in eight Iraqi deaths and calls by Iraqis to remove the "cold-blooded murderers" from the country. The Congressional report was highly critical of the State Department for not properly supervising Blackwater, which has been paid over $800 million for security services in Iraq and at other locations under a diplomatic security contract it shares with two other firms, DynCorp International and Triple Canopy (Broder 2007).

Critical Thinking

Should mercenaries be prohibited globally? Was Blackwater USA unfairly criticized because of its security activities in a war zone? Explain your answers.

GLOBAL PERSPECTIVE: THE GROWTH OF PRIVATE SECURITY IN THE EUROPEAN UNION

The following "global perspective" is from the work of Van Steden and Sarre (2007, 222–235). They point out that the publicly funded police agencies that evolved and grew during the nineteenth century never totally replaced private security that had preceded them. Over one million contract and in-house security employees work in the European Union (EU), and there is reliance on private security as part of public policing strategies. The private security/police ratio in the EU went from 0.43 to 1 in 1999 to 0.71 to 1 in 2004. In the United States, the ratio is generally agreed to be 2 or more to 1. (The EU is made up of most of the nations in Europe.)

Van Steden and Sarre write of the difficulty of measuring the private security industry in the EU and the use of different definitions for private security. Some security companies offer limousine services, and some accountancy firms offer investigative services, thus making classifications and counting difficult. Furthermore, most private firms are reluctant to release proprietary information on their market share, revenue, and number of employees. At the same time, Van Steden and Sarre were able to compile several interesting points concerning private security in the EU, as listed next.

- In comparison to other EU members, Denmark and Sweden have small private security industries and low ratios of security personnel per police officers (0.38 to 1 and 0.56 to 1, respectively). The Danish government is hesitant to cooperate with private security. Interestingly, Falck and Securitas, two of the largest multinational security firms, were founded in Denmark and Sweden, respectively.
- The nations where private security personnel outnumber police are Hungary (2.0 to 1.0), Poland (1.94 to 1.0), Ireland (1.67 to 1.0), Luxembourg (1.40 to 1.0), Estonia (1.36 to 1.0), and the United Kingdom (1.06 to 1.0).
- The five nations with the highest number of security personnel are Poland (200,000), Germany (170,000), the United Kingdom (150,000) France (117,000), and Spain (89,450).
- Many nations have enacted laws to regulate private security. For instance, in 2001, the English parliament passed the Private Security Industry Act as the first attempt to regulate contract and proprietary security, private investigators, security consultants, bodyguards, and other related specialists. The 2001 Act introduced licensing and an authority to monitor quality.
- Because of violence in South Eastern Europe, the following locations have had private security personnel accused of misuse of automatic weapons: Kosovo, Serbia, Montenegro, Bosnia, Herzegovina, Macedonia, and Albania. Additional issues relate to ineffective government oversight and rivalry between police agencies and security companies.
- The collapse of the Soviet Union resulted in tremendous growth of private security in Russia and limited accountability over the industry.
- Van Steden and Sarre conclude that private security enables privileged individuals to buy protection not available to the less privileged; engages in risk reduction, but takes advantage of crime panics; and is regulated differently among countries. In addition, many regulatory questions remain unanswered, and governments must coordinate private security and policing.

Critical Thinking

What are your opinions about Van Steden's and Sarre's concluding remarks that private security enables privileged individuals to buy protection not available to the less privileged and that the industry engages in risk-reduction, but takes advantage of crime panics?

GLOBAL PERSPECTIVE: OUTLAW PRIVATE SECURITY COMPANIES

Turbiville (2006, 561–582) provides research, as described here, of numerous cases of private security companies from around the world that were established for, or became involved in, criminal or terrorist agendas. *Public police, military, and private security practitioners should be aware of the threat imposed by outlaw private security companies.*

Turbiville writes that when a government becomes weak or loses legitimacy, or when war or ethnic or religious hate surface, an environment may develop that facilitates terrorism, insurgency, and organized crime. At the same time, private security or private military business may increase to support a government, corporations, or other organizations seeking protection in a dangerous environment. Iraq serves as one example, although the Western private protection businesses did not have a criminal or terrorist agenda. Turbiville uses the example of the rise of security businesses in the former Soviet Union in the 1990s. Prior to the collapse of the Soviet Union, when the state controlled all types of security, private security was unknown. Following the collapse, when public police and public security were weakened, organized crime grew, and private security filled a void to protect people and businesses that could afford protection. By 2005, there were 21,000 registered private security firms in Russia employing about 500,000 personnel with weapons. Legislation and the Russian Ministry of Internal Affairs failed at trying to regulate the industry, which had episodes of criminality while becoming part of the public safety environment.

The Al-Qaeda document entitled "Management of Savagery" covers infiltrating adversaries, including police forces, armies, and security companies. Turbiville describes advantages that terrorist and criminal groups see in becoming involved with private security. These include using a security company as a legitimate cover for surveillance, information acquisition, procurement (e.g., weapons, uniforms, and equipment), working with police and other government agencies, and providing "security" at potential targets!

Turbiville writes of criminal conduct by private security in specific regions. He not only refers to Russia, but also Bulgaria, Romania, Albania, and countries in Latin America, South America, and Africa. Criminal activities by private security and police are difficult to quantify for each country. However, the range of crimes includes murder, social cleansing through death squads (e.g., executing vagrants and street youths), robbery, and extortion. In addition, police and private security firms in certain countries may perpetrate crimes, such as kidnappings, so they can "solve" the crimes for monetary gain. (Is this similar to what Jonathan Wild did in England during the 1700s, as described in Chapter 1?)

Critical Thinking

Is it possible for outlaw private security companies to exist in the United States? Explain your answer.

Professionalism and Security Associations

Professionalism is "the conduct, aims, or qualities that characterize or mark a profession or a professional person" (Merriam–Webster 2008). It is also "the skill, competence, or character expected of a member of a highly trained profession" (Encarta 2008). In the security profession, as in other professions, members seek out avenues to grow professionally through training, education, adherence to codes of ethics, and applying "best practices" so that the work accomplished is of the highest possible quality. Certification programs are another avenue to enhance professionalism. Professional associations administer such programs. The requirements generally include specific education, training and experience, and successfully passing an examination prior to a person being awarded a professional designation. A certification typically requires a periodic renewal through training and education. *The best source to enhance professionalism is through those industry associations that are in themselves professional, maintain high standards of integrity, and are absolutely committed to advancing the profession that is served.* There are several associations in the security profession. Here we describe some of these associations and their characteristics. For the reader who is not a member, this may be a beginning point for considering which association(s) to join.

To simplify our discussion, if the reader seeks employment or is employed as a uniformed security officer or supervisor, the International Foundation for Protection Officers should be researched. For those interested in security management or related vocations, the target of research should be ASIS International. Individuals involved in the manufacture, sales, and service of security products and systems should consider the Security Industry Association or the National Burglar & Fire Alarm Association. Depending on the direction of one's career, other associations may be more appropriate and specialized, such as those that pertain to investigations, consulting, information security, or IT systems. In addition, associations serve professionals employed at specific types of sites, including hospitals, colleges, and retail stores.

International Foundation for Protection Officers

The **International Foundation for Protection Officers** (IFPO) was organized in 1988 as a nonprofit group to serve the training and certification needs of security officers and supervisors. The IFPO Web site is the source of the following information.

Several types of membership are available, each with specific benefits. Membership types are associate, introductory, corporate, and student. The benefits of membership include opportunities to network and learn from other members, a one-year subscription to *Protection News*, selection of one free security book, member exclusive Web site access, IFPO membership certificate, I.D. card and lapel pin, and a wide range of discounts for seminars, publications, and products.

The IFPO administers distance-delivery courses and certifications that include the Basic Protection Officer (BPO), the Certified Protection Officer (CPO) program, the Security Supervision and Management (SSMP) program, and the Certified in Security Supervision and Management (CSSM) program. Many entities have enhanced the professionalism and training of their security personnel through these programs.

ASIS International

ASIS International, originally known as the American Society for Industrial Security, is the largest organization of security managers and specialists. Its Web site offers the following description.

Created in 1955, ASIS International has over 36,000 members worldwide. It aims to facilitate professionalism while enhancing the competence, skills, and abilities of members through training and education programs, publications, and certifications.

Membership benefits include numerous paths for networking through over 200 chapters worldwide, more than 30 specialized councils, volunteer opportunities, many training and education programs, an annual seminar and exhibit, and regional seminars. ASIS publishes *Security Management* magazine, newsletters, a directory of members, books, security guidelines, and best practices. It also maintains an extensive library at its headquarters in Virginia and an online career center, both for members.

In 1966, the ASIS Foundation was incorporated. It supports a variety of academic, professional development, and research activities. ASIS administers three certification programs: the Certified Protection Professional (CPP), the Physical Security Professional (PSP), and the Professional Certified Investigator (PCI).

Security Industry Association

The **Security Industry Association** (SIA) is a nonprofit international trade association representing professionals from many sectors of the electronic and physical security business, from manufacturers to installers. The SIA's Web site notes that the group promotes growth and professionalism through education, research, standards, and advocating for member interests. The group is the sponsor of the International Security Conference and Exhibition, a major trade show.

Member benefits include discounts on networking events and educational products and courses, access to market research reports and a legislative tracking service on issues and regulations, exposure through SIA's online company profiles and other marketing techniques, SIA periodicals, and opportunities to participate in the development of standards.

The SIA established the Certified Security Project Manager (CSPM) Program to provide a nationally recognized professional accreditation for project managers who work on the design and installation of security systems. This credential is unique and specific. Candidates must be working as a project manager in the security industry and complete specific courses prior to an examination. Topics of study include project management fundamentals, CCTV and access control systems, codes, bidding, financial statements, and contracts.

National Burglar & Fire Alarm Association

The **National Burglar & Fire Alarm Association** (NBFAA) has many similarities to the SIA. The NBFAA Web site states that it is a nonprofit trade association and the largest one representing the electronic life safety, security, and integrated systems industry. Member companies are involved in manufacturing, sales, installation, service, and monitoring of systems. Member benefits include networking, marketing exposure on the NBFAA Web site, training programs, exclusive business insurance, employee recruitment services, and a variety of publications and updates.

Additional Associations and Certifications

The career direction of the reader will dictate which associations and certifications are most appropriate. Besides the ones cited previously, others exist to enhance professionalism. For those interested in white-collar crime and computer fraud, the Association of Certified Fraud Examiners offers the CFE. The Loss Prevention Foundation has the Loss Prevention Qualified (LPQ) designation for entry-level retail practitioners and a Loss Prevention Certified (LPC) designation for more advanced practitioners. The International Association for Healthcare Security & Safety offers the Certified Health Care Protection Administrator (CHCPA). In the financial industry, the American Bankers Association administers the Certified Financial Services Security Professional (CFSSP). The International Information Systems Security Certification Consortium offers the Certified Information Systems Security Professional (CISSP), among other designations. Several other certification programs are offered in the security profession, and each specialization may offer multiple certifications.

Ethics

Ethics is the study and analysis of what constitutes good or bad behavior. Morals and morality are what is judged as good conduct, as opposed to bad conduct or immorality. Professional ethics refers to the behavior of certain professions or groups (Pollack 1998, 6–7).

The "Report of the Task Force on Private Security" (U.S. Department of Justice 1976, 123) notes the following: "A code of ethics is a statement that incorporates moral and ethical principles and philosophies. It is a necessary prerequisite for any profession, providing guidance to its members so that their activities can be measured against a standard of behavior."

In the security profession, daily decisions are made on a host of topics, such as policies, procedures, laws, restricting people's movements, searches, use of force, and arrests. Examples of unethical behavior include lying to a customer, exaggerating facts of an incident for personal gain or to harm another, and avoiding job responsibilities. Unethical behavior can be a crime; examples are applying excessive force, falsifying an incident report, lying under oath (i.e., perjury), theft, and disclosing private information.

A code of ethics offers input for decision making. However, a code of ethics is the ideal. It describes a perfect world with perfect behavior, but humans are not perfect. We sometimes make errors in judgment, followed by mistakes in action or inaction (Figure 3.3). We also pay for our mistakes through an assortment of repercussions, such as harm to our reputation,

FIGURE 3.3 **Security personnel must never fall to the temptation of accepting something of value to compromise security and safety. There are manipulators in the world who benefit from the mistakes of others that can lead to disastrous consequences. (® Shutterstock.com. With permission.)**

lost sales, and being disciplined, demoted, fired, arrested, and sued. Thus, a professional must adhere to a code of ethics to the best of his or her abilities while making the best possible decisions.

Sources of codes of ethics are plentiful in the security profession. Web sites of security associations, such as ASIS International, contain codes of ethics. An accompanying box provides codes of ethics from the "Report of the Task Force on Private Security."

Mortman (2007, 22) offers an interesting and critical perspective on ethics requirements of security associations. He refers to doctors and lawyers and their participation in both refresher courses in ethics and continuing education requirements in ethics for recertification. Mortman calls for such requirements in security and an annual re-signing of a code of ethics. He claims that security associations tout ethics but "seem to use ethics requirements as more of an excuse to protect the certification rather than having any real interest in promulgating ethical behavior by their members or constituencies." Mortman argues for more transparency in the way in which ethics violations are handled. He notes that Web sites of security associations do not disclose information on disciplinary action, as in other professions (e.g., law), and the percentage of individuals who let their certification lapse as opposed to it being revoked.

Critical Thinking

In reference to Mortman's perspective, what is your opinion of the way in which security associations administer ethical standards?

DO NOT MAKE THIS MISTAKE

The Cost of Free Watches

At about 3:00 A.M., when the burglar alarm was activated at the Marsh Department Store, Security Officer Ted Moore rushed to the scene from the opposite end of the shopping mall. His supervisor met him. Two city police officers arrived a few minutes later. A glass door had been broken at the closed store. The store security manager was called, and she was on her way to the scene. When she arrived, a decision was made to search the store in case a burglar was present. Additional police arrived and a canine unit. As groups of two began the search, Security Officer Moore and Police Officer Ron Copeland decided to search together, since they had been close friends since high school. During the search, both Moore and Copeland passed the jewelry department, where they spotted some inexpensive watches on the sales counter. Copeland suggested that they each take a watch, since no one was in the area. Both concealed a watch in their respective pockets. At the same time, the store security manager and a police sergeant were in the security office reviewing earlier video recordings while a camera near the jewelry department was showing real-time video on a television monitor. Both the security manager and the sergeant witnessed the theft. Security Officer Moore was fired and Police Officer Copeland was placed on administrative leave without pay. Both were charged with larceny and Officer Copeland eventually lost his job. No burglar was found in the store that morning; however, two practitioners who were held at a high level of professionalism and trust were caught stealing.

> *Lessons:* Unethical or illegal behavior cannot be tolerated, especially in the security and criminal justice professions.

Critical Thinking

What do you think were the causes of the criminal behavior by Ted Moore and Ron Copeland?

Code of Ethics for Private Security Employees

In recognition of the significant contribution of private security to crime prevention and reduction, as a private security employee, I pledge:

1. To accept the responsibilities and fulfill the obligations of my role: protecting life and property; preventing and reducing crimes against my employer's business, or other organizations and institutions to which I am assigned; upholding the law; and respecting the constitutional rights of all persons.
2. To conduct myself with honesty and integrity and to adhere to the highest moral principles in the performance of my security duties.
3. To be faithful, diligent, and dependable in discharging my duties, and to uphold at all times the laws, policies, and procedures that protect the rights of others.
4. To observe the precepts of truth, accuracy, and prudence, without allowing personal feelings, prejudices, animosities, or friendships to influence my judgments.
5. To report to my superiors, without hesitation, any violation of the law or of my employer's or client's regulations.
6. To respect and protect the confidential and privileged information of my employer or client beyond the term of my employment, except where their interests are contrary to law or to this Code of Ethics.
7. To cooperate with all recognized and responsible law enforcement and government agencies in matters within their jurisdiction.
8. To accept no compensation, commission, gratuity, or other advantage without the knowledge and consent of my employer.
9 To conduct myself professionally at all times, and to perform my duties in a manner that reflects credit upon myself, my employer, and private security.
10. To strive continually to improve my performance by seeking training and educational opportunities that will better prepare me for my private security duties.

Source: U.S. Dept. of Justice (1976). "Report of the Task Force on Private Security." Washington, DC: U.S. Government Printing Office, p. 124.

Code of Ethics for Private Security Management

As managers of private security functions and employees, we pledge:

1. To recognize that our principal responsibilities are in the service of our organizations and clients, to protect life and property as well as to prevent and reduce crime against our business, industry, or other organizations and institutions; and in the public interest, to uphold the law and to respect the constitutional rights of all persons.

2. To be guided by a sense of integrity, honor, justice, and morality in the conduct of business; in all personnel matters; in relationships with government agencies, clients, and employers; and in responsibilities to the general public.

3. To strive faithfully to render security services of the highest quality and to work continuously to improve our knowledge and skills and thereby improve the overall effectiveness of private security.

4. To uphold the trust of our employers, our clients, and the public by performing our functions within the law, not ordering or condoning violations of law, and ensuring that our security personnel conduct their assigned duties lawfully and with proper regard for the rights of others.

5. To respect the reputation and practice of others in private security, but to expose to the proper authorities any conduct that is unethical or unlawful.

6. To apply uniform and equitable standards of employment in recruiting and selecting personnel regardless of race, creed, color, sex, or age, and in providing salaries commensurate with job responsibilities and with training, education, and experience.

7. To cooperate with recognized and responsible law enforcement and other criminal justice agencies; to comply with security licensing and registration laws and other statutory requirements that pertain to our business.

8. To respect and protect the confidential and privileged information of employers and clients beyond the term of our employment, except where their interests are contrary to law or to this Code of Ethics.

9. To maintain a professional posture in all business relationships with employers and clients, with others in the private security field, and with members of other professions; and to insist that our personnel adhere to the highest standards of professional conduct.

10. To encourage the professional advancement of our personnel by assisting them to acquire appropriate security knowledge, education, and training.

Source: **U.S. Dept. of Justice (1976). "Report of the Task Force on Private Security." Washington, DC: U.S. Government Printing Office, p. 124.**

Regulation of the Security Industry

As the private security industry grew during the twentieth century and increasingly became part of crime control efforts, government leaders saw the need to study this industry. The Rand Report (U.S. Department of Justice 1972, 30) is remembered for bringing attention to the problems of the security industry and the need for professionalism. The often-cited quote from this report is that "the typical private guard is an aging white male, poorly educated, usually untrained, and very poorly paid." Today, the situation in many respects is different because of the diversity of personnel in the security industry, and many security officers possess some education beyond a high school diploma. Certain security specialties have excellent training and pay well. At the same time, training and pay remain as issues in many security positions.

The "Report of the Task Force on Private Security" (U.S. Department of Justice 1976) was the first national effort to establish standards and goals for the security industry to enhance professionalism, competency, and effectiveness. The report recommended government regulation of the industry, including license and registration requirements for security industry businesses and employees. It also emphasized the need for improving screening of applicants, pay, and training. Two subsequent reports, funded by the U.S. Department of Justice, are known as the "Hallcrest Reports." The first one is entitled "Private Security and Police in America: the Hallcrest Report" (Cunningham and Taylor 1985). This report echoed the need for professionalism, but also stressed the contributions of both the public and private sectors in crime control. "Private Security Trends: 1970–2000, The Hallcrest Report II" (Cunningham et al. 1990) focuses on trends in the security industry, pointing out, for instance, that private security outspends public law enforcement and employs 2.5 times more personnel. In addition, this report anticipated the increased reliance on contract security services and systems.

The basic purpose of regulating the security industry, as with other industries, is to protect society and its citizens from, for example, errors and dishonesty. Industries are often unable to self-regulate, so government steps in to fill the void. Government regulation of the security industry varies among states and locales. Regulation occurs by requiring licensing and registration of contract and proprietary security organizations, registration of security officers, criminal history checks of applicants, and training. The government fees collected from security organizations helps to pay for the regulation. In essence, the security industry pays for its own regulation to protect against dishonesty and individuals with a criminal background.

The government agencies that regulate the security industry are bureaucracies that do the best they can with limited budgets and personnel. For those who work in the security industry, dealing with such a regulatory agency can result in frustration, especially in the contract security business where employee turnover is high and new applicants must be processed and trained according to government laws and regulations. Often housed in state police agencies, these government regulators respond to complaints; check the license, registration, and training of security organizations; and stop security officers on patrol or post to check credentials.

Davidson (2008, 4) reports on the example of California that shows the diversity of private security regulation by government agencies. Although California law requires proprietary (in-house) security officers to be registered, only two percent follow the law. The California Bureau of Security and Investigative Services (BSIS) reports that 4,200 proprietary officers, out of about 200,000, have completed a criminal background check and are registered. The BSIS has no way of tracking organizations that employ proprietary security officers, and there is no penalty for the violation. One strategy of the BSIS is to target specific businesses that are likely to staff their own officers, such as amusement parks, nightclubs, and major retailers. Another strategy is to emphasize the serious liability of an unlicensed security officer if an adverse event occurs. Stronger regulations are pending for proprietary officers. Davidson also reports that contract security firms are easier to regulate in California because of longstanding licensing and training requirements and a penalty of $5,000 for every unlicensed officer employed.

Although California faces challenges in regulating the security industry, other states face similar challenges, and still others maintain stricter regulations and enforcement. The need for regulation is especially important not only for unarmed officers, but for armed officers as well. Screening and training are vital. An excellent guideline is "Private Security Officer Selection and Training" (ASIS International 2004). It is useful for contract and proprietary security and government regulators. It sets forth minimum criteria for selection and training and includes definitions of terms and an extensive bibliography. The guideline recommends a regulatory agency in each state, state fees to support the regulatory process, liability insurance for security businesses, licensee requirements (e.g., education, experience, and written examination), and individual officer license and registration. The screening criteria for security applicants includes verifying name and social security number, requiring previous residential addresses and telephone numbers for the last seven years, high school diploma or GED, criminal history, fingerprint and previous employment check, drug screening, and submission of photographs. In addition, candidates must be 18 years of age for unarmed security positions and 21 years of age for armed positions. Forty-eight hours of training is required within the first 100 days of hiring.

The **International Association of Security and Investigative Regulators** (IASIR) works to promote the efficiency and effectiveness of government security regulators. Membership benefits include regular meetings; perspectives on what other states, locales, and nations are doing to regulate the security industry; and access to model statutes, regulations, and training. Its Web site offers a wealth of information on security regulations.

Another association, broader in scope than the IASIR, is the **Council on Licensure, Enforcement and Regulation** (CLEAR). It serves almost any individual or group interested in licensures, nonvoluntary certifications, and regulating occupations. Both public- and private-sector members discuss such issues as examinations, credentialing, enforcement, and discipline.

Before we leave this discussion of the regulation of the security industry, we will cover the federal government's role. Various attempts have been made by Congress to enact a national law for both applicant screening and training for the security industry. None has been successful. One recurring issue is the cost of training that would result from a national law mandating training. In the contract security business, turnover is often high, and investments in training may not show a return on investment, especially with contract companies that offer low wages and see employees depart within a short period. Without mandating training, Congress enacted the **Private Security Officer Employment Authorization Act of 2004**, which enables contract and proprietary private security organizations to send applicant fingerprints and other identifying information through a state agency or directly to the FBI for a criminal history check. This voluntary opportunity requires a fee, but enables the security employer to obtain results from a national check, rather than a check of the state in which the applicant presently resides.

It is important to note that the federal government issues comprehensive security regulations for certain vital industries, also referred to as critical infrastructure. Examples include the nuclear, airline, banking, and chemical industries. Since the 9/11 attacks, the federal government has been especially interested in enhanced security for critical infrastructure. (These topics are discussed in greater depth in later chapters.)

DO NOT MAKE THESE MISTAKES

"It's My Parking Space!"

Kyle Lubber, 24 years of age, was very enthusiastic about his job as a security officer at Mason Woods Mall. He took his job so seriously that he carried an illegal nightstick to work and gave people the impression that he was a public police officer. Upon driving into the workplace one day, a couple beat him to a parking space. His anger was overwhelming and an argument ensued. He yelled, "It's my parking space!" Then, Lubber flashed his illegal nightstick while showing the couple his handcuffs and the word "police" on his jacket. Lubber told the female driver that he was a police officer and he demanded her license, registration, and proof of insurance. The woman turned over all three documents, but requested to see his police ID. It turns out that the couple were police officers in another state. When Lubber failed to show the ID, the woman snatched back her documents and the couple departed. Lubber chased them in his personal vehicle, but the couple alerted police, who stopped Lubber and arrested him for impersonating a police officer and criminal possession of a weapon (Sullivan 2006).

Lessons: Training is essential prior to duty assignments. Security personnel must clearly understand their legal authority and what behaviors constitute abuse of authority and impersonating public police. They must also be instructed on permissible equipment and weapons. In addition, supervision of employees is vital.

Critical Thinking

Besides quality training and supervision, what else can an employer do to prevent these types of incidents?

Security Training

Training involves the acquisition of skills and behavior change. A key distinction between training and education is that the former is more hands-on and less theoretical, whereas the latter is less hands-on and more theoretical. Examples of training topics include how to handle customer complaints, use of a fire extinguisher, applying first aid, firearms qualification (Figure 3.4), and performing one's job safely.

FIGURE 3.4   **What is wrong in this photo of a security officer in training with his pistol? Firearms training is vital for armed security officers, but it must be conducted safely using precautions such as hearing and eye protection. (® Shutterstock.com. With permission.)**

Training is a major issue in the security industry, as covered previously. Its importance and benefits cannot be overstated. Through training, security personnel learn how to fulfill their job responsibilities, conform to law and company policies and procedures, respond to incidents, and help people. Training provides guidance to employees so that they can perform to the best of their abilities and improve judgment and behavior. In addition, it reduces liability. At the same time, training is costly, and it must show a return on investment. An organization that has high turnover will find it difficult to justify quality training. Traditionally, this has been a challenge for contract security businesses and other organizations that pay low wages and have high turnover.

> Many police officers who transition to the security profession view their police training as adequate for the private sector. However, the private sector is characterized by a culture (i.e., business) and strategies (i.e., emphasis on prevention) that are different from the public sector.

Methodologies for Preparing Instructional Programs

Several methodologies are available to help prepare instructional programs. Two popular methodologies are described next.

Instructional systems design (ISD) methods are used to develop training and education programs. There are many different ISD models, but most originate from the step-by-step ADDIE model, which means Analysis, Design, Development, Implementation, and Evaluation. Each is explained next (Kruse 2000).

Analysis: Instructional goals and objectives and desired behaviors are pinpointed. Students' existing knowledge and skills and the gap between what is desired are identified.

Design: This step includes planning learning objectives, assessment methods, content, exercises, lesson plans, and instructional media.

Development: This step follows through with the plans in the design stage by creating the learning materials and integrating technologies.

Implementation: The instructional program is delivered to the students.

Evaluation: The effectiveness of the instructional program is evaluated, and feedback is used to make improvements.

Another methodology helpful to prepare instructional programs is **job analysis** (Fine and Cronshaw 1999). It results in a description of the requirements of a job, the necessary skills and knowledge, and the duties performed. Besides assessing training needs, a job analysis can be used to write a job description, design employee work-performance evaluations and promotion systems, and plan compensation. A job analysis is conducted through interviews with employees, supervisors, and customers; questionnaires to these groups; group meetings; and observations on the job. The "Uniform Guidelines on Employee Selection Procedures," a federal publication prepared by multiple federal agencies, provides a professional and legal foundation for conducting job analyses.

Fay (2007, 226–229) offers a methodology for instructional programs from the perspective of preventing liability for alleged negligent training. His methodology is described next.

First, *validate training*. This entails applying an objective process to ensure that training is directly related to job duties and that instructional strategies are effective. One methodology to validate training is job (task) analysis.

Second, *administer training to specifications*. In other words, the training must be implemented according to the curriculum design. This auditing can be accomplished by examining test results, using student questionnaires of the instructional program, and visits to classes by instructional administrators. All three can be done with in-class and online training.

Third, *evaluate the trainee*. This includes testing of new knowledge through an examination and evaluating skills (e.g., interacting with an irate customer or firearms qualification).

Fourth, *maintain training records*. Various documents must be maintained to support the integrity of the training program. Examples are lesson plans, handouts, list of audiovisual materials, tests and results, and attendance records.

Fifth, *maintain instructor standards*. This may be set by state law and/ or the state agency that regulates the security industry. A training course may be required for certification as an instructor. Two major criteria for instructors are knowledge of the subject and ability to teach; these can be audited by observation (in-class or online), student questionnaires, and performance of trainees on the job.

Instructional Strategies

Although security training varies depending on the entity (e.g., nuclear plant, retail store), instructional strategies should be a mixture of approaches to serve the needs of the organization and the students. The lecture method of instruction has existed for centuries, but it has limitations, one of which is the difficulty of maintaining student attention. Consequently, to increase the effectiveness of training, lectures should be supplemented with a variety of additional instructional strategies. Examples include student opportunities to ask questions, participate in discussions, and work on assignments in groups. Technology serves to expand the range of instructional strategies through, for example, audiovisual presentations. Of significant importance is for instructional strategies to facilitate a connection from instructional material to practical application. In a training environment, for instance, if students are learning about fire extinguishers, they should have an opportunity to participate in a demonstration of their use. On-the-job training is also important.

Online learning has greatly expanded the range and flexibility of instructional strategies. Students can learn from almost anywhere, at any time, because of the Internet. The technology enables students to train at their own convenience according to their particular schedule. Cost savings result for students (e.g., transportation) and entities (e.g., a corporation can train large numbers of employees without a training facility).

Cordivari (2008, 15–16) writes that there is no one-size-fits-all training for today's workforce. He explains that baby boomers (born between 1946 and 1964) may be reluctant to embrace new technologies, while Generation X (born between 1965 and 1978) saw growth in digital technologies during their teen years and are thus more receptive to new technologies. Millennials (or Generation Y, born between 1979 and 2002), on the other hand, were born into digital technology and cannot imagine life without an iPod, MySpace, and YouTube. Consequently, large companies have the advantage of being able to invest in multiple instructional strategies to appeal to all generations. This can range from the traditional classroom lecture method to audio MP3 files that security officers can access and study at their own convenience and at their own pace.

Junginger (2008, 19–23) writes that the Millennial generation will be the largest generation in the past century, reaching 80 million people and surpassing Generation X. Interestingly, Junginger notes that the newer generations can process large amounts of visual information while possessing advanced motor, spatial, and strategy skills because of years of involvement with game technology. In addition, students frequently know more about certain technologies than their parents, teachers, and employers. These factors create challenges for instructors who must meet the learning needs of tech-savvy students. Junginger writes, "Millennials are team oriented and prefer a classroom setting that emphasizes group learning and problem solving, rather than one focused on lecture."

ASIS INTERNATIONAL TRAINING, EDUCATION, AND RESEARCH

ASIS International has put forth enormous efforts to train, educate, and professionalize security practitioners. As written earlier, the "Private Security Officer Selection and Training" guideline (ASIS International 2004)

---

recommends establishing a requirement that each security officer receive 48 hours of training within the first 100 days of employment. The topics include the role of security officers, security awareness, law, ethics, observation and reporting, communications, access control, information security, emergency procedures, and other topics, depending on site requirements.

ASIS International offers a variety of professional development courses through several mediums. These include traditional classroom programs in many cities; Webinars, which are fully interactive online education programs; and eLearning, available 24/7. The topics of these programs include assets protection, executive protection, security force management, CCTV, crisis management, and certification exam review. In addition, an annual seminar and exhibits provide more than 150 educational sessions attended by over 20,000 security professionals.

The ASIS Foundation has played a major role in security becoming a profession. It develops academic programs, encourages continuing education, sponsors research, and publishes reports. For example, research is conducted on strategies that can be applied to security challenges, such as preventing gun violence or dishonesty in the workplace. The ASIS Foundation also supports the annual Academic Practitioner Symposium, a forum that facilitates dialogue between practitioners and academicians to gain consensus on security topics and develop curriculum models.

Higher Education

During the last quarter of the twentieth century, the number of higher education programs in security began to increase. Prior to that period, the closest type of academic program to security was criminal-justice-related programs. Then, criminal-justice-related programs began to offer one or more security courses and certificates, and then bachelor and graduate degree programs in security increased in number. Through this development of academic programs in security, certain programs thrived, while others ended because of the difficulty of attracting students to the profession. A recurring problem in these academic programs and in training programs, even today, is the use of instructors with a police background to teach about security in a business environment.

Today, especially following the 9/11 attacks, there is heightened interest within organizations to protect people, assets, and operations. In addition, new academic programs have developed that are related to the security function. These include homeland security and emergency management.

Many security professionals and ASIS International (specifically publications of the annual Academic Practitioner Symposium) favor the placement of security academic programs in college and university business departments, rather than in criminal justice departments. This perspective is logical because security practitioners are often business executives with a specialization in security. In other words, they must understand the business environment in which they work, including knowledge of business management, business law, accounting, auditing, risk management, and global business. Although academic programs in business are hesitant to embrace security courses, the reader seeking a degree in security or a related field is wise to complete business courses, especially accounting.

The Web and security associations (ASIS International and IFPO) offer direction on academic programs in security. Ensure that the program of your choice is accredited by a reputable accrediting organization and that the academic program and accrediting organization have a long history.

The Benefits of a College Education

The pressure to attend college is pervasive within our society. The decision is a personal one based on many factors, and life *without* a degree can be rewarding. In fact, there are many people who never attend college, but are intelligent, happy, financially comfortable, and maintain a fulfilling life. At the same time, individuals, some with a college degree, view a college education as a waste of time and money. They view theory as "a bunch of B.S." Actually, organizations and practitioners in their work apply theories of security and criminal justice, as we will see in subsequent chapters. Here we list some of the general benefits of a college education.

- Entry into certain professions, and promotions, may require a college education.
- The employment market is competitive, and a college degree makes an applicant more competitive.
- A degree shows that an individual is capable of pursuing a long-term goal and has perseverance (i.e., the ability to pursue objectives in spite of difficulties).
- College graduates often earn higher salaries in their lifetime than nongraduates.
- Many people do not realize that a higher education helps an individual to learn how to learn and think. Examples are how and where to search for quality information, how to maximize reading and studying, how to think critically, and how to memorize information. This is especially important, since professionals are in a constant state of learning new skills and knowledge and must make crucial decisions.
- Besides improving reading comprehension to absorb more information, vocabulary is enhanced through a college education, and it is vital to understand what people are communicating. To illustrate,

in 1950, U.S. Senator Claude Pepper was challenged in a Florida campaign by George Smathers, who stated that Senator Pepper was a shameless extrovert, matriculated with co-eds when in college, engaged in nepotism with his sister-in-law, practiced celibacy before marriage, and had a sister who was once a thespian.

- Writing skills are improved, which are especially important for report writing and business correspondence. Many practitioners are promoted because of excellent report-writing skills; supervisors want accurate, clear reports of incidents.

- Verbal skills are improved. This is very important for succeeding in job interviews and general on-the-job duties, speaking with customers, testifying under oath, and being a trainer.

- Analytical and math skills are improved to solve problems, analyze crime statistics and other metrics, develop budgets, conduct risk analyses, and prepare crime scene and accident reports, among other duties.

- College courses offer knowledge and skills on a host of topics. For instance, courses in psychology help one to understand how various techniques can be used to manipulate people, as in advertising. Mental disorders are studied, and a practitioner will be better prepared when dealing with critical incidents involving a disturbed person. In addition, the study of psychology helps one to understand oneself, a prerequisite to successful interactions with others.

- The study of sociology helps us to understand diversity within our society, how groups interact, social problems, and the socialization process (e.g., training and examples set by others).

ISSUE

Security Periodicals: A Cautious Read

The discussion that follows can be applied to other professions, besides security. When we read security periodicals or research security topics, we must remind ourselves that a huge security industry is working to sell products and services through marketing and sales campaigns. These campaigns include periodical articles in security publications that subtly extol the advantages, return on investment, and enhanced security, whether accurate or not, from purchasing the product or service described. In the event that a security practitioner would make a purchase based upon such an article, the results could be disappointing.

A search of the Web for objective information on security products or services can be challenging. Vendors naturally praise what they are selling to increase sales. We should not necessarily discard the security periodicals that look somewhat like sales catalogs. These periodicals do contain technical data, security strategies, trends, and other helpful information. By piecing together information from multiple articles, issues, and publications, conclusions can be drawn about the security industry and professions. The key is to read cautiously with the following tips in mind:

- With a periodical article in front of you, quickly study the title and author and then go to the end of the article to check the background of the writer. Is the writer a vendor? Look for job titles containing words such as *marketing, sales,* or *community relations*. The editors of the periodical itself may also serve in a "sales role" by writing an article on a product or service.
- Read the last two or three paragraphs first to learn where the writer leaves the reader who spent time reading the whole article. Is it a summary of a "sales pitch"?
- If you decide to read the whole article, count the number of times a product or service is mentioned. The greater the number the more "repetition" is being applied as a technique to attract a customer.
- In the article, look for puffing, which refers to extravagant praise. Are claims of effectiveness, efficiency, or performance supported by scientifically sound research or testing from a neutral organization not affiliated or supported by the vendor or a group linked to the vendor?
- Finally, think critically about the article and draw conclusions cautiously.

Security journals are also considered periodicals. These publications contain articles that are much less biased when compared to articles in other security periodicals. Security journals publish scientific research and are an essential part of what makes security a profession. Scholarly journals are typically peer reviewed. This means that articles submitted for publication are screened by independent experts who approve or reject submitted articles based upon criteria of solid scholarship, such as competence of the research, structure, content, rigorously cited footnotes or bibliographies, and writing. Scholarly journals that are peer reviewed are identified by statements by the editorial staff in the journal itself or by checking online at *Ulrich's International Periodicals Directory.*

Two scholarly security journals are *Security Journal* (published by Palgrave Macmillan Journals with support from the ASIS Foundation) and the *Journal of Security Education* (official journal of the Academy of Security Educators and Trainers).

Answers to security challenges are also found in several disciplines outside of the security profession. The reader should look to publications in such disciplines as law enforcement, criminal justice, business, risk management, information technology, emergency management, fire protection, safety, and the behavioral sciences. The Web and a library are beginning points for research.

Critical Thinking

What is the value of security periodicals that look somewhat like sales catalogues?

Careers

The security profession offers many career options in the private and public sectors. Throughout this chapter, the huge private security industry is described; the reader can apply this information toward an understanding of the employment opportunities in security. In addition, most chapters in this book contain a "career box" describing a specialization in security.

The Web is an excellent source of career opportunities in security. The U.S. Department of Labor's Web site includes the "Occupational Outlook Handbook." It describes several employment categories relevant to security. Information from the handbook is contained within the career boxes in subsequent chapters. The ASIS International Web site offers a booklet entitled "Career Opportunities in Security." This excellent and comprehensive booklet describes entry-level and mid-level security management positions in the following security fields:

- Banking and financial services
- Commercial real estate
- Cultural properties
- Educational institutions
- Gaming and wagering
- Government industrial
- Healthcare
- Information systems
- Investigations
- Lodging and hospitality
- Manufacturing
- Retail loss prevention
- Security engineering and design
- Security sales, equipment, and services
- Transportation
- Utilities and nuclear

For employment openings in security, several sources are available. The Web is a major source of information. However, do not discount other sources, such as placement offices at educational institutions, educators, networking, professional associations, conferences and seminars, newspapers and other periodicals, bulletin boards in government buildings, libraries, and public and private employment agencies.

Summary

This chapter examines the profession and business of security. A professional performs a service to help our society, possesses specialized knowledge and skills, follows a code of ethics, and strives for self-improvement. Security associations are the main avenue to professionalism.

The security industry is huge, and this chapter describes the employment opportunities in this growing field. The security industry is challenged to regulate itself; consequently, government—especially on the state and local levels—typically requires licensing and registration of private security organizations and personnel. Government regulations include criminal history checks on applicants.

Training of security personnel is a major issue and is of the utmost importance prior to duty assignments. Personnel must know their job responsibilities and how best to protect people and assets while conforming to law and company policies and procedures. For those who choose to advance in a rewarding security career, a college education can be helpful, the most important benefit being the skill of learning how to learn.

The chapter content, and the Internet Connections at the end of this chapter, provide direction for further study of the business of security, careers, associations, and professionalism.

Discussion Questions

1. Is security a profession today? Why or why not?
2. Is privatization of government security a good or bad idea? Explain your answer.
3. What can be done globally to control outlaw private security companies?
4. What are the benefits of becoming a member of a professional security association?
5. Why do you think Congress has not passed a national law requiring mandatory minimum training for all private-sector security officers?
6. What is the value of a college education and degree?
7. What are the benefits and detriments of a security career?

Practical Applications

3A. If you had $25,000 to invest in the security industry, how would you invest this money?
3B. What are your career goals? How will you reach these goals?

3C. Access the Web and research two college degree programs in security. Compare the programs. Which program do you prefer and why?

3D. Conduct Web research of a security certification program. What are the requirements?

3E. As a contract security executive, how do you reduce the turnover of your security officers who are paid low wages and are required, by a combination of state law and the client, to receive 40 hours of training before duty assignments?

3F. As a global security investigator, how would you vet a contract security company in another country for a corporate client?

3G. Suppose you are the security manager at a multistory office building and an unexpected tornado strikes your geographic area. Your family resides only a few blocks away. The tornado strikes the office building and nearby neighborhoods, causing deaths, injuries, and destruction. You are unable to contact your family and you face an ethical dilemma of implementing emergency plans and assisting with the carnage at the office building or going home to check on your family. What is your decision? Explain your reasoning.

3H. In reference to the above scenario, what if you are a security officer? What is your decision? Explain your reasoning.

3I. As a security officer on assignment at an access point to a chemical facility, would you permit an unauthorized truck to enter the premises for $1,000 cash from the driver? Explain your answer.

3J. As a security officer, if you witnessed another security officer, a good friend of yours, steal an item in the workplace, would you report the officer? Explain your answer.

Internet Connections

Academy of Security Educators and Trainers: www.asetcse.org
American Bankers Association: www.aba.com
ASIS International: www.asisonline.org
Association of Certified Fraud Examiners: www.acfe.org
Association of Private Security Companies: www.bapsc.org.uk
British Security Industry Association: www.bsia.co.uk
Council on Licensure, Enforcement and Regulation: www.clearhq.org
Ethics Education Resource Center: www.aacsb.edu/resource_centers/EthicsEdu/default.asp
Federal Jobs Net: http://federaljobs.net/index.html
The Haworth Press, *Journal of Security Education*: www.haworthpress.com
International Association for Healthcare Security & Safety: www.iahss.org
International Association of Security & Investigative Regulators: www.iasir.org
International Foundation of Protection Officers: www.ifpo.org
International Information Systems Security Certification Consortium: www.isc2.org
Loss Prevention Foundation: www.losspreventionfoundation.org

National Association of Security Companies: www.nasco.org
National Burglar & Fire Alarm Association: www.alarm.org
Palgrave Macmillan Journals, *Security Journal*: www.palgrave-journals.com/sj/index.html
Security Industry Association: www.siaonline.org
U.S. Department of Labor: www.dol.gov

References

ASIS International. 2004. Private security officer selection and training. www.asisonline.org.

Bayles, M. 1995. *Professional ethics*. 2nd ed. Belmont, CA: Wadsworth.

Broder, J. 2007. Report says firm sought to cover up Iraq shootings. *New York Times* (October 2). www.nytimes.com.

Cordivari, R. 2008. One size fits all? *Security Executive* 3 (June/July):15–16.

Cunningham, W., et al. 1990. *Private security trends: 1970–2000, The Hallcrest report II*. Boston: Butterworth–Heinemann.

Cunningham, W., and T. Taylor. 1985. *Private security and police in America: The Hallcrest report*. Portland, OR: Chancellor Press.

Davidson, B. 2008. In California, proprietary security guards slow to get licensed. *Security Director News* 5 (September):4.

DeGeorge, R. 1990. *Business ethics*. New York: Macmillan.

Encarta. 2008. Professionalism. Encarta Encyclopedia. http://encarta.msn.com.

Erickson, D. 2008. 2008 legislative agenda: Follow the money. *Security* 45 (February):40.

Fay, J. 2007. *Encyclopedia of Security Management*. 2nd ed. Boston: Elsevier Butterworth–Heinemann.

Fine, S., and S. Cronshaw. 1999. *Functional job analysis: A foundation for human resources management*. Mahwah, NJ: Erlbaum Associates Publishers.

Freedonia Group, Inc. 2006. World security services: Industry study with forecasts to 2010 and 2015. www.freedoniagroup.com.

Freedonia Group, Inc. 2008a. Private security services to 2012. www.freedoniagroup.com.

Freedonia Group, Inc. 2008b. Electronic security systems: U.S. industry study with forecasts for 2012 and 2017. www.freedoniagroup.com.

Freedonia Group, Inc. 2008c. World security equipment: Industry study with forecasts for 2012 and 2017. www.freedoniagroup.com.

Glanz, J. 2008. Report on Iraq security lists 310 contractors. *New York Times* (October 28). www.nytimes.com.

Homeland Security Research. 2007. U.S. homeland security (government and private) market outlook: 2007–2011. www.homelandsecurityresearch.com.

Junginger, C. 2008. Who is training whom? The effect of the Millennial Generation. *FBI Law Enforcement Bulletin* 77 (September):19–23.

Kepner, M. 2008. Special report: NASCO's security summit and hill day. *Security Executive* 3 (June/July):10–12.

Kruse, K. 2000. *Technology-based training: The art and science of design, development, and delivery*. San Francisco: Jossey-Bass.

Merriam–Webster. 2008. Professionalism. Merriam Webster Online Dictionary. www.merriam-webster.com/dictionary/professionalism.

Mortman, D. 2007. Smoke & mirrors. *Information Security* 10 (July/August):22.

Pollock, J. 1998. *Ethics in crime and justice: Dilemmas and decisions*. 3rd ed. Belmont, CA: West/Wadsworth.

Singer, P. 2007. Can't win with 'em, can't go to war without 'em: Private military contractors and counterinsurgency. Brookings Institution policy paper no. 4 (September). www.brookings.edu.

Sullivan, J. 2006. Mall security guard arrested after fight over parking spot. *Times Herald-Record* (December 17). www.recordonline.com. (This news item and names were modified in the illustration in this chapter.)

Turbiville, G. 2006. Outlaw private security firms: Criminals and terrorist agendas undermine private security alternatives. *Global Crime* 7 (August–November):561–582.

United Nations Office at Geneva. 2008. UN Working Group on use of mercenaries says unregulated activities by private military security companies is major cause of concern (March 10). www.unog.ch/unog.

U.S. Department of Justice. 1972. Private police in the United States: Findings and recommendations 1. (The Rand Report.) Washington, DC: U.S. Government Printing Office.

U.S. Department of Justice. 1976. Report of the Task Force on Private Security. Washington, DC: U.S. Government Printing Office.

Van Steden, R., and R. Sarre. 2007. The growth of private security: Trends in the European Union. *Security Journal* 20:222–235.

Zalud, B., et al. 2008. The backbone: Security officers. *Security* 45 (February):72.

Section II

Protecting People and Assets

Chapter **4**

Security Methodology

Chapter Learning Objectives

After reading this chapter, you should be able to:

1. Define methodology
2. Explain the purpose and contents of a security business proposal
3. Explain the purpose and contents of a security master plan
4. Discuss the meaning and benefits of security-relevant criminology
5. List and explain at least four ecological theories of crime and the relevance of each to security
6. Describe crime mapping and its benefits and capabilities
7. Detail the risk-analysis process
8. Explain the purpose and contents of metrics in the security profession
9. Discuss the purpose of research and evaluation and how they are applied to security strategies

Terms to Know

methodology
security business proposal
return on investment

security master plan
theories
empirical validity
criminology
security-relevant criminology
ecological theories of crime
environmental criminology
Oscar Newman
defensible space
territoriality
natural surveillance
displacement
crime prevention through environmental design (CPTED)
C. Ray Jeffery
zoning ordinances
subdivision regulations
building codes
broken-windows theory
situational crime prevention
diffusion of benefits
rational-choice theory
routine-activity theory
crime-pattern theory
crime mapping
geographic information systems (GIS)
global positioning systems (GPS)
geographic profiling
high-definition mapping
vulnerability assessment
threat assessment
risk assessment
risk analysis
consequential event
direct losses
indirect losses
security survey
quantitative methodologies
qualitative methodologies
security standards
regulations
codes
metrics
layered security

scientific method
experimental-control-group design
pre-test
post-test
validity
reliability
multiple-group before-and-after research design

QUIZ

This quiz serves to prime the reader's mind and begin the reading, thinking, and studying processes for this chapter. The answers to all of the questions are found within this chapter.

1. Is criminology too theoretical to be applied to security planning?
2. Who is the father of the *defensible space* concept that had a profound affect on security?
3. What is *natural surveillance*?
4. What is the difference between pin maps and crime mapping?
5. Does a security survey typically concentrate on questioning people about their opinions of security?
6. Are quantitative methodologies used in the security profession?
7. What are security metrics?

Introduction

This chapter provides direction and methodologies to develop, plan, evaluate, update, and improve security programs. It offers theory, tools, and practical applications that can be applied in an effort to produce the best possible security programs while optimizing available resources and meeting business needs.

Security professionals are not only scrutinized about their security plans and budget, but they must also answer questions justifying their actions and inactions pertaining to organizational risks. Besides answering such questions for superiors, these same questions may have to be answered in court during litigation. This chapter helps security professionals to develop a framework and methodology to plan more efficiently and scientifically, to enhance planning and budgeting presentations, to answer difficult questions, and to explain *what they do, how they do it*, and *why*.

Methodology Defined

Methodology is a "body of methods, rules, and postulates employed by a discipline: a particular procedure or set of procedures." It includes "the analysis of the principles or procedures of inquiry in a particular field" (Merriam–Webster On-line Dictionary 2008). Not only does methodology refer to the study of methods of research, it also includes the rationale and philosophical assumptions that support and drive research. Other aspects of the methodology of a particular discipline are *theories* and *concepts*.

The security methodologies explained in subsequent pages are security business proposals, security master plans, theories, risk analysis, standards, metrics, and research and evaluation. These methodologies provide important and vital input to both security planning and the implementation of security strategies. These methodologies are by no means the "final word." The reader should seek out other sources, and expand and improve the proposed methodologies. Practitioners should apply the methodologies to enhance security programs to protect people, assets, and operations.

Security Business Proposals

A major avenue to develop and advance a security program and gain senior management financial support is through a **security business proposal** (SBP). This term has many meanings and definitions. In its most basic meaning, it refers to an offering from a seller to a potential buyer. Here, we are applying this term to an organization whose security executive is seeking senior management's approval of a security plan and budget. A vital prerequisite to an SBP, or planning security for a business, is an understanding of the business's strategic plans and objectives. What are the business projections over the next three to five years? Is domestic and/or international growth projected? What are the plans for facilities expansion and hiring? Or, will the business downsize and lay off employees?

Paquet (2005), writing from an IT perspective, provides noteworthy points to assist us in understanding SBPs. She writes that SBPs in organizations are often treated differently by senior executives when compared to proposals from other departments. She faults security executives for not providing enough financial justifications, while arguing that fear alone is often not convincing enough to generate support for an investment in security. Paquet favors SBPs with financials, because that is the language of business management. The "financials" approach is based on a common methodology that senior management uses to evaluate other business proposals, and budget approval is more likely for a security proposal that contains a financial analysis of the investment. According to Paquet, an SBP should include:

- Executive summary
- Purpose of security strategy
- Business objectives and strategic considerations

- Benefits, challenges, and impact of security strategy
- Security financials, including costs and benefits
- Alternatives and recommendations

An important component of financials for executives preparing an SBP is **return on investment** (ROI), which shows that an investment in a security strategy will result in financial and other benefits. For example, a security executive might show that investigative costs are well worth the added expense because they result in recovery of stolen items and/or court-ordered restitution that exceed investigative costs. Another approach might contend that investments in a security force to protect a facility are far less than the costs of potential loss of inventory or proprietary information, or losses from a lawsuit alleging negligent security. There is also the consideration that an increase in the level of protection from a security force should be offset by lower insurance premiums.

Ahrens (2007a), a security consultant, offers the following list of items to include in an SBP:

- The problem statement
- Methodology
- Proposed resolution
- Implementation plan
- Impact on budget
- ROI
- Return on investment over x years
- Statistical data

Another type of SBP is from the perspective of businesses selling security services or systems to businesses, institutions, and other clients. Examples of security services are contract security officers and investigative services. Examples of security systems are intrusion alarms and CCTV.

A contract security firm offering contract security officers to a potential client would prepare a proposal to provide security services that would include such information as the following:

- Introduction covering the contract firm and its history, clients, management, experience, and resources
- Administrative overview on such topics as recruitment and selection of officers, training, uniforms, appearance, supervision, and accountability
- Results from a security survey that shows the number of officers needed for protection as well as their assignments, scheduling, and hours
- Hourly billing rate and benefits
- Equipment and system requirements (e.g., vehicles, communications, card access system) and costs

- Certificate of insurance
- Contract

A company selling security systems would prepare a proposal that included such information as how the system meets the client's needs, system specifications and performance, system components, costs, installation schedule, project management, system testing, training, maintenance, warranty, and contract. Proposals vary considerably. (Chapter 7 provides information about purchasing security systems and services from the customer's perspective.)

We can see that there are various types, styles, and content requirements of SBPs. Proprietary security executives should seek guidance from coworkers for help in preparing the best possible business proposals that conform to organizational norms and business objectives. Security companies are also challenged to produce quality proposals in an effort to gain sales in a competitive business environment. An SBP requires research, preparation, and writing, which can be time-consuming. The present chapter, as well as subsequent chapters, offer tools, sources of information, and strategies that can serve as inputs for proposals.

Security Master Plans

Giles (2009) refers to **security master plans** (SMP) that contain elements of security business proposals. He defines an SMP as follows:

> A document that delineates the organization's security philosophies, strategies, goals, programs, and processes. It is used to guide the organization's development and direction in these areas in a manner that is consistent with the company's overall business plan. It also provides a detailed outline of the risks and the mitigation plans for them in a way that creates a five-year business plan.

Giles notes that an SMP assists a security executive (or the client of a security consultant) in gaining support for a security program and the budget to support it. In addition, a five-year plan that has been approved by senior management increases the likelihood that needed funding for security will be forthcoming—if not in the first year, then in subsequent years. Giles writes that the more the security executive can outline the specific funding needed to mitigate specific risks, the easier it will be to contain budget challenges.

Of particular importance in supporting the value of an SMP is ensuring that "security strategies are linked to the strategies of the business" and "in unison with the business" (Giles 2009, 1). This approach is assisted by engaging stakeholders—employees from across the business enterprise—who can provide valuable input and who will be affected by the change. Such individuals can generate support for the SMP. Depending on the organization, stakeholders can be representatives from manufacturing, information technology, engineering, human resources, risk management, and the legal department.

The initial step in developing an SMP, according to Giles (2009, xxii), is to collect information on the organization. Examples include general information on the business and its organization; security vulnerabilities and issues; security plans, policies, procedures, and post orders; security personnel; and physical security.

Giles (2009, 191) writes that an actual sample SMP is difficult to produce because such plans are extremely confidential. In addition, each entity's plan is different, which may mislead others in the development of their SMPs. Giles does offer an outline of what may be contained in an SMP, as listed below, but cautions that, depending on the entity, certain sections may not be applicable and other sections may have to be added.

- Purpose
- Introduction
- Executive summary
- Security philosophies, strategies, and goals
- Security organization's structure
- Security staffing and skills required
- Security technology plan
- Physical security
- Investigations
- Information security
- Emergency planning and crisis management
- Workplace violence prevention program
- Executive protection program
- Unique protection needs

Theories

Paulsen and Robinson (2009, 1) write that **theories** are statements, propositions, or hypotheses that relate two or more real-world things (e.g., concepts or variables) to explain or predict a phenomenon. They add that of the more than 100 theories of crime, most explain why criminal behaviors occur, and far fewer predict where and when crime is more likely to occur. Paulsen and Robinson note that criminological theory could be more useful if more emphasis was placed on predicting the "where and when" of crime, and this author agrees.

Paulsen and Robinson (2009, 4–5) wrote:

Although the word "theory" likely brings forth the conception of something that is "just theoretical" and "not practical," the truth is that theory is very useful in the real world…. Theory is aimed at explaining things we have observed. Theory thus allows us to make sense out of what we experience and of the world in general.

We evaluate theory through **empirical validity**, which is support of theory by real-world observations and data. In other words, theories are tested by collecting data through various types of observations (e.g., questionnaires or experiments) to see if empirical evidence does or does not support proposed hypotheses.

There are many more theories of crime than what is covered in the subsequent discussion. The major objectives here are to explain theory and draw out its relevance and practical application to security programs and strategies.

Criminology involves the study of crime, causes of crime, criminal behavior, victims, and the control of crime. Theories of crime tend to explain one or more types of criminal behavior, but no single theory can explain all types of crime. Criminologists study violent crime, property crime, other crimes, and a host of topics and issues related to the problem of crime. Security practitioners must deal with all types of crime, and criminologists offer many theories to explain and control crime.

Security-Relevant Criminology

Security-relevant criminology is theory that has practical applications for security programs and strategies. It is an essential component of security methodology, serving as a source of input for security business proposals, risk analyses, planning, budgeting, and justification. In addition, security practitioners should develop a mindset and habit of seeking out theory and research from a wide variety of disciplines, besides criminology and security. As this chapter progresses, and after theories are explained, the reader will see how theory can be applied to real-world security challenges.

Throughout the history of criminology, an emphasis has been placed on studying and researching the *individuals* who committed crimes and *why* they committed crimes. Such theories and research evolved primarily from the disciplines of biology, sociology, and psychology. An enormous number of research and publications have focused on internal causes of crime (i.e., biological and psychological), external causes of crime (i.e., sociological, including social forces that drive people to crime), and a combination of both. The typical criminology textbook offers many theories along these lines. A portion of these theories is without foundation and can be dismissed in a historical context under the banner, "This is what they believed back then." Even today, theories of crime generate controversy. On the other hand, another portion of criminological theories is supported by empirical research and withstands the tests of validity and reliability.

In the context of security-relevant criminology, an emphasis is placed on the environment (e.g., security features), criminal opportunities, and lifestyles of victims. Major questions are: Why did crime occur at a specific location? What can be done to prevent crime from occurring at the specific location?

Critical Thinking

Should criminology and government crime-control policies emphasize improving security and reducing criminal opportunities while forgoing criminal "rehabilitation" and related programs? Why or why not?

Ecological Theories of Crime

Ecological theories of crime are at the foundation of security-relevant criminology. For many years, sociologists have played a major role in the development of ecological theories of crime through their research that focused on demographics (i.e., characteristics of population groups) and geographics (i.e., mapping to pinpoint crime). The origin of ecological theories goes back to Adolphe Quetelet and André Guerry during the mid-1800s in Europe. Voit and others (1994, 222) write: "Quetelet introduced the use of statistics to calculate the different probabilities of crime occurring across regions and in relation to sociodemographic categories. Guerry was perhaps the first to plot the incidence of crimes on maps to discover high and low crime areas."

Ecological theories of crime are a major category of crime theory that has spawned a host of newer categories and theories. These include **environmental criminology** (also known as criminology of place), which looks to geographic location and physical features of buildings and grounds as important factors to consider in rates of victimization. Depending on the writer, the subsequent theories of crime may be categorized as either ecological or environmental. More importantly, the following ecological/environmental theories of crime make up the field of security-relevant criminology.

Defensible Space

Oscar Newman (1972), an architect, is the father of the defensible-space theory, which has had a profound effect on concepts of security. Although Newman's research focused on public housing, his concepts are applicable to other locations (Figure 4.1). He sought to reduce crime and fear of crime. **Defensible space** involves designs in architecture, landscape architecture, street layout, and land use that prevent crime by facilitating people's use of

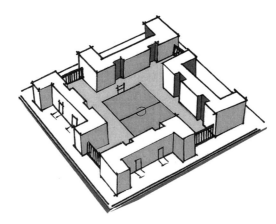

FIGURE 4.1 Oscar Newman, the father of defensible space, designed security features at public housing complexes to facilitate people's use of public places and to reduce crime. (Art by Julie Helms. With permission.)

public places and interactions with others to create a sense of community. Two types of social behavior encouraged from this theory are territoriality and natural surveillance.

Territoriality refers to a feeling of ownership of a location, an encouragement of legitimate activities, and efforts to keep away illegitimate activities. It also includes fences, hedges, and signs that establish both a physical and psychological barrier. In applying this theory to practice, when residents of a neighborhood know each other, their legitimate patterns of behavior, and what barriers residents customarily cross between public and private property, they are more likely to report suspicious behavior or events and notify police. This can also facilitate reporting through both Neighborhood Watch and Crimestoppers programs. In an environment of corporate security, a security executive should ensure that employees understand security policies and procedures and report suspicious activity. Employees should be provided with an easy, convenient, and anonymous way to report, such as a drop box, toll free number, or Web site. A variety of physical security features is applied in a corporate environment to prevent unauthorized access.

Natural surveillance results from design features of a building and the surrounding property that subtly facilitate people's observations of patterns of behavior and events, while limiting offender opportunities to remain undetected. This is accomplished through many strategies. For example, in the design of an apartment building, each apartment can contain a window at the kitchen sink overlooking the parking lot and playground, thereby allowing residents to watch children playing and residents' vehicles. Employees in an office building can also perform natural surveillance by viewing walkways and parking lots from office windows or from large windows in other areas of the building, such as in the cafeteria. The trimming of trees and hedges, quality lighting, and white, reflective paint facilities natural surveillance.

Paulsen and Robinson (2009, 73–74) point to criticisms of Newman's theory of defensible space. They describe the difficulty of proving that it reduces crime, including research methodology problems such as single-location research without a control group. In addition, they argue that the theory does not address the "root causes of criminality." Another criticism by Paulsen and Robinson is that of **displacement**, which means that potential crime may be "moved" and occur at a different, less-protected location. This is an interesting criticism of defensible space because one of the objectives of a security program is to design security at a site so that it appears formidable enough to cause an offender to avoid the site. The offender may seek an alternate target. Although displacement may not prevent crime in the area in which an offender operates, it may prevent crime at the site protected by a quality security program.

Critical Thinking

What are your views of a corporate security program that causes an offender to select and victimize a different company with less protection?

The issue of displacement is complicated by the multiple ways in which it can be measured. Worrall (2008, 17) refers to six types of displacement. The most popular type is spatial (i.e., crime moved to another location). Temporal involves an offender choosing a different time to commit a crime. Tactical refers to a different method. A different type of target may be selected, as well as a different type of crime. A sixth type occurs when apprehended offenders are replaced by new ones. Worrall notes possible evidence of the displacement of property crime. This would be a concern for security practitioners seeking to protect company assets at locations that are not as well protected as surrounding locations.

Crime Prevention through Environmental Design

Crime prevention through environmental design (CPTED) is defined by Clarke and Eck (2005) as "a set of principles for designing and laying-out secure buildings and public places." CPTED was developed through the work of **C. Ray Jeffery** (1977) in 1971. This theory is broader than Newman's defensible-space theory (Figure 4.2). Jeffery refers to preventing crime by addressing the "total environment." This includes changing the physical environment, increasing resident involvement and interaction, fostering proactive policing, and acting upon the root causes of crime, such as social, psychological, and biological factors.

FIGURE 4.2 The crime prevention through environmental design (CPTED) theory is broader than Newman's defensible space theory. Both theories contain security strategies, including natural surveillance (e.g., through windows) and controlling foliage. (® Shutterstock.com. With permission.)

Jeffery (1993, 303) was a biocriminologist who maintained an interest in crime prevention through biologically based programs. He favored pre- and postnatal care for pregnant women, monitoring children to reduce violent victimization, and biological research in prisons to identify causes of violence. Jeffery viewed antisocial behavior as a medical problem necessitating medical research on offenders.

Paulsen and Robinson (2009, 79–83) write that federal government funded research on CPTED began in the 1970s and concentrated on target-hardening measures (e.g., street lighting, residential locks and security systems, and architectural design changes). The results were moderately successful. It became difficult to pinpoint what works, where, and against what crime. In addition, as in studies of defensible space, it is difficult to draw generalizations from a study at a single site, especially when multiple security strategies are applied and firm conclusions about which ones are most effective become guesswork without an improved research design. Despite these challenges, Worrall (2008, 313) notes that environmental manipulation is one of the more effective strategies of reducing criminal opportunities and controlling crime. Consequently, quality research should aim to develop CPTED and pinpoint which strategies are successful and which ones are not.

Jeffery's CPTED is often referred to by the security literature and by practitioners because it is broad in scope and it includes defensible-space theory and practice. Today, CPTED is interdisciplinary, and it has many variations.

Timothy Crowe (2000), in his book, *Crime Prevention through Environmental Design*, writes that to implement CPTED, consideration must be given to the designation, definition, and design of a location. He offers the following questions:

Designation
- What is the purpose of the location?
- What was its original purpose?
- How well does the location support its current and future uses?

Definition
- How is the location defined?
- Is it clear who owns it?
- Where are its borders?
- Are there social or cultural definitions that affect how the location is used?
- Are legal or administrative rules clear, communicated, and reinforced?
- Is there adequate signage?
- Is there a conflict or confusion between the designated purpose and definition?

Design
- How well does the physical design support the intended function?
- How well does the physical design support the definition of the desired or accepted behavior?
- Does the physical design conflict with the productive use of the location?

Through answers to these questions, subtle security features emerge. In addition, the answers serve as input to plan enhanced security.

Randall Atlas, an architect and a Certified Protection Professional (CPP), offers guidance in applying Crowe's questions. Atlas (1993, 201) writes that CPTED seeks to

> eliminate any appearances that would suggest vulnerability of the inhabitants, and to promote deterrence by presenting appearances of unity and commitment against criminal activities. Poor building definition can create spaces that are not conducive to effective monitoring or intervention. Such spaces may be ideal for the burglar to effect a breaking and entering, the rapist to lie in wait for a victim.

Atlas adds that although parking lots, driveways, fences, walkways, shrubbery, and other features can be designed to remove spaces vulnerable to crime, quality design does not guarantee security and safety. He emphasizes that the key is the occupants who must assert their dominion over the location, and he refers to Neighborhood Watch and similar programs. As noted earlier, a security executive should recruit employees to assist security and safety efforts.

PUBLIC-SECTOR SITE-PLAN REVIEW PROCESS AND CPTED

The present chapter emphasizes *private*-sector security methodology. Here, a perspective on *public*-sector security methodology is presented. The following information is from Wright and Thomas (1993, 203–206), who wrote of the site-plan review process in Ann Arbor, Michigan.

In Ann Arbor, like most communities, when architects and developers seek to develop property, they research all relevant city ordinances and regulations. The ordinances and regulations fall under eight city departments in Ann Arbor. These are Planning (which guides the research), Building, Engineering, Housing, Police, Fire, Historic Commission, and Parks and Recreation. The Ann Arbor Police Department has been involved in hundreds of site petition reviews resulting in police comments on the impact of developments on crime. Experienced crime prevention officers refer to the work of Newman and Jeffery to formulate cost-effective suggestions on lighting, access controls, places of concealment, and other related issues. In addition, the development of property may necessitate the hiring of more police officers, the purchasing of more police vehicles, and other expenses such as training and equipment.

There is often a time gap between the initial plans and the completed development, including use by residents and employees. CPTED strategies may not work as well as planned. Possible reasons are that citizens may ignore or fail to use security precautions, they may need to be educated on the precautions, or maintenance of CPTED strategies may be lax. Another challenge is the differing priorities among the eight city departments involved in the site-plan review process. To ameliorate some of the challenges, cross-training is applied. Non-police planners are trained in CPTED, and they apply their new knowledge by differentiating various security strategies and identifying quality or poor CPTED plans. Crime-prevention officers receive training in city planning and the site-plan review process, plus they attend public hearings and plan review meetings. They also learn of the power of **zoning ordinances** for city planning as a way to regulate the use of private land to protect public health, safety, and morals. In other words, police influence decisions on planned land uses (e.g., a strip club) that may affect crime rates.

Subdivision regulations are somewhat similar to zoning ordinances. Besides regulating building setbacks, street locations and design, locations of schools and public facilities, and other things, several CPTED strategies (e.g., lighting and fences) are set in subdivision regulations.

Building codes are another avenue for introducing crime-prevention and security strategies into a city. These codes set requirements and minimum standards for construction features such as door and window sizes, locking hardware, and alarm systems, in addition to plumbing, electrical, and other installations.

Ann Arbor crime-prevention officers also gather crime analysis data, demographic data, and resident comments. A report of the findings is prepared, often in the form of a list of security concerns that are openly discussed at meetings of city planners and developers.

Wright and Thomas write that the site-review process can prevent poor security designs that can be expensive to correct later. In addition, they note the benefits of quality design and planning to prevent allegations of negligent security. *They see this process as applicable to the private sector, including industrial and commercial developments, health care facilities, and other projects.*

Broken-Windows Theory

Broken-windows theory (Wilson and Kelling 1982) claims that small problems (e.g., broken windows, graffiti, and public intoxication) in a geographic area, if not corrected, can lead to further problems and crime, decay in the physical environment, resident fear and withdrawal, and a general downward spiral of the geographic area. On the other hand, if residents play an active role in enforcing public order and compliance, neighborhoods will remain safe. Maintenance is an important related factor in curbing crime. This includes trimming overgrown vegetation, removing graffiti, and repairing physical security (e.g., locks) and other features of the built environment.

Situational Crime Prevention

Situational crime prevention seeks to *reduce opportunities for crime* (Figure 4.3) through a variety of techniques involving people and their behavior and the design of the environment (Clarke 1997). This approach is aimed at a specific crime, place, people, or times. It stresses a high degree of problem identification during security planning to increase the success of safeguards (Lab 2004). Situational crime prevention involves not only the environment, but also specific strategies to protect people and assets, and legal and management strategies. The five objectives of situational crime prevention are named and illustrated in Table 4.1. They are:

1. Increase the effort involved in committing crime
2. Increase the risks for the offender
3. Reduce the rewards
4. Reduce provocations that lead to criminal activity
5. Remove excuses that facilitate crime

TABLE 4.1 Twenty-Five Techniques of Situational Crime Prevention

Increase the Effort	Increase the Risks	Reduce the Rewards	Reduce Provocations	Remove Excuses
1. Harden targets • Steering-column locks and immobilizers • Anti-robbery screens • Tamper-proof packaging	6. Extend guardianship • Take routine precautions: go out in groups at night, leave signs of occupancy, carry phone • "Cocoon" neighborhood watch	11. Conceal targets • Off-street parking • Gender-neutral phone directories • Unmarked bullion trucks	16. Reduce frustrations and stress • Efficient queues and polite service • Expanded seating • Soothing music/muted lights	21. Set rules • Rental agreements • Harassment codes • Hotel registration
2. Control access to facilities • Entry phones • Electronic card access • Baggage screening	7. Assist natural surveillance • Improved street lighting • Defensible space design • Support whistleblowers	12. Remove targets • Removable car radio • Women's refuges • Prepaid cards for pay phones	17. Avoid disputes • Separate enclosures for rival soccer fans • Reduce crowding in pubs • Fixed cab fares	22. Post instructions • No Parking • Private Property • Extinguish camp fires
3. Screen exits • Ticket needed for exit • Export documents • Electronic merchandise tags	8. Reduce anonymity • Taxi driver IDs • "How's my driving?" decals • School uniforms	13. Identify property • Property marking • Vehicle licensing and parts marking • Cattle branding	18. Reduce emotional arousal • Controls on violent pornography • Enforce good behavior on soccer field • Prohibit racial slurs	23. Alert conscience • Roadside speed display boards • Signatures for customs declarations • "Shoplifting is stealing"

4. Deflect offenders
- Street closures
- Separate bathrooms for women
- Disperse pubs

5. Control tools/weapons
- "Smart" guns
- Disable stolen cell phones
- Restrict spray-paint sales to juveniles

9. Utilize place managers
- CCTV for double-deck buses
- Two clerks for convenience stores
- Reward vigilance

10. Strengthen formal surveillance
- Red-light cameras
- Burglar alarms
- Security guards

14. Disrupt markets
- Monitor pawn shops
- Controls on classified ads
- License street vendors

15. Deny benefits
- Ink merchandise tags
- Graffiti cleaning
- Speed humps

19. Neutralize peer pressure
- "Idiots drink and drive"
- "It's OK to say no"
- Disperse troublemakers at school

20. Discourage imitation
- Rapid repair of vandalism
- V-chips in TVs
- Censor details of modus operandi

24. Assist compliance
- Easy library checkout
- Public lavatories
- Litter bins

25. Control drugs and alcohol
- Breathalyzers in pubs
- Server intervention
- Alcohol-free events

Source: Center for Problem Oriented Policing, http://www.popcenter.org/25techniques.htm.

FIGURE 4.3 **Situational crime prevention seeks to reduce opportunities for crime. (® Shutterstock.com. With permission.)**

> In Chapter 5, the twenty-five techniques of situational crime prevention are applied to the problem of laptop thefts in commercial buildings.

Felson and Clarke (1998, 33) argue that, since opportunity is a cause of crime, crime-prevention policies by government should expand the strategy of opportunity reduction. They see opportunity reduction as closer to the crime incident and, thus, this increases the chances of curbing crime immediately. Bridging this theory to practice, preventive efforts by security and police are an essential component of crime control, besides "rehabilitation" and other programs and enforcement of criminal law.

Paulsen and Robinson (2009, 86) write of the criticisms of situational crime prevention theory. They note that it ignores the conditions in the environment (e.g., social problems) that increase the risk of crime. Except for altering opportunities to commit crime, the theory ignores programs to change offender behavior. On a positive note, they write that most research shows that displacement is not a reality resulting from situational crime prevention, and those crimes that are displaced do not equal those that are prevented. They also write of evidence of **diffusion of benefits**, meaning: "When efforts are made to prevent a single type of crime, other types of crime also are prevented." According to Clarke and Eck (2005), it also means "reducing crime beyond the focus of the prevention scheme; a multiplier of effectiveness."

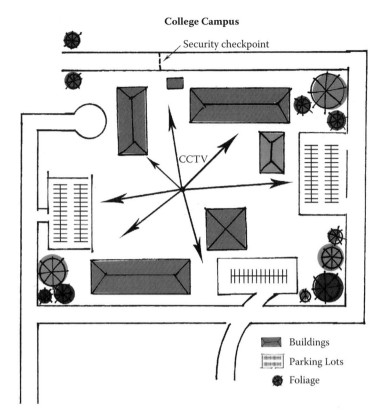

FIGURE 4.4   According to diffusion-of-benefits theory, although the CCTV camera installed on a pole in the center of the campus is unable to view parking areas blocked by buildings, offenders may not know of this limitation and thus avoid committing crimes in all the parking areas. (Art by Julie Helms. With permission.)

This is illustrated in Figure 4.4 from Clarke and Eck. They note other types of diffusion of benefits (similar to those applied earlier to displacement): temporal (i.e., additional prevention over time); target (i.e., additional targets protected); and tactical (i.e., additional methods thwarted).

Worrall (2008, 17) sees measurement challenges with displacement and diffusion of benefits. Measurement questions include the following: How do we know when each has occurred? How do we define the geographic area to which crime is likely to be displaced or into which diffusion occurs? These questions require research.

Rational-Choice Theory

Rational-choice theory, from Cornish and Clarke (1986), focuses on the *criminal who makes a conscious, rational choice of the crime to commit and the target of the crime.* The criminal considers opportunities, risks, costs, and benefits. This theory is aligned with situational theory because society can prevent crime by emphasizing situational factors (e.g., opportunities) that affect criminal behavior. For the security practitioner, security strategies should reduce opportunities and increase risks and costs for the offender.

Kitteringham (2007, 477) observes:

> If the reward is high enough, deterrents will not work.... Situational crime prevention works best with the amateur and least with the professional. The least skilled opportunist will be deterred by or unable to defeat standard crime prevention techniques and is likely to be caught in the attempt; the skilled and determined opportunist will not be deterred and may succeed in committing the act.

Routine-Activity Theory

Routine-activity theory, also referred to as "lifestyle theory," originated from Lawrence Cohen and Marcus Felson (1979, 588–608), who wrote that *lifestyles affect the volume and type of crime in society*. For instance, people who spend a lot of time away from their home may have higher rates of home burglary or victimization by strangers. Or, people who frequent strip clubs may have higher rates of victimization than people who frequent churches. The theory essentially points out that what people do in their routine, daily activities, and how they behave, will affect their risk of victimization. Cohen and Felson theorized that the convergence of three factors result in crime: a motivated offender, a suitable target, and the absence of a capable guardian (e.g., someone who is available to prevent crime, such as a witness or security officer).

Paulsen and Robinson (2009, 91) criticize routine-activity theory research, like situational crime prevention, for not measuring offender motivation. In addition, there is a need for measurements of the amount of time people spend in different places to link it to the risk of victimization.

Situational crime prevention, rational-choice theory, and routine-activity theory have been criticized for concentrating on individual choice without concern for the social factors (e.g., poverty, unemployment) that contribute to crime. Rational choice ignores the role of substance abuse in crime, a variable that has received much attention in research. Paulsen and Robinson (2009, 91) note the difficulty of researching the thought processes and observations of offenders as they decide whether or not to commit a crime.

Crime-Pattern Theory

Brantingham and Brantingham (1993) developed **crime-pattern theory**. It is a mixture of theories (as described previously), is multidisciplinary, and seeks to explain the process of how a crime event occurs, including criminal behavior, decisions, and patterns of crime. The process may begin, for instance, with an offender casing an office building on his way to work or recreation. He tests access controls to gain entry. Access to the building becomes an opportunity, as well as the observation of a pocketbook on a desk with no guardian. With no one in the area, and the available excuse of "picking up a package," the risks are low, the payoff can be substantial, and the opportunity triggers the theft.

The crime-pattern theory studies locations that offenders examine and their awareness of such locations as targets for crime. This theory has three main elements: *nodes* are where people travel to and from (e.g., home, work, recreation); *paths* are routes to and from nodes; and *edges* are the boundaries of nodes, such as neighborhood fringes. According to crime-pattern theory, crime risk is the greatest at edges.

Paulsen and Robinson (2009, 97) see crime-pattern theory as not widely tested, and its "empirical validity is not yet fully understood." As noted earlier, it is difficult to empirically verify the thoughts of an offender prior to committing a crime, although interviewing is one research method. Paulsen and Robinson see the potential of crime mapping to illustrate the elements of crime-pattern theory by mapping nodes, paths, and edges. They refer to analysis of offender site selection that, for example, helped to apprehend the Washington, D.C., area sniper in 2002. In fact, Paulsen and Robinson (2009, 102) argue that concepts from all of the theories cited here can be mapped to help explain crime risks among different locations with different characteristics. To map all the variables is challenging. However, such research and mapping assists in enhancing security.

The case of the pocketbook theft from an office building can be taken a step further, and security practitioners can use this case to inform employees of the consequences of not following basic security precautions. The criminal who stole the pocketbook telephoned the victim that night, from outside her home, claiming to be "Sgt. Smith" from the local police precinct. The criminal informed the victim that her pocketbook was recovered and she should pick it up. When she departed from her home, the offender used her keys to burglarize her home and steal more of her assets.

CRIME MAPPING

Crime mapping is defined by Clarke and Eck (2005) as "examining how crime is spread geographically by showing where it is occurring on maps." Guerry accomplished early crime mapping in the mid-1800s as he plotted crimes on maps (see earlier discussion). Since that time, police agencies have plotted all types of crimes on maps, as well as the residences of offenders. Colored pins, each color representing a specific type of crime, are pinned to a map when a crime occurs. This technique of using pin maps offers a look at where specific crimes are clustering, and planning is enhanced. Security practitioners can apply this same basic technique, although software is also available that offers sophisticated capabilities to analyze incidents and losses and to aid in planning. Criminal justice agencies, including police, have been applying a variety of software to improve efficiency and effectiveness. Police agencies use computer technology and software to study crime patterns, improve the deployment of police officers, analyze intelligence, and improve investigative capabilities. Crime mapping is available to the public on the Internet through Google.

Paulsen and Robinson (2009, 172–174) and Dees (2008, 68–71) write about the capabilities of **geographic information systems (GIS)**, **global positioning systems (GPS)**, crime mapping, and geographic profiling. GIS is a mapping technology that is of immense help to planners. It includes multiple databases in one display for a comprehensive view of a geographic area. Government agencies apply GIS to plot many items, from the location of fire hydrants to sites where business licenses have been issued. The private sector is also applying the technology in many industries. A retail security executive can plot the locations of robberies of stores in relation to nearby features (e.g., major highways or dense foliage that aids escape). A trucking company can plot the locations of loss incidents from trucks along roads to search for safe routes. GPS pinpoints locations on earth by triangulating a receiver's position using satellites. Among its applications, it can be applied to vehicles, cargo, people, and for our purpose here, the location of crimes.

Geographic profiling is a criminal investigation methodology based on environmental criminology that applies computer software to analyze locations of crimes and other data to decide on the most probable locations that an offender frequents. Police use geographic profiling to not only pinpoint crimes on a digital map, but also layer the map with a wide variety of other data such as the residences of offenders on probation or parole and their offenses; public transportation routes; the locations of victims, schools, and methadone clinics; and anything else that can help in identifying a pattern and solving crimes. Computer software is capable of analyzing a variety of data, comparing relationships among data (e.g., linked incidents), performing millions of calculations, and producing a geographic profile consisting of a three-dimensional map of the areas an offender is most likely to frequent (e.g., home and work).

An emerging use of both GIS and GPS is **high-definition mapping** that permits analysis of crime patterns in small areas. This is accomplished by creating a detailed base map, including streets, walkways, buildings, trees, and so forth. Then, crime events are mapped at their exact location. This technology has assisted organizations in identifying "hot spots" of crime and planning situational crime prevention. Advances in three-dimensional crime mapping (i.e., high-definition mapping that portrays locations within buildings), combined with GPS, hold promise as another aid to security planning.

As these technologies advance, answers to many security and safety questions will increase in accuracy. These questions include: Where are the likely targets of crime? When are crimes more likely? Where are the offenders? Where are security improvements needed? Which security strategies work best?

Risk Analysis Methodology

There are many different methodologies of risk analysis. Even the term itself is subject to debate. Variations exist among and within industries and government agencies. Practitioners and educators also differ in their opinions of methods of risk analysis, definitions of terms, metrics, and formats for reporting results. Another problem is that a risk-analysis methodology for one industry may not fit another. Straw (2008, 102) writes that the U.S. Department of Homeland Security originally sought a "one-size-fits-all" risk-analysis methodology, but then changed course because of the diversity of industry sectors (e.g., transportation, energy, and agriculture).

Whatever type of risk-analysis methodology is applied to an organization, internal and external stakeholders should be considered in the process. Internal stakeholders include senior management and their needs in fulfilling business objectives. In addition, managers involved in risk management, safety, fire protection, and other specializations linked to security should contribute to the risk-analysis process. External stakeholders include public-safety agencies that respond to incidents.

Here we define risk analysis and terms commonly associated with it. A **vulnerability assessment** focuses on weaknesses or opportunities for possible attack or harm against personnel, facilities, IT, operations, or anything else of value requiring protection. A **threat assessment** concentrates on sources or events that can cause harm. Examples are criminals and hurricanes. A **risk assessment** provides a probability of an adverse event occurring and an estimate of the damage and cost resulting from the event. A **risk analysis** (Figure 4.5) brings together vulnerability, threat, and risk assessments for a report on such topics as threats and hazards, vulnerabilities, risks, impact and costs of adverse events, priorities for protection, and costs/benefits and return on investment of protection.

General Security Risk Assessment Guideline

The "General Security Risk Assessment Guideline" (GSRAG) was prepared by ASIS International (2003, 1–22) through a consensus-based process. The GSRAG is a seven-step methodology, applicable to any environment,

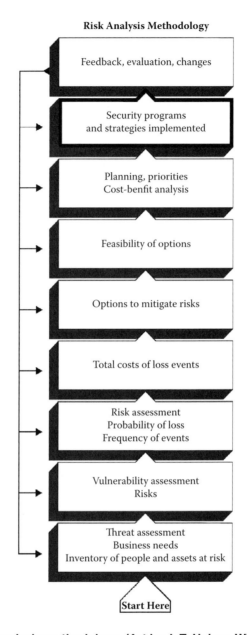

Risk Analysis Methodology

FIGURE 4.5   **Risk-analysis methodology. (Art by J. T. Helms. With permission.)**

for security practitioners so that they can identify risks and solutions, as described next.

1. *Understand the organization and take a comprehensive inventory of people and assets at risk.* This includes the types of products and/or services offered, hours of operation, and geographic location. People include employees, customers, visitors, vendors, and others. Assets are varied. Examples are land, buildings, equipment, IT systems, cash, securities, proprietary information, and brand.

2. *Risks and vulnerabilities.* This step identifies incidents or events that can cause harm. Major categories are crime and natural and human-made disasters. Specific occurrences are violence in the workplace, embezzlement, fire, accident, tornado, labor unrest, and electrical power failure. Metrics (e.g., crime rates) provide a source to analyze risks. This topic is covered later in the chapter.

   Another source of harm is a **consequential event**. This event occurs because of a direct or indirect relationship between organizations. For instance, if a subcontractor manufactures a defective component of a tool sold by a company, and customers are injured, then the company's reputation and sales may be harmed. China has been subject to criticism because it manufactured toys containing lead that were sold by major toy companies. China has also produced tainted milk products used to make chocolate that were linked to infant deaths and to chocolate manufacturers.

3. *Estimate the probability of loss risk and frequency of events.* There is no mathematical certainty here. Historical data (i.e., metrics) and similar events at similar entities provide input in estimating the probability of loss. Additional inputs are geographic characteristics and economic, social, and political conditions. As an illustration for this step, robberies are more likely at convenience stores and banks and less likely at nuclear plants, which face the possibility of diversion of nuclear materials, terrorist attack, and other risks. Gulf coast and eastern seaboard states are more likely to encounter a hurricane than California, which faces the risk of earthquakes.

4. *Determine the costs of an event.* For the sake of the security practitioner's value to the organization and employment status, the practitioner must demonstrate in clear, concise figures the direct and indirect costs of adverse events. Such financial reporting shows the harm of loss events and the importance of prevention through security. Examples of **direct losses** are death and injuries, psychological trauma, assets stolen, and damage (e.g., from a burglary or fire). **Indirect losses** include continued psychological trauma and medical expenses; reduced morale; lost productivity, sales, and customers; insurance, investigative, and administrative expenses; and negative publicity, and shareholder unrest.

5. *Prepare options to mitigate risks.* This step concentrates on the planning and development of a security program and strategies. The range of options includes management practices, policies, and procedures; personnel; and systems and equipment. Transferring a risk through contract terms to a security provider or to an insurer is also an option in mitigating risk. Risk assumption, also called "going naked," is another option whereby an entity accepts a risk and its

costs. This strategy is applied when the probability of an event occurring is low.

6. *Examine the feasibility of implementing options.* The many factors of consideration in this step include the impact on people and business operations; legal and regulatory requirements; practicality; total costs; feedback from preliminary plans; and evaluation (i.e., measurement of the success of each option).

7. *Cost-benefit analysis.* "The final step in conducting a security risk analysis is consideration of the cost versus benefit of a given security strategy" (ASIS International 2003, 15). It is not cost-effective to spend $100,000 on a safe for a retail store when other, less-expensive options are available, such as frequent bank deposits, armored-car money pickups, or a lower-cost safe for temporary deposits.

Applying Security-Relevant Criminology to Risk Analyses

When conducting risk analyses, the security practitioner should develop a mind-set that includes the theoretical and practical aspects of security-relevant criminology. Here we cover some illustrations through questions from which the reader can expand upon as researchers, writers, and practitioners further develop security-relevant criminology.

When a risk analysis (RA) is conducted, study what defensible space and CPTED features are in place. How can these features be enhanced in a cost-effective way to improve protection? From the perspectives of situational crime prevention and rational choice theory, where are the opportunities for offenders and how can the opportunities be reduced or eliminated? How can the risks for the offender be increased? How can the rewards for the offender be reduced? From routine-activity theory, can employees be guided toward safer behavior to reduce the chances of victimization as they go about their daily activities? Are crime and other loss events being "mapped" geographically to pinpoint "hot spots"? What technologies (e.g., GIS and GPS) can be applied to mapping to improve planning and security?

WHAT IS A SECURITY SURVEY?

A **security survey** in its most basic form is a checklist of physical features, security personnel and their duties, and policies and procedures to examine as a security practitioner walks through a facility to study the status of security. It provides input to a risk analysis. The survey should be conducted during the day and at night. A security survey can include the neighborhood, various organizational departments (e.g., IT), safety issues, information security, assets, and vulnerabilities. A security survey checklist should be in a constant state of development to fit the changing conditions and needs of the location being inspected.

A security survey should include the perspectives of adversaries. Try to think as an offender. How would they break into the facility? What methods would be applied by an adversary? How can outsiders and employee-offenders harm the organization? What security strategies can prevent harm?

Quantitative versus Qualitative Methodologies

Quantitative methodologies produce numerical measurements or metrics, such as the financial costs of an event (e.g., crime) or the probability of an event occurring. **Qualitative methodologies** produce subjective results that are an alternative to quantification because, for example, data may be lacking or a qualitative approach may be more appropriate. Examples are a researcher conducting a *case study* of a corporation's response to a workplace violence incident, the *interviewing* of all the people linked to the event, and a *focus group* (i.e., select people offering expertise) to suggest prevention strategies. The seven-step General Security Risk Assessment Guideline is another example of a qualitative approach.

An example of a quantitative approach to assist risk analysis is through the formula $ALE = I \times F$, where ALE means *annual loss exposure*; I is impact, meaning the cost of each event; and F refers to frequency. To illustrate, say that each employee-theft incident at a manufacturing company costs an average of $2,500 (total costs, direct and indirect) and 15 employees are caught stealing in a given year. Plugging in the numbers, the formula would show an ALE of $37,500 = $2,500 \times 15$. In planning security, many factors should be considered beyond the ALE. For instance, trying to figure (e.g., probability) the number of employees who stole but were not caught. In addition, the security strategies implemented to curb employee theft will likely affect (i.e., diffusion of benefits) other risks.

Straw (2008, 102) writes that the Department of Homeland Security (DHS), with the assistance of the Department of Defense and the Institute for Defense Analysis (IDA), applies a "familiar definition of risk as the factor of consequence, vulnerability, and threat ($R = C \times V \times T$) which is referenced in NIPP (National Infrastructure Protection Plan). The IDA methodology multiplies probability of attack (threat), by probability of success (vulnerability), by consequences (either monetary loss or mortality) to determine risk." The probability factors are figured by analysts and are "experientially based" and "empirical." In other words, based upon experience. This brings to the surface the question of whether risk analyses are an art or a science.

Straw notes that "gathering so-called hard quantitative data can be tricky." He refers to the challenge of determining the financial cost of adverse events, which is an important step in figuring the return on investment (ROI) from implementing security strategies. Straw writes, "Subjective calculations are inevitably involved in the assignment of cost when predicting potential damages, such as human casualties and business disruptions." Six major points from Straw's article, which covers interviews with risk-analysis specialists, are that:

- We are "not there yet" with precise risk analyses.
- Risk analyses are often a combination of quantitative and qualitative (or subjective) approaches.
- Although there are about 200 risk-analysis methodologies in use, the DHS does not favor any one.
- Homeland security analyses using computer models are enormously complex and are limited to regions and single scenarios.
- Consensus aimed at the DHS is to keep things simple and assess risk comparatively by applying qualitative but scientifically inexact rankings, such as high, medium, and low.
- There is a lack of consensus over many topics, such as the best methodologies and the feasibility of comparing risk across industry sectors.

SECURITY STANDARDS

An important component of security planning is **security standards**. These are a set of voluntary criteria and best practices developed through an unbiased and consistent methodology and used to improve the quality, performance, and reliability of services or products. Standards enhance professionalism in the security industry while assisting organizations and nations in improving their ability to face threats and hazards (Ahrens 2007b, 18–19; Geraci 2008).

Standards often develop from guidelines or best practices prepared by organizations such as ASIS International. Standards organizations, including the American National Standards Institute (ANSI) and the International Standards Organization (ISO), ensure that organizations develop standards in a fair and open manner and permit input from experts and other organizations. Then, the organization can be accredited as a Standards Development Organization (SDO), a designation ASIS International has received.

Many organizations produce security standards. These include the National Fire Protection Association (NFPA), the Security Industry Association (SIA), and Underwriters Laboratories (UL).

Two terms linked to standards are regulations and codes. **Regulations** are enforceable rules or laws enacted by government to promote an orderly and safe society. National scandals and world events have resulted in a flood of new laws and regulations, many pertaining to security. The Code of Federal Regulations (CFR) contains regulations resulting from numerous federal laws; it is the codification of rules published in the *Federal Register* by departments and agencies of the federal government.

Codes are standards that are adopted by government and enforced. These include building codes and fire codes. The NFPA 101 Life Safety Code, for example, has been adopted in many jurisdictions of the United States.

Metrics

Metrics are quantitative (i.e., numerical) measurements. For the security function, a host of metrics can be prepared to show the value of security, its performance, costs, losses, and other indicators. Many security planning questions can be answered with the assistance of metrics, and senior executives, in addition to security executives, need answers to such questions as: What are the most serious risks? How should the risks be prioritized? How much money and resources are needed to reduce individual risks? What is the return on investment? What is the effectiveness of individual security strategies?

Earlier in the chapter, under the heading "Security Business Proposals," we learned of the importance of "financials" (i.e., metrics, such as costs and benefits) to speak the language of business management and to ensure that security is competitive with other corporate units seeking investments from senior executives. Metrics are an essential part of the security business proposal.

Metrics are generated from many sources. Examples are incident reports, risk analyses and security surveys, loss forecasting, recoveries following property crime investigations, logs of various security and safety activities, customer satisfaction with security and safety, planned penetration attempts to test security, and turnover of security personnel.

Metrics are also available from sources outside of an organization. These include local crime statistics from police agencies, U.S. Department of Justice crime statistics (e.g., FBI "Uniform Crime Reports" and the Bureau of Justice Statistics "National Crime Victimization Survey"), U.S. Department of State publications on terrorism and safety in specific countries throughout the world, the National Counterterrorism Center, the National Fire Data Center, the Occupational Safety & Health Administration, industry associations, the risk management and insurance industry, universities, private firms, and other sources.

Security executives are responsible for the quality of security metrics. This means that metrics must be useful and accurate. A security executive can query senior management and peers in other organizations to ascertain the best possible metrics that are aligned with business goals and the security function supporting such goals. Campbell (2008, 18), a security metrics expert, adds: "Virtually all of the post-9/11 security-related regulations impose metrics to provide verifiable measures of compliance and thereby minimize the imposition of fines or other impact to shareholder value."

Metrics methodologies vary among organizations. The journal *Corporate Security* (Scribner et al. 2008, 1, 7) reported on a corporation's data-gathering system consisting of five separate metrics programs. One program is a Web-based incident-reporting system involving regional security managers and other staff who complete online incident forms requiring documentation of the incident type, location, date, time, narrative, and other facts. Monthly and yearly metrics expose the number of incidents in a specific category (e.g., burglary, robbery, and fraud) for each location. A second metrics program monitors the performance of security systems at each location and answers questions such as how long a system was out of service. A third program tracks individual security-officer activities (e.g., responding to incidents). Security officers are also monitored by another program that provides metrics on absences and turnover. A fifth program quantifies how well each company site complies with security policies (e.g., requirements of visitors and completing reports promptly).

Because metrics involve the gathering of statistics, methodological problems inevitably arise. Distortion can result from not reporting incidents, from differences in the way that personnel classify and report incidents, and for other reasons.

Practical Applications

This section of the chapter applies the theories of crime explained earlier to a real-world application of security for a special event. The intention is to assist the reader in bridging theory to practice. The discussion then moves on to address research and evaluation, followed by additional practical applications to security considerations at a special event.

Suppose you are a security consultant to an association of state fairs and this group hired you to improve security because of numerous shortcomings of certain member fairs that need and want assistance from their professional association. To the casual observer, a state fair may appear as a multiweek carnival that abruptly ends after about two weeks. However, the preparation, management, and operation of such a major special event are ongoing processes that last throughout each year. Fairs make up a large industry that has existed for many years. The International Association of Fairs & Expositions (IAFE) began in 1885 and today comprises 1,300 fairs/ members. It operates a Fair Management Institute, listing courses such as "Life Safety & Security" and "Emergency Planning." The IAFE offers the Certified Fair Executive (CFE) designation (International Association of Fairs & Expositions, 2005). Another fair industry group, the Western Fairs

Association, publishes "Industry Standards and Guidelines," which contains information on the importance of current emergency preparedness plans, substance-abuse management, and other topics (Western Fairs Association Industry Standards Committee, 1991).

As the security consultant, you conduct a risk analysis of one particular state fair in the Southwest as it is operating. You bring your expertise to the site and begin with a multipage security survey questionnaire. In addition, you learn the following through a review of records, documents, policies and procedures, emergency plans, interviews, and observations:

- About 40,000 customers attend the fair each day on the weekend (in the afternoons and evenings Friday through Sunday), and about half that number attend during the week (in the afternoons and evenings Monday through Thursday).
- The ratio of deputies to customers is about 1 per 1,000.
- According to the geographic distribution of deputies, twenty are assigned to the "midway" (i.e., the crowded area where rides are located), one at each of six gates, six near the stage for concerts, two on the walkways between the gates and the midway, four for backup, and two supervisors at the security office. Except at gates, deputies patrol in pairs. When serious crimes occur in the county (away from the fair), investigators working at the fair are called to the crime scene; this occurs almost every weekend evening at the fair.
- The fair is an annual event dating back about 120 years, with the local sheriff's department providing security without state police assistance. These "moonlighting" opportunities for deputies provide them with additional income paid to the deputies directly from the fair. The sheriff is able to reward the most loyal deputies with the highest number of work hours. This tradition and culture persists from one generation to the next, but results in antiquated, narrow-minded, and reactive event security.
- Security at the fair consists of personnel (i.e., deputies) without the application of security technology, numerous layers of protection, and a post-9/11 mind-set of improving security at special events. The risks to customers, employees, and assets are high.
- Calls for service from the fair do not go through the 9-1-1 system; the calls are handled within the fair site. No logs are maintained at the fair for calls for service. Deputies complete incident reports for arrests only; otherwise, calls for service do not result in an incident report.
- The fair lasts for two weeks, and during the previous two years the following arrests were reported through incident reports: assaults showed two reported during year one/four reported during year two; gang-related violence three/five; sexual assault one/three; drug arrests five/

four; disorderly conduct eighteen/eighteen; and public intoxication eleven/sixteen. During the most recent year, two arrests were made in two separate incidents involving the discharge of firearms; no injuries were reported. Gang graffiti was observed inside, and especially outside, of restroom buildings. Alcohol is not served at the fair.

- Medical-encounter forms from the on-site emergency medical services team showed that during the same two-year period, violent incidents were about three times higher than what was reported by deputies in incident reports. In addition, the fair Web site emphasized a high level of safety and security in a family-friendly environment.

- Deputies received no training for large special events. The sheriff's department viewed the police academy training as sufficient. Fair employees received no training on safety, security, and their protection role in conjunction with deputies. Employees did not know how to report a harmful incident.

- Security at the fair consists of four layers of security: parking lot patrols, deputies at gates, a perimeter chain-link fence with several holes in it, and patrols within the fair.

- The fair emergency-procedures manual is twenty-two years old and contains generic information not appropriate for a fair (e.g., protection from a tornado while in a building).

- While visiting the fair on a Saturday evening as the consultant, you walk about a quarter of a mile through the dimly lit, dirt parking lot containing pockets of overgrown foliage and do not see any deputies, but see a few patrons. You reach the main gate and do not see any deputies as you pay the admissions fee in cash and receive no receipt from the employee.

- While walking through the fair, deputies are observed patrolling. Four deputies are observed at one location speaking with each other for about 15 minutes. A group of six is observed at another location speaking for about 20 minutes. While maintaining a stationary position in the midway at the same location, time, and day when three violent incidents had been reported in incident reports, two deputies are observed patrolling through the location at intervals of 18, 17, and 19 minutes.

- While observing a rock concert at the fair, a mosh pit (i.e., where people slam into each other) formed, but deputies disbanded it without arrests.

- Upon leaving the fair, no deputies were seen at the main gate or in the parking lot.

From the perspective of a security consultant, the fair needs numerous security improvements, not all of which are covered here. What follows here are illustrations of the theory covered earlier applied to the security challenges of the fair.

To begin with, we are facing a delicate situation concerning the sheriff's department and its tradition and culture of providing security at the fair as a reward for its deputies. However, modern fair executives realize that the present state of security at the fair must change. Since the fair is in the jurisdiction of the sheriff's department, arrests are made and processed by this law enforcement agency, so negotiation and cooperation are required as security changes.

As covered earlier, a security business proposal is a practical tool to develop and advance security programs and gain management and financial support. We also know that the proposal relies on metrics. To obtain a more accurate picture of incidents and security activities at the fair, a log must be maintained of all calls for service, including the type of call, response time, who responded, duration of call, date, day, time, and other helpful metrics that can assist security planning and budgeting. And, responding deputies must complete incident reports (including how the incident was resolved), except for very minor calls that are defined by policy and procedure. Traffic accident reports are also important. Return on investment can be demonstrated through adverse publicity and lower attendance resulting from increasingly serious crimes. The cost of lawsuits from claims of inadequate security is another argument supporting increased investments in security.

Critical Thinking

Do you think that certain organizations within our society fail to report or record some crimes because of adverse publicity, harm to sales, and stockholder reactions?

By completing a risk analysis, many questions can be answered for the security business proposal and subsequent efforts to plan and implement security improvements at the fair. The information generated will be both quantitative and qualitative. One major issue important to the security business proposal is increasing the ratio of deputies to customers. Many other security issues will surface from the risk analysis.

In applying security-relevant criminology to the fair, ecological theories provide a foundation for mapping crime and other incidents at the fair. This helps plan resources and the geographical and chronological distribution of protection personnel.

In reference to defensible space and CPTED, several measures can be taken to improve security that should be part of the security business proposal. These include minimizing the foliage and improving lighting in the parking lots, repairing and improving the perimeter fence, installing signs that warn intruders who avoid paying for admission, and increasing surveillance by deputies through CCTV and raised security observation posts and/or deer stands. Fair employees can be recruited and trained to participate in a "watch," similar to a Neighborhood Watch, to increase the "eyes and ears" of deputies and to report incidents.

The broken-windows theory can be applied to the problems of public intoxication, holes in the perimeter fence, and the gang graffiti inside and outside of the restrooms. These problems must be corrected to authenticate fair management's business objective of creating a family-friendly environment.

Numerous applications of situational crime prevention and rational-choice theory can improve security and safety at the fair. As we know, these theories involve *reducing opportunities* for crime through specific strategies. The twenty-five techniques of situational crime prevention are illustrated in the following discussion.

TWENTY-FIVE TECHNIQUES OF SITUATIONAL CRIME PREVENTION TO REDUCE CRIME AT THE STATE FAIR

I. Increase the effort of the offender:
1. *Harden the target* by increasing physical security through, for example, improving the perimeter fence and access controls.
2. *Control access* by reducing the number of gates for entrance and, where necessary, ensuring that deputies are posted at gates to conduct searches for contraband.
3. *Screen exits* by posting deputies at gates to observe departing customers and employees.
4. *Deflect offenders* by refusing to admit those who wear clothes or colors representing gang affiliation. Conduct background investigations of job applicants.
5. *Control tools/weapons* with metal detectors at gates to check for weapons and cans of spray paint.

II. Increase the risks for the offender:
6. *Extend guardianship* by banning known offenders from the property, rewarding employees who help to control crime, and arresting law violators.
7. *Assist natural surveillance* through improved lighting and limited foliage.
8. *Reduce anonymity* by ensuring that deputies pay attention to and make eye contact with all entering customers.
9. *Use place managers* through the training of employees to report harmful incidents. Reward vigilant staff. Ensure adequate security coverage at "hot spots." Increase the ratio of deputies per 1,000 customers.

---

10. *Strengthen formal surveillance* through CCTV and observation posts.

III. Reduce the rewards:
11. *Conceal targets* by protecting, storing, and locking fair assets to prevent theft and carefully transporting fair bank deposits to prevent robbery.
12. *Remove targets* by making frequent bank deposits.
13. *Identify property* by marking it with the company name and using a method so that it cannot be removed.
14. *Disrupt markets* by checking pawnshops, Web sites, and street vendors. Work with public police to seize stolen property and arrest offenders.
15. *Deny benefits* by catching "gate crashers," immediately cleaning graffiti, and installing speed humps.

IV. Reduce provocations:
16. *Reduce frustration and stress* through customer-service training, expanded seating, and quick service.
17. *Avoid disputes* by responding quickly to verbal exchanges, fights, and mosh-pit activity.
18. *Reduce emotional arousal* by prohibiting gang-related clothing and colors, racial slurs, and antagonism among high-school rivalries.
19. *Neutralize peer pressure* through signs (e.g., "It's OK to say No") and by speaking with youth. Disburse unruly crowds.
20. *Discourage imitation* by quickly responding to incidents, expelling rule violators, and making arrests.

V. Remove excuses:
21. *Set rules*, investigate violations, and hold violators accountable.
22. *Post instructions* through signs listing rules and prohibited items, dress, and behavior.
23. *Alert conscience* through signs and training for employees.
24. *Assist compliance* through directions and signs, ample lavatories, training and awareness for employees, and rewards.
25. *Control drugs and alcohol* at access points and in parking lots. Assign undercover police and drug dogs to the entire site.

A popular strategy to improve security is through **layered security**. It refers to concentric circles of security that surround a site. Using the fair as an example, three layers are the parking areas, the access points (i.e., gates), and inside the fair. Each layer can be characterized by security personnel, undercover operations, a drug dog team, quality lighting, CCTV, signs, emergency call boxes, raised observation posts, and training all employees on security and safety procedures. Access points may be the only layer characterized by metal detectors and searches of belongings.

According to routine-activity theory (i.e., how the everyday behavior of people can result in their victimization), it would be in each customer's best interest to attend the fair in a group, rather than alone, because this theory rests on the convergence of a motivated offender, a suitable target, and the absence of a capable guardian.

According to crime-pattern theory, "edges" (i.e., the boundaries of home, work, and recreation) are the areas where crime risks are the greatest. However, most of the crimes at the fair occurred inside the boundary.

Research and Evaluation

Security executives have the responsibility of proving the success of security strategies that purport to protect people, assets, and operations. In addition, security strategies are costly, so it is to the security executive's benefit to evaluate a new strategy on a small scale (e.g., pilot or field test) prior to implementing the strategy corporate-wide with the possibility of learning later that the strategy is ineffective and a waste of money and resources.

Research and evaluation serve to measure performance and whether management objectives and industry standards were met. The results of research and evaluation are helpful to security planning, budgeting, and business proposals.

Continuing with the state fair for illustrative purposes, suppose state-fair executives request that you (the security consultant) prove, through research and evaluation, that investments in security are cost-effective and reduce crime at state fairs. With this task, we turn to the **scientific method** that consists of four steps: problem, hypothesis, testing, and conclusion. The problem is crime at state fairs. Bachman and Schutt (2008, 36) define hypothesis as "a tentative statement about empirical reality, involving a relationship between two or more variables."

There are various types of research designs for testing, such as experimental and control groups, survey, and interviewing. Applying the **experimental-control-group design**, you select two state fairs that are characteristically similar in terms of location, size, number of customers, when the fairs are held, crime rate, and other factors. The experimental group receives some type of special treatment or experimental manipulation. The control group, used for comparison, receives nothing new. You decide to concentrate on violent crimes, gang problems, and substance abuse. At one fair (the experimental group), the plan is to post two deputies with handheld metal detectors at each gate. In addition, signs are posted at gates listing rules on conduct, contraband, and prohibited dress (e.g., gang colors). The hypothesis is that violent crimes, gang problems, and substance abuse will be reduced at the fair through the assignment of two deputies with handheld metal detectors at each gate and the posting of signs. No additional security is implemented at the other fair.

Measurements of crime, especially related to violent crimes, gang problems, and substance abuse, are recorded at both fairs prior to the experiment and the opening of the fairs. This is called a **pre-test**. When the fairs end, measurements are recorded again. This is called a **post-test**. If crime drops at the experimental site, it is possible that the enhanced security was successful. However, caution is advised because other factors may have caused the decline. For example, a concert or other event at another location could have attracted offenders away from the fair when the experiment was conducted. The same type of event could have resulted in a decline in crime at the control group site. Another research challenge is to pinpoint which security strategies worked best. Although this is a simplified research design for illustrative purposes, improved designs and continued testing will strengthen research **validity** (i.e., asking the best questions and measuring what we intended to measure) and **reliability** (i.e., repeated measurement/research yields similar results).

Suppose, as the security consultant to the fair association, you are asked to design a security training program for protection personnel at fairs. You choose a **multiple-group before-and-after research design.** Two characteristically similar fairs are selected. The protection personnel of both are tested on their knowledge of security and safety. Then, one group (i.e., experimental group) receives the training program (based on a job analysis), while the other serves as the control group. (The previous chapter explains several methodologies to prepare instructional programs.) Following the training program, both groups are post-tested with the same test to measure any change in knowledge. If the experimental group shows increased knowledge of security and safety, and the control group's knowledge is the same, then the training program may be the cause, and it may be an effective training program. Here again, improved research designs and repeated measurements help to strengthen the training program.

It is important to note that enhanced security, training, and reporting of crimes at the fairs may appear to show that crime is rising. However, an improved security operation will likely result in improved investigations, reporting, and recording of crimes. It is ironic that "the harder they work, the worse they look." Eventually, the true amount of crime will likely surface through the metrics; hopefully, crime reports will level off and go down due to enhanced security.

The pace at which research and evaluation are being applied in the security industry varies widely. Besides government efforts (e.g., armed forces and national laboratories) and professional associations (e.g., ASIS International), the retail industry is one example of an industry searching for precise answers to security challenges. Hayes (2008, 40) writes about field-testing of a variety of security strategies (e.g., CCTV, security officers) at popular retail stores using pre-test, post-test, and control methodologies. A major goal is to test for cost-effectiveness prior to investments in security at many stores.

For research assistance, security professionals should contact employees in their own organization with graduate degrees, if available. Other sources are colleges, universities, and consulting firms.

YOUR CAREER IN SECURITY

Security Manager

A **security manager** is a leader in an organization's efforts to protect people, assets, buildings, and operations, while meeting the needs of the business. The title differs among entities, depending on such factors as type of industry, job requirements, level of responsibility, duties, and preference for a certain title. Examples of alternative titles are Loss Prevention Manager (or Director), Assets Protection Manager (or Director), and Vice President. The title of the superior to whom this manager reports also differs.

Nature of the Work

In general, managers plan, budget, organize, staff, direct, and control. At the foundation of a manager's duties is planning. It consists of advance thinking, forecasting, and applying analytical skills and select methodologies to reach objectives. A budget provides the funds to implement plans. Organizing entails communicating with superiors and subordinates to ascertain who is going to do what tasks according to a specific timeline and with what support (e.g., training or equipment). Staffing refers to human resources and includes screening applicants, hiring, and training. Directing guides employees toward objectives. Controlling serves to check or audit the work of others to ensure it was done correctly and, if not, corrective action follows (Purpura 1989).

The day-to-day activities of security managers, like other managers, include prioritizing tasks, meeting with supervisors and subordinates, completing organizational reports and forms, making and responding to telephone calls, reading and responding to e-mail, collecting information to assist with decision making, and attending training or providing training. Managers network with others in their profession to learn and to seek assistance.

Security managers not only work to prevent crimes, emergencies, and sensitive incidents (e.g., alleged sexual harassment), but they also respond quickly to such events. Their hours of work vary depending on the need to resolve problems, and they may travel frequently. As they investigate events, they interview employees, customers, victims, witnesses, suspects, and others.

Because government public safety agencies provide support to private-sector protection programs, security managers periodically meet with such practitioners to coordinate planning and operations, especially in the case of an emergency. If an arrest is made, law enforcement must be contacted, and security practitioners may be required to testify in court. Security managers are typically unarmed.

Security duties include managing a force of security officers and investigators, managing physical security systems, conducting security assessments of facilities, identifying specific security needs, meeting with vendors for security services and systems, and presenting security proposals to upper management to secure funds for implementation. Because of the convergence of physical and information technology (IT) security, practitioners from both groups must work together.

Security managers may be required to take on additional responsibilities to justify their value to a corporation. They may manage facilities, like safety in a building, traffic and parking, inventory, and the mail system.

Requirements

A security manager must possess excellent leadership and human-relations skills because a variety of people are linked to the security function. Equally important are written and verbal communications skills.

Many people do not realize that among the benefits of a college education is the skill of *learning how to learn*. Examples are reading with an enhanced ability to absorb useful information, understanding research, and critical thinking. In addition, as with other professions, security managers must be prepared to learn new skills and adapt and respond to a rapidly changing world.

Security managers are often referred to as "business people with a specialization in security." Consequently, students who major in security, criminal justice, criminology, and related fields should also enroll in business courses, such as management and accounting. Those who aspire to become a security manager will be at a competitive disadvantage without a bachelor's degree.

Employers may hire an applicant with limited experience, but with a college degree, as a security manager in training. Alternatively, an applicant with a college degree and several years of experience may be hired to perform security management duties immediately. As in the public sector, honesty and integrity are valued. A security manager must set an example and be beyond reproach.

The applicant screening process varies among businesses and institutions, and differs depending on whether the applicant is an internal candidate or an external candidate. Screening methods include interviews, background investigation, polygraph, drug test, medical examination, and psychological evaluation.

Once an applicant is selected as a security manager, an orientation program is typically conducted to assist the new employee in understanding the organization and its policies, procedures, and culture. Specialized in-house training may follow and consist of security-related topics and learning software used by the organization. Periodically, the manager will likely attend specialized training courses offered internally and externally.

Salary

The employment prospects for security managers are excellent. The world is becoming increasingly dangerous, and organizations demand protection. ASIS International research shows that the average compensation of security professionals in the United States was $108,000 in 2008, up about 8 percent from the previous year. This figure includes stock options (Moran 2008, 94). Whatever the base salary of a security manager, benefits may include stock options, performance bonus, insurance, retirement plan, company vehicle, and discounts on company products or services.

Advice

Study the advantages and disadvantages of working in the private sector versus the public sector. For example, the private sector may pay more than the public sector; however, job security is often better in the public sector. Conduct research on the Web, speak with people who are employed in each sector, and participate in college internship programs.

Summary

Senior executives are increasingly concerned about return on investment and the effectiveness and efficiency of security programs. Consequently, the security professional must utilize a variety of methodologies to meet these concerns. The security business proposal is a beginning point from which to advocate the need and value of security. It is a business document with financials to generate support for the security plan and budget. A security master plan goes beyond the security business proposal because it is a comprehensive description of the security program and includes security philosophies, strategies, goals, programs, and processes. Risk analyses, quantitative and qualitative methods, metrics, and research and evaluation are important inputs for the security business proposal and the security master plan. Prior to conducting a risk analysis, a security practitioner should have a clear understanding of security-relevant criminology, because such theory is practical and it assists in planning effective security and conducting enhanced risk analyses. This chapter ends with an illustration of the challenges of special-event security to draw out the methodologies that are explained here and apply them to practical problem solving.

Discussion Questions

1. What is a security business proposal and what are its purposes?
2. What is a security master plan and what are its purposes?
3. Of the numerous criminology theories we find in textbooks, why are ecological theories so helpful to security and other protection professionals in their work?
4. What are *displacement* and *diffusion of benefits*, and what is the impact of each on security?
5. Does a universally applicable risk-analysis or risk-assessment process exist? Explain your answer.
6. What are the purposes of security standards?
7. Is it possible that nonreporting and/or nonrecording of incidents by personnel can cause an organization to appear successful in reducing crime? Explain your answer.
8. Why are metrics important in security work?
9. What are the differences between quantitative and qualitative methodologies, and how is each applied in security work?
10. Is security planning an art or a science? Explain your answer.
11. Why are certain security professionals slow to embrace research and evaluation?

Practical Applications

4A. Research another type of business proposal, not covered in this chapter, that can help the security profession. Why is the business proposal that you researched beneficial to the security profession?
4B. Select a location (e.g., home, school, or work) and study and prepare a report on the defensible space and CPTED characteristics of the site.
4C. Conduct a risk analysis at the chosen site.
4D. You are a security executive who was recently assigned to a business planning committee. Your employer, a retail chain, is considering opening a store in the downtown area of two of the following three cities: Flagstaff, Arizona; Lexington, Kentucky; and Jacksonville, Florida. At a meeting next week, senior executives will be asking about crime rates in these cities. After researching and comparing the crime rates of each city, what are your findings?
4E. Study the following rules of data collection required of U.S. police agencies by the FBI Uniform Crime Reports: *hierarchy, hotel,* and *separation of time and place.* Why do you think such rules were established? Do you think a corporate security metrics program

would establish such rules of data collection? Why or why not? (On the Web, locate the FBI rules in the UCR Handbook at www.fbi.gov/ucr/ucr.htm or Congressional Research Service [2008], "How Crime in the United States is Measured," CRC Report for Congress, RL 34309, at www.fas.org/sgp/crs/misc/RL34309.pdf.)

4F. As a security consultant, refer to the state fair information covered in this chapter. Prepare a prioritized list of the top ten security recommendations you would make to management to improve security at the fair.

4G. Prepare a security business proposal, using a style of your choice, to improve security at the state fair described in this chapter.

Internet Connections

American National Standards Institute: www.ansi.org.

American Society for Industrial Security International: www.asisonline.org.

American Society for Testing and Materials: www.astm.org.

Center for Geospatial Intelligence and Investigation: www.txstate.edu/gii.

Center for Problem-Oriented Policing: www.popcenter.org/.

Federal Bureau of Investigation: www.fbi.gov.

Federal Regulatory Information: RegInfo.gov.

International Organization for Standardization: www.iso.org.

Loss Prevention Foundation: www.losspreventionfoundation.org.

National Crime Victimization Survey: www.ojp.usdoj.gov/bjs/cvict.htm.

National Fire Protection Association: www.nfpa.org/.

National Institute of Justice: www.ojp.usdoj.gov/nij/.

Regulations: http://standards.gov/standards_gov/v/Regulations/index.cfm.

Security Analysis and Risk Management Association www.sarma.org.

Security Industry Association: www.siaonline.org.

Standards: http://standards.gov/standards_gov/v/Standards/index.cfm.

Underwriters Laboratory (UL): www.ul.com.

References

Ahrens, S. 2007a. Security benchmarking. *Security Technology & Design* 17 (December):27.

Ahrens, S. 2007b. Security standards. *Government Security* 6 (October/November):18–19.

ASIS International. 2003. General security risk assessment guideline. www.asisonline.org/guidelines/guidelines.htm.

Atlas, R. 1993. Crime prevention through environmental design (CPTED): Defensible and offensible space. In *Encyclopedia of security management*, ed. J. Fay. Boston: Butterworth–Heinemann.

Bachman, R., and R. Schutt. 2008. *Fundamentals of research in criminology and criminal justice*. Los Angeles: Sage.

Brantingham, P., and P. Brantingham. 1993. Environment, routine, and situation: Toward a pattern of crime. In *Routine activity and rational choice*, ed. R. Clark and M. Felson. Vol. 5 of *Advances in criminological theory*. New Brunswick, NJ: Transaction.

Campbell, G. 2008. Demonstrate security's alignment with business objectives. *Security Technology & Design* 18 (February):18.

Clarke, R. 1997. *Situational crime prevention: Successful case studies*. 2nd ed. New York: Harrow and Heston.

Clarke, R., and J. Eck. 2005. Crime analysis for problem solvers: In 60 small steps. www.cops.usdoj.gov.

Cohen, L., and M. Felson. 1979. Social change and crime rate trends: A routine activity approach. *American Sociological Review* 44 (August):588–608.

Cornish, D., and R. Clarke. 1986. *The reasoning criminal: Rational choice perspectives on offending*. New York: Springer–Verlag.

Crowe, T. 2000. *Crime prevention through environmental design*. 2nd ed. Boston: Butterworth–Heinemann.

Dees, T. 2008. Crime mapping & geographic profiling. *Law Officer Magazine* 4 (December):68–71.

Felson, M., and R. Clarke. 1998. *Opportunity makes the thief: Practical theory for crime prevention*. London: British Home Office.

Geraci, M. 2008. Setting the standard. *Security Technology & Design* 18 (September):24.

Giles, T. 2009. *How to develop and implement a security master plan*. Boca Raton, FL: Taylor & Francis Group.

Hayes, R. 2008. Storelab: A concept whose time has come. *Loss Prevention* 7 (May–June):40.

International Association of Fairs & Expositions. 2005. About the IAFE. www.fairsandexpos.com.

Jeffery, C. 1977. *Crime prevention through environmental design*. Beverly Hills, CA: Sage.

Jeffery, C. 1993. Biological perspectives. *Journal of Criminal Justice Education* 4 (Fall).

Kitteringham, G. 2007. Crime control theories. In *Encyclopedia of security management*, ed. J. Fay. 2nd ed. Boston: Elsevier Butterworth–Heinemann.

Lab, S. 2004. *Crime prevention: Approaches, practices and evaluations*. 5th ed. www.lexisnexis.com/anderson/criminaljustice.

Merriam–Webster On-line Dictionary. 2008. Methodology. www.merriam-webster.com.

Moran, M. 2008. Raising the bar. *Security Management* 52 (August):94.

Newman, O. 1972. *Defensible space: Crime prevention through urban design*. New York: Macmillan.

Paquet, C. 2005. Security financials: The core element of security business proposals. www.ciscopress.com/articles/article.asp?p=379752.

Paulsen, D., and M. Robinson. 2009. *Crime mapping and spatial aspects of crime*. 2nd ed. Upper Saddle River, NJ: Prentice Hall.

Purpura, P. 1989. *Modern security & loss prevention management*. Stoneham, MA: Butterworth.

Scribner, M., et al. 2008. Security metrics may need complex system—Or, maybe not. *Corporate Security* 34 (February 15).

Straw, J. 2008. How vulnerable are we? *Security Management* 52 (August):102.

Voit, L., et al. 1994. *Criminology and justice*. New York: McGraw-Hill.

Western Fairs Association Industry Standards Committee. 1991. Industry standards and guidelines. www.fairsnet.org.

Wilson, J., and G. Kelling. 1982. Broken windows: The police and neighborhood safety. *Atlantic Monthly* (March).

Worrall, J. 2008. *Crime control in America: What works?* 2nd ed. New York: Allyn & Bacon.

Wright, J., and R. Thomas. 1993. Crime prevention through environmental design: The site plan review process. In *Encyclopedia of Security Management*, ed. J. Fay. Boston: Butterworth–Heinemann.

Chapter 5

Security Strategies

Chapter Learning Objectives

After reading this chapter, you should be able to:

1. Define *generic* and *specific* security
2. List and explain the seven objectives of security
3. Describe the three layers of defense
4. Differentiate security layers and security redundancy
5. Name and describe the five levels of security applied by the federal government
6. Explain the purpose of security maxims and provide five examples
7. Discuss the importance of force multipliers and provide three examples
8. Describe the problem of violence in the workplace, related theories, and countermeasures
9. Describe the problem of theft in the workplace, related theories, and countermeasures
10. Describe the problem of drugs in the workplace and drug-free workplace strategies

Terms to Know

generic security
policies
procedures
specific security
unpredictable security strategies
creature of habit
security layers
stand-off distance
redundancy
security maxims
force multipliers
Business Watch
workplace violence
predatory violence
affective violence
crime typologies
active shooter
Virginia Tech massacre
Mumbai attacks
mass notification
Clery Act
theft
larceny
burglary
fraud
embezzlement
robbery
Association of Certified Fraud Examiners
occupational fraud
amateur thief
situational inducements
professional thief
fence
Edwin Sutherland
Gresham Sykes
Donald Cressey
differential association
white-collar crime
occupational crime
social disorganization

fraud triangle
fraud scale
National White Collar Crime Center
Sarbanes-Oxley Act of 2002
Enron Corporation scandal
shrinkage
radio-frequency identification (RFID)
Anti-Drug Abuse Act of 1988
security consultant
marketing

QUIZ

This quiz serves to prime the reader's mind and begin the reading, thinking, and studying processes for this chapter. The answers to all of the questions are found within this chapter.

1. What event occurred with the USS *Cole* that has relevance to security?
2. Can an adversary conduct a risk analysis?
3. What is the meaning of *creature of habit* and what is its relevance to security?
4. What is the difference between *security layers* and *security redundancy*?
5. Do most violent crimes occur between people who do not know each other?
6. Does the Occupational Safety & Health Administration (OSHA) have law enforcement power to require employers to implement security to protect people from violence in the workplace?
7. What are the objectives of the Sarbanes-Oxley Act?
8. Are most illicit drug users employed?

Introduction

The previous chapter serves as a foundation for the present chapter by providing theories and tools for planning security strategies that are explained and illustrated in subsequent pages. First, generic strategies are presented that are commonly applied by practitioners to a host of protection challenges. Then, a variety of perspectives and suggestions are offered on how to think about security as it is planned prior to implementing specific security strategies. This chapter also includes security-relevant criminology and the workplace problems and security strategies pertaining to violence, theft, and drugs.

Generic and Specific Security

In Chapter 1, it was noted that security strategies develop from security methodology and focus on management application of human resources, information technology, physical security, policies and procedures, emergency response and recovery, investigations, and other components of security for optimum utilization and advantage. **Generic security** includes protection strategies that are general in nature and have broad application to numerous entities. *Three major categories of security are personnel, policies and procedures, and technology.* Examples of security personnel are security officers and investigators. Policies and procedures are prepared by management and guide the day-to-day duties of personnel so that they conform to the goals of the organization. **Policies** are requirements that must be fulfilled while performing job duties. **Procedures** are guidelines or steps to follow to conform to policies. An example of a policy is that all visitors to a facility must be accounted for and escorted. Procedures state that visitors must be "logged in," show photo identification, receive a temporary badge, and be escorted by either management or security personnel. Examples of security technology are access control systems, CCTV, and intrusion alarm systems (Figure 5.1). All of these strategies in the three categories are generic and applied at numerous locations in many industries.

Specific security is specially designed to meet the unique needs of a particular entity and its customers (e.g., employees, contractors, purchasers of products and services) and security challenges. In other words, security professionals must understand the business objectives and needs and then align the security program with these objectives and needs. In reference to the three major categories of security, an entity may organize a security force with specialized training, special equipment, and unique uniforms to meet specific organizational requirements. Policies and procedures can be designed to handle special problems, such as the security officer's role in physically controlling disruptive mental health patients at a hospital. Specific security technology fulfills distinctive requirements of businesses. Electronic article-surveillance systems that are now used in many industries to prevent theft and to maintain the accountability and location of merchandise were used primarily by retailers and libraries in the 1960s.

A threat, hazard, or adverse incident may result in changes in one, two, or all three categories of security. Following the successful terrorist attack against the USS *Cole*, a Navy destroyer, by a small bomb-laden watercraft in the port of Aden, Yemen, on October 12, 2000, in which 17 sailors were killed and 39 injured, the U.S. Navy reevaluated all aspects of specific security for U.S. Navy ships.

FIGURE 5.1   Three major categories of security are security personnel, policies and procedures, and technology. Quality security strategies prevent unauthorized access. (® Shutterstock.com. With permission.)

There is no clear demarcation between generic and specific security. Security planners and designers often begin with generic security and then tailor it to the specific requirements of a business. Or, they may innovate and develop something completely new to meet unique needs. Vendors of security systems or services may assist with the process of innovation. In addition, what was once thought of as specific security may become generic security, as illustrated with the present widespread use of electronic article surveillance.

Generic Security

There are many generic security strategies available. Each has a history, a cost, advantages, and disadvantages. This chapter is not an attempt to provide comprehensive information on these factors for all security strategies. Rather, *an emphasis is placed on how to think about and apply generic security strategies that may become specific security strategies specially designed to address the unique needs of businesses.* The following list provides examples of generic security strategies commonly applied by organizations. Most of these topics are covered in this book.

Personnel
   Security officers
   Security supervisors
   Security managers and executives
   Investigators
   Undercover investigators
   Physical security specialists
   Locksmiths
   K-9 specialists
   Training officers
   Consultants
   Others

Policies and procedures, for
   Applicant screening
   Training
   Attire
   Access controls
   Repair and maintenance of physical security
   Key control
   Traffic and parking
   Visitors
   Emergencies
   Bomb threats
   Evacuations
   Strikes and unions
   First aid
   Safety
   Fire protection
   Responding to alarms
   Responding to crimes and other incidents
   Reporting and recording incidents
   Access by government officials
   Media relations
   Investigations
   Questioning suspects
   Searches
   Contraband
   Use of force
   Arrests
   Inventory control
   Information security
   Illegal drugs and substance abuse

Weapons on the premises
Sexual harassment
Others
(*Note*: Some of the policies and procedures listed here reside in departments other than security, such as the human resources department.)

Technology
Locks and keys
Access control systems
Vehicle barriers
Fences and related barriers
Door and window protection
Blast protection
Intrusion-detection systems
Closed-circuit television (CCTV)
Control center
Protective lighting
Digital signs
File cabinets, safes, and vaults
Others

> A security strategy that works at one organization may not work at another, even in the same industry.

Objectives of Security

The objectives of security strategies are outlined next. These objectives do not adhere to any particular order of importance or placement at specific locations at a protected site. Each can play a role in the sequence of events involving a crime or attack.

Deter. This prevention-oriented objective is successful when an adversary conducts a "risk analysis" (through a quick decision, surveillance, intelligence gathering and open-source documents, inside information, or other means) and makes a "rationale choice" that the "opportunity" for crime is not ripe. This does not necessarily mean that an adversary would conduct as thorough a risk analysis as a security practitioner would. The offender may apply one or more risk-analysis steps and decide against committing a crime at the particular location. The offender may be unable to identify a personnel, physical, or virtual vulnerability of the organization; harm to the offender and/or his/her organization may be a real possibility; or the risks and costs may be too high. Deterrence works on the psyche of the would-be offender and creates anxiety. Formidable security limits "opportunities" for crime and sends a message to offenders that crime is unlikely to be successful. However, deterrence may not work!

The criminal justice system is plagued by problems with deterrence. Offenders and criminal-justice practitioners know that there is a limit to the effectiveness of criminal law sanctions. Although many criminal laws and penalties exist, and overcriminalization is an issue, offenders continue to commit crimes because the risks and chances of being caught are often not high. Consequently, if deterrence from either criminal sanctions or security strategies fails, other objectives of security may avert a criminal incident.

Critical Thinking

Do you think deterrence results in displacement of crime? Explain.

Deception. This security objective can be applied to make a facility appear to be "a more protected or lower-risk facility than it actually is, thereby making it appear to be a less attractive target. Deception can also be used to misdirect the attacker to a portion of the facility that is non-critical" (FEMA 2003, 5-3). Deception may not work if adversaries obtain inside information, conduct surveillance, or apply various aspects of risk analysis.

Detect. Suppose an offender chooses to target a particular entity because deterrence failed. In this case, security strategies should be in place to detect physical or virtual intrusion. An example includes an intrusion-detection system that senses the intrusion, notifies security and/or police personnel, and is followed by a response to apprehend the offender. Other detection strategies are CCTV, awareness among employees to report suspicious behavior, Neighborhood Watch, and intelligence. IT systems contain intrusion-detection software that detects hackers and others who seek to breach or who successfully breach IT access control systems.

Delay. An adversary may not be deterred or detected. However, an adversary may be delayed because of various security features. Examples are a strong door or window constructed of both high-security hardware and locks that cause the offender to be delayed in breaking-in. In such a scenario, as the time delay increases, so does the anxiety and frustration of the offender and the chances of detection or apprehension, or the offender may abort the crime. From the perspective of counterterrorism, properly designed landscape and architectural features can delay terrorists from reaching their target. This can be accomplished by, for example, designing an obstacle course or serpentine path for vehicles and creating a buffer zone between public areas and vital areas (FEMA 2003, 5-3).

Deny. An offender can be denied success in several ways. Examples are being apprehended, reaching the target to discover that the people or assets sought are missing, being unable to access the critical asset because of formidable security (e.g., a safe), or being duped into targeting a bogus location.

Mitigate. This objective lessens the impact of a crime event or attack when other security objectives fail. An example of this would be the practice of keeping a minimum amount of cash on hand in a retail store. In reference to a terrorist attack, structural hardening of a building can save lives, limit flying debris, facilitate evacuation and rescue, and prevent collapse (FEMA 2003, 5-3).

Respond. When security is notified of an adverse event, a response is necessary to help the injured, apprehend offenders, and protect assets. A response can occur at many points along the chain of events leading to the commission of a crime; for example, when someone is observed conducting surveillance of the entity, its personnel, assets, or operations, which would not necessarily justify an arrest; or when an offender breaches the perimeter, a door, or a window.

The objectives of security can be enhanced through **unpredictable security strategies**. This means that security should be designed to avoid, if possible, predictable patterns. Security officers should never become **creatures of habit** by patrolling the same locations, at the same time, on their shifts. Security supervisors should avoid inspecting security features in a similar, regular manner. This approach can be applied to variations in physical security (e.g., move a portable light, CCTV camera, or intrusion alarm system to different locations at unpredictable times) and policies and procedures (e.g., using extreme courtesy, periodically check vehicles, items, or people more thoroughly than what is the norm).

Security Layers and Redundancy

Security layers use demarcations (or concentric circles) of security that extend out from the site requiring protection (Figures 5.2 and 5.3). The Federal Emergency Management Agency (FEMA 2005, 2-2–2-10) describes three layers as follows:

The *first layer of defense* requires study of the characteristics of the surrounding area outside the site perimeter (Figures 5.2 and 5.3). What types of facilities and businesses are nearby? A high school would require different protection considerations than a chemical plant. Is the site within view of other buildings (unwanted surveillance) or close to adjacent dense foliage? In an urban area, the sidewalks, curb lanes, streets, and surrounding neighborhood require study (Figure 5.3). Security can include hardened planters, benches, trash bins, streetlights, and CCTV cameras. Geographic information systems (GIS) can be a valuable tool for studying layers of security.

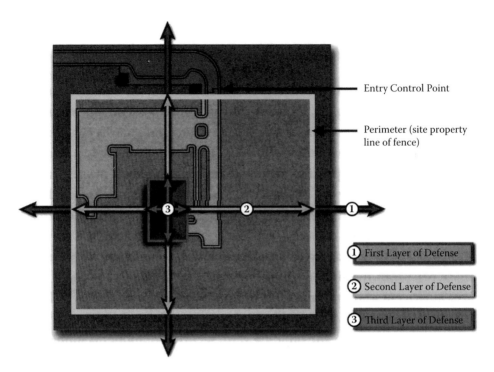

Entry Control Point

Perimeter (site property line of fence)

① First Layer of Defense

② Second Layer of Defense

③ Third Layer of Defense

FIGURE 5.2 Layers of defense. (*Source:* FEMA 2005).

The *second layer of defense* is between the site perimeter and the building (Figures 5.2 and 5.3). In urban areas, the building exterior is often the perimeter, which compounds security challenges. The second layer considers the three major categories of security: personnel, policies and procedures, and technology. It focuses on perimeter security, access points, loading docks, roadways, parking, walkways, natural and structural barriers, limiting foliage, protecting utilities and openings, lighting, intrusion-detection systems, CCTV, and security patrols. For protection against bombings, **stand-off distance** is important. The greater the distance from the detonation the better, which presents problems in dense, urban areas. Avoid straight roads to buildings and parking areas close to buildings. Prime considerations for the second layer are defensible space, CPTED, situational crime prevention, rational-choice theory, and other theories of security-relevant criminology.

The *third layer of defense* concentrates on the main asset itself, such as a building (Figures 5.2 and 5.3). If protection at the first and second layers fails, the third layer becomes especially important because it contains the lifeblood of an organization, namely people and physical and virtual assets. The third layer focuses on many of the same strategies considered in the second layer, but applied to a building. These include security personnel, policies and procedures, technology, and theories of security-relevant criminology.

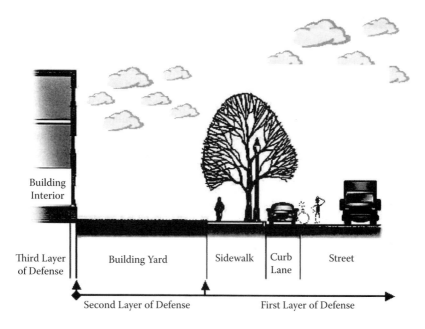

FIGURE 5.3   Layers of defense in an urban setting. (*Source:* FEMA 2005).

Violence is a serious concern at all three layers. Theft of assets becomes especially important in buildings where the most valuable assets are probably located. Appropriate security strategies for buildings include access controls, locked doors, CCTV, lighting, security officers, and internal intrusion-detection systems. The building should have emergency and evacuation plans and a fire protection system. To protect against terrorism, measures include blast-resistant construction and glazing, hardened mechanical and electrical systems, a HVAC system with efficient filtering and secure outside air intakes that are high above the ground, a smoke evacuation system, and strict access controls for an underground garage.

Johnston (2010, 65–69) extols the benefits of layering as a way to present the image of a facility as a hardened target and that the business takes security seriously. Depending on business needs and vulnerabilities, layering slows people and vehicles entering a facility, providing more time for security to observe suspicious behavior and objects. Johnston emphasizes the importance of critical thinking when planning layered security. This is to ensure that each layer is worth the expense, that a layer is not seen as a panacea, and that one layer of security does not interfere with another.

Redundancy means to back up. Whereas layered security consists of *different* types of security strategies, redundant security consists of two or more *similar* security strategies, for instance, two intrusion-detection systems along a perimeter. Prisons often have two or three fences along the perimeter to prevent escape. Nuclear plants typically contain redundant security systems besides redundant fire suppression and other safety systems. The purpose of redundant security is that if one system fails, the other performs the desired function. Another purpose, for instance with two intrusion-detection systems, is dual verification that an alarm is genuine and not false.

THE TRANSPORTATION SECURITY ADMINISTRATION (TSA) LAYERED APPROACH

The mission of the TSA, within the U.S. Department of Homeland Security, is to protect the nation's transportation systems while facilitating the movement of people and commerce. A major part of the TSA work is screening aviation passengers. However, TSA security goes beyond this strategy and includes twenty layers of security. The TSA notes that any one layer is capable of stopping a terrorist and, in combination, the layers yield formidable security. The TSA's twenty layers of security are listed here (Transportation Security Administration, 2006):

Intelligence
Customs and border protection
Joint Terrorism Task Force
No-fly list and passenger prescreening
Crew vetting
Visible intermodal protection response
Canines
Behavior-detection officers
Travel-document checker
Checkpoint/transportation security officers
Checked baggage
Transportation-security inspectors
Random-employee screening
Bomb-appraisal officers
Federal Air Marshal Service
Federal Flight Deck Officers
Trained flight crew
Law enforcement officers
Hardened cockpit door
Passengers

Security Levels

The federal government is a source of security standards and recommendations applicable to buildings used by federal government agencies. Although these standards and recommendations are not required for nonfederal buildings, they serve as a frame of reference and input for risk analyses and security planning in the private sector. The development of the following federal standards and recommendations began in earnest following the 1995 bombing of the Alfred P. Murrah Federal Building in Oklahoma City. The U.S. Department of Justice (1995), with the assistance of the U.S. Marshals Service, studied over 1,300 federal office buildings and developed security standards and levels of security. Many other federal government bodies are involved in security standards, including the General Services Administration as well as the Departments of Defense, State, and Homeland Security. FEMA (2005, 2-20–2-22) provides a description of the five levels of security and recommended security strategies, as described next.

- *Level I*: The typical location has ten federal employees, 2,500 square feet, low-volume public contact, and is a small "storefront." Security strategies include high-security locks, peephole, intercom at door, lighting with emergency backup power, and employee security training.
- *Level II*: This level is characterized by federal employees numbering between 11 and 150, 2,500 to 80,000 square feet, and moderate volume of public contact. The facility may be shared with the private sector. Security strategies include access controls for visitors and incoming and outgoing mail, CCTV, intrusion-detection and duress alarms (both with central monitoring), and security officers.
- *Level III*: The number of federal employees is between 151 and 450. The building is multistory, containing 80,000 to 150,000 square feet, and moderate to high volume of public contact. A mix of federal agencies shares the building, including law enforcement, courts, and government records. The security strategies are similar to Level II.
- *Level IV*: This level is characterized by 450 or more federal employees, multistory building, greater than 150,000 square feet, high volume of public contact, high-risk law enforcement/intelligence agencies, and district courts. The security strategies include an extended perimeter of concrete/steel barriers, hardened parking barriers, adjacent parking controls, security officers 24/7, and backup power system.
- *Level V*: This level is applied to principal department headquarters/ agencies critical to national security. The security strategies are comprehensive and extensive.

Security Maxims

Security maxims are critical-thinking statements about security that help professionals plan and develop strategies that are well thought out, practical, show value, and increase the likelihood of being effective. Roger Johnston (2006), of the Los Alamos National Laboratory Vulnerability Assessment Team, offers the following maxims:

- Security has no guarantees of success, especially because complacency, overconfidence, wishful thinking, and arrogance are not compatible with good security.
- Physical security is scarcely a "field." There is a shortage of models, fundamental principles, standards, critical thinking, and creativity. "Lots of snake oil salesmen."
- Effective security is highly multidisciplinary. Involve people in security from within who are smart, creative, and even those not part of the security force.
- The traditional performance measure for security is nothing happening.
- Security practitioners have trouble identifying vulnerabilities because they do not want them to exist.
- "There are an unlimited number of vulnerabilities, most of which will never be discovered (by the good guys or bad guys)."
- Adversaries need only find one vulnerability, but security practitioners must protect against all known ones.
- Beware of backdoor attacks. Most security devices and systems are subject to compromise through a few seconds of access at manufacturing, during shipment, or at installation.
- "The confidence that people have in security is inversely proportional to how much they know about it."
- The amount of critical thinking that goes into security is inversely proportional to the amount of high technology used in it.
- Low-tech attacks are capable of defeating high-tech security.
- Effective, simple, and low-cost countermeasures are available for most vulnerabilities.
- Try to be more creative and imaginative than adversaries.
- Although individuals are creative, rather than groups, groups can facilitate ideas, and they are necessary to fully explore threats and countermeasures.

Force Multipliers

Force multipliers refer to technology and nonsecurity people that enhance the resources and strategies of security. CCTV enables one person to watch multiple locations at one time from one location. Likewise, intrusion-detection systems installed at multiple points permit monitoring by one person from one location. The wise security executive understands the value and benefits of recruiting nonsecurity people into protection strategies. This is accomplished through new employee orientation programs, training, and special programs that generate awareness about security and reporting of events. Kotwica (2007, 20) suggests delivering security awareness through e-mails, a company intranet, posters, newsletters, meetings, and exercises/ drills. She notes that organizations often have to conduct security awareness and training programs to comply with government regulations under certain laws (e.g., Health Insurance Portability and Accountability Act). Furthermore, it is important to evaluate the effectiveness of awareness programs through periodic surveys, such as via an organizational intranet. In addition, the security executive should work cooperatively with executives in other departments in an organization (e.g., human resources, risk management, legal, and operations) to build support for security objectives.

Another avenue for awareness is **Business Watch**, derived from Neighborhood Watch. It facilitates ties between the private sector and public police, trains employees to report suspicious activities and crimes, promotes the use of traceable object identification tags, and instructs employees on self-protection and crime prevention. The ASIS Foundation received funding from the U.S. Department of Justice to promote Business Watch among ASIS members (ASIS International 2008, 1).

Force multipliers result from relationships with government agencies that are essential when adverse events occur. These agencies include police, fire, emergency medical services, hospitals, and emergency management units. A security professional should cultivate positive relations with government agencies long before an adverse event occurs. Mallery (2007, 44) writes: "One of the most critical aspects of a security professional's career is to establish strong relationships with public sector agencies—specifically law enforcement agencies." This is accomplished through face-to-face meetings when associations and other groups meet. Mallery encourages the building of relationships through mutual assistance, cross-training, and sharing intelligence and knowledge.

DO NOT MAKE THESE MISTAKES

Apartment-Complex Security

The Middleton Park apartment complex was built in the 1980s with a unique architectural style. Berms, valleys, and walls, combined with plentiful foliage, covered the grounds of the 400-unit complex. Residents were proud to live at the sightly complex. Over the years, however, the complex was bought and sold by several investors and managed by a variety of out-of-state property management companies. The landscape and apartments deteriorated because of poor maintenance. Crime steadily increased. The road running through the complex became a shortcut that resulted in traffic congestion, accidents, and an escape route for offenders.

Following an assault on one of the residents, a police crime prevention officer was invited by local Middleton Park management to conduct a free security survey. Several layers of security were recommended, including closing one of the vehicle entrances, trimming foliage, increasing lighting, using signs to warn trespassers, installing door viewers in each apartment entrance door, recruiting one or two public police officers to live at the complex in exchange for reduced rent, establishing a Neighborhood Watch, hiring a contract security company for patrols, and installing a fence, CCTV, and a card-access system and gate (at the entrance). When local Middleton Park management requested increased security from corporate headquarters based in another state, the request for security was denied.

One winter evening, a woman, who was living at the complex with her infant daughter, went to her vehicle with her daughter to begin a grocery-shopping trip. A man approached her as she was getting into her car. With a pistol, he ordered her to drive to her ATM to withdraw cash. He then ordered her to drive back to her apartment where he sexually assaulted her with her infant nearby. The woman retained an attorney, and a lawsuit was filed for alleged negligent security against the apartment owners and management.

The attorney hired an expert witness specializing in security who discovered that six violent crimes and numerous property crimes had occurred on the premises during the two years prior to the plaintiff's assault, and that management at corporate headquarters, with knowledge of the crimes, refused to improve security. Local management sent a request for increased security, with a copy of the police security survey attached, to corporate headquarters, and increased security was refused. A security survey by the expert showed that foliage was overgrown; numerous, dark hiding places were available because of the berms, valleys, and walls; illumination from a street light was blocked from a large oak tree that cast a shadow at night on the parking area used by the victim; several light fixtures on the apartment buildings required bulb replacement; and the Middleton Park Web site stated that the premises was safe and secure. In addition, police investigative reports of interviews of the offender revealed that he had committed a prior sexual assault at the complex that was not solved by police; he was able to easily "peep" into apartments because of the extensive use of window blinds (rather than curtains); he often masturbated while "peeping"; and poor illumination at night and the foliage helped him to avoid detection.

The security expert hired by the defense side found that two of the six violent crimes on the premises prior to the plaintiff's assault were domestic cases, and that most of the property crimes were vehicle break-ins. Also, two security officers were living at the complex when the plaintiff was assaulted, but neither were linked to security on the premises. Numerous public police preventive patrols occurred on the road running through the complex prior to the assault on the plaintiff. The defense security expert did not refute the findings of the plaintiff's expert on the need for improved security. Each side in the case also hired medical experts who studied the physical and mental trauma experienced by the victim. The case was eventually settled before trial for an undisclosed amount of money awarded to the plaintiff and paid for by the apartment complex's liability insurance policy.

> *Lesson:* Management at corporate headquarters refused to support and fund security that would have increased the security and safety of residents.

Critical Thinking

What security strategies would have increased the security and safety of residents?

DO NOT MAKE THESE MISTAKES

Theme-Park Security

The Rolling Rock theme park attracted hundreds of teenagers and families who paid an admission fee for access to rides, attractions, and live bands. Friday and Saturday evenings were especially busy for the theme park, and the greatest number of security officers was scheduled during these times. Officers were routinely assigned to patrol inside the theme park, at gates, along the perimeter, and in the parking lots. Periodically, illegal drugs, alcohol, and weapons were confiscated from youth. Arrests occurred each month for disorderly conduct, public intoxication, and assault and battery. Public police were summoned once an arrest was made. Although security was deployed throughout the premises, management repeatedly ordered officers off their posts and away from preventive patrol to check on employee whereabouts, operate rides (without training and certification), and run errands. The two security supervisors were assigned to count cash and prepare bank deposits in a back office. The supervision of security officers was haphazard.

One Saturday night during a concert and dance, two males, ages thirteen and eighteen, began arguing and pushing each other. A large crowd gathered, but the incident ended when their girlfriends interceded. Twenty minutes later, the confrontation erupted again, a large crowd gathered, and a fight ensued. Soon, the older teen was on top of the younger teen punching him into unconsciousness. Two additional fights erupted, as the crowd grew larger. Realizing the commotion required action by security, a theme-park worker contacted the security office. Ten minutes later, security officers arrived, dispersed the crowd, and contacted emergency medical services to care for the unconscious thirteen-year-old youth, who died two days later. The family of the deceased sued the theme park for alleged inadequate security. The lawsuit resulted in a settlement prior to trial, and the family of the deceased was awarded an undisclosed amount of money from the insurer of the theme park.

- *Lessons:* Management must understand the importance of security and that adequate security includes coverage of posts and patrols to ensure the safety of customers and quick response to incidents. In this case, security personnel were multitasking and improperly supervised, which resulted in gaps in security coverage and, essentially, inadequate security.

Critical Thinking

What recommendations would you make to improve security at this theme park? Compare this case with the previous case on apartment-complex security. What similarities and differences do you notice?

Violence in the Workplace

The Occupational Safety & Health Administration (n.d.) defines **workplace violence** as "any physical assault, threatening behavior, or verbal abuse occurring in the work setting." The work setting includes buildings, parking lots, field locations, clients' homes, and traveling to and from assignments. Examples of workplace violence are murder, robbery, assault, rape, intimidation (Figure 5.4), harassment, domestic violence, and bullying. Each year, on average, 1.7 million nonfatal, violent workplace incidents occur, and most are simple or aggravated assaults (FBI 2004). The U.S. Department of Labor (2007) reported 516 workplace homicides in 2006, a decline of over 50

FIGURE 5.4 **As a supervisor, how would you respond to this gesture from an employee following a verbal reprimand? As a security officer, how would you respond? (® Shutterstock.com. With permission.)**

percent from 1994. Certain occupations show a higher incidence of work-place victimization. These include law enforcement, mental health, retail sales, teaching, transportation, and medical. Besides the physical and psychological harm to victims, workplace violence costs about 500,000 employees 1,175,100 lost work days each year, lost wages of $55 million, plus billions of dollars in losses from lost productivity, legal expenses, property damage, diminished public image, and increased security (Occupational Safety & Health Administration n.d.).

Stories about workplace violence appear frequently in the media. In early 2008, in the St. Louis, Missouri, suburb of Kirkwood, a nine-square-mile community of 27,000 residents that is noted for high property values, quality schools, and safety, a disgruntled citizen killed six city officials and wounded the mayor during a city council meeting. The murderer was able to walk right into city hall, shoot the lone police officer, and take his service weapon to aid in the killing (Edelman 2008). In another case, a 25-year-old press operator, in Henderson, Kentucky, shot and killed five coworkers after arguing with his supervisor over not wearing safety goggles and using his cell phone while working. Wesley N. Higdon was so upset with his boss that he telephoned his girlfriend and told her that he wanted to kill him. The girlfriend provided no warning prior to the shootings. Higdon was known to carry a .45-caliber pistol in his vehicle, which is legal in Kentucky. Higdon turned the weapon on himself following the murders (Lenz 2008).

Critical Thinking

In reference to the Kirkwood and Henderson killings, how can such violence be prevented?

ISSUE

Are Fast-Food Restaurants Providing Adequate Security?

Horovitz (2007) describes the case of Mary Hutchinson, a manager at a Burger King and mother of three children. She had been pistol-whipped in a late-night robbery and lost hearing in one ear. Nine months later, while trying to deal with the fear and memory by seeing a therapist, she decided to fill in at a Burger King near Lindenhurst, Illinois. During one shift, while working alone at 4 a.m., her worst fears returned when a former employee barged through the back door and, during a robbery, stabbed her 21 times, killing her.

To increase profits, and because it is less expensive to extend hours than to build new restaurants, Burger King, McDonald's, Wendy's and other chains have expanded business hours. However, extended night hours increases crime risks for the 4 million workers in this industry, not only from murder, but also from more assaults, robberies, and other crimes. In addition, this industry is not subject to security regulations such as those in place for banks, airports, chemical plants, and other industries.

Horovitz's news story included an interview with Dr. Michael Witkowski, a security expert who teaches at the University of Detroit, Mercy. When asked about what will prompt the industry to enhance security, Witkowski replied: "The industry responds to jury verdicts. Whenever they are forced to pay significant court awards, that makes them rethink their policies. Unfortunately, that is what it takes."

Interestingly, *Security Law Newsletter* (Davis 2008, 127) reported that in the Hutchinson case, a lawsuit against Burger King and a franchisee was settled for $1.3 million. A lawsuit was also filed against Stand Guard, Inc., the security firm that provided the alarm system for the fast-food restaurant. The suit alleged that the alarm on the safe failed to activate when Hutchinson entered a code during the robbery.

Critical Thinking

What can be done to improve security at fast-food restaurants?

Theories of Violence

There are many theories that seek to explain violent crime. They span homicide, assault, sexual assault, robbery, and terrorism, among others. In the previous chapter, security-relevant criminology, specifically ecological theories of crime, were explained. It was noted that through the history of criminology, an emphasis was placed on biological, sociological, and psychological theories. Ecological theories differ by focusing on demographics, geographics, and physical features of locations where victimization occurs. Besides the importance of ecological theories to security planning, the traditional approach of studying the individual offender helps us to understand violence and other crimes. Helfgott (2008, 147–152), who has a background in criminal justice and psychology, offers the following comments and theory on violent crime. She writes: "Violence is a varied behavioral outcome of a complex web of motivational, situational, and contextual factors." Most violent crime involves people who know each other, and the event "is an emotional reaction, not diabolical, methodical, or predatory." Violence is shaped by biological, psychological, sociological, and cultural factors. Other factors influencing behavior and violence are the environments in which a child is raised, ethnic background, parenting style, and parents' socialization.

Helfgott (2008, 149) writes that the dynamics of violence (and other types of crime) can be understood at an interdisciplinary level by asking the following questions:

What internal and external factors and precipitating events led to the violence?

Why was the violence committed at this time and place and with this victim?

What was the relationship of the offender and victim?

What themes (e.g., motivation, opportunity, modus operandi, psychopathology, and/or fantasy) are linked to the crime?

Helfgott (2008, 150–151) explains the difference between predatory and affective violence as "an important theoretical tool in distinguishing violent crime from other types of crime and understanding the motivations of different types of violent offenders." **Predatory violence** is characterized by no perceived threat; no conscious experience of emotion; goal oriented, planned purposeful violence; and increased self-esteem. **Affective violence** is characterized by a perceived threat, conscious experience of emotion, goal threat reduction, reactive unplanned violence, and decreased self-esteem. As with many classification systems and typologies, there is overlap here, an offender can have a history of both predatory and affective violence.

Most violent incidents are affective. Examples are domestic violence, child abuse, barroom brawls, and the majority of murders. The offender has an emotional reaction to frustration, anxiety, confusion, anger, or other uncomfortable state and becomes violent.

Typologies offer additional input for our understanding of violence. **Crime typologies** are often used by criminologists to classify crimes according to particular categories, such as types of criminal offenses (e.g., robbery and assault), criminal motivations, criminal modus operandi (i.e., methods of committing a crime), or types of workplace violence. Although typologies generally have overlapping or nonexclusive categories, they help us to understand patterns of crime.

The FBI (2004) offers four typologies of workplace violence, as explained in subsequent paragraphs. These categories describe types of offenders, clues to what motivates them, types of crimes committed, and the circumstances of the crimes.

Type 1 involves offenders not linked to the workplace. An example is an armed robbery of a convenience store. Most workplace homicides fall in this category. Certain occupations are especially vulnerable within this category, such as taxi drivers and retail clerks, especially when both groups work at night.

Type 2 results from victimization of employees by those receiving a service. The offender may be a customer or a patient. Those working in criminal justice, security, and health care are more vulnerable and require specialized training. At the same time, many other occupations can be dangerous when rendering services and facing angry customers who may become violent.

Type 3 pertains to violence by an employee or former employee. Periodically, we hear in the media about multiple murders in the workplace committed by a disgruntled employee or former employee.

Type 4 workplace violence is characterized by an offender who is not an employee, but has some type of relationship with an employee. A common scenario is a male entering the workplace premises to assault a female because of a dispute in their relationship.

RESPONDING TO AN EMOTIONAL REACTION FROM OTHERS

On a practical note, since threats and violence can result from an emotional reaction to frustration, anger, and other uncomfortable states, employees should be trained to defuse dangerous situations. Here are suggestions when facing an angry person (Purpura 2003, 55):

- Do not take offensive remarks personally.
- Do not return offensive remarks.
- Since the first few seconds of an interaction are very important and set the tone for a calm resolution of the problem, offer to assist by showing genuine concern.
- Speak in a calm reassuring voice.
- Acknowledge the person's feelings. For example, "I know you are frustrated."
- State that you are here to help and that you need some basic information to resolve the problem.
- Show good listening skills and ask for explanations for statements you do not understand.
- You may have to call your supervisor if the person demands to see him or her.
- If violence is possible, stand at an angle and step back slightly to protect yourself. Call for assistance.
- The goal is to solve the problem peacefully.
- Report the incident to your supervisor.

Strategies to Counter Violence in the Workplace

Security executives must convince senior management of the importance of countermeasures against workplace violence. Avenues to enhance this effort are by gaining the support of other executives (e.g., human resources, safety) and preparing metrics from internal incidents (including verbal threats) and external sources (government and other organizations). Two other avenues relate to compliance and liability. The OSHA Act, Section 5(a)(1), requires employers to comply with the "general duty clause" to protect employees from "recognized hazards" that may cause injury or death, including violence. For repeated violent incidents, an employer can be found in violation of this Act and be fined and penalized.

In addition, a lawsuit for alleged negligent security is common against employers who foster inadequate security, especially in the face of mounting incidents. Legal principles involving workplace violence include premise liability (i.e., the responsibility of a property owner to protect people on the property from foreseeable violence), *respondeat superior* (i.e., the employer is responsible for the actions of an employee), a variety of negligence theories (e.g., negligent applicant screening, training, supervision, and retention), and a variety of types of harassment illegal under discrimination laws. Thus, employers should take steps to provide adequate security and show evidence of action. Although OSHA, state, local, and private organization guidelines on workplace violence are generally viewed as suggestions and typically do not have the force of regulatory law, complying with such guidelines provides a much improved defense from accusations of inadequate security (Blades 2008, 24–28).

In Chapter 4, security-relevant criminology was explained as theory that has practical applications for security programs and strategies. We should seek guidance from theories of violence and related research to help us plan strategies to counter violence in the workplace. A major objective here is to continue to develop a methodology and mind-set for planning and implementing the best possible security programs and strategies. As theory and research from multiple disciplines are published, security practitioners should extract the relevance to security. To illustrate, by studying the points Helfgott makes, we can better understand factors that can increase or decrease violence in the workplace and then apply this knowledge to prevention strategies. In reference to typologies of workplace violence, a security practitioner should pinpoint the types most relevant to the workplace at hand and design specific security strategies.

> As theory and research are published from multiple disciplines, security practitioners should extract the relevance to security.

Three sources of information for strategies against workplace violence are the Occupational Safety and Health Administration (1998), the National Institute for Occupational Safety and Health (NIOSH) (2002), and ASIS International (2005). Here are generic strategies, primarily from OSHA:

- Management commitment is essential for a successful program against workplace violence.
- Form an interdisciplinary committee (e.g., specialists from human resources, security, safety, law, operations) to plan and prepare policies and procedures.
- Adhere to legal requirements, including those that pertain to privacy, due process, discrimination, and labor agreements. Obtain quality legal assistance.
- Implement quality pre-employment screening and a drug-free workplace.
- Ensure that an Employee Assistance Program is available to help employees deal with personal problems early on before the problems become worse.
- Disseminate policies and procedures, train all employees, and ensure that all employees are involved. Employees should know the behaviors that signify the broad definition of workplace violence as specified by the organization and "best practices," how to deal with incidents, and reporting and documentation methods.
- Include policies and procedures on terminations, layoffs, prohibiting weapons on the premises, and searches.
- Assign responsibility and authority for the program.
- Include prohibitions of not only violence, including domestic violence, but also threats, intimidation, harassment of all kinds, bullying, and stalking.
- Communicate warning signs of violence. Examples are threats, reference to weapons, arguments with supervisors and coworkers, and desperation over personal problems.
- Take all violations seriously, quickly follow up with an investigation (e.g., interviewing) and corrective action, and care for victim needs.
- Crisis management plans for a variety of scenarios must be prepared early on.
- Conduct a worksite analysis to study factors that may increase dangers (e.g., contact with the public and exchange of money). The worksite analysis is similar to a risk analysis (see Chapter 4). Check past incidents and incident characteristics to improve planning.
- Since robbery is a serious risk to many organizations, *increase the effort* that an offender must expend by hardening the target (e.g., controlling access), *increase the risks* (e.g., CCTV), and *reduce the rewards* (e.g., limit the amount of cash on the premises).
- Enhance protection through a variety of security strategies. Examples are good lighting, CCTV, bullet-resistant enclosures, silent alarms, limited foliage, and a clear view into a store from the outside so

police or pedestrians can observe; lock doors not used by customers and ensure that the doors have a viewer.

- To improve a violence prevention program, track incidents (i.e., metrics), evaluate the program through research methodologies, and solicit feedback (i.e., survey of employees).

OSHA (1998, 4 and 6) reported on a variety of research projects that focused on reducing violence in retailing. Here is a summary of the research:

- Multiple studies found that the risk factors for robbery and sexual assault overlap (e.g., working alone, late at night, and in high-crime areas). Thus, security strategies that prevent robbery also may be effective in preventing sexual assaults.
- Research on convicted robbers showed that the stores most attractive to robbers had large amounts of cash on hand, an obstructed view of counters, poor outdoor lighting, and easy escape routes.
- Multiple studies found that robbers consider "opportunities" through environmental factors, such as ease of escape and low risk of detection (e.g., no CCTV and poor visibility from outside the store).
- Multiple studies found elevated risk of robbery during nighttime hours because of darkness and because fewer people are out.
- Behavioral and physical changes were made at an experimental group of 7-Eleven stores. The strategies included training employees, reducing cash on hand, and target hardening. The experimental group showed a 30 percent drop in robberies compared to the control group of stores. After implementing the program companywide, robbery at 7-Elevens dropped by 64 percent over 20 years.

ROBBERY PRECAUTIONS

Robbery is an especially dangerous crime because the offender may have a weapon and become violent. Here are guidelines for protection against robbery (Purpura 2003, 264):

- Security precautions against robbery should include a silent alarm (e.g., a special money clip in the cash register that signals an alarm when bills are removed), "bait" money (record denominations, series years, and serial letters and numbers), quality lighting, and CCTV.
- Ensure that employees are properly trained and clearly understand policies and procedures.
- The highest priority during a robbery is the safety of people.
- If a suspicious person enters the premises, call the police for a preventive patrol and visit.

- Once a robbery occurs, provide the robber with the assets demanded as quickly as possible so that he or she leaves quickly and does not become frustrated, resulting in violence.
- Trained police and security officers are unlikely to enter a robbery-in-progress scene when innocent bystanders are present. They are more likely to confront an escaping robber.
- If possible, make a mental note of the robber's unique physical features, statements, accent, and weapon.
- Avoid, as best as possible, the demand to accompany the robber as he or she departs.
- When the robber departs, cautiously observe direction of escape. If a vehicle is used in the escape, observe unique features and license tag. Immediately write as much as possible about the robbery.
- Notify public police following the robbery. Follow company policies and procedures.

To illustrate specific security strategies, rather than generic ones, NIOSH (2002) offers guidelines to prevent violence in hospitals that typically results from patients and occasionally from their family members who feel frustrated. In one case, an agitated psychotic patient assaulted a nurse, broke her arm, and scratched and bruised her. In another case, a family member was informed that his father had died in surgery. The assailant walked into the emergency room, shot to death a nurse and an emergency medical technician, and wounded a doctor.

In hospitals, violence is more frequent in psychiatric wards, emergency rooms, waiting rooms, and geriatric units. Risk factors include working with volatile people who may be influenced by drugs or alcohol, lack of staffing, long waits for service, transporting patients, and limited access controls. Prevention strategies are to have well-equipped and trained security officers, emergency signaling systems and alarms, training for all employees, metal detectors, CCTV, and escorts into parking lots. High-risk areas should be designed to minimize violence through bullet-resistant and shatter-resistant enclosures, enclosed nurses' stations, and careful placement of furniture and other objects to prevent their use as weapons.

At one Detroit hospital, stationary and handheld metal detectors prevented the entry of 33 handguns, 1,324 knives, and 97 defensive sprays during a 6-month period. In a New York City hospital, an access-control system, which involved the use of color-coded badges that limited visitor access to a specific floor and a maximum of two visitors per patient at any time, reduced reported violent crimes by 65 percent during an 18-month period.

Active Shooters

An **active shooter** is an individual, who may be accompanied by other shooters, who seeks to kill and wound as many random and/or specific people as possible by using firearms, explosives, and other weapons. Planning, coordination, surprise, and ploys (e.g., dressing like and using vehicles of first responders) often characterize active shooters. Their motivations vary (e.g., revenge, personal problems, and politics). The time line of the incident may be short (a few minutes) or it may extend over multiple days, with hostages. One or more sites may be targeted. The attackers either commit suicide, are killed by police or others, are taken prisoner, or escape.

On April 16, 2007, Seung Hui Cho, a mentally disturbed Virginia Tech student, began a one-day murder rampage by killing two students at a dormitory. His next step was to mail a package to NBC News in New York. It contained bitter and abusive statements, pictures of himself, and video clips. He then proceeded to a lecture building, where he chained exit doors closed from the inside, and in the subsequent 11 minutes he shot to death 30 more people and wounded 25 before killing himself. The **Virginia Tech massacre** holds the record at this point for the most deadly school shooting incident in U.S. history.

Not only did the Virginia Tech massacre bring to the forefront the challenge of dealing with an active shooter, the **Mumbai attacks**, in late 2008, added even more challenges to the problem. Mumbai is a city in India that is the country's financial capital and is also a haven for tourists. In a well-planned and well-coordinated attack, ten heavily armed terrorists arrived by small boat, scattered to several targets throughout the city—including a major hotel, a train terminal, and a Jewish center—and using explosives and automatic weapons, killed as many people as possible. Over three days, nearly 200 people were murdered, scores were wounded, and hostages were held before authorities prevailed.

Chudwin (2009, 50–55) wrote about the Mumbai attacks and lessons for first responders, as described next. Following the attacks, the *Times of India* and the Associated Press reported that police agencies in Mumbai had not participated in firearms practice for several years because of the absence of a firing range, ammunition, and weapons. In addition, few officers were armed during the attack. It was alleged that, during the attack, police ran or hid, and armed officers at the train terminal did not fire on two terrorists who methodically murdered over 50 men and women. A photographer said the terrorists were "sitting ducks" as they stood together talking and he took a photo of them. The terrorists were trained to operate in teams, and they used the buddy system, such that when one fired, the other reloaded. They were well equipped with backpacks and pants with numerous pockets running down their legs. They carried assault rifles, ammunition, explosives, and dried fruit and nuts—all to sustain them for a lengthy attack. Dressed in ordinary clothing, one team spotted a police van carrying seven officers, including a chief of counterterrorism; all but one of the officers were murdered, and then the terrorists drove off in the van. Indian commandos arrived hours after the assault began because they were based hundreds of miles away without their own aircraft. The commandos battling the terrorists at the Taj Mahal Palace & Tower Hotel lacked a floor plan, although the terrorists seemed to know the hotel's layout well.

For first responders, Chudwin, a police chief, emphasized the need to heed warnings. India's government was warned by the United States about a coming attack, possibly at luxury hotels. He wrote of the importance of the intelligence function to prevent attacks; the need for leaders to allow line officers to make decisions during chaotic events; the willingness to quickly respond with firepower, without waiting for special teams; the need for every patrol officer to have quick access to a rifle with ammunition capable of penetrating body armor; and the need for combat essentials, such as extra ammunition, wound bandages and a tourniquet, and binoculars.

Critical Thinking

As an unarmed security officer, how would you react to an active-shooter event?

A key question is: What can be done to protect people and assets from active shooters? With a huge inventory of soft targets available to disturbed individuals, terrorists, and other offenders, how can we protect ourselves? How can the public and private sectors provide security and safety from active shooters, whether a lone shooter or a group of shooters?

To begin with, violent events are difficult to predict, prevent, and stop. Simply put, the "bad guys" have the advantage of surprise; they can select the location and time, and bring with them their choice of weapons and equipment. The "good guys" need time to respond and bring adequate personnel, weapons, and equipment to match the threat. Where does this leave individuals who may be killed before help arrives? A list of suggestions follows, most of which are more applicable to employees in a building than civilians in public places. This list will grow as our society confronts the threat of active shooters.

- Early warning is vital. Public authorities and corporate executives must facilitate the reporting of suspicious behavior.
- Consider a behavioral intervention team (BIT) for the workplace. A BIT consists of representatives from various departments of an

organization (e.g., human resources, security, and legal) who review reports of individuals who may need counseling or intervention and recommend strategies for increased protection.

- Implement the best possible security program, including quality access controls.
- Plan and drill with local police and other first responders. Globally, police are increasing their planning and training to confront active shooters. Once an incident begins, they need time to respond. They know that by the time they arrive at the scene, people may be dead or bleeding profusely. In addition, hysterical victims may cling to or interfere with police before shooters are neutralized (Miller 2008, 58–63).
- Police should have detailed diagrams of the building and telephone numbers and e-mail addresses of occupants.
- Be aware that planning, drills, and policies and procedures are very important for employees to prepare for a violent incident. However, if the active shooter is linked to the organization, he/she is likely to be aware of methods of protection for employees, including access to "safe" areas and codes to signal police.
- If possible, evacuate the area immediately and seek safety. Otherwise, find a room or location that can offer protection and an escape path. Lock the door and barricade it. Turn lights off and close the blinds. Stay away from doors and windows. Contact authorities.
- Be creative, improvise, and maintain a survivalist mind-set.

Mass-Notification Systems

The Virginia Tech massacre brought attention to **mass notification**, which refers to one or more modes of communication to as many people as possible in a specific geographic area to warn them to take precautions to protect themselves from threats or hazards, or to assist authorities in investigative or public safety duties. Mass notification systems afford assistance with several types of events. Examples are bomb threats, fires, active shooters, tornados, tsunamis, hazmat emergencies, and abductions (e.g., Amber Alert).

In the Virginia Tech massacre, the university administration was criticized for not alerting students to the two earlier killings and encouraging them to stay in their dorm rooms. E-mail was finally used to send a warning. The school's siren was not considered because it was only used for adverse weather. A 2008 amendment to the **Clery Act** (requires crime awareness, prevention, and reporting of campus crime statistics) now requires "immediate notification" once an emergency has been confirmed, annual testing of the notification system, and publicizing of campus emergency procedures.

The U.S. Department of Defense requires mass notification in its facilities under its Unified Facilities Criteria. Instructions on what action to take for protection must also be communicated. In an increasingly dangerous world, more and more public and private organizations will become involved in mass notification systems.

What type of mass notification system is best? The answer is to use multiple paths of communication, because each type of technology has disadvantages. Sirens may not be heard in buildings; public-address systems may not cover all areas between buildings; messages to desktop computers and landline telephones do not help those not near one; digital signage cannot be placed everywhere; and cell phones may not be able to handle high-traffic situations, have dead spots in buildings, and may be on silent (Anderson 2008, 26–29). Consequently, using specialized software, messages can be sent to people listed in several databases through various technologies, such as cellular and landline phones, e-mail, computer displays, and instant messaging. In addition, consideration should be given to radio and television, computer pop-up messages, alert beacons, strobes, reverse 9-1-1, and 9-1-1 capabilities that can track a caller's location from a cell phone as well as from a landline.

Theft in the Workplace

Theft is a broad term and a popular name for larceny or stealing. Elements of **larceny** include knowingly taking property belonging to another, without consent, with the intent to deprive the owner of the property. Several terms are linked to theft. **Burglary** refers to breaking and entering of a dwelling with the intent to commit a felony. State statutes may not require a break-in; use of deception to enter may be included in a burglary statute. **Fraud** is the intentional misrepresentation of fact to induce another to part with something valuable or to give up a legal right. There are many types of fraud. Examples are check fraud, credit card fraud, computer fraud, and tax fraud. **Embezzlement** is a type of fraud whereby property entrusted to another is converted to one's own use. This usually occurs in an employer–employee relationship, such as when a bookkeeper in charge of a company's checking account writes checks for personal expenses (Black 1991).

Robbery contains the elements of force or fear during theft. It is in the category of *crimes against persons*, and other examples are homicide, rape, assault, and stalking. This category differs from *crimes against property*, as explained in the preceding paragraph.

In a business environment, theft can occur in many ways, and the crime can be committed by employees, outsiders, or a combination of both. Employees on an assembly line may steal one item per day and, in a large plant, create huge inventory losses. In another workplace, mechanics may steal tools periodically, thus requiring the replacement of tools. Shipping and receiving clerks may conspire with truck drivers to steal merchandise. A salesperson may pad an expense account to claim a higher reimbursement. "Theft of time" is a problem in many workplaces. It refers to employees falsely claiming hours worked or, while on the job, using an employer's equipment or systems (e.g., computers) to conduct personal business or operate a part-time business. Although most "theft of time" activities are handled as violations of policies and procedures in organizations, rather than crimes (e.g., fraud), the problem can result in expensive losses to productivity. Another type of theft in the workplace is stealing proprietary information and selling it to a competitor. A hacker, from the comfort of his or her home, may enter a company's IT system to steal inventory, personal identities, or proprietary information. A top executive in a company may embezzle millions of dollars in assets or commit fraud by falsifying financial statements to make the company appear profitable when it is not.

Theft in the workplace is a multibillion dollar problem (Figure 5.5). Hayes (2008, 4) writes: "Research has shown as many as 75 percent of all employees have stolen or otherwise harmed their employer." Research by Hollinger and Adams (2007) showed that retailers believe employees are the cause of 47 percent of inventory shortages. Shoplifters and paperwork errors are other causes of losses.

The **Association of Certified Fraud Examiners** (2008) periodically publishes a Report to the Nation on Occupational Fraud & Abuse. This group defines **occupational fraud** as "the use of one's occupation for personal enrichment through the deliberate misuse or misapplication of the employing organization's resources and assets." This definition is very broad and ranges from pilferage of company inventory to financial statement fraud. The 2008 report is based on 959 cases of occupational fraud investigated by Certified Fraud Examiners between January 2006 and February 2008.

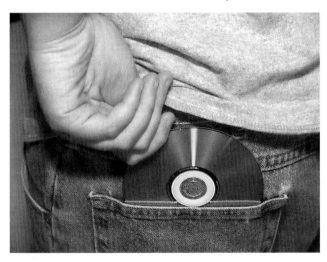

FIGURE 5.5   **Theft in the workplace is a multibillion dollar problem. (® Shutterstock. com. With permission.)**

"Participants in our survey estimated that U.S. organizations lose 7% of their annual revenues to fraud. Applied to the projected 2008 U.S. Gross Domestic Product, this 7% figure translates to approximately $994 billion in fraud losses."

Theories of Theft

Two typologies of thieves are the amateur and the professional (Glick and Miller 2008, 279). The **amateur thief** is an opportunist who steals occasionally without being part of a criminal lifestyle or possessing a criminal value system. He or she decides to steal with little or no planning when risks are low. **Situational inducements** are influences on an offender's behavior that increase risk taking. Examples are psychological factors (e.g., from financial pressure) or social factors (e.g., from peer pressure). Theft is often caused by a pressing situation, such as the need to pay a bill or purchase drugs. The **professional thief** is characterized by a criminal lifestyle and value system. They are skilled in committing crimes and are linked to a criminal subculture that supports their vocation through activities such as the sharing of information and the use of **fences**, who are brokers who deal in stolen goods.

Glick and Miller (2008, 279–280) refer to the work of **Edwin Sutherland** (1937), who studied the professional thief. He characterized the professional as devoting all working time and energy to larceny and other crimes, a careful planner, technically skilled, migratory, possessing status in the criminal subculture, and sharing common values with peers. Glick and Miller refer to the debate over whether the professional criminal is a dying breed. Is there a decline in professionalism and a consequent reduction in cohesion among professional thieves? **Gresham Sykes** (1978, 113–114) argues that the professional does not maintain full-time status as a thief, but steals as a moonlighting activity to supplement income from a low-paying job. In addition, criminals often work alone, are untutored, and do not belong to a criminal subculture. Glick and Miller note that, although debates continue in the field of criminology, there are "thieves who are amateurs and thieves who are professionals."

Critical Thinking

What is your viewpoint over whether the professional criminal is a dying breed? Do you think professional computer criminals work full-time in their work as offenders?

Helfgott (2008, 255–257) writes: "People steal first and foremost as a means of satisfying material wants and needs and steal for different reasons at different times. Theft is widespread and committed by all types of people with different motives and using a broad range of methods." She adds that theft is "dependent on situational factors and precipitators (e.g., target accessibility, absence of audience/onlookers, etc.)." Helfgott notes that theft may also result from mental illness or emotional need, although infrequently.

In Glick and Miller's (2008, 308) discussion of employee pilferage and theft, they cite the research of Clark and Hollinger (1983), who point to factors of the work environment that influence employee theft. They deemphasize economic factors as influencing theft and report that job dissatisfaction and feelings of exploitation more accurately influence employee theft.

Helfgott (2008, 259) writes that a lot of what is known about fraud is from the research of Edwin Sutherland (1937) and **Donald Cressey** (1973). Sutherland is famous for his theory of **differential association** that views criminal behavior as learned, like other behaviors, during interaction with others in a process of communication. He rejected many theories of criminology (e.g., biogenic and psychogenic) and sought an explanation as to why a normal person would commit a crime. Sutherland theorized that a white-collar criminal learns criminality just like other criminals (e.g., robbers), although their backgrounds may be different. The learning process includes techniques of committing the crime, rationalizations, and attitudes. **White-collar crime** means violations committed by individuals in professional, high-status occupations. (A more acceptable term is **occupational crime**, which is inclusive of all occupations.) Sutherland's theories point to the culture in workplaces that facilitate criminal behavior. This is referred to as **social disorganization**, in which certain business subcultures do not play a strong enough role in promoting norms that regulate ethical and legal conduct. When management scoffs at government regulations, makes unreasonable demands on employees, and "looks the other way," this culture facilitates crime. Dishonesty on Wall Street is just one example of this mind-set that permeates many workplaces.

Cressey's theory of fraud is known as the **fraud triangle**, which explains fraud and embezzlement as three points of a triangle: opportunity, pressure, and rationalization. Because employees are aware of vulnerabilities of the employing organization, an opportunity to exploit is identified by the employee thief. Pressure results from a private financial problem. Rationalization is an excuse to justify criminal behavior (e.g., not paid enough or just borrowing the valuables).

Helfgott (2008, 259–260) extends Cressey's work to the **fraud scale** from Albrecht and colleagues, as cited in Wells (2005, 22–23). This scale is based on research of internal auditors that identified *personal characteristics* of the offender and characteristics of the *occupational environment* that signal red flags for workplace fraud. The fraud scale supports Cressey's fraud triangle and reveals fraud as more likely when situational pressures and opportunities are high and integrity is low. Personal characteristics include living beyond their means, a strong desire for personal gain, high personal debt, a close association with customers, feelings of low pay, and a strong challenge to beat the system. Characteristics of the occupational environment include placing too much trust in key employees, lack of proper accounting controls and attention to details, inadequate disclosures of personal investments and incomes, and not enough internal audits.

Strategies to Counter Theft in the Workplace

Theft in the workplace is such a serious problem that it can result in the failure of a business. Security practitioners are at the front lines in preventing and investigating employee theft. They must convince management about its seriousness and gain their support.

The **National White Collar Crime Center** (2002) points out that the reasons for workplace theft are varied. Besides opportunity and financial need, the workplace environment (e.g., management setting a poor example), claims of inadequate compensation, and peer pressure all contribute to this universal problem. Thus, security strategies are important; however, a more comprehensive approach includes programs to ensure that employees are satisfied with the workplace. This means fair wages and benefits, honest management that sets a good example and is open to feedback, and initiatives to improve morale.

Legal requirements also play a role in supporting strategies to counter dishonesty in the workplace. For example, the **Sarbanes-Oxley Act of 2002** requires controls to prevent fraud and financial crime losses in businesses. Corporate scandals caused Congress to enact laws in an effort to prevent business crime. In 2001, the infamous **Enron Corporation scandal** resulted in employees and investors losing billions of dollars because senior executives hid billions of dollars in debt while they prepared fraudulent financial statements that showed profits.

Continuing with our mind-set and habit of seeking out security-relevant criminology as well as theory and research from multiple disciplines, we can see that the competence and behavior of thieves varies from amateur to professional. However, either one can destroy a business. Comprehensive strategies are necessary to counter theft in the workplace because it is widespread, the motives are many, and the methods of thievery are endless. What makes matters worse is that employee thieves, as insiders, are aware of security strategies, accounting controls, related weaknesses, and the most favorable times and places for opportunities to steal. The workplace environment and culture, and opportunities for theft, should be primary considerations in the design of countermeasures. In addition, a corporate culture may be so criminal, with senior executives "leading the pack," that the challenges for a security professional may be too overwhelming, and to avoid becoming part of the problem, alternative employment should be sought. Another product of research is the fraud scale covered earlier. It provides input for applicant screening, investigations, accounting controls, and security strategies.

The following are some generic strategies to protect against theft in the workplace:

- Management typically wants to avoid costly investigations and turnover. They want security to prevent theft and reduce theft opportunities.
- Basic strategies, as with other security challenges, include management commitment and support, a planning committee, risk analyses, metrics, policies and procedures, training, and applicant screening.
- Conduct a comprehensive inventory of all assets that can be subject to theft. This includes physical and virtual items, proprietary information, and anything else that, if stolen, can result in harm to the entity. An inventory should be maintained over merchandise for sale, raw materials, and related physical assets so that shrinkage can be investigated. **Shrinkage** refers to the difference between what is recorded in accounting records and what is physically present in inventory. It is expressed as a percentage rate. For example, 1 percent shrinkage (inventory missing) is better than 2 percent. Assets may be missing due to theft, shoplifting, sloppy recordkeeping, spoilage, or other reasons.
- Support an equitable employment environment.
- The "objectives of security," layers, redundancy, security levels, maxims, and force multipliers (as explained earlier) can be applied to several security challenges at the same time.
- Executives from security, human resources, risk management, legal, facilities, and other departments must work together on policies and procedures, union stipulations, searches, investigations, undercover investigations, public police involvement, prosecution, and other issues. (Chapter 10 provides guidelines on investigations.)
- Implement an awareness program so that all employees and others who enter the premises (e.g., contractors and delivery personnel) are mindful of the seriousness of theft. This program should also include IT personnel and systems and employees who are away from the premises on company business (e.g., salespeople, truck drivers, and those working from home).
- Place digital signs in the workplace that can be used for several types of threats and hazards. Periodically change the message to focus on a variety of security challenges.
- Employ security personnel: security officers who are stationed at posts or patrol to watch assets; investigators who respond to theft

incidents and gather facts to solve cases; and security executives who plan, implement, and evaluate strategies.

- Install physical security that assists personnel. Examples are many: fences, access control systems, intrusion-detection systems, locks, CCTV, lighting, and safes. (Chapter 7 covers physical security.)
- Bonding and insurance should be applied as a final layer of protection to be used as backup when other preventive layers fail. A fidelity bond entails a premium payment to the insurer and a background investigation of the employee to be covered to prevent theft; if theft occurs, the insurer indemnifies the employer. Crime insurance often focuses on crimes committed by nonemployees (e.g., burglary and robbery).

Marking and Tracking Assets

When a case of theft of company assets is investigated, and prosecution is a possibility, proof is required that the item belongs to the company. This can be accomplished through some unique feature of the item, the name of the company printed on the item, identifying numbers, a hidden code, a unique chemical mixture applied to the item, or some other method.

Tracking assets is important when assets are stationary, in transit, or upon being sold to customers. For instance, retail businesses use point-of-sale (POS) accounting systems consisting of bar codes or **radio-frequency identification (RFID)** tags on merchandise to maintain inventory records, to see which items sell better than others do, and to produce a variety of other business records. When merchandise is delivered to a store, added to a store's inventory, and sold, the assets are tracked via bar codes or RFID. In fact, asset tracking begins early in the supply chain, when raw materials are generated, and during manufacturing and transporting. The use of RFID is growing because it has so many applications. Besides tracking assets, it can track visitors, employees, and people who are institutionalized.

RFID systems contain tags, readers, and a computer. Each tag contains a microchip and a small antenna. The *passive* emitter tag is most common and is replacing bar codes. It has no internal power supply. A nearby reader powers these low-cost tags to transmit a signal containing data to the reader. The *active* tag contains a tiny battery and can transmit a signal to a reader or as far as a low-orbiting satellite. Tags vary in sophistication and expense. They can hold a variety of data, such as travel and time history and a serial number. Wireless technology enables the reader to pick up information from tags and transmit it to a central computer. These systems contain security features, including encryption, decryption, and user authentication. Inexpensive RFID systems without enhanced security are more vulnerable to hacking and tampering. It is important to note that the tag, like the bar code, is tracked, and problems can develop if a tag or bar code is placed erroneously or by design on the wrong item or person.

In Chapter 4, we explained global positioning systems (GPS) as a way to pinpoint a location on earth by triangulating a receiver's position using satellites. To apply this technology to tracking assets worldwide, a GPS device is attached to an item, and the user operates location and tracking technology. The applications are very broad (e.g., people, cargo, vehicles), and the use of these systems is growing. Assets can be tracked via the Internet during all forms of transportation. Enhanced systems that embed sensors in assets can monitor all types of data (e.g., intrusion, speed, and temperature), and remote management capabilities can perform a variety of functions (e.g., control access).

In one case, a seafood distributor based in Hawaii experienced huge theft losses of Alaskan king crab from the company's freezer. Over three months, the losses amounted to about $50,000, and the security manager of the company suspected one of the delivery drivers. To catch the suspect, a GPS tracking device was embedded in a container of fresh crab. The suspect stole the baited crab, and when the thief departed from the warehouse, the security manager was alerted. A Web-based system was used to monitor the location of the crab, and the suspect was caught selling through a fence. The evidence was provided to police, who issued arrest warrants (Weadock 2008, 16).

TWENTY-FIVE TECHNIQUES OF SITUATIONAL CRIME PREVENTION TO REDUCE LAPTOP THEFT

Here we apply the theory of situational crime prevention (see Chapter 4) to laptop theft in commercial buildings. The following techniques are from a study completed by the Building Owners & Manager's Association (BOMA), Calgary (2006). A sample of the techniques is presented here. The full range of techniques is available online. An important point here is that the twenty-five techniques can be applied to many other challenges facing security practitioners.

I. Increase the effort of the offender:
1. *Harden the target* through a variety of physical security measures, such as strong doors and locks and using laptop locking devices.
2. *Control access* through limited, secure access points and intrusion-detection systems.
3. *Screen exits* through RFID in laptops.
4. *Deflect offenders* by conducting background screening on all workers and never leaving laptops alone.
5. *Control tools/weapons* by not leaving bags around to carry laptops away and putting away cords, cables, etc.

II. Increase the risks for the offender:

6. *Extend guardianship* via policies that make employees responsible for theft; arrest offenders.
7. *Assist natural surveillance* by improving lighting and encouraging employee awareness and reporting.
8. *Reduce anonymity* by challenging visitors, using IDs, posting signs, and escorting visitors.
9. *Use place managers* by training all employees to report harmful incidents and rewarding vigilant ones.
10. *Strengthen formal surveillance* via security patrols, CCTV, auditing of laptops, and asset tracking (RFID).

III. Reduce the rewards:

11. *Conceal targets* by securing laptops after hours and storing vital information away from laptops.
12. *Remove targets* by considering locking laptops in vaults and conducting audits to ensure employees are following safeguards.
13. *Identify property* through markings on laptops and keep records of laptops (e.g., serial number, receipt).
14. *Disrupt markets* in conjunction with police (e.g., monitor pawnshops and online sales).
15. *Deny benefits* via passwords, biometric protection, and encryption software that encrypts only the data so that asset-tracking software is not hindered.

IV. Reduce provocations:

16. *Reduce frustrations and stress* through employee-assistance programs.
17. *Avoid disputes* through quality supervision.
18. *Reduce temptation* by locking away equipment when not in use.
19. *Neutralize peer pressure* by educating potential end users of stolen property.
20. *Discourage imitation* by seeking prosecution of thieves and using discipline when employees violate policies.

V. Remove excuses:

21. *Set rules* that are enforced and hold employees accountable.
22. *Post instructions* through signs.
23. *Alert conscience* by educating employees on their responsibility to protect company property.
24. *Assist compliance* through training and awareness.
25. *Control drugs and alcohol* that can lead to theft and other crimes.

Antifraud Controls

Research by the Association of Certified Fraud Examiners (2008) asked businesses victimized by fraud to list the antifraud controls in place at the time of the fraud. Fifteen controls were identified, and these appear in the following list. The first percentage in each line represents the percentage of victimized businesses that had the control in place when victimized. The association also analyzed the effectiveness of each of the fifteen controls by comparing median losses at organizations with each control to the median losses of organizations without each control. Two controls with the greatest impact on losses were surprise audits (66.2% reduction) and job rotation/mandatory vacations (61% reduction), although these controls were among the least commonly implemented. The second percentage in each line represents the percentage reduction in losses for each control.

- External audit of financial statement (69.6%/40%)
- Code of conduct (61.5%/45.7%)
- Internal audit or fraud examination department (55.8%/52.8%)
- External audit of internal controls over financial reporting (53.6%/47.8%)
- Employee-support programs (52.9%/56.0%)
- Management certification of financial statements (51.6%/29.5%)
- Independent audit committee (49.9%/31.5%)
- Hotline (43.5%/60.0%)
- Management review of internal controls (41.4%/45.0%)
- Fraud training for executives and managers (41.3%/55.9%)
- Fraud training for employees (38.6%/51.9%)
- Antifraud policy (36.2%/49.2%)
- Surprise audits (25.5%/66.2%)
- Job rotation/mandatory vacation (12.3%/61.0%)
- Rewards for whistleblowers (5.4%/28.7%)

Hotline Reporting

Despite an increase in antifraud controls following the Sarbanes-Oxley Act of 2002, the Association of Certified Fraud Examiners (2008, 4) reported that "occupational frauds are much more likely to be detected by a tip than by audits, controls or any other means." Research by the Security Executive Council and The Network, Inc., of 277,000 hotline incident reports from more than 650 organizations over a five-year period found the following: reports were made by employees, former employees, vendors, and the public; 65 percent were serious enough to warrant investigation; 50 percent concerned personnel management incidents; 16 percent involved company/professional code violations; 11 percent involved employment law violations; and 10 percent involved corruption and fraud allegations (Kotwica 2008, 20).

Hotlines appear to be a valuable strategy. Reporting methods include secure lockbox, toll-free telephone number, intranet, and the Web. Service firms are available that offer a hotline reporting program to organizations. To facilitate reporting, a reward and anonymity are used.

GLOBAL PERSPECTIVE

Strategies of the Oil Industry in Nigeria

Many factors influence the planning and implementation of security strategies in diverse regions of the world. These factors include culture, economic conditions, type of industry, political climate, level of corruption, and competence and strength of police and military forces. The oil industry of Nigeria illustrates the diversity of security strategies. The subsequent paragraphs are based on the work of Elliott (2007, 67–74).

Nigeria contains one-sixth of Africa's total population, with 130 million people. It is a haven of corruption and is Africa's largest crude oil producer. Sixty-five percent of the country's budgetary revenue comes from crude oil, in an economy with limited industry diversification, and it is the fifth largest provider of oil to the United States. The country's major oil and gas company is the Shell Petroleum Development Company of Nigeria (SPDC).

The problems of Nigeria are enormous. Residents are angered about not receiving a higher standard of living from the riches being made by foreign oil companies. Heavily armed rebels, who are viewed by the poor as Robin Hood was, are popular; they attack oil facilities and kidnap oil workers. The rebels call themselves the Movement for the Emancipation of the Niger Delta (MEND) and are supported by local communities. MEND maintains intelligence on the location of security forces and where an attack can do the most damage. Compounding the security challenges is Nigerian law, which requires multinational companies to hire Nigerians in numerous positions, increasing the risk of "inside jobs" and the loss of proprietary information. Theft of crude oil is rampant to fund MEND and to support corrupt officials and poor residents. The corruption includes international syndicates that have tankers waiting offshore for stolen crude oil. Corruption also permeates the ineffective government security forces who are supposed to protect the oil companies. The court system is too weak to prosecute offenders. "Finger pointing" between the government and the oil companies results from arguments over the issue of poverty in the oil-rich nation.

As is the case throughout history, when government is ineffective in protecting the private sector, the private sector must take action. In Nigeria, Shell has over 2,500 private security personnel. Most are at the main facility at Port Harcourt, while others are scattered along pipelines trying to curb theft. Shell has implemented a pilot program of three specific strategies.

First, gain the trust and aid of the thousands of communities along the pipelines by hiring residents to guard the lines and provide intelligence. Second, generate positive relations by building schools, clinics, and water projects. Third, launch a pilot program to investigate the viability of physical security consisting of CCTV cameras on tall towers (so the cameras are not stolen), underground sensing cables that send a signal to Port Harcourt for a response, and double fencing around key installations.

Critical Thinking

What are your suggestions for significantly reducing the theft of oil in Nigeria?

Drugs in the Workplace

Substance abuse is a serious and costly problem (Figure 5.6). Comprehensive security programs should consider the impact of drugs in the workplace and work with other internal departments (e.g., human resources) and outside agencies (e.g., alcohol and drug abuse; police) to plan and implement strategies to reduce this problem. The U.S. Department of Health and Human services (n.d.) offers the following figures and facts. About 14.8 million Americans are current illicit drug users, and 77 percent of these users are employed. Full-time, employed users tend to be between the ages of 18 and 25, less educated, male, never married or divorced, white, and low paid. However, many suspects fall outside of these characteristics. The industries with the highest rates of usage are food preparation workers, servers,

FIGURE 5.6   **Substance abuse is a serious and costly problem. (® Shutterstock. com. With permission.)**

bartenders, other service occupation workers, construction workers, and workers in transportation and material moving.

Substance abuse impacts the workplace in several ways. American businesses lose roughly $81 billion in productivity each year due to substance abuse; substance-abusing employees function at approximately 67 percent of their capacity. Up to 40 percent of industrial fatalities and 47 percent of industrial injuries can be attributed to alcohol use. Employees who abuse drugs are 3.6 times more likely to be involved in a workplace accident and five times more likely to file a workers' compensation claim. They cost employers about twice as much in medical claims in comparison to non-drug-using employees. Substance abuse increases absenteeism, tardiness, and turnover. In addition, turnover likely results in another employer hiring the substance abuser, unless the employer maintains quality drug screening. Violence and theft are also linked to substance abuse.

Drug-Free Workplace Strategies

Basic strategies of a drug-free workplace include a written policy, employee education, supervisor training, access to assistance, and drug testing. Such strategies are reinforced through the **Anti-Drug Abuse Act of 1988**, which requires federal contractors and grantees to establish a drug-free workplace. Regulated industries (e.g., transportation) are also required to promote anti-drug abuse programs.

The U.S. Department of Labor (n.d.) offers an online "Drug-Free Workplace Policy Builder" that enables employers to customize anti-drug abuse programs for the workplace. The interactive site consists of thirteen sections, each containing boxes to check for desired program components. Most of the subsequent paragraphs contain verbatim information from this site.

It is recommended that competent legal counsel review the final product prior to implementation. Consideration should be given to the following legally sensitive areas: confidentiality, communicating the policy to all employees, establishing procedures to investigate allegations, providing due process to employees, ensuring quality control of drug testing, conforming to union contracts, and following applicable federal and state laws.

Section 1: What is the purpose of the policy? Two objectives are to send a clear message that substance abuse is prohibited while encouraging employees to voluntarily seek help. Defensible objectives of the policy include health and safety, protection from theft, and compliance with federal and state regulations.

Section 2: Who will be covered by the policy? This can include all applicants and anyone who conducts business for the employer.

The range of individuals can be from top management to interns and volunteers.

Section 3: When will the policy apply? This question requires a thoughtful look at what constitutes "at work" or "on duty," use prior to work, and employer recreational activities that involve alcohol. A sample statement is: "Our drug-free workplace policy is intended to apply whenever anyone is representing or conducting business for the organization."

Section 4: What behavior is prohibited? A standard prohibition statement is: "It is a violation of our drug-free workplace policy to use, possess, sell, trade, and/or offer for sale alcohol, illegal drugs or intoxicants." Some employers include abuse of prescription and over-the-counter medications.

Section 5: Will employees be required to notify the employer of drug-related convictions? The Drug-Free Workplace Act of 1988 requires that any employee who is convicted of a drug-related offense in the workplace must notify the organization in writing within five calendar days of the conviction. Other employers, not subject to the Act, may choose to use this requirement as a standard in their drug-free workplace program.

Section 6: Will the workplace policy include searches? The Drug-Free Workplace Act of 1988 does not require covered employers to perform searches. Also, many states and some cities have legislation prohibiting or limiting searches. Seek legal consultation. If searches are to be a part of the program, set clear guidelines in a separate document and train all supervisory and/or security personnel. A sample policy is: "Entering the organization's property constitutes consent to searches and inspections. If an individual is suspected of violating the drug-free workplace policy, he or she may be asked to submit to a search or inspection at any time."

Section 7: How will drug testing be performed? Most employers are not required to drug test, and the Drug-Free Workplace Act of 1988 does not require that employers perform drug testing, although drug testing may be required under other federal regulations for employees in safety-sensitive and security positions. Many states have drug-testing laws and regulations that determine what types of testing are permissible and under what conditions. Federal agencies conducting drug testing must follow standardized procedures established by the Substance Abuse and Mental Health Services Administration (SAMHSA). While private employers are not required to follow SAMHSA's guidelines, doing so will help them stay on safe legal ground. Court decisions have supported following the guidelines and testing for only those drugs identified in them and for which laboratories are certified. As a result, many employers choose to follow them. Most employers use urine testing for drugs. Other methods include hair, saliva, sweat, and blood. Testing for alcohol is accomplished through an evidentiary breath-testing device.

Section 8: What will be the consequences if the policy is violated? Consequences vary widely and include progressive discipline, required rehabilitation, or termination. Ideally, employees should seek help. They may have special protections under the Americans with Disabilities Act (ADA) as well as under Section 503 of the Rehabilitation Act of 1973. They also may be eligible for Family and Medical Leave Act (FMLA) benefits.

Section 9: Will a return-to-work agreement be used? A sample policy is: "Following a violation of the drug-free workplace policy, an employee may be offered an opportunity to participate in rehabilitation. In such cases, the employee must sign and abide by the terms set forth in a Return-to-Work Agreement as a condition of continued employment."

Section 10: What type of assistance is available? A workplace drug-free program should encourage employees to seek help. Many employers have an Employee Assistance Program (EAP) that offers assistance (e.g., guidance, counseling, and referral) with a variety of personal problems. Assistance may be required under the ADA, the Rehabilitation Act of 1973, the FMLA, and other laws.

Section 11: How will employee confidentiality be protected? A sample policy is: "All information received by the organization through the drug-free workplace program is confidential communication. Access to this information is limited to those who have a legitimate need to know in compliance with relevant laws and management policies."

Section 12: Who is responsible for ensuring the success of the program? A sample policy is: "A safe and productive drug-free workplace is achieved through cooperation and shared responsibility. Both employees and management have important roles to play."

Section 13: How will the policy be communicated to employees? There are several avenues to communicate the policy and program to employees. These include providing a copy to employees, reviewing it during new employee orientation sessions or safety meetings, including it with paychecks, using an intranet, posters and brochures, and conducting training sessions for employees and supervisors.

YOUR CAREER IN SECURITY

Security Consultant

Security consultants have specialized knowledge, experience, and skills and offer these resources to businesses, government, and other organizations for a fee. Many consultants are self-employed, and others work for small or large consulting firms. Consultants offer numerous types of expertise. Examples are marketing, finance, information technology, manufacturing, engineering, international trade, safety, and law enforcement. Each general area of expertise may contain multiple specialties. For instance, security consultants may specialize in physical security and design, aviation security, chemical industry security, retail security, campus security, hospital security, or other specializations.

Nature of the Work

Security consultants are businesspeople. They must plan, budget, and organize their work. Two very important functions in consulting work are marketing and developing new business. These functions are challenging and a consulting business will not survive without success in these two areas. **Marketing** ascertains the needs of clients, and then a service (or product) is offered for a profit. Needs can be researched through a survey to potential clients, an electronic newsletter requesting feedback, networking, hiring a marketing consultant, and other methods. Avenues to develop new business include advertising, a Web site, speaking at professional conferences, word of mouth, and the methods just cited for researching needs. Many consultants have an excellent background, but they are unable to successfully market themselves and develop new business.

The consultant should consider liability insurance, errors and omissions insurance, and other insurance, depending on the type of work to be performed. An insurance agent or professional association can provide direction.

Depending on the locale and the type of security consulting conducted, a business license may be required and/or a private investigative license.

Once a consultant makes contact with a potential client, a proposal is prepared that outlines the work to be performed and the fees. If a client decides to hire a consultant, a contract follows that is based on the proposal and the agreement between the parties.

The actual work by a security consultant for a client varies considerably. A plant manager may request a one-day walk-through at a manufacturing plant to listen to verbal suggestions from the consultant, without a written report. Conversely, a client may request comprehensive services over multiple years that delve into all aspects of corporate security, such as policies and procedures, physical security, and training. Another client may request the presence of a security consultant when security vendors visit the client to sell services and systems, and then request that the consultant serve as a project manager to ensure that the new purchase results in success. This illustration points to the importance of the consultant being independent; in other words, not affiliated with any vendor so that an objective choice can be made for the client's benefit.

Because consultants are often involved with proprietary information as they serve their clients, such information must be protected from disclosure to unauthorized individuals. Clients often require that consultants sign non-disclosure statements to enhance the protection of proprietary information.

Requirements

Security consultants are generally unregulated among the states. Consumers should study credentials and research references prior to retaining a security consultant. A security consultant must excel in the following skills: security expertise, human relations, identification and analysis of complex problems, and verbal and written communications. Integrity and high ethical standards are essential. The desired background includes several years of relevant experience that serve to support expertise. A college degree is important because it is a foundation for learning and developing competencies and skills. Consultants often have a master's or doctoral degree and a record of publications.

Certifications are another valuable trait that provides competitive advantage and shows professionalism, knowledge, and competence. The security profession has several certifications. ASIS International offers three: Certified Protection Professional (CPP), Physical Security Professional (PSP), and Professional Certified Investigator (PCI). The International Association of Professional Security Consultants offers the Certified Security Consultant (CSC) credential.

Membership in professional associations is important because of educational and networking opportunities. In addition, each association requires members to adhere to a code of ethics; this is especially helpful in marketing consulting services, because potential clients often contact references who are familiar with a consultant's work.

Salary

Consulting services is one of the highest paying industries, with an average salary of $900 a week in 2006 (U.S. Department of Labor, 2008). Security consultants earn about $100 to $400 per hour, depending on their background and expertise. Information technology (IT) security consultants often earn the highest salaries.

Advice

It takes years to cultivate the background needed to become a security consultant. The profession is competitive, and practitioners may struggle to survive; many return to work in security positions that ensure a steady income. Others find their niche, maintain a strong client base, and profit from the services they offer.

Summary

Once security methodologies (Chapter 4) are understood, a foundation has been set for security strategies. In the present chapter, a major objective is to assist the reader in learning how to think about and apply generic security strategies that may become specific security strategies specially designed to address the unique needs of an individual entity. The concepts from the objectives of security, security layers, redundancy, security levels, maxims, and force multipliers all enhance the skill level of the security practitioner.

The final sections of this chapter concentrate on the serious workplace problems of violence, theft, and illicit drugs. Security-relevant criminology is explained to provide input for security strategies to counter workplace violence and theft. At the same time, the reader should look to other disciplines, besides criminology, for theories and research helpful to security. The violence section includes the issues of active shooter and mass notification. The theft section explains marking and tracking of assets, antifraud controls, and hotlines. In the section on drugs in the workplace, an emphasis is placed on the U.S. Department of Labor's strategies for a drug-free workplace.

Discussion Questions

1. Three major categories of security are personnel, policies and procedures, and technology. Which of the three do you view as most important and why? Which of the three do you view as least important and why?
2. What are your views of the success of deterrence as applied by private-sector security as opposed to the criminal justice system?
3. What are the differences among security layers, security redundancy, and security levels?
4. Which theories do you view as most useful for private-sector security strategies against violence? Which theories do you view as most useful for private-sector security strategies against theft?
5. What do you view as the five best generic strategies to counter violence in the workplace? How would you prioritize the list? Explain your justification for the priorities in the list.
6. What private-sector generic strategies are applicable to the active-shooter problem?
7. What do you view as the five best generic strategies to counter theft in the workplace? How would you prioritize the list? Explain your justification for the priorities in the list.
8. What do you view as the five best generic strategies to counter drugs in the workplace? How would you prioritize the list? Explain your justification for the priorities in the list.

Practical Applications

5A. Suppose you are on a security team planning security for a new FBI building in Chicago to be shared with other federal law enforcement agencies for a total of 450 employees. The building will be two stories, with two levels underground, totaling over 150,000 square feet. There will be an adjacent two-story parking garage. Each team member is to prepare an individual report to be evaluated by a panel; one plan, or a combination of plans, will be selected. Prepare a report of specific security strategies and include the following: objectives of security, layers, redundancy, government security level, and force multipliers.

5B. Refer to the box in the chapter entitled "Do Not Make These Mistakes: Theme Park-Security." Prepare a report of specific security strategies for the theme park and include the following: objectives of security, layers, redundancy, and force multipliers.

5C. Suppose that you are an armed security officer at a shopping mall; you are the first to respond to an active-shooter event; and you hear people screaming while shots are being fired. Do you wait for backup, or do you find the shooter and neutralize the threat? Before you have a chance to make a decision, three hysterical shoppers run to you, latch on to you tightly, and cry out for help. They do not appear to be physically harmed. What do you do?

5D. You are a security executive for a manufacturing corporation with plants in the United States and overseas. All the plants appear to be experiencing an increase in pilferage that is draining profits. Hundreds of employees are stealing finished products on a daily basis. The products are essentially metal tools and a wide variety of plastic household products. Prepare a report of specific security strategies and include the following: objectives of security, layers, redundancy, and force multipliers.

5E. As a security executive in a corporation, your employer has experienced revenue shortfalls and declining profits, and senior corporate executives are violating laws. You have factual information on falsification of financial statements and lying to government regulators, employees, and stockholders. What do you do?

Internet Connections

American Society for Industrial Security International: www.asisonline.org.
Association of Certified Fraud Examiners: www.acfe.com.
Bureau of Justice Statistics: www.ojp.usdoj.gov/bjs.
Bureau of Labor Statistics: www.bls.gov.

Institute for a Drug-Free Workplace: www.drugfreeworkplace.org/.

Institute of Management Consultants USA, Inc.: www.imcusa.org.

International Association of Professional Security Consultants: www.iapsc.org.

National Clearinghouse for Alcohol and Drug Information: http://ncadi.samhsa.gov/.

National Institute for Occupational Safety and Health: www.cdc.gov/NIOSH.

National White Collar Crime Center: www.nw3c.org.

Occupational Safety and Health Administration (OSHA): www.osha.gov.

OSHA: www.dol.gov/asp/programs/drugs/workingpartners/dfworkplace/dfwp.asp.

Substance Abuse and Mental Health Services Administration: http://workplace.samhsa.gov.

U.S. Department of Labor, Drug-Free Workplace Advisor: www.dol.gov/elaws.

References

Anderson, R. 2008. Communicating in an emergency. *Security Technology & Design* 18 (August):26–29.

ASIS International. 2005. Workplace violence prevention and response guideline. www.asis-online.org.

ASIS International. 2008. Foundation reaches out. *ASIS Dynamics* (January/February):1.

Association of Certified Fraud Examiners. 2008. Report to the nation on occupational fraud & abuse. www.acfe.com/documents/2008-rttn.pdf.

Black, H. 1991. *Black's law dictionary*. St. Paul, MN: West.

Blades, M. 2008. Workplace violence is your problem. *Security Technology & Design* 18 (October).

Building Owners & Manager's Association (BOMA), Calgary. 2006. Laptop theft in commercial buildings, 2006 Survey. Calgary, Alberta, Canada: BOMA Public Safety Committee.

Chudwin, J. 2009. Terror, again. *Law Officer Magazine* 5 (January):50–55.

Clark, J., and R. Hollinger. 1983. *Theft by employees in work organizations: Executive summary*. Washington, DC: National Institute of Justice.

Cressey, D. 1973. *Other people's money*. Montclair, NJ: Patterson Smith.

Davis, A. 2008. Security company sued over Burger King murder. *Security Law Newsletter* 28 (November):127.

Edelman, L. 2008. Workplace violence: Recent suburban tragedy can happen anywhere. *RiskVue* 10 (February). www.riskvue.com/fs0802b.htm.

Elliott, R. 2007. Crude oil and corruption. *Security Management* 51 (June):67–74.

FBI. 2004. Workplace violence: Issues in response. Quantico, VA: FBI.

FEMA. 2003. Primer for design of commercial buildings to mitigate terrorist attacks. *FEMA* 427 (December):5-3. Washington, DC: U.S. Department of Homeland Security.

FEMA. 2005. Risk assessment: A how-to guide to mitigate potential terrorist attacks against buildings. *FEMA* 452 (January). Washington, DC: U.S. Department of Homeland Security.

Glick, L., and J. Miller. 2008. *Criminology*. 2nd ed. Boston, MA: Pearson Allyn & Bacon.

Hayes, R. 2008. *Strategies to detect and prevent workplace dishonesty*. Alexandria, VA: ASIS Foundation.

Helfgott, J. 2008. *Criminal behavior: Theories, typologies, and criminal justice*. Los Angeles: Sage.

Hollinger, R., and A. Adams. 2007. *National retail security survey*. Gainesville, FL: University of Florida.

Horovitz, B. 2007. Late shift proves deadly to more fast-food workers. *USA Today*, December 12.

Johnston, R. 2006. How to conduct an adversarial vulnerability assessment. Speech for the National Security Institute's Impact 2006 Security Conference (April 3–5).

Johnston, R. 2010. Lessons for layering. *Security Management* 54 (January):65–69.

Kotwica, K. 2007. Is your security awareness program all it can be? *Security Technology & Design* 17 (September):20.

Kotwica, K. 2008. On the hotline. *Security Products* 12 (February):532.

Lenz, R. 2008. Kentucky gunman kills five co-workers. Associated Press, June 26.

Mallery, J. 2007. Security cooperation. *Security Technology & Design* 17 (September):44.

Miller, R. 2008. Active shooter response training: An alternative approach. *Law Officer Magazine* 4 (September):58–63.

National Institute for Occupational Safety and Health. 2002. Violence: Occupational hazards in hospitals. www.cdc.gov/niosh/docs.

National White Collar Crime Center. 2002. Embezzlement/employee theft. www.nw3c.org.

Occupational Safety & Health Administration. 1998. Recommendations for workplace violence prevention programs in late-night retail establishments. www.osha.gov.

Occupational Safety & Health Administration. n.d. Workplace violence prevention. www.osha.gov/dcsp/ote/trng-materials/wp-violence/wpvhealth.pdf.

Purpura, P. 2003. *The security handbook*. 2nd ed. Boston: Butterworth–Heinemann.

Sutherland, E. 1937. *The professional thief, by a professional thief*. Chicago: University of Chicago Press.

Sykes, G. 1978. *Criminology*. New York: Harcourt Brace Jovanovich.

Transportation Security Administration. 2006. Layers of security (April 4). www.tsa.gov/approach/layered_strategy.shtm.

U.S. Department of Health and Human Services. n.d. Drugs in the workplace. http://workplace.samhsa.gov.

U.S. Department of Justice. 1995. Vulnerability assessment of federal facilities. Washington, DC: U.S. Marshals Service.

U.S. Department of Labor. n.d. Drug-free workplace advisor. www.dol.gov/elaws/asp/drugfree/drugs.

U.S. Department of Labor. 2007. National census of fatal occupational injuries in 2006. Washington, DC: U.S. Department of Labor.

U.S. Department of Labor. 2008. Occupational outlook handbook 2008–2009. www.bls.gov.

Weadock, M. 2008. Business watch. *Security Products* 12 (November).

Wells, J. 2005. *Principles of fraud examination*. Hoboken, NJ: John Wiley & Sons.

Chapter 6

Personnel Security

Chapter Learning Objectives

After reading this chapter, you should be able to:

1. Define *personnel security* and explain what it entails
2. Define the *insider threat* and describe why it requires increased attention
3. List and describe typologies and characteristics of insiders who offend
4. Identify and describe at least eight strategies to counter the insider threat
5. Explain the importance of preemployment screening
6. Elaborate on legal guidelines for preemployment screening
7. List and explain at least five preemployment screening methods
8. Name and explain two theories of motivation
9. List and describe at least five methods of countering complacency and inattention by security practitioners
10. Explain at least ten strategies of executive and personnel protection

Terms to Know

personnel security

insider threat
critical infrastructure and key resources (CIKR)
globalization
preemployment screening
human resources (HR)
background investigations
record of arrest and prosecution (rap sheet)
Private Security Officer Employment Authorization Act of 2004
Fair Credit Reporting Act of 1971 (FCRA)
Federal Trade Commission
Fair and Accurate Credit Transaction Act of 2003 (FACT Act)
Title VII of the Civil Rights Act of 1964
Equal Employment Opportunity Commission (EEOC)
Federal Bankruptcy Act
Sarbanes-Oxley Act of 2002 (SOX)
Equal Pay Act of 1963
Age Discrimination in Employment Act of 1967
Americans with Disabilities Act of 1990 (ADA)
Financial Modernization Act of 1999
Health Insurance Portability and Accountability Act of 1996 (HIPAA)
diploma mill
fingerprint-based records
name-based records
infinity screening
socialization process
Theory X
Douglas McGregor
Theory Y
Abraham Maslow
complacency
electronic guard tour systems
executive and personnel protection
principal
express kidnapping
crisis management team
advance survey
identity theft
Identity Theft and Assumption Deterrence Act of 1998
personal protection specialist (PPS)
executive protection program
U.S. Secret Service
Bureau of Diplomatic Security
creature of habit

QUIZ

This quiz serves to prime the reader's mind and begin the reading, thinking, and studying processes for this chapter. The answers to all of the questions are found within this chapter.

1. Why is the insider the perfect "plant"?
2. What motivates insiders who offend?
3. Do most companies manage their insider risks?
4. What do the letters *HR* mean?
5. Prior to an external investigative service beginning an investigation of an employee, is the employer that requested the investigation required by law to inform the employee?
6. What is the next level of deceit by diploma mills?
7. Is it illegal for employers to visit social networking Web sites, blogs, and other online locations to screen job applicants?
8. What is the name of the U.S. Army general who was kidnapped by terrorists in Italy?
9. What is the approximate annual salary of personal protection specialists?

Introduction

ASIS International (2005, 8) defines **personnel security** as "ensuring the integrity and reliability of an organization's workforce," accomplished by conducting pre-employment screening and the "adjudication of results and granting security clearances and other information access privileges."

As odd as it may seem, an organization must protect itself from its own employees while providing security for the same employees. This chapter on personnel security concentrates on the insider threat, applicant screening, motivating personnel, and executive and personnel protection.

The Insider Threat

The insider threat can result in violence, theft, and an illicit drug problem. The insider threat is particularly ominous because the offender—an employee, contractor, or someone else linked to the workplace—has knowledge of the organization's security. The offender is familiar with policies and procedures, personnel, and technology (Figure 6.1). Like terrorists and other criminals, the insider can select the time, location, and target for victimization. In addition, the insider has other advantages, beyond those of the outsider. He/she is the perfect "plant," unlikely to be arrested for trespassing or questioned for conducting surveillance of the target. The insider can also manipulate an environment to facilitate a crime. Examples include leaving a

FIGURE 6.1 **The employee insider threat is familiar with policies and procedures, personnel, technology, and security. He or she may appear as a friendly coworker. (® Shutterstock.com. With permission.)**

window or door open, closing the door of a safe but not locking it, disabling an intrusion alarm system, or leaving a laptop computer unsecured.

The National Infrastructure Advisory Council (NIAC) (2008, 11), formed by the U.S. Department of Homeland Security (DHS) to provide the president and DHS with advice on the security of critical infrastructure, defines **insider threat** as follows: "The insider threat to critical infrastructure is one or more individuals with the access and/or inside knowledge of a company, organization, or enterprise that would allow them to exploit the vulnerabilities of that entity's security, systems, services, products, or facilities with the intent to cause harm." **Critical infrastructure and key resources** (CIKR) refer to vital industries and services that, if harmed, could create hardship and adversely affect our way of life, economy, and security. Harm to CIKR can result in loss of life and injuries, interruption of critical services to wide geographic areas, and psychological effects including loss of public confidence in industries, institutions, and government. CIKR are both physical and virtual (e.g., the Internet). Examples of critical infrastructure are agriculture and food, water, energy, transportation, banking and finance, and government and emergency services. Key resources are unique facilities such as national monuments, commercial centers, and sports complexes.

Typologies of Insider Threats

Kirkpatrick (2008, 55–64) writes about typologies of insider threats and argues that by increasing awareness of them, practitioners and researchers can improve their identification of indicators or "red flags" of each type. Although Kirkpatrick uses an inductive approach of using a few cases to develop general conclusions about types of insider threats, more research is needed to support and expand the proposed types that are explained and illustrated here from the work of Kirkpatrick.

One type of insider threat is to seek *revenge by harming or embarrassing* an organization. This may result from an employee not receiving a promotion or pay raise or being laid off. Violence may result, but other scenarios are possible. Justen Deal, a Kaiser Permanente employee, was frustrated over the company's electronic health record system. He e-mailed his concerns to 180,000 employees, and the e-mail resulted in the exposure of Kaiser's projected $7 billion in losses over two years. Deal was fired for sending the e-mail.

Another type of insider threat has a *nationalistic* basis. An employee may feel a sense of loyalty to his or her country of origin. Furthermore, nations may expect their citizens working or studying in the United States to assist the homeland by providing proprietary information on a host of topics, including research and development, which can be very costly to produce. Two distinguished employees of Lucent Technologies, Hai Lin and Kai Xu, legal U.S. resident aliens born in China, were indicted for stealing trade secrets for a Chinese company.

Another type of insider threat, *ideology*, can be linked to nationalist motivations. Terrorists fall within the ideology type. Amin Asmin Tariq was arrested because of his involvement in a fall 2006 plot to use liquid explosives to blow up passenger jets flying from England. He worked as a security officer at Heathrow airport.

The *individual benefit* motive is another type. Three variations are financial gain, career advancement, and beginning one's own business. Harold Worden, a retired Kodak manager, stole formulas, drawings, and blueprints that he sold to China. He recruited over 60 Kodak retirees who had access to proprietary information.

The NIAC (2008: 14) views the insider threat under three typologies: *psychologically impaired, disgruntled, or alienated employees*; *ideological or religious radicals*; and *criminals*. The NIAC notes the following:

- The development of insider typologies is important to understand their actions and to plan countermeasures.
- Insiders are very often identifiable by more than one typology.
- Motivations can be summarized as some combination of revenge, radicalization for religious or ideological objectives, or financial gain.
- Many employees with motivations and malicious intent never commit acts of betrayal. Inhibitions to betrayal include avoidance of adverse consequences and devotion to a specific individual.

- There is a subset to the typologies referred to as the passive or unwitting insider who is easily manipulated. They may be unaware of their exploitation or deceived into a compromising position.

Psychology of the Insider

The NIAC (2008: 15–16) cites Band et al. (2006), from Carnegie Mellon's Computer Emergency Response Team (CERT), in coordination with the U.S. Secret Service National Threat Assessment Center (NTAC), as conducting several research projects on insider threats. Models from the research showed significant commonalities between spies and IT sabotage cases, including personality traits and predispositions for insider betrayals. Characteristics of potential offending insiders noted from this research and the work of Post, Shaw, and Ruby (1998) show difficult or high-maintenance employees with personality issues, a history of rule violations, and possible substance abuse. Psychiatric or medical issues may also characterize the potential offender. These factors should be viewed not necessarily as a profile of offenders, but as a first set of indicators in a "critical pathway" when an individual faces stress in conjunction with a series of steps and events that can lead to offending behavior. The research shows that relying simply on the "disgruntled employee" reason for betrayal is limiting, because insider-threat psychology is more complex. In addition, oversimplification of the insider threat can restrict the scope of planning for countermeasures. The NIAC argues: "Despite the appearance of contrary evidence, there is no direct correlation between disgruntled workers and insider threats. The majority of disgruntled employees, even those with insider predispositions, never come close to betraying their employer."

The Challenges of Confronting Insider Threats

The NIAC (2008: 18–21) noted several challenges to consider in efforts to counter insider threats.

- Awareness and countermeasures vary greatly among CIKR sectors.
- "Industry at large is immature at detecting malicious insiders. Currently, most insiders are discovered after they have already committed a costly malicious act."
- The need for insider-threat countermeasures programs is escalating because of globalization and a globally distributed workforce, supply chain, and service providers.
- The employment of a worldwide workforce, and the collaboration of global business, compounds the challenges of screening job applicants and vetting new business partners.

- The world is becoming increasingly interconnected. Advances in business models, system management, and software tools have increased the reach of insider attack capabilities. Privileged system and network administrators can be located anywhere.
- Technology is affecting generational cultural issues. Younger, technologically savvy employees, with their connectivity to others and virtual-world needs, are facing IT security and corporate boundaries.
- Education and training must continue to address ethics. However, differences among global cultures make this task difficult.
- Global business encounters cultures with differing ethics, norms, and laws. In addition, there is conflict over allegiances among culture, nation, and corporate goals.

Research Needs

The NIAC (2008) recommended paths for research to mitigate the risks from insider threats. A primary issue involves risks from **globalization**. This term refers to world economics becoming increasingly interdependent in a global market. Goods and services produced in one country are sold in other countries, and this massive integration of economies has an impact on culture, labor, politics, and many other components of nations. Research on the insider threat has concentrated on domestic U.S. employers, and there is a need for further research pertaining to the international environment. CIKR operators of multinational businesses need research on global risks to guide them in their mitigation programs. For example, job applicant screening laws vary among nations, and employers may be limited in their opportunities to verify the identity and background of overseas employees. Additional topics for research recommended by the NIAC are the effects of outsourcing, global operations, and diversifying work forces; technological solutions to the insider threat, such as improved information protection technology and data correlation tools to identify threat-related behavior patterns in IT and physical access systems; and the intersection between a history of criminal convictions and employee behavior. The NIAC wrote: "Although there is lots of public debate on the relevance of criminal history records in employment suitability decisions, there is little solid evidence upon which to base these decisions."

Strategies to Counter the Insider Threat

Throughout history, organizations have emphasized perimeter security to keep unwanted outsiders from gaining access. This approach was, at times, at the expense of being oblivious to the insider threat. Such a mind-set still exists today at many organizations.

Owner-operators of CIKR vary in their understanding of the insider threat. According to the NIAC (2008: 18), surveys have shown that "corporate leadership neither completely appreciates the risk nor realizes the potential consequences. As a result, most companies do not actively manage their insider risk." Compounding the challenges for NIAC research is the stigma attached to an act of insider betrayal that can cause business partners, shareholders, and customers to lose trust in an organization. Consequently, owner-operators typically maintain secrecy over such events, which hinders research and a full understanding of the scope of the problem and risks.

The NIAC recommends that leadership for a national insider threat program come from the Executive Office of the President and that government establish a clearinghouse for CIKR operators to assist with assessment and mitigation. In addition, the NIAC strongly supports education and awareness, viewing these two strategies as showing the greatest potential return on investment to motivate CIKR operators and changing the corporate culture so that more resources are focused on the insider threat.

The NIAC (2008: 48–51) recommends a layered approach to protect against the insider threat. When initial strategies fail, such as applicant screening, succeeding layers of protection can prevent harm. The list that follows is primarily from the work of the NIAC.

- Owner-operators need improved information sharing, research, communication of threat information, and risk mitigation.
- Programs to counter insider threats should begin with risk management and risk analysis methodologies, especially because "preventing all insider threats is neither possible nor economically feasible." In addition, predicting future behavior is difficult.
- Controls such as policies, procedures, technologies, and organizational structures help to detect, prevent, and correct harmful events.
- Maintain quality employment applicant screening measures.
- Implement a cross-departmental insider threat approach and response team that includes human resources, legal, IT, and security.
- Establish a strong employee assistance program to help employees who need guidance when personal problems and stress develop. Maintain employee privacy.
- Maintain best practices for physical security and network/IT security.
- Use structured physical and IT access-control systems to minimize access risks. Use trust-based layers to control access to perimeter, outer, and inner layers. Coordinate these systems with human resources systems to account for the status of all workers, including contractors and others.
- Enhance accountability for crimes through prosecution and punishment.

- Since employers grant IT access to employees based on trust, compliance monitoring ensures that that trust is valid over time. When trust is violated, access should be revoked.
- Because of the threat of a combined physical-cyber attack, security against insider threats requires converged physical and IT security systems and procedures.
- Insider studies show that offenders are more likely to act when they believe they will not be caught. Successful security strategies entail clear accountability for actions and setting expectations and boundaries.
- Research shows that when betrayals occurred, management was well aware of offender issues in advance of the incident. Thus, intervention and mitigation are important to prevent harmful events.

Critical Thinking

Do you think the insider threat is a major problem or a minor problem? Explain your answer.

Preemployment Screening

Four questions are answered here pertaining to preemployment screening: What is it? Why is it important? What are relevant legal guidelines? What are preemployment screening methods?

Preemployment screening involves inquiries into the background of employment applicants, interviews of applicants, tests, and other screening methods to select the best possible candidates for an offer of employment. The **human resources** (HR) department in organizations, which manages a host of functions involving personnel (e.g., the personnel needs of the organization, job analyses, position descriptions, recruiting, hiring, training, motivating, retention, discipline, and employee benefits), plays a primary role in preemployment screening. This department typically receives employment applications, conducts initial interviews, and tests applicants. The department in the organization wherein the applicant will possibly work should be represented on the interviewing committee. Since HR functions are guided by numerous laws, court decisions, and government regulations, competent legal counsel is necessary.

Depending on the organization, internal and/or external security practitioners may play a role in the screening process, often through background investigations of applicants. **Background investigations** seek to verify information (e.g., education and experience) supplied by an applicant, check on anything detrimental in an applicant's background that can harm the organization, and help to study risk and level of trust.

Why Is Preemployment Screening Important?

The decision made by management to hire an applicant should be done carefully and never be taken lightly because of the potential negative consequences. Ideally, the best applicant should be chosen who would likely become a team player and assist the organization in reaching its objectives. Possible negative consequences from a poor hiring decision are many, and include the following:

- Increased risk from the insider threat
- Violence
- Theft
- Loss of proprietary information
- Illicit drug use
- Bogus background experience and/or education
- Harm to productivity and/or customer relations
- Costly lawsuits alleging negligent hiring, supervision, and retention
- Harm to a corporation's obligations to shareholders to properly manage the business
- False on-the-job injury claims
- Costly turnover of personnel and related costs of screening new applicants and training new employees

---

Management must do its best to hire an applicant who becomes an asset to the organization, rather than a liability.

DO NOT MAKE THESE MISTAKES

Company Police Department Becomes Magnet for Undesirables

In what turned out to be a magnet for undesirable applicants, a large shopping mall applied to its state attorney general's office to be certified as a company police agency and began hiring applicants with police experience to be certified as company police officers. Unbeknownst to mall management, the new chief, the new assistant chief, and the new lieutenant all had a background that would result in rejection from any organization that conducted a thorough background investigation.

Once the mall was certified as a company police agency, the lieutenant began organizing a police youth organization. His modus operandi was to distribute his business card to young females he met at the mall and at restaurants and invite them to weekly, evening meetings of the police youth group. At the end of meetings, he would discreetly request that a select female stay afterward for "a discussion," during which time the lieutenant would periodically commit statutory rape. The same crime occurred during weekend field trips. With an interest in one particular female, he asked her mother if the daughter could clean his apartment on a weekly basis for pay. The mother and daughter were more than willing to accept the offer, especially from a "trusted" law enforcement officer. The weekly "cleaning jobs" led to the young female's teenage sister accompanying her. When a love triangle blossomed, one of the sisters became upset and told her mother, who contacted the mall police chief. At about the same time, the lieutenant had a party at his apartment, and the attendees included members of the police youth organization and police and security officers employed at the mall. When a mall police captain showed up and saw underage drinking and an X-rated video, he made the mistake of his career by stating to all at the party that "this never happened" (prior to breaking up the party). He did not report the event to his superior.

Before the chief had a chance to react to incoming bad news, city police began an investigation. Eventually, parents sought attorneys for litigation. The result was that several mall police officers and security officers were fired. The lieutenant was successfully prosecuted and incarcerated for statutory rape. The captain was fired because he tried to cover up the party. Following a thorough investigation of the lieutenant, the assistant chief, and the chief, it was discovered that each had a record of on-the-job sexual improprieties during previous employment at police agencies. It was alleged that the previous employing police agencies maintained internal records of the sexual improprieties, but failed to report the conduct to the state standards commission—a source checked during background investigations. The mall should have checked the individual police agencies where the police officers had worked.

The colleges, hospitals, malls, and other entities in this state that become certified company police agencies, and employ company police officers, are required to meet the minimum preemployment and in-service training similar to other police in the state. The state standards commission conducts a background investigation for a fee charged to company police agencies. A police agency is required to report misconduct of an officer to the state standards commission. In addition, a liability insurance policy of at least $1 million is required of company police agencies.

> *Lessons:* The major lesson here is the importance of thorough background investigations. Also, the captain who showed up at the party should have reported what he witnessed. By not doing so, he became part of the problem and paid the price.

Critical Thinking

Do you think those organizations with weak background screening are magnets for undesirable applicants?

Legal Guidelines for Preemployment Screening

Employment law, including law pertaining to preemployment screening, is constantly changing. HR practitioners, and those linked to this profession (e.g., background investigators), keep up with changes while relying on competent legal assistance.

The NIAC (2008) studied the laws pertaining to CIKR applicant screening and referred to the "Attorney General's Report on Criminal History Background Checks" (U.S. Department of Justice, 2006). Much of the information in subsequent paragraphs is from this report, which was prepared in response to the Intelligence Reform and Terrorism Prevention Act (IRTPA) of 2004 that included Congress's interest in enhancing employer access to FBI fingerprint criminal history records. The NIAC noted that employers are increasingly using such records. Prior to the 9/11 attacks, the FBI processed fewer than 7 million noncriminal justice criminal history checks; today the number is over 9 million and growing. Certain regulated industries (e.g., nuclear, banking, aviation, securities, hazardous materials drivers, port workers, and care for children, the elderly and the disabled) are permitted access to federal and state criminal history records through federal statutes. Other employers must conform to state regulations and licensing and provide applicant fingerprints for similar checks. However, the majority of employers lack the legal authority to access fingerprint data and rely on service companies to conduct background checks on applicants.

Those industries with statutory access to federal government records submit applicant fingerprints, typically through a state identification bureau, to the FBI for a national criminal history check. One problem with these federal records for background checks is that the system was designed for the criminal justice system and not for noncriminal justice records checks. While a multistate view of an offender's **record of arrest and prosecution (rap sheet)** is provided, it often omits nonserious offenses available at the state and county level, and it may include information that was purged at the state and county level because of the adjudicative process. The federal data may be missing dispositions on arrests and not include whether arrests led to a conviction, acquittal, dismissal, or other decision. About 45 to 50 percent of FBI-maintained arrest records have final dispositions, compared to 70 to 80 percent of state-held arrest records (U.S. Department of Justice, 2006: 18).

Critical Thinking

Although federal criminal history records are the most comprehensive U.S. criminal history records available, missing dispositions in these records has resulted in concerns over privacy and fair-use issues. What are your suggestions to reduce this problem?

State statutes for access to state criminal history records, as well as the quality of the records, vary. Florida, for example, has about a million records that are not included in the FBI database, and only about 30 percent of the state's arrest warrants are in the federal system.

CIKR employers and other employers (e.g., retailers) who lack statutory access to federal or state criminal history data refer to private investigative firms, background-screening companies, and large consumer data companies that operate multistate criminal history databases gathered from public records available from county courthouses and other sources from across the United States. Since all criminal history information sources contain incomplete or inaccurate data, professional background investigators often double-check or cross-check information on applicants by, for example, running a credit report that shows past residences so that records in those jurisdictions can be investigated.

Public Law 92-544, passed in 1972, has been an avenue for noncriminal justice FBI criminal history checks by state agencies for licensing and employment checks. The state must have enacted a specific statute under PL 92-544 for access to ensure that a designated agency is responsible for screening based upon specific criteria. The Attorney General's Report noted that many states lacked resources to comply with the federal law and serve the needs of the private sector.

Although Congress passed laws to expand access to federal criminal history records for various industries, states often fall short in this effort because of their limited resources. For example, the **Private Security Officer Employment Authorization Act** (PSOEAA) **of 2004**, as part of the IRTPA, authorized private security companies to submit fingerprints to state identification bureaus to conduct FBI criminal background checks on security employment applicants. Unfortunately, state resources fell short again. This is a serious problem, because private security companies play a huge role in protecting CIKR. Federal criminal records contain information from multiple states that can be a better resource in comparison to a check of criminal records in only the state where the applicant applies for a security position. In addition, applicants may use false names and other background information that can be uncovered more comprehensively through a federal fingerprint check.

As noted previously, employers who lack statutory access to federal or state criminal history data often refer to private companies, often called Consumer Reporting Agencies (CRA), who specialize in background investigations and sell information. CRAs maintain files on people that include bill paying habits, lawsuits, arrests, and bankruptcy. A type of CRA is a credit bureau that sells information to employers, creditors, businesses, and others. Several federal and state laws regulate this industry and the use of information. A major law in this regard is the **Fair Credit Reporting Act** (FCRA) **of 1971**. The **Federal Trade Commission** regulates the FCRA and provides regulations and information on this act. Those companies that maintain their own in-house background investigation units, who are in the minority, and that do not use consumer reports, are not bound by the FCRA, but they must conform to other laws. The FCRA:

- Governs the use of criminal history and credit information by CRAs by promoting standards for privacy.
- Is intertwined with state laws that may be more restrictive.
- Requires an employer to notify an employment applicant that a background investigation is to be conducted through a service company, and written permission is required from the applicant.
- Prohibits CRAs from reporting to employers an applicant's bankruptcies after ten years and arrests, civil suits, and other negative information after seven years.
- Requires an employer who does not hire an applicant or who takes adverse action resulting from a criminal or credit investigative report to notify the applicant about these developments, provide a copy of the report and a copy of FCRA rights to the applicant, and offer the applicant an opportunity to explain inaccuracies in the report.

The FCRA was amended through the **Fair and Accurate Credit Transaction Act of 2003** (FACT Act). The FACT Act enhanced consumer rights in dealing with identity theft. It also removed the FCRA requirement that employers must inform an employee *prior to* a workplace investigation being conducted by an external investigative company for cases such as violence, harassment, and theft. The warning of an investigation could cause a suspect to destroy evidence or intimidate a witness.

Numerous federal and state laws, besides the FCRA and state CRA laws, prohibit employment discrimination in the use of background investigative reports. **Title VII of the Civil Rights Act of 1964** prohibits employment discrimination based upon race, color, religion, sex, or national origin. This law prohibits discrimination in numerous HR functions, including recruiting, screening, hiring decisions, pay scales, promotions, and firing. Monetary damages can be awarded for intentional employment discrimination. The **Equal Employment Opportunity Commission** (EEOC), a federal agency, enforces such laws and provides guidelines to employers. For criminal convictions, three factors are to be considered in hiring decisions: the nature of the crime, the time passed since the conviction, and the nature of the job. Lifetime disqualification should be applied only in special circumstances. Financial information (e.g., a credit report from a background investigation) is another potential discrimination concern of the EEOC. The information should be current, job related, show serious financial problems, and the applicant should be provided with an opportunity to explain the situation prior to a denial of a job or promotion. According to the **Federal**

Bankruptcy Act, discrimination is also prohibited against applicants who have a record of bankruptcy when bankruptcy is the sole reason underlying an employment decision.

Additional federal laws that prohibit discrimination and seek fair treatment in employment include the **Equal Pay Act of 1963**, which is enforced through the EEOC, and requires men and women to be paid the same wages when employed in similar jobs at the same location, unless seniority, quantity, and quality of work issues are justified. The **Age Discrimination in Employment Act of 1967**, enforced through the EEOC, prohibits discrimination in employment decisions based upon age. Amendments to this act have deleted a mandatory retirement age, except for reasonable justification. The **Americans with Disabilities Act of 1990** (ADA), also enforced by the EEOC, is like a "Bill of Rights" for people with disabilities. It prohibits discrimination and promotes access to services and jobs. "Reasonable accommodations" in the workplace is a requirement of employers.

The **Sarbanes-Oxley Act of 2002** (SOX), passed in response to corporate financial crimes, requires publicly traded companies to prevent fraud through internal controls that are the ultimate responsibility of senior executives. Many other types of organizations are following SOX guidelines to ensure accountability and good governance. SOX compliance includes background investigations on applicants who are seeking positions linked to financial reporting, corporate assets, proprietary information, and IT systems.

Laws and court cases involving preemployment screening emphasize that all applicant and promotional screening methods must be nondiscriminatory, job related, and valid.

Critical Thinking

Is it fair that employers may have to legally justify why they are denying employment or a promotion to an applicant with a criminal conviction or bad credit? Explain your answer.

Because the preemployment screening process involves the collection of personal and confidential information, privacy law must be considered. An organization must establish policies and procedures to protect such confidential information. This includes the use of the information and by whom, and its storage, security and destruction. The threat of identity theft is a related risk and another justification for controlling access to personal information. The **Financial Modernization Act of 1999** requires "financial institutions" (a broad term including insurance, securities, and credit reporting companies) to provide security over customer information. The **Health Insurance Portability and Accountability Act of 1996** (HIPAA) aims to improve information flow in the health care industry and protect patient information from unauthorized use. Many other federal and state laws pertain to privacy of personal information, and practitioners must seek competent legal assistance.

Preemployment Screening Methods

Two helpful sources for preemployment screening are the "Uniform Guidelines on Employee Selection Procedures" from the EEOC and the "Preemployment Background Screening Guideline" from ASIS International (2006). Both publications are available online.

Although preemployment screening methods vary among organizations and are based upon specific industries and needs, the importance of competent legal assistance cannot be overstated. Besides legal concerns, the foundation of preemployment screening consists of an HR executive, policies and procedures, a system for updating the screening process, and a multidisciplinary committee (e.g., HR, legal, risk management, operations, and security) to provide assistance.

An early step in the screening process is the employer reviewing employment applications (Figure 6.2) and/or resumes. Because applicants strive for

FIGURE 6.2 **Completing an employment application form in person or online is an early step in helping employers screen applicants. (® Shutterstock.com. With permission.)**

employment in a competitive world and may be under financial pressure and stress while seeking employment, exaggerations and false claims are common on applications and resumes and during interviews. Inaccurate information from applicants is a major reason supporting the need for thorough background investigations.

Employers often prefer a standard application for employment to a resume because it provides uniformity in the types of information requested. Typical information requested includes name, address, telephone numbers, social security number, employment history, education, skills, and criminal history, if any. Depending on the position, an application form may request extensive information, such as addresses and employers for the past several years. An important statement on the application requiring the applicant's signature pertains to false information being grounds for withholding an offer of employment or termination. The application should contain a statement requiring the applicant's signature for consent for the employer to conduct a background investigation. Under the FCRA, if an outside service is used for the investigation, then a separate, signed consent form is required.

Web-based recruiting is growing because of cost savings, because the applicant can receive more information about the employer, and because an application can be completed online. For job seekers, Web sites are available that offer the opportunity to post resumes reaching large numbers of employers and recruiters; however, identity theft is a risk, so applicants should never post a social security number, date of birth, address, or other personal information.

BOGUS COLLEGE DEGREES

The federal criminal case of Dixie and Steven K. Randock Sr., a couple from Colbert, Washington, as described in subsequent paragraphs based upon the work of Schemo (2008), illustrates the importance of checking employment applicants thoroughly. The Randocks operated a **diploma mill**, defined by Congress as "entities that award degrees for little or no coursework and that lack accreditation by any government-recognized entity."

When a retired military officer from Syria, a state-sponsor of terrorism, sought degrees in chemical engineering, useful for obtaining a visa to work in the United States, James Monroe University provided assistance. Upon payment of $1,277, the officer received degrees in chemistry and engineering from James Monroe University, which was actually one of 120 fictitious universities operated by the Randocks. The school had no faculty or courses. The retired Syrian officer was actually a U.S. Secret Service agent. A three-year investigation resulted in guilty pleas from the Randocks to mail and wire fraud. They generated over $7 million in revenue and supplied diplomas to over 10,000 customers in 131 countries.

The total number of diploma mills is difficult to pin down; however, such companies sell 100,000 to 200,000 phony degrees annually. In 2006, Congress made it more difficult to investigate diploma mills by eliminating a requirement that online institutions of higher education provide at least half their courses in "brick and mortar" classrooms. In addition, when states crack down on diploma mills, the offenders move to other states.

The U.S. Government Accountability Office found hundreds of federal government employees who had degrees from diploma mills, and more than half worked for the Department of Defense. The investigation of the Randocks showed that fourteen New York City firefighters had used false credentials to gain promotions and raises.

In Washington state, Gutierrez (2009) reported that ten state troopers obtained "questionable diplomas" to boost incentive pay. The troopers were placed on paid administrative leave during an investigation that could result in termination.

The Internet has assisted diploma mills in selling bogus degrees globally by flooding e-mail inboxes with spam without spending a lot on advertising. Modern technology also helps diploma mills appear authentic on the Web by "cutting and pasting" from legitimate sites.

The Randocks also supplied counterfeit degrees from legitimate universities and offered bogus transcripts and letters of recommendation. A special telephone line was established to "verify" credentials when employers called. Moreover, they created accreditation mills in an effort to give an impression of legitimacy to the bogus degrees. This is the next level of deceit, whereby an employer calls an "accreditation association" to seek "verification" that the degree is authentic.

Following a review of applications, an employer selects applicants for the interviewing process (Figure 6.3). Similar questions should be asked of all applicants in a standardized format. Questions can focus on the need for elaboration of education, experience, skills, and other employment-related topics. Employers often use a diverse group of interviewers. Care must be exercised to avoid illegal questions on both the application and during the interview. Examples are questions pertaining to race, religion, height, and weight. EEOC views any screening method, including questions, as having the potential to discriminate. Because certain minority groups are physically smaller than others are, questions pertaining to height and weight can be discriminatory. Questions about convictions are more acceptable than questions about arrests, since a person is innocent upon arrest, until proven guilty. Credit inquiries are another concern of the EEOC. Employers must justify the need to inquire into potentially discriminatory subjects.

FIGURE 6.3 The employment interview is a method of screening applicants. (®️ Shutterstock.com. With permission.)

The extent of a background investigation will vary depending on the type of position, regulatory or legal requirements, if any, the time available, and the cost. A primary objective is to verify the accuracy of information provided by the applicant. The checking of references is another related task; however, applicants usually provide references that are likely to state favorable comments about the applicant. Alternatives are to obtain references from references or query those who have had contact with the applicant, but are not listed as references. This can include interviews of neighbors, friends, and associates who can describe the applicant's character.

A background investigation can focus on many types of information. Examples are education, work history, driving record, credit report, property ownership, bankruptcy, civil suits, professional licenses, military record, criminal history, and sex offender lists.

For those entities that use the services of recruiters, it is important to realize that these people are in business to place job seekers for a fee and not conduct thorough background checks. These service firms do conduct some vetting, such as for education and experience; however, the thoroughness of the checks may be subject to criticism. In one case, a city government paid a recruiting firm $20,000 to locate an "ideal" candidate for city manager. Following a few months on the job, the new city manager was unable to perform his duties because of a lengthy substance abuse problem.

The NIAC (2008: 34) noted that federal and most state criminal history records are **fingerprint-based records**. This ensures positive identification. Those entities that use **name-based records** checks may encounter an applicant living under a different name (e.g., stolen identity), while trying to hide true identity because of a criminal record. This is a significant risk. In addition, the availability of high-quality false documents on the Internet makes verifying identity via fingerprints especially important. "In 1997, roughly six-hundred-thousand of the FBI's fingerprint checks conducted for employment and licensing purposes produced criminal record 'hits', and 11.7% of individuals screened for those hits provided names that were different than what was listed on their criminal history record. These records would have been missed by a name-only check."

The NIAC (2008) recommended that the federal government provide uniform statutory access for CIKR managers to federal fingerprint records to assist with risk assessments of CIKR applicants and employees. At the same time, the NIAC noted that a one-size-fits-all approach is not appropriate because of different risks and intensities of screening among CIKR. The NIAC also argued for the need to encourage, fund, and provide incentives for states to improve records accuracy and presentation.

Gordon and McBride (2008, 11–17) write that in our age of transparency, more and more of what people write or do ends up as a digital fingerprint online that never gets erased. In addition, employers are often Googling applicants before reading applications and resumes! Online resources include MySpace, FaceBook, digital photographs, Web sites, blogs, chat rooms, school and organizational activities, and media reports. With almost everyone having a cell phone with a camera or a digital camera, a photograph or video can be posted with ease without a person knowing his or her "interesting behavior" was captured. Gordon and McBride refer to 2007 research by Vault.com, a career information company, that found that 44 percent of employers visit social networking Web sites when screening job applicants. This figure is probably much higher today.

ASIS International (2006, 24) favors caution when employers use the above online sources because: Certain sites have privacy notices; use of such information must not violate privacy law; allegations of unlawful discrimination can surface if the online research reveals information that can potentially be used to discriminate against an applicant; and the online information may be inaccurate (e.g., false information or a person's head superimposed on a nude body holding contraband). The FCRA does not apply when employers use the Internet directly, without the services of a CRA.

Testing is another preemployment screening method. As with other screening methods, tests must be job related, valid, and nondiscriminatory. Examples of tests are cognitive ability tests, agility tests, medical examinations, personality tests, and drug tests. Honesty tests, which measure attitudes about theft and other topics concerning trustworthiness, are used with increasing frequency because of restrictions on the use of the polygraph (see Chapter 10). Psychological tests are employed for certain critical security positions, such as in the nuclear security field.

The difficulty of ensuring that a preemployment screening test is valid, reliable, and nondiscriminatory is illustrated through the work of Leeds et al. (2003, 63–78), who reported on a novel tool for selecting health-care security officers. This research team studied the use of situational judgment tests (SJTs) that present applicants with written or video versions of critical incidents followed by applicant selection of options to manage each incident. The SJTs in this research were specific to health-care security duties; in other words, they were job related. Although the research results showed "racial group disparity in test performance favoring White persons and Hispanics," this study serves as a model from which to refine and improve the fairness of SJTs for not only health-care security, but also other specializations in security, while improving predictions of job performance.

Another option in screening is to periodically rescreen the work force in an organization. Known as **infinity screening**, this strategy is important because employees may develop negative behavior while employed— behavior that may not have existed prior to their being hired. For instance, periodic driving record checks of employees with driving responsibilities may show unsafe behavior. Rescreening may discover information missed or unavailable during preemployment screening. Nixon (2008, 54–59) recommends developing relevant policies, identifying which sensitive positions to rescreen, following laws, and ensuring that a consent form is signed by employees. Nixon described the case of a woman who became a bookkeeper at a company following a background investigation that showed nothing negative. The company's infinity screening of her, which occurred several years after her hire date, checked her credit history and other records that revealed serious credit problems. This led to an audit that showed her books were being falsified. She had found a loophole in the company's financial tracking system and exploited it to embezzle funds.

Another type of screening is U.S. Department of Defense (DOD) personnel clearances. Armed forces members, federal workers, and defense industry employees must obtain security clearances to gain access to classified information categorized as top secret, secret, and confidential. The DOD maintains 2.5 million security clearances. Delay in determining eligibility is a challenge that can result in risk of loss of classified information, increased contract costs, and problems in attracting and retaining personnel. In 2007, it took 276 days to process a top-secret clearance and 335 days for renewal (U.S. Government Accountability Office, 2008).

SELECTING A PREEMPLOYMENT SCREENING SERVICE

Lester Rosen (2007, 90–92), an attorney and expert on preemployment screening, offers advice on an issue many employers face—whether to perform preemployment screening in-house or to outsource the task. The following guidance is from the work of Rosen.

There is a growing trend in businesses and organizations to outsource preemployment screening, among other functions, while concentrating on the core business. This approach saves employers money, time, and effort in hiring personnel. It also helps to avoid learning the many state and federal laws regulating preemployment screening, seeking legal assistance, and purchasing specialized software.

When selecting a preemployment screening firm, consider competence, experience, integrity, and price. These requirements can be studied through the firm's Web site and marketing materials and by speaking with clients. Check if the firm is a member of professional associations, which improve professionalism, competence, and ethics. Ask the firm if they have 50-state legal knowledge and keep clients updated on regulatory changes. Find out if the firm provides an account manager, rather than a customer service telephone number resulting in a different representative upon every call. The firm should be able to provide customer orientation and meet the needs of each industry, including technology solutions. Modern firms have online systems and options for integration with HR systems. Of particular importance is how the firm obtains up-to-date background information and how it is verified. In addition, because background information is confidential, the firm should have policies and procedures to ensure privacy and data protection.

Critical Thinking

If you were an HR or security executive in a company, would you favor internal or outsourced preemployment screening? Explain your answer.

ISSUE

Ex-Offender Reintegration

The NIAC (2008, 35) presented the issue of reintegration of offenders into society as productive law-abiding citizens. With calls for improved background screening for CIKR and other entities, an unintended effect is the exclusion of individuals with convictions or arrest records and "the creation of a very large class of disaffected, unemployed Americans." This issue is linked to potential discrimination, as covered in this chapter. The NIAC recommends minimizing the effect on ex-offenders and encouraging CIKR managers to consider risk, the type of position, and other factors.

> **Critical Thinking**
>
> What are your views on ex-offender reintegration versus barring ex-offenders from the workplace?

Motivating Personnel

Once preemployment screening is complete and an applicant becomes an employee, orientation and training (see Chapter 3) typically follow. The new employee (in any position) is guided to become a productive contributor to the organization and its objectives, including playing a role in protection.

Experienced coworkers, supervisors, and managers in the workplace participate in what sociologists refer to as the **socialization process**, whereby organizational culture is transmitted from one generation to the next. Macionis (1999, 121) defines socialization as "the lifelong social experience by which individuals develop human potential and learn patterns of their culture." In society, culture consists of values, beliefs, behaviors, material objects, technology, language, symbols, and norms. We see these same characteristics in businesses, institutions, and other organizations. A new employee learns corporate culture from coworkers, through training and study, and by other means. Specific subjects learned include corporate objectives, priorities, and values; policies and procedures; and internal "hot button" issues. Cultural characteristics vary from one organization to another, are unique, and can include answers to questions such as the following: "Who holds the real power in a company?" "What styles of dress are permitted?" "What time does the 10:00 A.M. Monday meeting typically begin?"

From a security perspective, management must ensure that the socialization process is positive and nurturing so that new employees, whether working in security or not, are motivated to assist with the many challenges facing security.

Theories of Motivation

How can management motivate security and nonsecurity personnel in fulfilling the objectives of protection programs? Theories of motivation offer insight into the answers to this question. The theories that follow apply to motivating all personnel, although security examples are presented. Fictitious names are used.

Rush Smith is a corporate security manager for the TECH Corporation, and he oversees 50 security employees. Generally, Rush is negative and cynical. He has a negative view of his security force, feels that they do not like work, and that they do not have initiative to "go the extra mile" with their assignments. Rush believes employees need to be coerced and threatened to complete tasks. Rush seeks tight control over employees and affords them limited discretion. He looks at feedback from anyone as criticism. At the same time, he is quick to find fault in subordinate work performance, and he criticizes them frequently. These views are referred to as **Theory X**, according to **Douglas McGregor** (1960). Contrast these views with those of Mary Ward, a security manager of over 50 security employees at the Clark Corporation. Mary is positive toward her security team, praises good work, and explains why their work is important. She believes her employees like their work, seek to do a good job, and that they can improve their job performance through good management, skill development, recognition, and rewards. Mary sees feedback not as criticism, but as valuable information to improve the customer services her team provides. She facilitates discretion and creativity in employee decision making. Mary motivates employees by working to meet their needs. These views fall under McGregor's **Theory Y**. It produces a management style that motivates employees to do quality work and unlocks their potential and creativity.

With enormous challenges facing security managers and supervisors, it is imperative that they seek introspection to learn their management style and how they treat and motivate employees. The success of a security program depends on motivated personnel.

Mary Ward relies on the work of **Abraham Maslow** (1954) to meet employee needs to motivate them. Maslow's theory of motivation contains a hierarchy of human needs requiring the fulfillment of lower level needs before an individual will seek upper level needs. At the bottom of the hierarchy are *physiological needs* that include food, shelter, and clothing. A paycheck serves to support these needs, as well as a workplace that contains heat and air conditioning and a cafeteria. Once these basic needs are satisfied, *security and safety needs* follow up the hierarchy. Employers provide insurance and other benefits and promote safety and security in the workplace. *Social needs* are next and include the need to interact in a group and have friends. Management can meet these needs through the socialization process, training, coaching, and strategies that promote a team effort and fellowship, such as through a company sports team or periodic picnic. *Psychological needs* are next in the hierarchy of human needs. Management satisfies these employee needs through praise, recognition, and listening to subordinate viewpoints. At the top of the hierarchy are *self-actualization needs*, whereby employees seek to reach their full potential. An employer helps employees satisfy this need through professional development, training, skill building, and promotions.

ATTRIBUTES OF A FLAWED SECURITY PROGRAM

Johnston (2006) lists several attributes of a flawed security program. Here are several of his attributes relevant to security personnel that affect the success of security programs and strategies.

- Insiders are not seen as a possible threat.
- Security managers are micromanaged by unqualified business executives.
- Security practitioners are not encouraged to think on the job and ask questions.
- Security practitioners are hesitant to report problems and vulnerabilities; when exposed, security managers cover them up.
- Security practitioners receive little training and are vague on their duties and responsibilities.
- Low-level security practitioners are treated poorly and are rarely recognized for above-average performance.
- Security practitioners are not briefed at the beginning of their shift, nor debriefed at the end of their shift.
- Relations with local first responders, neighbors, and the public are poor.
- Technology is seen as a silver bullet for security without interface with personnel.

Critical Thinking

What other attributes of a flawed security program can you formulate?

Countering Complacency and Promoting Reliability and Excellence

Complacency refers to "self-satisfaction especially when accompanied by unawareness of actual dangers or deficiencies" (Merriam–Webster, 2009). In the security profession, complacency can result in death, injuries, the loss of profits and assets, and other harm.

The ASIS International definition of personnel security (see the beginning of this chapter) contains a key word relevant to our discussion here. The word is *reliability*. The survival of an organization may very well depend on the efforts of managers and supervisors in countering complacency and promoting reliability and excellence among all employees. Here we focus on security personnel.

Security officers are often considered the backbone of a security program. They are often on the "front lines" acting as gatekeepers while protecting people, assets, and operations. Security officers may be at a stationary post, such as at an access point, or on patrol on foot or in a vehicle. Their basic duties are to observe and report events and to render services to customers.

Periodically, we read accounts of security officers shirking from their duties. WSMV.com (2008) reported that seven security officers were caught sleeping at the Y-12 nuclear weapons plant in Oak Ridge, Tennessee. This plant contains ingredients to make a "dirty bomb" and produces uranium parts for the U.S. nuclear arsenal. Three of the security officers were fired, and the rest were disciplined. Sleeping and inattention when on duty is a problem in the security industry. In another news item, 10News.com (2008) reported that an employee at the San Onofre nuclear power plant in San Diego falsified records for five years, deceiving others into thinking that hourly fire patrols were conducted when they were not. The U.S. Nuclear Regulatory Commission ordered the plant's management to expand its ethics training, develop training to prevent misconduct, conduct an independent assessment of the safety culture, and monitor the corrective action.

COUNTERING INATTENTION

Solutions for inattentive or sleeping security officers include quality applicant screening, orientation, and training; clear policies and procedures prohibiting such behavior; supervision; CCTV with sensors that detect no motion; rewards for excellent work; and discipline.

When officers are on patrol, **electronic guard tour systems** are an option. These systems consist of wands containing special software. A wand looks somewhat like an oversized pen. Another part of the system is buttons, which are computer chips enclosed in a steel case and placed along a patrol route. When an officer places the wand near a button, the wand reads a unique number encoded in the button, and the location, time, date, and officer are recorded. The wand is later downloaded to a computer for a record of the tour. Supervisors must ensure that buttons are secure so an officer does not "cheat" by picking up the buttons on the first patrol round, reading the buttons at one location during the shift, and then replacing the buttons to the original locations on the last patrol round. Anderson (2009, 36–38) writes of a more sophisticated system that applies GPS technology. It features patrol data that can be stored by the security company and the client. The system enables users to track a security officer in real time via the Internet; a password-protected Web site offers a satellite image of the premises and information of the security officer's movements. The officer carries a unit containing a GPS locator and programmable buttons for the input of codes representing various conditions (e.g., fire, burglary). The system can also be used for time and attendance data.

Asken and Paris (2008, 42–43) write about how to counter complacency in policing. Several of their suggestions are applicable to security practitioners. They note three sources of complacency: innate complacency that predates one's career; complacency learned over one's career; and situational complacency that results from the workplace environment. Asken and Paris argue that some practitioners bring too much ego or machismo to the job, causing a lax attitude toward vigilance and respect for policies and procedures. They claim that officers who overestimate their own ability or do not appreciate threatening situations because of ego or inexperience become more dangerous over time. Asken and Paris refer to "social loafing" as behavior characterized by slacking off because of the viewpoint that someone else will do necessary tasks, such as preparation and taking precautions. They argue that this can be a lethal assumption, because even if everyone else does their job, the complacent officer creates unsafe conditions for others. They add that rationalizations such as "it was fate" or "their number was up" are excuses that may be used to justify complacency. Here are measures to counter complacency from Asken and Paris:

- Communicate complacency awareness and acknowledge the importance of vigilance.
- Use reminders and creativity to keep the messages alive.
- Ensure that all personnel know that no one is ever fully trained or experienced.
- Instruct personnel on the duty mind-set using tactical performance imagery. This means to mentally rehearse possible actions when a call or service request is received.
- Use affirmations such as "I am not complacent; I am actively aware at all times when on duty."
- Use self-reviews to improve performance after rendering service or answering a call.

DO NOT MAKE THESE MISTAKES

Arming Security Officers

As president of a contract security company, one of your clients, a regional hospital, requests that you prepare a security business proposal and plan to arm security officers at the hospital. Your major concerns are that, although arming officers with firearms serves as a deterrent, it also increases both liabilities and costs for your company and the hospital. Management at the hospital states that senior executives and legal, risk management, and human resources personnel carefully considered their decision. They also conferred with management at other hospitals, and they are concerned about violence in the workplace, active-shooter incidents, and terrorism.

You are not sure if some of the officers you have assigned to the hospital are capable of qualifying on the firing range and handling firearms on the job. In addition, you are not exactly sure where at the hospital armed officers are needed the most. However, you conduct a risk analysis, prepare a security business proposal, submit it to the client, and it is approved.

Although a security supervisor at the hospital implores you to avoid arming two specific security officers, you overrule the recommendation and include them in training and arming because of their extensive longevity and loyalty. Subsequent to this decision and the arming of all security officers, a Saturday night scuffle at the hospital emergency room results in one of the security officers in question accidentally shooting and killing a nurse. A lawsuit follows.

Lessons: Carefully screen officers to be armed and place more emphasis on subordinate recommendations because they are often closer to certain problems and challenges.

Critical Thinking

What options would you have considered early on as president of this security company prior to arming the hospital security officers?

DO NOT MAKE THESE MISTAKES

Keys Locked in Vehicle

Security Officer Marc Fipps was patrolling the parking lot of the Centerville Square Mall when he spotted a subject near a vehicle. The subject requested assistance with keys locked in his vehicle. Officer Fipps knew he had a slim-jim (i.e., a lockout tool) stored in his company vehicle, but there were no liability forms available in his vehicle for the subject to sign in case the vehicle was damaged while he was trying to unlock the vehicle. Officer Fipps proceeded anyway, and while trying to unlock the door, the driver's side window broke. At about the same time, the true owner of the vehicle appeared.

Lessons: Prior to going on patrol, officers should have proper equipment, forms, and so forth. In addition, verify the owner of the vehicle by requesting identifying information.

Critical Thinking

As a security officer, what do you do if the owner of a vehicle needing assistance in unlocking their vehicle claims that their ID is locked in the vehicle?

DO NOT MAKE THESE MISTAKES

Was It a Burglary?

Roger Gault liked working second shift as a security officer at Miller Industries, because once he completed his duties, he had opportunities to study for college courses. Usually, he was the only person on the premises after 6:00 P.M. One summer evening, about 7:00 P.M., he was patrolling inside the huge warehouse when he heard someone toward the back of the warehouse. He quickly made his way to the front of the building to see if an employee had signed in, according to policy and procedure, and if another employee vehicle was in the parking lot. Upon seeing neither, he rushed back to the warehouse and continued to hear someone. Since he was unarmed, he picked up a shovel and slowly walked toward the back of the warehouse, until he heard the person walking toward him. Quickly hiding behind some large bins, Roger feared for his safety as he waited in the dim light of the warehouse. As the subject walked by, Roger struck the subject with the shovel on the side of the head, causing the subject to fall to the ground. Next, Roger checked the subject, who was unresponsive. Roger recognized him as Milton Vaught, the plant manager. Roger telephoned 9-1-1 for an ambulance. He also telephoned his supervisor.

Milton Vaught recovered from his injuries and sued the contract security company employing Roger. Roger was fired, even though he explained to his supervisor that he thought the plant manager was a burglar, that no one had signed in as required by policy and procedure, and that no vehicle was in the parking lot (except for his own). Milton Vaught's wife had dropped him off at the back of the warehouse, which explained why Roger saw no additional vehicle in the parking lot. Vaught used his master key to enter the warehouse.

Lessons: Once Roger suspected a burglar on the premises, he should have telephoned both 9-1-1 for police assistance and his supervisor. The plant manager should have signed in according to policy and procedure.

Critical Thinking

What can security managers and supervisors do to prevent the mistakes described here? Although security personnel are charged with protecting people and assets, in what ways can they harm protection efforts and what are the solutions to these problems?

Executive and Personnel Protection

Executive and personnel protection (EPP) consists of programs and strategies implemented by specialists who strive to protect employees, their families, and others linked to the organization. Executive protection focuses on senior leaders in an organization, whereas personnel protection concentrates on employees in general.

The threats of concern in this security specialization are numerous. The previous chapter covered violence in the workplace and countermeasures to protect *all* employees and those linked to the workplace. EPP extends beyond an organization's premises and is broader than protection against violence. A top executive's family, home, office, and travel plans may require protection. Murder, assault, kidnapping, robbery, and burglary are serious threats. Disgruntled employees, layoffs, and street criminals are additional security concerns. At the same time, an executive speaking at a university, for instance, may need protection from demonstrators or such nonlethal actions as eggs being thrown at the **principal** (i.e., the person being protected).

Because of international business, many employees and their families work and travel globally. The risks include civil unrest, terrorism, infectious diseases, and natural and human-made disasters that can also occur domestically. EPP should plan for possible emergency evacuation and medical emergencies. EPP specialists not only provide close personal protection, but also crime-prevention information, and they brief employees on security, safety, and health in the United States and in other countries.

As with violence in the workplace, an employer has a legal obligation to implement EPP programs and strategies that are reasonable and customary to ensure safety based on foreseeable events. (Chapter 9 explains *foreseeability*.) In addition, organizations should avoid concentrating on protecting only executives while neglecting employees in general. Sales people, truck drivers, and employees who work at home are examples of employees who should receive training and reminders on security and safety. Protection also includes organizational sites that are in varied geographic locations, while considering unique needs. A lawsuit alleging negligent security can result from harm to employees. A research company hired by Control Risks (2007) interviewed 1,040 business travelers in the United States (501) and England (539) and found that terrorism and natural disasters play heavily on their minds. The research showed that almost two-thirds of British companies and almost half of U.S. companies have no clear travel security policy. The survey results showed that over half of the employees in each country would consider litigation if an emergency event were not handled properly, and that nearly 90 percent of British and 80 percent of U.S. business travelers see their employers as having a legal obligation to advise and support them when abroad.

GLOBAL PERSPECTIVE: KIDNAPPING CASES

Jenkins (1985) offers interesting descriptions of kidnapping cases. He describes the 1976 case of Richard Oetker, age 25, and descendant of a German family owning a huge business fortune. Oetker was kidnapped after leaving a campus building in a small Bavarian town and kept in a small wooden crate. While in the crate, he assumed a bent and cramped position while connected to electrodes that ensured his death upon escape. Two days later, the family paid a ransom, and he was found in a forest. He was crippled for life because electrical shocks had cracked two breastbones and both thighbones; he had an irregular heart rhythm; and a lung collapsed because of shallow breathing in the cramped space. Two years later, an unemployed economist was arrested because a banknote from the ransom was used, and it was linked to him.

Jenkins also describes the 1981 kidnapping of U.S. Army Brigadier General James Dozier, in Italy, by Red Brigade terrorists. Dozier's security consisted primarily of an armed driver who traveled multiple routes to and from Dozier's apartment. However, other security precautions were not adopted. The terrorists disguised themselves as plumbers and gained access to Dozier's apartment in Verona, Italy. The terrorists subdued the general after a struggle, put him in a truck, and tied and gagged his wife. Four hours later, neighbors heard the general's wife and rescued her. The terrorists held him for 42 days, in a tent, in an apartment above a supermarket. He was handcuffed to a cot, earphones were placed over his ears, and he was permitted to eat and bathe. Although no military secrets were sought, he was interrogated, "tried" for "imperialism," and communiqués were issued from the Red Brigade. The terrorists intended to negotiate release of their members held in prison. An Italian antiterrorist police unit raided the hideout, and without bloodshed, Dozier was rescued.

Based upon good intelligence, Dozier was warned prior to the kidnapping. His response was (Jenkins 1985, 260): "Quite frankly I was so busy in the last months before the kidnapping that I paid no attention to those threats. I accept full responsibility for not heeding the warning." Jenkins added that, overseas, protection is enhanced through efficient local police and intelligence services and cooperation from the victim's own government. Jenkins noted the shortcoming of Dozier in not adopting residential and other security precautions, not screening visitors to his apartment, and continuing with a set routine.

Today, kidnapping is big business globally. Large worldwide corporations are especially vulnerable because they are known to pay large ransoms, backed up by kidnap insurance. The topics of executives being kidnapped, kidnap insurance, and ransoms paid for the return of captives are often secretive to reduce the incentive for future kidnappings. Many kidnappings are not reported, which presents problems for data collection, research, and planning countermeasures.

Barham (2008, 49–55) reports that Mexico is the top location for kidnappings, with two to three people being victimized in Mexico City every day and about ten abducted daily in other locations in Mexico. The problem is fueled by police inefficiency, corruption, and the drug war. He writes that **express kidnapping** is booming. It refers to victims being held for a few hours, until they withdraw money from their ATMs or other sources. Second on the list in top-ten locations for kidnapping is Brazil, followed by Columbia, Venezuela, Philippines, Nigeria, Chechnya, Afghanistan, Iraq, and Haiti.

Strategies of Executive and Personnel Protection

The costs of executive protection for one principal can be in the millions of dollars per year. Since protection may entail 24/7 coverage, and if each practitioner costs $150,000 annually (salary, benefits, equipment, training, travel, and other expenses), a four-person team can total $600,000 annually. If a spouse and children require protection, the cost rises. Another expensive cost can be the vehicle used to transport the principal. Depending on the level of protection installed in the vehicle, costs can reach several hundred thousand dollars. Physical security is another expense to protect the principal at home and at the office. Portable security systems (e.g., motion sensors and CCTV) are helpful for hotels and other locations away from home. GPS is another tool.

Several sources offer lists of tips for EPP. Oatman (2007) offers the following, with a leaning toward executive protection (EP):

- Establish a corporate **crisis management team** of executives and specialists (e.g., top executives, attorney, risk manager, and security) to prepare and respond to emergencies.
- Seek to understand the "big picture" of risks and consider simple and basic strategies.
- Plan for flight, not fight (Figure 6.4). Escape from the attack.

FIGURE 6.4 **An executive protection specialist must plan for an escape with the principal upon being attacked. (® Shutterstock.com. With permission.)**

FIGURE 6.5   An advance survey facilitates security and safety wherever a principal visits. (® Shutterstock.com. With permission.)

- Conduct threat assessments. Research what may attract offenders to the principal, crime rates, and threats against the principal and the organization. Assess travel habits, plans, and home and office security.
- Conduct an **advance survey** to assess travel and destination; evaluate mode of transportation, lodging, restaurants, and other sites the principal will visit (Figure 6.5). This includes many details, meeting with employees at destinations, and checking with first responders and medical facilities.
- Use private aircraft whenever possible to avoid busy, public airports and aircraft where someone may recognize the principal.
- Conduct countersurveillance. In other words, watch if anyone is watching.
- Stress the importance of planning. Offenders have the advantage of selecting the time, the place, the equipment, and the ploy. They will likely attack with their finger on the trigger of a firearm or a detonator. An EP specialist may not be able to pull out a firearm quickly when flight is a priority. This is why planning is so important. In addition, carrying firearms into other jurisdictions and countries presents challenges.
- Periodically brief the principal and his/her family on current threats and provide information on precautions.

Katz (2008) offers these tips:

- An important behavior of self-protection is learning to pay attention to the surroundings.
- If you see the same person or vehicle three different times, someone may be following you.
- If you notice surveillance or are being followed, go to a well-lighted and populated area, a police station, a hospital, a shopping mall, or the U.S. Embassy or the embassy of a friendly nation.
- When abroad, the U.S. Department of State recommends contacting the embassy or consulate as soon as possible upon suspecting you are being followed.
- Dress and act conservatively. Do not flaunt affluence.
- If renting a vehicle, remove rental information that would signal that you are a foreign visitor. Hide valuables from view.
- More Americans are killed abroad from traffic accidents than from all other causes combined.
- Seek a vehicle with a good crash rating and airbags.
- Request power locks and climate control (so the windows do not have to be down).
- Seek a safe hotel with security and a sprinkler system. Request a second-floor room because the first floor may be more subject to burglary. Never open a door to a stranger. Notify the front desk of the visitor.
- Call the embassy or consulate to find out the best and safest hotel. They probably did their homework in checking out the hotel.
- For conducting travel homework, check the following sources: U.S. Department of State: www.travel.state.gov; CIA: www.cia.gov/library/publications/the-world-factbook/index.html; and Centers for Disease Control: www.cdc.gov/travel/default.aspx.

The U.S. Department of State, Bureau of Diplomatic Security, offers an online publication entitled, "Personal Security: At Home, On the Street, While Traveling" (www.state.gov/m/ds/rls/rpt/19773.htm). It contains lists of tips on security at home, while traveling, and in hotels. Topics also focus on child safety, sexual assault prevention, letter and parcel bombs, carjacking, and surveillance. Another source is the Overseas Security Advisory Council (OSAC): www.osac.gov.

U.S. citizens traveling or residing in other countries can benefit from the services of the U.S. Department of State's Office of American Citizens Services. It provides emergency services to U.S. citizens in case of victimization, medical evacuation, death, arrest, and financial difficulty.

The Web and Identity Theft

An EPP team should use the Web to enhance security. To begin with, if a principal is affiliated with an organization, its Web site should be studied from the perspective of an adversary, and information helpful to an adversary should be brought to the attention of those in the organization in an effort to have it removed. As noted previously, in our age of transparency, a lot of information about people is in digital form online. This includes professional sites, media reports, blogs, and social sites. Conduct a wide search of the Web for information on the principal and his/her family, note harmful information, including items that can result in identity theft, and suggest that the items be deleted, if possible.

Identity theft refers to the illegal acquisition of another person's personal identifying information. Obtaining another person's identifying information is a crime under several laws, as is the use of such information for personal gain through fraud. The **Identity Theft and Assumption Deterrence Act of 1998** made this crime a federal offense, bringing federal personnel and resources into combating the problem. Subsequent amendments expanded the criminal elements to aggravated circumstances and terrorism, while increasing penalties.

Security practitioners in general, and those involved in EPP in particular, should be knowledgeable of the identity theft problem and work with the employees they serve on prevention strategies and steps to take when the crime occurs. This entails teaching employees through short talks and providing resources, possibly through an organization's intranet.

Efforts are ongoing to hinder the identity theft problem. It affects more than eight million people, according to the Federal Trade Commission (FTC). The federal government's Identity Theft Task Force formulated over thirty recommendations, including the reduction in the use of Social Security numbers, public awareness, guidance on data security for the private sector, and working with local police. Challenges include 14,000 variations of certified birth certificates. The federal government is seeking to share more information with organizations (e.g., motor vehicle departments) to prevent ID theft (Spadanuta 2009, 16–18).

For businesses, several strategies can be applied to the threat of identity theft. Here are some suggestions from Greene (2007): knowing what personal information is on hand and where it is stored, destroying what is not needed, using passwords to control access to sensitive data, and avoid collecting personal information unnecessarily (e.g., collecting Social Security numbers to identify customers). (More on information security in Chapter 8.)

The FTC Web site (www.ftc.gov) offers numerous lists of strategies for consumers to prevent and "fight back against identity theft." ID theft occurs through the following examples: stealing a wallet, purse, mail, personal garbage, or employer information; phishing, which entails bogus e-mails purporting to be legitimate businesses to cause a victim to release ID information; and skimming credit/debit cards through the use of a storage device when a victim makes a legitimate purchase. The FTC offers numerous recommendations. Examples are shredding personal documents before discarding them and not giving ID information out unless you are positive about who is requesting it and why it is needed.

An amendment to the Fair Credit Reporting Act requires each of the major nationwide consumer reporting agencies to provide consumers with a free credit report once every year. A report can be ordered from each agency from the following e-mail address: www.annualcreditreport.com, or call toll free at 1-877-322-8228.

YOUR CAREER IN SECURITY

Personal Protection Specialist

A **personal protection specialist (PPS)** protects an individual from physical harm and other threats. Several terms are applied to this profession, including bodyguard, close-protection officer, and executive protection specialist. The Web offers information on this profession and various associations that are actually businesses that provide training, networking, and protection services to clients.

The personal protection profession spans both the private and public sectors. Large corporations often maintain an **executive protection program** to ensure the security and safety of top executives wherever they may reside or visit. This protection extends to the executive's family. The program often includes a crisis response committee and plans, risk management, and kidnap and ransom insurance. Besides proprietary (in-house) personal protection programs, many people hire a PPS on a contract basis for short-term or long-term assignments. Such clients include celebrities, politicians, and wealthy individuals.

In the public sector, the **U.S. Secret Service** protects the president, the family of the president, and other officials. The U.S. State Department's **Bureau of Diplomatic Security** safeguards U.S. missions and related dignitaries and employees overseas. On the state and local levels, governors and large city mayors are protected by PPSs.

Nature of the Work

A PPS works long hours because the principal requires 24-hour protection. A team may provide relief from long shifts; however, the hours extend to evenings and weekends. Wherever the principal goes, the team goes, and the travel can lead to overseas locations.

A PPS must be attentive and alert at all times while protecting the principal. The ability to react quickly to a threat and utilize PPS skills is of the utmost importance, especially since an adversary is unlikely to provide a warning.

A professional in this vocation plans protection for the principal, conducts research, investigates, performs security assessments and advance surveys, and attends training courses. The protection of a principal must be based on a comprehensive plan that considers numerous vulnerabilities. A PPS seeks media reports of violence, protest, adverse weather, and other conditions. Individuals and groups, volatile locations, and certain technologies that present a threat must be identified. Resources include the Web, U.S. Department of State, peer networks, and private firms.

The office and residence of the principal require a constantly updated security assessment. Hotels, restaurants, office buildings, and other locations require advance surveys to check security, police protection in the area, parking, neighborhood, nearest hospital, and many other issues.

PPSs are often equipped with a radio, nonlethal and/or lethal weapons, and possibly a bullet-resistive vest. Training is of the utmost importance to offer the best possible protection and to optimize equipment usage.

One challenge facing the PPS is to avoid becoming a **creature of habit**. An individual is more vulnerable when predictable. If, each day, a principal travels the same route to work, arrives at the same exact time, and follows a precise pattern with other daily activities, then the planning of an attack becomes easier for an adversary. Another challenge for the PPS is to train the principle and his or her family in safe behavior, especially when the topic may be a lower priority than other thoughts and activities.

Requirements

Generally, the personal protection industry is unregulated in the United States. Consumers should study credentials and research references. Although a college education is desirable by employers, a heavy emphasis is placed on training and experience in personal protection from military, security, or police organizations. Applicants must be in excellent physical condition. PPSs may be specialized in multiple fields, such as weapons, explosives, martial arts, portable security systems (e.g., intrusion and CCTV), and technical surveillance countermeasures (i.e., defeating "bugs" and other spying equipment).

Besides government training programs, private PPS (or bodyguard) schools are available (see the Web). Training subjects include security, intelligence, countersurveillance (i.e., watching for adversaries conducting surveillance), crowd screening and control, defensive tactics, armed and unarmed combat, evasive driving, first aid, dress and appearance, and culture and languages.

Salary

According to Bodyguard Careers (2008), several factors influence the earnings of PPSs or bodyguards. These include prior experience, skills and training, level of risk, amount of travel, and type of client. Factors that can garner higher earnings are military, police, or security experience, fluency in multiple languages, and medical training. Former U.S. Secret Service agents are often in demand because of their experience and training. Earnings for PPSs can range from $350 to $700 per day. Experienced PPSs can earn $100,000 annually, plus bonuses. Many earn more than $70,000 annually.

Advice

The work of a PPS, as with many other occupations, can be interesting and exciting, but it can also be boring and tedious at times. Understand the challenges that face PPSs, study the vocation, and speak with practitioners. Do you like to travel? Can you accept working different shifts and during weekends and holidays, away from family and home?

Summary

Personnel security aims to ensure honest and reliable employees who benefit an organization. It includes efforts to counter the insider threat, preemployment screening, motivating personnel to enhance security, and executive and personnel protection.

The insider threat is receiving increasing attention from the public and private sectors because of the devastation it can cause. Insiders have tremendous advantages over outsiders when planning and executing attacks and other harm. For example, the insider is typically familiar with security and may even be embedded in the security force. The National Infrastructure Advisory Council (NIAC) is a rich source of information on the insider threat, especially in reference to protecting critical infrastructure and key resources (CIKR). The NIAC study of the insider threat, which is covered in this chapter, includes typologies and psychology of the insider, the challenges of confronting the threat, research needs, and countermeasures.

Preemployment screening is a major strategy to counter the insider threat, and it entails numerous complex issues. Examples are legal guidelines, antidiscrimination laws, deciding on the intensity of the screening, lawful access and use of public- and private-sector data, and deceptive practices of applicants.

An integral component of security is security personnel who are reliable and motivated. Complacency has no place in security. Security supervisors and managers must implement programs and strategies that promote reliability and excellence; the survival of the security organization, and the enterprise itself, depends on these efforts.

The last part of this chapter concentrates on executive and personnel protection (EPP). Such programs and strategies should be integrated with efforts that protect against workplace violence. However, EPP extends beyond the premises and is much broader than protection against violence in the workplace. Both types of programs entail employer legal obligations, and an employer should avoid concentrating on protecting only executives at the expense of employees in general (e.g., sales people and truck drivers). Executive protection often focuses on an executive and his or her family, their residences, the workplace, and while traveling. A broad perspective should always be maintained on EPP, including the Web and identity theft.

Discussion Questions

1. Why is the insider threat a serious concern of the federal government, besides other entities?
2. What challenges face the public and private sectors in confronting the insider threat?
3. Why would a company maintain secrecy over harm caused by an insider?
4. What do you view as the most important preemployment screening method? What do you view as the least important preemployment screening method?
5. Do you think laws pertaining to preemployment screening are unfair to employers? Explain your answer.
6. What are the best strategies to motivate employees?
7. Do you think employers overemphasize executive protection at the expense of protecting employees in general? Explain your answer.
8. What are the benefits and detriments of being a personal protection specialist?

Practical Applications

6A. As a security executive for a research and development company, your boss has requested a report from you that answers three questions: Why do we need a plan to counter the insider threat? What will be in the plan and what strategies are most appropriate to counter this threat? What are the approximate costs? Prepare the report for your boss who expects it in five business days.
6B. Through the Web, research the preemployment screening process of the FBI.
6C. Suppose you are a new security manager for a large manufacturing plant in the United States. Your top priority at this time is correcting the following problems of security officers: sleeping on third shift, inattention at access points, poor report writing, and a general lax

attitude about security duties. What are your plans and strategies to correct these problems?

6D. You are a personal protection specialist in charge of a four-person detail that protects a top executive of a large oil corporation. Your next assignment is to protect the executive during a trip to a major university to give a speech on energy. The executive will travel with her spouse on a private jet and stay in the university town for one night at a hotel. How will you protect these people on this trip?

6E. As a personal protection specialist, you are assigned the task of conducting research on Thailand, the next destination your protection team will visit while protecting a corporate executive. Prepare a report on Thailand and include the following topics: country description, entry and exit requirements, safety and security, crime, medical facilities and health information, road and aviation conditions, embassy location, and the Web sites you visited for the information.

Internet Connections

American Psychological Association: http://www.apa.org/.

ASIS International, Preemployment Background Screening Guideline: www.asisonline.org/guidelines/guidelines.htm.

Bodyguard Careers: www.bodyguardcareers.com.

Carnegie Mellon, Insider Threat Research: www.cert.org/insider_threat/.

Council for Higher Education Accreditation: http://www.chea.org.

Equal Employment Opportunity Commission: www.eeoc.gov.

Federal Trade Commission: www.ftc.gov/.

International Bodyguard Association: www.ibabodyguards.com.

National Association of Professional Background Screeners: www.napbs.com.

Overseas Security Advisory Council (OSAC): www.osac.gov.

Society for Human Resources Management: www.shrm.org.

U.S. Department of Education (database of accredited schools): http://www.ope.ed.gov/accreditation.

U.S. Department of Labor: www.dol.gov/dol/allcfr/Title_41/Part_60-3/toc.htm.

U.S. Department of State: www.state.gov.

U.S. Department of State, Bureau of Diplomatic Security: www.state.gov/m/ds/.

U.S. Secret Service: www.secretservice.gov.

References

10News.com. 2008. San Onofre nuclear plant caught falsifying records, January 14. www.10news.com/print/15047670/detail.html.

Anderson, T. 2009. Keeping tours on track. *Security Management* 53 (March):36–38.

ASIS International. 2005. *Career opportunities in security.* Alexandria, VA: ASIS International.

ASIS International. 2006. Preemployment background screening guideline. www.asisonline.org.

Asken, M., and C. Paris. 2008. Keep them sharp: 10 countermeasures to fight complacency. *Law Officer Magazine* 4 (March):42–43.

Band, S., et al. 2006. *Comparing insider IT sabotage and espionage: A model-based analysis.* Pittsburgh, PA: Carnegie Mellon University.

Barham, J. 2008. Outwitting the outlaws. *Security Management* 52 (December).

Bodyguard Careers. 2008. www.bodyguardcareers.com/bodyguard-salary/.

Control Risks. 2007. The Business Travel Report 2007. www.crg.com.

Gordon, G., and R. McBride. 2008. *Criminal justice internships: Theory into practice.* 6th ed. Newark, NJ: Matthew Bender & Co.

Greene, C. 2007. Identity theft is your business. *Fraud Alert.* www.mcgoverngreene.com.

Gutierrez, S. 2009. No charges in online diploma inquiry. *Seattle Post-Intelligencer,* February 2. http://seattlepi.nwsource.com.

Jenkins, B. 1985. *Terrorism and personal protection.* Boston, MA: Butterworth.

Johnston, R. 2006. How to conduct an adversarial vulnerability assessment. Lecture at the National Security Institute's IMPACT 2006 Security Conference, Falls Church, VA. April 3–5.

Katz, D. 2008. Protecting the international business traveler. *Loss Prevention* 7 (July-August).

Kirkpatrick, S. 2008. Refining insider threat profiles. *Security* 45 (September):56–64.

Leeds, J., et al. 2003. The development and validation of a situational judgment test for security officers. *Security Journal* 16:63–78.

Macionis, J. 1999. *Sociology.* 7th ed. Upper Saddle River, NJ: Prentice Hall.

Maslow, A. 1954. *Motivation and personality.* New York: Harper & Row.

McGregor, D. 1960. *The Human Side of Enterprise.* New York: McGraw-Hill.

Merriam-Webster. 2009. Complacency. *Merriam-Webster's On-Line Dictionary.* www.merriam-webster.com.

National Infrastructure Advisory Council. 2008. The insider threat to critical infrastructures (April 8). www.dhs.gov/xprevprot/committees/editorial_0353.shtm.

Nixon, B. 2008. Taking screening to the next level. *Security Management* 52 (March):54–59.

Oatman, R. 2007. Executive protection in a new era. In *Encyclopedia of Security Management,* ed. J. Fay. 2nd ed. Burlington, MA: Butterworth-Heinemann.

Post, J., E. Shaw, and K. Ruby. 1998. The insider threat to information systems: The psychology of the dangerous insider. *Security Awareness Bulletin* (June).

Rosen, L. 2007. Selecting a pre-employment screening solution. *Security Technology & Design* 17 (September):90–92.

Schemo, D. 2008. Diploma mill concerns extend beyond fraud. *New York Times,* June 29. www.nytimes.com/2008/06/29/us/29diploma.html.

Spadanuta, L. 2009. Identity theft loose ends. *Security Management* 53 (January). [p. 251].

U.S. Department of Justice. 2006. Attorney General's Report on Criminal History Background Checks. www.usdoj.gov/olp/ag_bgchecks_report.pdf.

U.S. Government Accountability Office. 2008. DOD personnel clearances: DOD faces multiple challenges in its efforts to improve clearance processes for industry personnel. www.gao.gov/news.items/d08470t.pdf.

WSMV.com. 2008. Feds: 7 napping guards at weapons plant since 2000 (January 17). www.wsmv.com/print/15067784/detail.html.

Chapter 7

Physical Security

Chapter Learning Objectives

After reading this chapter, you should be able to:

1. Define *physical security* and explain its challenges
2. Explain the importance of standards for physical security
3. Describe the relationship between *information technology* and *physical security*
4. List and explain at least ten strategies of physical security
5. List and explain at least five types of electronic security system sensors to prevent unauthorized intrusion
6. List and explain the three categories of electronic entry-control devices
7. Describe at least five characteristics of lock and key systems
8. Discuss how to protect doors and windows
9. Describe at least five characteristics of security lighting
10. Describe at least five characteristics of closed-circuit television systems

Terms To Know

physical security
security culture

climate for security
standards
consensus standards
regulations
codes
SAFETY Act
integrated systems
convergence
interoperability
open architecture
perimeter
perimeter security
perimeter barrier
metal chain-link fence
top guard
clear zone
metal detectors
contraband
canine unit
bollards
standoff distance
anti-ram vehicle barriers
electronic security systems
intrusion-detection systems
detection zones
exterior intrusion-detection sensors
boundary-penetration sensors
volumetric motion sensors
electronic entry-control systems
coded devices
credential devices
Homeland Security Presidential Directive 12
biometric devices
key-in-the-knob lock
dead-bolt lock
single-cylinder dead-bolt lock
double-cylinder dead-bolt lock
cylinder
mortise lock
unit lock
rim-mounted lock
padlock
fail safe

fail secure
electric strike
electric bolt
electric lockset
electromagnetic lock
electromechanical lock
Americans with Disabilities Act of 1990
key control
master key
interchangeable core lock
money safe
fire safe
delayed-egress device
glazing
balanced design
annealed glass
heat-strengthened glass
fully thermally tempered glass
wire-reinforced glass
laminated glass
security window film
polycarbonates
color rendition
footcandle
glare
illuminance
lamp
light trespass
lux
incandescent lamp
fluorescent lamp
high-intensity discharge lamp
sustainability
Leadership in Energy and Environmental Design (LEED)
Internet Protocol (IP)
video analytics
thermal security camera
videocassette recorder
digital video recorder
network video recorder
security operations center
central station

QUIZ

This quiz serves to prime the reader's mind and begin the reading, thinking, and studying processes for this chapter. The answers to all of the questions are found within this chapter.

1. With the formidable physical security of today, do you think offenders can penetrate it?
2. Is security officer turnover as high as 500 percent at many locations?
3. In which direction is physical security technology and systems heading, digital or analog?
4. What is the meaning of "wait and pounce" and "poke the system"?
5. What is interoperability and how is it related to physical security?
6. Is standoff distance the recommended safe distance between a security officer and a suspect?
7. Does egress mean "going in" or "going out"?
8. How does the Americans with Disabilities Act relate to physical security?

Introduction

Traditionally, physical security concentrated on hardware. Today, it consists of hardware and sophisticated electronics meshed with information technology (IT) systems. Physical security is becoming increasingly automated and "smart." This chapter covers the following topics: research directions, challenges of physical security, standards, IT and physical security, perimeter security, barriers, blast protection, electronic security systems, electronic entry-control systems, lock and key systems, doors, windows, lighting, closed-circuit TV, and security operations center.

Physical Security Defined

ASIS International (2005, 8) defines **physical security** as follows:

Physical security focuses on the protection of people, property, and facilities through the use of security forces, security systems, and security procedures. Physical security personnel oversee proprietary or contract uniformed security operations, identify security system requirements, assess internal and external threats to assets, and develop policies, plans, procedures, and physical safeguards to counter those threats. Physical security can include the use of barriers, alarms, locks, access control systems, protective lighting, closed-circuit televisions, and other state-of-the-art security technology.

The U.S. Government Accountability Office (2008, 3) states: "We defined physical security as the combination of operational and security equipment, personnel, and procedures used to protect facilities, information, documents, or material against theft, sabotage, diversion, or other criminal acts."

Physical security is a product and service resulting from the application of security methodology and the implementation of security strategies. It facilitates the objectives of security: deter, deceive, detect, delay, deny, mitigate, and respond. In physical security, we see generic and specific security, layers, redundancy, levels of security, and force multipliers (see Chapter 5).

Research Directions for Physical Security

Bitzer and Hoffman (2007, 2) write of the growing importance of physical security because of global threats and hazards. However, they note that there is limited research on physical security and that the research is fragmented among many disciplines. They see physical security as primarily an applied field (different from math and physics) with no distinct line of research. The research spans electronic engineering, mechanical engineering, computer science, chemistry, physics, criminology, sociology, and psychology. Bitzer and Hoffman add that too much multidisciplinary, fragmented research can be a disadvantage because researchers may miss each other's findings and ideas. They suggest the use of peer-reviewed journals and academic conferences.

Bitzer and Hoffman (2007, 3–4) propose several directions for research on physical security, as described next. To begin with, they argue that although most funding for research is for equipment and technology, the personnel behind it deserve increased attention (Figure 7.1). They offer two illustrations: Retired General Eugene Habiger, former commander of U.S. nuclear forces, stated that "good security is 20 percent equipment and 80 percent people." The second illustration describes the personal experience of one of the authors who walked his dog at the same time security officers patrolled near his apartment. On a regular basis, officers would drive to a fence, leave their patrol car, place a wand at a button attached to the fence (i.e., log the stop with an electric guard-tour system), quickly return to the patrol car, and drive away. Not once did an officer stop and ask the author if anything unusual was occurring in the area.

Critical Thinking

In the nearby illustration of the security officers using the electronic guard-tour system, what was the higher priority, supervisors monitoring officers on patrol or increasing security on the premises? Do you think the guard-tour system hindered security? Explain your answers.

FIGURE 7.1   The value, investment, and effectiveness of physical security depends on the personnel behind it. Personnel must be properly screened, trained, motivated, and supervised. (® Shutterstock.com. With permission.)

To facilitate research, Bitzer and Hoffman (2007, 5) divide physical security not only into two major topics (i.e., equipment/technology and personnel), but further divide personnel into two subsets: (a) the impact individuals and groups (e.g., organizations and societies) have on security and (b) how personnel interact with equipment/technology.

An example and topic for research within the first subset is security officer turnover. It can be as high as 100 to 300 percent at certain locations. Although this problem is pervasive in the security industry, Bitzer and Hoffman see specific remedies deserving more attention: personality testing, biodata, and realistic job previews. Relevant issues that affect the usefulness of such research include low pay and the need for a supervisor or manager to "fill a post with a body immediately."

Another direction for research pertains to **security culture** and **climate for security** (Bitzer and Hoffman 2007, 9). The former is defined as "organizational manifestations which reflect the importance that an organization places on securing physical, electronic, and information assets." The latter is defined as "employees' shared perceptions of what the organization is like in terms of security practices, procedures, routines, and rewards." The authors write that these concepts work together to influence employee security behaviors. This can extend to influencing job applicants (e.g., dissuade a criminal from applying). Bitzer and Hoffman point to needed testing pertaining to the security culture and climate to answer questions about the dimensions that comprise these concepts and ways to assess the concepts in a security context. Additional directions for research from the first sub-set, cited by these authors, are the insider threat, professionalism, screening, boredom, and performance appraisals associated with the job of security officers.

Research direction for the second subset, according to Bitzer and Hoffman, concentrates on a wide variety of security duties involving personnel interaction with equipment and technology. They write that security systems are not completely automated because personnel, for instance, must review and act once data is collected. When an X-ray machine shows an image on a screen at an airport or courthouse, person-nel must interpret the image and act. CCTV systems also require human observation and action, although increasingly "smarter" systems are assisting personnel by detecting and reporting anomalies. At the same time, the monitoring of screens and systems by personnel often results in fatigue and boredom.

Bitzer and Hoffman conclude that other mature disciplines have researched many of the issues they describe. They believe that with this pre-vious research as a base, an improved understanding of physical security will evolve, and they hope to spark further research.

Challenges of Physical Security

Roger G. Johnston (2004), an expert on physical security employed at Los Alamos National Laboratory, is a critical thinker about physical security issues. He writes that physical security is challenging because of the follow-ing reasons:

- Whereas an adversary may seek and find only one vulnerability, security practitioners must protect against all vulnerabilities.
- There is a general lack of useful performance measures for security. Success is often defined as no incidents occurring. However, such a measure does not support effective cost/benefit analysis and results in poor planning of resources and hysteria when an incident does occur, leading to huge spending on security that may be ineffective and wasteful.
- There are a limited number of standards.
- Physical security is often ambiguous and vague in terms of its goals and adversaries. The terminology is not used consistently.
- Although a strategy of security programs is to make security appear formidable to the outside world, a healthy security program exer-cises caution about being overconfident.
- Additional challenges, according to Johnston, include society's ambivalent attitudes toward security, the perceived low status of

certain security positions, boredom from routine duties, and the tendency of the profession to attract authoritarians and bureaucrats who are so focused on compliance and satisfying superiors and regulators that security and creativity may be compromised.

Challenges of Vulnerability Assessments

Johnston (2004) and his security team at Los Alamos have conducted vulnerability assessments on hundreds of different security devices and systems. This means that they study various types of attacks on these devices and systems to expose weaknesses for corrective action. Also important in these studies are the false alarm rate and the performance in detecting an adversary. Johnston names and defines the types of attacks next:

- *False alarming* is when an adversary causes random, multiple false alarms to hinder usefulness and confidence in the system.
- *Fault analysis* occurs when an adversary causes a system to perform differently from the way it was designed to collect information for advantage.
- *"Poke the system"* attacks activate the system to see what happens to collect information for advantage.
- *"Wait and pounce"* involves an adversary patiently waiting for an unexpected event or security personnel making a mistake and then acting quickly.
- *Social engineering* is a technique against personnel to defeat security through persuasion, trickery, impersonation, bribery, seduction, threats, force, or other means.

According to Johnston: Studying such attacks is difficult to observe, model, predict, and replicate; realism is a challenge; all vulnerabilities are never known; there is a frequent "shoot the messenger" mentality (i.e., vendors and security practitioners want to avoid problems); no useful guidelines or standards on vulnerability assessments exist; and time and budgets are limited. He adds that these assessments are more of an art than a science. Another point he makes is that physical security can fail not only because of hardware factors, but also because of human and organizational factors. Examples are errors, overconfidence, and poor training and communications. And, these variables are difficult to study.

Specific activities of a vulnerability assessment, according to Johnston, include the following: understand the objectives of the system and what it seeks to accomplish; study how the system is used by interviewing security officers, managers, and vendors; play with the system and brainstorm; begin with the simplest type of attack and demonstrate it, if practical; prepare countermeasures; and complete a report.

Johnston's suggestions for the content of a vulnerability assessment report include the following: whether the attack is theoretical or practical; the cost and time to demonstrate the attack from off-site and/or on-site; the personnel, skills, and equipment employed; inside and/or public information used; positive features of the system; and suggestions for change.

For enhanced vulnerability assessments of physical security, Johnston recommends that they be conducted from the early part of the design stage, not at the end of development, when changes are more difficult. They should also be done periodically once the system is implemented, and different assessors should be employed.

Security Standards

Chapter 4 explained the importance of security standards to improve quality, performance, and reliability of services and products. Standards also enhance professionalism. The term **standards** refers to criteria or avenues of measurement for comparison to others. It can be applied in various contexts. It can refer to uniform terminology and testing methods to gauge the performance of products and services in a particular industry. A corporation may produce internal standards that must be followed by all corporate branches. Professions typically promote standards for members to enhance professionalism and competence. Numerous types of organizations worldwide develop standards. Besides industry and professional standards, there are government standards and international standards.

The term **consensus standards** means that specialists in a particular discipline developed standards through a process of study and change. Organizations such as the American National Standards Institute (ANSI) and the International Organization for Standardization (ISO) offer standards to organizations that establish standards to ensure that the standards are developed in a fair and open manner. Then, the organization can be accredited as a Standards Development Organization (SDO). This is important, because organizations can be biased in establishing standards that favor a particular perspective on an issue, or a specific product or service.

Standards may evolve from an organization's development of *guidelines*, *recommended practices*, or *best practices*. These terms are used loosely in various disciplines. Standards do not have the force of law, unless adopted by government through legislative enactment on the local, state, or federal levels. However, if voluntary standards are practiced within an industry, such standards can be an issue in litigation, and if a judge decides so, a standard can be supported by case law and cited in subsequent cases as precedent.

Many organizations and industries develop standards to prevent laws from being enacted that force compliance with specific standards (which can be expensive). When government gets involved, which is the case with many industries, the terms *regulations* and *codes* are employed. **Regulations** are government laws or rules that require compliance, backed up by law enforcement and criminal and civil penalties. **Codes** are standards adopted into law and backed up by government.

When security is being planned or modified, or when new systems or hardware are being considered, planners must research applicable standards, regulations, and codes. This is a practice of architects, landscape architects, engineers, and other professionals. The National Fire Protection Association Life Safety Code (NFPA 101) is an illustration of a standard that is important to security planning. Although the NFPA is a private organization without enforcement powers, its NFPA 101 is used in all states, backed up by law. The NFPA 101 emphasizes emergency protection for occupants, and it includes building design features, adequate exits for escape, locks, alarm devices, doors, emergency lighting, and other topics relevant to physical security that must never interfere with NFPA 101 requirements for safety and ease of escape in case of emergency.

It is important to remember the varied sources from government that provide input for security planning. This includes the many publications on security from the Federal Emergency Management Agency (FEMA), the Department of Defense (DOD), the Government Accountability Office (GAO), the General Services Administration (GSA), and other government bodies. The FBI and Secret Service also provide input for security planning. In addition, federal-government-regulated industries, such as air transportation and nuclear power, are required to follow stringent security regulations. State and local governments also play a role in security regulations and standards through, for instance, the regulation of security businesses and security at courthouses.

Examples of standard-setting organizations, besides the NFPA, are listed next, and their Web addresses are given at the end of the chapter. Security practitioners should check these organizations to see if they provide standards, testing, or other information on a security product or service of interest. Alternatively, type the word *standards* following the item of interest in an Internet search engine.

- American Architectural Manufacturers Association (AAMA): The AAMA is involved with manufacturers of windows, doors, and related products to develop standards and influence codes.
- American National Standards Institute (ANSI): This group promotes and facilitates voluntary consensus standards among many groups.
- American Society for Testing and Materials (ASTM International): Its standards include those on security, fire protection, and safety.

- Builders Hardware Manufacturers Association (BHMA): This group develops performance standards for architectural hardware (e.g., locks, exit devices, and doors).
- Institute of Electrical and Electronics Engineers (IEEE): A leading association for the advancement of technology, the IEEE is a source of technical and professional information and standards (e.g., intrusion-detection systems).
- International Organization for Standardization (ISO): The ISO is the world's largest developer and publisher of international standards.
- National Electrical Manufacturers Association (NEMA): This trade association represents the electrical manufacturing industry and develops technical standards on many types of products (e.g., CCTV).
- Security Industry Association (SIA): This trade association provides educational programs, supports research, and develops technical and performance standards.
- Underwriters Laboratories (UL): Among its functions are testing and rating various products (e.g., locks, safes, and alarm systems).

ESTABLISH A METHODOLOGY FOR PURCHASING DECISIONS

If you speak with a veteran security practitioner, project manager, or someone linked to a history of purchasing physical security, the chances are they can tell you about a product, system, or service that was highly touted but did not live up to its expectations. The stories are endless—the fence that was easy to penetrate, the intrusion-detection system that had excessive false alarms, the CCTV system that produced unclear images, and the revolving door that did not revolve. Here are some tips that can help prevent errors that reflect on the security practitioner:

- Establish a methodology for purchasing. This can include a self-styled checklist and components of a security business proposal.
- Conform to organizational purchasing requirements.
- Base purchasing decisions on specific, well-thought-out needs, costs, and critical thinking.
- When possible, include input from a risk analysis with relevant metrics, as well as available research and product evaluations.
- Bring IT and other internal specialists into the decision-making process, if appropriate.
- Study standards and codes.
- Speak with people who are users of the product, system, or service.
- Speak with members of professional associations who are familiar with your needs.
- Observe the product, system, or service in action.
- Check on maintenance, warranty, and repair response time.

- Check on whether the system can be expanded.
- Check on training and personnel requirements.
- Speak with sales professionals, but expect puffing.
- Remain a critical thinker when speaking to references supplied by a salesperson.
- Remember that testing reports may reflect performance under ideal conditions (e.g., weather).

Lifrieri (2009, 16) brings to the surface another issue of consideration when purchasing physical security: installing SAFETY Act designated systems. The **SAFETY Act** is short for the Support Anti-Terrorism by Fostering Effective Technologies Act of 2002. This federal law, part of the Homeland Security Act, facilitates the development and deployment of antiterrorism technologies. It provides manufacturers and others involved in this business with limited liability if a system or product fails during a terrorist attack. The reasoning is that no system is foolproof and that a business can be ruined from the failure. To qualify, businesses submit information about their technology to the U.S. Department of Homeland Security. By installing SAFETY Act systems and products, a business owner essentially reduces liability.

Lifrieri notes that many manufacturers are not taking advantage of the act's benefits. One reason may be that proprietary designs are required to be shared with the government.

Information Technology and Physical Security

The history of physical security includes individual systems separate from one another within buildings. In other words, a separate intrusion-detection system, a separate access control system, a separate fire alarm system, and so on. Today, we see more of what is called **integrated systems**, meaning many systems are controlled at one computer-operated common point. For decades, architects and engineers have promoted "smart buildings," whereby security, safety, and fire protection systems; heating, ventilation, and air-conditioning (HVAC) systems; lighting; elevators; and other systems are managed by one mega system. The benefits include streamlined management and data, energy efficiency, greater convenience, and lower costs. Although the technical difficulties with hardware and software have been challenging, the push for integration remains because of its value and the increasing number of sensors in buildings. One challenge is to fully utilize, interpret, and act upon the data from the large number of sensors.

The integration trend includes the potential of Internet protocol (IP) and Ethernet networks to further assist in the integration of multiple systems. IP products (e.g., IP-based network cameras) are connected to existing LAN (local area networks connecting devices, often in the same building) and WAN (wide area networks connecting devices, possibly miles apart). Ethernet refers to a computer networking technology for LANs. In essence, physical security systems are increasingly being placed on enterprises' computer networks, and this is known as **convergence**. The benefits include monitoring physical security (and other systems) from almost any point globally, less travel and personnel expenses, and the use of only one access card per person for worldwide sites linked to the network.

Because physical security specialists and IT specialists are working together more often, it is to the benefit of the enterprise that they seek to understand each other and the agendas of each. For example, physical security specialists are concerned about back-up systems during IT maintenance or when the power goes out, storage and retrieval of video, activity logs, and upgrades. IT specialists are concerned about how a multitude of security systems (e.g., CCTV, access controls, intrusion detection) will affect the capacity of the network.

Verity (2008) offers a variety of scenarios, as described here, to illustrate how modern systems operate. A corporate security operations center located in the United States receives a fire alarm signal from one of its sites in Japan. The site shows fifteen employees are in the building. Besides a fire alarm being sounded in the building and the fire department being contacted, a cell phone text message is sent to each employee that states: "A fire has been detected in your facility. Reply '1' if you are safe and secure, and '2' if you require help." The system focuses on-site cameras on the fire and the emergency as it is unfolding, and the HVAC system is adjusted to reduce fire and smoke. In another scenario, the system in a building adjusts lighting and temperature as employees enter in the morning and use the card access system. At the same time, CCTV cameras detect too many employees waiting too long in the lobby for elevators, so additional elevators are pressed into service.

Verity shares a dose of reality when he writes that although cameras, access control card readers, and HVAC systems may share Ethernet networks in buildings, it does not mean that they can make sense of each other's data. He adds that various building automation vendors sell their own software or consoles for collecting, recording, and analyzing data from multiple sensors and devices, and they develop integration platforms designed to accommodate data encoded in different formats and translate it into a common format for analysis. The theory behind this technology is commendable, and "smart" buildings do offer value and convenience, but challenges remain. One challenge described by Regelski (2008, 10) is **interoperability**, which he defines as physical security customers "being able to purchase a product from any manufacturer and have it work seamlessly with any other product." To reach this goal, Regelski argues for continued emphasis on **open architecture**. This means that a manufacturer's hardware and software specifications are public, rather than proprietary, which enables other manufacturers to add new and improved compatible products to the original product. Regelski writes: "Industry-wide endorsement of this concept is the only way to solve customer concerns of upgradeability, ease of integration and better technical support."

> Security systems should be reliable, and this includes built-in redundancy; if one path or component fails, the system should continue to function.

Physical Security

To assist the reader in understanding physical security, the perimeter security at U.S. biosafety level (BSL)-4 labs is explained. **Perimeter** refers to outer boundary and **perimeter security** includes a variety of strategies at the perimeter that deter, use deception, detect, delay, deny, mitigate, and respond to threats. (See Chapter 5 under "Objectives of Security.") BSL-4 labs handle the world's most dangerous agents and diseases, as scientists work on vaccines. These labs contain agents that are so dangerous that if humans make contact with them, there is no cure or treatment. The threats include agent theft and terrorist attack. Under the U.S. Bioterrorism Act, these labs are registered with and regulated by the U.S. Centers for Disease Control and Prevention (CDC). The U.S. Government Accountability Office (GAO) (2008) was asked by Congress to conduct a security assessment of perimeter security at the nation's five BSL-4 labs. Fifteen perimeter controls were studied at each lab as listed here with the rationales (verbatim) for each security control. The insider threat and cybersecurity were not studied. Perimeter security leading up to the lab building points of entry were studied. In addition, there was no analysis of security controls to see if they worked as intended, and there was no study of training or inventory controls. The GAO found significant differences in security among the five labs, depending on which agencies were involved with the lab, other than the CDC. The names of the labs were not included in the GAO report for security reasons.

1. *Outer/tiered perimeter boundary.* There should be a perimeter boundary outside the lab to prevent unauthorized access. Examples include a reinforced perimeter security fence or natural barrier system that uses landscaping techniques to impede access to buildings. Outer/tiered perimeter also includes other structures that screen visibility of the lab.
2. *Blast standoff area (e.g., buffer zone) between lab and perimeter barriers.* To minimize effects of explosive damage if a bomb were to be detonated outside the lab, the perimeter line should be located as far as practical from the building exterior.

3. *Barriers to prevent vehicles from approaching lab.* A physical barrier consisting of natural or fabricated controls, such as bollards, designed to keep vehicles from ramming or setting off explosives that could cause damage to the building housing the BSL-4 lab.

4. *Loading docks located outside the footprint of the main building.* Because of areas where delivery vehicles can park, loading docks are vulnerable areas and should be kept outside the footprint of the main building.

5. *Exterior windows do not provide direct access to the lab.* Windows are typically the most vulnerable portion of any building; therefore, there should be no exterior windows that provide direct access to the lab.

6. *Command-and-control center.* A command-and-control center is crucial to the administration and maintenance of an active, integrated physical security system. The control center monitors the employees, public, and environment of the lab building and other parts of the complex and serves as the single, central contact area in the event of an emergency.

7. *CCTV monitored by the command-and-control center.* A video system that gives a signal from a camera to video monitoring stations at a designated location. The cameras give the control center the capability of monitoring activity within and outside the complex.

8. *Active intrusion-detection system (IDS) integrated with CCTV.* An IDS is used to detect an intruder crossing the boundary of a protected area, including through the building's vulnerable perimeter barriers. Integration with CCTV is integral to the IDS's ability to alert security staff to potential incidents that require monitoring.

9. *Camera coverage for all exterior lab building entrances.* Cameras that cover the exterior building entrances provide a means to detect and quickly identify potential intruders.

10. *Perimeter lighting of the complex.* Security lighting of the site, similar to boundary lighting, provides both a real and psychological deterrent, and allows security personnel to maintain visual-assessment capability during darkness. It is cost-effective in that it might reduce the need for security forces.

11. *Visible armed guard presence at all public entrances to lab.* All public entrances require security monitoring. This presence helps to prevent or impede attempts of unauthorized access to the complex.

12. *Roving armed guard patrols of perimeter.* The presence of roving armed guard patrols helps to prevent or impede attempts of unauthorized access and includes inspecting vital entrance areas and external barriers.

13. *X-ray magnetometer machines in operation at building entrances.* These machines provide a means of screening persons, items, and materials that may possess or contain weapons, contraband, or hazardous substances prior to authorizing entry or delivery into a facility.

14. *Vehicle screening.* Screening vehicles that enter the perimeter of the lab includes an ID check and vehicle inspection to deny unauthorized individuals access and potentially detect a threat.

15. *Visitor screening.* Screening visitors to the lab reduces the possibility that unauthorized individuals will gain access. Visitor screening includes identifying, screening, or recording visitors through methods such as camera coverage or visitor logs so that their entry to the lab is recorded.

To illustrate the range of security—from stronger to weaker—at the labs studied, verbatim descriptions of two labs are presented next:

Lab A: The physical security controls of Lab A presented a strong visible deterrent from the outside, with 14 of the 15 key security controls in place. Lab A was located in a complex of other buildings that was separated from an urban environment by a perimeter security fence reinforced with airline cable to further strengthen the fence and deter unauthorized access. A roving patrol of armed guards was visible inside and outside the perimeter fence, while other guards operated gated entry inspection points. The gates incorporated technical support for the guards to assist them with the inspection of both private and commercial vehicles. Guards conducted ID checks at the gates and searched vehicles that did not have the appropriate access decals. Further, all trucks were required to enter a single gate containing an X-ray screening device. Past this outer perimeter, a further fabricated barrier existed around the building containing the BSL-4 lab. Although Lab A had most of the security controls we focused on during our assessment, it did not have an active intrusion-detection system integrated with the CCTV network covering the facility. This reduced the possibility that security officers could detect and quickly identify an intruder entering the building perimeter.

Lab E: Lab E was one of the weakest labs we assessed, with 4 out of the 15 key controls. It had only limited camera coverage of the outer perimeter of the facility and the only vehicular barrier consisted of an arm gate that swung across the road. Although the guardhouses controlling access to the facility were manned, they appeared antiquated. The security force charged with protecting the lab was unarmed. Of all the BSL-4 labs we assessed, this was the only lab with an exterior window that could provide direct access to the lab. In lieu of a command and control center, Lab E contracts with an outside company to monitor its alarm in an off-site facility. This potentially impedes response time by emergency responders with an unnecessary layer that would not exist with a command and control center. Since the contracted company is not physically present at the facility, it is not able to ascertain the nature of alarm activation. Furthermore, there is no interfaced security system between alarms and cameras and a lack of live monitoring of cameras.

Customary in GAO reports on evaluations of agencies is an opportunity for the agency subject to study to comment on the GAO results. In this case, at the end of the GAO report, the CDC noted that lab security is risk-based and dependent on the type of research conducted at the lab. The CDC added that they would study security further and seek input from security experts and the scientific community. In questioning the appropriateness of the GAO's fifteen security controls, the CDC requested research references, the experts consulted, and whether the controls had been peer-reviewed. The GAO response, at the end of the report, referred to the GAO's security expertise and research of commonly accepted physical security principles. The GAO acknowledged that the fifteen controls are not the only strategies for perimeter security, but they do contribute to strong perimeter security.

Perimeter Barriers

Physical security at the perimeter often includes a barrier. The Federal Emergency Management Agency (FEMA) (2003a, B-15) defines **perimeter barrier** as "a fence, wall, vehicle barrier, landform, or line of vegetation applied along an exterior perimeter used to obscure vision, hinder personnel access, or hinder or prevent vehicle access." The decision as to what type of barrier or barriers to install depends on need following a risk analysis. Local ordinances should be researched, since they may contain restrictions on certain security features (e.g., prohibitions against barbed wire). In addition, civil engineers and landscape architects are examples of specialists who can provide input for barriers when, for example, issues such as landform, drainage, and foliage develop (Figure 7.2).

A commonly applied perimeter barrier is the **metal chain-link fence** (Figure 7.3). Its design varies. The American Society for Testing and Materials (ASTM) publishes standards for fences (ASTM F 567). Fences should be coated with a substance (e.g., zinc or aluminum) to resist deterioration. The height depends on site needs. For industrial settings, for instance, the height should be 8 feet with a top guard of 1 foot. The posts should be installed at a depth of about 3 feet in concrete. Since the typical top rail of a fence (located below the barbed wire and razor ribbon in Figure 7.3) is a security feature that assists offenders when climbing, it should be replaced with a

FIGURE 7.2 A fountain or pond can be applied as an aesthetically pleasing barrier, and trees can block surveillance from off the premises. (® Shutterstock.com. With permission.)

FIGURE 7.3 Metal chain-link fence topped with razor ribbon and three strands of barbed wire is an effective barrier. (® Shutterstock.com. With permission.)

tension wire to support the fence, not a person. The chain-link fence steel wire should be No. 9 gauge or heavier. The **top guard** often consists of three strands of *barbed wire* of No. 12 gauge supported by arms facing away from the perimeter at a 45-degree angle. If the fence is right on the property line, the arms should be facing inward due to liability issues. Again, to avoid assisting an offender, the supporting arms should be made of hard plastic, or another substance, to support the barbed wire, but not an offender climbing over the fence. Another option at the top of a fence, for increased security, is to install barbed wire in a V shape. This consists of three strands of barbed wire facing away from the perimeter at 45 degrees and three strands facing inward at 45 degrees. Razor ribbon at the top also increases security over the usual three strands of barbed wire.

Constructive criticism of traditional fencing is important because, unless it is well designed, a fence will serve to assist offenders. In addition, offenders attempting to penetrate a fence will seek to go over it, through it, or under it, unless thwarted by multiple security layers (e.g., fence disturbance sensors, CCTV, lighting, and security personnel).

Razor ribbon consists of razor-sharp barbs along a coiled wire that is secured at the top of a fence. *Concertina fences* are similar to the razor ribbon concept. Developed and applied by the military as a portable and quick barrier, these consist of coiled razor wire. Two coils stretched next to each other can form a base for a third coil to be secured on top.

A **clear zone** should be maintained on both sides of a fence to allow for ease of observation. Foliage or any other things blocking the view should be eliminated.

For increased security, *anticlimb fences* are available (Figure 7.4). These fences are constructed with mesh so close together on the fence that an offender is unable to grab or place a foot on the fence. This contrasts with a chain-link fence, with mesh that is 2 × 2 in. Another type of anticlimb fence consists of vertical bars supported with horizontal bars.

Walls are another barrier for perimeter security, although more expensive than a chain-link fence. In addition, visibility is hindered, which can be a disadvantage for seeing out; but at the same time, adversaries can be blocked from seeing in.

A perimeter at a site in an urban area may be close to a busy street. It may also consist of a wall with another tenant on the other side or a wall against an adjacent building. In such cases, specific security can include no parking zones and vibration detectors in walls and other intrusion-detection systems. The *roof* is another vulnerability of buildings that may serve

FIGURE 7.4 Anticlimb fence.

as an entry point for offenders. Roofs and roof openings must be protected with locks, lighting, intrusion-detection systems, CCTV, and other security strategies. Burglars repeatedly cut through roofs to enter buildings. Other points of entry requiring protection include basements, crawl spaces, vents, and utility openings.

Whatever type of perimeter security exists at a site, openings are required for access by people and vehicles. The least number of openings is best to control access. At a fence or wall, a *gate* is typically constructed and secured with a lock when closed. When open, this access point may be guarded by a security officer housed in a small building who checks people and vehicles for authorized access.

Screening of people, vehicles, mail, and packages at access points along a perimeter vary, depending on specific security needs. A security officer may check photo IDs and compare it with the individuals offering them. A card key, personal identification number, and biometrics (explained in subsequent pages) may also be part of the access control system. **Metal detectors**, consisting of walk-through or handheld devices, are often used to detect weapons, concealed electronic devices (e.g., hidden transmitters), and explosives having metal components. Since **contraband** (i.e., anything prohibited) can contain numerous plastic parts, metal detectors have limitations. Vehicles require inspection. At low-security sites, an ID may be checked along with a parking sticker. At high-security sites, multiple IDs may be checked in addition to a thorough vehicle inspection, including inside and under the vehicle. Mail and packages may contain many types of contraband (e.g., bombs and chemical, biological, and radiological materials) and should be screened near the perimeter at a stand-alone building. Besides metal detectors, screening technology includes X-ray scanners, devices that detect components of explosives, and radiological detectors. In addition, the use of a **canine unit** (e.g., bomb- or drug-sniffing dogs) is another option for screening. A canine unit is also an asset to patrolling high-security locations and along perimeters. Depending on the duties of the canine unit, planning includes selection of breed and handler, training, housing costs, and liability issues (Figure 7.5).

Signs are an important element of security. Along a perimeter, and at access points, signs should clearly send messages such as "private property," "no trespassing," "authorized access only," "no unauthorized weapons," and "people, vehicles, and items subject to search."

Senior management in businesses often favors security that does not make a site look like a prison. This can be challenging for designers. However, aesthetically pleasing security includes CPTED (crime prevention through environmental design), wrought iron fences, fences built on top of low walls, thick and/or thorny hedges, **bollards** (i.e., a vehicle barrier of steel or concrete that appears as a cylinder a few feet above the ground and is well secured underground), bollards hidden in foliage, large planters (made of concrete and steel), and fountains.

ASIS International (2009, 13) refers to bollards and planters available in crash-rated configurations that meet U.S. Department of Defense K-ratings: K4, K8, and K12. A K4-rated barrier is designed to stop a 15,000-lb. vehicle traveling at 30 mph. The K8 and K12 are designed to stop a vehicle of the same weight at 40 and 50 mph, respectively.

FIGURE 7.5 **Canine unit in training. Careful planning is required for canine units, including consideration of liability issues. (® Shutterstock.com. With permission.)**

CPTED AND SECURITY-RELEVANT CRIMINOLOGY

Crime prevention through environmental design (CPTED) was explained in Chapter 4. Here, a refresher is offered because of its importance and relevance to security planning. *Natural surveillance* refers to the placement of physical features, activities, and people to maximize visibility. *Territoriality* aims to use physical features, such as landscaping, buildings, fences, and signs to show ownership. *Access controls* involve the wise placement of entrances, exits, fencing, lighting, and other related features.

CPTED applied to commercial parking lots or structures can include lighting that avoids dark hiding spots, the painting of walls white to increase light intensity, open designs to facilitate natural surveillance, restrooms in busy locations for visibility, and signs and kiosks to assist customers.

CPTED applied to lobbies in office buildings uses barriers that direct people to a reception desk or checkpoint prior to access to elevators and stairs. At the desk, various technologies (e.g., IT, CCTV, elevator controls) are applied to control access.

Security-relevant criminology was also covered in Chapter 4. For example, *situational crime prevention* was explained as seeking to reduce *opportunities* for crime through people's behavior and the design of the environment. This includes increasing the efforts and risks of committing a crime through, for instance, employee policies and procedures and physical security.

Blast Protection

The application of blast protection strategies to a facility depends on such factors as the results of a risk analysis, the type of facility (e.g., embassy), and the location. For many facilities, blast protection is not practical or cost effective.

Since the 9/11 attacks, FEMA has published numerous manuals on protection of buildings against terrorist attacks. The following strategies are from FEMA (2008, 2003b).

Because the characteristics of explosives used in attacks cannot be predicted, the most effective strategy to protect buildings is to keep bombs as far away from buildings as possible by maximizing **standoff distance**, defined as the distance between an asset and a threat.

Anti-ram vehicle barriers prevent a vehicle from penetrating a perimeter and causing harm from a bomb or other threat. Two types are passive and active. *Passive vehicle barriers* are stationary and consist of bollards, walls, large planters, berms, and other obstructions. *Active vehicle barriers* can be retracted or moved away to permit passage at roadways or access points. Pop-up vehicle barriers are difficult to spot and rise up from the ground to block a vehicle. The U.S. Department of State Bureau of Diplomatic Security maintains requirements and certifies vehicle barriers.

The design of roads and driveways can also play a role in preventing vehicle attacks, while increasing traffic safety. Avoid straight roads that lead to checkpoints and buildings to prevent an opportunity for acceleration. Tight corners and speed bumps require slow driving.

Electronic Security Systems

The following information is paraphrased from FEMA (2003b). An **electronic security system** (ESS) is an integrated system that encompasses interior and exterior sensors; closed-circuit television (CCTV) systems for assessing alarm conditions; electronic entry-control systems (EECSs); data-transmission media (DTM); and alarm reporting systems for monitoring, controlling, and displaying various alarm and system information. Interior and exterior sensors and their associated communication and display subsystems are collectively called **intrusion-detection systems** (IDSs).

An ESS is used to provide early warning of an intruder. This system consists of hardware and software elements operated by trained security personnel. A system is configured to provide one or more layers of detection around an asset. Each layer is made up of a series of contiguous detection zones designed to isolate the asset and to control the entry and exit of authorized personnel and materials.

Detection Zones

After a perimeter has been defined, the next step is to divide it into specific **detection zones**. The length of each detection zone is determined by evaluating the contour, the existing terrain, and the operational activities along the perimeter. Detection zones should be long and straight to minimize the number of sensors or cameras necessary and to aid security officer assessment if cameras are not used. Entry points for personnel and vehicles must be configured as independent zones. This enables deactivation of the sensors in these zones, i.e., placing them in the access mode during customary working hours (assuming the entry points are observed by security officers) without having to deactivate adjacent areas. The specific length of individual zones can vary around a perimeter, but they should not exceed 300 feet. If the zone is longer, it will be difficult for an operator using CCTV assessment or for the response force to identify the location of an intrusion or the cause of a false alarm. If an alarm occurs in a specific zone, the operator can readily determine its approximate location by referring to a map of the perimeter.

Exterior Intrusion-Detection Sensors

Exterior intrusion-detection sensors are used outdoors to detect an intruder crossing the boundary of a protected area (Figure 7.6). They can also be used in clear zones between fences or around buildings and for

FIGURE 7.6 Exterior intrusion-detection sensor (dark column) applied between fences. CCTV and lights serve as additional layers of security.

protecting materials and equipment stored outdoors within a protected boundary. Because of the nature of the outdoor environment, exterior sensors are also more susceptible to nuisance and environmental alarms than interior sensors. Inclement weather conditions (e.g., heavy rain, hail, and high wind), vegetation, the natural variation of the temperature of objects in the detection zone, blowing debris, and animals are major sources of unwanted alarms. Several different types of exterior intrusion-detection sensors are available, as described here.

Fence sensors detect attempts to penetrate a fence around a protected area. Penetration attempts (e.g., climbing, cutting, or lifting) generate mechanical vibrations and stresses in fence fabric and posts that are usually different from those caused by natural phenomena like wind and rain. Four types of sensors used to detect these vibrations and stresses follow. *Strain-sensitive cables* are transducers that are uniformly sensitive along their entire length. They generate an analog voltage when subject to mechanical distortions or stress resulting from fence motion. Strain sensitive cables are sensitive to both low and high frequencies. Because the cable acts like a microphone, some manufacturers offer an option that allows the operator to listen to fence noises causing the alarm. Operators can then determine whether the noises are naturally occurring sounds from wind or rain or are from an actual intrusion attempt. *Taut-wire sensors* combine a physically taut-wire barrier with an intrusion-detection sensor network. The taut-wire sensor consists of a column of uniformly spaced horizontal wires up to several hundred feet in length and securely anchored at each end. Typically, the wires are spaced 4 to 8 inches apart. Each is individually tensioned and attached to a detector located in a sensor post. Two types of detectors are commonly used: mechanical switches and strain gauges. *Fiber optic cable sensors* are functionally equivalent to the strain-sensitive cable sensors previously discussed. However, rather than electrical signals, modulated light is transmitted down the cable, and the resulting received signals are processed to determine whether an alarm should be initiated. Because the cable contains no metal and no electrical signal is present, fiber optic sensors are generally less susceptible to electrical interference from lightning or other sources. *Capacitance proximity sensors* measure the electrical capacitance between the ground and an array of sense wires. Any variations in capacitance, such as that caused by an intruder approaching or touching one of the sense wires, initiates an alarm. These sensors usually consist of two or three wires attached to outriggers along the top of an existing fence, wall, or roof edge.

Buried line sensors consist of detection probes or cable buried in the ground, typically between two fences that form an isolation zone. These devices are wired to an electronic processing unit. The processing unit generates an alarm if an intruder passes through the detection field. Buried line sensors have several significant features:

- They are hidden, making them difficult to detect and circumvent.
- They follow the terrain's natural contour.
- They do not physically interfere with human activity, such as grass mowing or snow removal.
- They are affected by certain environmental conditions, such as running water and ground freeze/thaw cycles.

Microwave intrusion-detection sensors are categorized as bistatic or monostatic. Bistatic sensors use transmitting and receiving antennas located at opposite ends of the microwave link, whereas monostatic sensors use a single antenna.

Infrared (IR) sensors are available in both active and passive models. An active sensor generates one or more near-IR beams that generate an alarm when interrupted. A passive sensor detects changes in thermal IR radiation from objects located within its field of view. Active sensors consist of transmitter/receiver pairs. The transmitter contains an IR light source (such as a gallium arsenide light-emitting diode [LED]) that generates an IR beam. The light source is usually modulated to reduce the sensor's susceptibility to unwanted alarms resulting from sunlight or other IR light sources. The receiver detects changes in the signal power of the received beam. To minimize nuisance alarms from birds or blowing debris, the alarm criteria usually require that a high percentage of the beam be blocked for a specific interval of time.

Video motion sensors are available on most digital video recorders used in security applications. They can be programmed to activate alarms, initiate recording, or any other designated action when a security camera detects motion. Some digital video recorders can be programmed to monitor very specific fields of view for specific rates of motion in order to increase effectiveness and minimize extraneous detections. Video motion sensors can also greatly improve the efficiency of security personnel monitoring security cameras by alerting them when motion is detected.

Boundary-Penetration Sensors

Boundary-penetration sensors are designed to detect penetration or attempted penetration through perimeter barriers at buildings. These barriers include walls, ceilings, duct openings, doors, and windows.

Structural-vibration sensors detect low-frequency energy generated in an attempted penetration of a physical barrier by hammering, drilling, cutting, detonating explosives, or employing other forcible methods of entry. A piezoelectric transducer senses mechanical energy and converts it into electrical signals proportional in magnitude to the vibrations.

Glass-breakage sensors detect the breaking of glass. The noise from breaking glass consists of frequencies in both the audible and ultrasonic range. Glass-breakage sensors use microphone transducers to detect the glass breakage. The sensors are designed to respond to specific frequencies only, thus minimizing such false alarms as may be caused by banging on the glass.

Passive ultrasonic sensors detect acoustical energy in the ultrasonic frequency range, typically between 20 and 30 kilohertz (kHz). They are used to detect an attempted penetration through rigid barriers (such as metal or masonry walls, ceilings, and floors). They also detect penetration through windows and vents covered by metal grilles, shutters, or bars if these openings are properly sealed against outside sounds.

Balanced magnetic switches (BMSs) are typically used to detect the opening of a door. These sensors can also be used on windows, hatches, gates, or other structural devices that can be opened to gain entry. When using a BMS, mount the switch mechanism on the doorframe and the actuating magnet on the door. Typically, the BMS has a three-position reed switch and an additional magnet (called the bias magnet) located adjacent to the switch. When the door is closed, the reed switch is held in the balanced or center position by interacting magnetic fields. If the door is opened or an external magnet is brought near the sensor in an attempt to defeat it, the switch becomes unbalanced and generates an alarm. A BMS must be mounted so that the magnet receives maximum movement when the door or window is opened.

Grid-wire sensors consist of a continuous electrical wire arranged in a grid pattern. The wire maintains an electrical current. An alarm is generated when the wire is broken. The sensor detects forced entry through walls, floors, ceilings, doors, windows, and other barriers. An enamel-coated number 24 or 26 American wire gauge solid-copper wire typically forms the grid.

Volumetric Motion Sensors

Volumetric motion sensors are designed to detect intruder motion within the interior of a protected volume (Figure 7.7). Volumetric sensors may be active or passive. Active sensors (such as microwave) fill the volume to be protected with an energy pattern and recognize a disturbance in the pattern when anything moves within the detection zone. While active sensors generate their own energy pattern to detect an intruder, passive sensors (such as infrared [IR]) detect energy generated by an intruder. If CCTV assessment or surveillance cameras are installed, video motion sensors can be used to detect intruder movement within the area. Because ultrasonic motion sensors are seldom used, they will not be discussed herein.

> *Microwave motion sensors.* With microwave motion sensors, high-frequency electromagnetic energy is used to detect an intruder's motion within the protected area. Interior or sophisticated microwave motion sensors are normally used.
>
> *Interior microwave motion sensors* are typically monostatic; the transmitter and the receiver are housed in the same enclosure (transceiver).
>
> *Sophisticated microwave motion sensors* may be equipped with electronic range gating. This feature allows the sensor to ignore the signals reflected beyond the settable detection range. Range gating may be used to effectively minimize unwanted alarms from activity outside the protected area.

FIGURE 7.7 **Interior volumetric motion sensor (bottom); CCTV camera (top).**

Passive infrared (PIR) motion sensors detect a change in the thermal energy pattern caused by a moving intruder and initiate an alarm when the change in energy satisfies the detector's alarm criteria. These sensors are passive devices because they do not transmit energy; they monitor the energy radiated by the surrounding environment.

Dual-technology sensors. To minimize the generation of alarms caused by sources other than intruders, dual-technology sensors combine two different technologies in one unit. Ideally, this is achieved by combining two sensors that individually have a high probability of detection (POD) and do not respond to common sources of false alarms. Available dual-technology sensors often combine an active microwave sensor with a PIR sensor. The alarms from each sensor are logically combined in an "and" configuration (i.e., nearly simultaneous alarms from both active and passive sensors are needed to produce a valid alarm).

Video motion sensors generate an alarm when an intruder enters a selected portion of a CCTV camera's field of view. The sensor processes and compares successive images against predefined alarm criteria. There are two categories of video motion detectors, analog and digital. Analog detectors generate an alarm in response to changes in a picture's contrast. Digital devices convert selected portions of the analog video signal into digital data that are compared with data converted previously; if differences exceed preset limits, an alarm is generated. The signal processor usually provides an adjustable window that can be positioned anywhere on the video image. Available adjustments permit changing horizontal and vertical window size, window position, and window sensitivity. Units that are more sophisticated provide several adjustable windows that can be individually sized and positioned. Multiple windows permit concentrating on several specific areas of an image while ignoring others. For example, in a scene containing six doorways leading into a long hallway, the sensor can be set to monitor only two critical doorways.

Point sensors are used to protect specific objects within a facility. These sensors (sometimes referred to as proximity sensors) detect an intruder coming in close proximity to, touching, or lifting an object. Several different types are available, including capacitance sensors, pressure mats, and pressure switches. Other types of sensors can also be used for object protection.

Capacitance sensors detect an intruder approaching or touching a metal object by sensing a change in capacitance between the object and the ground. A capacitor consists of two metallic plates separated by a dielectric medium. A change in the dielectric medium or electrical charge results in a change in capacitance. In practice, the metal object to be protected forms one plate of the capacitor and the ground plane surrounding the object forms the second plate. The sensor processor measures the capacitance between the metal object and the ground plane. An approaching intruder alters the dielectric value, thus changing the capacitance. If the net capacitance change satisfies the alarm criteria, an alarm is generated.

Pressure mats generate an alarm when pressure is applied to any part of the mat's surface, such as when someone steps on the mat. One type of construction uses two layers of copper screening separated by soft-sponge rubber insulation with large holes in it. Another type uses parallel strips of ribbon switches made from two strips of metal separated by an insulating material and spaced several inches apart. When enough pressure is applied to the mat, either the screening or the metal strips make contact, generating an alarm. Pressure mats can be used to detect an intruder approaching a protected object, or they can be placed by doors or windows to detect entry. Because pressure mats are easy to bridge, they should be well concealed, such as placing them under a carpet.

Pressure switches. Mechanically activated contact switches or single ribbon switches can be used as pressure switches. Objects that require protection can be placed on top of the switch. When the object is moved, the switch actuates and generates an alarm. In this usage, the switch must be well concealed. The interface between the switch and the protected object should be designed so that an adversary cannot slide a thin piece of material under the object to override the switch while the object is removed.

ISSUE

Should Businesses or Government (i.e., Taxpayers) Pay for False Alarms?

Ever since intrusion-detection systems were invented and installed to protect businesses and homes, the false alarm problem has persisted. The term *false alarm* is subject to debate because if no offender is found by police at the site of the alarm, it is often assumed that no offender was ever present and that the cause of the alarm resulted from a system malfunction, poor installation, user inexperience, a train nearby, or a host of other possibilities. However, police response to an alarm could have caused an offender to take flight and escape.

The cost of responding to alarms nationally is over $1 billion annually. Chicago police, for example, respond to more than 300,000 burglar alarms each year, and 98 percent (a national average) are "false"; the resources expended are 195 full-time police officers (Sampson 2002). The problem is considered a serious waste of resources, and certain police agencies are lax in responding and may not even respond to an alarm. Local ordinances have been enacted across the country to fine businesses for excessive "false alarms." In 2009, Chicago's false alarm ordinance went from permitting three per year to "zero tolerance." When a "false alarm" is logged and a citation issued, a hearing date is automatically set. Businesses have seven days to pay a $100 fine or appear at the hearing. A defense consists of proving that a licensed alarm contractor was hired and that the system was inspected within the past 12 months (Gelinas 2009).

Critical Thinking

Who should pay for the "false alarm" problem? What can be done to reduce the problem?

Electronic Entry-Control Systems

FEMA (2003b) offers the following information on **electronic entry-control systems**. The function of an entry-control system is to ensure that only authorized personnel are permitted into or out of a controlled area. Entry can be controlled by locked fence gates, locked doors to a building or rooms within a building, or specially designed portals. These means of entry control can be applied manually by security officers or automatically by using entry-control devices. In a manual system, security officers verify that a person is authorized to enter an area, usually by comparing the photograph and personal characteristics of the individual requesting entry. In an automated system, the entry-control device verifies that a person is authorized to enter or exit. The automated system usually interfaces with locking mechanisms on doors or gates that open shortly to permit passage. Access controls include mechanical hardware (e.g., locking mechanisms, electric door strikes, and specially designed portal hardware) and equipment used to detect contraband material (e.g., metal detectors, X-ray baggage-search systems, explosives detectors, and special nuclear-material monitors).

All entry-control systems control passage by using one or more of three basic techniques: *what you know* (e.g., a password or personal identification number [PIN]); *what you have* (e.g., ID card or badge); and *who you are* (e.g., biometrics). Automated entry-control devices based on these techniques are grouped into three categories: coded, credential, and biometric devices.

Coded Devices

The first category, a **coded device,** operates on the principle that a person has been issued a code to enter into an entry-control device. This code will match the code stored in the device and permit entry. Depending on the application, all persons authorized to enter the controlled area can use a single code, or each authorized person can be assigned a unique code. Group codes are useful when the group is small and controls are primarily for keeping out the general public. Individual codes are usually required for control of entry to more critical areas. Coded devices verify the entered code's authenticity, and any person entering a correct code is authorized to enter the controlled area. Electronically coded devices include electronic and computer-controlled keypads.

Electronic keypad devices: The common telephone keypad (12 keys) is an example of an electronic keypad. This type of keypad consists of simple push-button switches that, when depressed, are decoded by digital logic circuits. When the correct sequence of buttons is pushed, an electric signal unlocks the door for a few seconds.

Computer-controlled keypad devices: These devices are similar to electronic keypad devices, except they are equipped with a microprocessor in the keypad or in a separate enclosure at a different location. The microprocessor monitors the sequence in which the keys are depressed and may provide additional functions such as personal ID and digit scrambling. When the correct code is entered and all conditions are satisfied, an electric signal unlocks the door.

Credential Devices

The second category, a **credential device,** identifies a person having legitimate authority to enter a controlled area. A coded credential (e.g., plastic card or key) contains a prerecorded, machine-readable code (Figure 7.8). An electric signal unlocks the door if the prerecorded code matches the code stored in the system when the card is read. Like coded devices, credential devices only authenticate the credential; it assumes a user with an acceptable credential is authorized to enter. The most commonly used types of cards are described as follows:

Smart card: A smart card is embedded with a microprocessor, memory, communication circuitry, and a battery. The card contains edge contacts that enable a reader to communicate with the microprocessor. Entry-control information and other data may be stored in the microprocessor's memory. Smart cards include proximity and encryption (i.e., to prevent hacking) capabilities. Wagley (2008, 72) writes that smart cards are popular because of serving multiple functions, "from financial transactions, time and attendance, tracking, and equipment and material checkout to healthcare processing and network logon."

FIGURE 7.8 Credential device (plastic card) to enter a controlled area. (® Shutterstock.com. With permission.)

The federal government has been a strong proponent of smart cards through legislation such as the Patriot Act, the Health Insurance Portability and Accountability Act, and the Gramm-Leach-Bliley Act. The aim is to reduce identity fraud and other crimes. Smart cards also received strong support from the 2004 **Homeland Security Presidential Directive 12** (HSPD-12), which mandates that federal executive departments and agencies issue one secure and reliable ID card to employees and contractors for multiple purposes.

Proximity card: A proximity card is not physically inserted into a reader; the coded pattern on the card is sensed when it is brought within several inches of the reader. Several techniques are used to code cards. One technique uses a number of electrically tuned circuits embedded in the card. Data are encoded by varying resonant frequencies of the tuned circuits. The reader contains a transmitter that continually sweeps through a specified range of frequencies and a receiver that senses the pattern of resonant frequencies contained in the card. Another technique uses an integrated circuit embedded in the card to generate a code that can be magnetically or electrostatically coupled to the reader. The power required to activate embedded circuitry can be provided by a small battery embedded in the card or by magnetically coupling power from the reader.

Magnetic-stripe card: A strip of magnetic material located along one edge of the card is encoded with data (sometimes encrypted). The data is read by moving the card past a magnetic read head.

Wiegand-effect card: The Wiegand-effect card contains a series of small-diameter, parallel wires embedded in the bottom half of the card. The wires are manufactured from ferromagnetic materials that produce a sharp change in magnetic flux when exposed to a slowly changing magnetic field. This type of card is impervious to accidental erasure. The card reader contains a small read head and a tiny magnet to supply the applied magnetic field. It usually does not require external power.

Bar code: A bar code consists of black bars printed on white paper or tape that can be easily read with an optical scanner. This type of coding is not widely used for entry-control applications because it can be easily duplicated. For low-level security areas, the use of bar codes can provide a cost-effective solution for entry control.

Biometric Devices

The third category used to control entry is based on the measurement of one or more physical or personal characteristics of an individual. Because most entry-control devices based on this technique rely on measurements of biological characteristics, they have become commonly known as **biometric devices**. Characteristics such as fingerprints, hand geometry, voiceprints, handwriting, and retinal blood-vessel patterns have been used for controlling entry. Typically, in enrolling individuals, several reference measurements are made of the selected characteristic and then stored in the device's memory or on a card. From then on, when that person attempts entry, a scan of the characteristic is compared with the reference data template. If a match is found, entry is granted. Rather than verifying an artifact, such as a code or a credential, biometric devices verify a person's physical characteristic, thus providing a form of identity verification. Because of this, biometric devices are sometimes referred to as personnel identity verification devices. The most common biometric devices are described as follows:

Fingerprint-verification devices: These devices use one of two approaches. One is pattern recognition of the whorls, loops, and tilts of the referenced fingerprint, which is stored in a digitized representation of the image and compared with the fingerprint of the prospective entrant. The second approach is minutiae comparison, which means that the endings and branching points of ridges and valleys of the referenced fingerprint are compared with the fingerprint of the prospective entrant.

Hand geometry: Several devices are available that use hand geometry for personnel verification. These devices use a variety of physical measurements of the hand, such as finger length, finger curvature, hand width, webbing between fingers, and light transmissivity through the skin to verify identity. Both two- and three-dimensional units are available.

Retinal patterns: This type of technique is based on the premise that the pattern of blood vessels on the human eye's retina is unique to an individual. While the eye is focused on a visual target, a low-intensity IR light beam scans a circular area of the retina. The amount of light reflected from the eye is recorded as the beam progresses around the circular path. Reflected light is modulated by the difference in reflectivity between blood-vessel pattern and adjacent tissue. This information is processed and converted to a digital template that is stored as the eye's signature. Users are allowed to wear contact lenses; however, glasses should be removed.

DO NOT MAKE THESE MISTAKES

Access Controls

Regina Byrd had worked in the Clinton County Clerk's office for three months as an office assistant. She was well liked, and her supervisor was pleased with her work. Unfortunately, Regina's boyfriend Max, and his brother Pete, were heavily involved in the illegal drug trade and violent crimes. One evening, Max asked Regina to smuggle a pistol into the Clinton courthouse, which maintained access controls for visitors, but not employees. Initially, Regina refused, but Max threatened her.

On the day Pete was to be tried on drug charges, Regina hid a pistol in her pants, entered the courthouse as she did each work day, met Max in an isolated, public area, and transferred the pistol to him. Max watched the detective who would testify against his brother enter the crowded courthouse. He waited until the detective reached the courtroom door, and then Max shot him twice in the head, killing him instantly.

Lessons: Both visitors and employees at a courthouse should be required to go through access controls to prevent crimes. Provide separate entrances for witnesses and other individuals important to cases. Conduct thorough background investigations on employment applicants.

Critical Thinking

If both visitors and employees are required to go through access controls at courthouses, are other avenues available for smuggling in weapons? What can employers do if they know that an employee, in such a position, has a relationship with a dangerous person? Explain your answers.

Lock and Key Systems

Locks have a long history dating back to the ancient Egyptians. Through centuries of development, locks have been refined and improved. In colonial America, blacksmiths crafted locks, but could not keep up with demand. When the Industrial Revolution occurred, mass production supplied the demand. Fredrick T. Stanley established the first factory to produce locks in 1831.

Today, this industry offers many types of locks. UL is a leader in setting standards and testing of locks. The NFPA is another source of standards, especially pertaining to safety and ease of escape during emergencies. ANSI, BHMA, and local ordinances are other sources for lock selection.

The basic purpose of a lock and key system is to prevent unauthorized entry. There are many types of locks with various levels of security. Three major types of locks are mechanical, electric, and a combination of both.

Beginning with mechanical residential locks, most people are familiar with the **key-in-the-knob lock** (bottom of Figure 7.9), whereby a key is

FIGURE 7.9   **Key-in-the-knob lock (bottom) with latch bolt and dead latch at edge of door. Double-cylinder dead-bolt lock (top) with bolt at edge of door.**

FIGURE 7.10 **Key-in-the-lever (bottom) lock and coded device (also called combination lock) (top). (® Shutterstock.com. With permission.)**

inserted in the keyway in the knob to unlock the lock. On the inside is the button that must be pushed or rotated for locking. For ADA compliance, we see increasing numbers of levers (Figure 7.10), rather than knobs, to open doors with greater ease. These mechanical locks have a spring-loaded latch bolt (bottom of Figure 7.9 at edge of door) with a beveled face (i.e., the bolt is cut at an angle) so that when the door is almost closed, the latch bolt retracts until the door is closed, upon which the latch bolt springs into the strike plate (to receive the latch bolt) attached to the door frame across from the lock attached to the door. The latch bolt affords limited security because a thin tool can be inserted at the door strike to push it back. To hinder this attack, manufacturers attach a dead-latch locking bar to the latch bolt (bottom of Figure 7.9 at edge of door).

To increase security, a **dead-bolt lock** is installed on a door so that a bolt (top of Figure 7.9 at edge of door) extends about 1 inch into the door frame to secure the door. A **single-cylinder dead-bolt lock** has a cylinder facing the outside, and it requires a key to retract the bolt into the door when entering; on the inside, this lock has a thumb turn that allows an individual to lock and unlock the door from the inside. If glass is nearby, an offender may be able to break the glass, reach in, and unlock this lock. A **double-cylinder dead-bolt lock** has a cylinder on both sides and affords increased security because a key is required to lock and unlock the door from either side (top of Figure 7.9).

However, fire authorities and codes may restrict the use of this type of lock because it may hinder escape in case of emergency. A resident should keep the key near the door. Residential locks typically afford limited security.

A major component of these locks is the **cylinder**, which includes the keyway and internal vertical pins, among other parts. When the correct key is inserted, the pins fall onto the cuts in the key, enabling the key to turn the cylinder and release the lock.

Another type of lock is the **mortise lock**, which is recessed into the edge of a door once a cavity is hollowed out. It is rectangular in shape and contains both a dead-bolt and a latch. These locks are often seen on building entrances and office doors. Security is limited.

A **unit lock** requires a rectangular cutout on the edge of a door followed by insertion of the lock. It is often used in place of a mortise lock for thin doors; it contains no exposed screws; and it affords good protection against attempts to remove the cylinder or the whole lock.

A **rim-mounted lock** is installed on the inside surface of a door, and it is used for supplemental protection. This lock is also designed with key operation from the outside, which requires installation of a cylinder that extends through the door.

Padlocks are manufactured for a variety of security levels. Two basic types are key-operated and combination-operated. A shackle (at the top of the padlock) serves to, for instance, hold chains together at a closed gate. Padlocks are commonly used with a hasp (Figure 7.11). A weak hasp can render a strong lock useless. More-secure padlocks are manufactured with hardened metal to prevent cutting at the shackle. Increased protection is afforded through a steel case that surrounds the shackle and the lock body (Fennelly 2004, 176–182; Elkins and Farrar 2000).

FIGURE 7.11   **Hasp secured with padlock to protect access point. (® Shutterstock. com. With permission.)**

Electric locks are compatible with automated access control systems. These locks are available with one of two features, known as fail safe or fail secure. **Fail safe** means that the lock opens during a power failure. **Fail secure** means that the lock remains locked during a power failure, in which case, safety becomes an issue. The design of an access control system must consider local and national fire, life safety, and electrical codes. Since the fail-safe approach creates a security vulnerability, policies and procedures should be in place to prevent unauthorized access.

The **electric strike** is a common electric lock. The strike, which is the electrically controlled portion of the lock mechanism, is mounted in a door frame (jamb) and does not require wiring through the door itself. The electronic strike contains a bolt pocket, which is the indent that holds the protruding latch bolt or dead bolt secure in the frame. To open, the strike rotates away from the pocket, providing a path for the bolt to escape. The **electric bolt** is fitted on or in the jamb or the door, and when activated, it protrudes (or in some models, swings) into a strike plate on the adjoining surface. The dead bolt will not give way with spring action, and once it is locked in place, it cannot be retracted until the electric signal is given to unlock. This device is used generally for interior door applications, because the electric bolt may not meet certain safety code regulations for egress doors. An **electric lockset** provides positive locking by pushing a solenoid-operated bolt or rotating bar into a hole in the door edge. Another option is the electronic key-in-the-knob (or key-in-the-lever) lock, which electrically releases the knob, allowing retraction of the bolt. The **electromagnetic lock** consists of an electrically powered magnet and a steel plate. The magnet is mounted to the door frame in alignment with the steel plate to provide a strong or hardened area in which to apply magnetic force. Most of these devices are inherently fail-safe, because power is interrupted to unlock, while some are fail-secure because they maintain power with a backup battery supply. **Electromechanical locks** are operated with a key (mechanical) or through electricity by receiving power to unlock once a correct credential (e.g., code or card) is presented (Elkins and Farrar 2000).

THE ADA

The **Americans with Disabilities Act of 1990** (ADA) has been referred to as the "Bill of Rights of disabled individuals." It promotes access to buildings and employment opportunities for people with disabilities. Physical features of buildings must not hinder or injure disabled individuals. This includes access controls, signs, and emergency systems.

Gross (2008, 112–115) writes that the U.S. Department of Justice, responsible for buildings under the act, selected the U.S. Access Board to develop the "Americans with Disabilities Act Accessibility Guidelines." Gross notes that after years of enforcing these rules, there are still complaints and lawsuits. He writes of several common mistakes, some of which are described next.

Individuals who have had a stroke, a neck injury, or other medical event may be unable to fully open their hands and grab a doorknob. Under the ADA, round knobs should not be in government and commercial buildings. Lever hardware is preferred.

As visually impaired people use a cane to walk, they cannot detect objects with a cane that are higher than 27 inches above the floor. Errors in design occur when objects protrude more than 4 inches from the wall. An impaired person may become injured from fire extinguishers, light fixtures, and other objects, unless they are recessed into the wall.

A third example pertains to signage. Door signs should not be on the door. If a sight-impaired person is reading Braille on a door swinging out, injury can occur. Room signs should be on the wall nearest to the door lever.

Key Control

Key control refers to the security and accountability of keys to prevent unauthorized use. Security is compromised when a key is stolen, lost, or duplicated without authorization. Such events may necessitate changing the locks to prevent losses.

A **master key** requires close protection because it can open locks within submaster systems. Each submaster key opens locks within, say, a floor of a building. A change key opens only one lock.

Control keys for changing the cores of locks also require close protection. **Interchangeable core locks** permit the changing of the keyway, tumblers, and springs rather than the whole lock. This enables a different key to be used.

Various software programs are on the market to track keys and users, prepare reports, interface with electronic locking systems to activate or deactivate locks remotely, and link key-cutting machines directly to computers.

Vulnerabilities of Locks, Keys, and Access Control Systems

There are many techniques of defeating security. Lock-and-key-system vulnerabilities are numerous. Throughout history, and today, the cat-and-mouse game continues: As security is enhanced, offenders devise ways to circumvent new security methods. Locks are subject to physical attack and lock picking. "Bumping" is a type of lock-picking technique that uses a bump key sold online. To counter this technique, manufacturers are producing locks that are resistant to bumping. Keys are vulnerable to many techniques. For example, an offender can press a key into putty or soap and then file a key from a blank.

Electronic access control systems are also subject to defeat. When authorized access is granted to one individual and another person quickly follows, this is known as *tailgating*. When one individual is granted access and passes back a card key or other credential so another person can enter, this is referred to as a *pass back*. To deal with these vulnerabilities, strategies include the use of a turnstile or rotary gate, sensors at openings to count and record (CCTV) those who enter, and security officers. Electronic access control systems are subject to hackers who seek to duplicate access cards, enter systems remotely and on site, and trick biometric devices.

SAFES

Businesses and institutions often purchase safes to protect valuables such as cash, important documents, jewelry, computer media, and so forth. Two major types of safes are money safes and fire safes. The **money safe** (burglary safe) is generally more expensive, heavier, and more solidly built than the fire safe. A **fire safe** has walls containing insulation in the form of powder that turns to steam during a fire to cool the contents (e.g., cash) of the safe as firefighters respond. Safes are available that protect against both burglary and fire.

Underwriters Laboratories (UL) tests and rates safes. As an example, the TL-15 class of burglary safe resists attack to the door for 15 minutes by common mechanical and electrical tools. At the other end of the spectrum, the much more secure TXTL-60X6, resists attacks to all six sides for 60 minutes by common mechanical and electrical tools, cutting torches, and up to 8 oz. of nitroglycerine.

Vaults and file cabinets are other secure locations for valuables. Security specialists must carefully research employer needs to ensure proper selection and ratings.

Doors

A door system includes the door, frame, and anchorage to the building. A door is an opening to a building and, thus, a weak point. Security design should consider that high-security door locks and hardware, and strong and secure walls, ceilings, and floors could be rendered wasteful if an offender is able to break through a weak door. Numerous standards are available for doors from several organizations (e.g., AAMA and NFPA).

Doors should be of solid wood or made of metal. Although many businesses have aluminum doors with full-length glass that is aesthetically pleasing, layered security should surround these openings. This includes glass-breakage sensors, contact switches recessed in the doorframe, motion sensors, and CCTV. Whenever possible, door hinges should be on the inside to avoid the hinge pins from being removed and the door taken off the hinges. Here again, one such vulnerability renders useless other security features. If hinges are on the outside, the pins can be spot-welded to prevent removal. Another option is the use of continuous hinges that run down the length of the door (Phillips 2008, 44). Every door of a building (e.g., garage, utility) should be protected.

Another security layer for doors is inspections. Security officers should check doors to ensure that they are actually locked. It is not unusual for employees to leave the premises for the night and leave a door closed but unlocked. Another vulnerability occurs when a door is propped open with a small rock or other object; the door looks locked, but it is not.

Safety and ease of escape in emergencies are major concerns in planning doors. The NFPA 101 Life Safety Code is the go-to source for guidance. Emergency escape must not be hindered at any door. Electronically controlled doors are typically linked to fire-protection and life-safety systems to facilitate immediate escape. Doors designed primarily for emergency escape present a security weakness because offenders may use them to depart or enter. One solution is the **delayed-egress device**. (Egress means going out.) This device delays egress for a period of time (e.g., 15 seconds) and an alarm is sounded once the hardware (i.e., a bar) is pushed. These devices must release immediately during an emergency.

The U.S. Department of Defense (2007) and FEMA (2003b) offer the following recommendations for doors, with an emphasis on protection against terrorist attacks. As part of a balanced design approach, exterior doors in high-risk buildings should be designed with consideration to withstand an explosive blast. Other general door considerations are as follows:

- Provide hollow steel doors or steel-clad doors with steel frames.
- Provide blast-resistant doors for high threats and high levels of protection.
- Limit normal entry/egress through one door, if possible.
- Keep exterior doors to a minimum while accommodating emergency egress. Doors are less attack-resistant than adjacent walls because of functional requirements, construction, and method of attachment.
- Ensure that exterior doors open outward from inhabited areas. In addition to facilitating egress, the doors can be seated into the door-frames so that they will not enter the buildings as hazardous debris in an explosion.
- Replace externally mounted locks and hasps with internal locking devices, because the weakest part of a door system is the latching component.
- Install doors, where practical, so that they present a blank, flush surface to the outside to reduce their vulnerability to attack.

- Locate hinges on the interior or provide concealed hinges to reduce their vulnerability to tampering.
- Install emergency exit doors so that they facilitate only exiting movement.
- Equip any outward-opening double door with protective hinges and key-operated mortise-type locks.
- Provide solid doors or walls as a backup for glass doors in foyers.
- Strengthen and harden the upright surfaces of door jambs.

Windows

Windows are another weak point in buildings. Offenders typically break through a window or door. A variety of standards are available from several organizations (e.g., AAMA, ASTM, General Services Administration, and UL) for windows and glazing. The term **glazing** refers to the numerous types of materials (e.g., glass) installed in a window frame.

As with other physical security features (e.g., doors), windows should have a **balanced design**. This means that the security feature should theoretically be integrated with the components it is attached or linked to for comparable strength and security, such that failure (e.g., from a burglar or a blast) occurs at the same time. For windows, this would include the glazing, the frame to which it is attached, and the anchoring of the frame to the building. Imagine a burglar seeing a formidable window with burglar-resistant glazing that is not properly secured to the building, whereupon the whole window is removed for access. Examples of security for windows are locks, screens, grilles, and bars; however, ease of escape is a top priority, as emphasized in codes. Glass-breakage sensors, contact switches recessed in the window frame, and motion sensors are applicable to window protection.

The following recommendations for glazing and windows, with an emphasis on protection against terrorist attacks, are paraphrased from FEMA (2003b). Four types of glass are commonly used in window glazing systems: annealed glass, heat-strengthened glass, fully thermally tempered glass, and polycarbonate. Of the four types, annealed glass and fully thermally tempered glass are applied most often at office buildings.

Annealed glass, also known as float, plate, or sheet glass, is the most common glass type used in commercial construction. Annealed glass is of relatively low strength and, upon failure, fractures into razor-sharp, dagger-shaped fragments. **Heat-strengthened glass** is about twice as strong as annealed glass of similar thickness; it fractures similar to annealed glass.

Fully thermally tempered glass (TTG) is typically four to five times stronger than annealed glass. The fracture characteristics are superior to those of annealed glass. Upon failure, it will eventually fracture into small cube-shaped fragments. Breakage patterns of side and rear windows in American automobiles are a good example of the failure mode of TTG. Current building codes generally require TTG anywhere the public can physically touch the glass, such as entrance doors. Although TTG exhibits a relatively safe failure mode for conventional usage, failure during a blast presents a significant danger. Results from blast tests reveal that a blast can propel the fragments at a high enough velocity to constitute a severe hazard.

Wire-reinforced glass is a common glazing material. It consists of annealed glass with an embedded layer of wire mesh. Its primary use is as a fire-resistant and forced-entry barrier. Wire-reinforced glass has the fracture and low-strength characteristics of annealed glass and, although the wire binds some fragments, it still ejects a considerable amount of sharp glass and metal fragments. Wire-reinforced glass is not recommended for blast-resistant windows.

Laminated glass is a pane with multiple glass layers and a pliable interlayer material (usually made from polyvinyl butyral) between the glass layers. Combining interlayer bonding materials with layers of glass produces cross-sections that perform well against blast, ballistic, and forced-entry attacks. The interlayer acts as the glue that bonds the multiple layers of glass. Laminated glass offers significant advantages over monolithic glass. It is stronger and, if failure occurs, the interlayer material may retain most of the glass fragments. In addition, if a projectile passes through the glass, most spalling glass fragments will be retained. Increased safety for fragment retention can be obtained in the event of catastrophic failure from an explosive blast by placing a decorative crossbar or grillwork on the interior of the glazing. However, note that crossbars must be mounted across the center of mass of each windowpane to be effective. Consider installing blast curtains, blast shades, or spall shields to prevent glass fragments from flying into the occupied space.

Another treatment used for mitigating the effects of an explosive attack is **security window film**. The polyester film used in commercial products is commonly referred to as fragment-retention film (FRF), safety film, security film, protective film, or shatter-resistant film. These films are adhered to the interior surface of the window to provide fragment retention and reduce the overall velocity of the glass fragments at failure. FRF combines a strong pressure-sensitive adhesive with a tough polyester layer. It behaves similar to thin laminated and polycarbonate glazing in terms of fragmentation. FRF can also provide protection from natural disasters (e.g., high winds) and graffiti, while reducing energy costs from solar heat (International Window Film Assoc. 2007, 26). As with laminates, increased safety can be obtained with window films by placing a decorative crossbar or grillwork on the interior of the glazing.

Polycarbonates are very strong and suitable for blast- and forced-entry-resistant window design. Monolithic polycarbonate is available in thicknesses up to 1/2 inch, but can be fused together to obtain any thickness needed. However, polycarbonate is expensive and subject to environmental degradation. Local building codes should be consulted when considering polycarbonates, as there are several fire safety issues associated with its use. Additionally, because of its strength, local fire codes may require a percentage of polycarbonate glazing to pop out for emergency egress.

The maximum strength of any window and anchorage system should be equal to the wall strength. This becomes particularly important in the design of ballistic-resistant and forced-entry-mitigating windows, which consist of one or more inches of glass and polycarbonate. These windows can easily become stronger than the supporting wall.

The pressures exerted on a building in a large explosion (e.g., a truck bomb) are often significantly greater than the pressures for which protected windows are designed. For these large events, the upgraded solutions may not be effective, except for windows on the sides of the building not facing the explosion or adjacent buildings. This is particularly true if structural damage occurs. Flying debris generated by structural damage typically causes more severe injuries than window damage alone; however, blast-mitigating window designs are expected to be effective for a large number of threats where the pressures are low. Two such scenarios include a package bomb near the building and a truck bomb that goes off a block away.

Consider using ballistic- and burglar-resistant glazing in high-risk buildings. Ballistic glazing, if required, should meet the requirements of UL 752 Bullet-Resistant Glazing at a level appropriate for the project; glass-clad polycarbonate or laminated polycarbonate are two types of acceptable glazing materials. Security glazing, if required, should meet the requirements of ASTM F1233 or UL 972, Burglary-Resistant Glazing Material. Resistance of window assemblies to forced entry (excluding glazing) should meet the requirements of ASTM F588 at a grade appropriate for the project.

Interior glazing should be minimized where a threat exists. The designer should avoid locating critical functions next to high-risk areas with glazing, such as lobbies and loading docks.

Critical Thinking

How would you answer the following questions about upgraded window protection to protect against a bomb blast at an office building? If an internal explosion occurs, will the upgraded windows increase smoke inhalation injuries by preventing the smoke from venting through windows that, if not upgraded, would normally break in an explosion? If a fire occurs, will it be more difficult for firefighters to break upgraded windows in order to vent the building and gain access to the injured? Will a window upgrade that is intended to protect the occupants worsen the hazards to passersby?

Lighting

Lighting is an essential component of CPTED. The question of whether lighting reduces crime has generated controversy and research. Improvements in street lighting have been studied, and the results are mixed. Two noteworthy studies were conducted in the U.K. by Painter and Farrington (1999), who used experimental-control-group designs and demonstrated that improved street lighting resulted in a reduction in crime. Clarke (2008, 12–13) studied eleven research projects on street lighting, eight in the United States and three in the U.K., including the Painter and Farrington studies. Of the eight studies in the United States, four showed a reduction in crime. The U.K. studies all showed lower crime.

Although these studies focused on street lighting, the critical thinking that surfaced from the research serves as input for planning specific security strategies. For example, Pease (1999) describes how improved lighting could *reduce crime* by deterring offenders, increasing natural surveillance, and enhancing pride and cohesiveness that may lead to reporting of crime. Alternatively, Pease argues that improved lighting could *increase crime* by escalating the visibility of potential victims, assets, and vulnerabilities; improving the surveillance capabilities and techniques of offenders; and helping offenders pinpoint the location of "capable guardians."

Clarke (2008, 11) notes the difficulty of evaluating the effects of lighting. Although he concentrates on street lighting, the variables he cites are applicable to research of security lighting in general. As an example, consider the effects on crime during the day or in darkness and for the experimental area as well as the control area. This would include the issues of displacement of crime and diffusion of benefits. Other variables are the effect on different types of crime, the effect on fear, type of lighting, and the interaction of lighting with other environmental improvements and security features (e.g., CCTV and security officers).

Lighting is a psychological deterrent, and it permits security officers, public police, and passersby to observe harmful events. Well-designed lighting can also improve sales by making customers feel safe when shopping at night, and it can draw customers to stores, merchandise, and sales events.

Lighting terms and definitions are listed here as an aid to understanding lighting:

- **Color rendition**: The differences among lamp light outputs that distort people's perception of color. Good color rendition facilitates revelation of suspect ID.
- **Footcandle** (fc): A unit of illuminance equal to 10.76 lux; it is also a measure of light 1 foot from its source.
- **Glare**: Excessive brightness that hinders visibility.
- **Illuminance**: Light intensity on a surface or object measured in units of lux or fc.
- **Lamp**: Another term for *bulb*.
- **Light trespass**: A type of light pollution that goes beyond its boundary and/or purpose, possibly causing harm (e.g., glare and problems with sleep and animal health).
- **Lux**: The international metric unit of illuminance equal to 1 lumen (light) evenly distributed over a surface of 1 square meter. One lux equals about 0.093 fc.

Here are examples of average illuminance at buildings and facilities according to the Illuminating Engineering Society of North America (2003):

- Interior lighting for patrolling security officers in unoccupied buildings: 10 lux (1 fc)
- Guarded entrances for inspections: 100 lux (10 fc)
- Open parking facilities: 30 lux (3 fc) on the pavement
- Parking garages and covered parking facilities: 60 lux (6 fc) on the pavement
- Convenience stores and gas stations: 60 lux (6 fc) on the pavement
- Common areas (e.g., hallways and stairways) of multifamily residences: 30 lux (3 fc)

The National Fire Protection Association (2005, 12) divides lamps into three categories—incandescent, fluorescent, and high-intensity discharge (HID)—as described next with the assistance of Fennelly (2004, 218–222) and the Illuminating Engineering Society of North America (2003, 17).

Incandescent lamps pass an electric current through a tungsten filament that glows and produces light in a glass tube containing a gas. These lamps are common in residences, are inexpensive, have a short life (750 hours), and are low in efficiency. Color rendition is good, except blue and green are dulled. *Halogen lamps* (or quartz iodide) are of the incandescent type, but have increased efficiency, and halogen gas is contained in a glass tube. The life is 2,500 hours. Blue and green colors are dulled.

Fluorescent lamps produce light by passing electricity through a glass tube containing gas. These lamps are more efficient than incandescent lamps. The life is 20,000 hours. Color rendition is good. These lamps do not project light over long distances.

High-intensity discharge lamps pass electricity through a gas and require starting and warm-up time of between 5 and 10 minutes to reach usable light output. *Mercury vapor lamps*, the first-to-be-developed HID lamp, pass electricity through mercury vapor, have good efficiency, and long life (24,000 hours), which is why they are commonly used as street lights. Green is dulled. *Metal halide lamps* are similar to mercury vapor lamps, but they produce better color rendition, although red is dulled. The life is 20,000 hours. These lamps, although expensive, produce close-to-daylight conditions and are used at sports stadiums. *High-pressure sodium lamps* are popular, efficient, penetrate fog, and are used at building exteriors and parking lots. The life is 24,000 hours. Red and blue are dulled, while yellow is enhanced. *Low-pressure sodium lamps* are more efficient than high-pressure sodium lamps, although expensive to maintain. The life is 18,000 hours. All colors are dulled, except for yellow, which is enhanced.

Another type of lighting gaining interest is light-emitting diodes (LEDs). These lights use a semiconductor chip that electricity runs through to produce light that can last for 50,000 hours. The light efficacy is touted as better than metal halide, incandescent, and compact fluorescent light bulbs. The downside is an expensive initial investment (Durant 2007).

FEMA (2003b) offers four types of security lighting, paraphrased next.

Continuous lighting is the most common security-lighting system. It consists of a series of fixed lights arranged to flood an area continuously during darkness, with overlapping cones of light. Two primary techniques of using continuous lighting are glare projection and controlled lighting. The *glare-projection security-lighting* method lights the area surrounding a controlled area with high-intensity lighting. It serves as a strong deterrent to a potential intruder because it makes him or her very visible while making it difficult to see inside the secure area. Security officers are protected by being kept in comparative darkness while being able to observe intruders at a considerable distance. This method should not be used when the glare of lights directed across the surrounding territory could annoy or interfere with adjacent operations. *Controlled lighting* is best when there are limits to the lighted area outside the perimeter, such as along highways. In controlled lighting, the width of the lighted strip is controlled and adjusted to fit the particular need. This method of lighting may illuminate or silhouette security officers.

Standby lighting has a layout similar to continuous lighting; however, the lights are not continuously lit, but are either automatically or manually turned on when suspicious activity is detected or suspected by security personnel or alarm systems.

Movable lighting consists of manually operated, movable searchlights that may be lit during hours of darkness or as needed. The system normally is used to supplement continuous or standby lighting.

Emergency lighting is a backup power system of lighting that may duplicate any or all of the previously described systems. Its use is limited to times of power failure or other emergencies that render the normal system inoperative. It depends on an alternative power source such as installed or portable generators or batteries.

ISSUE

Security versus Sustainability

Sustainability refers to humans using Earth's resources at a rate at which they can be replenished for future generations. The **Leadership in Energy and Environmental Design (LEED)** is the standard for building "green." It involves a Green Building Rating System developed by the U.S. Green Building Council for environmentally sustainable construction. The results are buildings that are more efficiently built, more energy efficient, and healthier. Individuals who pass an accreditation examination can use the LEED Accredited Professional (AP) acronym after their name. Two disadvantages of LEED standards are the need for additional research by designers and an estimated two percent higher investment in a building that can be recouped over the life cycle of the building (Wikipedia 2009).

Spadanuta (2008, 51–59) raises the security-versus-sustainability issue and sees an increasing number of security practitioners involved. She cites one example where a security designer told a contractor to remove trees because they blocked CCTV viewing. The contractor objected because the trees were needed to earn the building LEED points. Spadanuta recommends that security be involved with designers in the early stages of planning a building because the questions and issues concerning sustainability can also affect security considerations. For instance, many windows are favored in green design to bring natural light into a building and to decrease energy costs. However, at the same time, windows are an entry point for offenders; spies can use windows for surveillance; and during explosions, flying glass is a major cause of casualties. Indoor and outdoor light pollution is another concern that conflicts with lighting as a security strategy. Creative solutions and negotiation can resolve many of the developing issues of security versus sustainability.

Spadanuta (2009, 72) sees some solutions, the costs of which vary, such as using low-light-level cameras that do not need as much light as traditional cameras, using blast-resistant windows that also improve energy efficiency, using sensors that adjust lighting and HVAC depending on the presence of people, constructing grassy berms rather than installing bollards, and planting grass and other plant life on roofs to camouflage a building from above and make it look like a park (unless street-level or 3-D maps are available to the observer).

Critical Thinking

What other issues do you see on the horizon relevant to security and sustainability? What are your solutions?

Closed-Circuit Television Systems

Closed-circuit television systems (CCTV), also referred to as video surveillance systems, are a tremendous asset to security programs. They are applied at perimeters, outside and inside buildings, in public places, and at many other locations. Multiple locations can be observed by one individual thousands of miles away at an operations center or via laptop, cell phone, or PDA. Recordings are available as an aid to criminal and civil cases. CCTV systems have numerous capabilities. Referred to as "PTZ," cameras *pan* side-to-side, *tilt* up and down, and *zoom* in for a closer look. Tiny pin-hole-lens cameras assist investigators in gathering evidence against offenders. These cameras can be hidden in many places.

Fullerton (2009, 7) describes the broad application of CCTV systems that help justify the investment beyond protection needs. He writes of two examples. Retail stores use these systems to monitor customer behavior to optimize business by, for example, collecting information on traffic flow and items purchased from various locations in a store. Construction managers use CCTV systems to observe actual construction and adherence to safety regulations.

In the public sector, CCTV is applied to city streets and highways to prevent and watch for crime and traffic problems. Video transmissions are reaching patrol cars so police can watch crimes in progress as they plan and respond.

Studies have been conducted on the usefulness of CCTV in public places to reduce crime. A study conducted in San Francisco over several years by the University of California found that CCTV did not reduce violent crime, but succeeded in reducing burglary, pick pocketing, and purse snatching. The study found that CCTV was not integrated with other police strategies and the technology was inadequate (Selna and Bulwa 2009). A multiyear New York City study by New York University found no evidence of a drop in major crimes, but a drop in minor crimes. A study in East Orange, New Jersey, found a 50 percent drop in violent crimes; police had access to video and quick police reports, and electronic listening devices were installed in high-crime areas. Other studies showed mixed results (Lee 2009). At the same time, CCTV has served as a deterrent and an aid to solving crimes in both the public and private sectors.

Zalud (2008, 46) described how Walgreens used CCTV. Following an investment of over $30 million over one year to install networked digital video recorders, all stores aim to have at least four public-view monitors so all those who enter the store can see the TV monitors and know they are being watched (i.e., a deterrent). Walgreens' loss prevention supervisors are able to see live or recorded video at any time, and if police need a photo of an offender, it can be downloaded to the store photo lab for copies.

CCTV originated during the mid-twentieth century. By the 1960s, manufacturers introduced vacuum-tube television cameras, and in the 1980s, the introduction of the solid-state CCTV camera became a significant advancement in technology. As crime increased and CCTV technology improved, while prices dropped, these systems came into greater use. Low-cost videocassette recorders (VCR) complemented these early systems (Kruegle 2004, 237).

Today, CCTV technology has standards from several sources (e.g., SIA and ANSI). It has advanced significantly beyond the camera with a cable running to a television monitor. However, major questions facing decision makers involve when and how to make the switch to newer IP technology (digital video) without making costly errors. The trend is toward digital and away from analog. Simply put, analog signals are, for instance, on a tape in original form, whereas with digital, analog signals are sampled, turned into numbers, and stored digitally. This is a conversion to a format enabling data to be stored and transmitted through a computer network. **Internet Protocol (IP)** is a standard that permits computers to communicate across the Internet, which is the world's largest network. With IP cameras, data goes directly into the network; with analog cameras, the video must first be converted to IP.

Enman (2008, 45) writes: "IP video, in its simplest form, is real-time video surveillance—or the ability to view live feeds of video pictures that are transmitted across the Internet and your internal network. IP cameras use the same language or protocols (procedures, codes of behavior, set of rules, modus operandi) as all of the other IP products on the Internet."

The benefits of IP over analog include the transmission of almost-live video at great distances. Analog is appropriate when video is viewed at only one site. In new construction, network cables are less expensive than coaxial cables for analog systems. A disadvantage of IP is the system going down because of a network problem, a hacker, or maintenance. Another challenge with IP is problems with interoperability, meaning that customers are limited in their choice of products that work with their system; IP standards are being planned among manufacturers.

Elliott (2010, 48) refers to the hidden costs of IP surveillance and vendors selling such systems who may not take into account the true cost when providing a quote to customers. Although the cost of installing an IP-based system is typically described as being lower than an analog system, labor is required with the IP system "to configure the corporate network, the switches and routers, to support the required Quality of Service (QoS) features and bandwidth that an IP surveillance system will need." Another hidden cost is network redundancy. If a corporate network is without redundant connections, switch engines, and power supplies, a failure within the network can harm the operation of the IP surveillance system. The implications are serious for entities under legal and regulatory requirements to maintain 24/7/365 video surveillance and recording.

Ahrens (2008, 47) offers advice on the decision as to whether to switch from analog to digital video. Although IP is the trend and inevitable, he recommends a hybrid system of building an infrastructure that supports either analog or digital cameras and systems. The benefits include being able to switch back to analog if the change to digital is too complicated.

Enman (2007, 42) illustrates how design and installation of an IP video surveillance system can go wrong. A school district in Kansas City spent $400,000 to install 195 IP cameras and a digital video network to connect 16 facilities. With numerous break-ins, $80,000 in annual costs from vandalism, and a $1 million arson loss, the investment in the system was necessary. However, the system did not work as touted. It delivered still images rather than video, it did not operate properly for months, and the integrator was without a solution. Another, more competent, integrator was hired. Solutions included upgrading the 195 cameras' power supplies that were underpowered, resulting in downtime; implementing a new network video recording system; working with the school district's IT department on the amount of bandwidth required on the network for so many cameras; and raising some cameras that were too low and subject to being moved by students.

A growing tend in video surveillance is **video analytics** (VA), also called intelligent video. Nason (2008, 24) explains it as a combination of CCTV data and rules-based algorithms. He differentiates video motion detection and video analytics by writing that the former "simply provides an alarm based on changes in pixel gray-scale levels. VA takes it one step further and attempts to determine if these pixel changes represent unauthorized activity." The VA software sets off an alarm when established rules are broken, such as a vehicle stopping in a "no stopping" zone, an item abandoned, an intruder in an unauthorized area, too many people congregating at a location, certain behavior, and so forth. A major benefit of VA (and even video motion detection) is that the number of security personnel observing numerous television monitors connected to an even greater number of cameras can be reduced because the system alerts personnel to anomalies in real time. Nason suggests doing away with intrusion sensors because VA serves as the sensor and alerts personnel who can view the site of the anomaly and, thus, reduce false alarms. VA also assists with the fatigue personnel experience when watching monitors for multiple hours.

An option for development is integrating thermal security camera technology into VA. At night, when lighting is poor, or when fog or smoke are present, **thermal security cameras** permit security personnel to observe video that shows differences in heat among objects (e.g., human). Spadanuta (2009, 72) writes of other developing night vision technology such as continuous-wave lasers that provide light for long distances in a safe way; this technology directs a laser light to exactly the spot the camera is seeking to capture. Additional options for development are integrating radar and GIS into VA. Another type of camera option when light is not available is infrared (IR); this requires an IR light source.

The progression of recording video went from **videocassette recorder** (VCR), to **digital video recorder** (DVR), to **network video recorder** (NVR). The older VCR required the storage of numerous cassette tapes and the changing of the tape in the recorder. The old, less expensive VCR often has to be rebuilt or replaced after about two years, and there is the problem of image degradation caused by dirty heads. In the DVR, the moving parts are primarily contained in the hard drive. It will last longer than the VCR. Instant accessibility (even remotely over the Internet) is another advantage.

The DVR is capable of recording audio from a microphone in a camera to listen to and record offenders. However, legal advice should be sought to ensure employee rights are protected.

Capulli (2009, 39) writes about video recording technology:

> The "middle of the road" of video surveillance is upgrading by using a DVR. A DVR system is not truly fully IP-based, but is a step toward the more advanced IP technology. In actuality, a DVR system uses the same cameras and structures for cabling as the older CCTV analog systems, but the old VCRs and multiplexers have been replaced with DVR for storage of the data. The data is converted to digital so it can be stored on hard disks, but the quality of the images captured remains analog since this is how it originated. In other words, analog signals are fed from the cameras to the DVR, where they are converted into digital signals for storage and/or transmission over digital networks. However, in such applications, one must be very careful of image degradation. That is because analog and digital use different video display methods.

Madsen (2009, 32) distinguishes between the *stand-alone DVR* and the *PC-based DVR*. The former is a single unit containing a computer, software, hard drive, and other components. The latter is a PC combined with recording equipment; it contains a motherboard, a network card, a video board, a hard drive, video inputs for analog cameras, Ethernet ports for IP cameras, and other components. Madsen writes that stand-alones are much less vulnerable to hackers, viruses, and other attacks. In addition, the PC-based DVR is more expensive because of such needs as operating system updates, antivirus software updates, and patches.

A true, nonhybrid NVR involves digital transmission from camera to recorder on the network. The NVR is a computer storage system as opposed to the bulky DVR. However, analog and the nonnetworked DVR are more secure than the NVR, which is part of the network and thus subject to attack.

Critical Thinking

When Chicago Mayor Daley learned that security officers at the city's water filtration plants and state military posts were caught sleeping and had abandoned a post, the $13.3-million security contract was rebid, and the mayor said that the city needed to replace people with surveillance cameras. Daley said: "Technology is the key in all security. You don't need human beings sitting there anymore" (Main and Spielman 2007). Do you agree with the mayor? Explain your answer.

Security Operations Center

A **security operations center** (SOC) is a central point from which personnel, policies and procedures, and technology are applied 24/7 to daily security and safety operations and emergency events that may be local or global. SOC standards can be obtained from the NFPA, ANSI, UL, and other groups.

Because the SOC plays a crucial role in protecting people and assets from a variety of threats and hazards, it must be designed with survivability in mind so that it can be a focal point for responding to emergencies. At the same time, an alternate SOC site should be planned. Redundancy is also important, so that if one communication path or source of electric power is disabled, another one can take its place. Another important design consideration is the security and safety of the SOC itself. This entails quality access controls, doors, and locks. The level of security depends on need following a risk analysis. Windows should be kept to a minimum and, if used, consideration should be given to glass block walls for sunlight. The location of the SOC is subject to debate, and the answer depends on various factors, such as type of facility and business and potential threats. The SOC may be located in a secure underground bunker or in a lobby in view of everyone who enters. Design considerations include fire-resistant construction materials, fire protection, and bullet-resistant glazing.

An SOC often contains security personnel who monitor CCTV, access controls, and security, safety, and fire alarm systems. Mass notification systems are another component of SOCs. At SOCs, incoming calls for service are received, and security personnel (and even maintenance specialists) are dispatched. As systems and buildings become "smarter," more and more decisions will be made automatically without human intervention.

Organizations have the option of outsourcing the monitoring of security and fire-protection systems to what is referred to as a **central station**. This is a service business located away from the protected facility. When it receives an alarm signal, it contacts public police, other first responders, and the client.

YOUR CAREER IN SECURITY

Physical Security Specialist

Physical security is a multibillion-dollar industry offering a variety of products, systems, and services to protect clients. Employment ranges from small, local companies to large, global corporations. States and locales often require a license and registration for these businesses and their employees.

Careers in physical security are varied in this huge industry. Here, we focus on two types of positions: physical security technician (PST) and physical security systems specialist (PSSS).

Nature of the Work

A PST may work at residential sites or commercial sites installing and servicing intrusion detection, CCTV, fire, card access, communications, and other systems. The duties include following procedures, practices, and standards when working on systems; completing assignments in a timely manner; instructing and satisfying customers; completing company documentation; caring for tools, equipment, and a vehicle; and attending meetings and training.

A PSSS analyzes, develops, and recommends systems in conjunction with the operational plans of an entity. The work entails a lot of planning, research, budgeting, and coordination. A PSSS is knowledgeable of the state-of-the-art so that the best possible recommendations can be made to management on which systems to select. Responsibilities include installation, upgrades, and servicing of many types of physical security systems. Project planning and vendor relations and management are also part of the job. This work requires the application of standards, specifications, and policies to ensure the success of physical security and minimal business disruption if failure occurs. Another aspect of the work is to provide system solutions when problems surface from customers or audits. The PSSS is the point of contact for physical security during emergencies (Brennan and Walker 2008, 47).

Requirements

Depending on the employer and the complexity of assignments, a PST should have at a minimum a high school diploma or GED, with preference given to those with an associate or bachelor's degree in electronics or equivalent military training. Those with specialized training and certifications are more marketable. A few years of employment with an experienced technician while installing and servicing systems is often required. Additional requirements are computer proficiency, state and local low-voltage licenses, ability to work on a ladder, strong customer relations skills, ability to work independently or as part of a team, ability to travel, and a valid and clean driver's license. Many companies provide in-house training for technicians.

The National Burglar and Fire Alarm Association (NBFAA) provides standardized training to meet licensing requirements. The National Training School (NTS), a member service of the NBFAA, offers classroom and online training for those who sell, monitor, install, and service electronic systems. Almost 30,000 students have completed NTS courses, and thousands have been certified (National Burglar and Fire Alarm Association 2008).

Another professional association offering training and publications is the National Alarm Association of America (NAAA). It provides training and manuals for installers, service personnel, and those who design systems.

For the PSSS, Brennan and Walker (2008, 47) recommend a bachelor's degree relevant to security systems and more than six years of experience with such systems, security software, and IT systems.

ASIS International offers the Physical Security Professional (PSP) certification. To be eligible to take the PSP examination, candidates must have five years of experience in the physical security field, a high school diploma or GED, and a clean record.

Salary

According to multiple companies on the Web in 2009, PSTs earn $35,000 or more annually. Depending on the employer, additional compensation may result from overtime pay, incentives, and bonuses. Pay is often tied to production. Benefits (e.g., insurance, 401[k]) vary. Employers provide one or more of the following: training, company vehicle, laptop computer, cell phone, and tools. If technicians are successful in selling products or services, they may receive a commission and an offer to become a salesperson.

For the PSSS, Brennan and Walker (2008) see the salary at between $70,000 and $80,000 annually.

Advice

For those interested in a career as a physical security technician, electronics and computer skills are especially important, along with relevant education, training, and experience. This career is appealing to those who like to work with their hands and troubleshoot systems. Remember that an entry-level position may lead to advancement to supervision, management, sales, owning your own business, and other career options. Search the Web and speak with practitioners to learn more about this vocation.

For the PSSS, engineering and business degrees provide a foundation for the work and subsequent opportunities in management and consulting.

Summary

Physical security is in need of research as it faces challenges, vulnerabilities, and the development of standards. Physical security entails a wide range of devices and systems coordinated with policies, procedures, and personnel. There is an increasing merger of physical security and IT systems, and this convergence continues to encounter numerous challenges. Although both well-designed and operated physical security is formidable, it must be constantly evaluated and improved because offenders seek to challenge and defeat it.

This chapter explained and illustrated numerous physical security strategies, including perimeter barriers, electronic security systems, electronic entry-control systems, lock-and-key systems, doors, windows, lighting, CCTV, and security operations centers. Before selecting specific physical security strategies to apply, the security practitioner should develop a security methodology as a foundation for planning and implementation.

Discussion Questions

1. What research directions would you suggest for the physical security field?
2. What do you view as the most serious vulnerability facing physical security?
3. How do IT and physical security impact each other?
4. What security strategies would you recommend for a multistory office building located adjacent to a city street downtown in a major city?
5. What are your solutions for "false alarms"?
6. What are the vulnerabilities of lock-and-key systems, and what are your solutions?
7. How do you think physical security technology is affecting employment opportunities in the security profession today? What about the future?
8. In what ways can physical security be defeated? What countermeasures do you recommend?

9. Do you think the issue of security versus sustainability will disappear in a few years? Explain your answer.

Practical Applications

7A. You are a physical security specialist. Your new assignment is to prepare plans for perimeter security for a pharmaceutical plant that contains a facility for animal research. The research is controversial, and protests and internal sabotage are potential threats. Another security specialist will be planning strategies to protect against internal threats. The plant is located in an isolated, rural area ten miles from a medium-size city. What are your plans for perimeter security?

7B. You are a physical security specialist. You are assigned the task of researching the standards and testing of doors, windows, and passive and active vehicle barriers. Your focus is to protect against terrorist attack, among other threats and hazards. Conduct a search of the Web. List the organizations that prepare standards and test each of these items.

7C. As a security manager, you are preparing plans and a budget to purchase physical security for five similar convenience stores in an urban area that are open 24/7 and are experiencing an upsurge in robberies and internal theft. You will be purchasing five safes and five internal and external CCTV systems. Research the type of safe you will purchase and the costs. Research the type of CCTV system you will purchase, the number of cameras for each store, recording capabilities, installation, maintenance for one year, and total costs. Include all relevant information and costs in a security business proposal (see Chapter 4). Hypothetical information can be added for this application.

7D. You are on a physical security committee of a large nonprofit association of security professionals. The committee's present task is to prepare a report on the top challenges facing physical security in general and their solutions. What is your input? Prepare at least three challenges with solutions.

Internet Connections

American Architectural Manufacturers Association: www.aamanet.org
American Institute of Architects: www.aia.org
American National Standards Institute: www.ansi.org
American Society for Testing and Materials: www.astm.org
American Society of Landscape Architects: www.asla.org
ASIS International: www.asisonline.org

Builders Hardware Manufacturers Association: www.buildershardware.com
Central Station Alarm Association: www.csaaul.org
Illuminating Engineering Society of North America: www.iesna.org
Institute of Electrical and Electronics Engineers: www.iee.org
International Association of Lighting Management Companies: www.nalmco.org
International Organization for Standardization: www.iso.org
National Alarm Association of America: www.naaa.org
National Association of Building Owners and Managers: www.boma.org
National Burglar and Fire Alarm Association: www.alarm.org
National Crime Prevention Council: www.ncpc.org
National Electrical Manufacturers Association: www.nema.org
National Fire Protection Association: www.nfpa.com
National Lighting Bureau: www.nlb.org
Security Industry Alarm Coalition: www.siacinc.org
Security Industry Association: www.siaonline.org
Technical Support Working Group: www.tswg.gov
Underwriters Laboratory: www.ul.com
U.S. General Services Administration: www.gsa.gov
U.S. Marshals Service: www.usdoj.gov/marshals

References

Ahrens, S. 2008. Is IP the Wall Street of video? *Security* 45 (December):47.

ASIS International. 2005. *Career opportunities in security.* Alexandria, VA: ASIS International.

ASIS International. 2009. Facilities physical security measures guideline. www.asisonline.org.

Bitzer, E., and A. Hoffman. 2007. Psychology in the study of physical security. *Journal of Physical Security* 2:9.

Brennan, J., and S. Walker. 2008. Physical security systems specialist III. *Security Technology & Design* 18 (February):47.

Capulli, M. 2009. Going hybrid. *Security Technology Executive* 19 (January):39.

Clarke, R. 2008. Improved street lighting to reduce crime in residential areas (December). Washington, DC: U.S. Department of Justice, Office of Community Oriented Policing Services.

Durant, J. 2007. LEDs benefit general illumination. *Morning News* (August 15).

Elkins, E., and M. Farrar. 2000. *User's guide on controlling locks, keys and access cards.* Port Hueneme, CA: National Facilities Engineering Service Center.

Elliott, D. 2010. The hidden cost of IP surveillance. *Security* 47 (January):48.

Enman, C. 2007. Second time around. *Security Products* 11 (November):42.

Enman, C. 2008. A world of possibilities. *Security Technology & Design* 18 (January):45.

FEMA. 2003a. Primer to design safe school projects in case of terrorist attacks. FEMA 428 (December). Washington, DC: U.S. Department of Homeland Security.

FEMA. 2003b. Reference manual to mitigate potential terrorist attacks against buildings. FEMA 426 (December). Washington, DC: U.S. Department of Homeland Security.

FEMA. 2008. Incremental protection for existing commercial buildings from terrorist attack. FEMA 459 (April). Washington, DC: U.S. Department of Homeland Security.

Fennelly, L. 2004. *Handbook of loss prevention and crime prevention.* 4th ed. Boston: Elsevier.

Fullerton, E. 2009. The next step in convergence: Video enabling. *Security Director News* 6 (February):7.

Gelinas, D. 2009. Chicago moves to zero tolerance on false alarms. *Security Systems News* 12 (February).

Gross, J. 2008. Accessibility mistakes you don't want to make. *Buildings* 102 (October):112–115.

Illuminating Engineering Society of North America. 2003. *Guideline for security lighting for people, property, and public spaces.* New York: IESNA.

International Window Film Association. 2007. Window film basics. *Buildings* 101 (August):26.

Johnston, R. 2004. Effective vulnerability assessments. Proceedings of the Contingency Planning & Management Conference, Las Vegas, NV, May 25–27, 2004.

Kruegle, H. 2004. CCTV surveillance. In *Handbook of loss prevention and crime prevention*, ed. L. Fennelly. 4th ed. Boston: Elsevier.

Lee, J. 2009. Study questions whether cameras cut crime. *New York Times* (March 3).

Lifrieri, S. 2009. Leveraging liability to increase sales. *Security Systems News* 2009 (January):16.

Madsen, J. 2009. Standalone vs. PC-based DVRs. *Buildings* 103 (March):32.

Main, F., and F. Spielman. 2007. Asleep at military post. *Chicago Sun-Times* (October 24).

Nason, R. 2008. Analyze that. *Security Technology & Design* 18 (March):24.

National Burglar and Fire Alarm Association. 2008. National training school. www.alarm.org.

National Fire Protection Association. 2005. *NFPA 730 guide for premises security.* Quincy, MA: NFPA.

Painter, K., and D. Farrington. 1999. Street lighting and crime: Diffusion of benefits in the stoke-on-trent project. In *Surveillance of public spaces: CCTV, street lighting and crime prevention*, ed. K. Painter and N. Tilly. Monsey, NY: Criminal Justice Press.

Pease, K. 1999. A review of street lighting evaluations. In *Surveillance of public spaces: CCTV, street lighting and crime prevention*, ed. K. Painter and N. Tilley. Monsey, NY: Criminal Justice Press.

Phillips, M. 2008. Increasing the longevity of high-use doors. *Buildings* 102 (February):44.

Regelski, M. 2008. Supply and demand. *Security Products* 12 (July):10.

Sampson, R. 2002. False burglar alarms. Washington, DC: U.S. Department of Justice, Office of Community Oriented Policing Services.

Selna, R., and D. Bulwa. 2009. Study gives split verdict on crime cameras. *San Francisco Chronicle* (January 13).

Spadanuta, L. 2008. The greening of security. *Security Management* 52 (July):51–59.

Spadanuta, L. 2009. Shedding light on nighttime surveillance. *Security Management* 53 (March):72.

U.S. Department of Defense. 2007. DOD minimum antiterrorism standards for buildings. UFC 4-010-01 (January). Washington, DC: U.S. Department of Defense.

U.S. Government Accountability Office. 2008. Biosafety laboratories: Perimeter security assessment of the nation's five BSL-4 laboratories (September). www.gao.gov/new.items/d081092.pdf.

Verity, J. 2008. The smart, secure building. *Security Products* 2 (June).

Wagley, J. 2008. Trends in ID cards. *Security Management* 52 (July):72.

Wikipedia. 2009. Leadership in energy and environmental design. http://en.wikipedia.org/wiki/Leadership_in_Energy_and_Environmental_Design.

Zalud, B. 2008. High flying solutions. *Security* 45 (March):46.

Chapter 8

Information and Information Technology Security

Chapter Learning Objectives

After reading this chapter, you should be able to:

1. Discuss why information is a valuable asset
2. Name and describe four laws that pertain to the security of information technology and data
3. List and explain ten threats to information technology and data
4. Elaborate on cyber warfare
5. Detail ten strategies of information security
6. Name and explain five technical controls to protect information technology and data
7. Explain *communications security*
8. Differentiate *spying* and *competitive intelligence*

Terms to Know

classified information
copyright
data
data mining
information security

open-source intelligence
patent
proprietary information
reverse engineering
social engineering
trademark
trade secret
Uniform Trade Secrets Act
Economic Espionage Act of 1996
Sarbanes-Oxley Act of 2002 (SOX)
Government Information Security Reform Act of 2000
Health Insurance Portability and Accountability Act of 1996 (HIPAA)
Computer Fraud and Abuse Act of 1986
Electronic Communications Privacy Act of 1986
malware
Trojan horse
worm
virus
spoofed e-mail
patching
botnets
spam
denial-of-service attack
distributed denial-of-service attack
hackers
cyber criminal groups
exploit tools
logic bomb
phishers
sniffer
vishing
war driving
zero-day exploit
steganography
voice over Internet Protocol (VoIP)
cyber warfare
Federal Information Security Management Act of 2002
cyber reconnaissance
cybersecurity
cyberspace
cybersecurity policy
ISO/IEC 27000-series
classification system

nondisclosure agreement
Operations Security (OPSEC)
Overseas Security Advisory Council (OSAC)
technical controls
firewall
intrusion-detection system
wireless network footprint
encryption
cryptography
cryptanalysis
communications security (COMSEC)
TEMPEST
electronic soundproofing
technical surveillance countermeasures (TSCM)
electronic eavesdropping
wiretapping
bugging
keylogging program
Society of Competitive Intelligence Professionals
Chief security officer (CSO)
C-suite

QUIZ

This quiz serves to prime the reader's mind and begin the reading, thinking, and studying processes for this chapter. The answers to all of the questions are found within this chapter.

1. Is it large or small businesses that create the majority of technological innovations in the United States?
2. How can a marketer use data mining?
3. What is the difference between reverse engineering and social engineering?
4. What are the top three countries involved in theft of proprietary information?
5. What are botnets?
6. Is cyber reconnaissance illegal?
7. What is the difference between wiretapping and bugging?
8. What are the legal limits of investigating a business competitor?

Introduction

We live in an age where nations, armed forces, businesses, and other entities seek and retain power and superiority through information. The value placed on certain information is so great that illegal means may be applied to obtain it. This chapter begins by explaining the value of information and the terminology used to understand information security. Laws pertaining to the security of information technology systems and data offer a foundation from which legal action occurs while providing input for security planning. In this chapter, these laws are followed by relevant examples of federal criminal cases involving businesses and cases of espionage against the U.S. military. Laws requiring the protection of personal information are also covered. Finally, the variety of threats facing proprietary information, as well as information security methods and strategies, are explained.

Information as an Asset

Information is an asset that can be very valuable to an organization (and/or individual). The survivability of an organization or business may very well depend on certain information it possesses (Figure 8.1). Examples of such information include formulas to produce a product, production processes, technical drawings, customer lists, and marketing plans.

As much as 75 percent of the market value of a typical U.S. company resides in intellectual property assets (ASIS International 2007a, 1). U.S. losses of intellectual property due to data theft are estimated as high as $1 trillion (White House 2009, 2). *Business Week*, in 2005, estimated that the value of legitimate sales lost to intellectual property theft and related offenses are as high as $512 billion annually (Hayes 2009, 28–29).

FIGURE 8.1 **Research and development are expensive, and if a competitor can steal such proprietary information, the competitor can save enormous sums of money and sell a product at a lower cost. (® Shutterstock.com. With permission.)**

Hayes (2009, 28–29) writes of economic spies targeting small businesses, described as those businesses employing fewer than 500 employees. The U.S. Small Business Administration counted 26.8 million businesses in the United States, with 99.9 percent having fewer than 500 employees. Hayes adds that Census Bureau data on high-patent industries shows, for instance, that 98 percent of companies patenting telecommunications technology employ fewer than 500 people. The figure is 97 percent for the software publishing industry, 92 percent for aerospace products and parts, and 90 percent for pharmaceuticals and medical manufacturing. Hayes emphasizes that small businesses create the majority of technological innovation, and when economic spies victimize Fortune 1,000 companies, these larger businesses generally possess the resources (e.g., security, investigative, and legal) to confront the threat, while small businesses may not survive.

In Chapter 6, Personnel Security, the insider threat was explained. This threat includes economic espionage. The National Infrastructure Advisory Council (2008, 17) noted the

> large and growing threat of Nation-State economic espionage targeting critical technologies in U.S. critical infrastructure companies.... The potential for financial losses is enormous.... Unchecked, this threat would undermine the competitiveness of these companies and could potentially drive them out of business.
>
> Of the economic espionage threats, the threat posed by Nation-State actors seeking critical U.S. technologies is the most serious. Many countries have vast technical resources, highly sophisticated tools, deniability, and a significantly lower level of accountability than individuals or competing corporations. State-sponsored espionage often ties in with corporate espionage, feeding stolen technologies to domestic companies....
>
> Economic espionage is not always State-sponsored. Dynamics in workforce markets are raising the rates of employee turnover,... increasing exposure ... and the likelihood that their high-value institutional knowledge could be transferred to a competitor.

ASIS International (2007a, 2–3) research on proprietary information loss found the following:

- Deliberate and inadvertent actions of current and former employees are serious threats to proprietary information.
- Exploitation of trusted relationships (e.g., customers, vendors, contractors, and consultants) is a threat to proprietary information.
- Information in all forms (e.g., paper, electronic, oral, and prototypes) is being targeted.
- Data-mining software, the availability of open-source and public information, and social engineering present significant threats.

- Information compromises have caused losses to corporate reputation, image, competitive advantage, technology, and profitability.
- The top three offending countries are China, Russia, and India.

Slate (2009) argues that Chinese businesses, with Chinese government encouragement and support, are increasingly relying on illegal human and technical intelligence collection methods to acquire U.S. proprietary information. He writes that Chinese corporate intelligence programs are damaging the foundation of the American corporate world, specifically intellectual property. He adds that U.S. corporations have 75 percent of their value in such intangibles (98 percent for the U.S. technology sector).

Critical Thinking

Do U.S. companies and government agencies conduct economic espionage? Explain your answer.

TERMINOLOGY FOR INFORMATION SECURITY

The following terms and definitions assist the reader in understanding threats to proprietary information and information security.

- **Classified information:** sensitive information restricted by law or regulation to certain individuals who have gone through a background investigation.
- **Copyright:** provides the owner of an original work with the exclusive right to reproduce, distribute, perform, display, or license the work. The Copyright Office of the Library of Congress administers relevant law.
- **Data:** facts and statistics that are processed and analyzed to produce information that is more meaningful than raw data.
- **Data mining:** a process of obtaining information and patterns from data. Investigators can use data-mining software to establish links among people, their travels, and assets by using telephone records, credit card usage, and other data. It can be used for surveillance and to detect fraud. The process can generate patterns about companies and organizations to produce proprietary information. Marketers use data mining, for example, to learn what retail merchandise is sold more often on what day and the characteristics of the purchaser; this helps with ordering merchandise and pricing.
- **Information security:** the protection of sensitive information. Although it often refers to the protection of U.S. Government classified information, it also includes business proprietary information and intellectual property. Specific strategies of information security include who should access the data and how the data is stored,

controlled, marked, disseminated, and destroyed (ASIS International, 2005, 8).

- **Open-source intelligence:** the acquisition and analysis of a variety of types of information from publicly available sources. These sources include public government reports, official data, and contract awards; news media; Web sites, such as blogs, maps, and social networking sites; and professional and academic publications and conferences.
- **Patent:** a government grant of exclusive rights to an invention. The patent application must support the invention as new and useful (as in industry). A patent is a right to prevent others from producing, using, or selling the invention without permission. Such laws vary among countries.
- **Proprietary information:** a property right or other valid economic interest in data resulting from private investment. Protection of such data from unauthorized use and disclosure is necessary in order to prevent the compromise of such property right or economic interest (Title 48: Federal Acquisition Regulations System, 27. 402 Policy).
- **Reverse engineering:** the acquisition of a product (possibly of a competitor) and then dismantling it to learn of its composition and operation (possibly to manufacture a similar product).
- **Social engineering:** manipulating people through deception and trickery to gain sensitive information or to facilitate harmful action. It is often used to gain access to a building or computer system. Examples are as follows: using the Web to send phony e-mails to trick people into releasing information; an individual claims to be a repair technician to seek an access code; and dropping a USB flash drive or other device at a building in anticipation of a victim inserting it into their computer, resulting in sensitive information being sent to the offender. The ploys are endless, so employees must be reminded not to be gullible and to remain vigilant.
- **Trademark:** a unique symbol, phrase, or other indicator used by an organization or person to distinguish its product or service from others. Unauthorized trademark infringement can result in civil action against the alleged violator.
- **Trade secret:** a wide variety of business, scientific, and other types of information producing economic benefit that is not generally known to the public and is protected by the owner to maintain its secrecy.

Laws Protecting Proprietary Information

The **Uniform Trade Secrets Act**, adopted by approximately 46 states as the basis for trade secret law, imposes civil rather than criminal liability for misappropriation of trade secrets and creates a private cause of action for the victim. Remedies for misappropriation of trade secrets under the act include

injunctions (i.e., a court order restraining action), monetary damages, and reasonable attorney's fees. Another law protecting proprietary information is the **Economic Espionage Act of 1996** (18 U.S.C. Section 1831–1839). This act makes the theft or misappropriation of a trade secret a federal crime. This law contains two provisions criminalizing two types of activity: the theft of trade secrets to benefit foreign powers and the theft of trade secrets for commercial or economic purposes. Because the definition of a trade secret includes information the owner has protected from disclosure, the strength of the security methods used to protect a trade secret are weighed by courts in case decisions. In addition, employers must exercise care when hiring applicants of competitors, who may transfer trade secrets to a new job; an applicant may have signed a nondisclosure contract with a previous employer.

Several laws pertain to the security of IT systems and data. The **Sarbanes-Oxley Act of 2002 (SOX)** was enacted in response to corporate crime. It has been referred to as an investor-protection law for public companies; however, private and nonprofit organizations are applying its requirements. The act emphasizes responsibility and controls over the accuracy of financial reports. IT is affected because financial records reside on IT systems that must use standardized controls across the enterprise, and compliance with the act's requirements necessitates attention to detailed reporting from IT.

The **Government Information Security Reform Act of 2000** aims to improve government-agency IT and data security. It requires annual reviews, outside evaluations, and reporting to Congress. Reports must contain plans, budgets, staffing, and training.

The **Health Insurance Portability and Accountability Act of 1996 (HIPAA)** focuses on protecting health information. The act requires the health-care industry to ensure the privacy of personal medical information.

The **Computer Fraud and Abuse Act of 1986** is the foundation of numerous subsequent related laws. It has been amended several times and defines a variety of crimes such as those related to harm to IT systems, theft of government or private-sector information, and fraud. In addition, these laws specify punishments following successful prosecution. States have also developed relevant laws.

The **Electronic Communications Privacy Act of 1986** is a law that prohibits the unauthorized interception of wire, electronic, or oral communications. The act is a family of statutes covering such topics as interception and disclosure; manufacture, distribution, and use of intercepting devices; and authorization and use of intercepted communications by law enforcement agencies.

FEDERAL PROSECUTION OF THEFT OF TRADE SECRETS AND COMPUTER FRAUD

In Chapter 6, Personnel Security, the discussion of "Typologies of Insider Threats" provides examples of economic espionage against businesses. Here, we provide additional examples.

Press release from:
U.S. Department of Justice
United States Attorney
Eastern District of Michigan
Detroit, Michigan
July 5, 2006

Former Metaldyne Employees Indicted for Theft of Trade Secrets

A federal grand jury indictment was unsealed today in Detroit charging one former Vice President and two former senior employees of Metaldyne Corporation with plotting to steal and stealing Metaldyne Corporation's secret process for manufacturing heavy automotive parts from powdered metal, and providing this information to a Chinese competitor. Metaldyne Corporation is headquartered in Plymouth, Michigan, and is one of only two automotive parts manufacturers in the world to have developed a process to successfully fabricate powdered metal into large, heavy-duty automotive parts, such as connecting rods.

Charged in the 64-count indictment was Anne Lockwood, 53, formerly a Vice President for Sales at Metaldyne; her husband, Michael Haehnel, 51, formerly a senior engineer at Metaldyne, both of Rockford, Michigan; and Fuping Liu, 42, a former metallurgist for Metaldyne, of Westland, Michigan. Liu worked out of Metaldyne's Shanghai, China, office until April 2004.

According to the indictment, after Lockwood left her position at Metaldyne in early 2004, she began planning with Fuping Liu to develop Chinese powdered metal manufacturers who could displace Metaldyne as the supplier of various kinds of powdered-metal manufactured parts, including connecting rods, to U.S. auto and equipment manufacturers. A company set up by Lockwood, and also involving Fuping Liu and Michael Haehnel, was to receive commissions based on the expected sales by the Chinese companies.

While Lockwood and Fuping Liu negotiated with Chinese competitors, Michael Haehnel, Lockwood's husband, remained employed as a senior engineer with Metaldyne. According to the indictment, Haehnel used his position there to gain access to hundreds of confidential Metaldyne files, and copied them to compact discs for Lockwood. The indictment alleges that both Lockwood and Liu forwarded confidential Metaldyne information pertaining to its costs, designs, and processes for manufacturing parts from powdered metal to the Chinese manufacturer, Chongqing Huafu Industry Company, Ltd., or "Huafu." After Fuping Liu left Metaldyne in April 2004, he began working for GKN Sinter Metals' Shanghai, China, office. GKN Sinter

Metals also manufactures powdered metal parts, and is located in Auburn Hills, Michigan. The indictment also alleges that Fuping Liu provided confidential information belonging to GKN Sinter Metals to Lockwood, as well as to another Chinese auto parts manufacturer, the Liaoning Shuguang Automotive Corporation, or "SG Auto."

United States Attorney Stephen J. Murphy said, "Regardless of the highly competitive rough and tumble of today's global automotive industry, stealing is still stealing. And today's indictment alleges a case of former and current employees stealing secret and crucial information from a victim company and handing it over to a competitor overseas. The federal laws protecting trade secrets prohibit such conduct, and whenever it occurs, it warrants an aggressive law enforcement response. I commend the hard work of the FBI that led to these charges being unsealed today." Daniel D. Roberts, Special Agent in Charge, Federal Bureau of Investigation (FBI) Detroit, Michigan, advised "Theft of trade secrets is investigated by the Detroit Division's Cyber Crime Squad and Cyber crime is one of the top priorities of the FBI. In this case of global outsourcing and the highly competitive nature of the world-wide business environment, protecting trade secrets is absolutely critical and at the core of the survival of U.S. companies; therefore, it is imperative trade secrets remain private and confidential. The FBI will continue to aggressively pursue those individuals who intentionally breach such confidentiality by stealing such secrets and using them for personal gain or turning the information over to third parties."

An indictment is only a charge and is not evidence of guilt. A defendant is entitled to a fair trial in which it will be the government's burden to prove guilt beyond a reasonable doubt.

Source: http://www.cybercrime.gov/lockwoodind.pdf.

Press release from:
U.S. Department of Justice
United States Attorney
Northern District of California
San Francisco, California
December 22, 2005

Silicon Valley Engineer Indicted for Theft of Trade Secrets and Computer Fraud

The United States Attorney for the Northern District of California announced that Suibin Zhang, 37, of San Jose, California, was charged late yesterday by a federal grand jury in San Jose in a nine-count indictment alleging computer fraud; theft and unauthorized downloading of trade secrets; and the unauthorized copying, transmission and possession of trade secrets.

In particular, the indictment charges three counts of computer fraud in violation of 18 U.S.C. § 1030(a)(4); three counts of theft, misappropriation and unauthorized downloading of trade secrets in violation of 18 U.S.C. §§ 1832(a)(1), (2) and (4); two counts of unauthorized copying and transmission of trade secrets in violation of 18 U.S.C. §§ 1832(a)(2) and (4); and one count unauthorized possession of stolen trade secrets in violation of 18 U.S.C. §§ 1832(a)(3) and (4).

Mr. Zhang entered not guilty pleas to the charges this morning before U.S. Magistrate Judge Richard Seeborg, who released Mr. Zhang pending trial on a $500,000 bond. Mr. Zhang's next scheduled court appearance is January 23, 2005, at 9:00 a.m. before U.S. District Judge Ronald M. Whyte.

The indictment alleges the following:

Mr. Zhang was employed by Netgear, Inc. as an engineer, and later product development manager, from August 2000 until April 2005. Netgear, a Sunnyvale-based company that sells computer networking products, was a customer of both Marvell Semiconductor, Inc., and Broadcom Corporation. Both Marvell and Broadcom sell semiconductor chips for use in broadband communications devices. As a Netgear employee, and pursuant to a nondisclosure agreement and other restrictions, Marvell permitted Mr. Zhang controlled access to trade secret information about its products on Marvell's Extranet, a Web site for its customers.

On March 8, 2005, Mr. Zhang accepted a position at Broadcom in its network switching group, and announced his intention to leave Netgear. Immediately following that announcement, on March 9, 2005, and later on March 16 and 18, the indictment alleges that Mr. Zhang committed computer fraud by downloading dozens of files from Marvell's Extranet containing proprietary and trade secret information about Marvell's switches and transceiver products. The indictment alleges, for example, that between 9:52 a.m. and 10:43 a.m. on March 9, 2005, Mr. Zhang downloaded over 30 confidential documents from Marvell's Extranet concerning a broad range of Marvell products. A week later, between 10:38 a.m. and 10:45 a.m. on March 16, 2005, Mr. Zhang downloaded over 20 Marvell documents from the extranet. Finally, in a nine minute span on March 18, 2005, Mr. Zhang downloaded over a dozen additional documents containing confidential and trade secret information about Marvell's products.

On April 27, 2005, two days after beginning work at Broadcom, Mr. Zhang allegedly loaded many of the files containing Marvell's trade secrets onto a laptop computer that had been issued to Mr. Zhang by Broadcom. Later, on June 2, 2005, Mr. Zhang allegedly emailed certain Marvell trade secrets to other Broadcom employees.

The maximum penalties for each of the computer fraud counts is 5 years imprisonment, a $250,000 fine or twice the gross gain or loss and 3 years supervised release. The maximum penalties for each of the trade secret counts is 10 years imprisonment, a $250,000 fine or twice the gross gain or loss and 3 years supervised release.

An indictment simply contains allegations against an individual and, as with all defendants, Mr. Zhang must be presumed innocent unless and until convicted. The investigation was overseen by the Computer Hacking and Intellectual Property (CHIP) Unit of the United States Attorney's Office. Christopher P. Sonderby, Chief of the CHIP Unit, is the Assistant U.S. Attorney prosecuting the case. This prosecution is the result of an investigation by the FBI.

Source: http://www.usdoj.gov/criminal/cybercrime/zhangIndict.htm.

CASES OF ESPIONAGE AGAINST THE U.S. MILITARY

Here we focus on examples of espionage against the U.S. military from "Changes in Espionage by Americans: 1947–2007" (U.S. Department of Defense 2008). Much has changed over the first decade of the twenty-first century with regard to espionage. The eleven cases of study of espionage against the military, as described in this publication, show more offenders were naturalized citizens (i.e., a foreign national granted U.S. citizenship upon fulfilling specific requirements), and more had foreign relatives or friends, foreign business links, or foreign nationalistic ties than in earlier years. The offenders were equally divided between civilian and uniformed members of the military. There were twice as many nonwhites than whites, and most held security clearances. More than half of the cases involved terrorist groups. The most common motivation was divided loyalties. Disgruntlement was the second most common motive. Four offenders had serious mental or emotional problems. Ten of the eleven employed computer technology in espionage, illustrating how espionage techniques have changed over previous decades. A sample of these eleven cases is presented next.

Timothy Smith. In the early morning hours of April 1, 2000, Smith stole computer disks from the first officer's desk on the ammunition supply ship USS *Kilauea*. He was caught in the act, fought briefly against capture, and was subdued. Smith worked as a civilian seaman on the ship, which was docked in Bremerton, Washington, during the episode. At first, Smith was charged with espionage, theft of government property, and resisting arrest. A search found five more documents marked "Confidential" in his storage locker. He told investigators he intended to steal "valuable classified materials" in order to "take revenge on shipmates who had mistreated him," and he would "possibly sell them on the Internet to terrorists." In December 2000, in a plea bargain, Smith pled guilty to theft of government property and was sentenced to time served, 260 days, 3 years probation, and treatment for alcoholism and mental illness.

This case illustrates a typical ill-planned, impulsive theft of the most valuable commodity at hand, national defense information, to sell and, at the same time, to get vaguely defined revenge on shipmates. The new element in the case was Smith's apparently casual assumption that he could make contact with "terrorists" on the Internet, who he assumed would welcome his offer and pay him for his stolen documents.

Kenneth W. Ford, Jr. Ford worked for the National Security Agency (NSA) as a computer specialist from mid-2001 to the end of 2003. According to a press account of his trial, the prosecutor explained that "on his last day of work there, Ford packed up cardboard boxes with national security documents, left through an unguarded exit, and loaded them into his pickup." When the FBI searched his home in mid-January 2004 (acting on a tip from Ford's girlfriend), they found several boxes of top secret documents piled in the kitchen, and more classified documents in a bedroom safe and under the bed. Ford claimed he had taken the documents home to refer to them in his next job, which was to be with Northrop Grumman on a classified contract. Prosecutors responded that Ford did not have enough information about the new job to know what would be relevant to it, but they did not claim they had evidence that Ford intended or tried to sell the information. Having lost the Northrop Grumman job, Ford was warned by a judge at a hearing in August 2004 that if he applied for other work with classified materials while on bail, Ford would have to disclose on the Standard Form 86 (SF-86) that criminal charges were pending against him. Ford proceeded to apply for employment at Lockheed Martin, where he filled out an SF-86 claiming that there were no charges pending against him, that he had been falsely arrested by the FBI, and that he had no prior criminal record. His lies on that SF-86 earned Ford a second criminal charge: In addition to unlawful possession of classified information relating to the national defense, he was also charged with making false statements to a government agency. Ford was convicted of these offenses on December 15, 2005, and sentenced on March 30, 2006, to 6 years in prison, to be followed by 3 years probation.

In an otherwise mundane case of stolen classified documents, the ease with which Ford walked out of NSA with considerable quantities of classified documents is startling. This happened despite notorious recent examples of trusted employees taking classified materials out the exits of their agencies, including Jonathan Pollard in the mid-1980s, and Brian Regan in the mid-1990s. Ford underlined again in 2004 the need for vigilance and systematic physical security at exits, and better information security to track and account for classified documents.

Ariel Weinmann. Weinmann joined the U.S. Navy at age 22, an idealist and outspoken patriot, hoping for a promising naval career that would build on his conventional middle-class start in life. However, a series of disappointments in his first year soured him on military life, diverting him into ill-considered, increasingly desperate crimes. Once in the navy, he found there were no openings in the linguist rating he wanted. He settled for a fire-control-technician rating on a nuclear submarine, but he hated the petty corruption he found in the intensely competitive struggle for advancement and the indifference he felt the officers showed to the junior men. Next, his fiancée broke up with him and, at her parents' insistence, moved to Switzerland to go to school. Weinmann decided to desert from the navy that he was coming to hate and to follow his fiancée to Europe, hoping she would take him back. He carefully planned his escape and used his computer skills to leave with salable assets. Stealing a laptop computer, he downloaded files from classified databases onto CDs he thought would be salable, and he stored other classified files on external disk drives and memory cards. He took his life savings of $7,000 and deserted. Weinmann left in July 2005 and flew to Vienna, Austria, where he lived for the next 8 months.

Knocking about the city, mocked by acquaintances with whom he shared his amateurish spy plans, eventually he entered the Russian Embassy in Vienna and handed over his four classified manuals for the Tomahawk cruise missile system to the duty officer, who assured Weinmann that he would be back in touch with him. When he realized he had given away his only resource and gotten nothing for it, Weinmann decided to return to the United States, fly from there to Russia, and defect. Since his name appeared on a deserter's list, he was arrested at the Dallas–Fort Worth, Texas, airport on March 26, 2006. At his court-martial, he pled guilty in a plea bargain. The charges were desertion and espionage, including failure to secure classified information, making electronic copies of classified information, and communicating classified information to a person not entitled to receive it, as well as larceny for stealing and destroying the laptop. Two other espionage charges relating to attempts he made to sell classified information in Bahrain (before he deserted his sub) and Mexico City, Mexico (on his way back to the United States), were dropped in the agreement. Weinmann was sentenced to 12 years in prison, a dishonorable discharge, and forfeiture of all pay and benefits. He would be eligible for parole in 4 years. In the judgment of an examining psychiatrist, Weinmann was "immature, impulsive, and impatient," unable to respond to life's downturns with resilience, and under the impression that he did not have to follow rules.

Ahmed Fathy Mehalba. Mehalba immigrated to the United States from his native Egypt in the early 1990s, became a U.S. citizen, and settled in the Boston, Massachusetts, area. He held ten jobs in 10 years, and served briefly in the U.S. Army in 2000 until he was medically discharged for being overweight. During the decade he scrabbled for a living, he had married and divorced, declared bankruptcy in 1997, and been sued by one of his employers, the owner of a taxi company, who claimed that when Mehalba drove a taxi, he had not reported his traffic accidents. In 2002, Mehalba answered a newspaper ad for Arabic speakers to serve as translators, and after background checks by the contractor who supplied linguists to the federal government, Titan Corporation, and by the U.S. Army, he was sent to the interrogation center at Guantanamo Bay, Cuba, to do translation and interpretation.

Seven months later, Mehalba was arrested at Logan International Airport, Boston, Massachusetts, on September 29, 2003, while returning from several months of emergency leave to visit his family in Egypt, during which he had also married. Among over 100 computer disks in his luggage was one disk with 725 documents copied onto it, amounting to some 2,000 pages; 368 of the documents were classified "Secret" and had originated with the FBI, CIA, Department of Defense (DoD), or Department of Justice (DOJ). At the airport, Mehalba denied knowing about the documents or how they got onto the disk in his possession. He was charged with making false statements and with mishandling national security information by removing classified documents from Guantanamo Bay. The fact that he had an uncle in the Egyptian military intelligence was of considerable concern, as was his sale on eBay of a personal computer, which the FBI retrieved and found five classified documents still on its hard disk. In January 2005, Mehalba changed his plea to guilty and admitted copying and removing the 368 classified documents, claiming he wanted to work on them at home to do a better job. In exchange for his guilty plea, the government agreed to a reduced sentence based on the defense's claim that Mehalba had suffered from diminished mental capacity because—despite his diagnosis several years earlier of bipolar disorder, depression, and attention deficit disorder—he had received no medication for bipolar disorder or his other problems while at Guantanamo Bay. He received a 20-month sentence in February 2005; with time already served in jail and time off for good behavior, Mehalba had 22 days left to serve of his sentence.

In retrospect, Mehalba seems like a poster child for high security risk, since he had issues with many of the thirteen adjudicative guidelines that determine eligibility for access to classified information, including employment instability, mental health issues, past criminal record, bankruptcy and financial problems, divorce, computer security violations, and having close relatives living in a Middle Eastern country. Yet the government's demand for speakers of Arabic has been so great since 9/11 that Mehalba was hired on by Titan Corporation and sent to Guantanamo Bay. Once there, physical security against insiders was also trusting. When he left for his flight to Egypt, the facility did not regularly perform bag searches or computer searches of contractor employees like Mehalba; it began these security procedures after his arrest. Prosecutors did not prove he passed classified information to others, and although officials from the Joint Terrorism Task Force tried to trace his movements and contacts in Egypt, it is unclear whether he intended or attempted to pass his documents. His case illustrates a new type in recent espionage, one closely intertwined with the American response to terrorism and Islamic extremism.

Almaliki Nour, a.k.a. Noureddine Malki. Since this individual used at least five different aliases during his two or three decades in the United States (when he arrived in the country is in dispute), it is challenging to decide what name to use in discussing his case. He was prosecuted under the name FNU LNU (first name unknown, last name unknown), since authorities continue to be unsure of his actual name. On his application for naturalization in 1998 and on his applications for employment and a security clearance in 2003, he gave his name as "Almaliki Nour," so this is the name used here. Like Ahmed Mehalba, Nour also applied to be an Arabic translator for the U.S. Army in Iraq by seeking work with Titan Corporation. He was hired by Titan in August 2003. Since classified information is involved in the work, Nour filled out an SF-86 application for a security clearance. He received eligibility for access to secret and then for top secret information, and went to work in Iraq in the Sunni triangle, a particularly dangerous assignment, from late 2003 through the fall of 2005. In September 2005, security concerns appear to have led the FBI to interview Nour about whether he could keep his clearance; in October, personnel from the Joint Terrorist Task Force in New York searched Nour's Brooklyn apartment, and the FBI interviewed him again.

In November 2005, he was indicted for making false statements to government officials in three instances: on his naturalization application, on his SF-86 application for access to classified information, and during his interview with the FBI in September. He pled guilty to the falsification charges the following month. He had lied about his name, his birth date, his birthplace, his parents' religious background and location, the dates and his reasons for emigrating, and his marriage. In March 2006, Nour was indicted on additional charges: four counts of unauthorized possession of national defense documents that had been found in searches of his apartment and computer. While in Iraq, he had downloaded a thick classified file from the 82nd Airborne Division of the U.S. Army onto an unclassified thumb drive and then onto a CD, taken other hard-copy classified documents, and stored them in his Brooklyn apartment. The classified information described insurgent activities in Iraq in detail: routes pilgrims would take on their religious journeys to Mecca, Saudi Arabia, that would require protection; artillery positions for upcoming actions; and a photograph of a battle map Nour made on U.S. troop routes during the battle of Najaf, Iraq. Further details emerged in the case that called into question Nour's loyalties and his intentions for the classified information in his possession. Telephone numbers found in his address book led investigators to document that he had had e-mail contacts and placed over 100 phone calls to various Sunni sheiks, including Al Qaeda leaders, from whom he admitted taking bribes. Images found stored on his computer, which had been downloaded from the Internet, glorified Al Qaeda and the 9/11 attacks. Prosecutors did not claim to have evidence that Nour actually passed classified information to others. On February 14, 2007, Nour pled guilty to illegally possessing classified defense documents in addition to his earlier guilty plea on the falsification charges. He is presently serving a 10-year sentence in a federal prison.

On top of his warehousing stolen classified information and his unauthorized interactions with Iraqis, the scale of the lies Almaliki Nour told about himself to U.S. government officials makes his case startling. It highlights the near impossibility of checking background details for persons who were born and lived abroad. Because the demand to employ native speakers of Middle Eastern languages as interpreters has been urgent during the Iraq war, this security vulnerability has grown. Nour is another instance of the recent intertwining of espionage-related activities with potential terrorism by the Al Qaeda network.

Critical Thinking

Do you think there are cases of espionage that are unknown? Why or why not?

Threats to Information Technology and Data

Whitman and Mattord (2008, 39–41) see broad threats to information technology and data (Figure 8.2), as listed next with examples.

- Human error (e.g., accidents or mistakes)
- Compromises to intellectual property (e.g., piracy or copyright violations)
- Espionage or trespass (e.g., unauthorized access to steal data)
- Information extortion (e.g., blackmail to obtain information)

FIGURE 8.2 **Information technology and data are exposed to many types of threats and hazards. (® Shutterstock.com. With permission.)**

- Sabotage or vandalism (e.g., physical harm to systems or data)
- Acts of theft (e.g., stealing equipment or information)
- Software attacks (e.g., viruses or worms)
- Substandard quality of service from service providers (e.g., power issues or interruption of services)
- Forces of nature (e.g., flood or lightning)
- Technical hardware failures (e.g., equipment malfunction)
- Technical software failures (e.g., bugs or unknown loopholes)
- Technological obsolescence (e.g., outdated hardware or software)

Major cyber threats are described next from multiple sources, especially the "Emerging Cyber Threats Report for 2009" published by the Georgia Tech Information Security Center (2008). This report emphasizes that data will continue to be the primary motive behind future cyber crime that will target fixed and mobile IT systems.

Malware

Malware is slang for malicious software or code that is designed to disrupt an IT system. For example, a **Trojan horse** is a computer program that performs a useful function, but contains a hidden, harmful function. A **worm** is a malicious program that can replicate itself and send copies to multiple computers. A **virus** is a small software code that attaches itself to a legitimate computer program, and each time the program runs, the virus also runs to disrupt IT and reproduce itself (Newman 2010, 436–442).

The Georgia Tech (GT) report provides examples of malware attacks. In one scenario, a FaceBook message sent from one friend to another includes a link to a YouTube video. When the recipient clicks on the link supposedly sent by the friend, a prompt appears to install a new version of Flash Player to watch the video. When the "installment" is done, malware is actually installed. In another example, customers of a credit union may be targeted with a **spoofed e-mail** (i.e., a computer disguises itself as another) with a link to a news story of interest. When customers click on the bogus link, malware is installed that can log keystrokes and "mine" personal information.

According to the GT report, malware and botnet attacks are facilitated by failing to install **patching** or installing it after the harm has been done. (Patches are software upgrades that enhance computer performance, fix a problem, or improve security.) When a corporation, for instance, has all of its employees using a similar, standardized software application, it means that a single security failure at one point can result in an infection of corporate-wide computers. Today, many software companies are shipping auto-patch/update capability with new software for corporate and retail customers so users can remain up-to-date with patches and curb cyber threats.

Botnets

Botnets are groups of computers infected with malicious code and unknowingly controlled by a "master" (i.e., cyber criminal). The GT report estimates that 10 percent of online computers are controlled by botnets, and the percentage is growing because infection can result from ordinary use of a computer, such as clicking on a legitimate Web site or using e-mail. Once bots are installed, they remain inactive to avoid detection by antivirus and anti-spyware technology. Bots periodically communicate with a command and control server for updates (to avoid detection) and instructions. Since a bot uses http (i.e., a standard for information transfer on the Internet), it appears as normal traffic. Whereas traditional malware is for a single-purpose attack, bots remain in computers like an army waiting to attack with a lot of computer power. Bot activities include stealing data, delivering spam, and conducting denial-of-service attacks. **Spam** is unsolicited e-mail with hidden or false information to sell merchandise, conduct phishing, distribute spyware/malware, or harm an organization in some other way, such as through a denial-of-service attack. A **denial-of-service attack** comes from a single source that prevents system access by legitimate users by flooding the target computer with messages. This attack can prevent a system from exchanging data with other systems or using the Internet. A **distributed denial-of-service attack** comes from multiple computers and may make use of worms to spread to multiple computers in order to deny service (U.S. Government Accountability Office 2008b, 8).

As is typical for security in general, a "cat and mouse war" exists between computer security specialists and cyber criminals. To battle bots, new technologies can locate Internet communications between botnets and bot masters and close the links to prevent disruption of IT systems. Because antivirus and intrusion-detection security are limited in the battle against bots, behavior-analysis techniques are applied to search for anomalies in Internet connection duration, time of day, or type of information uploaded or downloaded.

The Variety of Threats

The U.S. Government Accountability Office (2008b, 7) sees cyber threats from hackers, cyber criminal groups, insiders, foreign intelligence services, terrorists, bot-network operators, phishers, spammers, and spyware/malware authors.

Hackers break into networks for the thrill of the challenge or for bragging rights in the hacker community. While gaining unauthorized access once required a fair amount of skill or computer knowledge, hackers can now download attack scripts and protocols from the Internet and launch them against victim sites. Thus, while attack tools have become more sophisticated, they have also become easier to use. According to the Central Intelligence Agency, the large majority of hackers do not have the requisite expertise to threaten difficult targets such as critical U.S. networks. Nevertheless, the worldwide population of hackers poses a relatively high threat of an isolated or brief disruption causing serious damage.

Cyber criminal groups seek to attack systems for monetary gain. Specifically, organized crime groups are using spam, phishing, and spyware/malware to commit identity theft and online fraud. International corporate spies and organized crime groups conduct industrial espionage, facilitate large-scale monetary theft, and hire or develop hacker talent.

The U.S. Government Accountability Office (2008b, 8) explains the following terms that increase our understanding of IT threats:

- **Exploit tools** are publicly available and sophisticated tools that intruders of various skill levels can use to determine vulnerabilities and gain entry into targeted systems.
- **Logic bomb** refers to a form of sabotage in which a programmer inserts code that causes a computer program to perform a destructive action when some triggering event occurs, such as terminating the programmer's employment.
- **Phishers** are individuals or small groups that execute baiting schemes (e.g., a message that appears as a legitimate bank) in an

attempt to steal identities or information for monetary gain. The term "phishing" is derived from "fishing" for information.

- **Sniffer** is synonymous with packet sniffer. A sniffer is a program that intercepts routed data and examines each packet in search of specified information, such as passwords transmitted in clear text.

- **Vishing** is a method of phishing based on voice-over-Internet Protocol technology and open-source call center software. This threat has made it inexpensive for scammers to set up phony call centers and criminals to send e-mail or text messages to potential victims, saying there has been a security problem and they need to call their bank to reactivate a credit or debit card, or send text messages to cell phones, instructing potential victims to contact fake online banks to renew their accounts.

- **War driving** is a method of gaining entry into wireless computer networks using a laptop, antennas, and a wireless network adaptor while patrolling a geographic area in a vehicle.

- **Zero-day exploit** is a cyber threat taking advantage of a security vulnerability on the same day that the vulnerability becomes known to the general public and for which there are no available fixes.

ISSUE

Should Government Regulate Private Use of the Internet?

The Georgia Tech Information Security Center (2008) explains that a debate has been going on over responsibility for security education and government regulation of online behavior. The issue is becoming more serious because of criminal exploitation of the decentralized and open nature of the Internet. Compounding the challenges of online security are the enormous number of users, the borderless nature of the Internet, the difficulty of verifying identity online, and the lack of standardization for protection. These factors make government regulation controversial. However, action is required because crime is seriously threatening the Internet. Some argue that mandatory antivirus software should be required, similar to the way government requires vehicle insurance. In addition, numerous entities (e.g., Internet-related industries and financial institutions) should reinforce security education, awareness, and personal responsibility.

Critical Thinking

Should government establish regulations for cyber security for private individuals and require related public education? Why or why not?

RESPONDING TO COMPUTER EMERGENCIES

Many organizations respond to computer and Internet emergencies. Here are the major ones. (Web addresses are listed at the end of the chapter.)

Federal Bureau of Investigation: The FBI plays a dominant role in cyber investigations and focuses on computer intrusions, Internet fraud, piracy/intellectual property theft, and online predators.

U.S. Secret Service: The U.S. Secret Service is noted for its Electronic Crimes Task Force that brings together not only federal, state, and local law enforcement agencies, but also prosecutors, the private sector, and academia, with the purpose of investigating and mitigating electronic crimes.

U.S. Department of Homeland Security (DHS), National Cyber Security Division (NCSD): The NCSD partners with public, private, and international entities to secure cyberspace and U.S. cyber assets. It operates the U.S. Computer Emergency Readiness Team (US-CERT). There are over 250 organizations that use the name *CERT* or a similar name and focus on cyber security. US-CERT is independent of these groups, but it may collaborate with them on security incidents (U.S. Department of Homeland Security, 2010).

Computer Emergency Response Team (CERT), Carnegie Mellon University: This federally funded research and development center coordinates communications among experts during computer and Internet emergencies and helps to prevent and mitigate such incidents through partnering, information dissemination, and training.

There are an endless number of ways in which data and information can be lost from IT systems and devices. Credant Technologies (2008) and Mallery (2009, 78–82) offer examples as follows.

An overemphasis on hi-tech information security solutions may miss low-tech methods of theft, e.g., a spy making a photocopy of proprietary information. However, low-tech methods of theft may require high-tech methods of detection, such as a digital record of all items photocopied. In another example, software can be used to identify an employee who is abusing his access rights by accessing a greater number of records for longer periods.

An employee may try to steal a copy of a database by attaching it to an e-mail. Another, more crafty method, one that attempts to avoid leaving a trail, is to upload the file to an external system, such as Yahoo, Hotmail, or a hosted document storage system. These online data storage sites are popular because people can have access to their data from almost anywhere. Google GMail e-mail accounts also contain file storage capabilities. Instant messaging is another threat that can be used to steal data.

FIGURE 8.3 **A PDA can be used to steal data and information as well as infect a computer or IT system. (® Shutterstock.com. With permission.)**

Lost or stolen devices (e.g., laptops, BlackBerrys, etc.) and media (e.g., flash drives, CDs, etc.), especially those containing unencrypted data, are other causes of lost data.

Data and information can be stolen through many types of devices and techniques (Figures 8.3 and 8.4). Examples are personal digital assistants (PDAs) such as BlackBerrys, iPhones, and Pocket PCs. CDs and DVDs can

FIGURE 8.4 **A flash drive, which can be disguised as a pen, watch or other ordinary item, can be used to steal data and information and infect a computer or IT system. (® Shutterstock.com. With permission.)**

be used to transfer enormous amounts of data out of an organization. Digital cameras can be used to photograph documents, drawings, models, the interiors and exteriors of buildings, and people. A camera can be connected to a computer via a USB port to receive data by file copying. Radio-based devices that permit a connection of PDAs or a cell phone to a computer network are another threat. Furthermore, devices and media can contain malicious code that can infect a computer or IT system (Brill 2007, 35).

COMPUTER BREACHES AND DATA LOSS

In 2008, the U.S. Department of Homeland Security reported that there were 5,499 known intrusions into U.S. government computers with malicious software. In 2006, the number was 2,172 (Associated Press, 2009).

The U.S. Government Accountability Office (2008c) reported:

- The Department of Veterans Affairs (VA) announced that computer equipment containing personal information on 26.5 million veterans and active-duty members was stolen from the home of a VA employee. Notices were sent out to all affected, the equipment was recovered, and forensic analysts concluded that it was unlikely the personal information had been compromised.
- The Transportation Security Administration announced that an external hard drive containing personal information on 100,000 employment records from 2002 to 2005 was discovered missing.
- The Census Bureau reported 672 missing laptops, of which 246 contained some degree of personal data. Of the laptops containing personal data, 104 were stolen, often from employee vehicles, and former employees did not return another 113.

The European Network and Information Security Agency (2008, 13) reported:

- USB flash drives containing U.S. Army classified military information were for sale at a bazaar near Bagram, Afghanistan.
- About 13,000 employees of Pfizer, Inc., had their personal information compromised when a company laptop and USB flash drive were stolen.
- About 8,000 Texas A&M University students had their personal information compromised when a mathematics professor, on vacation in Madagascar, lost a USB flash drive.

Mallery (2009, 78) explains that permitting employees to download iTunes and connect personal iPods to their computers may facilitate the downloading of proprietary information to the same iPods. He relates a case of a former employee who copied 45,000 files to an iPod prior to leaving her job. Mallery also warns about blogs. An employee might create a blog and use it to vent frustration by revealing employer business plans or other proprietary information. The internal threat must be viewed as a top vulnerability, especially because employees are already inside intrusion-detection systems, firewalls, and other methods of IT security.

Hines (2008) reports that cyber espionage is applied not only among nations, but also among businesses globally. The type of proprietary information sought is broad. For instance, if Company A is about to negotiate a partnership with Company B, A may pay hackers to enter B's IT system to gain information for an advantage in bargaining. The hacking may extend to B's attorneys, accountants, consultants, and suppliers. One technique hackers may apply is a "targeted spear phishing campaign" that tricks employees into opening tainted attachments that appear as if they came from a coworker. When opened, the virus-laden attachment infects the IT system and information is sought.

Border crossing points (e.g., on roads and at airports) in the United States and elsewhere are locations where access controls are intense, especially because of terrorists and other criminals. Not only are travelers subject to search, but also their belongings, including laptops, PDAs, cell phones, and so forth. In addition, devices are subject to viewing of contents and downloading. Consequently, travelers should review the data in their devices prior to departure to ensure that proprietary information is not compromised (Vijayan 2008).

Another possibility is that a virus or other malicious code could be covertly entered into the traveler's device for subsequent harm. In China, for instance, the government controls Internet services and wireless networks, and, thus, computers and other devices can be monitored and planted with malicious code remotely. Upon returning to the United States, travelers should have their devices checked for malicious code.

Steganography

Cole (2006, 36) writes of ancient methods of **steganography**, meaning the technique of hiding coded or secret information in a host. Julius Caesar would order servants' heads to be shaved and then tattooed with a secret message. The servants would then be held in solitary confinement until their hair grew to cover the secret message. Their mission would follow, and at their destination, their heads be would be shaved again to reveal the message. Another ancient technique was to carve a secret message on a finished board and cover it with thick wax to be melted off when the board was delivered.

Today, technology has enhanced the techniques of steganography. For instance, a sender can use one of a number of online commercial programs to hide an encrypted and password-protected message inside a host file; the receiver uses the password to access the secret message. A host file can be an e-mail, text message, or photo that appears unchanged because binary data is added. A photo of a beautiful mountain range could be hiding an image of a newly designed missile engine costing hundreds of millions of dollars to develop. A spy could post a vehicle for auction on the Internet, and although many people would see it, the contact would download the photo and extract the hidden information. Steganography can also be used to steal proprietary information via a laptop, DVD, CD, or USB device.

Cole (2006, 36–37) explains strategies to counter steganography, which is difficult to detect. He refers to stego-marking that flags sensitive files that can be detected by firewalls, intrusion-detection systems, and content filters. Forensic techniques can help to investigate the threat. For instance, an expert could scrutinize supposedly identical files for different binary compositions and search for characteristics of steganography use, since each tool manipulates a file in a particular way to hide data.

Cole sees legitimate applications of steganography, for example, when an executive travels to another country with proprietary information on his/her computer and electronic devices, or when communicating using various devices. A traveling executive's daily video conference with a supervisor at corporate headquarters could contain secret data through steganography.

ARE DATA BREACHES MORE COMMON FROM ELECTRONIC DOCUMENTS OR PAPER DOCUMENTS?

Research by the Ponemon Institute (2008) shows that despite widespread use of computers in the workplace, we are still dependent upon paper. Their research claims to dispel the myth that the cause of most or all data breaches is lost or stolen electronic documents. Respondents revealed that they had one or more data breaches in the past 12 months, and 49 percent stated that one or more of these breaches involved the loss or theft of paper documents. Respondents favored protecting paper documents to curb identity theft of customer and employee information, and to a lesser extent, proprietary information that may affect brand.

Voice over Internet Protocol and Cellular Phones

Voice over Internet Protocol (VoIP) refers to the technology applied to transmit voice communications over a data network. Voice is digitized, encoded, compressed into packets, and exchanged over networks. The GT report views VoIP technology as eventually rivaling landline and mobile communications in terms of reliability and quality. As with technology in general, criminals will try to exploit Internet telephony and mobile computing as these systems handle more and more data. Cyber criminals will seek to steal data, commit fraud, and engage in other crimes similar to the threats e-mail has experienced. Other threats include malware, denial-of-service attacks, and botnets.

Financial transactions are increasingly taking place over mobile devices. For example, people are ordering credit reports over their BlackBerrys, which places important financial and identity data at risk. The "digital wallet" is coming into greater use as consumers store personal identity, payment card information, and other data on smartphones. Increasingly, people (e.g., in Japan) are using their cell phones to make purchases.

In criminal cases, courts are recognizing that today's cellular phones are similar to small computers. Immense amounts of information and data (which may become evidence) are stored in cellular phones, including incoming and outgoing calls, address books, calendars, voice and text messages, e-mail, video, and photos.

The weight of case law supports warrantless retrieval of information from cellular phones by police incident to (i.e., during) arrest. Certain jurisdictions may require a warrant for such retrieval (Clark 2009, 25–32). Seized electronic devices should be placed in a Faraday bag, foil, or a metal can to prevent remote alterations or erasure of information and data.

Cyber Warfare

Cyber warfare involves intentional use of disruptive methods against an adversary's IT systems and computers to cause harm. Coleman (2008, 11) writes that what began with individual hackers has spread to organized criminals, terrorists, and nations. Because nations rely so much on IT systems and computers for infrastructure, militaries from throughout the world are refining their skills on electronic warfare, in addition to conventional methods of warfare (Figure 8.5). A "cyber arms race" appears to be gaining momentum.

The GT report referred to the 2008 Russian cyber attack prior to the air and ground attack against Georgia. The cyber attacks targeted Georgian media outlets and government communications systems. Georgian Internet traffic was blocked, data was stolen, and there was defacement and hosting of fake Georgian Web sites that showed misinformation.

Cyber warfare is advantageous because it is less expensive than a physical attack; the Internet affords "plausible deniability"; an adversary's cyber defenses may be inadequate; and there is a lack of rules among nations when such warfare unfolds. It can also be deadly. For instance, if malware enters a military computer system and causes friendly forces to appear as the enemy, these forces could be subjected to air or other types of attack (i.e., friendly fire).

FIGURE 8.5 **Conventional wars will increasingly be fought in conjunction with cyber warfare. (DoD photo by Petty Officer 2nd Class Kim Smith, U.S. Navy.)**

The U.S. Department of Defense is responsible for cyber warfare at military bases in the United States and overseas. The Department of Homeland Security is responsible for the threat in the United States, along with the U.S. Department of Justice, which has some authority outside the United States.

Because of the threat of cyber warfare and cyber terror, Congress enacted the **Federal Information Security Management Act of 2002**. The act ordered the Office of Management and Budget (OMB) to establish information security policies for all federal agencies and to audit compliance. The act also requires the National Institute of Standards and Technology to prepare standards and guidelines as aids for agency compliance to OMB policies. The private sector, likewise, must continue its efforts to protect its infrastructure and IT systems.

Fickes (2008, 13) writes about government cyber defense and, as with physical security, the concept of defense-in-depth. This entails layers of security that fall under three categories: *technical controls*, such as computer access controls; *managerial controls*, including policies and procedures; and *operational controls* that focus on physical security. Operational controls include contingency plans that are put into action in the event of a successful attack so that an entity can respond and recover.

The GT report noted that the U.S. government is preparing for inevitable cyber warfare by hosting exercises with states, foreign governments, and private companies. Cooperative efforts help to identify vulnerabilities and develop comprehensive countermeasures.

ISSUE

Should Government Restrict the Public's Use of Cyber Reconnaissance Technology?

Cyber reconnaissance is the viewing of satellite and/or street-level mapping and imagery that is available worldwide to anyone with a computer capable of accessing the Internet. Google Street View and Microsoft Virtual Earth are examples of this technology, which offers three-dimensional viewing of the Earth. Among the features of this technology is geo-tagging, which adds geographical information to the map as well as latitude and longitude. Although this technology offers numerous benefits to legitimate users, terrorists, spies, and other criminals also benefit. For instance, the physical features of a building or facility can be used to enhance proprietary information previously stolen. Or, an offender can use the technology to study how to gain access to or harm the people or assets on the premises. The Associated Press (2008) reported that the Pentagon banned Google Earth teams from taking street-level video recordings of U.S. military bases to produce panoramic maps accessible from the Internet. The Pentagon order followed an incident where a crew was permitted access to one base, and it came a few days after protesters in London supposedly used Google Earth to help plan access to the roof of the Parliament building.

Critical Thinking

What are your views of government restrictions on the public's use of cyber reconnaissance technology?

Information Security

Whitman and Mattord (2008, 2–3) write of an earlier age of computers when this technology was located in climate-controlled rooms of a data center and electronic data processing (EDP) was centralized. In the last twenty-five years, computer technology has moved beyond the computer room to just about every facet of the business environment, wherever it might be located. Because of this shift, computer security of the data center has evolved into the broader concept of information security that covers a wide range of issues, as explained in this chapter. Moreover, information security is not only focused on technology; it also includes nontechnical vulnerabilities and strategies of security. Examples are training employees to avoid being victimized by social engineering and ensuring that the trash collection system is protected from spies. Whitman and Mattord (2008, 3) add, "Information security funding and planning decisions involve more than just technical managers, such as information security managers or members of the information security team." They see three distinct groups of decision makers who work to find consensus on a plan to protect information assets:

- Information security managers and professionals protect the entity's information assets from a variety of threats.
- IT managers and professionals support business objectives by supplying and supporting IT appropriate to business needs.
- Nontechnical, general business managers and professionals prepare and communicate policies, objectives, and budget resources to the other groups.

The terms *cybersecurity*, *cyberspace*, and *cybersecurity policy* are explained here, although these terms are subsumed within the broader term *information security*. **Cybersecurity** refers to the protection of information technology and data.

The federal government defines "cyberspace" and "cybersecurity policy" as follows (White House 2009, 1–2):

> National Security Presidential Directive 54/Homeland Security Presidential Directive 23 (NSPD-54/HSPD23) defines **cyberspace** as the interdependent network of information technology infrastructures, and includes the Internet, telecommunications networks, computer systems, and embedded processors and controllers in critical industries. Common usage of the term also refers to the virtual environment of information and interactions between people.
>
> **Cybersecurity policy** includes strategy, policy, and standards regarding the security of and operations in cyberspace, and encompasses the full range of threat reduction, vulnerability reduction, deterrence, international engagement, incident response, resiliency, and recovery policies and activities, including computer network operations, information assurance, law enforcement, diplomacy, military, and intelligence missions as they relate to the security and stability of the global information and communications infrastructure. The scope does not include other information and communications policy unrelated to national security or securing the infrastructure.

In 2009, President Barack Obama directed a review to assess U.S. policies and structures for cybersecurity. The review report is entitled "Cyber Policy Review: Assuring a Trusted and Resilient Information and Communications Infrastructure." The review team of government cybersecurity experts engaged with and received input from a variety of individuals from industry, academia, the civil liberties and privacy communities, state governments, international partners, and the legislative and executive branches. Conclusions drawn from this review include the following statements (White House 2009, iii):

The globally-interconnected digital information and communications infrastructure known as "cyberspace" underpins almost every facet of modern society and provides critical support for the U.S. economy, civil infrastructure, public safety, and national security. This technology has transformed the global economy and connected people in ways never imagined. Yet, cybersecurity risks pose some of the most serious economic and national security challenges of the 21st Century. The digital infrastructure's architecture was driven more by considerations of interoperability and efficiency than of security. Consequently, a growing array of state and nonstate actors are compromising, stealing, changing, or destroying information and could cause critical disruptions to U.S. systems. At the same time, traditional telecommunications and Internet networks continue to converge, and other infrastructure sectors are adopting the Internet as a primary means of interconnectivity. The United States faces the dual challenge of maintaining an environment that promotes efficiency, innovation, economic prosperity, and free trade while also promoting safety, security, civil liberties, and privacy rights.

Standards and Guidelines

An excellent source of IT information security standards is the **ISO/IEC 27000-series** (also known as the ISMS [Information Security Management System] family of standards). It contains standards published jointly by the International Organization for Standardization (ISO) and the International Electrotechnical Commission (IEC). The series provides best-practice recommendations for information security management, risks, and controls. The series is broad in scope and includes more than just privacy, confidentiality, and IT or technical security issues. It applies to a variety of organizations. Because of the dynamic nature of information security, the series plans for continuous feedback and improvement activities. Examples of content include information security policy, access controls, physical security, personnel security, and business continuity (Wikipedia 2009).

ASIS International (2007b) offers a comprehensive approach to information security through its "Information Asset Protection Guideline." Early in the guideline, an emphasis is placed on the importance of an organizational information asset protection (IAP) policy that must be clear, practical, and communicated (e.g., through training and e-mail). Senior management who delegate authority to manage and audit policies should support those same policies.

Policies

Kennedy (2008, 45) espouses the importance of policies that address process, people's behavior, and technologies. Examples of such policies are as follows:

- Policies governing the use of external removable media (e.g., flash drives and DVDs)
- Policies that help to avert the opening of infected e-mail attachments or sending proprietary information outside an organization using an e-mail attachment
- Policies that prohibit the printing of proprietary information and stealing it
- Policies that prevent the downloading of malicious code from the Web
- Policies that prevent placing critical data on a laptop that may be stolen or lost

Piwonka (2008, 61–63) writes about the difficulty of managing the risk of removable storage devices (e.g., USB flash drives and iPods) in the workplace. He recommends developing metrics on the use and type of such devices in the workplace. Uncontrolled use can be risky, so a determination of business requirements can be made for departments or individuals. Acceptable usage policy has its limitations, since monitoring is required. At the same time, awareness training and enforcement of policy are important. Another strategy is a software solution that permits IT specialists to monitor compliance with policies.

Although we often hear about the importance of policies to strengthen security, do employees follow policies closely as ordered by management? Research by the Ponemon Institute, an IT research and consulting firm, found that employees routinely violate their employer's security policies. About half of 1,000 corporate respondents in a study say that both employees and management ignore data security policies. Policy violations include misuse of USB devices, personal e-mail use, use of Web-based e-mail accounts from work computers, sharing passwords, downloading free applications, turning off firewalls and other security settings, social networking, and loss of mobile devices containing corporate data. Lack of enforcement is a related issue (Higgins 2009).

Critical Thinking

What can be done about IT security policies not being followed by employees?

Classification Systems

An early step in IAP is to identify the information that needs to be labeled and protected. The information should be classified so that the most important information receives the greatest security. An example of a **classification system** is *highly restricted*, *internal use*, and *unrestricted*. The definition of such terms and the security for each category varies among entities.

Members of the armed services, federal workers, and those who work in defense industries must obtain security clearances to access classified information. Three levels of clearances are *top secret*, *secret*, and *confidential*. Each level details the type of security required for information and the harm that can occur from disclosure. Disclosure of top secret information can result in exceptionally grave damage, disclosure of secret information can result in serious damage, and disclosure of confidential information can result in damage (U.S. Government Accountability Office 2008a, 4). Two other classifications used by the military that are for less sensitive information are *sensitive but unclassified data* and *unclassified data*. Compromise of the former might adversely harm U.S. interests, whereas the latter is open to the public because it poses no risk to national security.

Once proprietary information is classified, labeled, and protected, employee access should be limited. Avoid unrestricted access to data. Use software and controls to restrict access to employees who "need to know" and limit what they can view. Monitor access behavior to flag anomalies.

Information protection includes accountability for and documenting of all transfers of proprietary information. Another aspect of information protection is ensuring that storage facilities meet codes and standards pertaining to fire protection, humidity, and other reasonable precautions.

ASIS International (2007b, 13) notes that entities often handle private information pertaining to employees, customers, and others. Thus, to meet legal and regulatory requirements, the protection of private information is important. This includes an employee responsible for managing the privacy program, policies, audits, investigation of breaches, notification of parties if a compromise occurs, and destruction of private information when no longer needed.

DO NOT MAKE THESE MISTAKES

IT Policies

Marlow Industries was having frequent accidents at their main manufacturing plant. One avenue to help identify problems, accident causes, and solutions was to utilize the extensive CCTV system at the plant that consisted of state-of-the-art IP-based network cameras. Safety managers, the chief security officer, and IT specialists met, and a decision was made to provide video clips of accidents to the safety department.

One particular accident of interest to safety investigators involved a forklift that ran into a robot on the manufacturing floor, injuring the forklift driver and two employees, and destroying equipment valued at $275,000. The total cost of the accident was approaching $800,000.

About one month after the video of the accident was provided to the Marlow Industries safety department, it appeared on YouTube and became a popular video attraction providing entertainment to viewers. Management at Marlow was livid and embarrassed. As a publicly traded company, stock-holders wanted answers. The problems grew worse when the news media printed a story about the video.

Later, investigators hired by Marlow Industries found that an employee of the safety department brought home an unlabeled CD of the accident. His teenage son viewed the video, thought it was humorous, and placed a copy on the Internet.

> *Lessons:* Training, policies, procedures, and discipline are especially important regarding sensitive information. The video and CD of the accident should have been labeled "sensitive information," along with the name of the company and a strong warning about unauthorized use. In addition, a log should have been maintained on who accessed the video and who made a copy. The copy should not have been taken off the premises. Once the video and copies are no longer needed, policies and procedures should guide destruction.

Critical Thinking

In what ways can management and security prevent such a fiasco as described here?

Destruction of Proprietary Information

ASIS International (2007b, 16–17) lists guidelines for destruction of proprietary information once it is no longer needed.

- Formulate and update policies and procedures on destruction.
- Ensure that in the planning of destruction, precautions are taken to prevent reconstruction by an adversary (Figure 8.6).
- Minimize the unnecessary retention of proprietary information, records, documents, and computer media by periodically reviewing such inventory.
- Post signs to ensure compliance with policies and procedures. For example, at printers, copiers, and fax machines, signs should be posted about security concerns.
- Shredders or collection bins should be located at printers, copiers, and fax machines.
- Protect items to be destroyed by using locked containers, seals, RFID tags, escorts, logs, vetted contractors, and other methods.
- Avoid discarding sensitive items in areas that can be accessed by internal and external adversaries.

Livingston (2007, 63–66) offers advice on data destruction. He argues that the average computer user has a false sense of security regarding their

FIGURE 8.6   Do you think an adversary can piece together the paper being shredded by this office shredder? (® Shutterstock.com. With permission.)

Recycle Bin (on Windows) or their Trash Can (on Macs). Neither feature thoroughly deletes data. He makes the same point with storage devices (e.g., USB sticks), smart phones, iPods, and other devices. Although paper shredders dominated data destruction in the past, digital media has overtaken (not replaced) paper and presents new challenges.

Livingston writes that the U.S. Department of Defense and NATO recommend overwriting data on computers three times to render the files unrecoverable. He notes that vendors offer programs that permanently erase files from hard drives, USB drives, memory cards, and other media. Remote data deletion technology is also available; this is helpful if a computer is lost or stolen. Certain models of shredding machines enable physical destruction of hard drives, CDs, DVDs, and other media.

Before data is destroyed, ensure that laws will not being violated, especially if civil and/or criminal action is pending. In one case, described by Livingston, an ex-CEO was sentenced to federal prison for 15 months because he used a software program to try to delete two child porn movies and 12,000 other files off his company-issued PC. He pled guilty to child pornography and obstruction of justice because he tried to eliminate the evidence (a violation of the Sarbanes-Oxley Act).

Tangible Assets

Strict access controls should protect research and development facilities, prototypes, models, laboratories, and other locations containing proprietary information. Security should include ID badges showing approved level of access, and consideration should be given to biometric controls. Visitor (e.g., contractor) accountability and control is also important and may require an escort. Unauthorized photography, drawing, and other means of recording information should be prohibited and signs posted explaining policies. *Security officers and other employees must be trained to beware of social engineering and other devious methods of acquiring information.*

Strategies of Information Security

- Conduct risk analyses of IT, data, and personnel. Include portable and personal devices.
- Applicant screening (for full-time, contract, etc.) is especially important to prevent hiring a spy who seeks to steal information to order. Another important strategy is to rescreen the workforce, known as "infinity screening" (see Chapter 6). In addition, ensure that ex-employees are barred from IT access.
- Ensure that information security conforms to the business's needs and strategies.
- Ensure that press releases and interviews by the media are handled through a trained, designated spokesperson only. Journalists may become too aggressive in trying to obtain information.
- Trade shows provide an opportunity for businesses to market their products and services. However, employees should be trained not to share proprietary information, while being aware of ploys used to collect information.
- Consider that building changes, orders from vendors, discarded packaging, scrap, modes of transportation, job announcements, and other information can be "pieced together" by an adversary for advantage. Prepare countermeasures and protection.
- Consider that potential business partners, customers, clients, and others may possess the ulterior motive of collecting proprietary information.
- Require all those working on sensitive projects to sign a **nondisclosure agreement** (i.e., a legal contract that defines what the parties are prohibited from disclosing outside of their work relationship).
- When a business outsources services so it can concentrate on its core business, proprietary information can be compromised. Contractors should ensure adequate security and sign a nondisclosure agreement.
- Monitor the Internet for breaches of information security, counterfeit products, or stolen assets.
- Maintain close ties to law enforcement agencies; be prepared with sound evidence of illegal activity, because these agencies typically have limited resources. Ascertain their specific evidence requirements before they prosecute a case.

- Research and consider government programs that help to protect proprietary information and intellectual property rights. For example, research the U.S. Customs and Border Protection.
- Consider government strategies to protect proprietary information. For instance, **Operations Security (OPSEC)** is a government-developed approach of thinking like adversaries and ascertaining their information needs. Once this is done, their needs must be denied. The process is akin to risk analysis, with an emphasis on knowing adversaries.
- Security practitioners employed by entities with overseas interests should consider involvement with the **Overseas Security Advisory Council (OSAC)**. This group, in cooperation with the U.S. Department of State, facilitates enhanced security through sharing information, publications, and planning. A major aim is to strengthen American businesses that face multiple threats.
- Groups overseas that may provide assistance on matters include the FBI's Legal Attaches, FBI National Academy Associates, the International Association of Chiefs of Police, and ASIS International.
- The FBI's InfraGard Program is a partnership between the FBI and the private sector to share information and intelligence to prevent hostile acts against U.S. interests.
- Install software that can detect devices that seek to connect with IT at the enterprise to steal data. For legitimate users with a valid reason to access data, the data should be encrypted while not impeding the IT system.
- Update firewall and antivirus software on IT systems and portable devices.
- Conduct unannounced audits of security methods.
- Conduct penetration tests to ascertain security weaknesses and then reduce vulnerabilities.
- Include IT and data security within emergency and business-continuity plans.
- Ensure that backup systems are available and maintain copies of software and data.
- ASIS International (2007a, 12) research found that when there is a loss of proprietary information, companies conduct investigations, perform damage assessments, reassess security, revise risk planning, initiate criminal and civil action, withdraw from business transactions, and redesign products.

Technical Controls

Whitman and Mattord (2008, 553) define **technical controls** as follows: "control measures that use or implement a technical solution to reduce risk of loss in an organization, as well as issues relating to examining and selecting the technologies appropriate to protecting information." Examples of technical controls that are explained in subsequent paragraphs are access controls, firewalls, intrusion-detection systems, remote access security, wireless networking security, and encryption (Whitman and Mattord 2008, 342–392; Newman 2010).

Information security combines the efforts of personnel, policy, procedures, awareness, training, education, and technology. This is a "layered" approach to security. *The role of technical controls is to facilitate the enforcement of policy where human behavior is difficult to regulate.* An example of this would be software controls that block computer usage unless passwords are changed periodically, contain mixed cases, and have not been previously used.

Access Controls

Access controls involve four processes:

- *Identification*: obtaining the identity of the person or entity requesting access to an IT system or physical area. Example: a person's name.
- *Authentication*: confirming identity. To validate identity, a variety of methods are applied: something you *know* (e.g., password), *have* (e.g., card or token), *are* (e.g., fingerprint or retina scan), or *produce* (e.g., voice or signature pattern).
- *Authorization*: determining which actions can be performed by the person or entity seeking access.
- *Accountability*: documenting the actions.

Firewalls

Firewalls are constructed in buildings from the basement to the roof by using concrete or masonry materials; the purpose is to prevent the spread of fire. In the context of IT systems, a **firewall** is "any device that prevents a specific type of information from moving between the outside world, known as the untrusted network (e.g., the Internet), and the inside world, known as the trusted network" (Whitman and Mattord 2008, 353). One type of firewall acts as a filter to screen data packets based on IP address, type of packet, port request, and other elements. Another type consists of a separate computer between the trusted network and the untrusted network that serves as a filter. The architectural configurations of firewalls can be mutually exclusive or combined. The way in which an organization uses its network, as well as budget restrictions, dictate the configuration.

Intrusion-Detection Systems

Intrusion-detection systems (IDSs), in the context of IT security, rather than traditional physical security, are "devices that inspect data communication flows to identify patterns that may indicate that hacking is underway" (Whitman and Mattord 2008, 548). When the system detects an intrusion, an alarm is activated and an administrator is notified via e-mail and numerical or text paging. In addition, an external service provider can also be contacted. Events are logged to help investigate the attack. As with firewalls, IDSs require complex configurations and a system of criteria, depending on the level of detection and response needed. A *host-based IDS* configures and classifies various categories of systems and data files and reports on changes in certain ones, while ignoring changes in others. A *network-based IDS* monitors patterns in network traffic, such as a denial-of-service attack. A *signature-based IDS* examines data traffic that matches an attack pattern; it is a form of antivirus software that must be continually updated. The *statistical anomaly-based IDS* (or behavior-based IDS) first collects data from normal traffic to compare it to activity outside the norm. The *intrusion-prevention system* is an evolving concept that combines the capability to respond to known methods of attack with the capability to create responses to previously unknown methods of attack.

Remote Access Security

Prior to the Internet (a public network), organizations established private computer networks that permitted people to connect to them via telephone dial-up or leased-line connections. Dial-up is similar to two humans connected for a conversation via a telephone line, except computers are connected at both ends of the line. Whereas firewalls provide security today between an organization and the Internet, dial-up access also requires security. Although many organizations have upgraded to Internet connectivity, dial-up access is still a security concern.

Dial-up is less complex than Internet connectivity, generally requiring user name and password for authentication. Innovations have improved security. For instance, the Remote Authentication Dial-In User Service (RADIUS) centralizes access decisions for improved management.

Considerations for dial-up include determining the number of dial-up connections, since an organization may be paying for services not needed and the connections to the network may be unmonitored. Special software can detect connections. Ensure that dial-up numbers remain confidential. Use *call-back*, if possible. It requires a user to be at a specific location. The user calls in, a disconnect occurs, and the user is called back prior to the connection to the network being allowed. This security method is problematic for travelers. A *token* is another security method that goes beyond user name and password. The device interacts with the computer to which access is requested, and access is granted based on an internal algorithm.

Wireless Network Security

A wireless network does not require the installation of cable and is less expensive than a wired network. However, security is important for the **wireless network footprint** (i.e., the geographic area containing sufficient signal strength for a connection). A balance must be maintained between a sufficient signal for the employees working in a specific area and a signal that has too much power and can allow those outside the area to connect. War driving, for example, as explained earlier, exploits wireless networks. Security for wireless networks includes virtual private networks (i.e., a private, secure network within a network that keeps messages hidden), encryption, and firewalls.

Encryption

Whitman and Mattord (2008, 374–375) define **encryption** as "the process of converting an original message into a form that cannot be used by unauthorized individuals. That way, anyone without the tools and knowledge to convert an encrypted message back to its original format will be unable to interpret it." Whitman and Mattord (2008, 375–387) further explain encryption as follows. The science of encryption is known as *cryptology* and it includes two disciplines: cryptography and cryptanalysis. **Cryptography** is from the Greek words *kryptos*, meaning "hidden," and *graphein*, meaning "to write." It is the science of encoding and decoding messages so that other individuals cannot decipher them. **Cryptanalysis** originates from the Greek word, *analyein*, meaning "to break up." It refers to deciphering an original message from an encrypted message without knowing the algorithms and keys applied to encrypt the original message. An *algorithm* is a mathematical formula. A *key* is information on how to encrypt an original message in conjunction with an algorithm. Newman (2010, 197) writes that a public key is used in conjunction with a corresponding private key, and when both are applied, it is called an *asymmetrical system*. He adds that, historically, secure message transmission depended on single-key encryption, whereby the sender and receiver relied on the same key for encryption and decryption. To prevent eavesdropping, new security had to be developed. One avenue is to encrypt messages using the public key and decrypt using a private key known only to the user.

Adversaries seek to crack encryption codes, so encryption strategies should be changed periodically, and key security is important. Encryption is a necessity in our age of Internet usage, business on-line, privacy of information, the protection of proprietary information, and use of portable laptops and other devices. *In addition, as physical security continues to converge with*

IT security and increasingly becomes part of computer networks, encryption becomes especially important to ensure the security of security systems.

Mallery (2009, 44–46) writes of the importance of encrypting data not only in transit, but also at rest on computers and a variety of devices. He warns that many people think that their laptop computers and devices are protected because they login and use a password. However, for example, if data is only protected by a Microsoft Windows username and password, it is possible to boot the computer using a bootable Linux CD that can enable an adversary to access data and copy it to a USB device. An adversary could also simply remove the hard drive and connect it to another computer.

WHAT TECHNICAL CONTROLS ARE APPLIED BY BUSINESSES?

Research by Price, Waterhouse & Coopers (2009) found the following technical controls applied by businesses, along with the percentage of respondents (i.e., business executives) who applied the specific control. The first percentage represents 2007 and the second percentage represents 2008.

Malicious-code detection tools: 80%, 84%
Application-level firewalls: 62%, 67%
Intrusion detection: 59%, 63%
Encryption, database: 45%, 55%
Encryption, laptop: 40%, 50%
Wireless handheld device security: 33%, 42%

Communications Security

Communications security (COMSEC) is a broad term encompassing the protection of a wide variety of means of sending communications. Transmission occurs through wire, fiber-optic lines, microwave signals, satellite, space radio (e.g., cellular telephones), and other methods. Thus, data and information can be intercepted in numerous ways.

Highly skilled electronic countermeasures specialists are required to deal with this threat. Countermeasures include policies, procedures, training, and awareness; a physical search for spying devices; and a variety of technical controls (e.g., encryption). The term **TEMPEST** (not an acronym) refers to U.S. Department of Defense standards that aim to reduce unintended radio frequency emanations from computers and other electronic devices that are sought by spies using electromagnetic field decoders. Such interceptions can pick up computer chip processing, disk data, keystrokes, and other activity. Although it is an expensive option, **electronic soundproofing** (i.e., encasing a room in metal) can be used to shield a room from releasing electronic emissions.

Technical Surveillance Countermeasures

ASIS International (2007b, 19) defines **technical surveillance countermeasures (TSCM)** as "the use of services, equipment, and techniques designed to locate, identify, and neutralize the effectiveness of technical surveillance activities (electronic eavesdropping, wiretapping, bugging, etc.)." TSCM is a category within communications security.

Electronic eavesdropping means to electronically intercept a conversation without the consent of at least one of the parties. **Wiretapping** is a type of electronic eavesdropping that permits one to covertly listen to telephone conversations. Because of alternatives to the traditional "land line" method of telephone communications—such as cellular, microwave, and satellite—conversations and data can be accessed in various ways.

Bugging is a type of electronic surveillance that employs a variety of transmitting devices that permit one to listen to conversations. Bugs are often small and covertly hidden in objects (e.g., lamps and calendars).

Interception threats also face IT systems, computers, local area networks (LAN), wide area networks (WAN), and all types of cables (e.g., fiber optic). One device, for example, a keystroke-capture device, is installed between a keyboard and a computer, captures keystrokes, and sends the data to an adversary through the Internet. This can also be accomplished remotely through what is called a **keylogging program**.

Methods of intercepting conversations or data through electronic means are illegal unless conducted by law enforcement personnel with a court order. The equipment to conduct such surveillance is readily available online and from electronics retailers. In addition, devices that are not intended to conduct covert listening can be converted to listening devices. Examples are wireless microphones/transmitters used by speakers, baby listening devices, and toys containing a microphone and a transmitter that can be picked up by an ordinary radio.

Because electronic means of intercepting conversations, information, and data are difficult to detect, the extent of such illegal acts is impossible to ascertain. Moreover, these methods are part of an arsenal of methods used by spies, as described in this chapter.

If electronic spying is suspected, the services of a TSCM specialist can be retained. Use a public telephone, away from the premises, to contact a specialist. These consultants should be thoroughly vetted prior to retaining their services. Inquiries and verification should be made regarding training, experience, references, equipment, and insurance. Quackery is a possibility with some "experts," and certain equipment may be useless. A consumer can hide an ordinary tape recorder with a microphone to see if it can be detected.

Prior to hiring a TSCM specialist, consideration can be given to "low-tech" methods of electronic surveillance countermeasures. For instance, physically search a building and rooms for bugs, taps, and small cameras. Seek the assistance of specialists already employed, such as engineers, electricians, and IT specialists. They would recognize something odd on a cable or equipment. When meetings and conversations pertaining to sensitive information occur, an option is to communicate at an alternative location. Another option is to keep certain sensitive information separate from the IT system, possibly in a safe.

Surveillance by electronic means is technologically sophisticated and varied, to the point of being difficult to counter and detect. Electronic countermeasures specialists face enormous challenges, and the unwary in the private and public sectors are extremely vulnerable. In addition, the stronger the communications security, of whatever type (e.g., TEMPEST and TSCM), the greater are the chances a spy will shift to easier avenues of acquiring information at vulnerable points.

Fiber-Optic Vulnerability

Fiber-optic transmission lines transport data through the use of light waves within an ultrathin glass fiber encased in a protective jacket. Although this method of transporting data has been touted as being more secure than standard wiring (e.g., copper) and airwaves, in reality, fiber cabling is just as vulnerable as other transmission methods. Miller (2006, 44–47) explains the vulnerabilities of fiber cabling. She offers examples of penetrations of fiber cabling and writes that, in 2003, an illegal eavesdropping device was found attached to Verizon's optical network to access sensitive financial information of a mutual fund. Early knowledge of the information was worth millions of dollars. Similar taps were found on police networks and the networks of pharmaceutical companies in Europe. Miller notes that high-profile intrusions result in few details being released, and many intrusions go unreported and undetected. She writes that tapping fiber cabling has also been linked to national intelligence, and she refers to the USS *Jimmy Carter*, the $3.2-billion submarine retrofitted to conduct tapping of undersea cables.

Miller (2006, 44–47) explains that although there are millions of miles of fiber cable globally, most is difficult to access for a tap. However, plenty of cable is accessible, and some cities post cabling maps online to lure entities to hook into their network. She writes that the equipment to tap into a fiber cable is readily available online. Once a hacker gains access to a fiber cable, a clamp is placed on the line to bend the cable to leak a small amount of light, which is then captured by an optical photo detector and converted to a signal for connection to a computer where software analyzes the signal. To counter this threat, entities should use encryption. Vendors are also developing security tools that detect both intrusion of the cable and optical events such as malicious intrusions and data-signal loss. Tapping into a fiber cable may be more difficult than acquiring information from many legal paths.

Competitive Intelligence

The **Society of Competitive Intelligence Professionals** is composed of specialists who seek information through legal and ethical means to analyze the strengths and weaknesses of business competitors. This group has a code of ethics that guides their vocation. Corporations often have such specialists on their staff or outsource the work. The purpose is to ascertain what the competition is doing. Competitive intelligence (CI) helps with business planning and avoiding errors and miscalculations. The sources of CI include business information databases (e.g., LexisNexis), public documents, publications, sales literature, speeches, and news releases. Such sources provide a foundation for analysis and conclusions. Mallery (2009, 82) writes that there are those who take CI to the "next level" and violate laws and ethics through, as examples, theft, electronic eavesdropping, and hacking.

WHAT ARE THE LEGAL LIMITS OF INVESTIGATING A BUSINESS COMPETITOR?

The following story and guidelines are from the work of Dekieffer (2009, 111–112). He describes a large food manufacturer that worried about the competition that one of its products would face from a new company. The manufacturer hired a consulting firm to conduct research on the competitor. The consultant's in-depth report contained the names, social security numbers, and home addresses of the competitor's management, as well as personal information. The report also included plans of the competitor's new manufacturing plant, the ingredients of the rival product, and bids from suppliers. The large manufacturer noticed that some of its suppliers were in the report, so the company contacted the suppliers, claiming that there was a conflict of interest and urging them to make a choice between the two customers. When the suppliers informed the competitor about the pressure to make a choice, litigation followed, and the consultant's investigative methods surfaced. These included paying a contractor for a look at the competitor's new plant, placing an investigator in the competitor's facility as a secretary to access proprietary information, searching through their trash system (often called "dumpster diving"), and investigating the personal lives of executives to "dig up dirt." The civil case was eventually settled out of court, and the consultant was charged with several crimes because of the methods used in the investigation.

Ethical and legal methods of intelligence gathering are of the utmost importance. Personal records, such as medical records and tax returns, as well as trade secrets and classified documents, are off limits. Possessing such documents can result in prosecution. Open-source intelligence provides a lot of information for investigators, and it is often a beginning point of an investigation. Interviewing is permissible as an investigative technique; however, no one can be forced to answer questions. Surveillance is permissible in public areas. Investigators must avoid trespassing, hacking, electronic surveillance, wiretapping, and other illegal acts.

YOUR CAREER IN SECURITY

Chief Security Officer (CSO)

ASIS International (2004) developed the "Chief Security Officer (CSO) Guideline." It serves as a foundation for the following information. The guideline is a model for entities developing a senior-level leadership function that provides for comprehensive, enterprise-wide security. Also helpful in developing this position is the ASIS International (2008) "Chief Security Officer (CSO) Organizational Standard."

The **chief security officer (CSO)** title has been applied in the information technology (IT) vocation for several years, and it refers to those individuals whose primary responsibility focuses on IT security. In this career box, the CSO position is described in a much broader context beyond IT security, and it includes all aspects of security in an organization.

Whitman and Mattord (2008, 48) provide definitions of organizational titles pertaining to IT. They refer to the chief information officer (CIO) as "the senior technology officer responsible for aligning the strategic efforts of the organization into action plans for the information systems or data-processing division of the organization.... The Chief Information Security Officer (CISO), sometimes called the Chief Security Officer, Security Manager, Director of Information Security, or a similar title, is responsible for the assessment, management, and implementation of securing the information in the organization."

The CSO position is important because risks are increasing in complexity on a global scale. Entities have a responsibility to identify all risks and take remedial action. The pressure to accomplish these objectives is derived from an organization's desire to survive and profit, its board of directors and shareholders, laws and regulations, the public, and other sources.

Nature of the Work

A CSO reports to the most senior-level executives within an organization, such as the chief executive officer (CEO) or chief financial officer (CFO). These senior corporate positions are referred to as the **C-suite** (or senior

C-level). The effective CSO works with the senior executive team to fulfill business objectives.

Besides the customary duties of a security executive (i.e., planning, budgeting, organizing, staffing, directing, and controlling), a CSO assesses information and metrics, studies the probability of security-related incidents, and plans preventive strategies and business continuity. The range of threats and hazards to consider as a CSO is very broad and enterprise-wide. A CSO focuses not only on the importance of people and assets, but also supply chain, intellectual property, trade secrets, reputation, major fraud, product tampering, and many other issues. Information security and security of IT are additional responsibilities of a CSO. Business-continuity planning is vital for critical systems (e.g., IT), and if failure occurs for whatever reason, operations must be restored. The CSO works with internal and external resources and government agencies to maintain business continuity.

A CSO directs a staff of managers who apply the best possible security methodologies. In addition, they implement policies and security practices, research and deploy state-of-the-art technology, and maintain comprehensive, global security throughout the organization.

Requirements

A CSO is a top leader with superior skills in business, security, human relations, and verbal and written communications. Zalud and Maddry (2008, 26) write that the CSO must be skilled in both IT and physical security because of the integrated security environment. They add the following: "Given the expansion in their responsibilities, CSOs must retool themselves and acquire the skills necessary to operate in an ever changing combined threat environment. It is no longer good enough to be a skilled practitioner in one area of security."

ASIS International (2004) lists CSO requirements as including demonstrated integrity and skills in analysis, strategic planning, and creative problem solving. In reference to experience requirements, the CSO must be a seasoned manager with a proven record of accomplishments across a broad range of corporate experiences. A CSO should have three to five years of experience in a significant leadership role and ten to fifteen years in a private- or public-sector security or related position.

Advanced degrees are desirable in the candidate, including majors such as business, accounting, law, IT, security, or criminal justice. Certifications are valued and illustrate professionalism and competence through education, training, and testing. Two certification examples are the Certified Protection Professional (CPP), demonstrating general security management expertise, and the Certified Information Systems Security Professional (CISSP), demonstrating knowledge of network and system security practices.

Salary

A CSO is a highly paid executive with enormous responsibilities. Base pay, performance bonus, stock options, and a variety of benefits can exceed $200,000 annually.

Advice

Not everyone has the ability to become a CSO. The position requires extraordinary skills and years of experience and education. At the same time, the work can be interesting and challenging because of the constantly changing risks facing organizations.

Summary

Information is a valuable asset that, if not protected, can result in serious harm to an organization. Because of such goals as power, superiority, and wealth from the acquisition of certain information, entities and individuals commit a variety of crimes to obtain targeted information. Various laws, such as the Uniform Trade Secrets Act and the Economic Espionage Act of 1996, provide a foundation for legal action against offenders who steal proprietary information. At the same time, there are many methods of acquiring information legally to gain a competitive advantage, such as through both the Internet and public documents. Laws also require organizations to protect personal information, as illustrated through the Health Insurance Portability and Accountability Act of 1996 (HIPAA).

The threats and hazards facing IT, data, and information are many. These include human error, natural disasters, malware, botnets, lost or stolen computers or other electronic devices, and electronic eavesdropping. Likewise, the spectrum of information security methods and strategies are broad. Examples are employment applicant screening, training and awareness, policies and procedures, classification, destruction, and technical controls.

Discussion Questions

1. What are the most serious threats to information technology, data, and information?
2. Do you think the U.S. government and businesses place enough emphasis on information security? Explain your answer.
3. Will the information security profession, in the public and/or private sectors, be capable of securing cyberspace in the future? Explain your answer.

4. What can employers do about protecting proprietary information from so many types of portable electronic devices in the workplace?

5. Should corporate security personnel be permitted to seize portable electronic devices if such devices are prohibited on the premises and relevant policies have been communicated to employees?

6. Is it possible for a nation to win a war through cyber warfare? Explain your answer.

7. Which technical controls (to protect information technology and data) do you view as most helpful, and which do you view as least helpful?

8. Would you be interested in a career in information security? Why or why not?

Practical Applications

8A. As a security officer on patrol at a corporate research and development site, you are approached by a visiting salesperson with a temporary ID who asks if she can walk around in a restricted area. You refuse, and then she offers you $5,000 cash if you let her into the restricted area. What do you do?

8B. As a security officer at a corporate site you are approached by two employees, and each hands you a USB flash drive that they state was found outside the building. Neither flash drive has identifying information. What do you do?

8C. As a chief security officer (CSO) for a corporation, what policies do you formulate for corporate scientists, engineers, and employees when they speak at outside functions such as conferences and symposiums.

8D. As a security manager at a hospital, you are assigned the task of correcting a growing problem of theft of hospital laptops on and off the premises. What are your plans and strategies?

8E. As a CSO for a corporation, you are on a planning committee working on establishing a wireless network for a corporate site. What are your security suggestions for the committee for the wireless network?

8F. As a corporate security manager, you learn that a vice president of research and development is soon to leave on a business trip to China. What information security guidelines do you provide to the executive?

8G. As a corporate security manager, how would you evaluate applicants applying for a technical surveillance countermeasures service contract with your employer?

8H. As a corporate security manager, your supervisor assigns you the task of developing guidelines for corporate employees investigating business competitors. Prepare at least five guidelines.

Internet Connections

Business Espionage Controls and Countermeasures Association: www.becca-online.org

Computer Emergency Response Team (CERT), Carnegie Mellon University: www.cert.org

Federal Bureau of Investigation (cyber investigations): www.fbi.gov/cyberinvest/cyber-home.htm

Information Security: http://informationsecurity.techtarget.com

InfraGard: www.infragard.net

International Association of Computer Investigative Specialists: www.iacis.com

National Association of Information Destruction, Inc.: www.naidonline.org

National Counterintelligence Center: www.ncix.gov

National Institute of Standards and Technology, Computer Security Resource Center: http://csrc.nist.gov

OPSEC Professionals Society: www.opsecsociety.org

Overseas Security Advisory Council: www.osac.gov

Society of Competitive Intelligence Professionals: www.scip.org

Spy Life: www.spylife.com

Spy World: www.spyworld.com

SysAdmin, Audit, Network, Security (SANS): www.sans.org

U.S. Department of Homeland Security, National Cyber Security Division: www.us-cert.gov

U.S. Secret Service (Electronic Crimes Task Forces): www.secretservice.gov/ectf.shtml

References

ASIS International. 2004. Chief security officer guideline. www.asisonline.org.

ASIS International. 2005. *Career opportunities in security.* Alexandria, VA: ASIS International.

ASIS International. 2007a. Trends in proprietary information loss (June). www.asisonline.org.

ASIS International. 2007b. Information asset protection guideline. www.asisonline.org.

ASIS International. 2008. Chief security officer (CSO) organizational standard. www.asisonline.org.

Associated Press. 2008. Pentagon bans Google teams from bases (March 6).

Associated Press. 2009. Cyber spying a threat, and everyone is in on it (April 10).

Brill, A. 2007. Protecting data sources from internal theft. Global Fraud Report 2007–2008. www.kroll.com.

Clark, M. 2009. Searching cell phones seized incident to arrest. *FBI Law Enforcement Bulletin* 78 (February):25–32.

Cole, E. 2006. More than meets the eye. *Information Security* 9 (November):36–37.

Coleman, K. 2008. Triggering a cyber war. *Government Security* 7 (January/February):11.

Credant Technologies. 2008. 15 ways to lose your data. www.credant.com.

Dekieffer, D. 2009. Investigating the competition. *Security Management* 53 (April): 111–112.

European Network and Information Security Agency. 2008. *Secure USB Flash Drives* (June). www.enisa.europa.eu/doc/pdf.

Fickes, M. 2008. Cyber terror. *Government Security* 7 (July/August):13.

Georgia Tech Information Security Center. 2008. Emerging cyber threats report for 2009. www.gtiscsecuritysummit.com.

Hayes, B. 2009. Small business secrets under siege. *Security Technology Executive* 19 (January):28–29.

Higgins, K. 2009. Study: Most employees disobey security policies. *Dark Reading* (June 9). www.darkreading.com.

Hines, M. 2008. Cyber-espionage moves into B2B. *InfoWorld* (January 15).

Kennedy, J. 2008. Protecting an organization's information from the inside risks. *Homeland Defense Journal* 6 (March):45.

Livingston, J. 2007. When "delete" is not enough. *Security Technology & Design* (September):63–66.

Mallery, J. 2009. Overlooked data leaks. *Security Technology Executive* 19 (March):44–46, 78–82.

Miller, S. 2006. Optical illusion. *Information Security* 9 (November):44–47.

National Infrastructure Advisory Council. 2008. The insider threat to critical infrastructures (April 8). www.dhs.gov/xprevprot/committees/editorial_0353.shtm.

Newman, R. 2010. *Computer security: Protecting digital resources*. Boston: Jones and Bartlett.

Piwonka, B. 2008. The data defenders. *Security Products* 12 (June):61–63.

Ponemon Institute. 2008. Security of paper documents in the workplace. www.ponemon.org.

Price, Waterhouse & Coopers. 2009. The global state of information security, 2008. www.pwc.com.

Slate, R. 2009. Competing with intelligence: New directions in China's quest for intellectual property and implications for homeland security. *Homeland Security Affairs* 5 (January).

U.S. Department of Defense. 2008. *Changes in espionage by Americans: 1947–2007*. Monterey, CA: Defense Personnel Security Research Center.

U.S. Department of Homeland Security. 2010. US-CERT. www.us-cert.gov.

U.S. Government Accountability Office. 2008a. DOD personnel clearances. www.gao.gov/new.items/d08470t.pdf.

U.S. Government Accountability Office. 2008b. Cyber analysis and warning: DHS faces challenges in establishing a comprehensive national capability (July 31). www.gao.gov/new.items/d08588.pdf.

U.S. Government Accountability Office. 2008c. Information security: Progress reported, but weaknesses at federal agencies persist. www.goa.gov/new.items/d08571t.pdf.

Vijayan, J. 2008. Travel group warns: Corporate data at risk from laptop searches at border. *Computerworld* (April 30). www.computerworld.com.

White House. 2009. Cyber policy review: Assuring a trusted and resilient information and communications infrastructure. www.whitehouse.gov/assets/documents/Cyberspace_Policy_Review_final.pdf.

Whitman, M., and H. Mattord. 2008. *Management of information security*. 2nd ed. Boston: Thomson.

Wikipedia. 2009. ISO/IEC 27000-Series. http://en.wikipedia.org/wiki/ISO/IEC_27000-series.

Zalud, B., and T. Maddry. 2008. What the CEO thinks. *Security* 45 (May):26

Chapter **9**

Security Law and Liabilities

Chapter Learning Objectives

After reading this chapter, you should be able to:

1. Explain federalism, law, and three theoretical models of law and society
2. Define and provide examples of substantive and procedural *criminal* law
3. Define and provide examples of substantive and procedural *civil* law
4. Detail arrest law for citizens, security officers, and public police
5. Name and describe the four weights of evidence and under what circumstances each is applied
6. Detail search-and-seizure law for public police and security officers
7. Explain electronic evidence and discovery of electronic information

Terms to Know

federalism
law
value consensus theory
pluralistic theory

class conflict theory
criminal law
civil law
adversary system
plaintiff
compensatory damages
punitive damages
substantive criminal law
elements
capital crime
felony
misdemeanor
infraction
procedural criminal law
booking
initial appearance
preliminary hearing
grand jury
arraignment
plea-bargaining
discovery
bench trial
motion
cross-examination
substantive civil law
tort
negligence
premises security claim
foreseeability
adequacy of security
vicarious liability
expert witness
interrogatories
deposition
subpoena
discovery
International Association of Professional Security Consultants
procedural civil law
civil complaint
summons
motion for summary judgment
pretrial conference
under color of law

arrest
Amendment IV
Amendment V
Amendment VI
Amendment VIII
Amendment XIV, Section 1
Burdeau v. McDowell 256 U.S. 465 (1921)
common law
statutory law
citizen's arrest
reasonable force
deadly force
use-of-force continuum
weights of evidence
reasonable suspicion
Terry v. Ohio 392 U.S. 1 (1968)
probable cause
affidavit
proof beyond a reasonable doubt
preponderance of the evidence
exclusionary rule
Mapp v. Ohio 367 U.S. 643 (1961)
warrantless searches
People v. Zelinski 594 P. 2d 1000 (1979)
State of Minnesota v. Beswell 449 N.W.2d 471 (Minn. App. 1989)
evidence
computer forensics
digital evidence
litigation hold
attorney-client privilege

QUIZ

This quiz serves to prime the reader's mind and begin the reading, thinking, and studying processes for this chapter. The answers to all of the questions are found within this chapter.

1. Are criminal law statutes found in the U.S. Constitution?
2. What is a capital crime?
3. What is the name of the type of money damages paid to the wronged party in a successful lawsuit to punish the defendant for wrongdoing?
4. Do juveniles have all of the same constitutional rights as adults?

> 5. Can an individual be arrested and sued for the same act?
> 6. What is a deposition?
> 7. Are public police prohibited from working part-time in security positions?
> 8. Do private security officers generally possess arrest powers equal to citizen arrest powers?
> 9. Which amendment of the Bill of Rights of the U.S. Constitution provides guidelines for arrest, search, and seizure?

Introduction

Law is essential for an organized society, and it guides conduct. Security practitioners learn through the law what they can and cannot do as they perform their duties. They are also guided by organizational policies and procedures, supervisors, and managers—although these sources of guidance are subservient to law. Legal terminology and theory are explained throughout this chapter, providing a broad picture of our legal system and how it functions. This chapter also covers liabilities common in the security profession, plus laws of arrest, search and seizure, and evidence.

The Development of Law

Federalism

The United States operates under a form of government known as **federalism**. It is a compromise between a strong central government and local needs within the states. Federalism was debated during the Constitutional Convention, in Philadelphia, in 1787. There was a realization of the need for a strong central government for national defense, foreign policy, trade, banking, currency, and taxation. The foundation of federalism is Article VI of the U.S. Constitution, which refers to the Constitution as the "supreme Law of the Land." The powers of Congress, the president, and the U.S. Supreme Court (Figure 9.1) are limited to powers granted in the Constitution. The Tenth Amendment provides that "[t]he powers not delegated to the United States by the Constitution ... are reserved to the States...." Thus, states govern needs at the local level, including the enactment of laws, which must conform to the U.S. Constitution (Gardner and Anderson 2010, 22).

Law Defined

Neubauer (2005, 25–26) defines the word *law* and explains each phrase of his definition. He defines **law** as "a body of rules enacted by public officials in a legitimate manner and backed by the force of the state." The "body of

FIGURE 9.1 U.S. Supreme Court Building, Washington, D.C. The U.S. Supreme Court is the highest court in the United States. (® Shutterstock.com. With permission.)

rules" is found in a variety of sources, including federal and state constitutions, statutes passed by Congress and state legislatures, ordinances passed by city and county councils, federal and state court decisions, and administrative regulations from federal and state regulatory agencies. "Enacted by public officials" is noteworthy because all organizations typically have rules and regulations that govern members; however, private rules are not law unless recognized by public officials, such as judges, legislators, and executives. "Legitimate manner" means that legislators follow laws and methods for enacting new laws, executives follow procedures for applying laws, and judges interpret laws. "Backed by the force of the state" refers to sanctions for those who do not conform to law.

Theoretical Models of Law and Society

Voigt et al. (1994, 58–60) describe three explanations of the development and function of law in society: (1) value consensus theory, (2) pluralistic theory, and (3) class conflict theory.

Value consensus theory is closely aligned with democratic ideals. The legal system seeks to be "value neutral" while working to settle differences according to public interests that reflect the general consensus and the larger public good. Law is viewed as representing values and norms, and the legal system is viewed as vital for the well-being of society.

Pluralistic theory views law as resulting from the struggles of competing interest groups who vie for legal protection of their economic, social, political, and other interests. Judges and legislators are seen as primarily responsive to those with wealth and power. Law frequently changes in response to well-organized groups who use their influence on the law making and law enforcement systems for their own advantage.

Class conflict theory views law and the justice system as tools of the dominant group to control other, less fortunate groups. Law is not applied to benefit society as a whole, as in value consensus theory. In contrast to pluralistic theory, which mobilizes pressure in the legal system when an interest group's dominance is in jeopardy, class conflict theory sees one dominant group maintaining power over legal and economic systems. Criminal law, law enforcement and judicial agencies, and prisons are used to maintain the status quo and prevent discontent over the unequal distribution of wealth.

Critical Thinking

Which of the three theoretical models of law and society do you view as existing in the United States today?

Criminal and Civil Law and Procedures

Criminal law is a body of written offenses and punishments that are applied by government to individuals who commit crimes against society. **Civil law** is a body of written rules that govern relationships and disputes among private individuals, businesses, and government. Our criminal and civil justice **adversary systems** each contain opponents who seek justice by convincing a judge and jury that their perspective is correct. In criminal cases, the prosecutor represents the state, and a defense attorney represents the accused. In civil cases, an attorney represents the wronged party (i.e., the **plaintiff**) who sues the defendant, who is defended by an attorney. In the criminal justice system, the guilty party is subject to a fine, probation, incarceration, or death. In the civil justice system, the wrongdoer is subject to civil remedies: **Compensatory damages** are ordered by the court to be paid to the wronged party; these damages cover actual losses suffered (e.g., medical bills and lost wages). **Punitive damages** are ordered by the court when the wronged party has been harmed in a malicious or willful manner (e.g., a security officer beat a suspect); the required payment is used to punish the wrongdoer. Other civil remedies include injunction (i.e., order from a judge to stop a person from taking certain actions) and declaratory judgment (i.e., court decision on rights of parties, as in a divorce).

Substantive Criminal Law

Both criminal law and civil law can be divided into the categories of substantive law and procedural law. **Substantive criminal law** focuses on specific definitions of crimes and related punishments. Each state and the federal government have written substantive criminal laws on many types of crimes. Each written crime contains **elements** specifying the conditions required to be proven for successful prosecution. Investigators and prosecutors must prove all the elements of the crime for which they are charging an individual. For instance, the elements of first-degree murder are often defined as follows: an unlawful killing, of a human being, intentionally, and with prior planning and determination.

Substantive criminal law can be categorized as follows:

- **Capital crime**. A serious crime such as murder, resulting in the penalty of death.
- **Felony**. A serious crime generally punishable by one or more years of incarceration. Examples are manslaughter, sexual assault, robbery, and grand larceny.
- **Misdemeanor**. A less serious crime generally punishable by incarceration of less than one year. Examples are disorderly conduct, public drunkenness, petty larceny, shoplifting, and trespassing.
- **Infraction**. This is the least serious of offenses, defined by state statute or local ordinance, and often punished through a fine. Examples are traffic offenses and littering.

Procedural Criminal Law

Procedural criminal law provides the rules and steps to be followed in the proceedings of criminal cases. It has been referred to as the "machinery of justice." Once evidence is gathered and an arrest is made, a suspect is taken to a police department or jail for **booking**. This is an administrative process of collecting information on the arrestee (e.g., name and charge), including photographing and fingerprinting. Without unnecessary delay, the defendant is taken to an **initial appearance**, before a magistrate, who informs the defendant of constitutional rights, the charges, and the status of bail. The initial appearance may be followed by a **preliminary hearing** (also called a probable cause hearing), whereby a magistrate decides if enough evidence exists to proceed to trial. Depending on the jurisdiction, the type of crime, and the strength of the evidence, a variety of options are available to criminal justice practitioners. A magistrate or prosecutor may decide that the case lacks sufficient evidence and the case is dropped, or the defendant is diverted to a "helping agency" for assistance with a substance abuse or domestic violence problem.

Depending on the state, grand jury action may be required if the case is to proceed to trial. A **grand jury** is a group of citizens who have been selected by law and are sworn to hear evidence in cases; sufficient evidence will result in an indictment of the accused. If an arrest warrant has not yet been issued, it will be following an indictment. The next procedural step is an **arraignment**, whereby the accused is informed of the charges and constitutional rights and enters a plea to the charges among the following options: guilty, not guilty, nolo contendere (i.e., does not admit guilt, but accepts a penalty), or not guilty by reason of insanity.

Earlier in the procedural process, prosecutors and defense attorneys are often involved in negotiation called **plea-bargaining**, whereby the defendant pleads guilty to a lesser crime and receives a reduced sentence in exchange for waiving the right to a trial by jury, which saves a lot of time and expense for the prosecutor, defense, and court. **Discovery** assists with the negotiation process. In criminal and civil cases, discovery (also called disclosure), backed by procedural law and case law, requires opposing sides to share their case files with the other side, when requested, to disclose points of dispute and to expedite justice. Most cases (criminal and civil) never make it to the trial stage, but are negotiated. Neubauer (2005, 286) reports that about 36 percent of murder cases and less than 10 percent of all other types of criminal cases go to trial.

If a defendant pleads guilty or nolo contendere, and a judge accepts the plea, sentencing follows. If a defendant pleads not guilty, or not guilty by reason of insanity, a trial is held. A **bench trial**, which is a trial before a judge without a jury, may be requested if issues are technical or emotional; the judge decides factual issues after hearing the arguments of opposing attorneys and then renders a decision on guilt or innocence.

A trial may be preceded by **motions**, which are requests to a judge. For example, a defense attorney may file a motion to suppress evidence seized unconstitutionally by police. Prior to trial, a jury is selected. Then, when the jury trial begins, the prosecutor and the defense attorney make opening statements to the judge and jury to explain what they intend to prove. Next, the prosecutor presents evidence (e.g., witnesses and physical evidence). The prosecutor examines (i.e., questions) witnesses (Figure 9.2), and then the defense attorney cross-examines the witnesses. **Cross-examination** means that a witness is examined to ensure accuracy and quality of evidence. After the prosecutor presents his or her case, the defense may file a motion for acquittal. If denied, the defense side presents evidence and examines witnesses. The prosecutor then cross-examines the witnesses. Each side has an opportunity to rebut evidence presented by the other side. As the trial ends, opposing attorneys present closing arguments to the jury, the judge provides directions to the jury on the charge and how to reach a verdict, and the jury deliberates prior to reaching a verdict. A guilty verdict will be followed by

FIGURE 9.2   Witnesses are a major source of evidence. (® Shutterstock.com. With permission.)

sentencing. A not-guilty verdict will free the defendant. A guilty verdict may also bring motions (e.g., for a new trial) and an appeal by the defense side.

JUVENILES AND JUVENILE JUSTICE

When public police and private security personnel encounter juvenile suspects, a different array of laws and procedures are required in comparison to adults. The terminology and philosophy of juvenile justice also differ from the adult system. Depending on the jurisdiction, a term such as *arrest* may be replaced with the term *petition of delinquency*, and the term *sentence* may be replaced with the term *disposition*. This softer approach includes an attempt to "guide and rehabilitate youngsters" so that they can mature and lead law-abiding lives. Although juveniles have the same constitutional rights as adults, except for a trial by jury (unless they are transferred to the adult system for a serious crime), they usually receive a determination of how they will be processed in the justice system by a juvenile intake officer who is employed by a department of juvenile justice. Security personnel should check with local public police for guidance in procedures for juveniles.

Substantive Civil Law

Substantive civil law defines duties owed among persons, and it is applied to settle disputes. Neubauer (2005, 36) describes five major areas of civil law: torts, contracts, property, domestic relations, and inheritance. Here we concentrate on torts.

A **tort** is a civil wrong, damage, or injury, other than a breach of contract. Management in all organizations and security practitioners should be aware of torts and potential lawsuits. In addition, persons are subject to being sued and arrested for the same offense. Notice that several of the following torts are also crimes.

Assault: causing fear in another person through an attempt or threat to harm.

Battery: harmful physical contact with another.

Trespass: an unauthorized entry on the property of another.

False imprisonment: confining a person within fixed boundaries against his or her will.

Malicious prosecution: initiation of criminal charges, without sufficient evidence and with malice, against another.

Intentional infliction of emotional distress: an outrageous intent to cause severe emotional distress in another.

Defamation: communicating false statements about another to harm that person's reputation. When this is done through the spoken word, it is referred to as *slander*. When done through writing, it is referred to as *libel*.

Invasion of privacy: causing harm by intruding into another's private life or communicating private information of another.

Critical Thinking

Since individuals can be sued and arrested for the same offense, why do we not see more offenders sued by victims?

Negligence

Negligence is a type of tort. Our system of law and justice recognizes a duty to adhere to certain standards to protect others against risk of harm. If a person (e.g., business) fails to adhere to a required standard, and the failure causes harm, then the party that is harmed has a foundation for a lawsuit for negligence. Because of an infinite number of possible scenarios, it is not possible to establish an exact set of rules for negligence. The *elements for a lawsuit for negligence* are: "(1) a duty or standard of care recognized by law, (2) a breach of the duty or failure to exercise the requisite care, and (3) the occurrence of harm proximately caused by the breach of duty." All of these elements must be proved by the plaintiff for a lawsuit for negligence to be successful. A jury must make a determination of whether the defendant acted as a reasonably prudent person would have facing the same situation (Schubert 2008, 502).

Negligent behavior by security officers, security investigators, security managers, or other security practitioners can result in various types of civil action. An example of *negligent hiring* results when a security officer at a hotel, who has access to rooms, enters a female's room and sexually assaults her. Hotel management did a poor job of screening the security officer, who had multiple charges for sexual assault. As another example, *negligent retention* results when a security investigator, who has been disciplined several times for threatening and assaulting employee theft suspects, retains his position and continues to assault employee suspects. *Negligent assignment and entrustment* results, for example, when security management assigns a security officer, who has a record of larceny and substance abuse, to a client's high-value storage area, and the security officer, in collusion with internal and external offenders, is arrested as an accessory to a burglary at the "protected" site. *Negligent training*, a serious problem, especially in security companies with high turnover, can occur when, for example, state-mandated training is not conducted, and a security officer abuses his/her authority by making a poor arrest decision. *Negligent supervision* can result when, for example, security officers fail to conduct patrols in a hospital parking lot and a nurse is assaulted. Alternatively, negligent supervision also occurs when security personnel customarily sleep in front of CCTV monitors and fail to observe and react to crimes.

Negligence also includes **premises security claims**. This involves a claim that management did not provide adequate security and safety for people (e.g., employees, customers, etc.) on the premises, and a person was victimized by a third party (e.g., robber, rapist, or murderer). The elements for a lawsuit for negligence apply. **Foreseeability** is an issue in premise security claims to determine whether a duty to protect existed. Kaminsky (1995, 9) explains that "to establish that a crime was or should have been foreseen by the defendant, the plaintiff must show that the defendant knew or should have known that the criminal act was likely to occur." He writes that strategies for establishing foreseeability include presenting evidence of prior crimes on or near the premises, that the premises is in a high-crime area, and that the conditions on the premises attracts criminals. **Adequacy of security** is another issue in such a case. Was the security on the premises adequate? Did it conform to what is reasonable security for the conditions on or nearby the site? Did the security conform to guidelines, standards, and/or regulations? In these cases, both plaintiff and defense, with the use of experts, typically conduct a thorough study of all aspects of security, which each side shares with the other side through discovery.

Vicarious Liability

Schubert (2008, 708) defines **vicarious liability** as follows: "Substituted or indirect responsibility, e.g., the responsibility of an employer for the torts committed by his employee within the scope of his employment." In the security realm, an employer, manager, or supervisor can be held accountable for the actions or inactions of a security officer or other security employee. The legal concept of vicarious liability is also referred to as *respondeat superior* (let the master respond). The master is liable for torts committed by employees within the scope of employment. This is why competent management, screening applicants, policies, procedures, training, and supervision are so important. If management hires an independent contractor, management may not be liable for torts committed by the contractor. However, the question of liability depends on the service contract, whether the duty is nondelegable, the type of action or inaction by the contractor's employee, and other exceptions (Nemeth 2005, 152).

DO NOT MAKE THESE MISTAKES

Shopping Mall Security

As Vanessa Smith completed her evening of shopping at the Mayville Central Mall, she returned to her vehicle in the dimly lit parking lot. While entering her SUV, she was kidnapped and then sexually assaulted and robbed. Following these crimes, the offender pushed her out of her vehicle ten miles from the mall, in an isolated area. Vanessa struggled to reach a rural farmhouse, and the owner telephoned 9-1-1. She endured a long recovery, and the emotional scars remained. The offender was not apprehended. She decided to sue the mall and the contract security company, Multi-Force Security, for inadequate security.

During discovery, attorneys for the insurer of the mall and the contract security company insisted that the mall had no records of security/safety surveys at the mall, crime rates at the mall, studies of lighting levels in the parking lot, and joint-meetings of mall management and management of Multi-Force Security.

As the case dragged on, the plaintiff's security expert found, among other items, the following statements on the Multi-Force Security Web site:

"As a foundation for quality and professional security at all of our client sites, Multi-Force performs an initial and quarterly security/safety survey and meets with the client to share the results.... Survey reports include ... lighting levels.

"Multi-Force carefully tracks crime incidents at all client sites and prepares monthly reports for clients.

"All clients of Multi-Force are visited quarterly by senior management for a complete report on security metrics and strategies to enhance security and safety for people and assets."

Three years of police records prior to Vanessa Smith's victimization, including 9-1-1 calls for service from the mall and incident reports completed by responding police, showed three sexual assaults, two shootings, and six armed robberies—all in the mall parking lots. Other offenses included simple assaults, drug possession and sale, and numerous property crimes. In addition, media reports exposed a gang problem at the mall.

During the time of Smith's victimization, three of the five security officers scheduled to work were on a meal break, leaving one to patrol the parking lot and one to patrol inside the mall.

When the preceding information was disclosed by the plaintiff's attorney to the defendants, a settlement was reached. Vanessa Smith received compensation.

Lessons: Company Web sites, brochures, and other (public) marketing publications should be reviewed by a company attorney for accuracy. In addition, parties involved in litigation are required by law to adhere to rules of discovery.
- When serious crimes occur on the premises, an evaluation of security strategies should occur, including a risk assessment.
- Careful planning is essential for the chronological and geographical distribution of security officers. Meal breaks for security officers should be planned to ensure maximum protection of people and assets.

Critical Thinking

Should victims of crime have the opportunity to sue entities for compensation? Why or why not?

YOUR CAREER IN SECURITY

Expert Witness

An **expert witness** is a person who is very knowledgeable in a specialized field and helps the parties in a legal case—attorneys, judge, jury, and others—understand technical aspects of the case. If a case is not settled prior to trial, a trial jury can apply knowledge and opinions from expert testimony in arriving at a verdict. Attorneys on both sides of a case may hire one or more experts so that each legal team has an improved understanding of the strengths and weaknesses of the case. The expertise and opinions of experts provide valuable perspectives on a case to assist attorneys in negotiating and settling, or deciding whether to proceed to trial. There are many types of cases, both civil and criminal, where experts may be helpful. Examples in civil litigation are accidents, wrongful deaths, and medical malpractice. In serious criminal cases, such as murder, experts may study the case and testify.

The types of expertise that experts offer are almost endless. If we focus on experts for accidents, there are automobile experts, truck experts, bicycle experts, lawnmower experts, hand tool experts, industrial experts, and so forth. In criminal cases, both prosecution and defense may seek experts to study a case and testify. Specializations include DNA, fingerprints, ballistics, bloodstain patterns, vehicles, computers, sexual assault, arson, and many other areas.

Nature of the Work

An expert witness studies the case file provided to him/her by the hiring attorney. Whichever side of a case an expert is hired by, the expert must be objective in studying the case and arriving at opinions.

Examples of items that may be in a case file of alleged negligent security are: the complaint filed in court by the plaintiff's attorney that explains the grounds for the lawsuit; police and security reports of the incident; police logs of 9-1-1 calls from the location or nearby for three years preceding the incident; police incident reports for the location and nearby for three years preceding the incident; maps and technical drawings of buildings; **interrogatories** (i.e., written questions prepared by one party to be answered in writing by the other party or someone else); **depositions** (i.e., a written record of verbal testimony based on questions from an attorney on either side of a case) of victims, witnesses, expert witnesses, security personnel, and others; company policies, procedures, and training manuals; and expert witness reports.

Expert witnesses may study and conduct security surveys of the location where the alleged negligent security occurred. Examples of subjects of study are the security force (e.g., screening of personnel, training, and supervision), security policies and procedures, logs, security planning, and physical security.

Once an expert has completed the study of a case file, and surveyed and studied the location of the victimization, a determination is made of the adequacy of security when the incident occurred. An opinion is then formulated by the expert based upon his/her experience, education, and training. A verbal and/or written opinion is presented to the attorney who hired the expert. The opposing attorney may subpoena the expert to question him/her. A **subpoena** is a court order requiring attendance at a deposition or trial to testify under penalty for failure to attend.

It is important to note that as each side of a case generates a case file, **discovery** (or disclosure) is required. This means that each side shares (i.e., copies) their case file with the other side. The purpose is to prevent protracted litigation by allowing each side to study the strengths and weaknesses of the case and to possibly negotiate a settlement and avoid an expensive and time-consuming trial. Most cases (civil and criminal) never reach the trial stage.

The **International Association of Professional Security Consultants** (2005) has issued a consensus-based and peer-reviewed "Best Practice:

Forensic Methodology." The publication is available on their Web site and serves as a guide for expert witnessing in security.

Requirements

An expert witness generally possesses extensive experience in the field of expertise, a college degree (frequently a graduate degree), and publications. The background of an expert must be impeccable. Honesty and integrity are of the utmost importance. Excellent analytical skills and objectivity are essential. The expert must also have excellent written and verbal communications skills. In addition, he/she must be able to testify under oath at deposition or trial and answer questions from opposing counsel. The judge in a case decides whether an expert is qualified to offer testimony at trial.

Salary

An expert may work on a case for a few weeks, months, or years, depending on such factors as the size of the case file and whether the case goes to trial. Experts command fees of about $150 to $400 per hour and a higher fee per hour ($250 to $500) for testifying at deposition or trial. Since the workload varies, many experts also work as consultants and educators.

Advice

Many years of work are required to develop expertise in a particular field. Generally, to become an expert witness, the preparation includes a college education, 10 to 20 years of experience, the development of relevant skills, and publications. Then, you may be contacted to serve as an expert.

Procedural Civil Law

Procedural civil law provides the rules and steps to be followed in the proceedings of civil cases. An attorney may recommend (to a client) informal means to settle a claim such as alternative dispute resolution (ADR), which is a generic term for several different methods of negotiating a settlement. Otherwise, when a plaintiff initiates a lawsuit, an attorney drafts a **civil complaint**, which is a pleading of facts, claims, and requested relief that is filed in the court jurisdiction where the alleged wrongful incident occurred. The defendant receives a copy of the complaint and a **summons**, which is a court order to appear in court to answer the complaint. If a defendant does not respond to a civil action, the defendant can lose the case and be forced to pay damages.

If the defendant's attorney identifies defects in the complaint or summons, motions may be filed to make changes or dismiss the case. The defense attorney typically plans a defense to the allegations and prepares a written response to the complaint. Throughout the case, even during trial, opposing attorneys negotiate in an attempt to settle. Pretrial discovery helps both sides evaluate the evidence and the strengths and weaknesses of each side. Once the facts of a case have been investigated, one or both sides often file a **motion for summary judgment**. This is an attempt to dispose of the case through a judgment (i.e., the judge's final decision) to avoid a trial. This motion is granted when both sides agree about facts in the case and then the judge applies applicable law to the facts before rendering a decision in favor of the deserving party. If a motion for summary judgment is denied and no settlement is reached, then a **pretrial conference** follows. This involves a meeting among the judge and opposing attorneys to discuss evidence, issues, and a settlement or trial. Depending on the jurisdiction, ADR may be required or encouraged at this point.

A bench trial is another option; there is no jury, and attorneys present evidence in an environment of relaxed rules of evidence. A judge decides factual issues, whether the plaintiff proved the case, and then a judgment is made. Although very few cases lead to a jury trial, this step requires jury selection. Then, as the trial begins, each attorney makes opening statements to the judge and jury to explain what they intend to prove. Next, the plaintiff's attorney presents evidence, such as witnesses and documents, to prove the case. Cross-examination by the defense follows. The defendant's attorney may file a motion to dismiss the case because of deficiencies in the evidence. The trial continues if this motion is denied. The defense then presents evidence, also subject to cross-examination. Each side has an opportunity to rebut evidence presented by the opposing side. As the trial ends, attorneys from both sides present closing arguments (Figure 9.3), the judge instructs the jury, and the jury's verdict follows. A dissatisfied litigant may appeal.

FIGURE 9.3 An attorney presenting a closing argument in a jury trial. (® Shutterstock.com. With permission.)

UNDER COLOR OF LAW AND MOONLIGHTING BY PUBLIC POLICE AS SECURITY OFFICERS

Under color of law refers to a misuse of power by someone working for the state and/or connected to state authority. Nemeth (2005, 100) writes that "to claim that security officers or other personnel are acting under color of state law requires objective proof of a racial, religious, or gender motivation, or at least a demonstration that the acts alleged and the injury inflicted were done under the auspices and approval of the state or other governmental authority." Legal arguments in a civil suit that a state action caused a personal loss, affront, or indignity under the auspices of color of state law are based on civil rights law, 42 U.S.C. Section 1983, and litigants claim civil rights violations and constitutional infractions. This post–Civil War law is aimed at state and local governments. An example of such a claim involving private security might be an alleged plan by public police and private security to target poor minorities for minor arrests in a downtown business district. Examples of claims against state actors under color of law are false arrest, assault and battery, malicious prosecution, and illegal search and seizure. The closer security personnel work with public police, the greater the likelihood of under-color-of-law claims.

Nemeth (2005, 185) writes that the majority of litigation and actions under 42 U.S.C. Section 1983 have been civil. However, he notes that Congress enacted law that attaches criminal liability to those acting under color of law.

Scarry (2006, 72) focuses on public-police liability when they moonlight (i.e., off duty work) in security positions. She asks: What if an arrestee sues the officer for violating his or her civil rights? Is the officer civilly liable for the offending action as a security officer or as a public police officer? State and local police may be sued for their actions and/or inactions, not only under 42 U.S.C. Section 1983, but also under state tort law. And, under certain conditions, they can be prosecuted criminally in federal and state courts. Police officers are acting under color of law when they are acting in their official capacity.

Scarry (2006, 74) offers cases where it was found that public police officers moonlighting as security officers were acting under color of law. In *Pickrel v. City of Springfield*, 45 F.3d 115 (7th Cir. 1995), a customer of a fast-food restaurant filed a lawsuit against a police officer, the City of Springfield, and the officer's private security employer. The police officer, in trying to get the customer and her father to leave a restaurant, pulled the female from a booth, threw her to the floor, and arrested both for trespass, obstructing a police officer, and resisting arrest. The charges were eventually dismissed. When the incident occurred, the moonlighting officer was wearing his police uniform, carrying his police badge and pistol, and drove his city police car to the restaurant. The court viewed these factors as acting under color of law.

In *Abraham v. Raso*, 183 F.3d 279 (3rd Cir. 1999), a female public police officer working part-time in security at a retail mall was asked to assist in the apprehension of a shoplifter. When the officer repeatedly told the suspect to stop, the suspect got into his car, and when he attempted to run over her, the officer shot and killed him. The suspect's estate filed a civil lawsuit alleging violations of constitutional rights. The court ruled that she was acting under color of law because she was wearing her police uniform and attempted to arrest him.

In *Bouye v. Marshall*, 102 F.Supp. 2d 1357 (N.D. Ga. 2000), a public police officer working in security at an apartment complex conducted a stop and frisk of a male dropping off his son at a babysitter's apartment. The male filed a civil suit alleging unlawful search and seizure. The court found that the officer was acting under color of law because he used his police authority to detain and search, wore a police sweatshirt and bullet-resistive vest, and displayed his police badge while patrolling and investigating suspicious behavior at the complex. The court ruled that the officer's actions were reasonable, while not violating the male's constitutional rights.

Scarry (2006, 74) recommends that public police officers recognize that, when they work in security jobs, they may be held civilly liable as public police officers rather than as security officers. They should look to their state's statute and/or case law on off-duty activities and departmental policy on secondary employment. In addition, they should obtain clear answers on who provides liability coverage for secondary employment.

Critical Thinking

As a public police officer, would you moonlight as a security officer to earn extra income? Why or why not?

Law of Arrest

An **arrest** involves seizing and detaining a person by lawful authority to bring the person before a court to answer criminal charges (Schubert 2008, 679). An arrest is a serious action that must be based on a sound foundation of consideration of several factors:

- Is the arrest legal?
- Does the arrestor possess the legal authority to make the arrest?
- Is the arrestor within the appropriate jurisdiction to make the arrest?
- Does the arrest conform to organizational policies and procedures?
- Does the arrestor possess the training, equipment, personnel assistance (i.e., backup), and organizational support for the arrest?
- Are the time and location of the arrest safe and practical? Would another time and/or location be better?

A comparison of the arrest authority of citizens, private security officers, and public police provides guidelines for arrests. One major, general distinction among these groups is that government, public sector (e.g., public police) action is heavily controlled by the Bill of Rights of the U.S. Constitution, whereas citizens and private security officers are less restricted by such constitutional protections.

AMENDMENTS OF THE BILL OF RIGHTS, UNITED STATES CONSTITUTION

The following constitutional amendments play a major role in criminal justice in the United States.

Amendment IV The right of the people to be secure in their persons, houses, papers, and effects, against unreasonable searches and seizures, shall not be violated, and no Warrants shall issue, but upon probable cause, supported by Oath or affirmation, and particularly describing the place to be searched, and the persons or things to be seized.

Amendment V No person shall be held to answer for a capital, or otherwise infamous crime, unless on a presentment or indictment of a Grand Jury, except in cases arising in the land or naval forces, or in the Militia, when in actual service in time of War or public danger; nor shall any person be subject for the same offence to be twice put in jeopardy of life or limb, nor shall be compelled in any criminal case to be a witness against himself, nor be deprived of life, liberty, or property, without due process of law; nor shall private property be taken for public use, without just compensation.

Amendment VI In all criminal prosecutions, the accused shall enjoy the right to a speedy and public trial, by an impartial jury of the State and district wherein the crime shall have been committed; which district shall have been previously ascertained by law, and to be informed of the nature and cause of the accusation; to be confronted with the witnesses against him; to have compulsory process for obtaining witnesses in his favor, and to have the assistance of counsel for his defense.

Amendment VIII Excessive bail shall not be required, nor excessive fines imposed, nor cruel and unusual punishments inflicted.

Amendment XIV, Section 1 All persons born or naturalized in the United States and subject to the jurisdiction thereof, are citizens of the United States and of the State wherein they reside. No State shall make or enforce any law which shall abridge the privileges or immunities of citizens of the United States; nor shall any State deprive any person of life, liberty, or property, without due process of law; nor deny to any person within its jurisdiction the equal protection of the laws.

The U.S. Supreme Court has been hesitant to extend the amendments to private-sector action. In **Burdeau v. McDowell 256 U.S. 465 (1921)**, the Court set a standard that has been upheld by subsequent decisions in that Fourth Amendment protections do not apply to citizens arrested or searched by the private sector or private parties. The topics of security officers not being required to read *Miranda* warnings (Fifth Amendment right to remain silent) to suspects, interviewing, and interrogations are covered in the next chapter.

Generally, private security officers have arrest powers equal to citizen arrest powers. However, exceptions are plentiful. For example, in South Carolina, security officers have arrest powers equal to public police, but only on the protected property; when the security officer steps beyond the property line, citizen arrest powers take hold. Since states vary on the law of arrest for citizens and security officers, it is imperative that security practitioners maintain a clear understanding of their arrest powers in their respective state. Private-sector personnel may be deputized or receive a special commission from a state statute or local ordinance that provides arrest powers beyond those of a citizen.

The foundation of private security arrest law is from common and statutory law. **Common law** evolved over many centuries in England as judges followed custom and community consensus to establish principles and precedents (i.e., a legal standard to follow) through case law. English common law has been a major contributor to the development of law in the United States. **Statutory law** refers to a law passed by a legislative body.

A **citizen's arrest** means that a person, who is not a sworn law enforcement officer, has taken action to restrict the movement of a subject who will be transferred to law enforcement authorities to answer criminal charges. During such an arrest, for safety reasons, a citizen is permitted to search an arrestee to locate and seize weapons. From a perspective of legal caution, a citizen should make a citizen's arrest for only a felony committed in his/her presence (i.e., in view) and avoid a citizen's arrest for a felony or misdemeanor not committed in his/her presence. State laws vary and permit broader citizen arrest powers than the above cautious approach. Nemeth (2005, 72) provides two examples, Alaska and New York:

"Alaska: A private person or peace officer without a warrant may arrest a person:

1. For a crime committed or attempted in the presence of the person making the arrest;
2. When the person has committed a felony, although not in the presence of the person making the arrest;
3. When a felony has in fact been committed, and the person making the arrest has reasonable cause for believing the person to have committed it" (Alaska, Section 12.25.030).

"New York: Any person may arrest another person:

1. For a felony when the latter has in fact committed such felony, and,
2. For any offense when the latter has in fact committed such offense in his presence" (N.Y., Section 140.30(1)).

Although many states permit citizens to make arrests for felonies not committed in their presence and for misdemeanors committed in their presence, caution is urged for several reasons. A private citizen usually does not possess the training, equipment, backup, insurance, and legal assistance afforded to a law enforcement officer. In addition, Nemeth (2005, 71) adds: "When compared to public officials' arrest rights, the private citizen has a heavier burden of demonstrating actual knowledge, presence at the events, or other firsthand experience that justifies the apprehension."

Judicious decision making on arrests is advised for private security officers as well. In comparison to private citizens, security officers possess varying levels of training, equipment, backup, insurance, and legal assistance, although generally less than law enforcement officers in all of these categories.

In essence, citizens, security officers, and public police all possess the authority to make felony arrests. The issue of arrest authority for misdemeanors is more complicated. Public police generally avoid misdemeanor arrests when the misdemeanor is not committed in their presence; however, there are exceptions to this generalization. For instance, consider the case of someone driving under the influence (DUI): A police officer arrives at a scene where a vehicle hit a tree; the driver smells of alcohol; and the officer did not see the driver operating the vehicle, but makes an arrest for DUI. Another exception is criminal domestic violence (CDV): Officers arrive at a home and a resident looks injured from a recent assault; although the assault was not witnessed by officers, they make an arrest for CDV. Although citizen and private security authority to make misdemeanor arrests is limited, there are exceptions. Shoplifting is an example; however, the arrestor must be an employee of the retail store. Citizens and security officers should be well versed on state law prior to making any arrest.

USE OF FORCE

When a citizen, security officer, or public police officer makes an arrest, if force is necessary, it must be **reasonable force** (Figure 9.4). This is the standard courts apply. If a subject initially resists an arrest, but then stops resisting, force must likewise stop, even if the subject had struck the arrestor. In the unlikely event of **deadly force** being applied, such action is restricted to when your life or someone else's life is about to be taken.

Public police have applied the **use-of-force continuum**, and it can serve as a guide for the security profession. It begins with the lowest possible level to gain compliance and progresses step-by-step to greater force, depending on the need to control a subject. The continuum begins with an officer's presence, followed by verbal commands, physical-weaponless methods, chemical agents, taser, impact weapons (e.g., baton), and then deadly force (i.e., firearms). Depending on the behavior of a subject, an officer may begin the continuum at any point. Whatever use-of-force policies and procedures are provided to security officers, and whatever weapons they are issued, management must ensure that officers receive quality training.

Critical Thinking

As a security officer trying to handcuff an arrestee who has just punched, kicked, and hurt you, do you think you can stop using force once the suspect is down and stops resisting? Explain your answer.

FIGURE 9.4 When a citizen, security officer, or public police officer makes an arrest, if force is necessary, it must be reasonable force. (® Shutterstock.com. With permission.)

Weights of Evidence

Here we explain **weights of evidence** to enhance our understanding of law. This term refers to classifications of strengths of evidence, each applied to a different aspect of the justice system.

Reasonable suspicion is evidence to suspect that an individual has committed, is committing, or is about to commit a crime. It is the evidence required by public police to conduct what is called a "stop and frisk" or "Terry-stop." *Personnel who are deputized or provided with a special police commission are likely to possess the authority to conduct a "stop and frisk." Security officers with arrest powers equal to the public police on the protected property are also likely to possess this authority; however, security managers must prepare relevant policies and procedures.*

This police power is derived from the U.S. Supreme Court case, ***Terry v. Ohio* 392 U.S. 1 (1968)**. The facts of this case began in October of 1963 when Cleveland Police Department detective McFadden noticed three men, one named Terry, acting suspicious near a liquor store. The men walked past the store and talked multiple times as if "casing" the store for a robbery. The detective became suspicious of the men, approached them, identified himself as a police officer, asked for ID, frisked them (i.e., patted down their clothing), located .38-caliber revolvers on two men, and arrested them for carrying a concealed weapon. Following convictions and on appeal, the U.S. Supreme Court was asked to answer whether the Fourth Amendment prohibition against unreasonable search and seizure was violated during the stop and frisk if the detective possessed reasonable suspicion that the men were armed and dangerous. The Court upheld the convictions of the lower court and provided guidelines for police when conducting a stop and frisk: (1) reasonable suspicion about a crime and that the suspect may be armed and dangerous; (2) police must identify themselves and make a reasonable inquiry; and (3) limited pat down of clothing to search for weapons. In *Terry*, the Court emphasized that an officer must have "specific and articulable facts" as a legal foundation for a stop. Since *Terry*, the Court has favored a "totality of the circumstances" test to judge whether a stop is supported by reasonable suspicion (Gaines and Miller 2009, 212). In other words, multiple factors are considered, such as a suspect being nervous, avoiding eye contact, and providing false information.

It is important to note that a "stop and frisk" may or may not result in an arrest. Subjects may be permitted to depart following a "stop and frisk" if no crime is evident. Case law notes that the time a person can be held for a "stop and frisk" must be reasonable. In *U.S. v Sharpe*, 470 U.S. 675 (1985), the U.S. Supreme Court ruled that a 20-minute detention was reasonable. Police are also permitted to handcuff the subject for their own protection and to prevent escape (*U.S. v Bautista*, 114 S. Ct. 1079, 1994). If contraband is seized during a frisk, it must be "immediately apparent" during the frisk that the item is contraband; otherwise, the arrest will be legally deficient (*Minnesota v. Dickerson*, 113 S. Ct. 2130, 1993). If police search pockets during a frisk, any contraband seized is likely to be excluded as evidence in the case (*Sibron v. New York*, 392 U.S. 40, 1968).

Probable cause is a greater weight of evidence than reasonable suspicion. It is stated in the Fourth Amendment and is required to make an arrest or to obtain an arrest or search warrant.

Nemeth (2005, 387) defines probable cause as based on a practical, common-sense decision, from a reasonable person, that there is a fair probability that a crime has been or is being committed by a suspect. He writes that probable cause is determined by a totality of the circumstances. The term *reasonable grounds* is synonymous with probable cause. In studying state statutes on arrest powers, Nemeth (2005, 77) notes that "reasonable grounds is the standard generally employed by statutes outlining a citizen's right to arrest," whereas "probable cause, the standard utilized for arrest, search, and seizure by public officials, is not commonly employed in the citizen's arrest realm."

If a bank robbery alarm is sounding and a police officer observes a man running with a pistol and a moneybag, probable cause is established and police pursuit and arrest are appropriate. Although an arrest warrant from a magistrate is required for all arrests, in this emergency situation, a warrant is obtained post-arrest. Police obtain arrest and search warrants from magistrates by demonstrating probable cause through a written and signed affidavit. An **affidavit** is a statement made under oath before a judge.

When security officers and citizens make an arrest, they should immediately contact public police, who will provide guidance on procedures to secure an arrest warrant. Public police will be very interested in who will support the probable cause for the arrest. Once this is settled, they will transport the prisoner.

Public police are protected from civil liability for false arrest when they can demonstrate that probable cause existed for the arrest. They make arrests with probable cause based on their own senses, a description of a suspect by a victim or witness, a police radio broadcast or other communications method describing a suspect, or knowledge of an outstanding arrest warrant on a subject.

Because a person may provide false information of a crime to cause another to face distress, a cautious approach prior to arrest is appropriate when a citizen reports a crime. Once a crime is reported, additional information should be gathered to verify information. Suppose, as a security officer at an office building, you are approached by a female executive who claims that a male executive hit her with an umbrella as they entered the building. You gather information on the incident, contact your supervisor, and ascertain the location of the male executive in the building. Do you have probable cause to arrest the male executive? At this point, refrain from an arrest. Collect additional information by interviewing witnesses and the male executive. As it turned out, witnesses claimed the two executives were arguing about domestic issues as they entered the building. No one saw the male strike the female. The male admitted that a domestic argument occurred when he and his girlfriend entered the building; however, he denied any violence. Upon returning to interview the female executive, she admitted to being angry with her boyfriend and fabricating the story of being hit with the umbrella. A security report was sent to the human resources department of her employer.

Suppose, as a security officer at a health-care facility, you are patrolling the parking lots in a security vehicle. As you drive around a hospital building and into another parking lot, you spot a young man breaking the window of a vehicle, reaching in and grabbing a computer, and running away. Do you have probable cause to make an arrest? After using your radio to report the incident, you are joined by two other security officers, and following a short foot chase, the subject is apprehended and arrested with sufficient probable cause. As in all arrests, the arrestee is legally subject to a search for weapons and other contraband.

Proof beyond a reasonable doubt is the weight of evidence required by the state to prove a defendant guilty of a crime at trial. Since *presumption of innocence* is a fundamental protection for U.S. citizens, defendants are not required to prove innocence (Neubauer 2005, 31). A prosecutor, representing the state, seeks to prove guilt beyond a reasonable doubt, whereas a defense attorney seeks to cast a doubt on the state's evidence so that the jury will not convict. Proof beyond a reasonable doubt is a weight of evidence greater than probable cause, but less weight than certainty.

Reasonable suspicion, probable cause, and proof beyond a reasonable doubt are weights of evidence associated with the criminal justice system. Now we turn to a weight of evidence associated with the civil justice system: **preponderance of the evidence**. This is the weight of evidence required to win a civil case (i.e., a lawsuit). It is more weight than probable cause and less weight than proof beyond a reasonable doubt. Thus, a criminal trial requires a greater weight of evidence than a civil trial, as illustrated in the accompanying example.

DOES A CRIMINAL OR CIVIL TRIAL REQUIRE A GREATER WEIGHT OF EVIDENCE?

The 1995–1996 criminal and civil trials of football great and media commentator O. J. Simpson offer an answer to this question. Simpson was charged with the murders of his ex-wife, Nicole Brown Simpson, and her friend Ronald Goldman, outside of her Los Angeles home in 1994. Following the murders, Simpson disappeared, but was soon observed on national television by millions who observed police pursuing him in an SUV before he was apprehended.

During his criminal trial of 37 weeks, which received intense media attention and was watched by millions on television, his defense team was unrelenting in attacking the prosecutors' evidence and the police detectives. The defense team argued that the evidence against Simpson was faulty and resulted from shoddy police work. One of the detectives presenting evidence was alleged to be motivated by racism. This allegation was supported by taped interviews the detective, Mark Fuhrman, had made years earlier with a screenwriter researching the Los Angeles Police Department. As the trial ended, the jury deliberated for four hours and then announced a verdict of not guilty. The defense team succeeded in casting a *doubt* on the prosecution's case that did not prove Simpson's guilt beyond a reasonable doubt.

The following year, O. J. Simpson was sued. However, in comparison to a criminal trial, in a civil trial, the rules changed. Whereas in the criminal trial he was charged with homicide, the civil trial focused on wrongful death (a tort). The plaintiff had to prove a preponderance of evidence, less weight of evidence than required by prosecutors in a criminal case, which requires proof beyond a reasonable doubt. Rather than having to prove criminal intent, the plaintiff had to prove negligence, a broader, easier to prove concept. Constitutional protections also differed for Simpson. In the criminal trial, he exercised his Fifth Amendment right to remain silent, and his defense attorneys did not call him to the witness stand to testify. However, in a civil case, a defendant can be forced to testify, as Simpson did. His deposition was taken prior to the trial by plaintiff attorneys, and he was called to the witness stand as a plaintiff witness. If Simpson were found guilty in the criminal trial, he would have received a prison sentence. In the civil trial, the outcome was in favor of the plaintiff. The civil jury ordered him to pay damages of $33.5 million to the Goldman family and to his ex-wife's estate. He was unable to pay most of the damages (Neubauer 2005, 32).

Search and Seizure: Public Police

Citizen protections against public-police searches are specified in the Fourth Amendment: "The right of the people … against unreasonable searches and seizures,… warrants shall issue, but upon probable cause, supported by oath or affirmation,… describing the place to be searched, and the persons or things to be seized." If public police seize evidence in violation of the Fourth Amendment (or other amendments of the Bill of Rights), the **exclusionary rule** applies. The landmark U.S. Supreme Court case, *Mapp v. Ohio 367 U.S. 643 (1961)*, set the precedent that illegally seized evidence will be excluded from all courts. Although public police are guided and constrained in their searches by the Fourth Amendment, they also possess numerous opportunities to search through **warrantless searches** (i.e., searches without a warrant), as listed next (Hall 2009, 347–383).

> *Incidental to a lawful arrest*: A warrantless search of an arrestee and the nearby area within arm's reach of the arrestee is permitted to seize weapons to protect the officer and to seize evidence before it is destroyed. Upon arrest of a subject in a vehicle, officers may search not only the arrestee, but also the entire passenger compartment and any containers without a warrant.
>
> *Consent search*: The subject has given permission for a search of their person, home, vehicle, or belongings. Consent must be voluntary. Officers are in an improved legal position when the subject signs a statement of consent to search.
>
> *Mobile vehicle*: Any mobile vehicle (e.g., car, truck, boat, and plane) is subject to a warrantless search when police have probable cause to believe the vehicle contains evidence of a crime. This is an important police power, because a mobile vehicle can depart quickly. An immobile vehicle would be a mobile home on cement blocks in a suspect's yard; these circumstances necessitate a search warrant.
>
> *Plain view*: Police may seize contraband without a warrant when they are lawfully at a location, the items are "immediately apparent" to be contraband and no further investigation (e.g., interviewing, searching, or moving items) is required, and the contraband was observed inadvertently without prior intent to look for it.
>
> *Emergencies*: If police are chasing a subject who enters a building, they can enter and search the building without a warrant during this "hot pursuit." If a victim is being attacked in a building, police can enter without a warrant to save the victim.

Other warrantless searches and seizures include *abandoned property* (e.g., luggage left unattended or items in a vacated hotel room), *garbage left on the street, "stop and frisk," vehicles entering U.S. borders, open fields* (i.e., private property away from a house, garage, and other buildings), and when an inventory is being taken of an *impounded vehicle*.

Search and Seizure: Private Security

To prevent a lawsuit, and whenever possible, security officers should avoid touching a suspect. With sound probable cause, security officers should consider contacting public police and let them conduct searches; this transfers search liability to them. However, security officers sometimes face confrontations with suspects where they are under pressure to conduct an immediate search and there is no time to wait for public police to arrive.

Inbau et al. (1996, 44) write that although state statutes are explicit about citizen arrest powers, there are limited guidelines for searches by citizens (and security officers). Compounding this problem, there are various situations that may require a search by security officers. The Private Security Advisory Council (U.S. Department of Justice 1979, 15) offers the following situations: incidental to a lawful arrest, consent, as a condition of employment or part of an employment contract, and incidental to valid conditions. Depending on the business and the product or service provided, an employer may seek to search employees, their belongings, and vehicles entering and departing from the premises. In addition, desks and lockers may be part of searches. Employers should require that, because of the nature of the business, employees sign a consent to search form as a condition of employment. Signs in the workplace and periodic reminders will help to communicate information on workplace searches. Management in businesses and institutions must establish policies, procedures, and training for a variety of search situations, one reason being to prevent litigation. Although the U.S. Supreme Court has not applied constitutional restrictions on private security searches (*Burdeau v. McDowell*), plaintiffs may sue because of alleged wrongful action.

In an unusual decision, the California Supreme Court, in **People v. Zelinski 594 P. 2d 1000 (1979)**, ruled against security officers at a retail store who seized drugs in the personal belongings of a shoplifting suspect while recovering store items. The California Supreme Court supported the citizen's arrest for shoplifting and a plain-view search for store items; however, the search of the belongings was ruled as an unreasonable search and seizure under the Fourth Amendment. In **State of Minnesota v. Beswell 449 N.W. 2d 471 (Minn. App. 1989)**, the court equated private security searches at a racetrack as a "public act." The defendant, a patron of a racetrack, was searched by security and cocaine was discovered. The court agreed with the appellant's argument that such private security searches are a public act and subject to constitutional constraints. Nemeth (2005, 87–88) writes that *Zelinski* and *Beswell* "manifest a voice of discontent" and "signify a slow evolution and a small rebuke to settled law."

ELECTRONIC EVIDENCE AND DISCOVERY OF ELECTRONIC INFORMATION

Evidence is proof offered to establish the existence or nonexistence of a fact in dispute (Neubauer 2005, 478). Examples include testimony of witnesses, victims, police officers, security officers, experts, and others; and physical evidence (e.g., tools used to commit a crime and fingerprints). Rules of evidence focus on admissibility, which ensures that appropriate and important evidence is introduced in a judicial proceeding, rather than evidence that is irrelevant, from an incompetent source, or in violation of constitutional safeguards or law. A judge in a case decides on the admissibility of evidence.

Increasingly, criminal and civil cases include electronic evidence and discovery of electronic information. ("Discovery" is used here to refer to opposing sides sharing their case files with each other as required by law to expedite justice.) Prosecutors and criminal defense attorneys, as well as plaintiff and civil defense attorneys, are becoming more and more skilled at applying electronic evidence and discovery of electronic information. Courtrooms are accommodating the digital revolution through computers, audiovisual devices, wiring, and equipment to enable the presentation of digital evidence to judge and jury. Police and prosecutors must continue to develop their expertise in **computer forensics**, which is the application of science and technology to answer legal questions pertaining to computer and digital evidence. In addition, they must defend their techniques in court. Private security practitioners, likewise, must continue to develop their expertise so their cases can be convincing to prosecutors, other attorneys, judges, and juries.

Investigators in both the public and private sectors often encounter electronic crime scenes containing **digital evidence**, defined by the National Institute of Justice (2008, ix) as "information and data of value to an investigation that is stored on, received, or transmitted by an electronic device." Electronic crime scenes are varied. They may contain a computer system, a laptop, external hard drive, removable media (e.g., disc), cell phone, digital camera, personal digital assistant (PDA), a flash storage drive, surveillance equipment, video camera, digital audio or video recorders, video game consoles, MP3 players, GPS, fax machine, printer, or other electronic devices. In addition, these devices may contain physical evidence (e.g., fingerprints). All evidence necessitates proper crime scene processing procedures.

The National Institute of Justice (2008, ix–x) notes that digital evidence must be handled by trained specialists because it can be easily destroyed, damaged, or altered. The proper legal authority must exist to seize the evidence, whether as public police or private security. Furthermore, special equipment is necessary to process, collect, document, and secure an electronic crime scene. For example, a Faraday bag or aluminum foil is important to hold/wrap cell phones and other devices to prevent the device from receiving a call, text message, or other signal that may alter or delete the digital evidence.

The Federal Rules of Civil Procedure, codified in 1938, require that parties in a lawsuit disclose the information they possess that may be used to support their claims or defenses. In 2006, the federal rules were amended to include discovery of electronic information. State rules have similarities to federal rules.

Field (2009, 50–56) writes of the fairness of discovery procedures for both sides, but notes that compliance can be burdensome, especially because information is in many digital formats and locations. The following guidelines for discovery of electronic information are from the work of Field (2009) and Mallery (2008, 42–44).

Once an organization is served with notice of litigation, and to avoid what can amount to millions of dollars in penalties by a court for discovery rule violations and loss of a lawsuit, it has a duty to preserve paper and digital information. This is termed a **litigation hold** (or preservation hold). A beginning step in this process is to determine which information could be discoverable and develop a map illustrating where and how the information is maintained and by whom. Examples (pertaining to those named in the lawsuit) are office computers, mailboxes on the mail server, and home directories on the network server. Such information can be copied to CDs or DVDs as "read only." Handheld devices also contain digital records. In addition, archiving CCTV camera video may also be necessary. Although the judge determines what is discoverable, organizations should assume that all information could be discoverable. A plan should be in place to recover deleted information, and document and information destruction must stop upon being served notice of a lawsuit.

The federal rules protect from discovery information under a recognized privilege. An example is the **attorney-client privilege**, whereby statements made in this relationship are protected from forced disclosure. Proprietary business information may also be protected by the court. Examples are a secret formula or a special manufacturing process. Private information, such as medical records, also necessitate protection. A party in a case may argue to the judge that certain information should be exempted from discovery because its production would be too burdensome and costly; the opposing party's counterargument may result in the judge setting conditions for its discovery.

Summary

The coverage of this chapter included underlying theory and principles of our legal system as well as arrest, search, and seizure law. The United States operates under a form of government known as federalism, in which power is shared between a strong central government and the states. Law consists of a body of rules enacted by government leaders and backed by law enforcement authorities. Two major systems of law in the United States are criminal law and civil law. Criminal law contains written offenses and punishments. Civil law contains written rules that are applied to settle disputes among private individuals, businesses, and government. Both systems contain procedural laws that are rules and steps to follow in the administration of law and justice.

Private security is restrained in its duties and conduct more so by tort and negligence law than by the constitutional safeguards afforded to citizens against public police action. At the same time, private security practitioners and public police are subject to both a lawsuit and arrest for transgressions.

Unless deputized or holding a special commission, security officers typically have arrest powers equal to citizen arrest powers, which permit felony arrests based upon probable cause, but restrict misdemeanor arrests. Search-and-seizure law pertaining to public police is well defined, and they have considerable power under certain restrictions of the Bill of Rights. Citizens and private security officers are permitted to search an arrestee incident to a lawful arrest; however, caution is advised for other types of searches, because the law is not well defined and varies.

Weights of evidence help us to understand the quality of evidence required for various actions taken against individuals by public- and private-sector authorities. Reasonable suspicion is required by police to stop and frisk a suspect. Security officers are less prone to conduct such actions. Probable cause, a heavier weight than reasonable suspicion, is required for an arrest and for police to obtain arrest and search warrants, as specified in the Fourth Amendment of the Bill of Rights. Proof beyond a reasonable doubt is the weight of evidence required to convict a defendant at a criminal trial; this is the heaviest weight of the four. A preponderance of the evidence is required to win a case at a civil trial—a weight heavier than probable cause, but less than proof beyond a reasonable doubt.

The use of electronic evidence in criminal and civil cases is growing. Crime scenes often contain digital evidence in computers and other devices that contain digital storage space. Investigators, in the public and private sectors, and prosecutors, are increasingly applying such evidence in cases.

Discovery requires each side in either a criminal or a civil case to share their case files with the other side to expedite justice. Discovery of electronic information is important, and practitioners in both the public and private sectors must be trained in relevant law and technology for efficient and effective case processing.

Discussion Questions

1. Should victims have the opportunity to sue organizations for alleged inadequate security? Explain your answer.
2. What is the purpose of discovery in criminal and civil cases?
3. Do you think the weights of evidence required in criminal and civil trials are fair for defendants? What about for prosecutors and plaintiffs? Explain your answers.
4. Why do most criminal and civil cases never make it to trial?
5. Can expert witnesses remain objective when studying a case and testifying at deposition or trial? Explain your answer.
6. Should private security officers possess arrest, search, and seizure powers equal to public police? Explain your answer.

7. What are the search and use-of-force powers of citizens and security officers following a lawful arrest?

8. How are warrantless searches applied by public police and private security?

Practical Applications

9A. In the state in which you reside, research the felony and misdemeanor arrest powers of citizens, security officers, private investigators, and public police. Does your state offer designations such as special police or offer special police commissions?

9B. As a security officer on the premises of a manufacturing company, an employee informs you that another employee stole company property. Do you make an arrest? Why or why not? Following your decision, what do you do as the security officer?

9C. As a security officer on foot patrol at an office building, you observe an employee run outside to his vehicle and place company property into the trunk of his vehicle. Do you make an arrest? Why or why not? Following your decision, what do you do as the security officer?

9D. As a security officer on the premises of a manufacturer, you observe a truck driver from a delivery service steal company property. Do you make an arrest? Why or why not? Following your decision, what do you do as the security officer?

9E. As a security officer on vehicle patrol at a shopping mall parking lot, you observe a young, white male grab a woman's purse and run. What do you do? If you were to catch the subject, can you make an arrest? Why or why not?

9F. Does the state in which you reside provide victim compensation? How much money is available for victims? Do the answers to these questions influence your view of victims?

9G. As an expert witness with expertise in security, you receive an inquiry from a plaintiff's attorney who requests your services for a case of alleged negligent security. The plaintiff's attorney explains that her client was assaulted in the parking lot of a restaurant, sustained serious injuries, was hospitalized for a week, and is homebound and unable to work. Except for two vehicle break-ins prior to the assault, no other crimes occurred on the premises or nearby in the last three years. Security at the site, when the assault occurred, consisted of CCTV coverage inside and outside, but no security patrols. Do you take this case? What is your response to the attorney? Explain your answer.

9H. As an expert witness with expertise in security, you receive an inquiry from an attorney who is working for a liability insurance company, the insurer of a retail convenience store that is a defendant in a case of alleged negligent security. The attorney explains that the plaintiff, parents of a teenage homicide victim, is suing the convenience store for inadequate security because the deceased was shot in the head while sitting in a vehicle in the parking lot at the store at 2 a.m. The convenience store had internal CCTV coverage as the only security at the time of the murder. Do you take this case? What is your response to the attorney? Explain your answer.

Internet Connections

American Bar Association: www.abanet.org

Duke University School of Law: www.law.duke.edu

Human Rights Watch: www.hrw.org

International Association of Professional Security Consultants: www.iapsc.org

Law and Legal Research: http://law.onecle.com/

Law Library of Congress: www.loc.gov/law/

Legal Information Institute, Cornell University: www.law.cornell.edu

Ohio Bar Association: www.ohiobar.org (click on "Public Resources")

Power to Arrest Training Manual (California): www.bsis.ca.gov/forms_pubs/poa.pdf

References

Field, M. 2009. Too much information. *Security Management* 53 (February):50–56.

Gaines, L., and R. Miller. 2009. *Criminal justice in action.* 5th ed. Belmont, CA: Thomas Higher Education.

Gardner, T., and T. Anderson. 2010. *Criminal evidence: Principles and cases.* 7th ed. Belmont, CA: Wadsworth.

Hall, D. 2009. *Criminal law and procedure.* 5th ed. Clifton Park, NY: Delmar.

Inbau, F. E., et al. 1996. *Protective security law.* 2nd ed. Newton, MA: Butterworth–Heinemann.

International Association of Professional Security Consultants. 2005. Best practice: Forensic methodology. www.iapsc.org.

Kaminsky, A. 1995. *A complete guide to premises security litigation.* Chicago: American Bar Association.

Mallery, J. 2008. Know what to keep: Preserving electronically stored Information for litigation and investigations. *Security Technology Executive* 18 (December):42–44.

National Institute of Justice. 2008. *Electronic crime scene investigation: A guide for first responders.* 2nd ed. www.ojp.usdoj.gov/nij.

Nemeth, C. 2005. *Private security and the law.* 3rd ed. Boston: Elsevier.

Neubauer, D. 2005. *America's courts and the criminal justice system.* 8th ed. Belmont, CA: Thomas Wadsworth.

Scarry, L. 2006. Moonlighting & civil liability: Are you acting under color of law? *Law Officer Magazine* 2006 (November/December):72–74.

Schubert, F. 2008. *Introduction to law and the legal system.* 9th ed. Boston: Houghton Mifflin.

U.S. Department of Justice, Private Security Advisory Council. 1979. *Scope of legal authority of private security personnel.* Washington, DC: U.S. Government Printing Office.

Voigt, L., et al. 1994. *Criminology and justice.* New York: McGraw-Hill.

Chapter 10

Investigations

Chapter Learning Objectives

After reading this chapter, you should be able to:

1. Explain the purposes of investigations and the foundation of successful investigations
2. Describe fraud, internal theft, shoplifting, and robbery investigations and the guidelines for each
3. Explain ten guidelines for interviewing suspects
4. Detail the priorities at a crime scene
5. List ten major sources of information for investigators
6. Discuss the varied purposes and types of surveillance, applicable equipment, and guidelines
7. Describe private-sector undercover investigations
8. Explain the characteristics of superior investigative reports
9. Detail guidelines for testifying
10. Describe how technology and forensic science are helpful to investigations

Terms To Know

investigation
proprietary investigation

contract investigation
workplace investigation
undercover investigation
litigation investigation
due-diligence investigation
fraud
board of directors
Foreign Corrupt Practices Act of 1977
general counsel
mens rea
actus reus
detention
chain of custody of evidence
civil recovery
interviewing
offensive interviewing
closed-ended question
open-ended question
rapport
rationalization
subpoena duces tecum
interrogation
Miranda warnings
NLRB v. J. Weingarten Inc., No. 251 (1975)
information brokers
pretexting
Gramm-Leach-Bliley Act of 1999
Telephone Records and Privacy Protection Act of 2006
traditional surveillance
stationary surveillance
mobile surveillance
prop
perjury
link analysis
neural net technology
Employee Polygraph Protection Act of 1988
lie detector
polygraph
forensic science
Alphonse Bertillon
Sir Francis Galton
Alec Jeffreys
CSI effect

QUIZ

This quiz serves to prime the reader's mind and begin the reading, thinking, and studying processes for this chapter. The answers to all of the questions are found within this chapter.

1. Can criminal cases be prosecuted successfully without the services of a crime laboratory?
2. What is a due-diligence investigation?
3. What are the definitions of *mens rea* and *actus reus*, and which one is generally more difficult to prove in a criminal case?
4. As a loss-prevention agent in an alleged shoplifting case, is it more prudent to confront the suspect as soon as the store item is concealed or when the suspect passes the checkouts?
5. Did the U.S. Supreme Court decide to prohibit interrogations by public police and private security?
6. Can private security conduct undercover investigations?
7. What is the name of the written, chronological description of an incident in an incident report?

Introduction

This chapter contains three major sections: (1) types of and guidelines for investigations, (2) techniques of investigation, and (3) technology and forensic science. Four major types of investigations (i.e., fraud, internal theft, shoplifting, and robbery) are described so that the reader can understand how these investigations are conducted while comparing and contrasting each. General techniques of investigation, such as interviewing and surveillance, are explained to provide a foundation for many types of investigations. The chapter ends with a discussion of technology and forensic science and the relevance to private security investigations. Contrary to what is depicted in television programs and movies, investigative work entails painstaking perseverance that can last for years for certain cases, adherence to legal and constitutional requirements, the likelihood that a case can be solved without the services of a crime laboratory (and if such services are needed, tests often require more than ten minutes), significant "paperwork," and the possibility that the defendant will go free.

Investigations

An **investigation** is an inquiry to gather and ascertain the facts of a case, and then a report is prepared for subsequent action or inaction. In the public sector, police agencies serve the public, conduct a variety of investigations (e.g., larceny, robbery, and murder), and work with prosecutors to develop evidence for possible prosecution and trial. Investigations in the private sector serve private-sector (e.g., business) interests and needs and take various paths, with or without public police involvement. For instance, a violent crime in the workplace requires public police involvement; however, a case of internal theft may result in the firing of the employee without contacting public police. If a security officer on patrol at a business discovers that a burglary or robbery has occurred or is in progress, public police are called.

McRae (2008, 406) writes of purposes of private sector investigations. He notes that investigations bring value to a business by providing insight into an organization, correcting problems, preventing losses, recovering property, preventing litigation, and saving money. A case of alleged sexual harassment in the workplace, for instance, if promptly investigated, can avoid a lawsuit. At the same time, a poorly planned and conducted investigation can create more problems than it is seeking to solve and result in litigation and losses to a business. In addition, investigators and their work (e.g., methods of investigation and reports) are subject to scrutiny prior to and during criminal and/or civil action.

Ferraro and Mathers (2007, 199–203) provide a foundation for successful investigations as paraphrased in the following list.

- At the base of successful investigations are management support, clearly defined objectives, well-conceived strategies, adequate resources, competent investigators and supervisors, and ethical and lawful execution. Also important is accuracy in gathering facts that are reflected in an investigative report that management uses to make crucial decisions.
- An investigation must be conducted in a way that is least disruptive to the business and its operations while resulting in a return on investment.
- Investigations must be conducted in a manner that withstands legal challenges, adheres to due-process rights, and treats individuals fairly. Although there are greater constitutional constraints on public police in comparison to private security, if a case is heard in criminal or civil court, a judge and/or jury may view the full power of the Bill of Rights of the U.S. Constitution as applicable to private security action.
- Investigators must have a comprehensive understanding of criminal, civil, and employment law. In addition, they must be skilled in interviewing, information sources, surveillance, safety, report writing, and testifying.
- Techniques of investigation include interviewing, physical surveillance, application of CCTV (closed-circuit TV), auditing of records, undercover investigations, and forensic analysis.

YOUR CAREER IN SECURITY

Investigator

Investigators work in the public and private sectors gathering facts and evidence. Public-sector investigators, also called detectives (or agents on the federal level), work for local, state, and federal agencies and typically focus on criminal cases. They may also conduct background investigations and investigate misconduct in office, ethical violations, conflicts of interest, accidents, and other subjects of inquiry that may or may not involve criminal activity. In addition, the military branches maintain investigative units.

Private-sector investigators work for businesses, institutions, other organizations, attorneys, and individuals on many types of inquiries. Examples are internal theft, financial matters, negligence, accident, insurance fraud, domestic disputes, and the background of job applicants. A private-sector investigator may work for a corporation as a proprietary (in-house) investigator or for a contract firm (e.g., private investigation [P.I.] company) that provides investigative services to clients for a fee. If a goal of a private-sector investigation is to seek prosecution, public police or a prosecutor must be contacted.

Nature of the Work

Investigators apply numerous methods to gather facts. They interview victims, witnesses, suspects, and others linked to a case. Stationary and moving surveillance are also useful methods. They search for evidence; collect, secure, and label it; and present it in court. Legal guidelines must be followed; otherwise, their case may fail, and they may be subject to civil and/or criminal action. Investigators rely on various software and information systems to identify suspects, collect information, and build cases. These systems may be proprietary to a corporation or trade group or restricted to government use only. The Web also serves as a source of information. Once information is collected, investigators spend a lot of time preparing reports to document their work.

The duties of an investigator can lead to stress and danger. Investigators may work various shifts or be called to a case late at night or early morning, and they are on call for emergencies. The work can take a toll on the personal life of an investigator.

Public police investigators are armed. Private-sector investigators are usually unarmed because they focus primarily on collecting information, rather than arresting offenders.

Public police investigators work with uniformed police to respond quickly to crime scenes. Top priorities are to render emergency assistance, apprehend offenders, protect the crime scene from evidence tampering or destruction, conduct interviews, collect physical evidence, and ensure justice. A record of the crime scene is prepared with various types of cameras and a sketch. Notes are recorded to be used for report preparation on standard organizational forms. Evidence is processed and secured to be presented in court later. Criminal investigators seek to identify the offender, make a legal arrest, and present quality evidence to the prosecutor and court.

Private-sector investigators perform many of the duties performed by public-sector investigators, such as interviewing, developing evidence, and report writing. Whereas public-sector investigators meet with prosecutors who decide whether to proceed with a case, private-sector investigators meet with management in a company to decide on the next course of action (e.g., fire or seek prosecution) following an investigation.

There are many specializations in the investigation field. Examples of specializations in the public sector are homicide, robbery, and fraud. Examples of specializations in the private sector are internal theft, fraudulent workers' compensation claims, and civil cases. Several types of crimes are investigated by both public- and private-sector investigators. Examples are fraud and computer crime. As another example, if a robbery occurs at a convenience store, public police will investigate, and if the business is large enough to maintain proprietary investigators, they will also collect facts on the crime.

Requirements

In general, investigators should be objective, open-minded, inquisitive, persevering, and assertive. They should have excellent interpersonal skills, since they interact with all types of individuals as they interview and gather facts. Other important traits are honesty, integrity, quality report writing, and excellent verbal communications skills for interviewing and testifying.

Depending on the government agency, individuals seeking a position as an investigator or detective are often required to serve as a uniformed police officer (i.e., "on the street") prior to being selected or permitted to begin an internal screening and testing process. With thousands of police agencies in the United States, the path to an investigative position varies widely in terms of years of police experience, training, skills, and education. Federal law enforcement agencies often require a bachelor's degree, as do certain state and local agencies.

Investigators typically attend many specialized training programs in their careers. New laws, techniques of investigation, technology, and types of offenders are constantly evolving.

Private-sector investigators often have some college and previous experience in a relevant field. Corporate investigators usually possess a bachelor's degree, often in business. Some have a master's degree, law degree, or are certified public accountants. Much of the work of private detectives and investigators is learned on the job. Most states require private detectives to be licensed. The requirements vary (U.S. Department of Labor 2008a).

Investigators have the option of being certified to enhance professionalism. ASIS International offers the professional certified investigator (PCI), the Association of Certified Fraud Examiners offers the CFE, and the National Association of Legal Investigators confers the certified legal investigator (CLI).

Salary

The U.S. Department of Labor (2008a) sees faster-than-average employment growth for private detectives and investigators. In 2006, the pay ranged between $19,720 and $64,380. ASIS International (2005, 19) provides a range of between $35,000 to $85,000 for entry- and mid-level management positions in the field of investigations.

Advice

Investigative work is interesting and rewarding, but it can also be tedious and boring. Stationary surveillance, for example, takes a lot of patience; however, the technique can produce results. There are many types of investigative positions. Speak with practitioners to learn about various specializations and the advantages and disadvantages of each.

Types and Guidelines of Investigations

Many types of investigations are conducted for various reasons, and investigations focus on criminal and noncriminal events. Here is a list of types of investigations in the private sector, followed by an elaboration of investigations of fraud, internal theft, shoplifting, and robbery—crimes common in business environments.

- **Proprietary investigation**: conducted in-house by a company investigator.
- **Contract investigation**: provided by a service firm for a fee charged to a client. Several large firms offer a full range of investigative and security consulting services for a variety of client needs. Solo private investigators (PIs) are more numerous and often work domestic, alleged insurance fraud, and missing persons cases.
- **Workplace investigation**: a broad term referring to numerous types of investigations in organizations. The focus of a workplace investigation may be on fraud, theft, threats, violence, sexual harassment, employment discrimination, pre-employment or promotional screening, an accident, or a fire.
- **Undercover investigation**: a secret investigation. A corporation, for example, retains the services of an investigative firm to conduct a secret investigation within its organization to focus on a problem that is difficult to investigate overtly.
- **Litigation investigation**: often conducted by PIs working for law firms, this type of investigation supports civil and criminal cases through the collection of facts, the interviewing of witnesses, the review of case files, and through testimony. Civil cases that fall under this category include personal injury (e.g., vehicle accident),

product liability (e.g., a defective lawn mower that causes an injury), medical malpractice, and wrongful death (e.g., a family hires a PI to conduct a more thorough investigation of a family member's death than a government agency).

- **Due-diligence investigation**: involves responsible and careful attention to details to prevent being liable for negligence. For instance, a corporation considering the acquisition of a company would conduct a due-diligence investigation to ensure that the company's financial statements and claims are accurate. Stockholders and government regulatory agencies expect due diligence. Another illustration of due diligence is in employment applicant screening, whereby an employer conducts a thorough background check to ensure that an applicant does not cause harm if hired. Otherwise, poor screening followed by harmful action by a new employee can result in a lawsuit alleging negligent hiring.

Fraud Investigations

Fraud is an intentional act of deception used by one individual to gain an advantage over another (Schubert 2008, 689). There are many types of fraud, as described in the following examples (Swanson et al. 2009, 458–465). *Insurance fraud* involves someone who fakes a theft, injury, accident, or other loss to receive money from an insurance company. This crime also includes those who exaggerate losses, and insurance companies themselves who overcharge customers for premiums or declare bankruptcy when they are unable to pay many claims following a disaster. *Health-care fraud* is a multitrillion-dollar problem. The most common scheme is billing for services not rendered. Another method is charging for unnecessary tests. *Arson for profit* is another type of fraud, whereby an asset is set on fire to collect on an insurance policy. This crime may be perpetrated because a business is failing or an individual is unable to make loan payments on an asset (e.g., vehicle or building). *Workers' compensation fraud* results when employees falsely claim injury on the job. The alleged injury may be faked or exaggerated, or it may really have occurred prior to reporting to work. *Vendor fraud* is a problem for businesses and government. These organizations depend on vendors to supply a variety of items (e.g., paper, technology, and vehicles) necessary for the workplace. Examples of vendor fraud include offering a bribe to an employee of a purchasing office in exchange for favoring the vendor, supplying inferior items, overstating time worked and/or materials used to complete a job, and submitting false invoices in anticipation of being paid. Other examples of fraud include *credit card fraud* and *check fraud*.

Chapter 5 explained definitions, theories, and strategies to counter theft in the workplace, plus antifraud controls. *Occupational fraud* was defined as the use of one's occupation for personal gain through the deliberate misuse or misapplication of organizational assets. *Embezzlement* was referred to as a type of fraud whereby property entrusted to another is converted to one's own use. Here we emphasize fraud investigations. The Association of Certified Fraud Examiners et al. (2008) offer guidelines for managing the risk of fraud in businesses, as described in subsequent paragraphs.

Most organizations experience fraud. It is a serious problem that has resulted in the demise of entire business enterprises, massive investment losses, legal costs, and imprisonment of executives. However, when it is confronted, a positive organizational culture is nurtured, leading to a strong, effective, and well-run business.

Various laws (e.g., Sarbanes-Oxley Act) in the United States and in other countries have increased pressure on executives to manage the risk of fraud. An organization's board of directors should take the lead to confront fraud. A **board of directors** is a group elected or appointed to oversee the activities of a company or other organization. In a corporation, the board is elected by stockholders and is at the top of the management hierarchy. The board establishes broad policies, reviews the performance of the chief executive, and is involved in financial decisions. Besides the board, employees at all levels of an organization should work to curb fraud. Such employees include management at every level and internal as well as external auditors.

Dealing with fraud includes responding to heightened regulations and public and stakeholder scrutiny, managing the risk of fraud, preventing and detecting fraud, investigating fraud, and taking corrective action. Fraud risk can be analyzed by studying incentives and pressures that may lead to fraud. Also, attention should be given to access and override of system controls. Prevention includes applicant background checks, policies, procedures, and training. Detection entails methods that recognize that fraud has occurred or is occurring, including auditing, software programs, and a process of receiving and responding to complaints and tips.

The Association of Certified Fraud Examiners (2008, 63) reported that fraudsters often display behaviors or characteristics that serve as red flags that fraud *may* be occurring. The group's research showed that the most frequently cited red flag was the fraudster living beyond his or her financial means (37 percent of cases/median loss at $250,000). The second most frequent red flag was financial difficulties (34 percent/$111,000); third, wheeler-dealer attitude (20 percent/$405,000); fourth, control issues and unwillingness to share duties (19 percent/$250,000); fifth, divorce/family problems (17 percent/$118,000); sixth, unusually close association with vendor/customer (15 percent/$410,000); seventh, irritability, suspiciousness, or defensiveness (14 percent/$180,000). (Percentages exceed 100 percent because several offenders exhibited multiple characteristics.)

Factors of consideration when planning a fraud investigation (Figure 10.1) include:

- *Time-sensitivity.* This depends on legal requirements, the necessity to quickly reduce losses, and insurance claim requirements.
- *Notification.* Depending on the alleged offense, notification may be required to regulators, law enforcement, insurers, and external auditors.
- *Confidentiality.* Case file information must be limited to those with a "need to know."
- *Legal privileges.* This covers legal protection from forced disclosure of, say, communication with an attorney. Involving an attorney early in the investigation safeguards attorney-client communications.
- *Legal requirements.* Investigators must comply with applicable laws on gathering information, interviewing, and developing evidence to ensure admissibility during legal proceedings.
- *Objectivity.* Investigators should not be linked to issues or individuals under investigation. An objective investigation should be conducted.

The tasks to complete during a fraud investigation include interviewing witnesses, coconspirators, and the accused. Internal evidence to collect may include personnel files, internal phone records, e-mail, computer files, financial records, CCTV video, and access-control records. External evidence to collect may include public records, customer information, and private detective reports. Investigative tasks may extend to computer forensic examinations and data analysis.

FIGURE 10.1 Investigations should be carefully planned and conducted. (® Shutterstock.com. With permission.)

Management should consult with legal counsel, human resources, risk management, and security prior to taking disciplinary, civil, and/or criminal action. In addition, an investigation can show the need for corrective action (e.g., internal controls and business processes) to prevent future losses.

A CEO'S INVESTIGATION DILEMMA

Here we take the reader to the top of a large corporation where a newly hired chief executive officer (CEO) faces a difficult dilemma over whether or not to initiate a corporate investigation of internal issues. At the end of this scenario, the reader will be asked to make the decision with the information at hand and justify the decision. This scenario is based on the work of Finder (2007, 47–52). Names have been changed.

The first week of Sharon Cooper's new job as CEO at the Miller-Stein Corporation (MSC) was anything but calm. She replaced the former CEO, who died of an aneurysm on a golf course while consummating a multibillion dollar deal with executives of a major corporation based in the Orient. The former CEO had a colossal ego and an office fit for a king that was lined with photographs of himself with VIPs.

At the beginning of the week, Sharon met with Larry Armstrong, head of the largest and most successful division of MSC. He was also the internal candidate for the position Sharon now held. When Sharon met with Larry, the small talk eventually led to the success of Larry's division. Sharon praised the success but also emphasized the importance of not violating any laws. She specifically mentioned the Foreign Corrupt Practices Act. (The **Foreign Corrupt Practices Act [FCPA] of 1977** is a federal law that requires accuracy and transparency in both accounting records and financial transactions. It also requires a system of accounting controls. Another major part of this act is the antibribery provisions that prohibit U.S. persons from making payments to foreign officials to obtain a business opportunity.)

Sharon was clear that she would not tolerate bribery to consummate deals. Larry was stunned by her statements and became defensive. When Sharon said she was considering an internal investigation, Larry took it as a threat and asked if she had any evidence to back up her claim. She reminded Larry that, at her previous employer, an executive had gone to prison for bribery; the CEO resigned; millions of dollars were paid to the government in penalties; and potential business losses were huge. Sharon stated that she would be working especially hard to ensure that no laws were violated by employees of MSC. Larry did not know that Sharon was close to gathering possible evidence of a slush fund at MSC; the administrative assistant to Sharon's predecessor was presently searching for documents of one of MSC's accounts and wire-transfers to an offshore bank. Larry argued that if an investigation occurs and the "word gets out," the company stock will plummet. He said to Sharon, "You are here only a week and you are aiming to destroy MSC!"

Sharon's next stop was Curtis Johnson, MSC's general counsel. (A **general counsel** is a lawyer who leads a legal department in a corporation or government agency.) When she completed her speech on law, ethics, and what she discussed with Larry, Curtis was most concerned about having to spearhead the internal investigation. Sharon assured him that it would be conducted by an outside law firm. He was relieved, but at the same time he argued that an investigation would be a mistake because it would harm MSC, it could not be kept a secret, and investigators would dig deeply into years of records and e-mails. In addition, once the board of directors was informed, they could be held personally liable for any corporate illegal conduct they became aware of and did not act upon. Curtis continued his argument by hinting that the board of directors would likely take control of the company, and she would have no power.

Later that day, and prior to making her decision on the investigation, Sharon remembered that quarterly filings were due to the government soon. The Sarbanes-Oxley Act requires her to approve corporate financial statements as being true and complete. If a slush fund existed at MSC, her signature on the financial statements could result in legal liabilities for herself. (The Sarbanes-Oxley Act [SOX] of 2002 resulted from accounting scandals, and it seeks to prevent accounting fraud in publicly traded companies. Its provisions also affect other types of organizations. SOX established standards of accountability on boards of directors. They are directly responsible for internal accounting controls. Board members are subject to incarceration and fines for accounting fraud.)

Critical Thinking

In the associated example, "A CEO's Investigation Dilemma," what would you do as the CEO? Justify your decision.

Internal Theft Investigations

Suppose that you are an investigator on patrol at an industrial site, and an employee states to you that they saw another employee, named Jeff Collins, steal company equipment. After collecting basic information, you provide the information to your supervisor. An in-house investigation is likely to follow. Subsequent paragraphs provide guidelines for an internal theft investigation of this incident.

Maintain an open mind about the alleged theft, because the incident may not be theft at all. It is possible that the suspect-employee, Jeff Collins, has permission to be in possession of the company equipment and holds a property pass. Other possibilities are that the equipment may really belong to the employee, or the informant may hold a grudge against the "suspect."

Interview informants at least two times, thoroughly, to ensure the accuracy of what they observed.

Proceed cautiously with the investigation and collect as much information as possible prior to interviewing the suspect. Check to see if the equipment is in inventory or was legitimately checked out. Ensure that the equipment supposedly stolen is, in fact, company property and that it can be identified as company property. If possible, locate the same type of equipment and see if company-identifying information or marks are on it and/or a serial number. Companies often mark their property as part of a theft-prevention program and to assist authorities in identifying the owner when a recovery of stolen property is made during an investigation. A company can mark their property in multiple ways. Examples are stamping the company name and/or a serial number on it so that it is difficult to remove, or hiding a special substance or microdots unique to the company on the property. Vendors are available that offer various techniques of marking property.

The issue of marking property and being able to identify and prove an item is company property is vital to a criminal case. The prosecution must prove intent: The defendant intended to take possession of *company property* and remove it from the premises for personal gain. A prosecutor must prove **mens rea**, which means guilty mind and intent to commit a crime (Hall 2009, 50). A prosecutor must have proof beyond a reasonable doubt—the weight of evidence required to succeed in a criminal case. The job of the defense is to cast a "doubt" in the prosecution's case in front of a jury. This can be accomplished in several ways, such as disproving that the company owns the property; that the defendant had legitimate possession of the property; that the defendant did not intend to steal, but made an error; or that investigative methods were faulty.

Another objective of the prosecution is to prove **actus reus**—the physical act of the crime (Hall 2009, 66). This can be proved through an eyewitness or a CCTV recording. Actus reus is generally easier to prove than mens rea because the latter requires an inference (i.e., conclusion) to be drawn about what was on the mind of the defendant when actus reus was observed. For example, the defendant may have made an error and did not intend to commit a crime.

Upon collecting as much information as possible on the case of the alleged stolen company equipment, investigating all avenues that would disprove a theft has occurred, and in consultation with the human resources department, an interview of Jeff Collins, the suspect-employee, is next. Because hidden errors in the investigation are always a possibility, caution is advised as the investigation proceeds.

The suspect-employee should be calmly asked to sit for an interview. The interview should take place in a private office and be conducted by an investigator with a witness present. In a union environment, a union representative may be present. Without harsh wording, threats, touching, or restrictions on the movement of the employee-suspect (who may want to abruptly depart), questions can be asked about the incident. For example: "Can you tell us about the equipment that you had in your possession on Monday at the loading dock?" "Where is that equipment now and who has possession of it?" Answers to basic questions can lead the investigation in several directions. The employee-suspect may have a reasonable explanation that ends the inquiry. If the suspect admits to a violation of policy and/or a crime, ask him/her to write out a statement of their actions and sign it. All those present should also sign the statement. Companies also ask the employee-suspect to sign a prepared form that states that no threat or force was applied during the interview. If the employee-suspect does not cooperate, refuses to answer questions, or leaves the interview, management must decide on the next course of action. Depending on available evidence, and attorney advice, examples of action include suspension, termination, and/or calling public police.

If public police are contacted, they will question management and/or security on the probable cause to support the case and an arrest. Probable cause is established when, for instance, an investigator observes an employee in a company building conceal company equipment, exit the building, and drive to the final exit gate of the premises. Probable cause has greater legal weight than a hunch or suspicion, but it is less than certainty. As written in the previous chapter, probable cause is stated in the Fourth Amendment, and it is required to make an arrest or to obtain an arrest or search warrant.

DO NOT MAKE THESE MISTAKES

Investigation

Alice Davidson had been an internal auditor for Hugemart Stores for 5 years. Her annual performance evaluations were good. However, management at the store where she was assigned suspected her of internal theft. It was brought to management's attention that when she completed her break in the canteen one day, merchandise from the sales floor was left on a table. Following this report, the store manager and his two assistants placed Alice under close surveillance. When the store manager requested a loss-prevention investigator from headquarters to handle the Davidson case, the request was denied because the regional investigator, who had resigned, had not yet been replaced. Upper management ordered the store manager and his assistants to conduct their own investigation, arrest Alice if necessary, and call the police.

Two weeks later, an assistant manager noticed that Alice was in a department outside of her assigned area. The assistant manager also noticed a bottle of perfume sticking out of Alice's pocket. He demanded that she accompany him to his office and she complied. The assistant manager and the store manager accused her of stealing the perfume, although she claimed to have a receipt at home. Alice was questioned for about an hour. Then police were called. The questioning continued until police arrived and they transported her to jail. During over an hour of questioning, she was refused the opportunity to leave, use the restroom, or telephone an attorney. In addition, the managers promised Alice that she would keep her job and they would cancel the call to the police if she signed a confession. She refused. Eventually, criminal charges were dropped because Alice produced a receipt for the perfume. A lawsuit followed.

Lessons: Ensure that employees conducting investigations are properly trained and experienced. They must clearly understand policies, procedures, suspect rights, arrest law, and evidence law.

Critical Thinking

Why do companies cut back on trained and experienced personnel and risk errors and lawsuits?

Shoplifting Investigations

Suppose that you are a nonuniformed loss-prevention agent for a retail drug chain, and one day while you are on patrol in one of the stores you observe a customer at the allergy/cold medicine aisle holding a box of medication. The customer, named Marty Bell, opened up the box, placed a tablet in his mouth, and then placed the box in his pocket. Would you stop this individual and make an arrest for shoplifting? In this case, Marty was arrested for shoplifting, asked to accompany the agent to a store office, and interviewed. Marty claimed that no theft had occurred, that the box of medicine was purchased earlier, and that he used his credit card to make the purchase. The agent continued to process the incident as a solid shoplifting case, and public police were called to transport Marty to jail. Marty refused to plead guilty and pay a fine. He chose to have his day in court. Months later, at a city court criminal trial, he showed his credit card bill that listed the purchase of the medicine prior to his arrest. Marty was acquitted and then a lawsuit was filed against the store. Prior to a scheduled civil trial, the case was settled out of court for almost $30,000.

Notice that the agent observed Marty holding the box of medication, but no statement was made about whether an observation was made of Marty taking the store's merchandise off the shelf. Marty claimed that when he walked by the allergy/cold-medicine aisle, it was a reminder to consume his allergy medicine that he had in his pocket.

The case of Mary Clark is another illustration of the caution required in suspected shoplifting incidents. Mary was in a major retail store with her three small children. As she was holding a box of baby formula, a bag of diapers, and other items, she picked up a glass thermometer off the store's shelf. She held it for a few seconds and then placed it in her pocket. Upon reaching the checkout, she paid for all of the items she held except for the thermometer. Two store loss-prevention agents waited for Mary to pass the checkout. This helps to establish *mens rea*. In other words, she had an opportunity to pay for the item and did not, which helps to prove criminal intent. When Mary was confronted, she was asked to accompany the agents to a store office. She explained immediately that she forgot about the thermometer in her pocket, that she could not locate a shopping cart to hold her items, and that she did not want the kids to hold the glass thermometer. She stated that she placed the thermometer in her pocket temporarily and was going to take it out and pay for it at the checkout. During her explanations, one of the agents took hold of her arm to pull her toward the loss-prevention office. Following a brief struggle, she accompanied the agents, with the children following. At the office, she restated her earlier explanations. She also stated that her arm, neck, and back were hurting from the struggle. Mary refused to answer questions or write statements. The agents called police, who transported Mary to jail on the shoplifting charge. The children were released to a relative after the department of social services was contacted.

Rather than plead guilty and pay a fine, Mary demanded a trial on the shoplifting charge. During her trial, the prosecution showed *actus reus* to the jury with no complications: a CCTV video showed Mary placing the thermometer in her pocket and passing the checkout without paying for it; and two loss-prevention agents observed and testified to the same actions by Mary. The proving of *mens rea* became more challenging for the prosecution, but they argued that she intended to shoplift because she completed her purchases and passed the checkout without paying for the thermometer. Did Mary intend to shoplift the thermometer? Did she have a guilty mind? What were her thoughts when she placed the item in her pocket and when she was at the checkout? The defense argued to the jury that Mary looked for a shopping cart, found none, was holding multiple items, and did not choose to give a glass thermometer to a child to hold, so she placed it in her pocket, intending to pay for it at the checkout.

The jury drew inferences from the prosecution and defense arguments. The defense was able to cast a doubt on the prosecution's case and argued that the prosecution did not prove the case beyond a reasonable doubt. Mary was found not guilty. A subsequent civil suit focused not only on the issue of the arrest, but also on issues of negligence and on the injuries Mary was alleged to have received during the shoplifting arrest. The case was settled for an undisclosed amount prior to a civil trial. This case illustrates that management should develop guidelines for cost-effective decisions for shop-lifting arrests. In other words, security practitioners should ask themselves, "How would a jury decide a case when the prosecution must show *proof beyond a reasonable doubt*?"

What follows here are guidelines for investigations involving suspected shoplifters. There are several similarities and differences with internal theft and shoplifting cases. To begin with, caution is advised for both types of investigations because a crime may not have occurred, or the case may be too weak for it to be tried successfully. From a safety perspective, retail loss-prevention agents may be in a more dangerous situation when confronting a suspected shoplifter when compared to company investigators confronting a suspected internal thief in, say, an industrial environment. Loss-prevention agents are unlikely to know if shoplifting suspects are armed, or their background or behavioral tendencies. On the other hand, company investigators often possess background information on employee-suspects and their tendencies. In addition, layers of security (e.g., metal detector) on the premises may prevent a weapon from being brought into the workplace. However, extreme caution is advised when confronting any suspect.

Upon approaching a shoplifting suspect, loss-prevention agents should show their security identification and politely ask the suspect to accompany them to an office to discuss a store item. Avoid loud, accusatory language. The initial contact with the suspect requires trained and experienced agents because a variety of behavioral reactions can result from the suspect. Examples can range from willing compliance and cooperation, to reacting in a loud and boisterous manner, to bolting, becoming violent, or signaling gang members to intercede to facilitate escape.

Prior to approaching a shoplifting suspect, ensure that a valid legal foundation has been established. Make sure that a reliable employee or agent saw the suspect take store merchandise off a shelf or rack and conceal it. The item may also be worn or held, or a price tag may be changed. Individual state shoplifting statutes provide specifics on elements of the crime and requirements for a valid shoplifting arrest; probable cause is a typical legal requirement. Without losing sight of the suspect, who may ditch the item, wait until the suspect passes the last possible checkout without paying for the item, prior to the stop. Local prosecutors may require the suspect to be stopped at the door or even right outside the door to strengthen *mens rea*. (Checking with local prosecutors on their requirements can be an immense aid to planning a quality anti-shoplifting program.) Once the suspect reaches the door or is outside the door, he or she may run; this results in another safety issue. Employees and agents should refrain from chasing a suspect, because harm may come to themselves and customers. In one case, a male cashier chased a suspect into the parking lot, and the frantic suspect quickly drove away, hitting and killing a customer. The item shoplifted was a $14.00 steak. If a suspect bolts, obtain a description of the suspect and any accomplices and vehicles and immediately contact public police.

Once the suspect is in an office for an interview, he or she should be asked for photo identification, which may be bogus. (Positive identification is more likely if police fingerprint the suspect during booking at a jail following arrest.) During the store interview, the suspect should be asked for the concealed merchandise and a receipt. If the suspect refuses to give up the concealed merchandise, call the public police so that they conduct the search, thereby transferring potential search liability to them. If possible, loss-prevention agents should avoid touching the suspect throughout the whole confrontation. If use of force occurs, it must be reasonable; when the suspect stops resisting, force must stop. In the unlikely event of deadly force being applied, it is restricted to when your life or someone else's life is about to be taken. Retail loss-prevention agents are rarely armed with firearms, unless they are public police who are moonlighting.

State statutes on shoplifting may refer to a merchant's privilege to detain a shoplifting suspect to investigate (i.e., question) the ownership of merchandise. A **detention** is characterized by the suspect not being turned over to police, as in an arrest. Guidelines for detention are found in state statutes and case law that serve as a foundation for retail company policies and procedures. Besides the typical requirement of probable cause for the stop, "reasonableness" is also required in detaining the suspect for a period of time to interview, recover property, and document the case. The interview must be voluntary, without coercion or force. The suspect has the right to remain silent. Standard company forms may include a form for the suspect to write a confession (without guidance or coercion from agents), a form stipulating that no force or coercion was applied, and a form stating that the suspect will not file a lawsuit, nor return to the store for one year. The signing of these forms does not necessarily bar a lawsuit. Once the suspect signs all the forms, the suspect is released from the detention. An uncooperative suspect can lead from the initial detention to the calling of public police and ultimately to an arrest. The loss-prevention agent will sign a criminal complaint containing the facts of the case.

Most shoplifting defendants plead guilty and pay a fine or serve a short sentence. Repeat offenders or serious cases of shoplifting may lead to plea-bargaining and a longer sentence. In addition, there is the possibility of a criminal trial, which necessitates sound case processing for all cases.

If a shoplifting case goes to criminal trial, preparation by loss-prevention agents and the legal team is essential. This includes a thorough review of all relevant documents and evidence (e.g., recovered merchandise, video of events, and statements of all parties). The initial stages of a case, when evidence is being collected and processed, are the time to begin strict **chain**

of custody of evidence. This means that evidence is properly documented (e.g., name of the person who collected the evidence, date, time, and location), labeled, and securely stored prior to its introduction into a trial. The defense side typically attacks evidence presented by the prosecution to cast a "doubt" in the prosecution's case. For instance, upon cross-examination, a defense attorney will seek to destroy a loss-prevention agent's testimony and try to make him or her look like an incompetent buffoon in front of the jury. Alternatively, numerous questions will focus on video evidence to suggest (directly or indirectly) that the video does not show the full story, suffers from technical problems, or was doctored.

Retail store policies and procedures vary on the crime of shoplifting. Prevention is a popular strategy, whereby customer service, physical security, and signs seek to deter shoplifting. Furthermore, when a suspect conceals an item, he or she is approached by multiple agents in anticipation of the suspect placing the store item back on the shelf and leaving the store. Other stores maintain an aggressive arrest and prosecution policy, the effectiveness of which is debatable. Whatever approach is used, it should be cost effective, because retail businesses exist to make a profit and not operate a "mini-criminal justice system."

Civil recovery is another variable in the planning of a retail company's shoplifting polices and procedures. State statutes hold shoplifters liable for expenses incurred by retailers in dealing with the problem of shoplifting. Civil penalties seek to recover a variety of expenses resulting from shoplifting (e.g., security and legal costs). Retailers have the option of contracting this collection effort to service firms, who retain a percentage of funds recovered. The reality of civil recovery is that many shoplifters are poor and/or unwilling to cooperate, even following court intervention.

Robbery Investigations

As covered in Chapter 5, robbery is a dangerous crime, necessitating training and precautions for employees. A security officer's response when observing a robbery in progress, say, at a mall, depends on numerous factors. What type of training has the officer received? Is the officer armed with a firearm? Did the robber(s) spot the officer? Are customers, besides employees, at the scene? Is cover available for the officer? Robbery incidents are all different; however, as a security practitioner, a few general guidelines should be remembered as a foundation for action. First, the safety of people must be a high priority. Avoid entering the scene, even if armed, while a robbery is in progress. Seek cover, call public police, and let the robber(s) flee from the store to reduce the chances of injuries or deaths. Obtain a description of the offenders, the direction of travel, and a description of their mode of transportation. Take notes and provide as much information as possible to police when they arrive. If properly trained, render first aid to any injured parties after calling emergency medical services.

The characteristics of robbers and robberies vary. A robber may be wearing a bullet-resistive vest and possess greater firepower than a security officer. As an armed security officer without a bullet-resistive vest, would you confront an armed robber leaving the scene? Without adequate training, equipment, firepower, and backup, seek cover and observe and report the incident. What if the robber takes a hostage and demands your weapon and/or vehicle keys? Maintain a slow, calm conversation with the offender to stall until police arrive. Avoid giving up anything, since it can make the situation worse.

Following a robbery, the crime scene must be protected until police arrive. Keep onlookers and the media back. Police will arrive and perform several duties, including the following (Swanson et al. 2009, 414):

- Ensure that no threat still exists at the scene and search for any offenders close to the scene
- Care for the injured
- Protect the crime scene
- Interview victims and witnesses
- Search for physical evidence and process it
- Provide a description of the robbers to other police
- Record descriptions of assets taken (e.g., serial numbers)
- If a cellular phone was taken, identify the number, subscriber, and carrier
- When and where convenient, display a photographic lineup of suspects to victims and witnesses
- Follow up leads and re-interview victims and witnesses
- Review MO (modus operandi) and other departmental files
- If suspects are identified, contact the prosecutor, obtain arrest warrants, and prepare and distribute wanted fliers

When a robbery occurs in the workplace, public police are contacted so that their resources can be applied to apprehending the offender, saving others from potential victimization, and recovering assets. Both security practitioners and public police fulfill their respective roles following a robbery. Public police take the lead, and security personnel should share information on the case. Corporate investigators seek as much information as possible about the incident as input for improving security and safety. They may learn, for example, about a vulnerability at a store that was victimized and apply corrective action to other corporate locations. By maintaining metrics about each robbery—and by recording personnel, physical, and other characteristics present during each robbery and the MO of offenders—protection can be enhanced, and the information can be used in investigations to apprehend offenders.

Security executives of retail chains and other organizations often discover that robberies frequently have an internal connection. Examples include a manager who falsely claims robbery on the way to the bank, or an employee or former employee who participates in or offers aid in a robbery.

Techniques of Investigation

Interviewing

Types of Interviewing

Although many crimes would never have been solved without scientific crime detection and crime laboratories, cases can also be solved without "hard science." **Interviewing** (Figure 10.2) is a basic investigative strategy that has a long history. Swanson et al. (2009, 742) define it as "the process of obtaining information from people who have knowledge that might be helpful in a criminal investigation." This chapter takes a much broader view of interviewing in that it is helpful for many types of inquiries (e.g., access controls, background investigations, accidents, and sexual harassment), besides those related to crime.

Amotz Brandes (2007, 10) maintains strong views on the power of interviewing and its role in security. He argues that we emphasize a lot of defensive security (e.g., physical security, policies, procedures, and firearms in a tactical response to an attack), as opposed to offensive security. Brandes further notes that security personnel often go through several hours of training without learning "to effectively use the one weapon readily available and that affords the most powerful impact in terms of protection—a good question."

FIGURE 10.2 **Interviewing is a basic investigative strategy used to collect information and evidence. (® Shutterstock.com. With permission.)**

He favors **offensive interviewing**, which can be described as maximizing the interviewing process through questions that elicit useful information to further the objectives of security. It is not meant to be rude. Brandes provides reasons for the limited investment in training for interviewing: the risk of being invasive; not trusting personnel to ask questions effectively; and feeling comfortable with the traditional, defensive approach.

Brandes offers practical techniques of offensive interviewing. He refers to **close-ended questions** versus **open-ended questions**. The former require a short answer, such as "yes" or "no." For instance, "Were you at the scene of the loss last evening?" The latter require an elaboration and produces improved results, such as: "What were your activities last evening?"

In reference to questions asked by security personnel at access points, Brandes uses the example of a question asked at certain defense and government facilities: "Are you a U.S. citizen?" Brandes would ask: "Where were you born?" The answer leads to subsequent questions. Since criminals often use fake IDs and fictitious backgrounds, Brandes recommends asking questions that go from the general to the specific to expose false statements. If individuals are asked where they work and what they do, subsequent questions can delve deeper into their occupations. For example, if an individual says that she works for government social services, she can be asked the criteria for receiving aid. Such offensive interviewing can catch a deceptive person off guard, since there is a limit to the depth of cover stories.

In the private sector, besides interviewing at access points, interviewing typically takes place following an adverse incident. Examples of adverse incidents in the private sector that commonly require an interview are employee theft, fraud, violence, sexual harassment, accident, and fire. These incidents can be categorized as occurring from internal threats and hazards. Robbery, burglary, and shoplifting result from external threats. However, internal and external threats may overlap. Consider, for example, a fast-food store manager who plans a robbery of the store with a nonemployee from the outside. Each type of incident requires an investigator to be knowledgeable and skilled in interviewing, law, policies and procedures, and investigative objectives of the particular type of incident at hand.

Techniques to Enhance Interviewing

Interviews are often conducted of suspects, witnesses, and victims. Here the emphasis is on suspects; however, several of the techniques explained next are applicable to witnesses and victims.

At the beginning of the interviewing process, an investigator should identify himself or herself and show identification, then briefly state the purpose of the questioning.

Plan the interview, including the location and the questions to be asked. If a crime is being investigated, know the elements that must be proved; see the penal code. Since memory wanes over time, interviews should be conducted as soon as possible following an incident. In addition, prompt interviewing prevents suspects from planning an alibi or false stories, or conspiring with others. Ensure that the interview is conducted in a quiet office free of distractions. An interviewee may request an interview in a neutral location off the premises at a public location. Whenever possible, include a witness in the interview, especially one that is of the same sex as the interviewee. Avoid, for instance, a male investigator interviewing a female in an office without a witness present.

When possible, record (audio/visual) the interview. Public police do this, even without the interviewee's knowledge.

The beginning of the interview is a time to set the interviewee at ease and develop **rapport**, which refers to cooperative interaction between the interviewer and interviewee that facilitates communication. This can be accomplished by showing interest in the interviewee and by asking or making statements of a general nature about the weather, sports, or the interviewee's work. At the same time, study the demeanor and level of nervousness of the interviewee. These characteristics can be compared to behavior occurring when questions about the case are asked.

Body language of the interviewee provides clues as to the truthfulness of statements. Perspiration, excessive nervousness, avoidance of eye contact, and change in tone of voice, *may* signal deception. Nonverbal clues are often very helpful to investigators. However, cultures vary on the nonverbal clues exhibited (e.g., eye contact), and the investigator must know the cultural background of the interviewee.

One avenue to test the veracity of an interviewee is for the investigator to ask questions in which the answers are known. Another point is that a victim or witness may really be the offender.

An investigator must act in a professional manner when conducting an interview. Control of the interviewing process by the interviewer is essential, rather than the suspect controlling the interview. Objectivity is also important. Maintain an open mind, in that the suspect may be innocent. Seek lines of questioning that show innocence. For instance, if the suspect has an alibi, gather relevant facts to follow up.

When the interviewee is speaking, listen carefully, maintain eye contact, and avoid interrupting. When the interviewee stops speaking, maintain a few moments of silence. This may cause the interviewee to feel uncomfortable and begin speaking again. If this technique does not work, ask an open-ended question to continue the interview.

An investigator should ascertain if the interviewee has a disability that impairs the senses. Such a factor can distort facts. For instance, a witness who has a hearing problem may distort facts about what they heard during an incident. A vision problem is another example.

Rationalizations are excuses presented to an interviewee-suspect to minimize the seriousness of harmful behavior so resistance can be overcome and a confession can be obtained. Examples are as follows: "You are not the only employee who has participated in such activity." "Take advantage of this opportunity to help yourself and make things right."

Another avenue to possibly elicit a confession, when excellent evidence is available, is by inferring that the suspect committed a more serious offense. For instance, if $1,000 in assets was stolen, the investigator may argue that $10,000 in assets is missing. To avoid being charged with a more serious offense (e.g., grand larceny), the suspect may argue that he or she only stole $1,000 in assets so that the charge is for a less serious offense (e.g., petty larceny).

Another technique to enhance the success of interviewing is to elicit responses from interviewees that expose other offenders and threats. This can be akin to a "broad fishing expedition aimed at a captive audience—the interviewee." The inquiry should be broad because knowledge of any insider threat is vital information. Rather than, "Who else is stealing from the company?" ask, "Who else is harming the company and in what way?"

Whenever possible, a suspect should be permitted to write a confession and sign it. The investigator should not assist the suspect with sentence structure, spelling, and so forth. The suspect should also sign a statement that no force or coercion was used, and that the confession was voluntary.

Investigators should keep accurate records of interviews for reference and for case preparation. At the same time, these records may be subpoenaed. Whereas a subpoena is a court order requiring a person to appear at a specific place and time to provide testimony, a **subpoena duces tecum** is a court order requiring a person to provide specific documents and items relevant to a case.

Attorneys often guide investigators during investigations. An important rule in this relationship is the attorney-client privilege. It essentially means that communications between the investigator and the attorney in this relationship are privileged, and there is a choice not to disclose confidential communications. A human-resources executive may also play a role in guiding investigations.

INVESTIGATOR ACCUSED OF MAKING SEXUAL ADVANCES

In one case of bank fraud, a female suspect refused to be interviewed in the investigator's office, but agreed to an interview in the investigator's vehicle in the parking lot of a restaurant. During the interview, the suspect confessed to embezzling $40,000, but stated that if the investigator brought charges against her, she would claim that he made sexual advances toward her. Months later at the criminal trial, she made such an accusation while testifying on the witness stand. The prosecution asked the judge for a recess. A

---

meeting took place in the judge's chamber, at which time the investigator played an audio recording of the woman's threat that was recorded during the interview in the restaurant parking lot. When the trial resumed, the woman was also charged with perjury.

Investigative Questions

Many employment positions in the security and criminal justice professions involve the collection of *facts* that serve as a foundation for decision making for arrests, elimination of suspects, and many other reasons. Facts serve to describe and understand an incident, while also providing evidence to prove a case. Universally accepted and applied investigative questions to gather facts have been an essential component of investigations through history. These basic questions are reflected in the standard investigative forms that are completed by investigators in all organizations.

To illustrate, suppose an incident of theft occurred at a hotel. A customer placed her luggage outside her room at 6:30 A.M. as directed by her tour director, prior to departing to the next destination. Upon boarding the bus, the customer noticed that her luggage was missing. She reported the loss, and a hotel investigator began an investigation. The investigator began to collect facts by recording *what* occurred, a description of the luggage, and *who* suffered the loss. The victim's name, address, telephone numbers, and subsequent itinerary were recorded, along with similar facts on the tour director. A hotel supervisor was questioned for facts as to *who* handled the luggage from outside the hotel room to the bus and *who* else was working at the time. The investigator noted *when* the luggage was placed outside the room, other relevant chronological events, and *where* each event occurred or was alleged to have occurred.

Once basic facts were collected and recorded, the investigator began to formulate hypotheses (i.e., in this context, tentative thoughts of what may have occurred) that needed to be proved to explain the loss and identify the responsible party. The investigator walked the path that the porter supposedly walked with the luggage as it was being carried to the bus. The walk began with a thorough search of the hotel room, but nothing unusual was seen. During the walk, the investigator noted a locked closet near the ground-floor elevator. CCTV video from the hotel's NVR system was checked for any unusual events. Digital records of electronic access controls at doors were also checked, as well as electronic guard-tour records. The walk and the check of the security systems were made to try to find out the "Who? What? Where? When? How? and Why?" of the case. The investigator was also seeking others to question. In addition, if evidence was found, it could be shown to management, and possibly public police, along with suspect information. Questions of concern included the following: "Was an external thief on the premises, or was it an inside job?" "Was the luggage misplaced?" "Is the victim the offender?" (e.g., possible insurance fraud).

The check of all the security systems showed no anomalies. With the porter a high priority for interviewing, the investigator interviewed him. He stated that he took all the luggage to the bus and did not know anything about the missing item. When asked about the locked closet near the ground floor elevator, the porter became nervous, avoided eye contact, and was evasive with answers. A telephone call to the maintenance department revealed that the locked door led to a storage room. The investigator, the porter, and the maintenance supervisor met at the storage room door. The maintenance supervisor unlocked the door and the missing luggage was located. With further questioning by the investigator, the porter stated that he regularly saw the storage room key lying around. One day he quickly pressed it into a bar of soap, and then, at home, he filed a copy from a blank key. The porter stated that it was "the first time" he stole luggage. Further questioning revealed other thievery. The investigator completed the investigative report and provided it to management, who fired the porter and did not contact public police.

Critical Thinking

In the case of the stolen luggage, do you think management should have notified public police? Why or why not?

The six basic investigative questions are: Who? What? Where? When? How? and Why?

During an interview of an employee–suspect, the following questions may serve to gain information:

- Who else caused losses?
- Who is the most knowledgeable person about true losses in the workplace? Who is the next most knowledgeable person?
- What losses are occurring and who is involved?
- What groups are involved in losses? Who is in each group?
- What methods are being used to overcome security? Who is involved? What losses are occurring?
- Who is disgruntled?
- At the end of the interview, a general, open-ended question should be asked, such as, "Is there anything else that you can add to what you told me that is related to what we discussed?"

Interrogations and Suspect Rights

Becker (2009, 189) distinguishes between interviews and **interrogations**. He writes that "interviews are the pathways to interrogations" and provide a foundation for interrogations. During the interview, investigators learn about the suspect who answers a variety of questions. During the interrogation, the primary objective is to secure a confession, rather than seeking information and listening to fabricated or erroneous information from the suspect that occurs during the interview.

Because the term *interrogation* is often stereotyped and linked to "third-degree tactics" (i.e., use of force during questioning to gain a confession), security practitioners should favor the term *interviewing*. Suppose a lawsuit results from a private-sector investigation. Think of the effect the term *interrogation* will have on a jury, as opposed to the term *interview*. Private-sector investigators can use interrogation techniques that are legal and ethical, but term them *interview techniques*.

Nemeth (2005, 201) writes: "Constitutional protections apply to government action only. Extending warnings prior to custodial interrogation in private security settings has generally not been required though the climate for change alters according to abuses." In other words, **Miranda warnings** (i.e., right to remain silent, right to speak with an attorney and have one present) are only required to be read by law enforcement authorities; otherwise, all evidence obtained through the illegal questioning will be excluded from the criminal case. (There are exceptions to this general rule.) The U.S. Supreme Court has yet to require private security personnel to read the warnings prior to questioning suspects. However, a segment of private-sector practitioners employs Miranda-type warning and documents to strengthen their case in the event the case is challenged. If private security personnel work with public police on a case, or if public police work part-time in security (i.e., moonlighting), then Miranda rights are advisable for suspects in custody and about to be questioned (Inbau, et al. 1996, 74).

Nemeth (2005, 201) writes of the case of Cumberland Farm convenience stores in Boston. It was alleged that security personnel who accused employees of theft used the following procedure with multiple employees. Employees were escorted individually to a back room, seated on a milk crate, accused of theft, and threatened with public humiliation or prosecution if they did not sign a confession. Finally, several employees sued Cumberland.

Although constitutional protections have a limited effect on private security investigations, other means are available to control private security actions. These include fear of a lawsuit for negligence and violation of a variety of torts, criminal charges filed against security personnel, and loss or suspension of a security license by state or local regulatory agencies. In a union environment, private security investigators should realize that an employee is permitted to have a union representative present during an interview that may result in discipline when the employee requests such representation. This was the ruling of the U.S. Supreme Court case, ***NLRB v. J. Weingarten Inc., No. 251 (1975)***. The National Labor Relations Board, the government body that regulates management–labor issues, has reversed direction multiple times on whether *Weingarten rights* apply to non-union employees.

Protecting the Crime Scene

When a private security practitioner encounters a crime scene, top priorities are to ensure that no threat exists and to care for the injured. Training is required prior to rendering medical care. Prompt calls must be made for backup, public police, and emergency medical services. The suspect should be handcuffed and searched for weapons and evidence; this action constitutes an arrest. Once these priorities are accomplished, the crime scene must be protected.

The size of a crime scene can vary. It may be a small office or a large area inside or outside of a building. Security practitioners should keep unauthorized people away from the crime scene so that evidence is not disturbed, touched, or taken away (or items added to the scene). Once evidence is picked up, it cannot be placed back exactly where it was found originally.

As soon as possible, following the preceding prioritized tasks, the security practitioner should begin taking notes that cover the date, day, and time of arrival at the scene and what was observed and heard. By following the six basic investigative questions, a variety of facts should be recorded so they are not forgotten.

A major thought in the mind of investigators is that an offender typically leaves something at a crime scene (e.g., fingerprints, blood, shoe prints, tools) *and takes something with them* (e.g., stolen items, blood on their clothes from the victim, paint chips from a door or window, soil from the ground). An investigator searches the crime scene for evidence left by the offender, among other things. When suspects are interviewed and/or search warrants executed, items taken from the crime scene are sought. The objective is to link the suspect to the crime scene.

As soon as public police arrive at a crime scene, security practitioners turn the investigation over to them and offer support and information. Police crime scene technicians are trained to collect, document, maintain the chain of custody of evidence, and testify in court. Police investigators interview security personnel, witnesses, victims, and suspects and confer with crime scene technicians and prosecutors to solve crimes.

Sources of Information

There are many sources of information for investigators as they develop their cases or prepare reports for management decision making. Thus far, we have learned about witnesses, victims, and suspects who can supply information through investigative interviewing. In addition, crime scenes are a rich source of information and evidence. Other major sources include internal documents and records, anonymous tips from an internal reporting program or outside sources, informants, surveillance, undercover investigations, public police, databases, and government agencies. As we know, the Internet contains a wealth of information. By placing keywords in a search engine, an enormous amount of information is available on people, organizations, news events, history, and so forth.

Investigators often rely on Internet **information brokers.** These are service companies that offer databases to anyone willing to pay a fee. The databases contain a vast amount of personal information on individuals and information on businesses. Investigators use these databases to locate an individual, conduct a background check, and obtain information on a host of topics such as criminal records, lawsuits, assets, bankruptcies, and death. Caution is advised when using information brokers/databases because the information may be inaccurate, incomplete, outdated, secured from a limited geographic area, and obtained illegally.

Here is a sample of firms that offer information and services for a fee:

- LexisNexis: This company offers customers billions of searchable documents from more than tens of thousands of legal, news, and business sources. It helps professionals locate people and assets, authenticate identity, and conduct background checks. http://global. lexisnexis.com.
- Dun & Bradstreet: This firm is noted for offering a variety of information and services to businesses. www.dnb.com.
- US Search: This company offers people searches, background checks, property searches, court records, and phone searches. www.ussearch.com.

Refer back to Chapter 6, Personnel Security, for guidelines on investigating employment applicants, including topics on online resources, problems when checking criminal records, and people with bogus backgrounds.

ISSUE

Should All Pretexting be Prohibited?

Pretexting is an issue that is associated with the collection of information by investigators. There are many definitions of the term, and it is used in various contexts. The term refers to presenting a false identity or false information to someone to obtain information. Ferraro (2008, 18–20) argues that "pretexting is not about gathering *personal information*; it is about gathering information which is often unavailable by other means." At the same time, a lot of information is available as public records, and pretexting is not necessary. Examples of public records include home ownership, real estate taxes paid, or bankruptcy. However, not all information is readily available, and numerous laws protect privacy and restrict access (e.g., financial, medical, and telephone records).

The **Gramm-Leach-Bliley Act of 1999** prohibits pretexting to obtain a person's financial information, either directly from a financial institution or from a customer of a financial institution. The 1999 Act also prohibits pretexting through the use of forged, counterfeit, lost, or stolen documents to obtain a person's financial information. Through the **Telephone Records and Privacy Protection Act of 2006**, Congress banned pretexting to fraudulently obtain telephone records—for instance, pretending to be a customer requesting a previous month's calling records. The Federal Trade Commission views pretexting as illegal when it is used to obtain personal information to help commit a crime. In addition, states have laws that bar pretexting.

Investigative groups, such as the California Association of Licensed Investigators, see pretexting as a valuable investigative tool and advocate against laws to curb its use. In the context of undercover investigations, pretexts are necessary. Undercover investigators must conceal their true identity and purpose in order to gather information.

In the context of public policing, just about every driver violates traffic laws eventually. Should this be justification for a stop motivated by multiple reasons? For example, what if an officer stops a vehicle not only for a traffic violation, but also because the officer views the driver as the type of person that may be carrying illegal drugs or other contraband? Although this discussion relates to the issue of racial profiling, officers must have legal justification for stopping a vehicle. The courts play a role in controlling the use of pretexts by public police.

ASIS International (2008) offers interesting perspectives on the issue of pretexts. This group is not opposed to pretexting and favors its appropriate use. They note that Congress has made exceptions to allow it for certain types of investigations, such as insurance fraud and the collection of child-support judgments. Some investigators, who are also members of ASIS, have asked ASIS to advocate against banning pretexting by legislative bodies. The response from ASIS is that it is unable to offer assurances to legislators that investigators who abuse pretexting will face professional penalties. Thus, ASIS would like to see industry standards for the gathering and use of information by private investigators, including sanctions for violators.

Surveillance

Surveillance has been used throughout history as an investigative strategy to collect information (Figure 10.3). It can be explained from multiple perspectives. **Traditional surveillance** refers to the "good guys" covertly watching the "bad guys." This can entail **stationary surveillance**, whereby an investigator is at one location covertly watching someone or something. **Mobile surveillance** means that an investigator is covertly following someone on foot or in a vehicle. Multiple investigators may be applied to surveillance in a team approach. Technology provides the foundation for electronic surveillance (e.g., bugging), and it is available to both the "good guys" and the "bad guys," although its use is subject to legal restrictions, as explained in Chapter 8. Another type of surveillance that has existed for centuries, but is causing increasing concern, is covert surveillance of the "good guys" by the "bad guys." Since the 9/11 attacks especially, countersurveillance has increasingly become part of security planning because terrorists, besides other criminals, study a target prior to attacking. Consequently, a variety of organizations have begun or enhanced countersurveillance through personnel and technology.

Traditional surveillance, as applied in the private sector, focuses on many types of cases. For example, a P.I. conducts surveillance of a spouse in a divorce case, follows the spouse to a hotel parking lot, and uses photographic equipment to record the spouse embracing and kissing a lover. In another case, a P.I. sits in a truck with a bogus construction company name on it and tinted windows as she watches an alleged malingerer's house, waiting for the suspect to leave the house and work in his yard. Following three days

FIGURE 10.3   **Surveillance is an investigative strategy. (® Shutterstock.com. With permission.)**

of patient, tedious surveillance, the suspect is observed in his yard digging a hole to plant a tree. The P.I. uses both a video camera and a digital camera to record the physical abilities of the suspect. The evidence serves to avert an expensive workers' compensation claim. In a third example, a corporate investigator follows a corporate engineer to a restaurant to meet a competitor, who receives proprietary documents from the engineer. The meeting is photographed by the investigator, who uses the photographs to build a case against the engineer.

Investigators who conduct surveillance must be extremely patient and diligent while blending into the surroundings and being resourceful. Surveillance can be boring, and this state of boredom can last for many days or until the operation is successful or terminated. Resourcefulness is important, because detection is always a possibility during surveillance. How would you respond to the accusation, "Are you a P.I. watching me?" Previously rehearsed answers (i.e., the cover story) are helpful.

Prior to conducting surveillance, a plan is necessary. What are the objectives? What is the cover story for the investigator? Did investigators carefully study the subject of surveillance? What equipment is needed? How will communications be maintained? What is the budget and timeline?

Equipment applicable to surveillance includes cameras, binoculars, telescopes, night-vision devices, parabolic microphones for hearing from a distance, pinhole-lens cameras to covertly observe and record violations of company policy and law, and cell phones and other communication equipment. A vehicle tracking system enables an investigator to follow a vehicle without losing it. The investigator installs a transmitter on the vehicle to be followed and uses a receiver to pick up signals from the transmitter. Never should an investigator enter private property to install a device.

Surveillance vans are another aid to investigators. These vans can be customized with a variety of features, depending on need and budget allocations. Examples of equipment are multiple cameras to view any direction outside the van, a periscope/camera for observation, recording capabilities for all cameras, night vision and video motion-detection equipment, computers/monitors for video, communications equipment, a small refrigerator, and a toilet. Because a surveillance van may be spotted by an adversary, an alternative, unsuspecting vehicle may have to be employed (Figure 10.4).

In Chapter 4, we covered crime mapping, geographic information systems (GIS), and global positioning systems (GPS). GIS can assist investigators in investigations and in planning surveillance. If, for example, a suspected art thief lives in a particular city, Google Maps can be brought up on a computer and then "museums" and "art galleries" can be entered, followed by the suspect's zip code. Other suspect characteristics can be researched to develop information. Computer-generated crime maps perform similar functions, with locations of interest on a map linked to other information, such as

FIGURE 10.4 Unsuspecting surveillance vehicle. (® Shutterstock.com. With permission.)

locations of art collectors, pawnshops, methadone clinics, or other locations or data that may assist an investigation. As written in Chapter 5, GPS identifies a location on Earth by triangulating a receiver's position using satellites. By attaching a GPS system to people, vehicles, cargo, or just about anything, global tracking can be done worldwide, and it can be done online via the Internet. Chapter 5 also explained retail point-of-sale accounting systems in conjunction with bar codes and radio-frequency identification (RFID) tags. This is another way to track assets and an avenue to investigate theft. RFID tracking applications are broad and include vehicles, employees, visitors, and patients. In addition, items found at a crime scene or in possession of a suspect can possibly be traced back to a source (e.g., store and customer) if a bar code or RFID tag is attached to the item.

GUIDELINES FOR SURVEILLANCE

- Practitioners who conduct surveillance must be carefully selected, trained, and supervised.
- Plan surveillance and include safety as a top priority.
- Include code words and hand signals in safety planning.
- Prior to conducting surveillance, review plans, equipment, and safety precautions.
- Consider necessities such as food, water, and the elimination of waste. It is not unusual for an investigator to include a bucket as part of equipment for stationary surveillance from an unusual location.
- Memorize a cover story for the possibility of being challenged.

- Consider that a target of surveillance may be in a heightened state of vigilance and may plan to deceive the investigator. The tricks of subjects are endless. Examples include quickly boarding or exiting a bus or train at the last moment, or dressing as a member of the opposite sex.
- Surveillance can be enhanced by using multiple investigators and vehicles, especially for moving surveillance. This enables investigators to rotate their positions to prevent detection.
- Consider that an investigator may be exposed and that the subject may follow the investigator without the investigator being aware of it.
- Avoid assuming things; it may by a ruse. If a subject enters a store or restroom, the subject may escape out a rear door or window. Do not assume that a subject will not use the same methods you use. For example, a subject may use store windows as mirrors or pretend to read a newspaper with a small hole cut in it to view covertly.
- Less experienced investigators can learn a lot from more experienced investigators who develop and refine their skills over many years.
- A **prop** generally means to support or sustain, but it also refers to theater property. Because surveillance may require an investigator to blend in with the surroundings, consider the following props: a clipboard and a hard hat, a pizza box, a cardboard sign and a cup, a shopping cart and the look of a street person, or a dog for walking (Figure 10.5).

Critical Thinking

As an offender, what props would you use to disguise yourself while conducting surveillance of a potential target?

Undercover Investigations

An undercover investigation is a secret inquiry initiated to obtain information and evidence that is difficult to obtain from an overt investigation or other investigative methods. An undercover investigator (U.I.) typically takes on a false background and then infiltrates a group and/or befriends individuals to gain their confidence and trust so that information and evidence is shared with the U.I. The public and private sectors apply such investigations globally as an often-successful investigative technique. This technique is not only applied to expose criminal activity, but also to check on customer service (i.e., the investigator plays the role of a customer), as in "secret shopper services" offered to retail and other businesses. Here, an emphasis is placed on private-sector undercover investigations.

FIGURE 10.5   A dog for walking can be used as a prop. (® Shutterstock.com. With permission.)

Although U.I. service firms may offer their undercover operatives under the guise of management consultants, states often prohibit such practices and require all undercover investigators to possess a P.I. license. Consumers of these services should ensure that the service firm is not only bonded, but also insured to the point of naming the client, in writing, as part of the insured party. The client should also have legal representation in the investigation to prevent liability and errors. As examples, the U.I. should not investigate or report on union activities, nor make drug buys without public police approval. In addition, if the private-sector U.I. works with public police on an investigation, this is considered "under color of law" in the legal system, meaning that suspect rights (e.g., Miranda rights) increase because of government involvement.

Once a U.I. gathers sufficient information and evidence, often in a three-month investigation, suspects are interviewed to obtain a confession, recovery of losses and possibly the costs of the investigation. Management in the client firm often decides to fire the employee–thief and avoid criminal prosecution. Attorneys should be involved in decision making.

Undercover work is dangerous, and the U.I. must be prepared for a variety of uncomfortable and risky situations. Because a U.I. is playing a role with a fictitious background, he or she must act in a convincing manner without overdoing the part. The U.I. must be prepared for unexpected questions and accusations of being a P.I., "cop," or spy. Surprise and a statement such as, "They would never hire somebody with my background," could deflect an accusation. Illegal drugs may be offered to the U.I., and a possible response is, "I had an abuse problem." To prevent exposure, the U.I. should avoid using a vocabulary at a level different from coworkers and not ask questions pertaining to criminal conduct, but lead subjects to provide information. In one case, a U.I. strongly disagreed with a coworker who claimed that other coworkers were dishonest. The more the coworker was told that he was "full of it," the harder he worked at supporting his position—by supplying an enormous amount of information on theft and illegal drugs in the workplace.

Safeguarding Undercover Investigators

Krause (2008, 1–8), an FBI expert on safeguarding and improving the success of public police U.I.s, writes that U.I.s experience stressors that set them apart from their overt counterparts and place them at increased risk. Consequently, managers should be proactive in developing policies and procedures to safeguard U.I.s. This in turn will improve the results of undercover investigations and the well-being of U.I.s.

Krause explains critical functions and strategies that are applicable to private-sector U.I.s. Although there are similarities and differences between public- and private-sector U.I.s and investigations, Krause's critical functions and strategies are likely to become more a part of private-sector undercover investigations as they become more professional. These critical functions and strategies are explained next.

1. *Selection*: Management must apply existing research of personal and professional qualities that exemplify the best U.I.s in order to choose the best candidates. This can be aided through psychological tests that assess traits and skills, by in-depth interviews, and by role-playing that exposes skills and competence.
2. *Training*: Topics of training include the qualities and traits of effective U.I.s, the stressors they face, how to manage these stressors, pitfalls of the work, and the skills and abilities for success. U.I.s participate in classroom instruction and role-playing scenarios.
3. *Inoculation*: A proactive approach by the safeguard team emphasizes open and frank discussions of the self-awareness and mental preparation needed for undercover work.
4. *Support and monitoring*: Once a U.I. is trained and certified, the U.I. is referred to the safeguard process at the beginning, midpoint, and

end of every covert operation. This consists of psychological tests and one-on-one interviews at about six-month intervals to assess changes in stress levels and personality.

5. *Debriefing and reintegration*: U.I.s often face adjustment and difficulties upon termination of their undercover roles. Such problems can impair interpersonal relations with family and coworkers. Managers should pay attention to negative feelings, divided loyalty (i.e., identification with offenders), and other expressions from the U.I. Negative feeling should be resolved sensitively and directly prior to subsequent assignments.

6. *Risk management and liability mitigation*: The safeguard process is a commitment to the well-being of U.I.s, and it serves as a risk-management function.

Besides the six critical functions, Krause promotes critical features to support the safeguard process.

1. The safeguard process is based on empirical research.
2. The safeguard team requires access to internal and external sources of training.
3. Confidentiality must be maintained for information gleaned from the safeguard assessments. It should be a legally protected medical record separated from the U.I.'s personnel file and released only with written permission from the employee, except under criminal involvement. Since discovery and disclosure issues are possible in cases, management should use medical-record best practices.
4. The safeguard process addresses specific questions on the fit between the U.I. and the assignment.
5. By utilizing two independent opinions (i.e., psychologist and U.I. counselor), a more objective assessment is facilitated.
6. Decisions are made from multiple sources (e.g., interviews, testing, and role-playing).

DO NOT MAKE THESE MISTAKES

Undercover Investigation

Joey Plyer had been an undercover investigator for two years. He completed a bachelor's degree program in criminal justice and began working for Corbin P.I., Inc., following graduation. His supervisor was demanding and expected five typed reports and two telephone calls each week. On each three- to four-month assignment, Joey felt constant pressure to produce information on workplace theft, illegal drugs, security issues, production problems, and other facts helpful to executives of client companies that retained the services of Corbin P.I., Inc.

Working out of Corbin's Atlanta office, Joey headed to Mobile, Alabama, for his next assignment. As in other assignments, he retained his name but used false background information and references. When Joey reached Alabama, he went to the department of motor vehicles to obtain Alabama license plates to blend in better. His next stop was at Starquest Components, a manufacturer of specialized electronic parts for computers and appliances. The plant manager was the only one at the plant aware of Joey's status as an undercover investigator. Executives at Starquest corporate headquarters suspected internal theft and illegal drug usage at the plant. When Joey arrived at the plant, he completed an employment application, was interviewed, and was offered a position in shipping and receiving. The next day, he began work, and that night he e-mailed his first report to his supervisor. As in earlier assignments, initial reports provided basic information about the plant and its operations and employees, as well as security, safety, and production issues. Within one week, coworkers asked Joey to join them for bowling on Friday night. Joey joined the group, and a party at a coworker's house followed the bowling. Because Joey was affable, he was able to make numerous contacts in the workplace and with people in the community. After work each day, and on the weekends, he was usually involved in activities with coworkers, and he even had a girlfriend he had met at the plant.

Although Joey was successful at infiltrating the informal employee organization and keeping his undercover status a secret, his investigative supervisor was angry at Joey for not reporting any theft, illegal drug usage, production problems, or any other information helpful to the client. Joey's response was that he simply had neither suspects nor evidence of wrongdoing. His supervisor continued to pressure him for something substantial in his reports because the client was hinting at terminating the undercover investigation; this would result in Joey returning to Atlanta for another assignment.

Finally, Joey reported that he observed an employee in the shipping and receiving department place a box of electrical components near the dumpster close to the shipping-and-receiving dock, retrieve the box at the end of the day, place it in his (the suspect's) vehicle, and leave the premises. Joey was ordered to collect additional information on the suspect and carefully follow him after work to try to find out if the components were being sold. He was also ordered to research any companies in the area that could use such components and check the Web for sales of the stolen components.

Unfortunately for Joey, his supervisor, Corbin P.I., Inc., and the client, when the plant manager learned of the theft, she checked the work schedule of the suspect employee and discovered that the employee had the day off when he was alleged to have stolen the components. After Joey's investigative supervisor was informed of the discrepancy, Joey was questioned and admitted to his supervisor that he had fabricated the theft incident because of the pressure to produce results and because he was enjoying the assignment and his friends. The client terminated the investigation and refused to pay the balance of the bill for investigative services. Joey was terminated upon returning to Atlanta.

Lessons: Private- and public-sector investigators are often under pressure to produce results and solve cases. The pressure may be so intense that some investigators may violate ethical standards and laws. They may fabricate information, wrongly accuse individuals, and commit perjury. Such behavior must not be tolerated, and it can result in an investigator being prosecuted and sued. In addition, the organization, and the supervisors of such an investigator, suffer a variety of negative consequences.

A combination of pressure from his supervisor and Joey becoming too close to those around him probably led Joey to fabricate information. Supervisors are challenged by applying pressure on subordinates to produce results without applying excessive pressure that results in exaggerations and fabrications.

Obviously, the longer a contract undercover investigation lasts, the greater the income for the investigative firm. Supervisors must resist the temptation to exaggerate and fabricate as they receive reports from investigators and prepare reports for clients.

Critical Thinking

What methods can be used to prevent exaggerations, fabrications, and perjury by private and public investigators?

If you were Joey, would you return to Mobile, Alabama, to visit or live? If so, what would you tell your friends and your girlfriend in Mobile?

Report Writing

Report writing reflects directly on the writer. Security practitioners (and police officers) are often promoted to an investigative position because of excellent report-writing abilities. A variety of people may read a security investigator's (or security officer's) report. These include an immediate supervisor, a security executive, clients, victims, insurers, police, prosecutors and other attorneys, and expert witnesses.

The foundation of a report is often on-the-scene rough notes pertaining to the six basic investigative questions. Following an incident, when time permits, an officer will use the rough notes to prepare a formal report of the incident. Organizations typically have a standard form (i.e., incident report) for report writing, and the officer fills in the required information. Such a form often contains several lines for a narrative, which is a chronological description of the incident by printing or typing sentences. Two aids to the narrative are an outline and a dictionary (book or computer). The outline provides the order of topics to be covered in the narrative. A report and narrative should be neat; complete; concise; characterized by good grammar, sentence structure, and spelling; devoid of opinions; objective; factual; accurate; proofed by the writer; secured; and turned in on time. These are characteristics of superior reports. In addition to the incident report, there are several other types of reports employed in security work, depending on organizational needs. Examples are daily reports of activities, accident reports, visitor logs, summaries of reports, and reports on security surveys.

Testifying

The criminal and civil justice systems seem to move at "glacial speed." A security practitioner may be subpoenaed to testify at a deposition or trial long after an incident occurred and was investigated. A deposition is testimony provided by a witness so that each side of a case can evaluate the evidence within the testimony prior to trial. Depositions typically occur in an attorney's office while the deponent is under oath, and the testimony is recorded. Since memory wanes as time passes, practitioners typically rely on notes and reports completed earlier, around the time of the incident in question, to refresh their memory prior to and during testimony. Under rules of discovery, notes and reports must be shared with both sides in criminal and civil cases, and they are likely to become part of the evidence in the case.

Preparation is an important prerequisite to testifying. This includes studying the case file to refresh memory, ensuring that evidence is available to support testimony, reviewing possible questions that may be asked, and meeting with the attorney on your side of the case. Prior to testifying, a witness takes an oath (with his or her hand on a bible) to be truthful or affirms that he or she will testify truthfully. Lying under oath while providing testimony is referred to as the crime of **perjury**. During a trial, as an investigator or security officer, an attorney on your side or the other side of the case will call you to the witness stand to be examined (i.e., questioned).

Here are some guidelines helpful for presenting testimony:

- Study the testimony and courtroom behavior of experienced investigators.
- Present a neat, conservative appearance. Avoid flashy clothes, jewelry, or sunglasses.
- Keep your body still and your hands away from your face when testifying.
- Calm yourself by taking deep breaths without being obvious.
- Tell the truth.
- Think carefully prior to answering questions.
- If you are unclear on a question, politely request that it be repeated.

- Answer only the questions asked. Avoid elaborating beyond what each question asks.
- Never guess. If you do not know an answer, say so.
- Time and distance answers should be preceded by the word *approximately.*
- Avoid anger and do not argue.

When undergoing cross-examination, a variety of techniques may be used by an opposing attorney. Here is a sample of techniques with countermeasures.

- Applying a variety of techniques to get you to lose your temper. Examples are shouting at you and acting hostile toward every answer. Remain calm and answer one question at a time. Let the jury develop a dislike for the attorney's obnoxious behavior.
- Asking a compound question (i.e., two questions in one long sentence). Avoid answering. Request one question at a time.
- Making a suggestion through a question to trick you into agreeing to the suggestion. Adhere to facts and avoid being manipulated.
- Firing rapid questions to prevent you from thinking before answering. Break the rhythm of this technique by pausing and thinking before answering each question and asking for questions to be repeated.
- Repeating your answers, but incorrectly, to confuse you. Provide the correct information.
- Trying to engage you in conversation. Avoid conversations with opposing attorneys prior to, during, and following court proceedings. In addition, do not fall for the ploy of "Let's talk off the record." No conversations are "off the record."

Technology

Technology is a great aid to investigations. Earlier in this chapter, you learned of several tools helpful to surveillance—from night-vision devices to GIS and GPS. You also learned about the wealth of information available through the Internet. Here, we expand on technology for investigations. Because of the enormous amount of data available to investigators in this age of computers, efficient methods and software are necessary to detect patterns among individuals and their activities and assets. **Link analysis** helps to make visual sense out of data; it is the process of charting chronological and other data to uncover and help interpret relationships and patterns in the data (Swanson 2009, 226, 743). **Neural net technology**, also referred to as *nonlinear statistical data modeling*, is used to detect fraud before significant fraud can occur. It can track the spending behavior of credit card users and expose unusual patterns. For example, if a customer uses a credit card to purchase only food and gasoline and then purchases of building products suddenly appear in the data, this change would be red-flagged for further investigation (Gordon and McBride 2008, 160).

As covered in Chapter 9, public- and private-sector investigators often encounter electronic crime scenes containing digital evidence. In addition, suspects and arrestees typically have electronic devices (e.g., cellular phone and PDA) containing digital evidence on their person, and investigators should be trained and equipped to secure such evidence when legally appropriate.

So-called lie-detector and polygraph technology, described in the accompanying example, are additional tools applied by public and private sector investigators. These devices are subject to controversy and must be applied legally and with caution because of potential liabilities. The accuracy of these devices is a major issue. The University of Utah reported that the polygraph could be over 90 percent accurate (U.S. Department of Justice 1978, 8); however, it is often stated that its accuracy depends on the training, experience, and competence of the polygraph examiner. Public police use voice stress analysis (VSA), also called psychological stress evaluation (PSE), as another type of "lie detector." Damphousse (2008, 9) wrote: "VSA software programs are designed to measure changes in voice patterns caused by the stress, or the physical effort, of trying to hide deceptive responses." These software programs interpret changes in vocal patterns and purportedly show deception or truth on a graph. However, the National Institute of Justice (2008) funded research on two of the most popular VSA programs in use by police agencies in the United States; the results of their study concluded that the devices are "no better than flipping a coin." On the other hand, the study also noted that the mere presence of the device might deter an interviewee from giving a false answer (Damphousse 2008, 8).

EMPLOYEE POLYGRAPH PROTECTION ACT OF 1988

The following information is from the U.S. Department of Labor (2008b) and the U.S. Chamber of Commerce (2008). The Department of Labor administers and enforces the **Employee Polygraph Protection Act of 1988** (EPPA) through the Wage and Hour Division of the Employment Standards Administration. The 1988 Act generally prevents employers engaged in interstate commerce from using lie detector tests either for pre-employment screening or during the course of employment, with certain exemptions. Since the act became effective, polygraph testing of job applicants has been virtually eliminated by private employers. Behavioral or psychological testing has become more popular.

The act became effective on December 27, 1988. Under the act, the Secretary of Labor is directed to distribute a notice of the act's protections, issue rules and regulations, and enforce the provisions of the act. The act empowers the Secretary of Labor to bring injunctive actions in U.S.

district courts to restrain violators and to assess civil money penalties up to $10,000 against employers who violate any provision of the act. Employers are required to post notices summarizing the protections of the act in their places of work.

Definitions

- A **lie detector** includes a polygraph, deceptograph, voice stress analyzer, psychological stress evaluator, or similar device (whether mechanical or electrical) used to render a diagnostic opinion as to the honesty or dishonesty of an individual.
- A **polygraph** means an instrument that records continuously, visually, permanently, and simultaneously changes in cardiovascular, respiratory, and electrodermal patterns as minimum instrumentation standards and is used to render a diagnostic opinion as to the honesty or dishonesty of an individual.

Prohibitions

An employer shall not:

- Require, request, suggest, or cause an employee or prospective employee to take or submit to any lie detector test.
- Use, accept, refer to, or inquire about the results of any lie detector test of an employee or prospective employee.
- Discharge, discipline, discriminate against, deny employment or promotion, or threaten to take any such action against an employee or prospective employee for refusal to take a test, based on the results of a test, for filing a complaint, for testifying in any proceeding, or for exercising any right afforded by the act.

Exemptions

Federal, state, and local governments are excluded. In addition, lie detector tests administered by the federal government to employees of federal contractors engaged in national security intelligence or counterintelligence functions are exempt. The act also includes limited exemptions where polygraph tests (but no other lie detector tests) may be administered in the private sector, subject to certain restrictions:

- To employees who are reasonably suspected of involvement in a workplace incident that results in economic loss to the employer and who had access to the property that is the subject of an investigation
- To prospective employees of armored car, security alarm, and security guard firms who protect facilities, materials, or operations affecting health or safety, national security, or currency and other like instruments

- To prospective employees of pharmaceutical and other firms authorized to manufacture, distribute, or dispense controlled substances who will have direct access to such controlled substances, as well as current employees who had access to persons or property that are the subject of an ongoing investigation

Qualification of Examiners

An examiner is required to have a valid and current license if required by a state in which the test is to be conducted, and must maintain a minimum of $50,000 bond or professional liability coverage.

Employee/Prospective Employee Rights

An employee or prospective employee must be given a written notice explaining the employee's or prospective employee's rights and the limitations imposed, such as prohibited areas of questioning and restriction on the use of test results. Among other rights, an employee or prospective employee may refuse to take a test, terminate a test at any time, or decline to take a test if he/she suffers from a medical condition. The results of a test alone cannot be disclosed to anyone other than the employer or employee/prospective employee without their consent or, pursuant to court order, to a court, government agency, arbitrator, or mediator.

Under the exemption for ongoing investigations of workplace incidents involving economic loss, a written or verbal statement must be provided to the employee prior to the polygraph test that explains the specific incident or activity being investigated and the basis for the employer's reasonable suspicion that the employee was involved in such incident or activity.

Where polygraph examinations are permitted under the act, they are subject to strict standards concerning the conduct of the test, including the pre-test, testing, and post-test phases of the examination. Under federal law and under some state laws, a copy of the notice informing job applicants of the polygraph testing prohibitions, exemptions, and the rights provided to test takers under the law must be posted in the workplace. Notices should be posted in a conspicuous location in the workplace where job applicants will have access to the notice.

Civil actions may be brought by an employee or prospective employee in federal or state court against employers who violate the act for legal or equitable relief, such as employment reinstatement, promotion, and payment of lost wages and benefits. The action must be brought within 3 years of the date of the alleged violation. Some states place additional restrictions on how lie detector tests can be administered and what can be asked.

Administering the Test

If you administer lie detector tests to applicants and employees, the 1988 Act requires that the following documentation be retained for three years from the date a polygraph exam is conducted or requested:

- A copy of the statement that sets forth the specific incident or activity
- Records specifically identifying the loss or injury in question and the nature of the employee's access to the person or property that was the subject of the investigation and was the basis for testing that particular employee
- The questions asked during the test
- All opinion lists and other records relating to polygraph tests of such persons and any charges stemming from them

---

GLOBAL PERSPECTIVE: TRANSNATIONAL INTERNAL INVESTIGATIONS

Hillis (2009), an attorney, writes of the legal pitfalls of transnational internal investigations, as described in the following paragraphs. Major issues are the legal guidelines for a public company headquartered in the United States investigating a citizen of another country working at an overseas operation.

In one case, a U.S.-based corporation asked a U.S.-based investigative company to conduct a polygraph examination of an employee, a citizen of another country, working at a corporate overseas facility, to verify a fraud accusation. Although the corporation knew of no prohibition of administering a polygraph examination in the country containing the overseas facility, the corporation was concerned about the U.S. Employee Polygraph Protection Act of 1988 (EPPA) and its applicability to overseas business operations. Hillis (2009) writes:

> The EPPA covers not only operations of all companies—foreign and domestic—within the United States, its provisions also "extend to any actions relating to the administration of lie detector ... tests which occur within the territorial jurisdiction of the United States, e.g., the preparation of paperwork by a foreign corporation in a Miami office relating to a polygraph test that is to be administered on the high seas or in some foreign location." Based on this language, it seems that the U.S. planning of the polygraph in Singapore may have been enough to trigger EPPA coverage.

In another example, although hypothetical, Hillis describes a U.S. parent company of a European subsidiary receiving an anonymous tip that embezzlement is occurring at a facility in Europe and that evidence can be located on the suspect's corporate e-mail account. The Sarbanes-Oxley Act of 2002 requires that the parent company investigate the allegations. This can be accomplished by reading the suspect's e-mail. The parent company and the subsidiary share the same e-mail system on the same server, based in the United States. The e-mail will be read in the United States, where U.S. courts have decided that employees generally have no expectation of privacy when using an employer's e-mail system. However, European laws may provide greater privacy, which can prohibit the viewing of the e-mail. Depending on the jurisdiction, employers may be restricted from viewing personal communications. European Union privacy directives should also be researched to establish how the directives are applied by governments and interpreted by courts.

Forensic Science

Forensic science applies scientific methods to the examination, evaluation, and explanation of evidence within a legal framework. The fundamentals of forensic science are from the scientific method. Investigators often apply the scientific method, unconsciously or haphazardly, rather than intentionally and systematically, to reconstruct the past within an investigation, as described next (Becker 2009, 1–4).

- An investigator describes the *problem* by identifying what crime may have been committed.
- A *hypothesis* (i.e., tentative thoughts about solutions to the alleged crime) is formulated based on information and evidence.
- *Data collection* involves the gathering of records, evidence, and corroborative or uncorroborative information.
- The hypothesis is *tested* by repeatedly reviewing all facts and evidence, whether consistent or inconsistent with the hypothesis. Interview suspects.
- Continue to collect data, information, and evidence.
- As the investigation focuses on a particular suspect, gather additional corroborative information.
- Arrive at a *conclusion* and *theory*. When probable cause has been attained, private security would interview to obtain a written confession and/or contact public police.

Forensic science grew through the work of many individuals. In 1879, **Alphonse Bertillon**, a French clerk, while searching for a way to identify unique features of criminals, decided that no two individuals had the same physical characteristics, and that if enough measurements of individuals could be taken, individual identification could be established. Bertillon's method became known as *anthropometry* or *Bertillonage*, and it was widely adopted in the United States. Unfortunately, the method was short-lived because it lacked the capability of positive identification.

A new system was needed. Henry Faulds, a physician working in Japan, observed pottery and documents being identified through handprints and fingerprints. By 1892, **Sir Francis Galton** published *Finger Prints*, which explained a system of classifying fingerprints. The method was adopted globally (Becker 2009, 25). A third method of identification developed during the last part of the 20th century was DNA matching. Deoxyribonucleic acid (DNA) is contained in all human cells; it is the foundation of life; and its configuration is determined by heredity. Becker (2009, 26) writes:

> Based on the work of **Alec Jeffreys** at the University of Leicester, a method was developed to extract DNA from a specimen of blood, semen, or other tissue, slice it into fragments, and tag the fragments with a radioactive probe so that they would expose X-ray film. The resulting pattern of stripes on the film is as distinctive as a fingerprint, and Jeffreys and his colleagues named the process of isolating and reading DNA markers *DNA fingerprinting.*

DNA fingerprinting has been an immense aid to investigations, including "cold cases" from earlier years when this method was unavailable but the evidence was saved and is available for testing. Offenders can leave DNA at a crime scene in so many ways, such as through sweat (i.e., touching something), saliva, blood, and semen. In addition, a victim can leave DNA on an offender before he or she departs, which can tie the offender to the crime scene.

FORENSIC SCIENCE AND PRIVATE SECURITY

What is the significance of forensic science for private security investigators? Although investigations in the private sector (and public sector) often rely on interviewing and confessions to solve cases, the technology of our modern age requires more sophisticated methods of confronting crime. For example, digital forensic analysis is a growing specialization for gathering, analyzing, and presenting digital evidence from a host of devices (e.g., cell phones, MP3 devices, digital cameras, and computers).

In the future, private security personnel are likely to become more involved in fingerprint and DNA evidence, and the processing of other evidence at crime scenes, in conjunction with public police. Limited public police resources may facilitate this trend. The CSI effect (described in an accompanying box) may also affect this trend if jurors expect forensic evidence in more and more cases. In addition, if courts rule that private security personnel must advise suspects of Miranda-type rights prior to questioning, and more suspects remain silent, then forensic science will increase in importance, as it has with public police.

Critical Thinking

What are your views of the role of forensic science as an aid to private-sector investigations?

CSI EFFECT

CSI are the initials for *crime scene investigation*. The **CSI effect** means that jurors who watch television programs like *CSI* are influenced by these programs and wrongfully acquit guilty defendants when prosecutors present no scientific evidence. Television programs containing crime stories involving scientific evidence are blamed for the CSI effect, and prosecutors argue that such programs influence jurors into thinking that scientific evidence (e.g., DNA test) is needed for every case. This issue has resulted in varied opinions.

Although Shelton et al. (2008) believe that a "tech effect" exists that influences juror expectations and demands, their research did not support a CSI effect. The researchers surveyed 1,000 jurors prior to their participation in trial processes. Questions focused on television viewing habits, expectations for scientific evidence for specific types of crimes, and guilty or not-guilty decisions for 13 scenarios. The research results showed that 46 percent of respondents expected to see some type of scientific evidence in every criminal case. *CSI* viewers had higher expectations for scientific evidence than non-*CSI* viewers did. However, these expectations had little effect on decisions to convict. (Further research is warranted.)

Critical Thinking

What are your views on the CSI Effect?

Summary

An investigation seeks to gather facts. There are several types of investigations, and each type requires adherence to specific guidelines and law to improve the chances of success. This chapter emphasized fraud, internal theft, shoplifting, and robbery investigations. Although we can compare and contrast different types of investigations, several techniques can be applied across the various types. As covered in this chapter, these include interviewing, protecting the crime scene, developing sources of information, surveillance, undercover investigations, report writing, and testifying.

Technology has been an immense aid to public- and private-sector investigators who apply many tools, such as assorted camera equipment, GIS, GPS, and investigative software. Forensic science is another aid that has helped public police for many years. The private sector will increasingly turn to forensic science as investigations and the legal environment become more complex.

Discussion Questions

1. Which type of specialized investigation would you prefer to conduct as a vocation and why?
2. What do you view as an appropriate background (e.g., education, experience, training, and certification) for the specialization selected in the previous question?
3. Which type of confrontation with a suspect is more difficult and dangerous, internal theft or shoplifting? Why?
4. What do you view as the top eight prioritized guidelines of caution you would observe as a private-sector investigator to protect yourself and others from physical harm and to prevent a lawsuit resulting from your investigations?
5. What do you view as the top five prioritized guidelines for conducting interviews in private-sector investigations?
6. Under what circumstances are private-sector undercover investigations appropriate?
7. Should the use of the polygraph and other "lie detector" devices be expanded? Why or why not?

Practical Applications

10A. As an in-house investigator for a manufacturing company, you receive a report from a department manager that a production worker is stealing items off the production line. What do you do? Prepare a prioritized list of ten steps you will follow.
10B. As a female loss-prevention investigator for a retail store, you make a shoplifting apprehension, and the suspect willingly accompanies you to your office. The suspect refuses to show ID, answer questions, or give up store merchandise you observed her conceal in her chest area. What do you do?
10C. As a P.I. conducting surveillance of an alleged malingerer in a case of workers' compensation fraud, you are sitting in your pickup truck on a residential street about 100 yards from the backyard of the suspect. Your pickup truck has tinted windows and the name

of a bogus construction company on its side. While you are conducting surveillance, you are surprised at your window by the suspect, who cannot see you but knocks at the window. What do you do?

10D. As an investigator for a global corporation based in the United States, you are assigned to travel to Brazil to investigate alleged fraud and internal theft at a corporate plant. How do you conduct this investigation? What legal challenges do you face? What resources do you rely on? What helpful resources do you locate online?

10E. You are a manager of investigations for a security company, and you learn that one of your investigators is claiming to be a government official while on the telephone seeking information. What do you do? Do you permit this technique to continue? Why or why not?

10F. As a loss-prevention investigator at a retail store, one of your male coworkers brags to you about a pretty and shapely shoplifting suspect who cried and begged to be released without being reported to police. He stated that when the suspect stated that she would do anything to be released, he pointed to his crotch. Then, he stated that she complied with his suggestion, that he released her without documenting the case or calling police, and that he sees her occasionally. What do you do?

10G. Prior to graduating from college, one career path on your mind is private investigations. Research the requirements in your state to become a P.I. If there are experience requirements, how would you gain experience?

Internet Connections

American Institute of Certified Public Accounts: www.aicpa.org

ASIS International: www.asisonline.org

ASIS International, Professional Certified Investigator: www.asisonline.org/certification/pci/pciabout.xml

Association of Certified Fraud Examiners: www.cfenet.com

Council of International Investigators: www.cii2.org/news/news002.shtml

International Association of Computer Investigative Specialists: www.iacis.info/iacisv2/pages/home.php

International Private Investigators Union: www.ipiu.org/

International Society of Forensic Computer Examiners: www.isfce.com/

National Association of Legal Investigators: www.nalionline.org/

Overseas Security Advisory Council (OSAC): www.osac.gov/

The Institute of Internal Auditors: www.theiia.org

United States Department of State: www.state.gov/

United States Professional Investigators Network: www.thepigroup.com/

World Association of Professional Investigators: www.wapi.com/

References

ASIS International. 2005. Career opportunities in security. Alexandria, VA: ASIS International.

ASIS International. 2008. Letters to the editor: Pretexting debate. *Security Management* 52 (September):20.

Association of Certified Fraud Examiners. 2008. Report to the nation on occupational fraud & abuse. www.acfe.com/documents/2009-rttn.pdf.

Association of Certified Fraud Examiners et al. 2008. Managing the business risk of fraud: A practical guide. www.acfe.org.

Becker, R. 2009. *Criminal investigation.* 3rd ed. Boston: Jones and Bartlett.

Brandes, A. 2007. The most powerful weapon? Asking a good question. *Homeland Defense Journal* 5 (December):10.

Damphousse, K. 2008. Voice stress analysis: Only 15 percent of lies about drug use detected in field test. *National Institute of Justice Journal* 259. Washington, D.C.: U.S. Department of Justice.

Ferraro, E. 2008. Letters to the editor: Pretexting debate. *Security Management* 52 (September):18–20.

Ferraro, E., and B. Mathers, B. 2007. Workplace investigations. In *Encyclopedia of Security Management,* ed. J. Fay. Burlington, MA: Elsevier.

Finder, J. 2007. The CEO's private investigation. *Harvard Business Review* 85 (October):47–52.

Gordon, G., and R. McBride. 2008. *Criminal justice internships: Theory into practice.* 6th ed. Newark, NJ: Matthew Bender & Co.

Hall, D. 2009. *Criminal Law and Procedure.* 5th ed. Clifton Park, NY: Delmar.

Hillis, M. 2009. Potential legal pitfalls of transnational internal investigations. *Global Fraud Report* 2009 (January):14. www.kroll.com.

Inbau, F., et al. 1996. *Protective Security Law.* 2nd ed. Boston: Butterworth–Heinemann.

Krause, M. 2008. Safeguarding undercover employees: A strategy for success. *FBI Law Enforcement Bulletin* 77 (August):1–8.

McRae, G. 2008. Insights on investigations. *Security Management* 52 (December):134.

National Institute of Justice. 2008. Voice stress analysis not effective in field test. *National Institute of Justice Journal* 259. Washington, D.C.: U.S. Department of Justice.

Nemeth, C. 2005. *Private security and the law.* 3rd ed. Burlington, MA: Elsevier Butterworth–Heinemann.

Schubert, F. 2008. *Introduction to law and the legal system.* 9th ed. Boston: Houghton Mifflin.

Shelton, D., et al. 2008. The CSI effect: Does it really exist? *National Institute of Justice Journal,* 259. Washington, D.C.: U.S. Department of Justice.

Swanson, C., et al. 2009. *Criminal investigation.* 10th ed. Boston: McGraw-Hill.

U.S. Chamber of Commerce. 2008. Lie detector tests. https://business.uschamber.com/PO5_1035. www.uschambersmallbusinessnation.com/toolkits/guide/.

U.S. Department of Justice. 1978. Validity and reliability of detection of deception. Washington, D.C.: U.S. Government Printing Office.

U.S. Department of Labor. 2008a. Occupational outlook handbook 2008–2009. www.bls.gov.

U.S. Department of Labor. 2008b. Fact sheet no. 36: Employee Polygraph Protection Act of 1988. www.wagehour.dol.gov.

Section III

Risk and All-Hazards Protection

Chapter 11

Enterprise Risk Management and Resilience

Chapter Learning Objectives

After reading this chapter, you should be able to:

1. Define risk management and explain its value
2. Compare and contrast risk management in the private and public sectors
3. Define enterprise risk management and explain its value
4. Define enterprise security risk management and explain its value
5. Describe the characteristics of and precautions for three natural disasters
6. Describe the characteristics of and precautions for three human-made events/disasters
7. Differentiate business continuity and enterprise resilience
8. Describe emergency management, life safety, and fire protection

Terms To Know

risk management
risk
mitigation
resilience

loss prevention

deductibles

SWOT analysis

U.S. Government Accountability Office

risk communication theory

Chief Risk Officer

enterprise

enterprise risk management

enterprise security risk management

natural disaster

Richter Magnitude Scale

Saffir-Simpson Hurricane Wind Scale

pandemic

human-made event/hazard

workers' compensation laws

Occupational Safety and Health Administration Act of 1970

HAZMAT

Local Emergency Planning Committee

Superfund Amendments and Reauthorization Act of 1986

Emergency Planning and Community Right-To-Know Act of 1986

OSHA Hazard Communication Standard

safe area bombing

suicide bomber

business continuity

NFPA 1600 Standard on Disaster/Emergency Management and Business-Continuity Programs

Implementing Recommendations of the 9/11 Commission Act of 2007

enterprise resilience

availability-related risks

operational risks

ASIS SPC. 1-2009

emergency management

interoperability

life safety

true first responders

NFPA 101 Life Safety Code

shelter-in-place

fire prevention

fire suppression

standpipe

QUIZ

This quiz serves to prime the reader's mind and begin the reading, thinking, and studying processes for this chapter. The answers to all of the questions are found within this chapter.

1. What is risk management?
2. What hurricane was the most expensive in U.S. history?
3. What is OSHA and what is its function?
4. What is HAZMAT?
5. What is NFPA and what is its function?
6. What is enterprise resilience?
7. About how many fires occur in the United States each year?
8. What are two classes of fire that should not be extinguished with water?
9. What is a standpipe?

Introduction

Security is linked to the profession, methodologies, and strategies of risk management. A security practitioner's understanding of risk management provides insight into how risk is addressed by senior executives in business and government and how their decisions affect security duties, functions, planning, and budgets in both sectors. At the same time, risk management methodologies can be applied by security practitioners to help them think as a businessperson while planning and implementing security strategies. This chapter explains that, whereas risk management advanced strategic thinking in insurance planning, enterprise risk management takes risk management to the next level of strategic thinking. The latter sections of this chapter describe natural disasters and human-made events/hazards and the methods applied to manage and mitigate these risks.

Risk Management

Risk management (RM) is an important, practical management tool applied in both the private and public sectors to mitigate losses from harmful events (e.g., embezzlement, fire, and terrorism). It entails the planning and implementation of RM strategies prior to harmful events occurring in order to promote resilience. **Risk** is exposure to harmful events, and it includes measuring the probability, frequency, and severity of such events. **Mitigation** refers to reducing the severity of harmful events. **Resilience** is characterized by adaptability and survivability when facing harmful events, so that previously planned organizational goals can be attained.

Risk Management in the Private Sector

Here we begin an explanation of RM from private-sector (i.e., business) perspectives, followed by public-sector (i.e., government) perspectives. Leimberg et al. (2002, 1–2) write that RM is "a preloss exercise that reflects an organization's postloss goals ... comprised of five distinct steps" (somewhat similar to a risk analysis).

Step 1: Identify the risks facing the organization.
Step 2: Quantify and analyze risks relative to the impact on the organization. Explain risks, losses, and strategies in financial terms.
Step 3: Evaluate RM strategies.
Step 4: Implement RM strategies.
Step 5: Monitor RM strategies and make adjustments as needed.

Leimberg et al. (2002, 2) note that "the degree to which risk is mitigated must be defined by the goals of the organization." They offer the following illustrations: Company A favors minimum RM controls. Its postcatastrophic-loss goal is to remain in business without regard for the number of lost customers or employees laid off, as long as the company survives and avoids bankruptcy. In contrast, Company B seeks to retain all customers and employees and plans for minimum downtime following a harmful event. Because of its postloss goals, Company B will incur greater preloss RM costs than Company A will. In either case, senior executives justify and show the value of their RM plans, plus the impact on profits. These illustrations show us how companies differ on how they perceive and manage risks.

Leimberg et al. (2002, 1) trace the growth and development of RM to the early 1960s. Prior to this period, insurance was the dominant and narrow strategy of handling risk. It was purchased by a hodgepodge of managers (e.g., treasurer, purchasing manager, and safety manager) within organizations. Outside insurance brokers have a long history of meeting the insurance needs of businesses, especially when no insurance specialist is employed by an entity. Today, brokers are still active in assisting customers.

If an organization is large and it can afford to hire a risk manager, their duties focus primarily on somewhat of a balancing act. By applying their expertise, methodologies, and strategies, they seek to manage risk by purchasing enough insurance and implementing adequate RM strategies to place the entity in a favorable position in case of loss, while not overspending and wasting funds on excessive insurance coverage and excessive RM strategies. Risk managers are "designated worriers" who plan insurance needs and interact with insurance company representatives for the best possible coverage for the lowest cost. They also review insurance policies with attorneys to ensure that insurance coverage is clearly understood. The risk manager's tool chest includes the use of loss prevention strategies and deductibles. **Loss prevention** is a broad concept of many types of strategies that prevent and control loss from harmful events. It can be applied as an investment with a return by, for instance, reducing insurance premiums. Examples are installing sprinklers in a building to reduce loss from a fire, and requiring security officers to patrol a facility to observe and quickly report harmful events so that they can be mitigated immediately. **Deductibles** refer to an insured party paying for low-cost losses up to a specified amount, at which point the insurer pays for the more costly losses up to a specified ceiling.

Among the knowledge and skill sets of a risk manager is the need to be attuned to legal requirements. For instance, insurance coverage of a business may be required by law, as with workers' compensation and vehicle liability insurance. The Sarbanes-Oxley Act of 2002 is another consideration that requires public corporations to manage risks effectively or face sanctions. In addition, risk managers must ensure that their employers are protected from a host of liability risks and litigation.

Critical Thinking

Do you think risk management is similar to gambling? Why or why not?

Callahan (2008, 16–28) presents a common challenge for risk managers and business-continuity professionals: securing funds from senior executives for RM strategies. He argues that many people think of risk as a "bad" topic; however, it should be perceived in a positive light. As a foundation for Callahan's argument, he explains that risks must first be *identified* and *prioritized* prior to planning and applying RM strategies such as the following:

- *Avoid*: Eliminate the risk through planning or discontinue the process.
- *Substitute*: Choose a less risky alternative to do the same function.
- *Transfer*: Let someone else handle liability for the risk (e.g., through insurance).
- *Reduce*: Implement strategies (e.g., fire prevention and fire suppression) to prevent loss.
- *Accept*: Plan to accept the risk, but be aware of consequences.

Callahan sees not only the harm that can result from risks, but also the opportunities that can be exploited and lead to improved outcomes for businesses. In other words, rather than risk managers, business-continuity professionals, or security professionals sounding like scaremongers, they should promote RM as adding business value that is explained in financial terms. This positive perspective is a key factor that can enhance the chances of receiving funding for RM initiatives.

In operating a company, senior executives must decide on acceptable levels of strategic risk to incur for the company to make a profit from a product or service offered for sale. Some business ventures flop, while others may yield a profit. Just as senior executives must decide what to do about risks that can result in harm, they also make decisions on opportunities from strategic risks. The decision-making process includes the following (Callahan 2008, 18):

- *Pursue*: High-return opportunities can result in greater shareholder value.
- *Partner*: If necessary, seek outside expertise and resources to enhance opportunities.
- *Develop*: Leverage internal expertise and resources to enhance opportunities.
- *Disregard*: Take no action because the opportunity is unlikely to result in benefits.

Callahan sees threats and opportunities facing organizations and the need to use business strategy tools (i.e., methodologies) to evaluate both. As an example, he refers to **SWOT analysis** (i.e., strengths, weaknesses, opportunities, and threats) to evaluate internal and external organizational factors to minimize weaknesses and threats while maximizing strengths and opportunities. He recommends that those in the protection profession apply the same methodologies employed by senior executives. Callahan provides an example through pandemic (i.e., spread of a disease) planning and the need to prevent workforce disruption (e.g., employees unable to go to the traditional work site) by increasing computer network connectivity choices (e.g., wireless). If a risk manager, business-continuity professional, or security professional proposes the need for increased connectivity because of the threat of a pandemic, this traditional approach does not present as much influence as a proposal that argues much more, such as business value, including opportunities for connectivity for employees from hotels, airports, and other locations. The words "reduced downtime," "increased employee productivity," and "closer customer contact" are more pleasing to senior executives than "we need increased network connectivity because of the threat of a pandemic."

ISSUE

Are Certain Types of Risk Managers More Important than Others?

Coffin (2009) differentiates two different groups who use the term *risk management*. He calls one group "operational risk managers." They manage the insurance needs of entities as well as prevention and response to a variety of harmful events such as crimes, accidents, fires, and environmental contamination. The other group is referred to as "financial risk managers," who focus on credit and currency risk, financial portfolio risk, market risk, and other related risks. Coffin argues that these two major types of specialists call themselves risk managers, but they do not communicate well, are in competition with each other, and the financial risk managers appear to have the upper hand for access to senior executives and resources. Issues such as turbulence in the financial markets play a role in fostering the increased influence of financial risk managers. Coffin writes that RM with two different voices is harmful to a business and that unification is needed through an enterprise-wide RM approach that considers all risks.

Critical Thinking

Do you think there are advantages or disadvantages of having two types of risk managers in a business? Explain your answer.

Risk Management in the Public Sector

Increasingly, all levels of government are employing RM methodologies and strategies for more efficient operations and to prevent and control losses. The range of RM initiatives in government is broad, with similarities to the private sector. Examples are requiring safety-belt usage for all employees using government vehicles, requiring safety training and equipment (e.g., hardhats) at hazardous sites, and promoting programs to eliminate tobacco usage.

The **U.S. Government Accountability Office (GAO)** is a federal government entity directed by Congress to evaluate government programs and expenditures. It views RM as an important component of government planning, and Congress agrees with this view. The GAO conducts studies, audits, and undercover investigative operations. It issues legal opinions and makes recommendations. GAO specialists report to Congress and testify at hearings on a broad array of issues, leading to new initiatives and laws and more efficient and effective government. GAO reports and testimony are available on-line at no cost.

As an example of GAO's facilitation of RM in government, it published "Risk Management: Strengthening the Use of Risk Management Principles in Homeland Security" (U.S. Government Accountability Office 2008). The following information is from this report. On page one, the GAO defines risk management as "a strategic process for helping policymakers make decisions about assessing risk, allocating finite resources, and taking actions under conditions of uncertainty." Risk is defined as "a function of threat, vulnerability, and consequences, or, in other words, a credible threat of attack on a vulnerable target that would result in unwanted consequences."

The GAO RM framework adheres to industry best practices and divides RM into five major phases: (1) setting strategic goals and objectives, and determining constraints; (2) assessing risks; (3) evaluating alternatives for addressing these risks; (4) selecting the appropriate alternatives; and (5) implementing the alternatives and monitoring the progress made and results achieved.

The GAO noted that integrating RM into government decision making is challenging, especially for the U.S. Department of Homeland Security, with its diverse responsibilities ranging from natural disasters to industrial accidents and terrorist attacks. Although the history of natural disasters provides experts with historical data to assess risk, the asymmetric and adaptive nature of terrorists complicates the application of RM.

Of particular importance is that RM principles can assist state and local governments and the private sector in planning homeland security. The private sector owns over 85 percent of critical infrastructures (e.g., food sources, electric power, and modes of transportation) and works with government on protection issues. Congress has directed federal agencies to foster better information sharing with these partners to improve resiliency in critical infrastructures following a catastrophic event. The federal government favors a shared national approach to manage homeland security risks.

With the use of a forum of experts, the U.S. Government Accountability Office (2008) identified three key challenges to strengthening the application of RM to homeland security: risk communication, political obstacles to making risk-based investments, and a lack of strategic thinking.

Risk communication theory focuses on communication perceptions of experts and lay citizens. Experts seek to simplify safety information for citizens, but safe behavior may not follow. Researchers in this specialization study citizen perceptions of risk and variables that influence behavior (e.g., cultural, social, psychological, and political). This research is important because it serves as a foundation for educating and preparing citizens for harmful events. For example, when citizens are apathetic about impending disasters and do not evacuate, casualties may rise. Government authorities must communicate risk as accurately and convincingly as possible (Purpura 2007, 236, 248). The forum assembled by the U.S. Government Accountability Office (2008) noted important risk-communication challenges:

- Citizen lack of understanding of homeland security risks due to media sensationalization
- The need for government–citizen dialogue on risks that explains the probability of various events occurring and risk-based resource-allocation decisions

and offered recommendations for action:

- Educate elected officials
- Establish a common vocabulary that defines RM terms
- Develop a new risk-communication system to alert the public during an emergency

In reference to political obstacles to making risk-based investments, the forum voiced concern about politicians addressing the public's perceived risks that are often based on inaccurate information. This creates less incentive to invest in long-term solutions to reduce risks.

Although the federal government has prepared national strategies for homeland security (see Chapter 2), the forum recommended an improved national strategic planning process to guide investments in homeland security. The forum noted fragmentation at all levels of government with respect to managing security risk and the need for government-wide guidance on applying RM principles. One example mentioned is that each branch of the armed services within the Department of Defense has its own perception of risk.

Another point here is that although government is driving homeland security, the private sector owns much of our infrastructure that is affected by government planning, laws, regulations, and policies. There is a need for improved communications, interaction, and shared decision making between both sectors.

As stated in Chapter 2, it is important to note the vital and major role of local and state governments in homeland security, protecting critical infrastructure, and responding to emergencies. Every day, local police, fire, emergency medical, and other services respond to calls for service to save lives, care for victims, and protect property. These local, public safety agencies are more likely to be on the scene of a disaster much faster than federal agencies.

Comparing and Contrasting Private and Public Sector Risk Management

The U.S. Government Accountability Office (2008) compared and contrasted private and public sector RM. The private sector manages risk by, for example, diversifying risk through insurance and creating incentives for lowering risk (e.g., reduced premiums if the insured takes certain steps to prevent loss). The public sector takes similar actions. In addition, the public sector manages risk by, for example, regulating land use and establishing building codes; organizing disaster protection, response, and recovery measures; and setting regulatory frameworks. Whereas the private sector can avoid certain risks in cases where RM costs are excessive, the public sector has less flexibility because government has wide responsibility to prepare for, respond to, and recover from all natural and human-made disasters, while being accountable to the public. At the same time, both sectors must make choices and prioritize protection against risks.

In the private sector, businesses may employ a **Chief Risk Officer**, an executive focused on RM and reporting to senior executives. In the public sector, this concept is more difficult to implement because of multiple branches of government. However, there is a need for a single risk manager in the federal government for central leadership and responsibility and coordination on spending decisions.

Government appears to be playing catch-up with the private sector in quantifying RM return on investment. The GAO reported that homeland security investments are often not valued in monetary terms. The private sector is quicker and more flexible in changing than the public sector, where flexibility is often described as like "bending granite."

Enterprise Risk Management

The word *enterprise* has become a buzzword. It is combined with words such as "risk management" and "security," often to signify, and drive evolution to, the next level of such disciplines. The definition and meaning of *enterprise* and the words with which it is combined differ with the source. Merriam–Webster's Online Dictionary (2009) defines **enterprise** as "a project or undertaking that is especially difficult, complicated, or risky; readiness to engage in daring or difficult action; and a unit of economic organization or activity." Here viewpoints on "enterprise risk management" (ERM) and "enterprise security risk management" (ESRM) are offered.

Coffin (2009, 2) writes: "Just as risk management as we know it today was the future of insurance management, ERM is the future of risk management." He adds that ERM "entails a quantum leap forward in how risk awareness factors into the tactical and strategic decision-making of any enterprise."

Makomaski (2008) defines ERM as "a decision-making discipline that addresses variation in company goals." Her concise definition is based on her research of RM professionals, who offered numerous perspectives on risk and ERM. She noted that the responses were "all over the map." Major points stated by respondents were that ERM manages:

- "the choice of losses or gains by addressing probabilities"
- "the deviation from goals with target and performance management"
- "uncertainty with increased business intelligence"
- "adverse events with business continuity programs"
- "expected losses with prudent budgeting and transfer mechanisms"

Makomaski (2008) tests her definition by explaining that risk is measured by the variation of business goals over a specific time. Her illustration is as follows: Say a company goal is to spend only $200 million in operating costs to meet earnings targets; risk is expressed by the deviation from the $200 million. Anticipated costs between $198 to $201 million could be considered low risk, while a range of between $183 and $245 million could be unpalatable and show an entity's risk tolerance. The spread in costs is the risk affected by an infinite number of positive (e.g., favorable economy, superb business intelligence) and negative (e.g., high inflation, explosion at a manufacturing plant) events. Metrics provide a risk measure from which to base ERM decisions.

An excellent source for a comprehensive explanation of ERM is "Enterprise Risk Management—Integrated Framework" from the Committee of Sponsoring Organizations of the Treadway Commission (2004). This commission comprises representatives from various accounting organizations, such as the American Accounting Association and the American Institute of Certified Public Accountants. The commission defines **enterprise risk management** as "a process, affected by an entity's board of directors, management and other personnel, applied in strategy setting and across the enterprise, designed to identify potential events that may affect the entity, and manage risk to be within its risk appetite, to provide reasonable assurance regarding the achievement of entity objectives." ERM encompasses the following characteristics, paraphrased from the commission:

- Enterprises face a variety of risks affecting different parts of the organization and ERM plans for responses to interrelated risks.
- Operational surprises and losses are minimized through ERM.
- Alternative RM responses are applied. Examples are risk transfer and risk avoidance.
- Management considers the risk appetite of the entity and seeks to balance risk with business goals. How much risk will the entity accept in efforts to grow the business?

The commission wrote that ERM is aligned with an entity's objectives that are within four categories:

- *Strategic*: high-level goals aligned with and supporting the business's plan and mission (e.g., manufacturing a useful product that yields a profit)
- *Operations*: effective and efficient application of resources
- *Reporting*: reliability of reporting (e.g., financial reporting)
- *Compliance*: following laws (e.g., Sarbanes-Oxley) and regulations (Laws and professional associations require and/or encourage RM.)

CASE STUDIES OF ENTERPRISE RISK MANAGEMENT

The following cases of ERM are paraphrased from "The Convergence of Physical and Information Security in the Context of Enterprise Risk Management" (The Alliance for Enterprise Security Risk Management 2007, 44–48).

Case Study 1, General Energy Group

Issue

As an old and well-established utility company, General Energy Group (GEG), owns and operates 35 fossil fuel power plants and 3 nuclear plants. The company employs 11,000 full-time employees and 2,000 contract employees. Jason Morris, director of enterprise security at GEG, was hired to manage operational risks following the Enron scandal and to prepare for increasing government regulation. Jason concentrated on two goals: deliver the status of the entity to senior executives whenever needed and prove that his team was delivering value.

Solution

The GEG enterprise security group falls into the larger ERM group that reports directly to a chief risk officer/VP. There are four operational units that report to Morris: information risk, enterprise operation, access management, and regulatory compliance management. Morris emphasized three factors that he viewed as keys to the success of enterprise security:

Communication: People are informed about what is happening and why at every stage.

Collaboration: Appropriate senior managers are on board and support enterprise security to facilitate its success.

A dynamic team of security professionals: Personnel are aligned with business units that match their qualifications and skills.

Results

Senior executives receive real-time operational and financial information of the entity's risks.

Case Study 2, National Consumer Goods

Issue

National Consumer Goods (NCG) is a producer and distributor of consumer goods. It had an ERM program that was "going down a road to nowhere." NCG needed an evaluation of its current ERM initiatives compared to best practices to gain senior executive support for changes.

Solution

- Develop ERM that is more integrated with the executive management process.
- Use specific industry and cross-industry knowledge and experience to create executive buy-in.
- Demonstrate to executives the value added through ERM.
- Facilitate a culture of communication and collaboration among business units relative to ERM.
- Develop and deploy tools to identify and mitigate risk.

Results

Following the above activities, NCG was able to:

- Offer a plan and recommendations to improve ERM, including organizational structures, leadership involvement, and project management.
- Identify a methodology that results in action when critical issues surface and are presented to senior executives and the board of directors.
- Ensure that the needs of executives are identified and that there is follow-up with them.
- Integrate the cycle of risk identification, assessment, response, and monitoring into the organization's strategic planning and budgeting process.

ISSUE

Can Enterprise Risk Management Prevent Litigation?

Nichter (2008, 108–118) explains the story of a young woman out with her friends at a Las Vegas nightclub when a fight occurred. As she fled to avoid the violence, the combatants fell on her and continued the fight on top of her until security personnel interceded. The young woman sustained spinal injuries and sued.

In studying this case of litigation, Nichter viewed the defendant business as lacking ERM, since each organizational department connected to the incident was managed separately without an understanding of interdependencies. His description of this case and the parties involved follows.

The depositions of security officers who worked at the nightclub revealed a need for additional officers because of recurring fights and hostile customers. Adequate training was also lacking. The training supervisor testified in her deposition that she had never worked at a nightclub and knew little of nightclub issues. Her previous experience was as a junior high school teacher.

The defendant's risk manager focused on claims management and interaction with the insurer, while playing no role in risk analysis for the nightclub because it was the responsibility of the security director. The risk manager also testified that he and the security director rarely met. He stated that he was not knowledgeable of the number of times fights erupted at the club, nor the number of times police were summoned. Fights and other incidents were brought to his attention when claims resulted. The security director testified about not maintaining metrics about incidents at the club because he thought it was done by the risk manager. His deployment of security officers was based on what he "felt" was adequate. He never conducted a study of security at other similar clubs to develop "best practices."

Critical Thinking

How would you apply ERM and other methodologies to the case of the nightclub to improve management and security?

Enterprise Security Risk Management

Enterprise security risk management (ESRM) is an evolving concept requiring study, research, and guidelines. Johnson and Spivey (2008, 1) explain factors that influence the development of this term, its meaning, and utility. They write that security and RM professionals struggle with the difficulty of quantifying a nonevent and become frustrated when senior management reduces security funding because "nothing happened." They ask: "Is the absence of incidents the result of effective security and risk management? Or is it the absence of risk itself?" Although these questions are difficult to answer, Johnson and Spivey offer input for seeking answers to these questions. They begin with the convergence of physical and IT security, along with RM and business continuity, into ESRM as a component of a comprehensive ERM model. Johnson and Spivey propose the following definition (although lengthy) of **enterprise security risk management**:

The component of an enterprise risk management model focused on the security perspective for identification, assessment, and mitigation of those events that impact an organization's ability to achieve its business goals and objectives, ESRM concentrates on organizational activities relating to the planning, prevention, response, resiliency, recovery and resumption of events; creating physical, technical and administrative mitigation controls that provide for the deterrence, detection, assessment and response to such events. ESRM is a holistic risk management process that aligns organizational drivers affecting strategy, processes, people, technology and knowledge to protect key assets in accordance with governance, risk, and compliance (GRC) requirements.

ESRM requires cross-functional collaboration within the backdrop of ERM between multiple management disciplines including, but not limited to physical and logical security, safety, legal, risk management, crisis management and business continuity planning.

To facilitate ESRM, Johnson and Spivey look to ASIS International efforts at professionalism and competence in the security industry. They also cite ASIS obtaining designation as "certified technologies" for ASIS guidelines and professional certifications under the SAFETY Act of 2002 (see Chapter 7), which provides for limited liability in the event of terrorist acts. In other words, companies can not only enhance professionalism and competence, but also reduce liability by applying ASIS methodologies and obtaining ASIS professional certifications.

In addition, guidelines and standards come from several other organizations that are an immense aid in improving security and reducing risk. Examples are the National Fire Protection Association (NFPA) and Underwriters Laboratories (UL).

Davidson (2009, 56–61) offers additional perspectives on ESRM through interviews with security practitioners. She defines ESRM as a subset of ERM that encompasses traditional security risks and broader issues, such as safety, IT, and brand integrity. Davidson writes, "Security professionals who know how to facilitate ESRM and fit it within the broader ERM landscape will have a permanent seat at the C-suite table." Her interviews with security practitioners produced the following points:

- Models for ESRM are diverse and specific to individual companies.
- Models for ESRM must ensure that risks are identified, prioritized, and mitigated. The process must show value to the business when reviewed by an entity's board of directors.
- The models require constant review to ensure that they are relevant to company goals and needs.
- Commonalities among models include identification of critical processes, alignment of security strategies and objectives to the business, and risk mitigation.
- ESRM often faces challenges, such as cost cutting, that can reduce security and controls while increasing risks. However, security professionals must meet such a challenge by optimizing available resources and "deliver the right information to the appropriate level of management so that executives can prioritize and make appropriate choices."
- ESRM is in a constant state of evolution, and subject-matter experts are needed as partners to "define the skills, training, standards and guidelines, benchmarks, policies, and procedures that are needed to shape a robust ESRM strategy."

Risks

As explained earlier in this chapter, risk refers to exposure to harmful events, while risk management involves planning and implementing strategies to promote resilience so that an organization can survive and continue to meet its objectives following a harmful event. The range of risks facing businesses and government is very broad. Examples include natural disasters (e.g., hurricanes and flooding), human-made events (e.g., accidents and bombings), and technological events (e.g., electrical service outage). Chapter 2 describes a variety of threats and hazards that are risks facing organizations.

Natural Disasters

A **natural disaster** is the human, environmental, and/or financial impact from a natural hazard, such as a tornado. Numerous Web sites offer a wealth of information on natural disasters. These include the sites of the Federal Emergency Management Agency (FEMA) and the Centers for Disease Control (CDC). The CDC (2009) Web site lists the following "natural disasters and severe weather" conditions: earthquakes, extreme heat, floods, hurricanes, landslides and mudslides, tornadoes, tsunamis, volcanoes, wildfires, and winter weather events. Some of these natural disasters are explained next from the FEMA and CDC Web sites.

Earthquakes

Earthquakes strike suddenly, violently, and without warning (Figure 11.1). FEMA offers a risk chart by state and territory, with a classification of "moderate risk," "high risk," and "very high risk." Very high-risk states are Alaska, California, Hawaii, Idaho, Montana, Nevada, Oregon, Washington, and Wyoming. The **Richter Magnitude Scale** is a mathematical device to compare the size of earthquakes. The magnitude of an earthquake is expressed in whole numbers and decimal fractions. As examples, whereas an earthquake with a magnitude of 3.5 to 5.4 is felt and rarely causes damage, an earthquake of 6.1 and above can be destructive, and one between 7.0 and 7.9 is considered a major earthquake. The Richter scale has no upper limit.

FEMA and the CDC offer suggestions of what can be done prior to, during, and following an earthquake. For instance, prior to such an event, check for hazards such as large objects that can topple and cause injury or death, and secure the objects by using strapping or bolting them to the floor. In addition, identify safe places (e.g., inside, under sturdy furniture, or outside away from anything that can fall), learn about this hazard and what can be done for increased protection, and prepare emergency supplies. During an earthquake, try to minimize movement and watch out for falling objects and downed power lines. If trapped, do not light a match (a gas leak could

FIGURE 11.1 Building destroyed by earthquake. (® Shutterstock.com. With permission.)

result in an explosion) and tap on a pipe or other object to signal rescuers. Following an earthquake, prepare for aftershocks, listen to emergency information by using battery-operated devices, watch for falling objects, and check damage.

Floods

Floods are one of the most common hazards in the United States (Figure 11.2). The impact can be local or regional—across multiple states. Floods may develop slowly, but flash floods are extremely dangerous. Flood hazard maps show different degrees of risk and help to determine the cost of flood insurance.

Avoid building in a flood-prone area. Educate yourself about floods. Secure valuable assets and papers. During a flood, listen to emergency broadcasts; evacuation may be necessary. Six inches of water can cause loss of control of vehicles; a foot of water can result in a vehicle floating. After a flood, beware of contaminated water, downed power lines, and damaged structures. The U.S. Army Corps of Engineers works with communities that are flooded frequently.

Hurricanes

The intensity of a landfalling hurricane can cause extensive loss of life, injuries, and property damage. The **Saffir-Simpson Hurricane Wind Scale** is a 1 to 5 categorization. Category 5, the most severe, means that winds are greater than 155 mph. It results in catastrophic damage: Homes and industrial buildings are likely to lose roofs; buildings may be blown down or away; mobile homes will be destroyed; all signs are blown down; windows

FIGURE 11.2 Flooded office building. (® Shutterstock.com. With permission.)

in high-rise buildings may become airborne; and trees will be snapped or uprooted. Flying debris will kill and injure. Electricity will be unavailable for weeks and possibly months. Hurricane Camille, in 1969, which reached 190 mph at landfall in Mississippi, and Hurricane Andrew, in 1992, which reached 165 mph at landfall in Southeast Florida, are examples of Category 5 hurricanes. The Southeast is more susceptible to this natural hazard. Hurricane Katrina, in 2005, was the most expensive natural disaster in U.S. history (see Chapter 2).

Prior to a hurricane, secure property by using, for instance, window shutters and straps. Prepare an evacuation plan and supplies. During a hurricane, listen to emergency broadcasts, stay indoors, seek protection by sturdy objects, and beware of flying debris. Following a hurricane, maintain safe behavior, evaluate damage, and seek assistance.

Tornadoes

Tornadoes are nature's most violent storms and can cause quick devastation and deaths in seconds. Winds can reach 300 mph, and the damage path can be over 1 mile wide and 50 miles long. Every state is at risk.

Prior to a tornado, listen to emergency broadcasts and look for an approaching storm. Danger signs include a dark sky, large hail, and a loud roar, similar to a freight train. If under a tornado "warning," go to a shelter, safe room, basement, or the lowest level of a building. Go under a sturdy table and use your arms to protect your head. If outside, lie flat in a ditch or depression and cover your head. Watch out for flying debris. Following a tornado, apply similar suggestions as with a hurricane.

Pandemics

A **pandemic** is the spread of an infectious disease among humans over a wide geographic area. The 1918–1919 Spanish influenza pandemic has been referred to as the mother of all pandemics. It infected about one-third of the world's population, causing about 50 million deaths worldwide. The reasons as to why it was so fatal have not been determined, and almost all influenza A pandemics since that time have been caused by descendants of the 1918 virus (Taubenberger and Morens 2006).

The U.S. Government Accountability Office (2009) reported that pandemic planning and exercising has occurred at all levels of government, but gaps remain. Further action must address response and recovery, including increased space capacity for patient treatment, and the acquisition and distribution of medical and other critical supplies, such as antivirals and vaccines. The GAO emphasizes that an influenza pandemic continues to be a serious risk facing the United States and the world. Unlike threats and hazards that are usually bounded by space and time, a pandemic is not a single event, but more likely to arrive in waves that last for weeks or months across many geographic areas simultaneously.

Two organizations, the CDC and the World Health Organization (WHO), monitor global influenza outbreaks. The CDC serves as a hub for coordinated planning and prevention and the research and production of vaccines.

Besides the human toll from a pandemic, the monetary costs are very high. Because of the possibility of restricted travel and quarantine enforcement, the operation of critical infrastructure could be affected. The CDC estimates that a severe pandemic could result in 200,000 to 2 million deaths in the United States. In 2006, Congress authorized supplemental funding of $5.62 billion for pandemic preparedness (U.S. Government Accountability Office 2009, 5, 11).

For businesses and other entities, planning for a pandemic is essential. How can customer contact be maintained? How can employees do their jobs if they are unable to travel to work, must care for a sick family member, or get sick themselves? "Guidance on Preparing Workplaces for an Influenza Pandemic" (Occupational Safety and Health Administration 2007) is a publication that offers numerous recommendations for organizations. It covers planning, preparedness, infection control, and several other topics pertaining to employers and employees.

Human-Made Events/Hazards

A human-made event/hazard is the human, environmental, and/or financial impact resulting from error, negligence, criminal intent, or failure of a component or system.

The FEMA (2009) Web site lists a combination of natural disasters and hazards. It lists the following topics, besides the natural disaster topics listed on the CDC Web site (see previous section): chemical, dam failure, fire, hazardous materials, nuclear power plant emergency, and terrorism. Here, the following human-made events/hazards are covered: workplace accidents, hazardous materials, and bombings.

Workplace Accidents

Workplace accidents are a serious risk and hazard. In 2007, there were 5,657 fatal occupational injuries and 4 million cases of nonfatal workplace injuries and illnesses in the United States. Workplace illnesses accounted for fewer than 6 percent of the 4 million injury and illness cases (Bureau of Labor Statistics 2009).

For centuries, government and industry have been working to prevent and control workplace accidents. The Industrial Revolution in England during the eighteenth century, was an era when government leaders saw the need for improved safety in the workplace because of accidents and the exploitation of child labor. The United States followed the example of England, and states passed laws on workplace safety. A major type of law enacted in both countries was **workers' compensation laws** that require companies to pay for losses incurred by workers due to accidents. Businesses generally abhorred these laws because of the costs and the prevailing view that workers were expendable. Government leaders viewed these laws as a way to facilitate increased safety to reduce costs from accidents. To assist businesses, insurance companies began to offer workers' compensation insurance.

Using one state as an example, Greenhouse (2009) writes that a century ago, when New York created a workers' compensation system, the aim was to establish a no-fault insurance program to resolve injuries without litigation; today, litigation is common. The following descriptions of workers' compensation are from the research of Greenhouse. He reports that employers see the system as extremely expensive and riddled with fraudulent claims. A single injury can result in a cost of several hundred thousand dollars when an injured worker draws benefits for life. One executive with a company in Buffalo spent $4,900 per employee in 2007 for workers' compensation for 220 workers. This amounted to $1,078,000, ten times what the cost would be in North Carolina. The bill represented 2.5 percent of revenues, and the plant had a profit margin of 3 percent. Now, the executive no longer relies on an insurance company, self-insures, and pays compensation costs that total

$850,000 for medical expenses for current workers, replacement wages for those workers, and a state assessment to support the compensation system.

Many companies provide incentives to promote safety in the workplace. "Safety bucks" are coupons that look like cash and can be redeemed at Home Depot, Red Lobster, and other locations. "Safety bingo" is another incentive program. The longer the workforce goes without a reported accident, the greater the incentives. Employers view the incentives as much less expensive than costly accidents. However, there is pressure on workers not to report accidents because of the incentives and employer costs. In one case, a worker crushed her thumb in a forklift accident. Her medical attention required a bone graft and the insertion of six pins in her thumb. She claimed that her employer pressured her to not report a loss-time accident to OSHA, so she reported back to work directly from the emergency room, was not given days off to recuperate, and was ordered to spend her workdays in the plant's break room.

Critical Thinking

As an employee at a manufacturing plant, what would you say and do if you injured yourself on the job and a coworker says, "You son of a bitch, don't report the injury or everybody will lose safety bucks!"

DO NOT MAKE THESE MISTAKES

Hearing Protection

John Cooper had worked as a uniformed security officer at Network Industries for two years. He was a retired postal worker and liked his part-time job as a security officer. Because production areas inside Network created hazardous noise, John was required to wear hearing protection, as were other employees. One day, as John was patrolling the outside shipping docks, he failed to remove his hearing protection. A truck proceeded to back up, and an audible warning signal was transmitted; however, John did not hear it. He was crushed between the truck and the dock, sustaining fatal injuries.

Lessons: The obvious lesson here is that John should have removed his hearing protection when he exited the plant. Policies and procedures involving day-to-day, routine duties can result in complacency.

Safety management should select hearing protection that reduces hazardous noise while permitting voice and signal frequencies to be heard.

Critical Thinking

Can you think of any other safety methods that can become dangerous when not properly used?

Occupational Safety and Health Administration

The **Occupational Safety and Health Administration Act of 1970** is a major national law promoting safety in the workplace across a broad number of occupations in the United States. This law is administered through OSHA, a government agency within the U.S. Department of Labor. OSHA prepares legally enforceable safety standards, offers publications and training, conducts workplace inspections, and issues citations for safety violations. Its focus is broad and includes workplace fatalities, injuries and illnesses, violence in the workplace, vehicle accidents involving employees, and emergencies at work. An emphasis is placed on preventing accidents and assisting employers. OSHA's Web site offers an enormous amount of information.

OSHA's reach does not extend to workplaces under safety requirements of other federal agencies, those who are self-employed, and family-operated farms. Employers under OSHA's jurisdiction must maintain OSHA workplace records and report fatalities and certain injuries and illnesses. Employers are also required to post both OSHA materials pertaining to employee rights and citations for safety violations. OSHA's Whistleblower Program seeks to ensure that employees report safety issues without retaliation.

OSHA is a government law enforcement agency. Thus, Fourth Amendment protections against unreasonable search and seizure are afforded to employers. Unless an employer gives consent to search to an OSHA inspector, the inspector must obtain a warrant based on administrative probable cause.

Safety Programs in the Workplace

Because employers face enormous costs from accidents in the workplace, they often implement safety strategies to prevent accidents (Figure 11.3). These strategies include establishing a safety committee, hiring a safety specialist, adhering to government safety regulations and insurer loss-prevention recommendations, issuing policies and procedures, conducting safety training, establishing safety incentive programs, investigating accidents promptly, and correcting safety hazards.

Perdue (2008, 73–79) emphasizes the need for creating a safety culture. He recommends that this approach begin at the CEO's desk and spread throughout the enterprise to facilitate awareness and safe behavior. He also suggests conducting site audits to spot hazards and then work toward mitigation.

FIGURE 11.3   **Safety is important to prevent accidents. Welder welding a vehicle part. (® Shutterstock.com. With permission.)**

OSHA ENFORCEMENT CASES

Press release from:
U.S. Department of Labor, OSHA
Region 4
June 22, 2009

OSHA proposes over $1.1 million in penalties to Milk Specialists Co. in Whitehall, WI

OSHA has cited Milk Specialists Co., a research and manufacturing firm, with violations of federal workplace safety and health standards and proposed $1,145,200 in penalties. In December 2008, OSHA responded to a complaint alleging safety hazards at the plant. Inspections revealed untrained employees entering confined spaces to perform maintenance and cleaning on electrical equipment without protection from hazards. Seventeen willful violations were noted. "A willful violation is one committed with plain

---

indifference to or intentional disregard for employee safety and health." Other citations included uninspected fire extinguishers and lack of exit route lighting and signage.

Source: http://www.fdrsafety.com/OCA615.pdf.

Press release from:
U.S. Department of Labor, OSHA
Region 2
June 18, 2009

OSHA finds Metro North Commuter Railroad Co. retaliated against employees

Whistleblower investigations by OSHA found that Metro North Commuter Railroad Co. retaliated against four employees who reported work-related injuries. OSHA ordered the railroad, which provides commuter rail service in NY, NJ, and CT, to take corrective actions. The four employees sustained on-the-job injuries in 2007 and 2008. They complained to OSHA alleging that the railroad disciplined them for reporting their injuries and interfered with their medical treatment and/or reclassified their injuries from occupational to non-occupational. OSHA investigated, found merit to the allegations, and ordered the railroad to: expunge the disciplinary action; compensate the employees for lost wages, medical expenses, and attorney's fees; pay them $75,000 in punitive damages; and post the rights of whistleblowers (e.g., to report incidents without retaliation).

Source: http://www.osha.gov/pls/oshaweb/owadisp. show_document?p_table=NEWS_RELEASES&p_id=18068.

Hazardous Materials

Chemicals are found almost everywhere. They are used in manufacturing, to purify drinking water and increase crop yields, and serve as fuel for vehicles. If not safely produced, stored, transported, used, or disposed of, injuries and death can occur. Hazardous materials (**HAZMAT**) can be in the form of explosives, flammable and combustible substances, poisons, and radioactive materials. Harmful events most often occur with these substances because of transportation or manufacturing accidents. The U.S. Department of Transportation (2009) reported 424 "serious" HAZMAT incidents in 2008 in the United States, resulting in 9 deaths, 84 injuries, and costing almost $40 million. "Serious" is defined as resulting in a fatality or major injury, the evacuation of 25 or more persons, the closure of a major transportation artery, the alteration of a flight path, the release of radioactive material, or the release of over 119 gallons or 882 pounds of a hazardous material.

FIGURE 11.4   Police line and preparation for decontamination at a HAZMAT incident. (® Shutterstock.com. With permission.)

Many communities have **Local Emergency Planning Committees (LEPCs)** resulting from the **Superfund Amendments and Reauthorization Act of 1986**. A LEPC focuses on the development of an emergency plan, and testing of the plan, to prepare for and respond to chemical emergencies in a specific community. The plan includes the identification of local facilities and transportation routes where hazardous materials are present, procedures for immediate response to an accident, notifying the community, and if necessary, evacuation and decontamination (Figure 11.4). The **Emergency Planning and Community Right-To-Know Act of 1986** requires that information on hazardous substances in or near communities be available for citizens at their request. Stiff penalties and lawsuits can result from noncompliance by companies.

Prior to a hazardous materials disaster, FEMA (2009) recommends that citizens include the following items in their disaster kit: plastic sheeting, duct tape, and scissors. If such a disaster strikes, seek information on whether to evacuate. If staying indoors, turn off HVAC (heating, ventilation, and air-conditioning); close windows, vents, and other openings; seal around windows and doors with wet towels or plastic sheets and duct tape; and go to a preselected shelter room. If outside, stay upstream, uphill, and upwind. Cover your mouth and nose with a cloth. Following an incident, seek medical assistance if contact has been made with a hazardous substance, find out how to clean up your property, and ventilate buildings.

HAZMAT safety at industrial facilities, transportation systems, and throughout communities is facilitated through numerous federal and state laws and regulations. For example, the **OSHA Hazard Communication**

Standard (1910.1200) requires that all chemicals produced or imported be evaluated, and that information concerning their hazards be communicated to employers and employees. This standard requires labeling, warnings, training, and material safety data sheets (MSDS). MSDS contain numerous topics, such as identification of the substance, hazards, ingredients, first-aid measures, handling and storage, and personal protection methods.

Bombings

Bombings are a serious domestic and international risk. The U.S. Bomb Data Center reported that, in 2006, in the United States, there were 3,445 explosive incidents, 135 injuries, and 14 fatalities. The metrics for 2005/2004 are as follows: 3,722/3,790, 148/263, and 18/36, respectively. "Explosive incidents" refer to bombings, attempted bombings, stolen explosives, and other categories (U.S. Bureau of Alcohol, Tobacco, Firearms and Explosives [ATF] 2008). The National Counterterrorism Center (2009, 21) reported 7,424 bombings worldwide in 2008.

Bombings have historically been a favorite tactic of terrorists because of the high number of casualties, extensive property damage, and intense media attention. Bombers are typically creative and crafty, as described in Chapter 2. They devise novel ways of getting a bomb to a vulnerable location. They may attempt to bring components of a bomb to a building or mode of transportation and assemble it prior to detonation. Another ploy, the **safe area bombing**, begins with a bomb threat at a building to see where evacuees gather; later, another bomb threat is called in, and when evacuees gather at the prearranged location, a bomb is detonated at the prearranged spot (Purpura 2007, 55–56).

Whereas a bomber can detonate a bomb from a safe distance, avoid injury, and flee the area, a **suicide bomber** typically dies in the explosion after precisely delivering a bomb to a target by making quick changes, if necessary, while traveling; the challenges of escape, interrogation, and incarceration are obviated. A suicide bomber could be anybody in any disguise (e.g., woman, child, and police officer or soldier in uniform). MacVicar (2009) reported that, in August of 2009, the head of Saudi Arabia's counterterrorism operations and others were wounded when an Al-Qaeda suicide bomber detonated a one-pound explosive he had inserted, including a detonator, into his rectum.

The Federal Emergency Management Agency (2003, 2–3) notes that thousands of deliberate explosions occur every year in the United States, with most having a weapon yield of less than five pounds. Large-scale vehicle weapon attacks using hundreds of pounds of explosives are very few in number. The chance of large-scale terrorist attacks occurring is extremely low. A smaller explosive attack is far more likely. At the same time, vehicle bombs are capable of delivering large quantities of explosives to cause casualties and structural damage to a building. Small, hand-delivered bombs can also cause loss of life and serious damage, especially when delivered to the "best" location. Each security layer can function as a sieve, reducing the size of the weapon. Chapter 7 covers blast protection for buildings, access controls, mail screening, and other related topics.

Although most bomb threats are hoaxes, each threat must be taken seriously. Planning is essential. Employee training is also essential, so that when a threat is received, whether by telephone or other means, information about the threat is recorded. Federal agencies (e.g., ATF) can supply a standard bomb-threat form containing questions such as: When will the bomb explode? Where is the bomb? Although bombers are unlikely to answer all the questions on a bomb-threat form when they communicate a threat, at the same time, they are unpredictable and may provide vital information. Employee training should include reporting suspicious activity, evacuations, not touching anything suspicious, bomb search procedures, and contacting public safety agencies.

Business Continuity and Enterprise Resilience

Business Continuity

ASIS International (2004, 7) defines **business continuity** (BC) as "a comprehensive managed effort to prioritize key business processes, identify significant threats to normal operation, and plan mitigation strategies to ensure effective and efficient organizational response to the challenges that surface during and after a crisis."

Kaye (2008, 38–39) describes a case study of a devastating fire at a crucial manufacturing facility that provided printed circuit board components to other company plants and to two lucrative contracts. Although no one was injured, the facility suffered extensive damage. When fire and other public safety agencies departed, management stood in the parking lot and had to answer the following questions:

- Who would be in charge and empowered to make decisions?
- Where would the team relocate to begin plotting the way forward?
- Who would brief employees, the press, and the board?
- Would damaged equipment on-site be difficult to replace?
- Where and how quickly could production resume?
- Which customers would receive standing inventory?
- Were there liability risks and contractual obligations to the firm's partners?

This case illustrates both the types of difficult questions that emerge when unexpected harmful events occur and the importance of a BC plan. Kaye recommends four essential needs of the BC planning process: (1) management expertise from all key functional areas; (2) a planning methodology; (3) availability of all participants throughout the planning process; and (4) placement of a project management structure so that participants understand tasks and due dates.

Kaye views BC as including, but not limited to, the following elements:

- *Emergency response plans* that cover initial actions to protect people and assets following a serious incident
- *Crisis management and IT incident management plans* that facilitate an effective response and strategic positioning following recovery
- *Crisis communications plans* to keep internal and external stakeholders informed about the crisis and recovery
- *IT disaster recovery plans* that restore IT systems and, if necessary, coordinate IT recovery with external assistance
- *Business function recovery plans* that seek to reestablish critical business functions with, if necessary, external assistance

Pitcher (2010, 28) supports the value of BC plans by arguing that a plan can save money and show a return on investment. He suggests leveraging the BC plan to assist a business in negotiating lower insurance premiums. Pitcher recommends communicating this strategy to senior executives and insurers; ensuring that the BC plan is up-to-date; and sharing information on the frequency of tests, the results of the BC plan, and research showing that risks are mitigated.

GLOBAL PERSPECTIVE: BUSINESS-CONTINUITY PLANNING IN ENGLAND

On July 7, 2005, during the morning rush hour, London was attacked by terrorist suicide bombs targeting public transportation. Four British Muslim men, against Britain's involvement in the war in Iraq, set bombs off on three underground trains and one bus. Fifty-six people were killed, including the four bombers, and about 700 were injured. Infrastructure damage included London's transit system and the country's mobile communications system. When such events occur, there is a heightened state of concern for the possibility of other attacks and emergencies.

The following business-continuity plan recommendations are for a medium-sized business with 50 to 250 employees (London Resilience Partnership/UK Government, 2008).

The planning process should begin with senior management support and be directed by someone with an overview of the whole business enterprise in cooperation with a team representing all functional areas of the organization. Plans vary, depending on the size of the organization, the type of business, and needs. One avenue is to prepare subplans for each department and then incorporate them into a comprehensive plan. The following five-step guide provides a foundation for planning:

Step 1 Analyze the business. Three important questions are: What functions are most vulnerable? What are the worst-case scenarios? With these questions in mind, what needs to be planned for employees, customers, suppliers, systems and processes, partnerships, and buildings?

Step 2 Assess the risks. There are three aspects to every risk facing a business: How likely is it to happen? How concentrated is the risk? In other words, for example, are multiple mission-critical activities located in the same area of a building? What effect will the adverse event have on the business?

Step 3 Develop strategies. Steps 1 and 2 serve as a basis for formulating strategy. The plan should contain a statement of purpose and a statement of support by senior management. It should also address the structure of the crisis team, business recovery, work-area recovery, technology recovery, public relations, and employee involvement in the plan. Finally, it should contain a description of the premises for evacuation, a copy of which should be provided for the insurer.

Step 4 Develop the plan as an ongoing planning process. Plan for action immediately following an event and action beyond the first hour or so after an event. Maintain contact with outside entities for assistance in planning and to seek help during an emergency. These entities include first-responder agencies, insurers, utility companies, and neighboring businesses.

Step 5 Train employees and test the plan. Train the team in detail to increase their efficiency. Ensure that feedback is shared. Try to reproduce authentic conditions and use what-if scenarios. Revise the plan regularly.

Balaouras (2009) reported on research of BC specialists conducted by Forrester Research and the *Disaster Recovery Journal*. The survey used a self-selected, nonrandom group of 295 respondents who provided insight into how businesses use BC programs. The BC respondents were primarily from North America and were employed by companies of various sizes and industries. Here is a summary of the findings:

- Only 23 percent felt that BC was a critical priority for senior executives at their company.
- When asked to select the top three BC challenges, there was a two-way tie for the top challenge: "inadequate funding" and "implementing a

BC program corporate-wide." These answers were followed by "the scope of our BC program is ill-defined."

- Fifty-four percent of respondents never validated or investigated the BC readiness of their strategic partners.
- Companies with fewer than 1,000 employees typically have one or two full-time BC specialists. Companies with a few thousand employees have between two and five full-time BC specialists. Large companies often have five or more.
- BC standards are influential, but not overwhelmingly so. Respondents were asked about three standards, and the most influential one was the NFPA 1600, followed by ISO 27001/27002 (Security Information Management), and then the British Standard 25999.
- Fifty percent of respondents have invoked their BC plans during the previous five years. The most common reason was extreme weather and natural disasters, followed closely by power outages, IT failure, telecommunication failure, and fire.
- The top three lessons from their invocations were: (1) not enough training and awareness across the enterprise; (2) plans did not adequately address internal communications and collaboration; and (3) plans did not adequately address workforce continuity.

The above research noted **NFPA 1600 Standard on Disaster/Emergency Management and Business-Continuity Programs**. This standard has been acknowledged by the U.S. Congress, the American National Standards Institute, and the 9/11 Commission. It has been endorsed by FEMA, the National Emergency Management Association, and other organizations. It has been referred to as the "national preparedness standard" for government and businesses. This standard contains information from BC and emergency management because of the convergence of these two disciplines resulting from lessons learned that show the vital interdependencies of private and public sectors during disasters. NFPA 1600 contains terms and definitions, lists of resources, and standards for program management, risk assessment, mitigation, training, logistics, and other topics (Purpura 2007, 262).

Another factor for consideration by organizations is a federal law entitled **Implementing Recommendations of the 9/11 Commission Act of 2007**. This law, specifically Title IX of Public Law 110-53, calls for the development of a voluntary private-sector all-hazards preparedness accreditation and certification program. The U.S. Department of Homeland Security will coordinate this effort in consultation with key stakeholders. Best practices and standards will be applied. In fact, the law refers to NFPA 1600; however, other standards will serve as input.

Enterprise Resilience

Earlier in this chapter, *enterprise* was explained as a term that has been combined with other terms to signify, and drive evolution to, the next level of certain disciplines (e.g., enterprise risk management). *Enterprise* refers to a unit of economic organization undertaking risky action and requiring boldness and perseverance to reach objectives. **Enterprise resilience** (ER) involves a corporate culture, plans, and strategies that emphasize organization-wide adaptability and survivability when facing harmful events so that previously planned goals can be attained. ER is broader and bolder than traditional business-continuity planning, which will evolve and merge with ER.

Zawada (2009, 12–16) writes of expanding traditional BC expectations and value. He explains that traditional BC is charged with preparing entities for risks and hazards by ensuring that people, workplaces, technology, equipment, and supplies are available following a disruptive event. This has been commonly called **availability-related risks**. At the same time, progressive BC professionals are addressing **operational risks** with BC implications. Examples are supply-chain issues (e.g., a fire at the site of a major supplier), the inability to replace skilled retiring workers, and nationalization of certain industries in another country.

Zawada (2009, 12–16) applies critical thinking and poses the following question: Why do BC professionals often avoid operational risks with BC implications? He answers this question as follows:

- Many BC professionals would say we have enterprise risk management programs to handle operational risks. However, Zawada asks whether such programs have "deep risk analysis and control-based assessment experience?" He goes on to write that BC professionals are positioned to partner with risk managers to perform a value-added role and leverage their expertise, an approach that is often lacking in a risk manager. Additionally, ERM may be a part-time assignment of a risk manager. On the other hand, many BC professionals lack the skills necessary to analyze financial issues relevant to BC.
- A BC program may be based on a regulatory mandate to address natural and human-made disasters and technological failures. Zawada writes, "Unfortunately, regulatory demands are often treated by many organizations as the definitive end goal, not the means to creating a business-aligned program that adds value to internal and external stakeholders." He adds that many executives are so busy that they do not see BC risks that have nothing to do with adverse weather, fire, and so forth.
- BC professionals, like other professionals, should continue to learn and apply new skills. This includes reading about new disciplines

(e.g., business and finance), attending educational programs, and speaking with peers.

Zawada refers to a standard approved by the American National Standards Institute (ANSI) that focuses on operational risks: **ASIS SPC. 1-2009**. The full name of this standard is "Organizational Resilience: Security, Preparedness, and Continuity Management Systems—Requirements with Guidance for Use." This standard incorporates guidance from the ASIS International "Business Continuity Guideline: A Practical Approach for Emergency Preparedness, Crisis Management, and Disaster Recovery, 2005." The ASIS SPC. 1-2009 does not state specific performance criteria, but provides generic auditable criteria for organizational resilience so that organizations can develop their own specific performance criteria. This standard encourages a process approach that emphasizes:

- Understanding an organization's risk, security, preparedness, response, continuity, and recovery requirements
- Using controls to manage risks within the context of an organization's mission
- Monitoring and reviewing performance and effectiveness
- Using objective measurements to continually improve organizational resilience

ASIS SPC. 1-2009 requires an organization to establish policy, identify enterprise-wide risks, adhere to applicable legal requirements, identify priorities, plan, control, monitor, prevent, and adapt to change. The standard's focus on operational risks is illustrated through the following statements (ASIS International 2009, 18):

> An unmanaged disruptive incident can taint an organization's image, reputation, or brand in addition to resulting in significant physical or environmental damage, injury, or loss of life.
>
> This *Standard* provides organizations of all sizes and types with the elements needed to achieve and demonstrate proactive risk reduction and organizational resilience performance related to their physical facilities, services, activities, products, supply chains, and operational (business) continuity.

Critical Thinking

Do you think that business-continuity professionals should become involved in operational risks or remain focused on only availability-related risks? Explain your answer.

Emergency Management

"**Emergency management**, originating from government, focuses on preparation for potential emergencies and disasters and the coordination of response and resources during such events" (Purpura 2007, 232). Whereas business continuity is associated with the private sector, emergency management (EM) is associated with the public (i.e., government) sector. EM is a politically charged, fluid term because of changes in threats and hazards and the way in which government responds. These changes throughout history include, as examples, the threat of nuclear attack during the Cold War, terrorism, and hurricanes. The Katrina disaster in 2005 showed the difficulty of government planning and response to major catastrophes. Hurricane Katrina decimated Gulf Coast states, flooded New Orleans, killed 1,833 people, and displaced most of the city's population (as covered in Chapter 2). Federal, state, and local governments failed in their response, and each blamed the other. Consequently, *citizens and organizations must take the initiative and prepare for threats and hazards, because government assistance following an event may not be available initially.*

Refer to Chapter 2 for a refresher on government topics such as homeland security, federal legislation, all-hazards protection, FEMA, the National Response Framework, the National Incident Management System, and other topics. Next, EM functions are explained so that the reader can make a comparison to business continuity and enterprise resilience.

Bullock et al. (2006) view EM as consisting of several components: mitigation, prevention, preparedness, response, recovery, and communications.

- *Mitigation* entails many methods and strategies aimed at reducing the risk and severity associated with hazards. For example, the National Flood Insurance Program is a federal program providing property owners with the opportunity to purchase flood insurance in exchange for adhering to government regulations (e.g., construction specifications) that reduce flood damage.
- *Prevention* includes action to avoid an incident and to protect people and property. Examples are intelligence and security, inspections, public health and agricultural surveillance and testing, immunizations, and quarantine.
- *Preparedness* is planning and readiness to immediately respond to an emergency, assist people, and protect property. Examples are disaster planning, training, drills, ensuring that equipment and vehicles are available for a response, and coordinating roles and functions with multiple organizations.
- *Response* to an emergency is usually local; however, larger events necessitate a response from state and federal agencies. Also, private-sector entities (e.g., Red Cross and Salvation Army) may be called

to action. Local responders include police, firefighters, a HAZMAT team, and emergency management personnel. Once an incident occurs, the value of mitigation, prevention, preparedness, planning, cooperative arrangements, and other before-the-fact activities becomes evident.

- *Recovery* involves assisting people, businesses, organizations, infrastructure, and the community in returning to a pre-disaster state. The process includes a host of needs, such as food and water, housing, physical and mental health services, and economic support. Recovery may require weeks, months, or years and special government appropriations.

- *Communications* includes government communicating among all levels of government and with all of its partners (e.g., Red Cross and industries), and especially citizens. Brochures, checklists, the Internet, and other media are avenues for government to help citizens learn about threats and hazards and how to prepare and recover. Warnings are also communicated via various media. Government is continuously working to improve communications by seeking to use common terminology. Another method is through **interoperability**, which is multiple agencies communicating with each other during an emergency by using similar technology.

Critical Thinking

How does emergency management compare with business continuity and enterprise resilience?

Life Safety

"**Life safety** pertains to building construction design that increases safety, what organizations and employees can do in preparation for emergencies, and what they can do once an emergency occurs." Life safety is vital because of the delay in government response and "the **true first responders** are the victims of an unfortunate event." "Public safety involves primarily government employees who plan, train and equip themselves for emergencies. They respond as quickly as possible to the scene of an emergency to save lives, care for the injured, protect people and property, and restore order" (Purpura 2007, 273). When an emergency occurs at an office building, for example, security officers, floor wardens, and other trained employees perform duties (e.g., guiding evacuees, fighting a fire, and rendering first aid) until first responders (e.g., police, firefighters, emergency medical services) arrive. Then, the duties of proprietary personnel *merge* with first responders, who take on the lead role at the site of the emergency, which may be a

FIGURE 11.5   How many life safety/fire protection features can you identify in this photograph?

crime scene. Because of this mutual involvement in safety, the private and public sectors should cooperatively plan, train, and conduct exercises, which is often the case.

Numerous standards and regulations promote life safety (Figure 11.5). Examples are the NFPA 1600 standard and regulations from OSHA. OSHA regulation 1910.38 Emergency Action Plans, for instance, calls for a written emergency plan, training, procedures for reporting an emergency, an alarm system, evacuation plans, first aid, and other requirements. OSHA regulation 1910.39 Fire Protection Plans requires a written fire protection plan, a list of fire hazards, HAZMAT procedures, fire protection equipment, and other requirements.

The **NFPA 101 Life Safety Code** is widely adopted by governments in the United States as an enforceable code. Its topics include egress (i.e., going out of a building) in case of emergency evacuation, fire drills, construction characteristics, fire protection equipment, and building contents and furnishings. It features standards for high-rise buildings and educational, health care, correctional, lodging, apartment, residential, industrial, and other facilities.

SHELTER-IN-PLACE

Not every emergency requires evacuation of a building. **Shelter-in-place** refers to taking immediate shelter, no matter where you are, to protect yourself from a chemical, biological, or radiological contaminant. (This is different from seeking a safe place when a storm approaches.) Emergency authorities—via communications over radio, television, or other mass-notification methods—may provide guidance for sheltering-in-place. FEMA, Red Cross, and other Web sites provide a variety of suggestions. For instance, an emphasis is on staying in an interior room with few or no windows, turning off HVAC and vents, and sealing all openings (e.g., doors, windows, and vents) with duct tape and plastic sheeting. During a chemical incident, an interior room above ground (i.e., second floor) is best, because certain chemicals are heavier than air and may enter the lowest floor or a basement. Early preparation is important for sheltering-in-place, and this includes availability of food, water, communications equipment, and supplies. During such an emergency, listen for emergency broadcasts for guidance.

Fire Protection

Fire is a serious problem. The U.S. Fire Administration (2008) reported that, in 2007, fire killed more Americans than all natural disasters combined. In addition, an estimated 1.6 million fires occurred, resulting in 3,430 civilian and 118 firefighter deaths, 17,675 civilian injuries, and direct property loss at about $14.6 billion. Although 84 percent of civilian fire deaths occur in residences, the threat remains for retail businesses, industrial facilities, schools, hospitals, modes of transportation, and so forth.

Imagine being an employee of a business located in a 50-story office building. You are working on the 10th floor and a fire occurs on the 2nd floor. The elevators return to the 1st floor and are inoperable (standard procedure in a building fire). The stairways are blocked by debris and thick smoke. What do you do? Did you attend life-safety and fire-protection training previously offered by building management? Did you participate in fire drills and mock emergency exercises? Do you know how to use a fire extinguisher and the standpipe hose system? Do you know how to increase your chances, and your coworkers chances, of survival in this totally unexpected, life-threatening emergency? The value of emergency preparedness, life safety, and fire protection become evident when an individual is placed in such a situation.

Fire protection can be divided into fire prevention and fire suppression. Both components of fire protection include specialists and numerous strategies and technologies. The National Fire Protection Association (NFPA) is a rich source of information on relevant standards. Moreover, enforceable codes in locales are often based on the NFPA.

Fire prevention includes strategies and technologies implemented by personnel to avert fire. Examples are management support through an adequate budget, policies and procedures, and training and drills. The design of buildings plays a role in preventing fire through enforceable codes that specify design requirements to reduce the risk of fire, such as masonry construction. The proper storage of hazardous materials is another way in which fire can be prevented.

Fire suppression applies personnel, strategies, and technologies to extinguish a fire once it begins. Modern buildings use computer-based integrated fire response and suppression systems to detect smoke and fire, pinpoint its location, notify occupants and the fire department, shut down certain electrical systems, activate emergency lighting, return elevators to the first floor, and suppress the fire through activation of a water or chemical sprinkler system. Multistory buildings often contain a standpipe and hose system. A **standpipe** is a vertical pipe constructed in a building to enable water to reach upper floors that contain a fire hose in a wall cabinet so people can fight a fire.

Once a fire begins, the investment in training and drills proves valuable. In a high-rise building, for example, rapid evacuation is essential. If employees are trapped in upper floors, strategies include communicating with first responders to ensure that they are aware of the location of trapped people; closing doors and placing wet towels at edges to reduce the spread of smoke; going to windows for observation by rescuers; and, since smoke rises, breathing at floor level with a wet towel over the mouth and nose.

Employees should be trained to use portable fire extinguishers, which should be inspected and charged to ensure proper functioning. Portable extinguishers are often of the Class ABC type, contain a dry chemical, and avoid the need for a person to frantically decide which extinguisher to use in an emergency if various types are deployed at a site, as listed next.

- Class A: to suppress a fire of paper, wood, and other ordinary combustible materials
- Class B: to suppress a fire of flammable liquid (e.g., gasoline)
- Class C: to suppress a fire of electrical components
- Class D: to suppress a fire of combustible metals
- Class K: to suppress a fire of cooking fuels (e.g., animal fat)

A water-type of extinguisher is available for a Class A fire, but applied to a Class C fire it could create an electrical hazard, because water conducts electricity. The same type of extinguisher applied to a Class B fire could cause a flammable liquid on fire to float on the water and spread the fire.

Widmer (2009, 32) writes, "When a portable fire extinguisher is used, it puts out the fire 94 percent of the time—typically within the first 2 minutes." However, he emphasizes that it should only be used once the fire department has been contacted and everyone is safe. Because a fire can spread rapidly, "every second counts," and the fire department should be contacted immediately. NFPA 10 provides guidance on portable fire extinguishers.

YOUR CAREER IN SECURITY

Business Continuity/Emergency Management Specialist

The business continuity/emergency management (BC/EM) specialist assists an organization in preparing for emergencies and disasters and takes an active role in recovery from such events. *Business continuity* is more of a private-sector term, whereas *emergency management* is more of a public-sector term. The duties of practitioners in each of these fields have many similarities. Here, an emphasis is placed on business continuity because this book is oriented more toward the private sector than the public sector.

BC Management (2008) reports that the business-continuity profession has varied job titles among companies. Examples are planner, coordinator, administrator, manager, assistant vice president, project manager, vice president, director, and consultant.

Security practitioners who seek a career in BC/EM must develop their background for this specialization through a combination of education, training, and experience. BC/EM specialists come from a variety of backgrounds as they fine-tune their niche. Their resumes may show experience in risk management, IT, business, government first-responder services, security, and the military.

Nature of the Work

Not only do BC/EM programs reduce the impact of crises on organizations, these programs make good business sense and are often required by government regulations and insurance policies. BC/EM specialists must integrate the BC/EM plans throughout a business enterprise, including risk management, IT, audit, security, and other corporate functions.

A BC/EM specialist is knowledgeable of both business objectives and needs, while understanding the regulatory environment from codes, regulations, and laws. With this foundation, a BC/EM plan is formulated that focuses on such objectives as the safety of people; the protection of assets, facilities, and operations; the need for backup systems; and quick recovery. The duties of the job also include risk analyses, updating the BC/EM plans, testing of plans, enhancing awareness of the plans, training, and providing expertise to management.

Requirements

Because the survival of an organization and its employees may depend on a BC/EM specialist, the requirements of this position are extensive. A bachelor's degree is generally required in a related field, such as business continuity, emergency management, or risk management. Other majors may be acceptable, depending on experience, training, and certifications. An applicant should have 5 to 10 years of related experience. A certification is often required from the Disaster Recovery Institute International, the Business Continuity Institute, or some comparable organization. Additional requirements include excellent written and verbal communications skills, the ability to serve as part of a team, and knowledge of emerging technologies and IT systems. Federal government positions may require U.S. citizenship and a secret clearance (Job Openings 2008).

Salary

Research by BC Management (2008) showed 2007 average total compensation was $101,554 annually for BC/EM specialists. Contractors in the same profession, in 2007, earned an average of $138,326 annually. The research also showed that 75 percent of 1,987 respondents were certified and 25 percent were not. In addition, certification enhanced income.

Advice

Preparation for a career in BC/EM takes several years. The career path can begin with a security position; however, relevant education, training, and experience are mandatory. Learn the background of BC/EM practitioners to understand the diverse career paths that led to their positions. They may have degrees and experience in BC/EM or shifted their skills from risk management, IT, government public safety, security, the military, or other vocations, to BC/EM.

Summary

Risk management improves an organization's resilience following a harmful event. The methodologies and strategies of risk management are applied in both the private and public sectors, although with variations. Enterprise risk management (ERM) advances risk management to the next level by applying a broad-based perspective on risks that are organization-wide and include, as a top priority, the entity's objectives. Enterprise security risk management, a component of ERM, is also comprehensive and organization-wide, while identifying, assessing, and mitigating security risks by including multidisciplinary perspectives and serving organizational needs.

Throughout this book, numerous types of risks are explained. This chapter added explanations and mitigation methods for the following risks: earthquakes, floods, tornadoes, hurricanes, pandemics, workplace accidents, HAZMAT incidents, bombings, and fires. Formalized programs to address these risks were also presented. These included business continuity, enterprise resilience, emergency management, life safety, and fire protection.

Discussion Questions

1. How can the discipline of risk management assist security executives in their work?
2. What are the differences between risk management and enterprise risk management?
3. Would you like to be a risk manager? Why or why not?
4. Do you think the present risk of terrorism in the United States is low? Explain your answer.
5. Should all regions of the United States prepare for natural disasters in the same way? Why or why not?
6. Do you think OSHA meddles too much in the operations of businesses? Explain your answer.
7. What are your views of "safety bucks" as an incentive to reduce accidents in the workplace?
8. What are the differences between business continuity and enterprise resilience?
9. What are the similarities and differences between emergency management and business continuity/enterprise resilience?
10. Do you think our nation places enough emphasis on life safety in buildings? Explain your answer.

Practical Applications

11A. As a security manager, you are preparing a proposal for new access control and CCTV systems for a large manufacturing facility. Rather than accentuate scare tactics related to losses from crime if the new systems are not installed, prepare a positive perspective (as described by Callahan earlier in the chapter) by emphasizing value to the business. Prepare a statement of business value that you will include in your proposal. Include hypothetical information, if necessary.

11B. As an assistant to the director of corporate security, your next assignment is to research and report on the topics of enterprise risk management and enterprise resilience. The director requests that you summarize what these terms mean, relevant methodologies, how the security department is linked to the application of these methodologies in a business environment, and the value of these methodologies to security and the business.

11C. You are a risk manager for a company based in Oklahoma City at a high-rise building. Your next task is to review business-continuity plans in case of tornado. What resources do you rely on to review the present plans? What are five major topics that should be in the plans?

11D. You are a security specialist who was recently assigned increased responsibilities by serving as acting coordinator of business continuity. Your employer, a major corporation, is expanding business to Buffalo; New York; Los Angeles; and Charleston, South Carolina. At a meeting next week, executives will be asking about overall crime rates in these cities and natural hazards. What are your findings that you will report?

11E. As a corporate investigator, the corporate risk manager asks for your recommendations to correct a growing problem: Metrics shows that an increasing number of employees are claiming work-related injuries on Monday mornings, soon after arriving at work. The risk manager thinks that a portion of the injuries may be from weekend activities and not work-related. The problem is getting increasingly expensive, and the risk manager wants action. What are your recommendations?

11F. As a corporate safety specialist and member of the corporate business-continuity team, your next assignment is to prepare a safety report on a chemical that will soon be introduced into the workplace in a new manufacturing process for a new product. The chemical is benzene. What sources and organizations do you rely on for the report? Focus on safety, transportation, storage, regulations, and related topics. Prepare a two-page summary and include a bibliography.

11G. As a sergeant in the security department at a college, you have been asked by your superior to prepare recommended policies and procedures for bomb threats and explosions to be presented to the college safety committee. Prepare the recommended policies and procedures.

11H. As the new director of security and safety for a high-rise office building, you will be conducting evacuation drills in the near future. Your top priority at this time is to increase participation in life safety training and related volunteer positions by the numerous tenants in the building. What are your plans to increase participation?

Internet Connections

American Insurance Association: www.aiadc.org
American National Standards Institute: www.ansi.org
American Red Cross: www.redcross.org
American Risk and Insurance Association: www.aria.org
ASIS International: www.asisonline.org
Building Owners & Managers Association: www.boma.org
Business Continuity Institute: www.thebci.org
Business Resilience Certification Consortium International: www.brcci.org
Centers for Disease Control: www.bt.cdc.gov
Disaster Recovery Institute International: www.drii.org
Emergency Management Accreditation Program: www.emaponline.org/

Emergency Management Institute: http://training.fema.gov

Federal Emergency Management Agency: www.fema.gov

International Association of Emergency Managers: www.iaem.com

International Code Council: www.iccsafe.org

International Risk Management Institute: www.irmi.com

National Emergency Management Association: www.nemaweb.org

National Fire Protection Association: www.nfpa.org

National Institute for Occupational Safety and Health (NIOSH): www.cdc.gov/niosh/homepage.html

National Safety Council: www.nsc.org

Occupational Safety and Health Administration (OSHA): www.osha.gov

Public Risk Management Association: www.primacentral.org

Risk and Insurance Management Society: www.rims.org

Risk World: www.riskworld.com

Security Analysis and Risk Management Association www.sarma.org

State Risk and Insurance Management Association: www.strima.org

Surety Association of America: www.surety.org/

The International Emergency Management Society: www.tiems.org

U.S. Department of Health and Human Services: www.hhs.gov

U.S. Department of Homeland Security: www.dhs.gov

U.S. Department of Homeland Security (site for business-continuity planning): www.ready.gov

U.S. Government Accountability Office: www.gao.gov

References

The Alliance for Enterprise Security Risk Management. 2007. The convergence of physical and information security in the context of enterprise risk management. www.aesrm.org.

ASIS International. 2004. Business continuity guideline. www.asisonline.org.

ASIS International. 2009. Organizational resilience: Security, preparedness, and continuity management systems—Requirements with guidance for use. American National Standard. www.asisonline.org.

Balaouras, S. 2009. The state of business continuity preparedness. *Disaster Recovery Journal* 22 (Winter).

BC Management. 2008. Business continuity-USA, 2007 compensation report. www.bcmanagement.com.

Bullock, J., et al. 2006. *Introduction to homeland security.* 2nd ed. Burlington, MA: Elsevier Butterworth-Heinemann.

Bureau of Labor Statistics. 2009. Injuries, illnesses, and fatalities. http://data.bls.gov.

Callahan, J. 2008. The (not so) dark side of ... risk. *Disaster Recovery Journal* 21 (Spring):16–28.

Centers for Disease Control. 2009. Emergency preparedness and response. www.bt.cdc.gov/disasters.

Coffin, B. 2009. The way forward: Rethinking enterprise risk management. *Risk Management* (April). www.rmmagazine.com.

Committee of Sponsoring Organizations of the Treadway Commission. 2004. Enterprise risk management—Integrated framework (September). www.coso.org.

Davidson, M. 2009. Managing risk across the enterprise. *Security Management* 53 (July):56–61.

Federal Emergency Management Agency. 2003. Primer for design of commercial buildings to mitigate terrorist attacks. FEMA 427 (December). Washington, DC: FEMA.

Federal Emergency Management Agency. 2009. Disaster information. www.fema.gov/hazard.index.shtm.

Greenhouse, S. 2009. In workplace injury system, ill will on all sides. *New York Times*, April 2. www.nytimes.com.

Job Openings. 2008. *Disaster Recovery Journal* 21 (Spring):96.

Johnson, M., and J. Spivey. 2008. ERM and the security professional. *Risk Management* (January):1. www.rmmagazine.com.

Kaye, B. 2008. Leading business continuity: A guide for senior executives. *Disaster Recovery Journal* 21 (Spring):38–39.

Leimberg, S., et al. 2002. *The tools & techniques of risk management & insurance*. Cincinnati, OH: The National Underwriter Co.

London Resilience Partnership/UK Government. 2008. Business continuity. www.london-prepared.gov.uk.

MacVicar, S. 2009. Al-Qaeda bombers learn from drug smugglers. *CBS Evening News*, September 28. www.cbsnews.com/stories/2009/09/28/eveningnews/main5347847.shtml.

Makomaski, J. 2008. So what exactly is ERM? *Risk Management* 2008 (April):2. www.rmmagazine.com.

Merriam–Webster's Online Dictionary. 2009. Enterprise. www.merriam-webster.com.

National Counterterrorism Center. 2009. 2008 report on terrorism. http://wits.nctc.gov.

Nichter, D. 2008. Betting on enterprise risk management. *Security Management* 52 (September):108–118.

Occupational Safety and Health Administration. 2007. Guidance on preparing workplaces for an influenza pandemic. www.osha.gov/Publications/OSHA3327pandemic.pdf.

Perdue, M. 2008. How to cultivate a safety culture. *Security Management* 52 (June):73–79.

Pitcher, E. 2010. Profiting from a business continuity plan. *Disaster Recovery Journal* 23 (Winter):28.

Purpura, P. 2007. *Terrorism and homeland security: An introduction with applications*. Burlington, MA: Elsevier Butterworth–Heinemann.

Taubenberger, J., and D. Morens. 2006. 1918 influenza: The mother of all pandemics. *Emergency Infectious Disease* 12 (January). www.cdc.gov/ncidod/EID.vol12no01/05-0979.htm.

U.S. Bureau of Alcohol, Tobacco, Firearms and Explosives. 2008. U.S. Bomb Data Center, fact sheet. www.atf.gov.

U.S. Department of Transportation. 2009. HAZMAT summary by incident state for 2008. www.phmsa.dot.gov.

U.S. Fire Administration. 2008. The overall fire picture. www.usfa.dhs.gov.

U.S. Government Accountability Office. 2008. Risk management: Strengthening the use of risk management principles in homeland security (June 25). www.gao.gov/new.items/d08904.pdf.

U.S. Government Accountability Office. 2009. Influenza pandemic: Continued focus on the nation's planning and preparedness efforts remains essential (June 3). www.goa.gov/new.items/d09760.pdf.

Widmer, J. 2009. Ensuring that fire extinguishers work. *Buildings* 103 (February):32.

Zawada, B. 2009. Reconsidering the business continuity professional's boundaries. *Disaster Recovery Journal* 22 (Summer):12–16.

Chapter **12**

Protection of Critical Infrastructures and Key Resources

Chapter Learning Objectives

After reading this chapter, you should be able to:

1. Define critical infrastructures and key resources
2. Explain the importance of critical infrastructures and key resources
3. Trace the history of critical infrastructure protection
4. Describe the National Infrastructure Protection Plan
5. Discuss the methodologies and challenges of assessing the vulnerabilities of critical infrastructures and key resources
6. Name and describe at least ten critical infrastructures/key resources
7. Explain the cascade effect

Terms To Know

infrastructure
critical infrastructure (CI)
key resources (KR)
protection

all-hazards
CIKR partner
Federal Civil Defense Act of 1950
National Infrastructure Protection Plan (NIPP)
sector-specific agencies (SSA)
sector-specific plans (SSP)
Infrastructure Data Warehouse
U.S. Department of Agriculture (USDA)
Food and Drug Administration (FDA)
Public Health Security and Bioterrorism Preparedness and Response Act of 2002
Project BioShield Act of 2004
Robert T. Stafford Disaster Relief and Emergency Assistance Act of 1974
tabletop exercises
Environmental Protection Agency (EPA)
penetration test
cascade effect
medical surge
U. S. Department of Health and Human Services (HHS)
Pandemic and All-Hazards Preparedness Act of 2006
Joint Commission on Accreditation of Healthcare Organizations
DHS, Office of Infrastructure Protection
Defense Production Act of 1950
Department of Defense (DOD)
National Industrial Security Program
National Communications System
U.S. Department of Energy (DOE)
Maritime Transportation Security Act of 2002
Transportation Security Administration (TSA)
Aviation and Transportation Security Act of 2001
U.S. Department of the Treasury
Bhopal, India
Texas City, Texas
Chemical Facility Anti-Terrorism Standards
Atomic Energy Act of 1946
Nuclear Regulatory Commission (NRC)
access point database check
loss-prevention agent

Introduction

Critical infrastructures and key resources (CIKR) sustain our way of life and are essential for our economy, prosperity, security, and defense. Damage to just one sector (e.g., energy)—through a natural disaster, accident, technological failure, or act of terrorism—can cause other sectors (e.g., communications, IT, banking, and commercial businesses) to be harmed, major inconveniences for large population groups, and multibillion dollar economic losses. Because of numerous threats and hazards facing CIKR, and the dependencies and interdependencies of sectors, our nation must work with its internal partners (e.g., governments at all levels and the private sector), and those overseas, to plan and implement protection and resiliency for CIKR. This chapter covers early critical infrastructure protection in the United States, the National Infrastructure Protection Plan, assessing vulnerabilities of critical infrastructures, and the characteristics and protection strategies of eighteen CIKR sectors.

TERMS FROM THE NATIONAL INFRASTRUCTURE PROTECTION PLAN

To assist the reader in understanding this chapter and the protection of CIKR, the following terms are presented verbatim from the "National Infrastructure Protection Plan, 2009" (NIPP) (U.S. Department of Homeland Security 2009a, 109–111).

Infrastructure: The framework of interdependent networks and systems comprising identifiable industries, institutions (including people and procedures), and distribution capabilities that provide a reliable flow of products and services essential to the defense and economic security of the United States, the smooth functioning of government at all levels, and society as a whole. Consistent with the definition in the Homeland Security Act, infrastructure includes physical, cyber, and/or human elements.

Critical infrastructure (CI): Systems and assets, whether physical or virtual, so vital that the incapacity or destruction of such may have a debilitating impact on the security, economy, public health or safety, environment, or any combination of these matters, across any federal, state, regional, territorial, or local jurisdictions.

Key resources (KR): As defined in the Homeland Security Act, key resources are publicly or privately controlled resources essential to the minimal operations of the economy and government.

Protection: Actions or measures taken to cover or shield from exposure, injury, or destruction. In the context of the NIPP, protection includes actions to deter the threat, mitigate the vulnerabilities, or minimize the consequences associated with a terrorist attack or other incident. Protection can include a wide range of activities, such as hardening facilities, building resiliency and redundancy, incorporating hazard resistance into initial facility design, initiating active or passive countermeasures, installing security systems, promoting workforce surety, training and exercises, and implementing cyber security measures, among various others.

All-hazards: A grouping classification encompassing all conditions, environmental or human-made, that have the potential to cause injury, illness, or death; damage to or loss of equipment, infrastructure services, or property; or alternatively causing functional degradation to social, economic, or environmental aspects.

CIKR partner: Those federal, state, local, tribal, or territorial governmental entities, public and private sector owners and operators and representative organizations, regional organizations and coalitions, academic and professional entities, and certain not-for-profit and private volunteer organizations that share in the responsibility for protecting the nation's CIKR.

Protection Challenges

"The National Strategy for The Physical Protection of Critical Infrastructures and Key Assets" (White House 2003a, 9) identified the following protection challenges:

Critical assets:
Agriculture and food
Water
Public health
Emergency services
Defense industrial base
Telecommunications
Energy:
    Electricity
    Oil and natural gas
Transportation:
    Aviation
    Passenger rail and railroads
    Highways, trucking, and busing
    Pipelines
    Maritime
    Mass transit
Banking and finance
Chemical industry and hazardous materials
Postal and shipping

Key assets:
National monuments and icons
Nuclear power plants
Dams
Government facilities
Commercial assets

The U.S. Government Accountability Office (2008a, 4) provides examples of the extent of CIKR in the United States: 55,000 community drinking water systems, 30,000 wastewater treatment and collection facilities, 4 million miles of roads, 26,000 miles of commercially navigable waterways, 11,000 miles of transit lines, 500 train stations, and 19,000 airports.

Government Web sites and many publications often note that the private sector owns and operates about 85% of the nation's critical infrastructure (U.S. Department of Homeland Security 2009b). The following statistics of the U.S. Government Accountability Office (2008a, 4–5) provide some specifics related to this often-cited statistic; however, comprehensive research is needed on CI ownership.

- CI is primarily owned and operated by state and local governments and the private sector.
- The federal government owns a limited amount of CI. For example, the federal government owns and operates the nation's air-traffic control CI.
- About 97 percent of the nation's roads and highways are owned by state and local governments, with local governments owning approximately 77 percent of the miles of roadway.
- About 98 percent of bridges and most transit systems are owned by state and local governments.
- Most freight railroads are owned by the private sector. The federal government owns about 650 miles of Amtrak's 22,000 miles of rail.
- Many ports are publicly owned and privately operated.
- Most commercial service airports are owned by state and local governments.
- About half of the nation's drinking water systems and 20 percent of wastewater systems are privately owned.
- The majority of dams in the United States are privately owned. The federal government owns and operates about 5 percent of the nation's dams.

Early Critical Infrastructure Protection

The U.S. Constitution, Section 8, was the beginning point of government's role in protecting CI. It requires the federal government to construct and protect roads to ensure the delivery of mail. As transportation systems grew with railroads, canals, shipping firms, and private roads—often through the private sector—so did the need to protect these vital modes of transportation for government and commerce. Early on, the U.S. Army played a major role in protecting transportation systems and, at the same time, the protection role of state and local governments (e.g., public police) grew (Brown 2006). In addition, as explained in Chapter 1, because of the limited ability of government to protect CI, private security expanded in the 1800s. Allan Pinkerton and his companies protected railroads and other industries; Henry Wells, William Fargo, and Washington Perry Brink protected valuables in transit; Edwin Holmes began a company offering electronic protection; and William J. Burns established a firm to protect banks.

The growth of railroads and unions had a significant impact on the protection of CI. Railroad security developed to meet the need of protecting crews, passengers, and cargo during westward expansion during the 1800s. Criminal gangs victimized railroads with ease because local law enforcement was reluctant to cross into other jurisdictions to chase train robbers. Eventually, states enacted laws to permit railroad companies to establish private security forces with full arrest powers and the legal authority to cross jurisdictional lines to apprehend train robbers. Railroad companies eventually saw the need for sworn law enforcement officers because proprietary and contract security organizations were unable to significantly curb crime against railroads. States began to enact laws to regulate railroad police departments, and Pennsylvania passed the first Railroad Police Act in 1865. By 1914, railroad police numbered about 14,000, and during World War I, they were deputized by the federal government to protect this CI sector. The Omnibus Crime Control Act of 1990 provides increased power to railroad police by enabling them to "enforce the laws of any jurisdiction in which the rail carrier owns property," including the crossing of state lines. Today, railroad police are professional, specialized, and work with local, state, and federal law enforcement agencies. CSX railroad, for example, developed a rapid response team of highly skilled and cross-functional counterterrorism law enforcement specialists trained in HAZMAT and explosive detection and supported by canine teams (Domzalski 2009; Purpura 2008).

Chapter 1 covered union activities and the use of strikes to force change. Bork (n.d.) writes that, between 1933 and 1937, there were about 10,000 strikes in the United States that involved some 5,600,000 workers. The confrontations between unions and companies were violent. Industries maintained the goal of continuing production and relied on the services of private security and public police forces. For example, in 1937, at a Republic steel plant in Chicago, when a strike occurred, management brought in food and cots for housing nonunion employees and maintained close contact with the Chicago police to ensure that production continued. When management saw the need to clear the site of union men, police entered the plant, and when a picket line formed outside, twenty-three persons were arrested for refusing to move. Soon after, a bloody confrontation resulted in what became known as the Memorial Day Massacre: Four marchers were fatally shot and many more injured, including police officers. The union movement across America, and many related violent confrontations, facilitated an increase in security at businesses and CI.

When wars occurred, there was a heightened urgency for preparedness and protection of vital industries and transportation systems. For example, the Council of National Defense (CND), established by President Woodrow Wilson in 1916, consisted of top cabinet secretaries (e.g., Army, Navy, Interior, and Commerce) who advised the president and agencies of government on vital goods and services needed during World War I, coordinated the work of state and local defense councils and women's committees, and studied the problems of postwar readjustment. The CND was suspended in 1921 and reactivated between 1940 and 1941. The women's committee of the CND worked on a variety of projects in support of war efforts, such as "Americanization activities," patriotic education, and the employment of women (National Archives 2009).

Because the CND lacked sufficient power to increase the production of military equipment, President Wilson also created the War Industries Board (WIB) in 1917. He augmented the powers of the WIB because various business executives refused to work with each other and the military. Under the leadership of financier Bernard Baruch, the WIB facilitated increased cooperation among industry groups and the Army and settled crippling strikes. The WIB ran the U.S. economy during World War I and ensured that military supplies and equipment received first priority at industrial sites. About one-quarter of U.S. production went to the allies in Europe during the war. The WIB set a foundation for the New Deal and the mobilization for World War II (Leuchtenburg 1993).

During the Great Depression (1930s), President Franklin Delano Roosevelt's New Deal era provided many jobs through public works projects. These construction projects built roads, bridges, dams, airports, shipyards, defense plants, and other structures. The issue of protecting CI was debated, and military leaders sought to divorce themselves from this responsibility as they prepared for the U.S. role as a superpower and the possibility of another war. As written in Chapter 1, World War II necessitated increased security for CI. Defense contractors were required to maintain security to protect classified materials and war supplies. More than 200,000 "plant watchmen" were granted the status of auxiliary military police by the federal government by the end of World War II. Eventually, the National Industrial Security Program was established, in 1993, to assist defense contractors in protecting classified information and deterring and detecting espionage. This program replaced industrial security programs operated by various federal agencies.

The Cold War (1945–1991) was an era of tension and potential nuclear war between the United States, the Soviet Union, and the allies of each of these nations. The **Federal Civil Defense Act of 1950** was a minimally funded federal effort to protect U.S. citizens from nuclear attack. Rather than spend huge sums of money to build a bunker system in the United States, a less expensive program of educating citizens to "protect themselves" in case of attack became the priority of civil defense policy. Meager funds were used to produce films and pamphlets on how to build family shelters and how to stock food and supplies. The federal government viewed military and diplomatic strategies as the best ways to deal with the potential of nuclear war.

In 1961, President John F. Kennedy created the Office of Emergency Preparedness to focus on natural disasters. FEMA was created in 1979 to consolidate a hodgepodge of disaster and emergency management programs that changed depending on perceived risks and the administration in power.

As the threat of terrorism increased as the twentieth century ended, and following the Oklahoma City bombing, President William J. Clinton signed Presidential Decision Directive (PDD) 39 which emphasized national policy and federal government agency direction on counterterrorism, plus initiatives for critical infrastructure protection (CIP). These initiatives included the U.S. Department of Justice performing risk analyses at government buildings and making security recommendations. PDD 39 also resulted in the Critical Infrastructure Working Group (CIWG), a multiagency panel to study physical and cyber CIP. The CIWG recommended the formation of an Infrastructure Protection Task Force (IPTF) and the President's Commission on Critical Infrastructure Protection (PCCIP). Presidential Executive Order 13010 established the PCCIP, and while it was conducting its analysis and preparing recommendations for the president, the IPTF worked to increase coordination efforts on protection among CI sectors.

The PCCIP included senior-level government officials, private-sector executives, and academic leaders. After fifteen months of study, the commission published its findings in 1997 entitled "Critical Foundations: Protecting America's Infrastructure." It reported on vulnerabilities of CI, the dangers of interdependency among CI networks, and offered recommendations, many of which were in the 1998 PDD 63, "Protecting America's Critical Infrastructure." PDD 63 was a major strategy to protect CI, and it was supplemented with other executive orders and directives and provided a foundation for subsequent government action to protect CI. It facilitated cooperation among all levels of government and the private sector and promoted a National Infrastructure Protection Plan, among other activities.

National Infrastructure Protection Plan

The **National Infrastructure Protection Plan (NIPP)** has gone through updates since 2006 as our nation learns more about how best to protect CI. The following information is from the "National Infrastructure Protection Plan, 2009" (U.S. Department of Homeland Security 2009a). It replaces the 2006 NIPP.

The Homeland Security Act of 2002 (a law enacted by Congress) provides a legal foundation for the Department of Homeland Security (DHS) responsibilities for the NIPP. The NIPP addresses the requirements President George W. Bush set forth in Homeland Security Presidential Directive 7 (HSPD-7) for a *single national program* of CI protection within a risk-management framework. (An HSPD is law.) The aim of the NIPP is to ensure the resiliency of CIKR of the United States as an essential component of the Nation's security, public health and safety, and economy. The NIPP is oriented toward "all-hazards" protection, which includes terrorist attacks, accidents, natural disasters, and other emergencies.

A "risk analysis and management framework" is applied by the NIPP to promote continuous improvements by focusing on efforts to: set goals and objectives; identify assets, systems, and networks; assess risks; establish priorities; promote return-on-investment; implement protective and resiliency strategies; and measure effectiveness.

The NIPP seeks to facilitate the sharing of information about threats and hazards among partners, build partnerships to implement protection programs, implement long-term risk management, and maximize the efficient use of resources for protection, restoration, and recovery. It works in conjunction with the National Preparedness Guidelines (NPG) and the National Response Framework (NRF) to provide a comprehensive approach to homeland security. The NPG set national priorities, doctrine, and roles and responsibilities for disasters, while the NRF concentrates on incident management.

HSPD-7 established a federal policy whereby the Department of Homeland Security is to lead CIKR protection efforts by identifying and prioritizing protection needs and assigning responsibility for CIKR sectors to federal **sector-specific agencies** (SSAs). The goals of SSAs are to coordinate protection among all relevant partners (i.e., government at all levels and the private sector) and develop **sector-specific plans** (SSPs). SSPs include defining sector partners and regulatory bases; identifying sector-specific methodologies, risks, and priorities; and establishing goals, objectives, and protection strategies. The SSAs and assigned CIKR sectors are noted throughout this chapter.

The NIPP states that all federal departments and agencies function as partners with the DHS and SSAs. These include the Department of State, which works with foreign governments and international organizations to strengthen CIKR protection; the Department of Justice, which includes the FBI that investigates and prosecutes cases of alleged terrorism; and the Nuclear Regulatory Commission, which works to protect nuclear reactors.

Additional partners to protect CIKR are: state, local, tribal, and territorial governments; boards, commissions, authorities, and councils that perform regulatory, advisory, policy, or business oversight functions related to CIKR; CIKR owners and operators; and academic and research centers that study CIKR protection issues and technology.

DHS maintains an inventory of assets, systems, and networks of the nation's CIKR. It is known as the **Infrastructure Data Warehouse** (IDW). The goal of the IDW is to provide information when serious events occur and to help in understanding relationships, dependencies, and interdependencies of CIKR. Sources for the IDW include SSAs, voluntary submittals from CIKR partners, trade associations, regulatory bodies, and studies of high-risk sites. DHS is responsible for protecting the IDW from unauthorized use.

Another component of the NIPP is personnel and organizational capability development. The NIPP "establishes a framework to enable awareness, education, training, and exercise programs that allow people and organizations to develop and maintain the core competencies and expertise required for effective implementation of the CIKR protection mission" (U.S. Department of Homeland Security 2009a, 82).

HSPD-7 establishes national policy to enhance the protection of CIKR through the nation's research and development capabilities. To encourage technology development and use by CIKR partners (e.g., businesses and their customers), Congress provided liability protection through the Safety Act (see Chapters 7 and 11).

The NIPP criteria for risk assessments seek to facilitate cross-sector risk comparisons through the following principles. The methodology and assessment must clearly show through documentation how a risk estimate is generated. Assumptions, weighting factors, and subjective judgments must be transparent to a user or audience of the methodology. The methodology must be reliable, produce comparable and repeatable results, be technically sound, and free of omissions and errors. Uncertainty about estimates of risk, vulnerabilities, and consequences must be communicated.

The NIPP measures its effectiveness through performance metrics that enable the DHS and the SSAs to quantitatively show results of efforts at CIKR protection and resiliency. Risk analyses help sectors establish priorities, and performance metrics enable partners to track progress against the priorities. Performance metrics facilitate sound management, accountability, and feedback for planning improvements. Examples are the number of protective programs established in a fiscal year, the number of sector entities exchanging CIKR information, and the number of entities that responded to a call for information on assets for planning purposes.

Recommendations are offered by the NIPP to private-sector owners and operators to improve the efficiency and effectiveness of their CIKR protection programs. These recommendations are based on best practices applied by various sectors as summarized next (U.S. Department of Homeland Security 2009a, 167–169).

- Incorporate the NIPP framework into assets, systems, and networks.
- Voluntarily share CIKR information with partners.
- Apply performance metrics and risk and vulnerability assessments.
- Apply personnel screening strategies.

- Protect IT systems and information.
- Partner with local first responders and state and federal agencies.
- Collaborate with other CIKR owners and operators on protection issues of mutual concern and be aware of interconnectedness and interdependencies of multiple infrastructures (Figure 12.1).
- Maintain business continuity and resiliency plans and participate in local, state, and federal exercises. Create a culture of preparedness throughout the enterprise.
- Utilize NFPA 1600 if the sector has not developed its own standard.
- Develop and maintain a comprehensive security program.
- Enhance security awareness and capabilities through training and drills in conjunction with public safety agencies and neighboring facilities.
- Identify and resolve supply-chain issues.
- Participate in accreditation and certification protection programs.

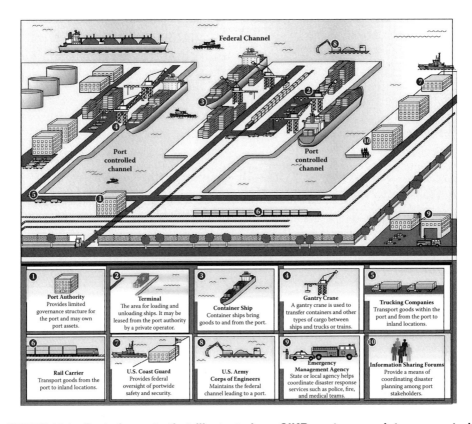

FIGURE 12.1 **Port elements that illustrate how CIKR sectors are interconnected and interdependent. (*Source:* U.S. Government Accountability Office, 2007, "Port Risk Management," p. 13; http://www.gao.gov/new.items/d07412.pdf.)**

ISSUE

Should Terrorism be the Major Focus of Critical Infrastructure Protection?

Colcher (2008) argues that terrorism presents a more worrisome threat to CI than "normal accidents" or natural disasters. He writes that CI is resilient to random failures, but very vulnerable to attacks because terrorists can take their time in studying a CI target to identify points of attack that can result in the most damage. And, terrorists can plan sustained attacks to cause lasting damage. Colcher goes on to note that we are very dependent on CI, and its disruption can harm public confidence in government and result in a breakdown of law and order. Compounding the threat of terrorism is the possibility of the media being unavailable because of infrastructure collapse and resultant rumors and misinformation. Another point made by Colcher is that because most of the CI is owned by the private sector, a large number of companies would have to work together with local, state, and federal government agencies. He argues that although patriotism is a factor during an emergency, for competitive and financial reasons, full cooperation is unlikely among companies. Colcher supports the views that it is impossible to prevent all terrorist attacks and that initiatives should go beyond preventive measures and increase the resilience of CI.

The U.S. Department of Homeland Security (2009a, 11), in the NIPP, points out that terrorists are "relentless, patient, opportunistic, and flexible, learning from experience and modifying tactics and targets to exploit perceived vulnerabilities and avoid observed strengths." In addition, domestic and international CIKR afford numerous targets for terrorists, and as security is increased at more predictable targets, terrorists are likely to shift their interest to less protected targets. This threat is complicated by a "vast and diverse aggregation of highly interconnected assets, systems, and networks" that can magnify vulnerabilities for cascading failure among multiple critical infrastructures, resulting in enormous human and economic harm.

As we know, the NIPP argues for CIKR protection and preparedness in an all-hazards context. It refers to Hurricanes Katrina and Rita, the Northridge (CA) earthquake, floods, the *Exxon Valdez* oil spill, and the need to protect the cyber infrastructure. The government's major avenue in facing threats and hazards is though a CIKR risk-management program.

Critical Thinking

What are your views of the threat of terrorism being the major focus of critical infrastructure protection?

Assessing Vulnerability of Critical Infrastructures and Key Resources

McCreight and Renda-Tanali (2007, 42–46) argue that DHS has placed responsibility for assessing the vulnerabilities of CIKR and preparing protection plans on states and locales, but there is incomplete information on the effectiveness of these assessments as benchmarks for preparedness. In addition, they write of the limited effort to share and consolidate relevant best practices and methodologies as states and locales apply various approaches that make sense to them. With less than a perfect formula, and the necessity to experiment with different approaches, McCreight and Renda-Tanali favor a practical blend of both nonscientific and scientific methods for assessing vulnerability.

It is important to note that although McCreight and Renda-Tanali (2007) emphasize state and local government CIKR vulnerability assessments, businesses and institutions are part of these efforts. Also, as we know, businesses and institutions typically have their own programs of protection, and they should continue to "look beyond the property line" and work with partners in the community, including government.

According to McCreight and Renda-Tanali (2007), the *nonscientific approach* is applicable to large and small cities. It involves certain key elements and steps: *First*, the team conducting a vulnerability assessment should include major interests in the community, such as public safety, business, education, and health care, to be led by the best leaders. *Second*, an advisory committee should be formed from the state government and neighboring cities to review assessments and provide feedback and suggestions. *Third*, an academic perspective is also helpful from the disciplines of engineering, public health, homeland security, and other related departments. The aim of all of these groups is to study CIKR and the locale's capacity to respond effectively to the most likely risks. Basic questions include: Who owns and operates CIKR? Who can restore it? In what time frame? What are alternative plans if the damage cannot be repaired within a few weeks?

McCreight and Renda-Tanali (2007) offer three "soft" approaches to CIKR vulnerability assessment:

- *Approach 1*: Focus on the top three CIKR (e.g., water, food, and energy).
- *Approach 2*: Focus on all CIKR. This facilitates prioritization of CIKR because capabilities of protection are limited.
- *Approach 3*: Blends approaches 1 and 2 with Emergency Assistance Compacts between local governments to share resources, such as training and equipment.

Each approach is subject to debate. However, McCreight and Renda-Tanali (2007) write that the different approaches build progressively on prior steps, lead to plans for dealing with each risk, and culminate in exercises to test plans against realistic scenarios to make refinements.

McCreight and Renda-Tanali (2007) write of *scientific approaches* to CIKR vulnerability assessments and note that there is no shortage of such quantitative methodologies. They see quantitative risk assessment as being based on three questions: (1) What can go wrong? (2) What is the likelihood? (3) What are the consequences? They define risk as "a measure of the probability of occurrence and severity of adverse events." Here is a summary of their comments on the scientific approach:

- Probabilistic risk analysis techniques, used to try to find answers to the above questions, entail many types of statistical and forecasting methods, some of which involve expert judgment. Event trees, for example, are applied to show a sequence of possible outcomes of an event and expected losses, often expressed monetarily.
- A comprehensive quantitative risk-assessment approach involves first measuring system risks as is, without protection and mitigation, calculating the probabilities of both harmful events occurring and system failures, and estimating expected losses. A second step is to introduce protection and mitigation and then recalculate failure probabilities. A third step is to measure the cost of protection and mitigation. A cost-benefit analysis is then applied to determine the return on investment.
- Complicating CIKR vulnerability assessments are the interconnectedness and interdependencies of multiple infrastructures. In fact, our understanding of these relationships is in need of further study. In addition, because of the difficulty of accurately modeling or simulating various scenarios, complicated by interconnectedness and interdependencies, a multidisciplinary approach is best, utilizing the expertise of engineers, mathematicians, and system operators.

McCreight and Renda-Tanali (2007, 46) write:

Using scientific methods, it is vital to grasp that sheer reliance on them, as intrinsically "superior" because of their apparent mathematical objectivity versus the more subjective non-scientific approaches, is not always wise. The key issue is whether a blend of both the mathematically rigorous and more subjective approaches could be blended in ways that might yield better results.

Critical Infrastructures and Key Resources

Agriculture and Food Sector

The protection of the nation's agricultural and food sector is a huge responsibility shared by all levels of government and the private sector. Threats and hazards to this sector are broad and include disease, pestilence, adverse weather, acts of terrorism, and attacks by hostile nations.

Various acts of deliberate contamination of food with a chemical or biological agent have been documented from across the globe. Here are a few examples from the James Martin Center for Nonproliferation Studies (2009):

- In October 2006, 350 police officers became ill because of a mass poisoning at a cafeteria located outside of Baghdad. Eleven deaths were reported. The symptoms included bleeding from the ears and nose. Cyanide was suspected as the causative agent. Suspicion focused on Sunni insurgents.
- Between 2003 and 2005, in eleven regions of Italy, one or more individuals injected bleach, acetone, or ammonia into commercial drink containers. A "copycat" theory evolved because of the wide area of victimizations. Thirty-three casualties resulted in significant economic losses for the bottled-water industry in Italy.
- In September of 1984, in Dallas, Oregon, members of the Rajneeshee cult poisoned salad bars in ten restaurants and one supermarket with salmonella bacteria to prevent citizens from voting in an election and to gain control of posts in the Wasco county government. About 750 people became ill. Several cult members were arrested, convicted, and imprisoned.

Although cases of foodborne illnesses are not usually intentionally caused, this problem is a serious health concern. The Centers for Disease Control (CDC) (2009) estimates that about 76 million U.S. residents get sick, 325,000 are hospitalized, and 5,000 die each year from foodborne illnesses. Salmonella infection, for example, has been estimated to cause about 1.4 million foodborne illnesses each year. However, only about 40,000 laboratory-confirmed cases of salmonella are reported to the CDC annually.

Foodborne illnesses are difficult to investigate and require scientific expertise. Two major challenges are detection and pinpointing the cause of tainted food. Surveillance (e.g., at hospitals) helps to link dispersed cases with common factors and symptoms.

Although terrorist attacks are a serious threat to critical infrastructures and key resources, we must continue an "all-hazards" approach to protection.

An all-hazards approach to protecting the U.S. agriculture and food sector is an enormous undertaking. This sector is capable of feeding and clothing people beyond the needs of the United States. The agriculture and food sector is almost all under private ownership and includes about 2.1 million farms, 880,500 firms, and over 1 million facilities. It is dependent on the water sector for clean irrigation and processed water, the transportation sector for movement of what it produces, energy for farming and production, and banking and other sectors. The agriculture and food sector accounts for roughly one-fifth of the nation's economic activity, and it is regulated at the federal level by the **U.S. Department of Agriculture** (USDA) and the U.S. Department of Health and Human Services' (HHS) **Food and Drug Administration** (FDA). These government bodies are sector-specific agencies (SSAs) for the agriculture and food sector, as specified in HSPD-7. Among the many duties of the USDA, it is responsible for the safety of meat, poultry, and egg products, as well as agricultural health. The FDA is charged with regulation and safety for 80 percent of the food consumed in the United States, including domestic food valued at $417 billion, imported food valued at $49 billion, roughly 600,000 restaurants and institutional food service providers, and about 235,000 grocery stores. State and local government bodies also regulate this industry, and receive guidance from the FDA (U.S. Department of Homeland Security 2007a, Part II, 1).

Laws that support the protection of the agriculture and food sector include the Homeland Security Act of 2002 that created the DHS and efforts to protect CIKR against, for example, agroterrorism. The **Public Health Security and Bioterrorism Preparedness and Response Act of 2002** (the Bioterrorism Act) supports the FDA's identification of domestic and foreign food suppliers, inspections, and requirements that the food industry keep records of the "chain of possession" of food to aid in investigations. Under HSPD-9, the USDA, the U.S. Department of Health and Human Services (HHS), and the Environmental Protection Agency (EPA) were directed to enhance plans for prevention, surveillance (e.g., maintaining data on outbreaks of diseases), and response to adverse events. The **Project BioShield Act of 2004** focuses on the need to improve planning for the distribution of vaccines and other medical assistance to counter bioterrorism. The **Robert T. Stafford Disaster Relief and Emergency Assistance Act of 1974** authorizes government leaders to distribute food to any area of the United States subject to a disaster.

Within the USDA is an Office of Inspector General (OIG) that is the law enforcement arm of the USDA. OIG special agents, often in cooperation with other agencies, conduct investigations of criminal activity related to USDA-related laws, regulations, and programs; execute search warrants; make arrests; and carry firearms. They investigate fraud, bribery, smuggling, assaults on employees, and other crimes. A major objective is the health and safety of the public. Investigations may also focus on, as examples, a case of a meat packer allegedly selling tainted products, food tampering, or agroterrorism (U.S. Department of Agriculture 2009).

The FDA, in cooperation with other government bodies, performs its public health and safety duties under several laws. FDA personnel inspect establishments, execute search warrants, make arrests, carry firearms, order recalls of products, seize products, conduct laboratory research of foods, and issue regulations. FDA special agents typically investigate counterfeit, unapproved, or illegally diverted drugs; product tampering; fraudulent health treatments; and fraud in new drug development (U.S. Food and Drug Administration 2008).

To assist with sector partnerships, in 2004, the Food and Agriculture Sector Coordinating Council (FASCC) was formed, composed of public and private sectors. The FASCC hosts forums for coordination of agriculture security and food defense strategies.

Another protection effort is the Strategic Partnership Program Agroterrorism (SPPA) Initiative, a joint assessment program of the FBI, DHS, USDA, and HHS/FDA. The purpose of these assessments is to support the requirements of the NIPP/SSP and HSPD-9. SPPA assessments were conducted on a voluntary basis on products and commodities in the food chain to study vulnerabilities, security, and mitigation to produce generic strategies. Other initiatives include a sector-specific assessment tool, **tabletop exercises** (i.e., a simulated emergency scenario in which participants discuss issues, roles, procedures, or responsibilities), and online training (U.S. Department of Homeland Security 2009c).

Water Sector

Water is essential for human survival. The water sector is vulnerable to attack by bioterrorism/chemical contamination and cyber threats. The interdependencies of the water infrastructure with other infrastructures are a serious concern of the NIPP. The water sector depends on electricity to operate water facilities, chemical plants to manufacture chlorine to purify water, and transportation systems to ship the chemicals. In August of 2003, for instance, the electricity blackout in the northeastern United States resulted in, among other problems, wastewater treatment plants in Cleveland, Detroit, New York, and other locations discharging millions of gallons of untreated sewage into waterways. In addition, the power failure at many drinking-water plants resulted in boil-water advisories (Congressional Research Service 2005, 1).

Our nation depends on the water sector for critical services. These include firefighting and health care. At the same time, the agriculture and food sector, among other sectors, relies on the water sector for operations and production.

According to the U.S. Department of Homeland Security (2009c), the water sector is composed of both drinking water and wastewater utilities; there are about 160,000 public drinking-water systems and over 16,000 publicly owned wastewater treatment systems in the United States. Notice that these figures differ from those cited from the GAO at the beginning of the chapter. This illustrates the difficulty of defining and counting CIKR, such as for the Infrastructure Data Warehouse.

The **Environmental Protection Agency** (EPA) is the SSA for the water sector, as specified in HSPD-7. Other laws that promote the protection of the water sector are as follows: HSPD-8 focuses on all-hazard preparedness and state grants for planning and training. HSPD-9 facilitates a national policy to defend the water, agriculture, and food systems; enhance monitoring and surveillance for early detection of disease, pest, and poisonous agents; develop a nationwide laboratory network; and enhance intelligence capabilities. HSPD-10 covers biodefense, and related to this topic is the Bioterrorism Act. The water sector is governed by numerous environmental laws that regulate drinking water and wastewater utilities. State governments often have direct jurisdiction over the water sector and foster security. However, to maintain primacy, states and tribes must adopt regulations for contaminants that are no less stringent than what the EPA requires in regulations.

As with other government departments and agencies, a variety of specialists are necessary for EPA operations, including administrators, accountants, IT personnel, and so forth. And, similar to the USDA, the FDA, and other federal government bodies, EPA special agents are fully authorized law enforcement officers. They investigate violations of environmental laws.

The EPA not only works with the DHS to implement the NIPP, it also works with other government bodies (e.g., USDA, FDA, and CDC). EPA partners include the states, local drinking water and wastewater utilities, and national organizations (e.g., American Water Works Association).

The EPA has established several programs to protect the water sector. For example, the Water Security Initiative pursues a contamination warning system to minimize damage to public health and economic impact from harm to a water system. It covers detection, response, testing, and training. As with other SSAs, the EPA promotes risk management, risk assessments, incident reporting, a culture of security, training, tabletop exercises, partnering, and information sharing (U.S. Department of Homeland Security and Environmental Protection Agency 2007).

DCS/SCADA

Digital control systems (DCS) and supervisory control and data acquisition (SCADA) systems enable many industries to control and monitor equipment remotely, even from great distances. The Internet and IT systems facilitate the control of sensitive processes that were controlled manually on site in earlier years. CIKR sectors that use such systems include food processing, water, transportation, energy, and manufacturing, among others. Serious harm can result if adversaries access these systems. In one attack, an engineer applied radio telemetry to access a waste management system to discharge raw sewage into a public waterway and onto the grounds of a hotel. The "insider" engineer worked for the firm that supplied the DCS/SCADA system to the waste management company. In another example, a **penetration test** (i.e., authorized attempt to access a system or physical site to study defenses) resulted in access to a utility's DCS/SCADA system within minutes. Operators drove to a remote substation, spotted a wireless network antenna, and from their vehicle, they operated their wireless radios and connected to the network. Following 20 minutes of work, they had mapped both the network and the SCADA equipment and accessed the business IT system. CIKR sectors must protect against this type of vulnerability. Helpful security strategies include access controls, encryption, virus protection, data recovery procedures, and manual overrides (Purpura 2007, 370).

The functioning of our society and lives depends on an interconnected web of sectors and dependencies, and if one sector is disrupted, others may falter like dominos. This is referred to as the **cascade effect**.

Health-Care and Public Health Sector

Imagine a city of, say, 100,000 people exposed to a bioterrorism attack, and everyone in the city is in need of medical assistance. Do you think the health-care and public health sector in this city will be capable of meeting the residents' medical needs? The volume of patients would exceed medical staff, beds, medicine, equipment, and supplies.

Small-scale and large-scale medical surges can result from a wide variety of human-made and natural disasters. A **medical surge** is "the ability to provide adequate medical evaluation and care during events that exceed the limits of the normal medical infrastructure of an affected community." The concept of medical surge is essential to preparedness planning for major events requiring medical services (U.S. Department of Health & Human Services 2009).

The U.S. Census Bureau (2009) reports 7,569 hospitals in the United States that employ 5.1 million people, including 819,000 physicians, 2.4 million registered nurses, and other staff. There are about 110 million visits to hospital emergency rooms annually (39 for every 100 people).

The U.S. Department of Homeland Security (2009c) reports that the health-care and public health (HPH) sector constitutes about 15 percent of the gross national product, with roughly 85 percent of the assets privately owned and operated. Health care is typically delivered at the local level, and public health is managed across all levels of government. The HPH sector is highly dependent on several other sectors: transportation, agriculture and food, energy, water, emergency services, and IT and communications.

The SSA for the HPH sector is the **U.S. Department of Health and Human Services** (HHS). The **Pandemic and All-Hazards Preparedness Act of 2006** designated the secretary of HHS as the lead official for all public health and medical emergencies, including medical surges. States have the responsibility for developing emergency preparedness plans in coordination with other levels of government. In addition, the DOD and the Department of Veterans Affairs are expected to assist state and local entities in emergencies through their hospital facilities. HSPD-21, Public Health and Medical Preparedness, issued in 2007, promotes the establishment of a national strategy for catastrophic health events. The Bioterrorism Act of 2002 noted that hospital emergency rooms are an important component of the nation's response to terrorism and diseases. This 2002 Act promotes surveillance systems at emergency rooms, public health departments, and the CDC to detect a medical emergency. The CDC is within HHS and serves in a leadership capacity during such an event.

When serious medical emergencies occur, health-care facilities experiencing a surge must be prepared through prior planning and training for a variety of scenarios (Figure 12.2). Otherwise, the health-care site can become a disaster site subject to mob violence, with medical workers themselves becoming victims and patients. OSHA has provided guidelines to health-care personnel on personal protective equipment and HAZMAT. Security officers also need training, since unruly victims of a medical emergency can disrupt medical care when they may first need to be quarantined and decontaminated (depending on the nature of the emergency).

HHS partners with the DHS to implement the NIPP. Numerous public-private sector councils meet to address a variety of issues, such as workforce sustainability during an emergency and surge. Various programs seek to enhance this sector's capabilities. Examples involve early detection of infectious diseases and other threats to health, vulnerability assessments, preparedness, and IT security (U.S. Department of Homeland Security 2009c).

FIGURE 12.2 Health-care facilities must be prepared for many types of emergencies.

Critical Thinking

The U.S. Government Accountability Office (2008b 26) reports that HHS estimates that in a severe influenza pandemic almost 10 million people would require hospitalization (a volume that would exceed current capacity). Almost 1.5 million of these people would require care in an intensive care unit (ICU), and about 740,000 would require a ventilator (to mechanically move oxygen into and out of the lungs of a patient who is unable to breathe on his or her own). What criteria would you establish to decide who is to receive a hospital bed, care in an ICU, and a ventilator?

Besides the challenges faced by the HPH sector just cited, from a strictly security perspective, the challenges are numerous. Health-care facilities often have limited access controls to permit patients to receive visitors who are often issued a visitor pass. Emergency rooms are subject to violence from causes such as intoxicated patients, irate patients and family waiting to be assisted, domestic situations, and gangs. Security strategies for emergency rooms include signs prohibiting weapons, access controls, metal detectors, and armed security officers. Security at nurseries is vital because of the threat of infant abduction. Applicable strategies are stringent access controls, ID cards for workers, closed-circuit TV (CCTV), and radio-frequency identification (RFID) bracelets for infants. Other areas of health-care facilities requiring security are the pharmacy, parking lots, locker rooms, and the morgue.

The **Joint Commission on Accreditation of Healthcare Organizations** (JCAHO) promotes professionalism in this field, and compliance with its standards is required for government funding. Security plans and programs are required under JCAHO standards. The International Association for Healthcare Security and Safety is another group that facilities professionalism. It offers publications, training, standards, and certifications. Guidance for professional operations at health-care facilities can also be found through OSHA, NFPA, HIPPA and other sources.

Emergency Services Sector

When a resident of a community, a business, or other organization telephones 9-1-1, or another emergency number, to report a serious incident, a dispatcher will ask specific questions about the emergency so that a decision can be made as to what services will be dispatched (Figure 12.3). The range of services includes police, fire, emergency medical, bomb squad, special weapons and tactics (SWAT), HAZMAT, search and rescue, and emergency management. These services comprise the Emergency Services Sector (ESS).

In the United States, there are over 17,000 local, state, and federal police agencies, most (about 13,000) on the local level. These agencies employ over 1,000,000 sworn and nonsworn personnel. The fire service is made up of about 31,000 local fire departments and over 1 million firefighters, of which 750,000 are volunteers. Emergency medical service responders number approximately 500,000 (Purpura 2007, 289–299).

The ESS is the primary protector of CIKR. An essential system of response and recovery, it is decentralized and local across the United States. This sector

FIGURE 12.3 **A variety of services and assets are available from the emergency services sector.**

consists of professionally trained and tested personnel who seek to save lives and mitigate property damage. Mutual-aid agreements among different jurisdictions enable multiple agencies to assist a locale that is dealing with an emergency which is straining its personnel and resources. Examples are a vehicle chase, a child abductor crossing jurisdictions, or a massive fire.

The **DHS, Office of Infrastructure Protection**, is the SSA for the ESS. The U.S. Department of Homeland Security (2009c) states:

> The ESS SSA engages stakeholders and coordinates ESS initiatives through the existing network of sector associations that extend to the 10 Federal Emergency Management Agency regions, the DHS/Office of State and Local Coordination, and the DHS/Office of Grants and Training. Additionally, the Emergency Management and Response Information Sharing and Analysis Center (EMR-ISAC) serves as a principal mode to coordinate sector plans and collect and share information with the ESS and other sectors.

The important role of local and state ESS should be clearly understood, as emphasized by the U.S. Conference of Mayors (Purpura 2007, 137): "When you dial 9-1-1, the phone doesn't ring in the White House … those calls come in to your city's police, fire, and emergency medical personnel … our domestic troops."

Defense Industry Base Sector

The Defense Industry Base (DIB) sector includes the Department of Defense, other government bodies, and the private-sector worldwide industrial complex. The mission of the DIB is to provide for the needs (e.g., weapons) of the military. Tens of thousands of companies and their subcontractors, including domestic and foreign entities, support these needs. The DIB depends on energy, communications, IT, and transportation, among other sectors. For national security, protection is an obvious necessity for the DIB and the sectors it depends on.

The legal foundation that supports the DIB includes the **Defense Production Act of 1950**, Executive Order 12919, and the DOD Directive 5000.60. HSPD-7 identified the DIB as a critical infrastructure sector and designated the **Department of Defense (DOD)** as the SSA.

The Critical Infrastructure Partnership Advisory Council enables private-sector owners and government officials to collaborate on issues and protection activities. A major issue and protection challenge is that the DIB exists in an open, global environment that compounds the difficulty of securing assets and classified information (U.S. Department of Homeland Security 2009c).

The DIB SSP uses a risk-management framework, like other SSPs, and applies these steps: set security goals, identify infrastructures and assets, assess risks, prioritize, implement protective programs, and measure effectiveness through metrics and evaluation methodologies. This SSP emphasizes a "layered, defense in depth" approach to protection (U.S. Departments of Homeland Security and Defense 2007).

The DIB faces a serious insider threat (see Chapter 6), especially from foreign intelligence services seeking U.S. technology to improve their military and economy. Besides private security at DOD contractor sites, another strategy to counter the insider threat is through the DOD **National Industrial Security Program** (NISP), administered by the Defense Security Service (DSS). This program focuses on information, personnel, and physical security to protect classified information held by businesses under a DOD contract. Private security at DOD contractor sites must adhere to NISP requirements.

The U.S. Government Accountability Office (2008c) has been critical of the DSS in multiple reports. Specific criticism points to DSS not properly using metrics to identify patterns of contractor security violations and inadequate training of staff in overseeing foreign contractors. *The GAO has designated the protection of critical technologies as high risk.*

Communications Sector

Imagine if you were unable to use your cellular phone or access the Internet. A serious disruption in the communications sector (CS) would be an enormous inconvenience and a shock to our culture of technology. We have become so dependent on the CS that we find it difficult to imagine life without this technology.

The CS is an essential component of our economy and supports the operations of businesses, government, including public safety agencies, and other organizations. The CS is composed of an interconnected industry of wire line, satellite, and wireless transmission systems. Several sectors are linked to the CS. As examples, the energy sector provides power to operate cellular towers and other communications systems; the IT sector provides control systems and Internet infrastructure; the banking and finance sector relies on the CS for the transmission of transactions and operations of financial markets; and the ESS relies on the CS for receiving 9-1-1 calls and coordinating responses to emergencies.

The SSA for the CS is the **National Communications System** within the DHS. It is responsible for implementing the NIPP pursuant to HSPD-7 and bringing together public and private sectors in a coordinated protection strategy. This government-led protection effort is supplemented and integrated with private-sector initiatives. The private sector owns and operates most of the CS and is primarily responsible for its protection. The CS concentrates on reducing risk by working to ensure that the U.S. communications networks and systems are secure, resilient, and quickly restored following a disaster (U.S. Department of Homeland Security 2009c).

The CS has been subject to not only HSPD-7, the Homeland Security Act of 2002, and the "National Strategy for the Physical Protection of Critical Infrastructure and Key Assets" (White House 2003a), like other sectors, but also "The National Strategy to Secure Cyberspace" (White House 2003b). This document states that a top priority is awareness of infrastructure interdependencies and improving the physical security of cyber systems and communications. In addition, besides executive orders from the president that emphasize the need for reliable communications during an emergency, the Communications Act of 1934, amended by the Telecommunications Act of 1996, is the primary law governing the CS, which is regulated by the Federal Communications Commission (FCC) (U.S. Department of Homeland Security 2007b).

The companies that operate the CS have a history of factoring in natural disasters, accidental disruptions, and cyber attacks into network architecture, business-continuity planning, and resiliency. The interconnected and interdependent nature of the CS has fostered information sharing and cooperative responses among companies, because a network problem of one company often impacts networks owned by other companies. As with other sectors, a risk-management approach is applied by the CS. Protection emphasizes response and recovery, besides physical and cyber security (U.S. Department of Homeland Security 2007b).

Information Technology Sector

The information technology sector (ITS) is essential to our world today and functions in conjunction with the communications sector to provide the Internet. The DHS is the SSA for the ITS. Private- and public-sector councils represent interests in this sector and collaborate on protection. Because all sectors rely on the ITS, resiliency is a top priority.

Several laws and authorities promote the ITS. Examples are HSPD-7, Executive Order 13231 (protection of IT for CI and emergencies), the Clinger-Cohen Act of 1996 (strengthens IT management in government operations), and the Cyber Security Enhancement Act of 2002 (improves sentencing for crimes such as computer fraud and unauthorized access to IT systems).

There are numerous government and private-sector IT protection units and programs. The following are examples: FBI Cyber Crimes Division (focuses on offenders who spread malicious code and child pornography and engage in computer fraud and theft of intellectual property), U.S. Department of Justice Computer Crimes and Intellectual Property Section, National

Counterintelligence Center, and U.S. Secret Service Electronic Crimes Task Force. The U.S. Computer Emergency Readiness Team (US-CERT) helps to protect the Internet by analyzing and reducing cyber threats and vulnerabilities, disseminating warnings, and coordinating incident response. National cyber exercises conducted by the DHS identify, test, and improve coordination of incident responses (U.S. Department of Homeland Security 2009c; U.S. Department of Homeland Security 2007c). Chapter 8 offers coverage of threats to IT systems and protection strategies.

Energy Sector

Virtually all sectors have dependencies on the energy sector (ES). When a blackout occurs and electricity is unavailable, the effect on people and the economy is huge. Imagine working on the 50th floor of an office building when a blackout prevents elevators from working and generators are unavailable. Do you think you can make it to the ground floor via the stairs? If you reach the ground floor, how will you get home? Public transportation often relies on electricity. If you drive a vehicle, inoperable traffic lights can lead to massive gridlock. Businesses suffer enormous losses during a blackout because the ES powers IT systems that record business transactions, telephones may be unusable, and so forth. Although emergency operations centers, hospitals, and other essential services typically have backup generators, a blackout can literally stop the everyday activities of a city and region.

Penetration-testing consultants have been probing CIKR defenses for many years to expose and correct vulnerabilities. Green (2008) reported that a team was able to hack into a power company's network overseeing power production and distribution. Initially, SCADA systems were closed systems, but eventually intranets and Internet access were added, and vulnerabilities increased. In this case, the team tapped into the distribution lists of SCADA user groups, where they harvested e-mail addresses of power company employees. Then, they sent them an e-mail stating that their employee benefits would be cut and they should click on a link to a Web site to learn more. When the employees clicked on the link, malware was downloaded, thereby providing the team with control over the SCADA system and an opportunity to create a power outage. The power company stopped the test as soon as the team gained control of the SCADA system. For improved security, the team recommended that the software be better engineered, that the network be segmented so that a breach via the Internet cannot reach the SCADA system, and that employees complete training on the prevention of social engineering.

Over 80 percent of the U.S. ES is owned by the private sector. The ES consists of three interrelated segments: electricity, petroleum, and natural gas, as explained next from the U.S. Departments of Homeland Security and Energy (2007).

The electricity segment contains more than 5,300 power plants. About 49 percent of electricity is produced by combusting coal (usually transported by rail), 19 percent from nuclear plants, and 20 percent by combusting natural gas. The remaining sources of electricity are from hydroelectric plants (7 percent), oil (2 percent), and renewable (e.g., solar and wind) sources. Over 211,000 miles of high-voltage transmission lines are used to transmit electricity from power plants. Voltage is stepped down at substations prior to being distributed to 140 million customers via millions of miles of lower voltage lines. The highly automated ES is controlled by SCADA systems.

The petroleum segment involves exploration, production, storage, transport, and refinement of crude oil. The crude oil is refined into petroleum products (e.g., gasoline and jet fuel). About 66 percent of crude oil required for the U.S. economy is imported. In the United States, there are over 500,000 crude-oil-producing wells, thousands of miles of pipeline, 133 operable petroleum refineries, and other components of the petroleum segments, which also rely on SCADA systems.

Natural gas is also produced, piped, stored, and distributed. There are over 448,000 gas wells, over 550 gas processing plants, in excess of 1 million miles of pipelines, and about 400 underground storage fields.

The **U.S. Department of Energy** (DOE), designated as the SSA for the ES, is charged with coordinating an ES SSP that is part of the DHS's NIPP. The DOE also coordinates information sharing with organizations in the ES. Numerous coordinating councils involving private- and public-sector groups share information, plan exercises, address issues, and discuss SSP updates.

Several laws and presidential directives affect multiple segments of the ES. These include HSPD-7. Another example is the Energy Policy Act of 2005 that was enacted to require mandatory electricity reliability standards for the United States.

The protection challenges for the ES are enormous. Emphasis is placed on preparedness, resiliency, and cyber security, with a risk-management framework that considers enterprise-wide protection (U.S. Departments of Homeland Security and Energy 2007).

Transportation Sector

We depend on the transportation sector (TS) for reliable, quick, and efficient service. The importance of this sector is often realized when we get stuck in traffic on a roadway for long periods of time, wait for a bus or train that is delayed, or learn that our flight has been delayed or cancelled. For consumers and business purposes, the transportation sector is the way in which goods are moved throughout the country and overseas.

FIGURE 12.4 **Commercial airports are subject to intense security.**

Six key subsectors or modes of the TS are as follows (U.S. Department of Homeland Security 2009c):

- *Aviation* includes 450 commercial airports (Figure 12.4), 19,000 additional airfields, aircraft, and air traffic control systems.
- *Highways* cover over 4 million miles of roadways.
- *Maritime transportation system* includes roughly 95,000 miles of coastlines, 361 ports (Figure 12.5), and over 10,000 miles of navigable waterways.

FIGURE 12.5 **Because of the threat of terrorism, security at ports has been enhanced. (® Shutterstock.com. With permission.)**

- *Mass transit* consists of multiple-occupancy vehicles, such as transit buses, trolleybuses, vanpools, ferryboats, monorails, subway and light rail, and cable cars.
- *Pipeline systems* refer to a vast network of pipelines that cover hundreds of thousands of miles throughout the nation, carrying natural gas, hazardous liquids, and various chemicals.
- *Rail* consists of hundreds of railroads, over 143,000 miles of track, more than 1.3 million freight cars, and about 20,000 locomotives.

Besides HSPD-7, many other directives and laws affect the multitude of transportation subsectors. For instance, the **Maritime Transportation Security Act of 2002** promotes port and ship security through the U.S. Coast Guard (USCG) in cooperation with other government bodies and the private sector. The transportation subsectors are subject to many government regulations from a variety of agencies that specialize in a specific mode of transportation. Examples include the Federal Aviation Administration (FAA), within the U.S. Department of Transportation (DOT), which regulates civil aviation, and the DOT's Federal Motor Carrier Safety Administration that regulates commercial trucking (e.g., driver requirements and size and weight of trucks).

The **Transportation Security Administration (TSA)** is the SSA for the TS. The TSA was formed following the 9/11 attacks through the **Aviation and Transportation Security Act of 2001**. Originally in the DOT, with an emphasis on airline security, the TSA was shifted to the Department of Homeland Security and now sees the need to protect all modes of transportation. The USCG is the SSA for the maritime subsector.

TS SSAs work together using the NIPP Sector Partnership Model. There are separate government–private sector coordinating councils for each subsector (e.g., aviation, highway) of the TS. Federal government bodies with transportation security responsibilities that are represented on these councils include the TSA; USCG; DOT; Department of Justice, FBI; and DOD. Additionally, the TS works with state, local, and international governments and organizations.

The risks and vulnerabilities of the TS are global and encompass supporting infrastructure and the people and goods moving through it. In addition, the TS has significant interdependencies with other sectors. For instance, the TS and the energy sector directly depend on each other to transport fuel to a variety of users and to support all forms of transportation.

Priorities of the TS are to prevent and deter terrorism against all modes of transportation, enhance resiliency, and improve the cost-effective use of resources for security. Each transportation subsector has unique protection challenges and specific, rather than generic, security strategies are designed to reduce risks. For example, access controls at airports are much tighter than for mass transit.

ISSUE

Is Aviation Security Adequate?

The DHS, TSA, FAA, other government bodies, and the private sector (e.g., airlines) have been involved in numerous initiatives to enhance security in the aviation industry. The scope of security strategies is broad and includes access controls at airports for people, vehicles, luggage, and cargo; trained TSA security screeners; physical security; TSA canine teams to detect explosives and other contraband; aircraft security and crew training; and the Federal Air Marshal Service (i.e., trained personnel who appear as passengers on flights to detect and defeat hostile acts against air carriers).

Despite massive aviation security expenditures, especially following the 9/11 attacks, security vulnerabilities remain and will never be totally eliminated (as with other CIKR). For instance, TSA security screeners at airport access control points are periodically subject to penetration tests. *USA Today* (Frank 2007) obtained one classified report on a series of tests, and the results showed the number of tests conducted and the percentage of fake bombs and related materials not detected. For three airports, the metrics showed Los Angeles International Airport at 70/75 percent, Chicago O'Hare International Airport at 75/60 percent, and San Francisco International Airport at 145/20 percent. Interestingly, the San Francisco screeners worked for a private firm and not the TSA.

The Congressional Research Service (2009), from which the following information is derived, reported on various vulnerabilities of the aviation industry and how terrorists may still choose to use aircraft to attack CIKR, as in the 9/11 attacks. Moreover, as ground-based security is improved globally—with such strategies as standoff distance to protect against bombs, bollards, access controls, and so forth—terrorists may see aircraft as the avenue to overcome high security at sites. On April 29, 2003, Pakistani authorities arrested Waleed bin Attash, the suspected mastermind of the USS *Cole* bombing, and other Al-Qaeda operatives, in Karachi, Pakistan. Following the arrests, authorities discovered plans to crash a small plane loaded with explosives into the U.S. consulate office in Karachi. Two aircraft thefts in the United States, in 2005, added more concern to this vulnerability. On June 22, 2005, a 20-year-old man stole an aircraft from a Danbury, Connecticut, flight school and went on a "drunken, three-hour joyride" with two teenagers before landing at a Westchester County, New York, airport. On October 9 of the same year, a 22-year-old Georgia man stole a Cessna Citation VII corporate jet, in which he served as a copilot, but was not trained to fly on his own, from the St. Augustine, Florida, airport. He and his friends went on a joyride and landed the jet at an airport near Atlanta. Although such thefts are rare, others have occurred.

The challenge of protecting general aviation, in addition to commercial aviation, is daunting. General aviation refers to flights other than commercial airline and military flights. It includes gliders, flight training aircraft, private flying, and the very large air cargo sector, among other categories.

Most flights in the world are within general aviation. The U.S. Department of Homeland Security, Office of Inspector General (2009), reported that general aviation accounts for 77 percent of all flights in the United States. Such flights often occur near airline flights at large commercial airports and at over 5,000 public-use airports, most of which are general aviation airports. The U.S. Department of Homeland Security, Office of Inspector General, determined that general aviation presents only limited threats to security, and those owners and managers at these airports have enhanced security in a positive and effective manner. In addition, the TSA provides guidelines and alerts. It was also noted that significant regulation of this industry would require considerable federal funding. The author of this book views the threat differently and sees general aviation as a serious threat to security. More security is needed through such strategies as improved TSA guidelines and training courses.

Another issue is the use of an aircraft to crash into a nuclear reactor. One research report notes that of the 103 reactors in the United States, 21 are located within 5 miles of an airport, and that 96 percent of reactors are not designed to withstand the impact of even a small plane. Another report views reactors, because of their sturdy design, as resistant to an aircraft attack. This is a contentious issue.

Critical Thinking

Does our nation place too much emphasis on aviation security, at the expense of mass-transit, ports, other CIKR, borders, and soft targets such as shopping malls and schools? Explain your answer.

GLOBAL PERSPECTIVE: INTERNATIONAL CIKR PROTECTION

Many U.S. CIKR are interconnected with a global infrastructure that supports modern economics. Each CIKR sector is linked directly or indirectly to global energy, transportation, communications, IT, and other infrastructures. The global economy not only results in benefits and efficiencies, but also interdependencies, vulnerabilities, and complex security challenges. Because of the risk of global disruptions and cascading, the NIPP and SSPs must also consider protection from an international perspective. The NIPP strategy for international CIKR protection concentrates on facilitating cooperation among global security partners, implementing current agreements, including cross-border programs, and addressing global issues such as cyber security. Examples of key partners and agreements include the 2001 Smart Border Declaration with Canada and the 2002 Border Partnership Declaration with Mexico. Both agreements address strategies to enhance security and expedite crossings at borders. The DHS formed a group with the United Kingdom to focus on a wide variety of homeland security issues. The "Group of Eight" (i.e., a forum of eight major nations, including the United States, U.K., Canada, France, Italy, Germany, Japan, and Russia) concentrates on sharing information on terrorists who cross borders, transportation security, and best practices for rail and metro security. In addition, the North Atlantic Treaty Organization (NATO) addresses CIKR protection through an emergency planning committee (U.S. Department of Homeland Security 2009d).

Note: Although the United States engages in collaboration and agreements with other nations pertaining to security, challenges remain because of each nation's perspective on security issues and the changing methods and strategies of terrorists.

Banking and Finance Sector

Owned primarily by private interests, the banking and finance sector (BFS) is the backbone of the economy and consists of an assortment of over 29,000 financial firms. These include banks, credit union, insurance companies, and securities firms.

The reach of BFS dependencies is global because of international financial markets. The BFS has identified four vital sector dependencies: energy, IT, communications, and transportation. A 2007 pandemic flu exercise allowed the BFS to study weaknesses in operations and dependencies that may occur in such a crisis (U.S. Department of Homeland Security 2009c). Vulnerabilities also point to cyber crime, power blackouts (that can disrupt financial transactions), and terrorism (because this sector is a symbol of power, wealth, and capitalism).

HSPD-7 designates the **U.S. Department of the Treasury** as the SSA for the BFS, and in this capacity, it has formalized the collaboration of BFS regulators, associations, and industry subsectors. Committees and councils assess risks and vulnerabilities and prioritize needs that often focus on the protection of IT and communications. The Financial Services-Information Sharing and Analysis Center (FS-ISAC) is a private-sector group that shares protection information and best practices of incident response.

Regulation of this industry by federal and state laws and government agencies is complex and challenging, especially in light of well-publicized scandals and fraud (e.g., Enron and the Madoff Ponzi scheme) and criticism of weak government regulatory authorities (e.g., Securities and Exchange Commission) and related law enforcement.

Major laws that influence the BFS are: the Sarbanes-Oxley Act of 2002 (requires accounting controls and accuracy in financial reporting); the USA Patriot Act of 2001 (contains anti-money-laundering provisions and strategies against financing terrorism); the Gramm-Leach-Bliley Act of 1999 (pertains to protecting the privacy of customer information); the Anti-Drug Abuse Act of 1988 and the Bank Secrecy Act of 1986 (both focus on anti-money-laundering and financial reporting requirements); and Regulation H, code of Regulations (pertains to bank security and anti-money laundering).

The BFS is involved in broad-based global protection initiatives. Examples are information and intelligence sharing, vulnerability assessment methodologies, crisis communications systems, emergency exercises, business continuity planning, and redundancy and backup for transactions (U.S. Departments of Homeland Security and Treasury 2007).

Chemical Industry Sector

Chemicals are essential to our lives, but they can be very dangerous if not safely manufactured, stored, transported, and applied. Accidents can occur, as well as terrorist or military attacks using chemicals.

The worst chemical disaster, thus far, occurred in **Bhopal, India**, in 1984, when a Union Carbide pesticide plant released toxic gas. There was no emergency response. The death toll reached almost 4,000 people, according to the Indian government. However, other estimates put the number of deaths at between 8,000 and 10,000. There were mass funerals and mass cremations. Bodies were also disposed of in the Narmada River. About 170,000 people were treated at hospitals for burning in the respiratory tract and eyes, breathing problems, stomach pains, and vomiting. It is estimated that 20,000 people have died since the disaster of related complications, and another 100,000 to 200,000 have permanent injuries. Following the leak, a variety of animals were collected and buried, food became scarce, fishing was prohibited, and leaves on trees turned yellow and fell off. Theories on the cause of the disaster include poor maintenance, lax safety, accident, and sabotage by a disgruntled worker. The health, environmental, and occupational rehabilitation of the area continues (Wikipedia 2009a).

In the United States, the worst chemical and industrial accident occurred in 1947, in **Texas City, Texas**, when a fire detonated about 2,300 tons of ammonium nitrate on board a ship in the city's port. At least 581 people were killed, including all 28 Texas City firefighters who were aboard the ship when it exploded and a nearby crowd who watched the fire from what they thought was a safe distance. Over 5,000 people were injured. Almost all the ships in the harbor were sunk and nearly 1,000 buildings in the area were leveled. Two airplanes flying in the area were destroyed and windows were shattered in Houston, 40 miles away (Wikipedia 2009b).

Chemicals are pervasive within our society, communities, workplaces, and homes. The chemical industry sector (CIS) is an integral component of the U.S. economy, privately owned, earning revenues of about $637 billion per year, and employing nearly 1 million people. A variety of chemicals are produced, including basic chemicals, specialty chemicals, agricultural chemicals, pharmaceuticals, and consumer products. The CIS is dependent on (or depended on by) the following sectors: transportation, energy, water, agriculture and food, IT, health-care and communications (U.S. Department of Homeland Security 2009c).

The DHS is the SSA for the CIS. The chemical industry formed a council composed of trade associations that work with the DHS to ensure that private-sector interests are considered in federal action. Federal government bodies that work with the CIS also formed a council to coordinate activities. These include the Environmental Protection Agency (EPA) and the Departments of Commerce, Justice, and Transportation.

Numerous laws and regulations affect the CIS, and the EPA plays a dominant role in enforcing safety and antipollution regulations in this industry. The Emergency Planning and Community Right-to-Know Act of 1986 followed the Bhopal disaster. This 1986 Act requires chemical plant management to be involved in planning for emergencies and sharing information, such as a leak. The Clean Air Act Amendments further reinforce the role of the EPA to ensure that plant operators prevent and mitigate environmental hazards. For chemical plants along U.S. waterways, the Maritime Transportation Security Act of 2002 requires assessments of risks to waterways. State and local governments are also involved in regulating the CIS.

The DHS views the risk of terrorist attack, theft, and diversion of hazardous chemicals as top-priority concerns. In 2007, the **Chemical Facility Anti-Terrorism Standards** (CFATS) became the first regulatory program that concentrates on security for high-risk chemical facilities. Section 550(a) of the act provides the legal authority for the DHS to require high-risk chemical facilities to complete security-vulnerability assessments and site-security plans and implement protection strategies that meet risk-based performance standards (RBPS) prepared by the DHS (U.S. Department of Homeland Security 2009c).

Congress directed the DHS to develop RBPS to facilitate flexibility at chemical facilities because each site has unique protection challenges. RBPS, rather than prescriptive standards (that are generic), are viewed as enhancing security because security strategies that differ among facilities complicate the plans of adversaries. A facility's risk is based on the consequences of an attack, the likelihood of a successful attack, and the likelihood that an attack would occur at the facility. The DHS has prepared methodologies and tools to assess risk. Certain facilities regulated by other laws and government bodies are exempt from CFATS.

Once chemical facilities complete a security plan, the DHS will review it for approval. Updated plans, training, testing, and exercises are also required. An inadequate security plan can result in a fine and a shutdown of a plant.

Postal and Shipping Sector

Every sector of the economy depends on the postal and shipping sector (PSS). It employs more than 1.8 million people, has revenues of over $213 billion per year, and moves in excess of 720 million messages, products, and financial transactions daily with the use of over 50,000 vehicles. This sector is different from general cargo operations because it moves small items and is operated by just a few providers, such as the U.S. Postal Service and United Parcel Service (U.S. Department of Homeland Security 2009c).

The PSS is subject to a wide variety of protection challenges. These include internal theft and customers shipping prohibited items (e.g., illegal drugs, hazardous materials, or weapons of mass destruction [WMD]). Chapter 2 recounts the 2001 anthrax attacks through the Postal Service.

The TSA is the SSA for this sector, and it concentrates on broad protection programs. At the same time, owners and operators in this sector maintain specific, proprietary security programs and strategies. The PSS has an informal council comprising the major providers in this business. Federal agencies that have also formed a council include the TSA, DHS Office of Infrastructure Protection, DHS Customs and Border Protection, CDC, and FDA. The private and public councils collaborate with each other on needs and issues.

For entities on the receiving end of items from the PSS, several security precautions should be implemented. Examples include the preparation of policies and procedures for screening mail, training employees on precautions, isolating the mail receiving area in a building separate from major operations, and applying technology to screen mail.

Critical Manufacturing Sector

HSPD-7 notes that the sector designations identified in 2003 could change as the threats and hazards facing our nation are continuously evaluated. In 2008, the DHS established the critical manufacturing sector (CMS) and designated the DHS Office of Infrastructure Protection as the SSA for this sector. Because an attack on certain parts of the manufacturing industry could disrupt multiple CIKR, the DHS, with guidance from HSPD-7, identified manufacturers of the following products for placement in the CMS: primary metals (e.g., iron and steel), machinery, electrical equipment, and transportation equipment (e.g., motors and aerospace products). For collaboration on protection issues, a government council comprising the DHS, the FBI, and several government departments formed, as well as a council of manufacturing companies (U.S. Department of Homeland Security 2009c).

National Monuments and Icons Sector

The National Monuments and Icons Sector (NMIS) consist of federally owned physical structures that represent U.S. heritage, traditions, or values. Located throughout the United States, these resources serve as points of interest for visitors and educational activities. Protection is required for visitors, staff, and the structures themselves. Destruction of these symbols can affect the national psyche. There are minimal cyber and communications protection issues associated with this sector (U.S. Department of Homeland Security 2009c).

The U.S. Department of the Interior (DOI) is the SSA for the NMIS. The DOI relies on voluntary compliance and cooperation because its statutory or regulatory authority is limited (except for assets under the National Park Service) for sharing asset information, conducting risk assessments, or implementing protective programs. The legal authority for the preservation and protection of assets in the NMIS is derived from laws such as the Antiquities Act of 1906, the National Park Service Act of 1916, and federal statutes. The assets in this sector have their own dedicated police or security force and may rely on state and local police. The FBI is granted investigative authority of this sector through 28 U.S.C. 533 and the USA Patriot Act.

A government coordinating council enables partners to share information and best practices. Because of the public nature of this sector, security strategies must be unobtrusive and include crime prevention through environmental design (CPTED). WMD detection systems are necessary at certain sites, as well as civil aviation restrictions (U.S. Departments of Homeland Security and Interior 2007).

Nuclear Sector

The nuclear sector (NS) represents about 20 percent of the nation's electric power from 104 commercial nuclear reactors licensed to operate in the United States. This sector includes nuclear power plants; nuclear reactors used for research, testing, and training; nuclear materials applied in medical, industrial, and academic settings; nuclear fuel fabrication; decommissioning reactors; and the storage, transportation, and disposal of nuclear material and waste. The interdependencies of this sector involve energy (as a supplier), transportation (to move radioactive materials), chemical (HAZMAT at fuel-cycle facilities), health care (nuclear medicine), and government facilities (that use radioactive materials for various purposes) (U.S. Department of Homeland Security 2009c).

The **Atomic Energy Act of 1946**, and subsequent amendments, established government control and management of U.S. atomic energy, whether owned by the government or the private sector. HSPD-7 assigned the DHS to protect the NS in cooperation with the **Nuclear Regulatory Commission (NRC)** and the Department of Energy (DOE). The NRC was created by Congress as an independent agency in 1974 to protect people and the environment from the use of radioactive materials. It regulates commercial nuclear power plants and other uses of nuclear materials. It has strong regulatory authority over this sector, especially with regard to licensing, safety, fire protection, security, and emergency preparedness. The DOE has a broad mission of advancing the national, economic, and energy security of the United States; ensuring environmental cleanup of the nuclear weapons complex; and enhancing national security through military application of nuclear energy. It is involved in a variety of protection issues, such as WMD, security of facilities and transportation of radioactive materials, and emergency preparedness.

The DHS established government and private-sector councils for collaboration and to share approaches to protection. The government council consists of representatives from the DHS, NRC, DEO, EPA, FBI, and Department of State, among other government bodies. The private-sector council consists of representatives from the nuclear industry (U.S. Department of Homeland Security 2009c).

YOUR CAREER IN SECURITY

Nuclear Security Officer

Nuclear power plants and related facilities and materials are an essential part of infrastructure that are vital to the economy and serve electricity needs. A successful attack, sabotage, theft, or other negative event against these facilities can have extremely serious consequences, possibly resulting in mass casualties, long-term environmental harm, disruption of electric service, and costly recovery.

The Nuclear Regulatory Commission (NRC), empowered by Congress, not only regulates nuclear plants and the transportation, storage, and disposal of waste, but also security and safety in this industry. The NRC requires strict adherence to security regulations to protect against internal and external threats. Security in this industry is extensive and demanding on personnel.

Nature of the Work

Nuclear security officers work to protect nuclear facilities by maintaining a secure perimeter; operating stationary posts at access points; checking and searching people, vehicles, and items; monitoring CCTV and alarm systems;

---

and patrolling by foot or vehicle. Officers check people and things to ensure that they are not carrying firearms, explosives, and other prohibited items. They process visitors and escort them to authorized areas. Officers respond to threats and other harmful events. The job requires a lot of checking and documenting to ensure adherence to the NRC-approved security plan and strict policies and procedures. Drills and training are another important part of the job. Officers work a variety of shifts and weekends and holidays.

Requirements

Because of the extensive security required at nuclear facilities, the requirements for the position of nuclear security officer are demanding. Depending on the employer, requirements include the following: three years of U.S. military, police, or armed security experience; proficiency with a handgun and rifle; no serious convictions; valid driver's license; high school diploma or GED; good communications skills; the ability to perform duties in a calm manner during tense situations; and integrity.

Besides a thorough background investigation, the applicant must pass the following tests: drug, psychological, physical, physical fitness, firearms qualification, and examinations after training.

Salary

In 2008, employer Web sites showed a salary range of between $42,500 and $54,700 per year, plus benefits, for armed nuclear security officers. ASIS International (2005, 16) describes entry-level management positions in the utilities and nuclear security field as requiring an associate's degree and five years of related experience, with a salary of $50,000 to $70,000 per year.

Advice

Because of close regulation of the nuclear industry by the NRC, extensive documentation of security activities is required. The work can be tedious and demanding, and at the same time, security officers must remain alert. Individuals who seek work in this field should understand the strict regulatory environment, the importance of policies and procedures, and the evaluating and testing of security to ensure compliance. This vocation can be very rewarding to those individuals who are capable of protecting nuclear facilities within the regulatory environment.

Dams Sector

The dams sector (DS) includes dams, navigation locks, levees, hurricane barriers, and other related water retention and/or control structures. The dependencies and interdependencies of the DS are broad: water for agriculture, waterways for transportation, water for drinking and firefighting, and energy through hydroelectric power. This sector is used to prevent flooding, facilitate wildlife habitat, and serve recreational needs.

The failure of a dam or other component of this sector from natural disaster, terrorism, or other cause can result in massive loss of life, property damage, and long-term consequences affecting other sectors. Protection is afforded through the Office of Infrastructure Protection, within the DHS, which serves as the SSA for this sector. Councils from both the private and public sectors collaborate to enhance protection. Numerous assets within this sector necessitate prioritization in planning protection. Security strategies for the DS include boat and vehicle barriers, access controls, CCTV, alarm systems, protection for SCADA, emergency planning, and security personnel (U.S. Department of Homeland Security 2009c).

Government Facilities Sector

The government facilities sector (GFS) is very broad and includes buildings owned or leased by federal, state, territorial, local, or tribal governments. These facilities are in the United States and overseas. The federal government alone controls over 3 billion square feet of space and more than 650 million acres of land, as well as embassies, consulates, and military bases located all over the world. The GFS also covers assets managed by 87,000 local governments in the United States (U.S. Department of Homeland Security 2009c).

Many government facilities have limited access controls to enable the public to conduct business. At the same time, other government facilities (e.g., military bases) maintain strict security controls. In addition, the security of information and IT is a major concern of the GFS. The terrorist threat is another concern, because the GFS represents symbolic value. (Chapter 5 provides federal government security standards and recommendations developed following the Oklahoma City bombing.) Protective measures must also consider all hazards based on the characteristics of the geographic location of the assets.

The DHS Federal Protective Service (FPS), as part of Immigration and Customs Enforcement (ICE), is the SSA for the GFS. The FPS coordinates a council of representatives from government entities who share information and ameliorate protection challenges. The FPS also works with the commercial facilities sector because of government leasing of space in commercial buildings (U.S. Department of Homeland Security 2009c).

Critical Thinking

Increasingly, people who seek to enter government buildings (e.g., courthouses, schools, correctional facilities, and military bases) must undergo an **access point database check**. This entails a scan of a driver's license, or providing a Social Security number, name, or date of birth. The purpose is to check if a person is "wanted" by police, has a criminal record, is a sex offender, has not paid traffic citations, and other concerns. What are your views on such database checks at access points?

Commercial Facilities Sector

The commercial facilities sector (CFS) is very broad and includes the following subsectors (U.S. Department of Homeland Security 2009c):

- Public assembly (e.g., stadiums, arenas, convention centers, zoos, and museums)
- Sports leagues (e.g., professional sports)
- Resorts (e.g., casinos)
- Lodging (e.g., hotels and motels)
- Outdoor events (e.g., amusement parks, fairs, and parades)
- Entertainment and media (e.g., motion picture studios and broadcast media)
- Real estate (e.g., office/apartment buildings and condominiums)
- Retail (e.g., retail centers, districts, and shopping malls)

Most of the CFS is privately owned and operated, with limited government regulations, especially in terms of security requirements. Government fire, safety, health, and other codes do apply to this sector. In addition, professional associations and trade groups, representing subsectors of the CFS, develop best practices, guidelines, and standards to enhance protection. Because the CFS accommodates access by the general public, with no or minimal access controls, this sector is often viewed as a "soft target" for terrorists (Figure 12.6).

The DHS is the SSA for the CFS and has organized a private-sector council representing all of the subsectors. A related government council was also formed, and both councils share information with each other and work on protection challenges.

Daily protection operations in each business of the CFS are handled individually by management. Local first responders serve as backup. The federal role is to provide threat indications and warnings and develop guides, self-assessment tools, and courses for various subsectors (U.S. Department of Homeland Security 2009c).

FIGURE 12.6 **The commercial facilities sector contains many "soft targets."**

YOUR CAREER IN SECURITY

Loss-Prevention Agent

A **loss-prevention agent** is generally employed by a retail company to thwart crime and other losses against the retailer. Alternative titles of this position are store detective, asset-protection officer, or investigator. A loss prevention (LP) agent may also be employed by a contract security firm that services retail stores. If a contract security firm offers the services of LP agents to retailers, such services are likely to be regulated by state or local government. Primary challenges facing LP agents are shoplifting, organized retail theft, internal theft, shrinkage, protecting company assets, and improving safety in stores.

Nature of the Work

LP agents usually work covertly and blend in with retail customers to watch for suspected shoplifters. The work requires a lot of standing and patrolling within a store. Hence, the antiquated and unprofessional term *floor walker* emerged. LP agents also watch CCTV monitors in a security office; such assignments should be limited to a few hours, since fatigue may cause an agent to fall asleep.

LP agents look for behaviors that may indicate that a customer may shoplift. An example of such behavior is repeatedly looking around to see if anyone is nearby or watching. Once evidence of shoplifting has occurred (e.g., concealing an item and passing the last point of sale), the LP agent confronts and detains the suspect, interviews, possibly makes an arrest and contacts the police, and, if necessary, testifies in court.

Agents may be required to perform a wide variety of duties. Examples are assisting with the opening and closing of the store, conducting security or safety audits, participating in audits and inventories of store merchandise, and serving on a shrinkage-reduction team.

Agents work varied schedules, evenings, and weekends. During major sales events and holidays, agents can expect to work long hours, since stores will be busy with shoppers.

Requirements

Basic requirements for the position of LP agent are varied and include a high school diploma, no criminal record, and relevant work experience. Individuals with police or military experience are more marketable in this vocation, as well as college students and graduates with majors in security, criminal justice, and similar fields.

A LP agent must understand the needs and objectives of the business and be able to interact with a diverse population. They must be knowledgeable of laws, company policies and procedures, and how to avoid errors and liability when confronting suspects. Other requirements are good interviewing and report-writing skills. In addition, an agent must have the ability to remain calm and make good decisions in tense situations.

Because this vocation is becoming increasingly professional, an employer may require the certification known as LPQualified from The Loss Prevention Foundation (2007).

Salary

The salaries of LP agents vary because they work in part-time or full-time positions. According to the National Retail Federation (2008), the starting salary is $8 to $14 per hour with varied benefits and store discounts.

ASIS International (2005) lists a salary range of $25,000 to $38,000 per year for entry-level LP management positions that require a bachelor's degree and three to five years of LP experience.

Top LP executives earn well over $100,000 per year, plus a bonus and benefits.

Advice

Many college students and recent graduates begin their careers in retailing. This work provides an excellent opportunity to learn about business operations, interacting with coworkers, customer service, and protecting

> people and assets. Retailing is a beginning point to develop skills and work experience.
>
> Because retailing is increasingly going on-line and via television programming, there is some shifting of LP positions, for example, from a store to a large distribution facility.

Summary

Critical infrastructures and key resources are essential to support our everyday activities, our economy, and our homeland and national security. The protection of CIKR is not a new initiative; it began during the early days of our nation's history with the protection of roads and the delivery of mail. As commerce and industry expanded, and especially during times of war, the protection of CIKR became increasingly important. Today, the National Infrastructure Protection Plan (NIPP) is a unified, single, national plan to protect CIKR. It applies a risk-management and all-hazards protection approach while seeking to bring together all levels of government, the private sector, and international partners.

The assessment of vulnerabilities of CIKR is an ongoing process of refining methodologies to improve assessments. One avenue is to blend both scientific and nonscientific methodologies, because each approach has advantages and disadvantages.

The CIKR sectors covered in this chapter have similarities and differences. Although vulnerabilities vary among the sectors, dependencies and interdependencies can result in a cascading effect that can cause massive disruptions to our way of life and harm our economy and security. The protection of each sector is facilitated through a designated federal government body known as a sector-specific agency (SSA) that coordinates a public-private sector-specific plan (SSP). Laws and regulations are an important part of the planning process. In addition, collaboration is essential within each sector and among all sectors because of numerous stakeholders and public and private interests.

We must forge ahead to protect CIKR. This is an enormous undertaking that is essential to protect our way of life and for our survival. It is a task for government, the private sector, and all citizens.

Discussion Questions

1. Since most of the critical infrastructure in the United States is owned by the private sector, why does the federal government play such a huge role in fostering its protection? Do you think the federal government meddles too much in private-sector security? Explain your answers.

2. Do you think the federal government works closely enough with state and local governments to facilitate protection of CIKR? Explain your answer.

3. How would you assess the vulnerabilities of CIKR?

4. What do you view as the five most important CIKR sectors? Prioritize and justify your answer.

5. Do you view any CIKR sectors as receiving excessive protection while other sectors receive less protection? Explain your answer.

6. If the energy sector suffered a major power outage in one or more states, what effect would this event have on other sectors? Name each sector and describe the impact. How would this event affect you personally?

7. Why is international collaboration important for protecting CIKR?

8. What two sectors would you find most interesting as a career? What two sectors would you find least interesting as a career? Explain your answers.

Practical Applications

12A. As a terrorist, how would you attack a city transit system (i.e., subway and buses) to create the most casualties and gain the most publicity for your cause?

12B. As a city transit security specialist, what are your security strategies to prevent and mitigate the attack described in your answer to 12A?

12C. As a terrorist, how would you attack a shopping mall to create the most casualties and gain the most publicity for your cause?

12D. As a security specialist for a corporation that owns shopping malls, what are your security strategies to prevent and mitigate the attack described in your answer to 12C?

12E. As a terrorist, how would you attack one CIKR sector so that the attack harms at least two other CIKR sectors, creating a cascading effect?

12F. As a security specialist for the DHS, what are your security strategies to prevent and mitigate the attack described in your answer to 12E?

12G. Suppose you are the chief security officer for a large corporation in the city (or nearest city) in which you live. By applying an all-hazards risk-management approach, what do you view as the most serious natural hazards facing this local corporation based on the history of this region? Justify your answer.

12H. Suppose you are a security specialist for a high-risk chemical facility. What federal security regulations are required?

Internet Connections

Airports Council International: www.airports.org

American Association of State Highway and Transportation Officials: www.transportation.org

American Bankers Association: www.aba.com

American Bus Association: www.buses.org

American Chemistry Council: www.americanchemistry.com

American Public Transportation Association: www.apta.com

American Trucking Association: www.truckline.com/index

American Water Works Association: www.awwa.org

ASIS International: www.asisonline.org

Association of American Railroads: www.aar.org/

Centers for Disease Control and Prevention: www.cdc.gov

Federal Emergency Management Agency: www.fema.gov

Food Products Association: www.gmaonline.org/

Government Web sites on food safety: www.foodsafety.gov

Information Systems Security Association: www.issa.org

The Infrastructure Security Partnership: www.tisp.org

International Association for Healthcare Security & Safety: www.iahss.org

International Association of Chiefs of Police: www.theiacp.org

International Information Systems Security Certifications Consortium: www.isc2.org

Joint Commission on Accreditation of Healthcare Organizations (JCAHO): www.joint-commission.org

The Loss Prevention Foundation: www.losspreventionfoundation.org

Metropolitan Transportation Authority, State of New York: www.mta.nyc.ny.us

National Association of Emergency Medical Technicians: www.naemt.org

National Infrastructure Protection Plan: www.dhs.gov/nipp

National Retail Federation: www.nrf.com

North American Transportation Management Institute: www.natmi.org/index.cfm

Nuclear Regulatory Commission: www.nrc.gov

U.S. Coast Guard: www.uscg.mil/default.asp

U.S. Customs and Border Protection: www.cbp.gov

U.S. Department of Agriculture, Food Safety and Inspection Service: www.fsis.usda.gov

U.S. Department of Defense: www.defenselink.mil

U.S. Department of Energy: www.energy.gov

U.S. Department of Health and Human Services: www.hhs.gov

U.S. Department of Homeland Security: www.dhs.gov

U.S. Department of Transportation: www.dot.gov

U.S. Department of Transportation, Maritime Administration: www.marad.dot.gov

U.S. Department of Treasury: www.ustreas.gov

U.S. Environmental Protection Agency: http://cfpub.epa.gov/safewater/watersecurity/index.cfm

U.S. Food and Drug Administration, Food Safety, Defense, and Outreach: www.fda.gov/Food/default.htm

U.S. Immigration and Customs Enforcement: www.ice.gov

U.S. Secret Service: www.secretservice.gov

U.S. Transportation Security Administration: www.tsa.gov

References

ASIS International. 2005. Career opportunities in security. www.asisonline.org.

Bork, W. n.d. Massacre at Republic Steel. The Illinois Labor History Society. www.kentlaw.edu/ilhs/republic.htm.

Brown, K. 2006. *Critical path: A brief history of critical infrastructure protection in the United States.* Fairfax, VA: George Mason University.

Centers for Disease Control. 2009. CDC congressional testimony, July 31, 2008. www.cdc.gov.

Colcher, D. 2008. Personal perspective: Terrorism risk to critical infrastructure. Institute for Crisis, Disaster, and Risk Management. Crisis and Emergency Management Newsletter Website. www.seas.gwu.edu/~emse232/april2008_6.html.

Congressional Research Service. 2005. Terrorism and security issues facing the water infrastructure sector (April 25). www.ndu.edu/library.

Congressional Research Service. 2009. Securing general aviation (March 3). http://ncseonline.org.

Domzalski, D. 2009. Authority of the railroad police. *Police Chief* 77 (March).

Frank, T. 2007. Most fake bombs missed by screeners. *USA Today*, October 17. www.usatoday.com/news/nation/2007-10-17-airport-security_N.htm.

Green, T. 2008. Experts hack power grid in no time. *Networkworld* (April 9). www.networkworld.com.

James Martin Center for Nonproliferation Studies. 2009. Chronology of chemical and biological incidents targeting the food industry 1946–2006. http://cns.miis.edu/cbw/foodchron.htm.

Leuchtenburg, W. 1993. *The perils of prosperity, 1914–32.* Chicago: University of Chicago Press.

Loss Prevention Foundation. 2007. Gain the knowledge you need to succeed in loss prevention. *L.P. Magazine* 6 (November-December).

McCreight, R., and I. Renda-Tanali. 2007. Assessing vulnerability: Using both the "soft-non-scientific" path and the scientific approach to measuring critical infrastructures. *Homeland Defense Journal* 5 (December):42–46.

National Archives. 2009. Records of the Council of National Defense. www.archives.gov/research/guide-fed-records/groups/062.html#62.5.

National Retail Federation. 2008. LP information. www.lpinformation.com.

Purpura, P. 2007. *Terrorism and homeland security: An introduction with applications.* Burlington, MA: Elsevier Butterworth–Heinemann.

Purpura, P. 2008. *Security and loss prevention, an introduction.* 5th ed. Burlington, MA: Elsevier Butterworth–Heinemann.

U.S. Census Bureau. 2009. Facts (April 17). www.census.gov.

U.S. Department of Agriculture. 2009. About OIG Investigative Division. www.usda.gov/oig/invest.htm.

U.S. Department of Health & Human Services. 2009. Disasters and emergencies. www.hhs.gov/disasters/planners/mscc/chapter1/1.1html.

U.S. Department of Homeland Security. 2007a. Agriculture and food (May). www.dhs.gov.

U.S. Department of Homeland Security. 2007b. Communications (May). www.dhs.gov.

U.S. Department of Homeland Security. 2007c. Information technology (May). www.dhs.gov.

U.S. Department of Homeland Security. 2009a. National infrastructure protection plan, 2009. www.dhs.gov/xlibrary.assets/NIPP_Plan.pdf.

U.S. Department of Homeland Security. 2009b. Critical infrastructure sector partnership. www.dhs.gov/files/partnerships/editorial_0206.shtm.

U.S. Department of Homeland Security. 2009c. Critical infrastructure and key resources. www.dhs.gov/files/programs/gc_1189168948944.shtm.

U.S. Department of Homeland Security. 2009d. International issues for CI/KR protection. www.dhs.gov/xlibrary/assets/nipp_international.pdf.

U.S. Departments of Homeland Security and Defense. 2007. Defense industry base. www.dhs.gov.

U.S. Departments of Homeland Security and Energy. 2007. Energy (May). www.dhs.gov.

U.S. Department of Homeland Security and Environmental Protection Agency. 2007. Water (May). www.dhs.gov.

U.S. Departments of Homeland Security and Interior. 2007. National monuments and icons (May). www.dhs.gov.

U.S. Department of Homeland Security, Office of Inspector General. 2009. TSA's role in general aviation security (May). www.dhs.gov.

U.S. Departments of Homeland Security and Treasury. 2007. Banking and finance (May). www.dhs.gov.

U.S. Food and Drug Administration. 2008. FDA law enforcers protect consumers' health. *Consumer Health Information* (August 4). www.fda.gov/consumer.

U.S. Government Accountability Office. 2008a. Physical infrastructure: Challenges and investment options for the nation's infrastructure. www.gao.gov/new.items/d08763t.pdf.

U.S. Government Accountability Office. 2008b. Emergency preparedness: States are planning for medical surge, but could benefit from shared guidance for allocating scarce medical resources. www.gao.gov/new.items/d08668t.pdf.

U.S. Government Accountability Office. 2008c. Department of Defense: Observations on the National Industrial Security Program. www.gao.gov/new.items/d08695t.pdf.

White House. 2003a. The national strategy for the physical protection of critical infrastructure and key assets (February). www.whitehouse.gov.

White House. 2003b. The national strategy to secure cyberspace (February). www.whitehouse.gov.

Wikipedia. 2009a. Bhopal Disaster. http://en.wikipedia.org/wiki/Bhopal_Disaster.

Wikipedia. 2009b. Texas City Disaster. http://en.wikipedia.org/wiki/Texas_City_Disaster.

Section IV

The Future

Chapter **13**

Twenty-First Century Security

Chapter Learning Objectives

After reading this chapter, you should be able to:

1. Write a definition of futures studies
2. Describe at least five characteristics of a futurist perspective
3. List and explain at least five methodologies for anticipating the future
4. Explain how at least three methodologies for anticipating the future can each be applied to security
5. Discuss at least five predictions from the World Future Society and other sources
6. Discuss at least five emerging security technologies
7. Describe security officers of the future in terms of the technology they will employ and their role in security programs
8. Discuss at least five emerging law enforcement technologies

Terms To Know

futures studies
artificial intelligence
trend analysis

extrapolation
cyclical pattern analysis
environmental scanning
cross-impact analysis
Delphi
scenarios
simulations and games
technological forecasting
impact assessments
intuition forecasting
proliferation
water stress
globalization of hazard
Behavior Transmitter-Reinforcer
image sensors
multitower triangulation
Bluetooth technology
Bluetooth scanners
infrastructure-to-vehicle communications
optically variable devices
touch DNA
desorption electrospray ionization
Mini-Buster secret compartment detector
nonintrusive cargo inspection technology

QUIZ

This quiz serves to prime the reader's mind and begin the reading, thinking, and studying processes for this chapter. The answers to all of the questions are found within this chapter.

1. Do humans have the power to help shape the future?
2. Do futurists (i.e., people who study future possibilities) assist corporations, government (including the military), and other organizations?
3. What is trend analysis and extrapolation, and how can these methodologies assist security?
4. Can a security practitioner study both internal metrics and external metrics to identify cyclical patterns?
5. Is it true that the World Future Society forecasts that seawater will eventually replace oil as a source of energy for vehicles?
6. What is the meaning of proliferation in reference to WMD?
7. What is globalization of hazard?
8. What is infrastructure-to-vehicle communications?
9. What is touch DNA?

Introduction

This chapter provides basic information for anticipating the future. The definition of futures studies is presented, as well as characteristics of a futurist perspective. Methodologies for anticipating the future are explained, along with practical examples relevant to security. Predictions from the World Future Society and others are presented. Emerging security and law enforcement technologies, and the role of security officers and the technology they will apply in the future, are also covered.

Futures Studies

Futures studies (or futurology) refer to "the philosophy, science, art, and practice of postulating possible, probable, and preferable futures and the worldviews and myths that underlie them." This discipline aims to understand what is likely to continue, what may change, and what is new. The methodologies supporting futures studies seek a "systematic and pattern-based understanding of past and present" and an estimate of the likelihood of future trends and events (Wikipedia 2009b). The term *futures* is used here because there are many possible futures, and these include those futures influenced by the actions (e.g., pollution versus protecting the environment, war versus preventing war) or inactions (e.g., doing nothing or not enough to control pollution or prevent war) of humans.

Groff and Smoker (1996), futures educators, offer characteristics of a futurist perspective that most futurists would agree on, as described next.

- Change is the norm, and it is speeding up.
- Events are interrelated within a systems context.
- There are many alternative futures.
- The goal is to make preferable futures more probable by visualizing what we want to create and then working to create that future world.
- There are consequences to what we do or do not do.
- Ideas, values, and positive visions are important in creating an improved future world.
- We must empower people to act responsibly in the present, because those actions will help shape the future.

Key subjects and issues studied by futurists are numerous and include the following (Groff and Smoker 1996):

- Global population growth
- Food and world hunger
- Energy sources
- Pollution
- Climate change

- Peace, conflict, and war
- Economic haves and have-nots and technological haves and have-nots
- Economic trends
- Political trends
- Technology
- Workplace trends
- Educational/learning trends
- Changing cultures
- Religious trends

Critical Thinking

In what ways do you think the "characteristics of a futurist perspective" and the "subjects and issues studied by futurists" affect security practitioner planning and security programs in entities?

ISSUE

Will Machines Outsmart Humans and Create Dangerous Consequences?

Markoff (2009) reports that scientists are becoming increasingly concerned about the machines we are creating and the eventual consequences. Advances in **artificial intelligence** (i.e., an intelligent machine that interacts with its environment and takes action) might result in losses in human control over computer-based machines which are making more and more decisions that were once handled by humans (Figure 13.1). When we have robots that can open doors and find electrical power for recharging; computers that can produce unstoppable computer viruses; systems that can kill autonomously; and technology that results in the wholesale elimination of a wide range of jobs, causing tremendous social disruption, then humans are in trouble. The debate continues as to whether we are "there" yet. Scientists are especially concerned about criminals exploiting artificial intelligence systems; this has been an unfortunate factor in the advancement of technology.

Although scientists agree that we are a long way from Hal, the computer that took control of a spaceship in *2001: A Space Odyssey*, we should also consider the writings of Vernor Vinge, who espoused the view that smarter-than-human machines will result in rapid change and the end of the human era. The challenge for humans *now*, and in the future, is to guide research and technological developments to improve society rather than cause a technological disaster.

FIGURE 13.1 How do you think robots will affect security in the future?
(® Shutterstock.com. With permission.)

Critical Thinking

Do you think smarter-than-human machines will result in rapid change and
the end of the human era?

Methodologies for Anticipating the Future

There are many quantitative and qualitative methodologies applied to
studying what may occur in the future. Each has been criticized, and none
can accurately predict the future. Although commendable efforts are made
by futurists to remain objective in their work, subjective judgments enter
into futures methodologies and futures studies. At the same time, futurists have much more credibility than those who claim to have a crystal ball
with the skill to predict the future. Futurists apply various methodologies
that offer us an improved understanding of possible future events so that we
can decide and plan on various courses of action. In fact, the methodologies
applied by futurists are also applied in the insurance industry and other
professions to estimate future risks. Examples are the Delphi methodology
and simulations (soon to be explained).

Futurists assist corporations, government (including the military), and other organizations in preparing for future events. In the security profession, anticipating future events is an immense aid to risk management, business-continuity planning, resiliency, all-hazards protection, and security in general.

Here we explain common futurist methodologies. It is important to note that not only are there many futurist methodologies, but each type has variations that have been developed from numerous disciplines such as business, science, engineering, and the social sciences.

Trend Analysis

Trend analysis (TA) relies on historical information to pinpoint patterns that signify change. It is applied in many fields and used to study, for example, changes in technology, social patterns, and fashion. In project management, for instance, TA uses a mathematical technique that looks to historical results to estimate future outcome (Wikipedia 2009c).

Extrapolation is a technique of TA whereby historical information is charted on a graph that extends into subsequent years to provide an estimate of events in the future. However, caution is advised because unanticipated events and variables often affect the future. In addition, changes in one particular direction or another are unlikely to continue indefinitely over time.

To illustrate, a security executive at an IT company shows, through TA and extrapolation, that over multiple years, an increase in the use of contract workers by the company has resulted in increases in losses of proprietary information, and projections show serious losses continuing into the future. Furthermore, through investigations, the security executive links all such losses that have occurred to contract workers. In this case, the metrics and graphs of TA and extrapolation can influence senior management's decision on whether to continue to use increasing numbers of contract workers and whether to support security strategies proposed by the security executive. Many outcomes are possible for this company. For instance, senior management may ignore the trends and requests for enhanced security strategies, and the company may close because of serious losses of proprietary information.

In another illustration, a retail company shows shrinkage increasing 0.5 percent each year. TA and extrapolation are used to chart shrinkage as follows: 2006 at 2.0, 2007 at 2.5, 2008 at 3.0, 2009 at 3.5, 2010 at 4.0, 2011 at 4.5, and 2012 at 5.0.

A retail security executive may also show that as the number of loss-prevention agents employed goes down, the number of security-related lawsuits goes up because store managers and assistant managers, without training and investigative experience, are responding to internal theft and shoplifting incidents. Such a trend projected over future years can show a return on investment by retaining loss-prevention agents.

Cyclical Pattern Analysis

Cyclical pattern analysis (CPA) is a broad term that refers to events that occur in cycles or recurring patterns. The ups and downs of the economy serve as a major example of a cyclical pattern. A booming economy during multiple years is typically followed by an economic slowdown (e.g., recession) that is then followed by improvements in the economy, and the cycle continues. Security executives should be aware of these ups and downs and try to incorporate these variables into multiyear security planning. CPA can be applied to study many phenomena, such as diseases, human behavior, and weather. In reference to the security profession, the internal metrics that a security executive collects related to the organizational security program can be analyzed to spot cycles. For instance, crime incidents may rise during high unemployment and go down during low unemployment. High unemployment may also show less turnover of security staff, while low unemployment shows higher turnover. During the Christmas holiday season, an increase in robberies of businesses may occur, which is often the case in many locales. Following this season, robberies of businesses often decline. Besides internal metrics, a security practitioner should study external metrics to identify cyclical patterns that may impact his or her employer. Such sources include government statistics on crime (e.g., FBI's "Uniform Crime Reports" and OSHA's reports on violence in the workplace), fires (FEMA), accidents (OSHA), and disease (CDC).

Environmental Scanning

"**Environmental scanning** [ES] is a process of gathering, analyzing, and dispensing information for tactical or strategic purposes" (Wikipedia 2009a). It seeks both factual and subjective information on the environment in which an organization operates or intends to operate. The methodologies of ES are applicable to businesses, the public sector, and many types of entities.

Specific techniques of ES involve searches of the Web and news media and other periodicals for emerging trends and issues that can serve as input for strategic planning. Scanning can occur periodically in response to major events in the news, on an annual basis, or continuously. Because our world is constantly changing at an accelerated pace, continuous ES is probably the most advantageous of the three approaches because it enables a business to act quickly, engage opportunities ahead of competitors, meet threats and hazards aggressively to mitigate harm, and survive.

The issues of interest in ES are numerous and include a particular industry as a whole, the economy, suppliers, competitors, consumer behavior, the political climate, present and proposed laws and regulations, threats and hazards, changes in technology, infrastructure, environmental concerns, demographic factors, labor supply, and trends. National and international perspectives are also important for ES. Each issue should be rated on two dimensions: the potential effect on the company and the probability of occurring. When a major issue is important enough to address, six options are as follows (Wikipedia 2009a):

- Seek to influence the environment to mitigate the impact.
- Adapt marketing plans for the new environmental conditions.
- Seek an advantage through a quick response.
- Redeploy assets to another market or industry.
- Apply contingency strategies within a broad range of responses.
- Avoid action and continue ES and further study.

From a security perspective, ES can be applied in various circumstances, such as the following: to identify political unrest in a country containing a corporate site so precautions can be implemented to protect people and assets; to anticipate the rise in price of a precious metal that requires increased security; to learn of new laws or regulations or changes in the criminal justice system that affect security; or to study new security technology and the most appropriate time to introduce it within an organization.

Critical Thinking

In what ways is environmental scanning similar to and different from competitive intelligence gathering (see Chapter 8)?

Cross-Impact Analysis

Cross-impact analysis is applied to show the effects of one variable on another variable. A matrix is used in this technique to identify interactions by labeling variables along horizontal and vertical axes. Intersections of variables within the matrix, such as trends and events, can be studied for impact and the likelihood of occurrence. For instance, an automated factory would require fewer employees, possibly fewer security employees, and a rethinking of security technology in comparison to a fully staffed factory. Changes in security technology requirements would affect the energy and IT needs of the automated factory. In another example, cross-impact analysis can be applied to the cascading-effect vulnerability of critical infrastructures. How does the failure of each infrastructure sector affect every other infrastructure sector? All sectors can be placed along both horizontal and vertical axes of a matrix so that each sector can intersect every other sector for study.

Delphi

The **Delphi** methodology seeks the opinions of experts to develop a consensus of what can be expected in the future. It begins with a topic. Examples are threats and hazards facing businesses in the future, or weapons likely to be used by terrorists in the future. The Delphi method was developed during the 1950s by the RAND Corporation while under contract for the U.S. Air Force, to study how many atomic bombs the Soviets would need to destroy U.S. munitions production.

The Delphi method is systematic and interactive, which is an improvement over an unstructured or individual approach. Independent experts answer questionnaires in one or two rounds. A facilitator providing a summary of experts' forecasts, including justifications, follows each round. A statistical summary of the group's opinions is also provided. Responses are kept anonymous to encourage the sharing of ideas. Once summaries are completed following a round, participants revise their earlier forecasts; this is supposed to narrow the range of answers. One criticism of the Delphi method is that there are many variations of it, which makes research on its advantages over other methods of forecasting difficult (Rowe and Wright 1999).

Additional Methodologies

Groff and Smoker (1996) explain several methodologies for studying change and the future, as summarized next.

- **Scenarios.** This technique is applied to show a possible sequence of events that could occur in the future based upon initial factors of consideration. Multiple scenarios are prepared about a selected topic. The scenarios can emphasize, for instance, best case and worst case.
- **Simulations and games.** In this approach, multiple variables from reality are used to create a computer model or game to observe how the variables interact with each other. Humans can initiate what-if events by making choices and then studying the consequences.
- **Technological forecasting.** The focus of this methodology is to try to forecast what technological breakthroughs are going to occur and when. Because technology is so important in our lives, we should anticipate the changes it may cause.
- **Impact assessments.** This approach seeks to understand how change, new developments, and technology affect society and the environment.

- **Intuition forecasting.** This refers to what has been called a *sixth sense* in which a person's knowledge, experience, and creativity brings to the surface an idea or patterns and relationships among things that were not seen earlier. Because our world is changing so rapidly, we may not have enough time or complete information to make a decision, and intuition helps to fill in the gaps.

Evaluating Futures Research

As an aid to planning, a security professional may conduct futures research or refer to the futures research of others. Such input to the planning process can be beneficial, but caution is advised. As we know, we have not advanced to the point of accurately and consistently predicting the future. Although futures research applies both quantitative methods (to enhance objectivity) and computers (that perform computations faster and more accurately than humans do), human judgments and subjectivity have an influence on all methodologies applied to futures research. We should also understand the faults of each methodology applied. For instance, extrapolation should not be relied upon for an extended look into the future. When intuition forecasting is applied, our intuition could be in error. In addition, predictions for the future are often incomplete. Security professionals should look for unanticipated intervening variables and liberally apply critical thinking.

Critical Thinking

Should a security practitioner focus on only one methodology of futures studies or apply multiple methodologies? Explain your answer.

Predictions from the World Future Society

The World Future Society publishes an annual "Outlook Report" that contains forecasts and ideas from the group's *The Futurist* magazine. The report covers business and economics, demography, energy, the environment, health and medicine, resources, society and values, and technology. All of these topics have relevance to security. The list that follows offers a sample of forecasts from the "Outlook Report" (World Future Society 2008).

- Currency counterfeiters are gaining the advantage over preventive methods because of state-of-the-art optical scanning devices. This is driving the shift toward a cashless society.
- The United States will see a shrinking, qualified labor force and growing income disparity. There will be a continuation in the move

away from manufacturing jobs as service and high-technology jobs increase in number. Training for the new jobs will be expensive and possibly unaffordable for many families.

- World population by 2050 may grow beyond expectations to 9.2 billion because of advances in health care. Most of the growth will take place in countries that are least able to grow food.
- Global oil production will peak soon, and the oil era will continue in its final phase. By 2020, 30 percent of energy worldwide will likely be derived from alternative energy sources. At the same time, global consumption of crude oil will grow, especially in the United States.
- Alternative energy sources, such as biofuels and ocean-current power, will gain increasing attention.
- Water will replace oil in terms of value, intense need, and limited supply. Water shortages and drought conditions are prompting an increase in desalination plants.
- Overfishing will cause a collapse in the global fishing industry, but a recovery will occur.
- The spread of surveillance technology (e.g., closed-circuit television [CCTV], cell-phone cameras, digital cameras, and YouTube) will reduce privacy.
- Terrorism will become more common and more deadly.
- Online education and training will continue to increase from colleges, school districts, businesses, government agencies, and other entities.
- Communications technology is altering human behavior. Increased availability of communications devices is causing use at inappropriate times and places. This is resulting in problems with decorum, a distracted population, and safety issues.
- Technologies are creating an increasingly complex world. In our personal lives and workplaces, our competencies are not keeping pace with technologies, and errors and disasters are more likely. Consequently, artificial intelligence and other systems will make certain decisions for us. Artificial intelligence will eventually evolve to surpass human intelligence.

Predictions and Issues

The list that follows offers additional insights from multiple sources on the challenges we may face in future years. The student and practitioner should look to these possibilities as input for understanding and planning security and one's career.

- As our world becomes more complex, so will security. Protection challenges will tax the intelligence and creativity of security professionals.

- Threats and hazards will remain. Crime will continue, as well as terrorist attacks, cyber crime, natural disasters, and technological mishaps (e.g., power outage). Some of these events will be massive and devastating, killing scores of people, injuring many, and causing extensive property damage and economic loss.
- The threats described in this book will continue in the future. Espionage and theft of proprietary information will remain as serious problems, as well as the insider threat. Transnational crime will also continue, examples being counterfeiting and money laundering.
- Security will continue to respond to the changing workforce. Challenges will result from an expansion in vulnerabilities from the traditional workplace to the home office and in between.

"The Report of the Commission on the Prevention of WMD Proliferation and Terrorism" (Graham et al. 2008), a Congress-initiated study to assess WMD (weapons of mass destruction) risks and countermeasures, concluded that unless the world community acts decisively and quickly, a WMD terrorist attack will occur somewhere in the world by the end of 2013. The commission views a biological attack as more likely than a nuclear attack. Recommendations include more aggressive actions by the United States and international partners to limit **proliferation** (i.e., the spread of WMD) while increasing prevention efforts (e.g., work globally to secure dangerous pathogens).

Analysts at all sixteen U.S. spy agencies point to global warming as likely to increase illegal immigration, cause humanitarian disasters, and destabilize governments. Africa, Central and Southeast Asia, and the Middle East are most vulnerable to warming that can cause drought, flooding, extreme weather, and hunger. **Water stress**, meaning a shortage of water (Figure 13.2), will become an increasingly serious issue among nations (Hess 2008).

Revkin (2009) reports on studies that point to an increased risk of disasters and deaths because of significant increases in urban populations in developing countries. The combination of dense populations with the risk of floods, earthquakes, and other hazards is creating a growing potential for catastrophes (Figure 13.3). In China, for example, economic growth has brought tens of millions of people to the coast, which is prone to flooding and cyclones. The United States and other countries face similar risks. Governments must take responsibility for protecting citizens through building codes, warning systems, and other methods. Security practitioners, especially those involved in business continuity, must understand global and local issues.

Hudson (2009) writes about the **globalization of hazard**, also called the export of risk, in which developed countries with enforceable safety, health, and environmental regulations export hazardous activities (e.g., manufacturing processes) and substances (e.g., industrial waste) to less developed

FIGURE 13.2 **Purification plant for drinking water. Water stress necessitates increased security of the water sector. (® Shutterstock.com. With permission.)**

countries with limited enforceable regulations. Examples are the Bhopal accident in India, the scrapping of ships on the beaches of Bangladesh and India, and the relocation of factories from the United States to right over the border in Mexico, from which air pollution, sewage, and contaminated food are "exported" back to the United States. In other words, "what goes around, come around." The future implications of these problems relate to nations and businesses taking responsibility for risks, hazards, pollution, illegal dumping, possibly catastrophic climate change, and related issues.

Another major point Hudson makes is that the tremendous growth in international travel facilitates the spread of diseases. He notes that, in 1950, there

FIGURE 13.3 **Densely populated areas increase the risk of catastrophes. (® Shutterstock.com. With permission.)**

were 25 million international passenger arrivals (globally); today the number is over 600 million annually, and the number will increase in the future.

Geewax (2008) reports on the concerns of U.S. government leaders that certain foreign governments, wealthy from sales of oil and manufactured goods to the United States, are increasingly investing in American companies. Such investments are in the multitrillion-dollar range, and it is a growing national security issue. The risks include a hostile nation gaining control of infrastructure sectors for political or military advantage. For instance, foreign control of the U.S. energy sector would be of great concern, or control of U.S. financial firms could affect trade. The issue gained prominence in 2006 when a company linked to the Dubai government sought to operate some U.S. ports.

Technology

Technology has done wonders for our lives. Every day we rely on technology to accomplish objectives unimaginable by earlier generations. At the same time, technology has its advantages and disadvantages. For instance, although the Internet has enabled us to access an enormous amount of information and communicate easily with many people, users are vulnerable to fraud and disruptions of service that can be traumatic to many and costly.

The use of technology is influenced by politics, social forces, and other variables. Just because certain technology is available does not mean that it will be accepted by our society and applied. For example, Quinney (1975, 250) wrote about the **Behavior Transmitter-Reinforcer** that is worn by a convicted offender, tracks the location of the offender in the community, transmits information about his or her activities, enables offenders and a control center to communicate, and modifies behavior by reward and punishment. Another, different technology is placed inside of an offender and monitors blood pressure, heart rate, oxygen levels, and other offender characteristics to monitor behavior in the community. These technologies reduce correctional system costs. Today we apply electronic monitoring and global positioning systems (GPS) to offender supervision in the community. In one case, a parolee, with an attached GPS device, saw his parole officer one morning and committed a murder in the afternoon. During the murder investigation, police learned that the suspect was on parole, so they contacted a parole agent, who informed the police that the suspect was being monitored by a GPS device. It was used to trace the parolee's movements to the parole office in the morning and to the murder scene in the afternoon. The device also helped authorities locate the suspect, who was quickly arrested. Although unruly defendants are controlled in court with remote shocking devices, we have not implemented remote punishment of offenders under supervision in the community.

Taking this technology further, one could argue that customers who enter a retail store, or employees at a job site, could wear such devices to prevent theft. In fact, everyone could wear such a device to reduce crime. These crime control strategies would obviously face constitutional roadblocks and societal opposition.

Critical Thinking

What are your views of the Behavior Transmitter-Reinforcer?

Security Technology

Each year, *Security* magazine gathers information on emerging security technologies (Zalud 2009a, 30–40). This reporting is derived from end users and vendors. Understanding the need to evaluate new technology, the magazine offers suggestions for a methodology of assessing new technology. These suggestions begin with a market analysis to identify promising technologies and their applications. Next, a financial evaluation helps to show a return on investment and competitive advantages. Also suggested is a risk analysis (see Chapter 4). (Chapter 7 of this book offers guidelines for establishing a methodology for purchasing decisions.)

The following comments from interviewed security practitioners add fuel to the need for a methodology of evaluating and purchasing new technology and the application of critical thinking (Zalud 2009a, 32):

- "There … is the gap between expectations and deliverables."
- "Their capabilities will always be overstated by vendors and over-anticipated by end-users."
- "There never will be a single technology that is a panacea."

Here is a summary of some of the technology covered in the *Security* magazine article.

- Traditionally, security systems consisted of burglar and fire alarm sensors, detectors, and control panels. A newer related technology is called **image sensors** that convert an optical image to an electric signal and are used in digital cameras. This technology includes megapixel and high-definition image sensors. Another example of image sensors is the three-dimensional image sensor that is being developed to work with access-control systems to detect tailgating at access points. The applications also point to counting people, elevator capacity, and automatic doors, among other uses.
- The marriage of GPS, wireless communications, and the Internet for asset management is promising. Charts, reports, and dashboard

views supply information for analysis and to facilitate making decisions at, say, construction sites. Google Maps serve as a background to identify sites and track construction assets. Such technology can be supplemented by video and intrusion-detection systems.

- An alternative to GPS for tracking people and vehicles is **multitower triangulation**. This technology involves measuring power levels and antenna patterns while applying the concept that a cell phone communicates wirelessly with the closest base stations. Such systems identify the sector containing the cell phone and an estimate of the distance from the base stations. As this technology advances, we may see identification, location, and tracking components built into cell phones.

- **Bluetooth technology** is the "open wireless protocol for exchanging data over short distances from fixed and mobile devices, creating personal area networks" (Zalud 2009a, 40). This technology has been used to track moving objects in real-time. In one research project, the traffic patterns of attendees at a festival were tracked by placing about thirty-six **Bluetooth scanners** throughout the venue (e.g., along roads and at bus stops). The scanners tracked Bluetooth-equipped mobile phones' media access control (MAC) addresses, a number that identifies a device on a network. The applications include tracking movement of customers, suspicious people, and employees evacuating during an emergency.

- Advanced driver-assistance systems (ADAS) enable vehicles to "read" road signs and traffic patterns and take appropriate action. In the future, underpasses could inform truck drivers if their vehicle's height will not fit through an underpass. Some call this technology **infrastructure-to-vehicle communications**. This developing technology will permit signage to communicate with vehicle drivers and pedestrians for security and safety purposes.

- To enhance countermeasures against counterfeiting, **optically variable devices** (OVDs) are an emerging technology. This method consists of visual security, obvious to the naked eye, revealing a multitude of visual effects as the object is moved. The visual effects include changing colors, holography, and liquid-crystal technology. Multiple visual effects applied at the same time result in formidable security to prevent counterfeiting that would otherwise require expensive and complex expertise and equipment.

- **Touch DNA** is a growing ID method that permits an analysis of seven or eight skin cells from offenders who touched victims, weapons, bombs prior to detonation, or other things at a crime scene. This method can also be applied to ink fingerprint cards. In other words, an offender's DNA found at a crime scene can be matched with DNA on a fingerprint card completed during a prior arrest. Another emerging fingerprint technique, **desorption electrospray ionization**, reveals identity and detects small amounts of substances remaining in a fingerprint. It produces the chemical composition (i.e., molecular compound) of what a person recently touched (e.g., drugs, explosives, or industrial chemicals). This technique also distinguishes among overlapping fingerprints from multiple individuals. Both public and private sectors can benefit from these advances.

Security Officers

Zalud (2009b, 42–46) interviewed security industry executives and recorded their predictions about the roles of security officers and the technology that they will apply in the future. His research is summarized next.

- Although the security officers of today often use cellular telephones and electronic guard-tour systems, and some travel around via Segways, the cost of new technology is a major factor in decisions on upgrades. At the same time, certain entities find that risks necessitate the most advanced technology for officers.
- In the future, security officers will have communications and surveillance equipment built right into their uniforms that will enable them to perform many functions, such as check-in and check-out, read e-mail and post orders, check on threats and hazards, and provide language translation.
- Uniforms will be designed for unique needs and contain resistive qualities (e.g. HAZMAT), sensors (e.g., for radiation), and tracking devices. This technology is available today, and future uniforms will become increasingly sophisticated.
- A multiuse device will permit sniffing for HAZMAT and drugs, sweeps for bombs, observation inside compartments, testing of substances, and other specific functions as required for a site.
- Devices and systems will become increasingly voice activated rather than touch activated.
- Armed, private security officers will increasingly supplant the duties of public police officers.
- Newer, less-than-lethal weapons used by police agencies will also be used by security officers.
- The use of sophisticated security robots will increase.
- Security officers will possess more skills and be required to successfully complete more training and education programs, and have more certifications and government clearances, as they perform increasingly complex roles in security programs.

Law Enforcement Technology

Reed (2008, 25–21) writes of emerging technologies in law enforcement. Such innovations are frequently applicable to the private sector. The **Mini-Buster secret compartment detector**, developed by the Counterdrug Technology Assessment Center (CTAC), is a handheld device that senses density in solid objects. When scanned over a vehicle or other object, it can pinpoint hidden compartments that may contain contraband. Another CTAC project is **nonintrusive cargo inspection technology** that signals the presence of contraband in a sealed container and identifies the contents (e.g., weapons, biological agents, or drugs) without the time and costs of searching by hand. Other technologies being developed by government units include the following: specially designed tactical uniforms (an alternative to large, plastic, HAZMAT suits) that offer improved maneuverability and resistance against firearms and WMD; liquid body armor; wearable computers; data mining (i.e., the use of computer technology to analyze a lot of data to search for patterns); artificial intelligence; wireless interoperability systems; and unmanned aerial vehicles (UAVs), the size of a small bird, that observe suspects from the air for long periods of time.

Dees (2008, 74–77) writes about the movie *RoboCop* that was released in 1987. It is a fictional story of a fallen police officer whose head is attached to a mechanical body. The setting is Detroit, whose police department is operated by a private corporation. *RoboCop* has impressive capabilities, such as body armor, an automatic firearm that expends a massive number of rounds to "kill the bad guys," and visual overlays that permitted *RoboCop* to link what he sees to online databases. As is the case with numerous science fiction writers, their creative visions often intersect with reality. Dees writes that University of Washington researchers are developing a contact lens that contains electronic circuitry and light-emitting diodes (LEDs) that constitute a data display. Pilots, vehicle drivers, and those needing visual aids can use the device. Police can employ the device instead of the mobile data terminal in their vehicle. The lens is made from layers of metal a few nanometers thick (1 inch = 25,400,000 nanometers), and power is derived from solar cells and the radio waves that carry data to them. An officer can use a microphone and speech-recognition software to make a data inquiry and see the results on the contact lens. Dees (2008, 77) writes, "If you were too young to have seen *RoboCop* in a theater, by the time you are ready to retire you will be taking for granted technology no one has even imagined yet—without having to remove your head from your body."

By applying law enforcement technology to private security, we can see various possibilities. The inspection technology developed by the CTAC can be used at all sorts of access points to prevent and detect prohibited items from going into or leaving a site. UAVs can provide 24/7 surveillance of corporate facilities and vehicles and complement executive protection.

Summary

We often wonder about what will occur in the future. What will our personal lives be like? What trends and challenges will we face in our vocation? For security practitioners, anticipating threats and hazards as well as changes in technology, economic conditions, and world events are major subjects that provide input for planning security. In this chapter, we learned about futures studies and that change is the norm. However, we have some power in shaping the future by our actions and inactions. Several methodologies are available for anticipating the future to assist numerous professions. In the security profession, trend analysis and extrapolation, for example, use historical information to chart anticipated events.

The World Future Society publishes an annual report containing forecasts. Many specialists from many professions also publish their forecasts. The reader should study such forecasts as a critical thinker and develop a methodology for evaluating futures research. This chapter suggests understanding the faults of each methodology, considering the subjective nature of forecasts, looking for unanticipated intervening variables, and realizing that predictions for the future are often incomplete.

As we know, technology has done wonders for our lives, but criminals exploit it. At the same time, the application of technology must be balanced with constitutional rights; this is especially important in the security profession, because technology is a major strategy of security.

Discussion Questions

1. What is the value of futures research to the profession of security?
2. Among the methodologies for anticipating the future, which two do you view as most helpful to the security profession and why?
3. Among the methodologies for anticipating the future, which two do you view as least helpful to the security profession and why?
4. What are four guidelines for evaluating futures research?
5. What are your views of the predictions from the World Future Society?
6. What do you anticipate for the future of the world? Support your answers.
7. What do you anticipate for the future of security? Support your answers.

8. What do you anticipate for the future of security technology? Support your answers.

9. What do you anticipate for the future of security officer functions and duties? Support your answers.

Practical Applications

13A. Select a security vocation that is of interest to you. Conduct research and apply the contents of this chapter to help you anticipate what the vocation will be like ten years from now. What additional skills will be required? What technology will be used? How do you think the working conditions will change?

13B. Select a type of crime. Conduct research and apply the contents of this chapter to help you anticipate how this crime will change in the next ten years. What methods do you think offenders will apply to this type of crime? What technology will they employ? How do you think the public and private sectors will respond to the changes you describe?

13C. Select a major type of security technology. Conduct research and apply the contents of this chapter to help you anticipate advances in this technology. How do you think the newer technology that you anticipate will affect the security profession? In the application of the technology, do you perceive any privacy or constitutional issues? Do you have any ideas on completely new security technology that does not exist today?

Internet Connections

Central Intelligence Agency: www.cia.gov
Department of Homeland Security, Science & Technology: www.dhs.gov/files/scitech.shtm
Society of Police Futurists: www.policefuturists.org
World Future Society: www.wfs.org
World Futures Studies Federation: www.wfsf.org

References

Dees, T. 2008. One step closer to robocop. *Law Officer Magazine* 4 (March):74–77.

Geewax, M. 2008. U.S. worried about foreign investments in U.S. firms. *Atlanta Journal-Constitution* (March 6). http://ajc.com.

Graham, B., et al. 2008. *World at risk: The report of the Commission on the Prevention of WMD Proliferation and Terrorism.* New York: Random House.

Groff, L., and P. Smoker. 1996. Introduction to futures studies. www.csudh.edu/global_options/IntroFS.html.

Hess, P. 2008. Report: Climate change linked to national security. *USA Today* (June 25). www.usatoday.com.

Hudson, R. 2009. The costs of globalization: Producing new forms of risk to health and well-being. *Risk Management* 11. www.palgrave-journals.com.

Markoff, J. 2009. Scientists worry machines may outsmart man. *New York Times* (July 26). www.nytimes.com.

Quinney, R. 1975. *Criminology: Analysis and critique of crime in America*. Boston: Little, Brown and Company.

Reed, B. 2008. Future technology in law enforcement. *FBI Law Enforcement Bulletin* 77 (May):15–21.

Revkin, A. 2009. 2 studies tie disaster risk to urban growth. *New York Times* (May 17). www.nytimes.com.

Rowe, G., and G. Wright. 1999. The Delphi technique as a forecasting tool: Issues and analysis. *International Journal of Forecasting* 15. www.forecastingprinciples.com.

Wikipedia. 2009a. Environmental scanning. http://en.wikipedia.org/wiki/Environmental_scanning.

Wikipedia. 2009b. Futurology. http://en.wikipedia.org/wiki/Futurology.

Wikipedia. 2009c. Trend analysis. http://en.wikipedia.org/wiki/Trend_analysis.

World Future Society. 2008. Outlook 2008. www.wfs.org/forecasts.htm.

Zalud, B. 2009a. Innovations and technology report. *Security* 46 (September):30–40.

Zalud, B. 2009b. Tech-armed officers on future's watch. *Security* 46 (September):42–46.

Appendix: Security Assessment or Self-Assessment Document

Introduction

The questions in this document are intended to assist in the determination of security status of a site or location. I consider security to be a process that is broken into four subprocesses: emergency planning, incident management, information protection, and physical security; therefore, the checklist is organized in that manner.

This document was developed to assist a security professional in assessing the security status of a site. Because a question appears in this document, it does not imply that it is a necessary protection requirement in all situations; it depends on the identified risks for this location. This is why it is mandatory that this document be utilized only by security professionals.

Site Information

Please provide the following information:

Site or Location Name _____

Security Manager _____

Senior Location Manager _____

Date of This Review _____

* This Appendix used with permission from *How to Develop and Implement a Security Master Plan* by Timothy D. Giles, ISBN: 1-4200-8625-1, © 2009, CRC Press,Taylor & Francis.

Summarize your environment, highlighting pertinent business facts, and cite any unique security problems and any special concerns or dependencies:

_____

_____

_____

_____

_____

_____

List all location tenant organizations, site population, and percentage of total site. Include all noncompany tenants in multitenant facilities.

Organization	Population	Percent of Total

_____

_____

_____

_____

Identified Security Risks

List all security risks that have been identified previously and attach a copy of your plan to mitigate the risks.

Subprocess	Risk
Emergency Planning	_____
	_____
	_____
	_____
Incident Management	_____
	_____
	_____
Information Protection	_____
	_____
	_____
	_____
Physical Security	_____
	_____
	_____
	_____

Emergency Planning

Crisis Management Team

List all current and alternate members of your crisis management team by title (CMT position and company position) and work location.

Name	Alternate	CMT Position	CO. Position	Location
_____	_____	_____	_____	_____
_____	_____	_____	_____	_____
_____	_____	_____	_____	_____
_____	_____	_____	_____	_____

Have the CMT and alternates been trained on their roles and responsibilities?

_____   _____

Yes   No

If yes, list the training date(s) during the past 12 months.

_____

_____

Crisis Management Rooms

	Primary	Alternate
Location:	_____	_____
Equipment:	_____	_____
	_____	_____
	_____	_____
Documents:	_____	_____
	_____	_____
	_____	_____

Emergency Planning Manual

Does your emergency planning manual (EPM) include the following elements?

	Yes	No
Natural and Human-Made Disasters	____	____
Hurricanes and Typhoons	____	____
Flood	____	____
Fire	____	____
Chemical Spill	____	____
Gas Explosion	____	____
Earthquake	____	____
Other	____	____

Threats or Acts of Violence	_____	_____
Bomb	_____	_____
Political or Civil Disturbance	_____	_____
Emergency Shutdown or Evacuation of Facility	_____	_____
Designation and Staffing of Primary and Alternate Emergency Control Headquarters	_____	_____
Designation of Coordinator for Overall Response	_____	_____
Designation of CMT and Alternates	_____	_____
Designation of Management Succession	_____	_____

Process for Coordination with the Following Groups:	Yes	No
Health, Safety, and Environmental Protection Personnel	_____	_____
Nearby or Adjacent Company Facilities	_____	_____
Landlord or Other Noncompany Occupants of the Building	_____	_____
Community Emergency and Law Enforcement Services	_____	_____
Company Communications for Response to Media	_____	_____
Human Resource Department	_____	_____
Legal Function	_____	_____

Will the following be provided?	Yes	No
Armed Off-Duty Law Enforcement Officers	_____	_____
Facility Protection	_____	_____
Fire Protection or Fire Brigade	_____	_____
Hazardous Material Emergency Response (if required)	_____	_____
Vital Services and Supplies	_____	_____
Emergency Alert System	_____	_____
Rescue Teams	_____	_____
First Aid Teams	_____	_____
Emergency Equipment	_____	_____
Emergency Transportation	_____	_____
Communication Capabilities	_____	_____
Medical Personnel and Supplies	_____	_____
Contact Numbers for Emergency Services	_____	_____
Plans or Blueprints with Office Phone Numbers	_____	_____
Current Personnel Listings	_____	_____

Date of the last two EPM updates:

_____   _____

List the holders of the EPM. Indicate if they have hard or soft copy.

Person	Hard	Soft
_____	_____	_____
_____	_____	_____
_____	_____	_____

Training

List all CMT training and testing that has occurred in the previous 12 months: threat management, demonstrations, and natural disasters.

_____

_____

_____

_____

List all training provided to managers in the last 12 months regarding emergency planning:

Date	Type of Training	Comments
_____		
_____		
_____		
_____		

List all training provided for floor wardens or emergency response personnel in the last 12 months:

Date	Type	Subject
_____	_____	First Aid
_____	_____	Bomb Search
_____	_____	Evacuation
_____	_____	Firefighting
_____	_____	Other _____
_____	_____	_____
_____	_____	_____

List threat call training provided for the following:

	Date	Comments
Receptionist	_____	_____
Telephone Operators	_____	_____
Mailroom Personnel	_____	_____
Control Center Operators	_____	_____
Other	_____	_____

Testing

List the dates that each element of the emergency plan was tested with the CMT in the last 24 months:

Date	Type of Test	Element Tested
_____	_____	Fire _____
_____	_____	Demonstration _____
_____	_____	Natural Disaster _____
_____	_____	Threat: Bomb _____
_____	_____	Threat: Personnel _____

List all corrective action(s) to correct deficiencies that resulted from tests.

_____

_____

_____

_____

List the dates that each element of the emergency plan was tested with the floor wardens or emergency response teams in the last 12 months:

Date	Type of Test	Element Tested
_____	_____	Fire _____
_____	_____	Demonstration _____
_____	_____	Natural Disaster _____
_____	_____	Threat: Bomb _____

List all corrective action(s) to correct deficiencies that resulted from tests.

_____

_____

_____

_____

Incident Management

Incident Reporting

Describe the process for employees to report incidents to security.

_____

_____

_____

_____

Has this process been communicated to management and employees?

	Yes	No
	_____	_____

If yes, describe how it was communicated.

_____

_____

Is there a process to categorize incidents?

	Yes	No

If yes, describe the process.

_____

_____

Is there a process to ensure each significant incident is fully investigated?

	Yes	No

If yes, describe the process.

_____

_____

For serious personnel incidents, who conducts the investigation?

Name   Title

_____

_____

Are noncompany employees (i.e., contract security) allowed to investigate minor incidents?

	Yes	No

If no, describe how minor incidents are investigated and by whom.

_____

_____

If yes, does a company employee maintain responsibility and accountability for investigation?

	Yes	No

If yes, describe the process.

_____

_____

Are major incidents analyzed to determine the underlying causes?

	Yes	No

If yes, describe the process.

_____

_____

Have appropriate actions and controls been implemented to mitigate reoccurrence of significant incidents that occurred during the past 12 months?

	Yes	No

If yes, describe the actions.

_____

How are incident reports and files classifieds and protected?

_____

_____

Management Notification

How is location management notified of incidents and incident trends?

_____

_____

Information Protection

List the process and dates during the past 12 months that the following were communicated to management and employees.

Baseline Security Education

_____

Basic Classification and Control Requirements for Every Employee

_____

Security Requirements for Every User of Computer Systems

_____

Security Requirements for Every Manager

_____

Site Services Security Education

_____

New Employees Education

_____

New Managers Education

_____

Does security have a process to ensure the adequacy of site services security education and training?

Yes _____   No _____

If yes, describe the process.

_____

_____

Does security have a process to ensure the adequacy of the baseline security education and training?

	Yes	No
	_____	_____

If yes, describe the process.

_____

_____

If no, list the exceptions.

_____

_____

Has verification of compliance to information protection controls been conducted during the past 12 months in the following areas?

	Date	Comments	Yes	No
Information/Systems	_____	_____	___	___
Procurement	_____	_____	___	___
Telecommunications	_____	_____	___	___

After-Hours Review Program

Summarize the security and management after-hours security program for ensuring that classified information is properly secured. Provide site data for the previous 12 months.

_____

_____

Use of Supplemental Employees and Onsite Contractor Personnel

Supplemental Employees, Contractors, and Part-Time Employees

What security education was provided to new supplemental employees and part-time employees during the past 12 months?

_____

_____

What security education was provided to onsite contractor personnel during the past 12 months?

_____

_____

Release of Company Confidential Information

What process exists to ensure all company confidential information given to vendors is approved by the authorized manager and is released on transmittals?

_____

_____

Receipt of Other Companies' Confidential Information

What process exists to ensure confidential information received from other companies is approved by the authorized manager and is properly protected within the company?

_____

_____

Vendor Security

List the vendor security reviews you have conducted or directed with purchasing in the past 12 months for vendors that have confidential information.

_____

_____

Telecommunications Security: PBX and CBX

Does your company have telecommunications security guidelines?

	Yes	No
	_____	_____

If no, list the reasons or exceptions.

_____

_____

Exit Interviews for Transfers and Terminations

Are exit interviews conducted for employees who transfer, terminate, or obtain a leave of absence?

	Yes	No
	_____	_____

Are key employees interviewed by legal and reminded of their confidentiality agreement?

	Yes	No
	_____	_____

Are debriefing forms completed and submitted to the human resources department?

	Yes	No
	_____	_____

If yes, describe how this is validated.

	Yes	No
	_____	_____

Physical Security

Lock and Key Control

Is there a daily accountability for grand master or building master or core keys?

	Yes	No
	_____	_____

If no, list reasons or exceptions.

_____

_____

List all holders of all grand or building master and core keys by name and function:

Name	Function	Key Type
_____	_____	_____
_____	_____	_____
_____	_____	_____
_____	_____	_____

Is there documentation on file by security management for master keys in excess of five?

	Yes	No
	_____	_____

List the reasons why there are more than five.

_____

_____

Is there documentation on file that demonstrates that keys are recovered from exiting employees?

	Yes	No
	_____	_____

Exterior Space

Is the perimeter controlled to vehicle access during an emergency or site closure?

	Yes	No
	_____	_____

Is there perimeter fencing around the property?

	Yes	No
	_____	_____

If yes, is it randomly inspected and properly maintained?

	Yes	No
	_____	_____

Are all building perimeter doors and interior restricted space doors equipped with anti-shim plates or anti-shim bolts or latches?

	Yes	No
	_____	_____

Are all perimeter doors and interior restricted space doors monitored by access control system (ACS) or an alarm system to deter and detect unauthorized access into the building or restricted area?

	Yes	No
	_____	_____

If no, list the reasons or exceptions.

_____

_____

Are less obvious points of building entry designed to prevent access into the building or vandalism to the utility system?

	Yes	No
Grills	_____	_____
Grating	_____	_____
Manhole Covers	_____	_____
Area Ways	_____	_____
Utility Tunnels	_____	_____
Roof Vents	_____	_____
Other	_____	_____

Do all building perimeters have an unobstructed line of site? (Shrubbery, plantings, etc., are at least four feet away from the building.)

	Yes	No
	_____	_____

Is all property properly posted with easily identifiable but nonspecific signs?

	Yes	No
	_____	_____

Is fencing provided for critical areas (chemical, electrical, communications, emergency power facilities, etc.)?

	Yes	No
	_____	_____

Is fencing properly installed and maintained?

	Yes	No
	_____	_____

Are surveillance cameras or alarms provided for the following:

	Yes	No
Chemical Tank Areas	_____	_____
Electrical Substations	_____	_____
Communications Facilities	_____	_____
Emergency Power Facilities	_____	_____
Parking Lots and Garages	_____	_____
Building Exteriors	_____	_____
Other	_____	_____

Is the lighting level adequate to provide for the safety and security of employees?

	Yes	No
Vehicle and Pedestrian Entrances	_____	_____
Property Perimeters	_____	_____
Pedestrian Walkways	_____	_____
Building Perimeters	_____	_____
Building Entrances	_____	_____
Parking Lots and Garages	_____	_____
Critical Facilities	_____	_____
Areas of Concealment	_____	_____

Are the trees and shrubbery maintained properly to provide for the safety and security of employees by not obstructing lighting or cameras?

	Yes	No
Building Perimeters	_____	_____
Parking Lots and Garages	_____	_____
Critical Facilities	_____	_____
Areas of Concealment	_____	_____

Interior Space

Is shatter-resistant glass or mylar film installed on exterior windows in the following areas (applies to high-risk facilities and areas only):

	Yes	No
Lobbies	_____	_____
Conference Rooms	_____	_____
Cafeteria	_____	_____
Open Office Landscaping	_____	_____
Passageways Connecting Buildings	_____	_____
Other	_____	_____

Is the lighting level adequate to provide for the safety and security of personnel and property. If no, explain.

_____

_____

Have all areas where bomb devices might be concealed been eliminated or sealed?

	Yes	No
Lobbies	_____	_____
Restrooms (in nonsecure areas)	_____	_____
Docks	_____	_____
External Concealment Areas (newspaper boxes, trash cans, etc.)	_____	_____
Other	_____	_____

If no, explain.

_____

_____

How many areas at the location are identified as "Restricted Space"?

_____

_____

Have they documented the requirements for "Restricted Space"?

	Yes	No
	_____	_____

Are all identified "Restricted Space" areas documented and in 100 percent compliance with established controls?

	Yes	No
	_____	_____

If no, list reasons or exceptions for each area.

_____

_____

Mailroom Controls

Does the mailroom have the following controls (as applicable):

	Yes	No
Access Restricted to Authorized Individuals	_____	_____
X-Ray Equipment Installed	_____	_____
Mail Bomb and Hazardous Substances Training Every 12 Months	_____	_____
Transportation of Mail: Auditable Process	_____	_____
Safe for Locking Classified and Valuable Mail After Hours	_____	_____

If no, explain._____

_____

Cashier or ATM

Are cashier or ATM facilities monitored by a third party for robbery or burglary?

Yes	No
_____	_____

If no, explain.

_____

_____

If yes, is the third-party response reported to their security?

Yes	No
_____	_____

Does a written emergency response procedure exist for location security?

Yes	No
_____	_____

Do you have a parallel alarm monitoring of cashier or ATM alarms?

Yes	No
_____	_____

Medical Facilities

Does your location have company medical facilities?

Yes	No
_____	_____

If yes, does the medical facility have the following in place:

	Yes	No
ACS between Reception and the Rest of the Medical Facility	_____	_____
Concealed CCTV in the Reception Area and Outside the Entrance	_____	_____
Panic Alarms in the Following Locations:		
Reception — With One-Way Audio	_____	_____
Physicians' Offices	_____	_____
Exam Rooms	_____	_____
Other	_____	_____
Secondary Egress from the Medical Area	_____	_____
Exterior Window Design to Prevent Direct Observation	_____	_____
Separate Locking System for Storage of Controlled Substances	_____	_____

Central Employment Offices

Is the employment office located adjacent to the building lobby?

	Yes	No
	_____	_____

If no, explain.

_____

_____

Does the employment lobby have the following:

	Yes	No
Capability to Verify Identity Prior to Unlocking/Locking Exterior Door	_____	_____
Separation of Lobby from the Staff Work Area	_____	_____
Panic Alarm	_____	_____
Do interview rooms include the following:		
Doors with Side Glass View Panel	_____	_____
Panic Alarm	_____	_____

Is there a rear exit from the staff work space?

	Yes	No
	_____	_____

Do written emergency response procedures for security exist?

	Yes	No
	_____	_____

How often are all security devices tested?

_____

Classified Waste

State the process for classified waste disposal at your location. Include how waste is protected during collection and prior to pickup by the vendor. Has the waste vendor had an unannounced security review?

	Yes	No
	_____	_____

If yes, list date.

_____

Panic Alarms

Do all panic alarms simultaneously activate audio and video, which is remotely connected to a constantly monitored location?

	Yes	No
	_____	_____

If no, describe.

_____

_____

Date training was provided to receptionist (and others as required) on use of panic alarm:

_____

How often are all lobby and other panic alarm devices tested?

_____

Lobbies

Does the lobby have the following:

	Yes	No
Remote Control Locking and Unlocking of Interior and Exterior Door(s)	_____	_____
Electronically Controlled Access to Interior Space	_____	_____
Audio and Video Panic Alarm to Security	_____	_____
Elevator Recall	_____	_____
Are all of the above items activated and deactivated by one activation device?	_____	_____
If no, describe alternative controls.		

_____

_____

Are all lobbies designed and furnished to eliminate potential for concealment of persons or packages?

	Yes	No
	_____	_____

Do remote control capabilities for locking and unlocking interior and exterior doors from the staffed lobby exist?

	Yes	No
	_____	_____

Loading Docks

Do the loading docks have the following:

	Yes	No
Remote Control Locking and Unlocking of Interior and Exterior Door(s)	_____	_____
ACS Controlled Access to Interior Space (Secondary Perimeter: Can Be Exterior Fence)	_____	_____
Audio and Video Panic Alarm to Security	_____	_____

Are All of the Above Items Activated and
  Deactivated by One Activation Device?   _____   _____
Separation of Shipping, Receiving, and
  Trash Removal Activities   _____   _____
Written Emergency Procedures   _____   _____

Access Control System Operations

Are badge supplies and duplicate photo files properly controlled?

Yes	No
_____	_____

Do ACS controls limit noncompany employees access to only their authorized working hours?

Yes	No
_____	_____

If no, explain.

_____

_____

Are ACS area reports distributed every 60 days for all area managers and contractors? (Area manager: The person responsible for approving access to an area.)

Yes	No
_____	_____

Are ACS area reports for contractors and "Restricted Space" 100 percent return audited to security every 60 days?

Yes	No
_____	_____

Are ACS backup tapes and disks of system data stored in an area that will not be affected by a primary disaster?

Yes	No
_____	_____

List the storage location(s):

_____

_____

What method is used to validate the ACS database?

_____

_____

How often is the database validated?

_____

_____

List ACS operator authorization levels for the following:

	Level
Contract Guards	_____
Guard Supervisors	_____
Contract Guard Manager	_____
Company Security	_____

Do all ACS alarms have a response defined on the appropriate alarm screen?

Yes _____   No _____

Control Center

Is all control center equipment, alarms, CCTV, ACS, etc., tested every 30 days for proper function?

Yes _____   No _____

Is all control center equipment on battery backup and emergency backup power?

Yes _____   No _____

Parking

List the parking controls for the location.

_____

_____

Are parking facilities properly illuminated?

Yes _____   No _____

Are parking facilities monitored by CCTV?

Yes _____   No _____

Are parking facilities provided with emergency call stations?

Yes _____   No _____

Contractor Controls

Do contractors exchange a company ID for a contractor badge?

Yes _____   No _____

List all service contracts. Do they have a confidential disclosure agreement (CDA)?

	CDA	
Contractor Name	Yes	No
_____	_____	_____
_____	_____	_____
_____	_____	_____
_____	_____	_____
_____	_____	_____
_____	_____	_____

What security education is provided to contractors?

_____

_____

Do all service contracts contain a requirement that no drugs, alcohol, or weapons are allowed onsite?

| Yes | No |
| _____ | _____ |

What action is taken to ensure the contractor complies with these clauses?

_____

_____

Contract Security

Does the guard contract contain the following:

	Yes	No
Background Check Requirements	_____	_____
Education Requirements	_____	_____
Training Requirements	_____	_____
Skills and Experience Prerequisites	_____	_____

How often are audits conducted to verify compliance with the above contract requirements?

_____

_____

List the last two audit dates and results.

Date	Results
_____	_____
_____	_____

Do all posts have current post orders?

| Yes | No |
| _____ | _____ |

Do contract security personnel act as receptionists? If so, what specific training have they received?

_____

_____

How is billing reconciled and verified?

_____

_____

Is overtime authorized? If so, under what circumstances?

_____

_____

Are any security services provided by the building landlord?

	Yes	No
	_____	_____

If yes, describe.

_____

_____

Company (Proprietary) Security Employees

List the security training provided to security personnel during the last 12 months.

Date	Training
_____	_____
_____	_____
_____	_____
_____	_____
_____	_____
_____	_____

Gatehouse Operation

What are the hours of attended gatehouse operations?

_____

_____

What factors determine the need for continual gatehouse operation?

_____

_____

Education and Awareness

Are education and awareness programs in place to cover the following:

	Yes	No
Drugs and Alcohol	_____	_____
Weapons	_____	_____
Cameras and Photography	_____	_____
Threat Policy	_____	_____
Display of ID Badge	_____	_____
Building Entry Procedures (Tailgating)	_____	_____

If no, explain.

_____

_____

Security Officer and Contract Guard Posts

Description	Hrs/Days	Worker/Years	Yearly Costs
_____	_____	_____	_____
_____	_____	_____	_____
_____	_____	_____	_____
_____	_____	_____	_____
_____	_____	_____	_____
_____	_____	_____	_____
_____	_____	_____	_____

Index